TRAVEL, TOURISM, AND HOSPITALITY RESEARCH

A Handbook for Managers and Researchers

TRAVEL, TOURISM, AND HOSPITALITY RESEARCH

A Handbook for Managers and Researchers

EDITORS

J.R. BRENT RITCHIE

University of Calgary
Calgary, Alberta, Canada

CHARLES R. GOELDNER

University of Colorado
Boulder, Colorado

John Wiley & Sons
New York   Chichester   Brisbane   Toronto   Singapore

Library of Congress Cataloging-in-Publication Data:

Travel, tourism, and hospitality research.

    Includes bibliographies and index.
    1. Tourist trade—Research.   I. Ritchie, J. R. Brent.
II. Goeldner, Charles R.
G155.A1T6578   1987   380.1′459104′072   86-13235
ISBN 0-471-84225-7

Printed in the United States of America

10 9 8 7 6 5 4 3 2 1

CONTRIBUTORS

JAMES ABBEY   Associate Professor, College of Hotel Administration, University of Nevada, Las Vegas, Nevada

BRIAN H. ARCHER   Head, Department of Management Studies for Tourism and Hotel Industries, University of Surrey, Guildford, Surrey, England

LYONNEL J. BARCLAY   Research Associate, American Graduate School of International Management, Glendale, Arizona

JAY BEAMAN   Director, Socio-Economic Division, Program Management, Parks Canada, Ottawa, Ontario, Canada

UEL BLANK   Emeritus Professor, University of Minnesota, *Residence:* 3209 Crawford Street, Columbia, Missouri 65201

JOHN C. CANNON   Chief, Housing Surveys Branch, Demographic Surveys Division, Bureau of the Census, Washington, D.C.

CAROLYN CAREY   Manager, Market Research, Knott's Berry Farm, Buena Park, California

ROBIN A. CHADWICK   Senior Advisor, National Task Force on Tourism Data, Statistics Canada, Ottawa, Ontario, Canada

JOHN D. CLAXTON   Faculty of Commerce, University of British Columbia, Vancouver, B.C., Canada

SUZANNE D. COOK,   Assistant Director, U.S. Travel Data Center, Washington, D.C.

LOUISE CRANDALL   Program Evaluator, National Capital Commission, Ottawa, Ontario, Canada

LAWRENCE F. CUNNINGHAM   Associate Professor, Marketing and Transportation Department, College of Business and Administration, University of Colorado at Denver, Denver, Colorado

THOMAS LEA DAVIDSON   Davidson-Peterson Associates, Inc., New York, New York

DAVID L. EDGELL   Director, Office of Policy and Planning, U.S. Travel and Tourism Administration, United States Department of Commerce, Washington, D.C.

RANDYL D. ELKIN   Chairman and Professor, Department of Industrial and Labor Relations, West Virginia University, Morgantown, West Virginia

JANE R. FITZGIBBON   Vice-President, Director of Research and Development, Ogilvy & Mather, New York, New York

DOUGLAS C. FRECHTLING   Director, U.S. Travel Data Center, Washington, D.C.

CHARLES R. GOELDNER   Editor, *Journal of Travel Research*; Director, Business Research Division, University of Colorado, Boulder, Colorado

CLARE A. GUNN   1602 Glade, College Station, Texas 77840

FRED HURST   Supervisor, Economic Analysis, Port Authority of New York and New Jersey, New York, New York

MARTINUS J. KOSTERS   Deputy Director, Netherlands Institute of Tourism and Leisure Studies, Breda, Netherlands

WILBUR F. LAPAGE   Director, Department of Resources and Economic Development, State of New Hampshire, Concord, New Hampshire

TYRRELL C. MARRIS   Assistant Director, Head of

Research Services, English Tourist Board, British Tourist Authority, Hammersmith, London, England

GORDON H. G. MCDOUGALL Professor, School of Business and Economics, Wilfrid Laurier University, Waterloo, Ontario, Canada

SCOTT MEIS Manager, Socio-Economic Division, Program Management, Parks Canada, Ottawa, Ontario, Canada

LISLE S. MITCHELL Professor, Department of Geography, University of South Carolina, Columbia, South Carolina

GEORGE H. MOELLER Assistant to Deputy Chief for Research, U.S. Forest Service, U.S. Department of Agriculture, Washington, D.C.

HUGH MUNRO School of Business Administration, Wilfrid Laurier University, Waterloo, Ontario, Canada

ROBERT P. OLSON Department of Habitational Resources, University of Wisconsin—Stout, Menomonie, Wisconsin

KAREN I. PETERSON President, Davidson-Peterson Associates, Inc., New York, New York

MICHAEL D. PETKOVITCH Research Assistant, University of Minnesota, Minneapolis, Minnesota

ABRAHAM PIZAM University of Central Florida, Orlando, Florida

STANLEY C. PLOG Plog Research Inc., Reseda, California

J.R. BRENT RITCHIE Faculty of Management, University of Calgary, Calgary, Alberta, Canada

LINDA K. RICHTER Associate Professor, Department of Political Science, Kansas State University, Manhattan, Kansas

RANDALL S. ROBERTS Employee Relations Manager, Louie Glass Company, Inc., Weston, West Virginia

STUART N. ROBINSON Stuart N. Robinson and Associates, Inc., Richmond, Virginia

ILKKA A. RONKAINEN School of Business Administration, Georgetown University, Washington, D.C.

JAMES M. ROVELSTAD Director, Center for Survey and Marketing Research, University of Wisconsin—Parkside, Kenosha, Wisconsin

PETER SHACKLEFORD Chief of Studies, World Tourism Organization, Madrid, Spain

ELWOOD L. SHAFER Chairman, Recreation and Parks Department, Pennsylvania State University, University Park, Pennsylvania

GORDON D. TAYLOR Manager, External Liaison Research Program, Tourism Canada, Ottawa, Ontario, Canada

PETER W. WILLIAMS Department of Geography, Ryerson Polytechnical Institute, Toronto, Ontario, Canada

E.D. WOHLMUTH 210 Locust Street, Philadelphia, Pennsylvania 19106

ARCH G. WOODSIDE Malcolm S. Woldenberg Professor of Marketing, Tulane University, New Orleans, Louisiana

DON WYNEGAR Director, Office of Research, U.S. Travel and Tourism Administration, U.S. Department of Commerce, Washington, D.C.

INTRODUCTION

In the short span of some 40 years, the travel, tourism, and hospitality industry has achieved international and national recognition as one of the major social and economic forces of our time. Despite this reality, those of us in the industry are well aware that its rapid growth during this period has not been matched by the development of a solid foundation or an infrastructure on which to sustain and enhance the industry's future. In particular, we are only too well aware that the information base on which decisions are being made in tourism throughout the world is fragile and, in many cases, simply unreliable.

The reasons for this situation are several. The very nature of the industry itself is, of course, a major factor. The large number of organizations involved in tourism and their relatively small size mean that efforts to collect data from them and for them are both costly and time-consuming. This is in marked contrast to other major industries, such as banking or automobile manufacturing, where information is concentrated in the hands of a much smaller number of firms and where government regulations for reporting requirements greatly facilitate the development of reliable data bases.

The second factor is the nature of the travel experience itself and the difficulties that are inherent in understanding consumer behavior and expenditure patterns within this travel experience. As has been pointed out (Ritchie, 1975)[1], research efforts in travel and tourism face a number of difficulties which are unique to the field and which go beyond the normal data collection concerns encountered in other fields. These difficulties decrease the reliability of our data, make it more costly to gather, make it more difficult to

[1]Ritchie, J.R. Brent (1975), "Some Critical Aspects of Measurement Theory and Practice in Travel Research," *Journal of Travel Research*, Vol. 14, No. 1.

interpret, frequently render it out of date before it is reported, and often cause it to be nonrelevant to management issues faced by individual users.

A third factor is perhaps less obvious but more pervasive. Because tourism is a relatively new industry, it has not had the opportunity to establish the educational infrastructure necessary to systematically attract and train its fair percentage of the best minds and most ambitious, most effective managers. Historically, individuals have entered the travel industry for a broad range of reasons, a great many of which have had little to do with a conscious decision to pursue a professional career in the tourism industry. As a result of this lack of formal education for a career in the industry, there has been little perceived need for systematic research and information systems on which to base management decisions.

All this has changed substantially over the last decade. During this period, world competition in tourism has grown dramatically as more and more countries and regions realize both the desirability and the necessity of including tourism as a major component of their social and economic structure. During this period, the tourism industry has been gradually "getting its act together" by becoming a more cooperative and more coordinated force. In parallel, and on another front, progress has been made in developing research techniques which improve the reliability of travel and tourism data, thus enhancing our understanding of consumer behavior and consumer spending patterns in tourism. While much progress yet remains to be accomplished, there is little doubt that the level of sophistication in tourism research is much higher than it was and that there will be continued pressure for even more rigorous information gathering, analysis, and interpretation systems.

Finally, the last decade has also seen meaningful

progress in the development of programs designed to enhance the education and training levels of those entering the industry as well as those currently employed in it. Tourism has not, of course, yet achieved the funding or the prominence in education of that attained by other sectors of the economy such as manufacturing or agriculture, but progress is being made. However, as this occurs, it will further fuel the demand for more and better research.

The Need for the Handbook

It was against this background that the preparation of the present handbook was undertaken. It became evident to the editors that while advances were being made in the preparation of textbooks and other teaching materials for tourism at the level of introductory courses, little was being done to consolidate the rapidly expanding knowledge base related to research in the field of travel, tourism, and hospitality. Again, the reasons for this situation are several in number. Perhaps the most important is the diversity of the knowledge base and the difficulty facing any single individual who attempts to master the many skills involved.

The second underlying cause was perhaps the failure of many to realize the extent of the strides which had been taken in the field of travel/tourism/hospitality research in recent years and the perception that existing journals adequately captured available knowledge. In retrospect, this view appears to suffer from two shortcomings. First, as many are aware, the number of publications in travel, tourism, and hospitality research has increased substantially over the past ten to fifteen years. The pioneering *Journal of Travel Research* and *Journal of Leisure Research* have been complemented by more recent publications such as the *Annals of Tourism Research*, *Leisure Sciences*, *Tourism Management*, *Hospitality Management*, and *Leisure and Society* to name only a few.

In addition, there has been a failure to take into account much of the valuable work and the many research skills which exist outside of the framework tapped by formal publications. This is particularly true in the field of travel, tourism, and hospitality where, because of the lack of a formal research training system, individuals and firms have been forced to develop their own abilities.

Given this situation, it was felt that the most effective and most appropriate response was to prepare a research-oriented handbook which would draw upon the knowledge and skills found among both educators and practitioners. The goal of the editors was to identify for each topic included in the handbook that individual judged by his or her peers to possess the most expertise in relation to each of the defined topics. This was done, and in most cases we believe we have succeeded by various means to convince leading experts in various aspects of travel and tourism research to provide us with the benefits of their knowledge and experience.

Philosophy and Orientation of the Handbook

From the very beginning, the philosophy and orientation of the editors has been to develop a major reference book that will be of use to:

A Managers in tourism who have a need to use research as a means of providing information for improving their managerial effectiveness;

B Beginning researchers who require an overview of available research methods in a single source combined with an associated basic bibliography, which will permit them to pursue more in-depth work when required.

It is also hoped that the handbook will prove useful to more experienced researchers who have a developed expertise in a given area but who may wish to refresh their memories or review research topics with which they have had little or no direct experience. Finally, it is hoped that the handbook will also be found valuable for use in introductory courses in tourism research methods.

The above philosophy and orientation was communicated to prospective authors from the outset and it has colored both the review process and the subsequent revising and editing of each chapter. It should be emphasized that this desire to achieve readability on the part of managers and beginning researchers was constantly balanced by an equally strong desire to maintain as much rigor as possible in each author's presentation. This balance was certainly not easy to achieve and each reader will undoubtedly come to his or her own conclusions concerning the extent to which the goal has been attained. Undoubtedly, our success in this area has been varied. In particular, there will be cases where academic authors may not have achieved the managerial relevance some might desire. In others, practitioners may not have achieved the sophistication in presentation that an academic might desire. It is hoped, however, that readers will find that we have been able to achieve a reasonable mix and balance in this regard across the entire contents of the handbook.

Structure and Contents of the Handbook

Given the diversity of the travel, tourism, and hospitality industry, it is not surprising that related research also contains numerous, complex elements. As such, a major task facing the editors was to decide upon what to conceptually include in the handbook and how to structure the material eventually obtained. The first step in this process was to review existing literature in an attempt to identify various substantive and methodological topics addressed by previous researchers. As a result of this process, some 55 topics were initially identified and tentatively designated as a handbook chapter. Since the present version of the handbook contains 43 chapters, we clearly did not succeed totally in our efforts. In certain cases, we were simply unable to identify an author who was capable of or willing to prepare the chapter in question. In others, individuals found they were unable to complete the task due to a lack of available information or other personal reasons.

Concerning the structuring of those chapters which were successfully completed, there were clearly several models that might have been chosen. The manner in which the handbook was finally structured was a reflection of the overall philosophy of the handbook, current industry practices, existing academic orientations, and the desire to regroup items likely to appeal to a similar audience. As a result, the handbook contains eight major parts.

Part One, entitled "A Managerial Perspective," has been designed to clearly emphasize that research must be viewed as a tool to assist management in improving the quality of planning and decision making. This approach reflects the philosophy of the handbook and emphasizes that management must lead and direct the research process.

Part Two of the handbook intentionally switches very quickly to a presentation of fundamental concepts and approaches for travel, tourism, and hospitality research. The point being made is that, while research must serve managerial purposes, it must also be conducted with rigor and from a sound conceptual and theoretical base.

As the reader moves into Part Three of the handbook, he or she returns to a more managerial setting, albeit the specialized world of the public sector. In the case of this section of the handbook, an effort has been made to provide insight and understanding concerning the nature and extent of research within national, regional, and municipal tourism organizations. The purpose of Part Three is to demonstrate how research is used at each of these levels and to clarify the nature of information requirements for decision making at different levels of aggregation/disaggregation.

Parts Four and Five of the handbook are intended to be distinct yet complementary. Part Four provides a view of tourism research as perceived from a disciplinary perspective. The intent here is to demonstrate and emphasize that tourism is a multidisciplinary field of study which draws extensively on a number of disciplinary roots for the great majority of its concepts and research methods. Unfortunately, the number of disciplines it was possible to cover was limited. Indeed, the treatment of all relevant disciplines would merit a book in itself. In contrast, Part Five reflects the practical structure of the tourism industry itself. In this case, it has been possible to obtain chapters covering the research needs of most important segments of tourism. Again, however, this coverage is not complete. For example, we were not able to obtain a chapter of research for hotel management. Hopefully, such gaps will be rectified in the future.

The latter three parts of the handbook focus on more specific research approaches and methods. Part Six contains six chapters all dealing with various aspects of estimating the impact of tourism on both the host community as well as the tourists themselves. Part Seven discusses the nature and application of some very specific planning and data collection techniques. Finally, Part Eight outlines some research approaches which are particularly applicable to various marketing tasks which are faced frequently in the field of tourism.

Using the Handbook

There are clearly a variety of ways in which a handbook containing as much material as the present one might be used. The reader, however, should keep in mind that the present document has been prepared primarily to fulfill its main mission; that is, to provide a working reference book for managers using research and for beginning researchers. It is anticipated that for such applications individuals are unlikely to read the handbook from cover to cover at a given point in time (as might be the case with a textbook). Rather, it is envisaged that users will selectively read chapters containing information having a direct bearing on the particular issue or problem they are currently facing. Given this type of usage, the handbook has been prepared so that each chapter can be read on its own. As such, no one chapter is entirely dependent on others in the handbook. While an attempt has been made by the various authors to refer specifically to other chapters related to their discussion, we have intentionally permitted a fairly substantial amount of duplication and overlap where this was appropriate and where it facilitated the ease of use and understanding of a given chapter.

The second way in which we anticipate the handbook will be used is as a textbook for tourism research courses and seminars. From a course perspective, students will clearly run into a certain amount of repetition when reading from cover to cover. It is our hope and indeed our belief that such repetition may prove highly beneficial from two perspectives. First, it should provide reinforcement of a number of important concepts. Second, it will provide the student with alternative perspectives on various topics which different authors felt to be important.

The use of the handbook for specialized seminars roughly parallels its use as a working reference document. As such, the approach of preparing compartmentalized stand-alone chapters, we feel, makes the handbook particularly appropriate for this type of application. However, in this regard, it is expected that instructors will probably want to provide participants with additional in-depth material, the identification of which is facilitated by the rather extensive bibliographies which most authors have provided.

As many others have found out, the preparation of a publication such as this handbook was much more demanding than originally envisaged. Despite a high degree of cooperation from our authors, the sheer size of the project and the limited resources available meant that it was not always possible to achieve our goals as quickly as we might have liked. However, we were determined to produce a useful, high-quality reference document which would reflect the integrity and the knowledge of our authors and which would be a positive contribution to the development of the tourism industry. The extent to which this has been achieved must be judged by others.

J.R. BRENT RITCHIE
CHARLES R. GOELDNER

ACKNOWLEDGMENTS

This handbook represents the culmination of a long process involving the support of many individuals. Because of the involvement of so many, we hesitate to acknowledge only a limited number of persons for fear of overlooking someone who has provided significant input or assistance. At the same time, we would be remiss if we did not formally acknowledge certain individuals and groups.

First, and most important, we wish to thank the authors for their cooperation, their contributions, and their patience. The process of preparing the handbook, in which we were dealing with some fifty authors concerning diverse topics over an extended period of time under the constraint of limited resources, meant that communication could only be on an "as necessary" basis except for periodic status reports. Thus, for their positive support, for their enthusiasm, and above all, for their quality contributions, we are most appreciative to each and every author whose work appears in this handbook.

While a number are also authors, we are extremely grateful for the support and assistance received from our associate editors. In this capacity, these individuals were responsible for assisting us in identifying prospective authors for a given topic, for soliciting their contributions, and, most importantly, for reviewing and commenting upon the original manuscripts which were submitted. Each manuscript was reviewed by two, and frequently three, associate editors so as to provide suggestions for improving both the practical relevance and the academic rigor of each chapter. While our recognition of the efforts of our associate editors is a small reward for their efforts, we hope they will accept our thanks in the sincere manner intended.

We also would especially like to thank Robin A. Chadwick, our senior associate editor. His commitment and support of our efforts throughout the process of compiling and editing the handbook went far beyond the normal professional contribution that was reasonable to expect. Indeed, without this support at particularly critical points in the preparation of the handbook, it is entirely possible that the project would not have been completed. Thus, to Mr. Chadwick and to his employer, Statistics Canada, who permitted his contribution, we express our deepest gratitude.

We also must, of course, recognize the organizational support which we received from two main sources. First, from the Travel and Tourism Research Association (TTRA), we received both moral and financial support. The moral support was particularly critical at the early stages of the project as a means of confirming the potential value of the handbook and for providing encouragement to initiate such a substantial long-term task with some confidence that it would eventually be published. The assurance of financial support was also critical to its successful completion. While attempts were made to keep direct expenses to a minimum, there were, nevertheless, significant costs for which no other funding was available. Finally, we must express our appreciation to the Faculty of Management at the University of Calgary which indirectly, and sometimes directly, provided considerable administrative support for the preparation of the handbook. In particular, we express our appreciation to Linda Anderson, who transformed manuscripts of varying physical quality into a well organized, well presented and easily readable format. We are also most grateful to Gerda Mann for the rigorous editing of the final manuscript and for ensuring we met publication deadlines.

J.R.B.R.
C.R.G.

CONTENTS

CHAPTER 6 63
Planning a Tourism Research Investigation
Abraham Pizam

CHAPTER 7 77
Demand Forecasting and Estimation
Brian Archer

CHAPTER 8 87
Scaling and Attitude Measurement
in Tourism and Travel Research
Gordon H.G. McDougall
Hugh Munro

CHAPTER 9 101
Issues in Sampling and Sample Design—
A Managerial Perspective
John C. Cannon

PART THREE
National, Regional, and
Municipal Perspectives

CHAPTER 10 117
Research in National Tourist Organizations
Gordon D. Taylor

CHAPTER 11 129
Tourism Research in European
National Tourist Organizations
Martinus Jan Kosters

PART FOUR
Some Disciplinary Perspectives

CHAPTER 30   363
Evaluating the Human Resource
(Employment) Requirements and
Impacts of Tourism Developments
Randyl D. Elkin
Randall S. Roberts

CHAPTER 31   373
The Social Impact of Tourism on Developing
Regions and Its Measurement
Louise Crandall

CHAPTER 32   385
Evaluating Environmental Impact and
Physical Carrying Capacity in Tourism
Peter W. Williams

PART SEVEN
Data Collection Methods
of Particular Relevance

CHAPTER 33   401
Enroute Surveys
Fred Hurst

CHAPTER 34   417
The Delphi Technique: A Tool for Long-
Range Tourism and Travel Planning
George H. Moeller
Elwood L. Shafer

PART EIGHT
Special Marketing Applications

TRAVEL, TOURISM, AND HOSPITALITY RESEARCH

A Handbook for Managers and Researchers

PART ONE

A MANAGERIAL PERSPECTIVE

This introductory section of the Handbook is intended to emphasize the fact that travel, tourism, and hospitality research must be viewed from a managerial as well as a technical perspective. It is a well recognized truism that managers and researchers in virtually all sectors of industry experience some degree of difficulty in working together effectively. While the reasons for this situation are many and varied, part of the difficulty stems from a lack of understanding of each other's purposes and priorities. Recognizing this reality, an attempt has been made in the four chapters which comprise Part One of this reference book to sensitize both managers and researchers (but particularly researchers) to the need for a managerial perspective in the planning, execution, and use of research.

Chapter 1 has been written by one of the most respected pioneers in tourism research, Clare Gunn. In this chapter, entitled "A Perspective on the Purpose and Nature of Tourism Research Methods," Dr. Gunn positions the field by examining a number of key dimensions which are required for an understanding of both the scope of research in tourism, the range of contributions which can be anticipated, and the complexities which must be dealt with in bringing together research from various sources and disciplines.

In contrast to Chapter 1, which has a philosophical and informational orientation, Chapter 2 attempts to provide both managers and researchers with an understanding of the various research approaches available and the manner in which each approach serves a different role in the overall managerial process. The author, J.R. Brent Ritchie of The University of Calgary, argues that the type of research method employed must reflect the level of decision making within an organization, the stage of the decision-making process for which research is conducted, and the functional problems being addressed by management. Based on this analytical framework, it is seen that information needs to be met by research can vary substantially within an organization. As a result, care must be taken to select a research approach which is appropriate to the data collection task at hand.

Chapter 3, "The Formulation of Tourism Policy—A Managerial Framework," has been prepared in an attempt to provide a transition from the more general considerations of the first two chapters to the more specific concerns of tourism planners and managers. In this chapter, David Edgell of the U.S. Travel and Tourism Administration explains the process of tourism policy formulation as an aid to the overall planning and management of tourism. As the chapter clearly demonstrates, the process of policy formulation is a complex one in which many groups and many types of information must be gathered and assessed. Since the role of research is to provide a systematic and objective approach to providing this information, it is critical that those responsible for the research have an appreciation for the uses to which it will be applied from a policy perspective.

In the final chapter of Part One, Jay Beaman and Scott Meis of Parks Canada address an important topic which is frequently overlooked in the travel, tourism, and hospitality research literature, namely, "Managing the Research Function for Effective Policy Formulation and Decision Making." The authors contend that, to be effective, research managers must spend much of their time on two main activities, research planning and research coupling. Research planning involves establishing a process in which areas of research are identified and prioritized in the light of existing resources, in which appropriate research methods are selected, and in which research is monitored during execution and evaluated for effectiveness upon completion. Research coupling, on the other hand, includes communication and organizational structuring activities directed towards stimulating and facilitating dialogue between researchers and user groups. It is perhaps this latter area which has been most severely neglected by all concerned in the execution and use of travel, tourism, and hospitality research. Hopefully the suggestions made by Beaman and Meis will be acknowledged and acted upon by readers of this volume.

In brief, it is hoped that these introductory chapters will serve to encourage a common perspective among managers and researchers with respect to the nature and roles of the research process as a vehicle for providing assistance for decision making. It is only with such a common perspective that research can be truly effective.

1

A Perspective on the Purpose and Nature of Tourism Research Methods

CLARE A. GUNN

Professor Emeritus
Recreation and Parks
   Department
Texas Agricultural Experiment
   Station
Texas A&M University
College Station,
   Texas   77843

Tourism research, while no substitute for superior management practices, provides objective, systematic, logical, and empirical foundations for such management. Tourism, because of its great complexity of social, environmental, and economic aspects, requires research input from many disciplines—marketing, geography, anthropology, behavior, business, human ecology, history, political science, planning and design, futurism, and many others. While the scientific method is basic to virtually all research, the several disciplines have slightly different approaches important to tourism. The value of such research lies in better development, management, policy-making, and education in this important and growing field.

The two most commonly asked questions posed by tourism practitioners are: (a) in a field dominated by skills and practices (such as hotel management), what can research do for me, and (b) beyond research for marketing, of what value is research? These questions have many implications, not the least of which is the generally low regard or suspicion of research held by most practitioners of tourism. These questions also imply a "show me" attitude that indicates a desire to know more about what the role of research in tourism might be. They also demonstrate a lack of communication between practitioners and researchers. In recent years, the amount and quality of research has improved greatly. Perhaps the following discussion will offer a perspective on the purpose and nature of tourism research.

RESEARCH VERSUS PRACTICE

For many individuals in business and in government, the primary career philosophy is that of experience,

not research. One regularly reads and hears about the need for high-quality management, astute decision making, and the need for innovation in a changing tourism world. These, they say, are subjective qualities of the art of management, not of science, the main focus of research. Their arguments rest firmly on a tradition of individuality in business and on the physical evidence of thousands of hotel rooms, restaurant seats, and airline seats that have resulted largely from subjective decision making. Or so it would seem. Little understood is the great amount of objective research that has gone into even the present tourism system.

For example, objective research and technology in electronic communication have revolutionized hotel and airline reservation and management systems. Research and development created new generations of jet air equipment. Environmental research of natural resources has changed the planning and management of natural resource areas in tourist destinations. Behavioral research has increasingly provided greater understanding of the tourist. All this, and more, has come about through application of objective research studies designed to provide new information and to solve tourism problems. With tourism growing into a major element of society throughout the world, tourism research offers one of the most challenging and exciting fields of endeavor open to young people today. With the increased domestic and international complexities of tourism, certainly tourism research is in even greater need than ever before.

So, it is not a matter of choosing *between* research and the art of good management but of creating a better system of tourism by using both. The purpose of this volume is to demonstrate how objective research can provide valuable information for better quality tourism throughout the world.

ROLE OF OBJECTIVE RESEARCH

Tourism knowledge today is building through a variety of means. Some means are more exacting than others. Some have been more popular than others. It may be useful at this point to paraphrase Kerlinger's (1973) identification of four ways of knowing, based on earlier work of Buchler, Cohen, and Nagel.

First, tourism practitioners know certain things because of *tenacity*. Certain "rules of thumb," known by those in the several facets of tourism, are passed from one to another as truths merely because they are held as truths. For example, the role of high occupancy for years has been the truth of hoteliers everywhere. Research, however, has demonstrated that many other factors in addition to occupancy can contribute to success and even 100 percent occupancy may not necessarily prove profitable. Sometimes, beliefs of certain truths prevail in spite of new objective research that proves them wrong.

Second is the method of *authority*. In some countries and in some aspects of tourism, certain tourism information is believed because it has been stated by an accepted authority. Even the courts recognize the strength of statements by experts. Such authority can come from several sources. It may come from public acceptance, from one who is reputed to have superior knowledge, or by governmental decree.

A third form of gaining tourism knowledge is by means of *intuition*. We accept certain information about tourism because it just seems right to do so. Beliefs, such as that tourism has no impact on resources or that tourism is always an economic good, are believed because they seem right to believe, especially by all those who believe in tourism. It "stands to reason" that these statements are correct.

The fourth way of gaining knowledge is through *science*, obtained by means of objective research. Built into this form of identifying information is one quality that does not appear in the others. This is the matter of questioning and systematic check. The others may produce, by chance, correct information but there is no questioning or check upon its correctness. In scientific research, there are many points along the way of investigation that force critical examination. Objective research is systematic, logical, and empirical and can be replicated (Tuckman 1972). As a result, the information is more dependable. "By testing thoughts against reality, science helps to liberate inquiry from bias, prejudice, and just plain muddleheadedness" (Hoover 1976). It is in the context of science that many new truths of tourism are developing.

PROPRIETARY VERSUS UNIVERSAL

In the field of tourism, and within objective research, a distinction must be made between *proprietary* (private) research and what might be called *universal* (public) research. Proprietary, as used here, refers to research that is done to solve problems privately within an agency or business but the results are not revealed to others. Universal research, on the other hand, is directed toward general or specific problems and the results are made public through technical journals or popular literature.

The intent here is to emphasize that in both instances, private and public, it is the quality of the research that must be maintained. In both types the researcher must let the results of the research dictate the conclusions. If a researcher is bound to produce results that management or a buyer prefers, it has lost its credibility and objectivity. For example, a hotel owner may hire a research consultant to prepare a feasibility study for a site but the study is to be used primarily for convincing a lender to provide financial support. The researcher in this case is not free to provide true results of his study, especially if it proves that the site is poor for this business.

While proprietary (private) research has a legitimate place in the field of tourism, it often suffers from poor objectivity because it does not have adequate built-in checks. When results are biased and are not published, a variety of outside researchers are unable to review the work and voice opinions on its quality. Scholarly (universal) research articles must pass through critical review of peers even before publication. After works are published, they can be reviewed by buyers and sellers of research as well as by research educators, providing them with opportunity of constructive criticism not possible in the case of private research that is kept secret.

An increasing amount of universal tourism research is being performed by large organizations, governments, and universities and is being made available to everyone interested. Subsequent researchers and their own research can build upon such studies and make further proof of their precepts or even disprove them. Eventually, through continued scientific research, precepts are developed into theory—laws that govern and explain the many aspects of tourism.

RESEARCH APPROACHES

For tourism, a few approaches are more popularly used today and vary in how they are performed and what they can accomplish. Four approaches, not necessarily mutually exclusive, are described in the following discussion. Sometimes one, such as description, leads to another, such as testing. (See the Suggested Sources of Information for resource materials and examples of tourism research.)

TO DESCRIBE AND INVENTORY

One approach in tourism is not to prove new relationships or to demonstrate the value of new practices but merely to describe. While some scholars denigrate the value of descriptive research, tourism knowledge is in such a stage of infancy that descriptive research is valuable and necessary today. The many facets of the complicated phenomenon we call tourism have not even been described adequately. Basic inventory and description is also often helpful in decision making.

For example, individual tourism businesses of some portions of Texas have long recognized the value of tourism to them and to their areas. However, this knowledge was not generally known nor accepted by other businesses or agencies. The Texas Tourism Development Agency contracted the U.S. Travel Data Center to obtain descriptive data for all counties. These data included expenditures, taxes paid, employment generated, and payrolls generated by travel. As a result of these research findings, several counties were surprised to discover the great importance of travel and stepped up their efforts to provide better service and to organize more formal efforts to promote tourism.

Throughout the United States, State Comprehensive Outdoor Recreation Plans (SCORP), sponsored by the former Heritage, Conservation and Recreation Service, employed descriptive research to inventory recreational facilities. These reports cataloged items important to tourism, such as campgrounds, picnic facilities, playgrounds, swimming areas, golf courses, boating areas, and other recreational development.

Also important to tourism are time series descriptive studies, such as those prepared by the U.S. Bureau of Census. Every five years that agency prepares a census of travel and a census of selected services. These provide base data, important to both the public and private sector.

Individual tourism businesses regularly develop statistics on their operations. Data on rooms rented, revenues obtained, costs of maintenance, and other facts are determined to describe the characteristics of the business. Descriptive data on markets are commonly compiled. Descriptive studies about certain tourism businesses, such as camping (Bevins, LaPage and Wilcox 1979), are being produced.

TO TEST

Experimental research, used for generations in scientific laboratories and field experiments, has application to tourism. It is especially useful in experimenting with changes in practices. It is more difficult, but is sometimes used, in testing physical development.

For example, food services may experiment with various menu combinations and portions before arriving at standardized menus and portion control. Maintenance managers may run experiments on the most cost-effective maintenance strategies and equipment for taking care of large properties. Airlines may run experiments on special price–destination packages. Experiments in obtaining opinion response from varying content and presentation of advertising copy and illustrations are often made before deciding upon advertising layout.

The experimental methods of research are very productive for certain types of tourism research.

TO PREDICT, FORECAST

Of interest to many tourist businesses is increasing the ability to make forecasts. Decisions on the purchase of new generations of equipment, new sites, and new technology may rest on predictions of increased demand for a specific tourism service or product. One of the fundamental problems in forecasting is the lack of basic data. Descriptive research can provide this foundation. Another problem is assuming that the external factors of influence will remain the same in the future. It is one thing to obtain research data on the past but quite another to assume that new factors will not change their arrangement or importance in the future. Predictability and forecasting are more reliable in the physical sciences than in social science, the realm of tourism behavior. At present there is an increasing amount of research on the factors that influence forecasting. Research of these factors, relating psychological and social factors to the economics of tourism, is seen as a major need in the field of tourism (Archer 1976).

TO MODEL, SIMULATE

One approach to research is to set up hypothetical situations, establish mathematical relationships between factors, and study controlled changes. In a way, this represents the creation of a scenario patterned after real world situations. However, the scenario does not utilize measures of existing situations but rather assumptions of these situations. The process of modeling forces the researcher to assume a set of conditions and to state explicit relationships. When the data are assigned quantifiable language, the computer is able to assist greatly in making rapid calculations regarding the influence of changes in relationships.

Simulation and modeling have been useful approaches in outdoor recreation demand studies. Some of the types used have been gravity models (relationships between origins and destinations), linear programming (optimal acquisition of resources), Acar model (policy regarding recreational opportunities), systems theory (recreational camping and boating), and comprehensive simulation modeling (state recreation plans) (Analysis 1977).

THE VARIETY OF TOURISM RESEARCH NEEDS

The breadth of the concept of tourism forces tourism research into a very broad scope, especially for the private sector. There is need for new understanding of people and their characteristics important to travel. Developers of resorts, destination attractions, tour circuits, and tour packages and marketers of tourism increasingly seek information on people's activities and on the factors that influence these activities. Providers of transportation increasingly realize the need for information on linkages between elements of the system, on increasing accessibility, and on improvements in consumer service. Impacts of fuel costs and supply are important areas of research study. Providers of the many services within tourism—accommodations, food, entertainment — seek improved information on both the internal operational factors of their business and behavioral characteristics of travelers.

The great array of natural and cultural resource agencies of governments and nonprofit organizations seek new and better information on analysis of resource assets, impacts of development and use, and management and control systems. Those elements of the tourism system engaged in promotion, advertising, publicity, guidebooks, and travel writing are looking for research facts on the value of their efforts. Policymakers in government increasingly support research studies that provide foundations for legislation and policy in the growing field of tourism. Educators seek better information for research and the training and education of young people and adults who are choosing careers in this important field.

This brief review touches only lightly upon the great variety of tourism research needs and suggests that the methods and techniques of research must be tailored to these specific needs. In order to do this, the body of known techniques must be surveyed and the several disciplinary approaches must be examined for possible assistance and enlightenment.

MANY DISCIPLINES INVOLVED

The breadth and complexity of the field of tourism demand the use of any and all disciplinary approaches that are most useful in the solution of problems or the provision of new information. This statement is contrary to the popular belief that only one discipline, such as marketing, is needed or useful in the field of tourism. The emphasis, instead, should be placed on the nature of the information to be gathered and the problems to be solved; then, to tap every resource, technique, and method appropriate for the purpose. Frequently, tourism problems demand team research involving several disciplines providing interaction as well as special input. The following discussion describes several disciplines and their relevance to tourism research. (See the Suggested Sources of Information for resource materials and examples of tourism research.)

MARKETING

By far the most active discipline in tourism, marketing, is an application of behavior, business, and economics with its own set of research approaches. Marketing research "is an *instrument* of decision-making" (Wentz 1972). Therefore, it is an applied field directed toward a specific function within the firm. Wentz identifies five types of marketing research: market and sales, distribution, product, business-economics, and advertising.

Adapting the scientific method to marketing, secondary data and survey research methods are used most frequently. Both experimental and nonexperimental designs are employed. Churchill (1976) emphasizes that the design must stem from the problem and classifies research into three categories: exploratory research (discovery of ideas and insights), descriptive research (frequencies, trends in consumption), and causal research (cause-and-effect relationships).

Because the emphasis is the solution of a problem, marketing research follows generally the scientific method: formulation of the problem; determination of sources of information and the research design; preparation of data-collection forms; design of the sample and collection of the data; analysis and interpretation of the data; and preparation of the research report (Churchill 1976).

A special subset within the study of marketing, very important to tourism, is that of *consumer behavior*. This topic has been the focus of scholars for several years, building upon the mix between psychology, sociology, and economics. Consumer behavior forms the foundation for much of marketing decision making. It also provides information and insight into social policy in consumer affairs, and it affords better information of direct value to the consumer (Kassarjian and Robertson 1973).

Consumer behavioral research could be classified into several emphases. One emphasis is that of consumer perception of brand, price, and the influences of levels of learning. Then, studies of motivation and personality are important as they relate to decisions to purchase. Of equal concern to marketers of tourism is research in attitude and attitude change. The social realm, such as role of the individual within the family or social class, has become an important area of study. These and many other emphases have great importance in application to tourism. Some have already begun; other applications show great promise.

GEOGRAPHY

Few disciplines are as tightly related to tourism as is geography, the science of spatial analysis with its several subfields. "It is the major discipline that is concerned with the identification, analysis and interpretation of spatial distributions of phenomena and their areal associations as they occur on the surface of the earth" (Haring and Lounsbury 1975). Clearly, geography and geographers have much to contribute to tourism research.

Many geographers employ the basic rules and procedures of scientific research. While experimental research is possible, it is more common to find the normative and historical types in geographic studies relating to tourism. The normative type, well suited to redistribution patterns of people during vacation and leisure periods, includes observation of events and evaluation to determine relationships or norms. "The historical method relies on source detection, evaluation, and analysis of findings in determining solutions or conclusions to research problems" (Haring and Lounsbury 1975).

The usual steps taken in research in geography are: (1) formulation of the research problem, (2) definition of hypothesis, (3) determination of the type of data to be collected, (4) collection of data, and (5) analyzing and processing the data. In addition, geography often relies on field techniques and mapping. Aerial photography, remote sensing, and hand cartography are often added to survey research techniques for the gathering and display of data.

ANTHROPOLOGY

The field of anthropology, because it is the science of man and culture, has strong ties with tourism, an important component of man and culture. Whereas other disciplines are more specific, anthropology seeks to identify, describe, and explain holistically the many manifestations of mankind.

The most conspicuous subdivision of anthropology related to tourism is that of *archeology*, providing information and sites of great value as tourist attractions. Of equal value to tourism is *sociocultural* anthropology, which studies human social and cultural life. Two other subdivisions of anthropology, *biological* (physical) and *linguistic*, may have potential contributions to make.

Anthropology utilizes both exploratory descriptive study and hypothesis-testing research. Descriptive studies, often using participant observation and informal interviewing as tools, frequently provide foundations for more highly focused hypothesis testing later on. Hypothesis testing is basically scientific research methodology but for anthropology may be directed along one or more of four paradigms: (1) pretest-posttest, (2) static-group comparison, (3) nonequivalent control group, and (4) control group (Brim and Spain 1974).

Because tourism is increasingly a worldwide phenomenon and crosses many cultures, there is need for better understanding of these cultures and the impact of tourism upon such cultures. "Anthropology has important contributions to offer to the study of tourism, especially through a neo-traditional approach that includes the basic ethnography and its national character variant, as well as the acculturation model and the awareness that tourism is only one element in culture change" (Smith 1980).

BEHAVIOR

Psychology and sociology, while different disciplines, have for years provided research insight into human behavior and how it is organized. Research techniques are increasingly employed to provide information and explanation of what activity takes place, as well as how, when, and where. The more difficult question of why it takes place continues to stimulate probing into factors influencing behavior, such as psychographic studies in tourism. Since tourism is dependent upon people's propensity, habits, and desires, behavioral research is a major element in building new knowledge and solving tourism problems.

In the behavioral sciences, two basic approaches are made in utilizing the scientific method: experimental and nonexperimental (Kerlinger 1973). The desire is to engage in experimental research whenever possible— whenever important variables can be manipulated, such as changes in management practice, room type, or transport vehicles. Other variables, however, are less amenable to manipulation, such as religious values, honesty, taste and esthetics, and many others.

The process of behavioral research often uses methods of survey research and follows the basic steps of the scientific method: (1) defining the problem, (2) identifying hypotheses, (3) selecting methodology, (4) collecting data, (5) analyzing data, and (6) presenting results and conclusions.

BUSINESS

Business, as a discipline, increasingly recognizes the value of research and therefore the business sector of tourism has much to gain from research. Emory (1976) identifies four areas of research interest by business. First are those research studies that *report*, basically in statistical form. The research design may be simple but the products may be very valuable to management for decision making. Second, business research is often *description*, including comparisons and relationships beyond mere reporting. By adding certain facts and assumptions, a third form of research, that of *prediction*, is performed. Finally, when *explanation* of the forces that account for the phenomenon is included, usually more sophisticated research is required.

Frequently, the term research and development is associated with business. Actually, while some experimental and survey research methods are utilized, this is more directly in the area of technology—the handling of engineering and technical problems. In business, operations research is closely related and usually emphasizes production and goods-handling. However, in actual business organization, it may become merged with marketing research and research and development departments.

According to Gearing *et al*. (1976), operations research in tourism is closely allied to economic analysis but places greater emphasis on decision-making situations that arise from real life. Operations research involves three steps: (1) structuring into a mathematical model, (2) exploring systematic procedures, and (3) developing solutions with optimal values.

Adaptation of the scientific method to business research often results in the following research process: (1) exploration of the situation, (2) development of research design, (3) collection of data, and (4) analysis and interpretation of results (Emory 1976). The two most frequent research designs used in business are experimental and simulation.

HUMAN ECOLOGY

Popularly known is the contribution of the science of ecology—the biological study of the relationships between organisms and their environments. This emphasizes the concept of niche, that organisms adapt to their environments. Human ecology, however, defines man as set apart from all other animals in his ability to reverse this relationship. "Man has decided that he shall manage all the resources of the planetary life-support system" (Sargent 1974). "Most important of all, therefore, is the notion that culture and biology, in man, are conceptually inseparable" (Johnston 1974). Human ecology, therefore, is the study of man's role in reshaping the environment, including the development of areas for leisure—recreation and tourism.

The study of human ecology, and therefore the research methods, taps many other disciplines in the use of the scientific method. Environmental physiology, medicine, and physical anthropology, as well as sociology and economics, are drawn upon to study human ecology. A case has been made (Murdock 1979) for the use of human ecological research in assessment of environmental impacts. And, even the urban ecosystem has been studied, resulting in a typology as related to urban landscapes (Brady *et al*. 1979).

The discipline of human ecology holds promise of providing new insights into the provision of and evaluation of tourism resource development.

HISTORY

History, previously preoccupied with chronological documentation, has increasingly applied scientific methods to describe and explain the past. The discipline of history is making many valuable inputs to tourism. Documentation of the past development and growth of the many facets of tourism provides the context for evaluation of today's tourism. Case histories of tourist businesses and tourist destination areas contribute to tourism decision making today. Greatly expanding historical restoration and interpretation, as tourist attractions, demand accurate research of past events and details of sites and architecture. Modern tourists require increasingly sophisticated description and presentation of historic places.

In addition to the gathering of primary source data, a very important task of the research historian is that of criticism and verification of data (Hockett 1949). It is for this purpose that new hypotheses are formed and new research is designed. The discovery of new evidence sometimes refutes earlier conclusions from historical research.

Historical research is so dependent upon statements that the aim of much research is to verify and substantiate these statements about the past. Some of the key steps of criticism, as outlined by Hockett (1949), are: (1) external criticism (determination of circumstances attending the production of a document, question of original form of document), (2) internal criticism (positive criticism, negative criticism), and (3) determinable facts (allusions, contemporary statements, cross-check of statements, fit).

Shafer (1969) emphasizes the importance of collecting and using historical evidence in a systematic manner, and identifies the following as essential elements of use: analysis and synthesis; the working hypothesis; bias and subjectivity; facts as values, ideas, objects; relevance; and final synthesis.

POLITICAL SCIENCE

Increasingly, tourism is being recognized as having important political implications. Developed countries seek new policies to protect and maintain present levels of tourism and developing countries promote policies of expansion. Less well known is political science research and the opportunity it holds for tourism.

The basic tenets of the scientific method are followed in political science research. However, the nature of the field requires special problem identification along three lines: "(1) simple description of the phenomenon, (2) relational analysis of various aspects of the phenomenon, or (3) causal interpretation of the phenomenon, its antecedents and its consequents" (Leege and Francis 1974). In general, the research designs of social science are used, but Leege and Francis identify the following as important to political science research: case study; one-group pretest-posttest; static-group comparison; pretest-posttest control group; Solomon four-group; posttest only control group; nonequivalent control group; separate sample pretest-posttest: counterbalanced; time series; multiple time series equivalent time samples; and mixed designs.

PLANNING AND DESIGN

Planning and design (urban and regional planning, architecture, landscape architecture, engineering, interior design) are distinct professions with many subdivisions. Yet they have some common elements, such as creating new physical environments for human use—in this case, tourism. Today, all these professions are seeking new and better data upon which to base their plans and creative designs. This research is not along any common lines of strategy but generally reflects the scientific method by seeking objective information and solution to problems.

In the land use and landscape analysis field, for example, many techniques are being experimented with. These represent aerial photography, hand graphics, and computer techniques of inventorying and evaluating physical land factors of importance to planners of recreation and tourism developments. Occasionally, studies are made of developed facilities to gain insight into how well the designed environment functions are planned.

Some sources of landscape analysis techniques are particularly important to tourism. Many studies have been produced by the U.S. Department of Agriculture, Forest Service. The *Proceedings of Our National Landscape: A Conference on Applied Techniques for Analysis and Management of the Visual Resource* (1979) contains many papers on topics such as: field trip simulation; descriptive approaches; computerized and quantitative methods; psychometric and social science approaches; and applications to recreation and tourism.

FUTURISM

While traditionalists may scoff at the notion of futurism as a distinct discipline, the field has risen to the level of considerable importance and relevance to tourism. Philosophers, scientists, technicians, and planners have joined in making insightful studies of trends, not necessarily to predict but to identify future possibilities. Futuristics can be defined as "applied history" (Cornish 1977).

Emerging among the futurists are many approaches toward gaining insight into the future. Some key approaches, used with varying degrees of success, are: (1) trend extrapolation, (2) scenarios, (3) use of experts (Delphi technique), and (4) models, games, and simulation. Already, several worldwide organizations and future-oriented research institutes have been organized and are producing research studies. Tourism, extremely vulnerable to many factors of the future, may look more and more to the works of these scientists involved in future-oriented research.

INPUT FROM OTHER DISCIPLINES

The complexity of tourism demands research input from many disciplines. Those discussed above are merely a start on a long list of disciplines applicable to the development of new information for tourism or to the solution of tourism problems.

For example, leisure and recreation studies are building a distinct area of interest with special research approaches and literature involving very important aspects of tourism. Park and resource management research, involving land use as well as behavior, has direct bearing on tourism. Engineering research is a vital component of many businesses directly related to tourism products and equipment. The field of communications is frequently identified as a distinct discipline and is having tremendous impact on many elements of tourism. Wildlife, fisheries, and forestry are often considered discreet disciplines and their research has direct bearing on tourism, especially in the planning and management of attractions. Probably the greatest amount of outdoor recreation research in the United States has been sponsored by the several experiment stations of the U.S. Department of Agriculture, Forest Service. Marine engineering and oceanography, with their many concerns over coastal development, are important to coastal tourism. The field of law is of increasing importance to the many facets of tourism everywhere. Medicine, health, and nutrition are at the very foundation of many concepts of personal fitness and use of leisure. The leisure implications of veterinary medicine are great, including the control of pet disease and management of zoos as tourist attractions. And, of course, studies in tourism economics are needed in order to go beyond the impact of the firm.

CONCLUSION

More and more, the many social, environmental, and cultural, as well as economic, implications of tourism are being recognized. Even this brief review of a few disciplines demonstrates current and potential input of varied research that is valuable to tourism. Future businesses, organizations, educational institutions, and governments have the opportunity of harnessing many ways of gaining new knowledge and solutions to problems of tourism.

While the several disciplines appear to utilize different research approaches, there is more fundamental similarity than difference. Throughout, the basic aim is to perform objective, systematic, logical, and substantive research. Specific problem-solving research is becoming an integral part of many tourist-oriented businesses. At the same time, universally applicable research is increasingly assisting nations, states, provinces, cities, organizations, and educational institutions in gaining greater insight into tourism.

Techniques and methodologies vary somewhat across disciplines but all seem to desire quantifiable methods whenever applicable. For some topics, it is sufficient to have the opinions of key leaders or specialists. However, more generalizable research, applicable to large masses of population, requires representative sampling designs. Because tourism does not have a long history of research, today descriptive and exploratory studies are providing worthwhile data.

The main conclusion is that tourism is a complex phenomenon and therefore the research of tourism must utilize all the disciplinary approaches that will be most useful in solving problems and in providing new information.

SUGGESTED SOURCES OF INFORMATION

The following sources are a sampling of research studies relating to the several disciplines. Further contact with the separate disciplines or agencies supporting such disciplinary research should provide other titles of interest.

GENERAL

Analysis Methods and Techniques for Recreation Research and Leisure Studies (1977), Ontario Research Council, Ottawa, Canada: Environment Canada.

Goeldner, Charles R. (1975), "Where to Find Travel Research Facts," *Journal of Travel Research*, (13) 4, 1–6.

Identifying Traveler Markets, Research Methodologies (1978), U.S. Department of Commerce, U.S. Travel Service, Washington, D.C.: U.S. Government Printing Office.

MARKETING

Archer, Brian H. (1976), *Demand Forecasting in Tourism*, Bangor Occasional Papers in Economics, No. 9, Bangor, Wales: University of Wales Press.

Churchill, Gilbert A., Jr. (1976), *Marketing Research: Methodological Foundations*, Hinsdale, Illinois: Dryden Press.

Johnston, Warren E., and Garry H. Elsner (1972), "Variability in Use among Ski Areas: A Statistical Study of the California Market Region," *Journal of Leisure Research*, (4) 1, 43–49.

Kassarjian, Harold H., and Thomas S. Robertson (1973), *Perspectives in Consumer Behavior*, Glenview, Illinois: Scott Foresman.

Mayo, Edward J. (1973), "Regional Travel Behavior, Research for Changing Travel Patterns: Interpretation and Utilization," *Fourth Annual Conference Proceedings*, The Travel Research Association, Salt Lake City: University of Utah, pp. 211–217.

Wentz, Walter B. (1972), *Marketing Research: Management and Methods*, New York: Harper & Row.

GEOGRAPHY

Haring, L. Lloyd, and John F. Lounsbury (1975), *Introduction to Scientific Geographic Research*, Dubuque, Iowa: W.C. Brown.

Van Doren, C.S., and Larry Gustke (1979), "Spatial Analysis of the U.S. Lodging Industry," *Tourism Planning and Development Issues*, Proceedings of the International Symposium on Tourism in the Next Decade, Washington, D.C.: George Washington University, pp. 321–332.

Williams, Anthony V., and Wilbur Zelinsky (1970), "On Some Patterns in International Tourist Flows," *Economic Geography*, (46) 4, 549–567.

ANTHROPOLOGY

Brim, John A., and David H. Spain (1974), *Research Design in Anthropology*, New York: Holt, Rinehart & Winston.

Kottak, Conrad Phillip (1978), *Anthropology: The Exploration of Human Diversity*, (2nd ed.), New York: Random House.

Lange, Frederick W. (1980), "The Impact of Tourism on Cultural Patrimony: A Costa Rican Example," *Annals of Tourism Research*, (7) 1, 56–68.

Pelto, Pertti J., and Gretel H. Pelto (1978), *Anthropological Research* (2nd ed.), London: Cambridge University Press.

Richter, Dolores (1978), "The Tourist Art Market as a Factor in Social Change," *Annals of Tourism Research*, (5) 3, 323–338.

Smith, Valene L. (1980), "Anthropology and Tourism," *Annals of Tourism Research*, (7) 1, 13–33.

BEHAVIOR

Darden, William R., and William D. Perreault, Jr. (1975), "A Multivariate Analysis of Media Exposure and Vacation Behavior with Life Style Covariates," *Journal of Consumer Research*, (2) 2, 93–103.

Darden, William R., William D. Perreault, Jr., and Michael T. Troncalli (1975–1976), "Psychographic Analysis of Vacation Innovators," *Review of Business and Economic Research*, (11) 2, 1–18.

Kerlinger, Fred N. (1973), *Foundations of Behavioral Research*, (2nd ed.), New York: Holt, Rinehart & Winston.

Levy, John (1977), "Transactional Analysis and the Airline Ticket Counter Transaction," *Eighth Annual Conference Proceedings*, The Travel Research Association, Salt Lake City: University of Utah, pp. 163–165.

Schewe, Charles D., and Roger J. Calatone (1978), "Psychographic Segmentation of Tourists," *Journal of Travel Research*, (16) 3, 14–20.

BUSINESS

Bevins, Malcolm I., Wilbur F. LaPage, and Daniel P. Wilcox (1979). *The Campground Industry*, Technical Report NE-53, Broomall, Pennsylvania: Northeastern Forest Experiment Station, U.S. Forest Service.

Crawford, William D., and E.C. Nebel (1977), "Travel Activity in the New Orleans Economy," *Louisiana Business Survey*, (8) 3, 2–5.

Emory, C. William (1976), *Business Research Methods*, Homewood, Illinois: Irwin.

Gearing, Charles E., William W. Swart, and Turgut Var (1976), *Planning For Tourism Development*, New York: Praeger.

Musselman, Vernon A., and Eugene H. Hughes (1973), *Introduction to Modern Business: Analysis and Interpretation* (6th ed.), Englewood Cliffs, New Jersey: Prentice–Hall.

Survey of the Labor Situation in the Accommodation and Food Services Sector of the Alberta Tourism Industry (1974), Prepared by Underwood, McLellan and Assoc., Calgary, Alberta, Canada: Travel Alberta.

HUMAN ECOLOGY

Brady, R.L., *et al.* (1979), "A Typology for the Urban Ecosystem and Its Relationship to Larger Biogeographical Landscape Units," *Urban Ecology*, (4) 11–28.

Filani, M.O. (1975), "The Role of National Tourist Associations in the Preserving of the Environment in Africa,"

Journal of Travel Research, (13) 4, 7–12.

Johnston, Francis E. (1974), "Human Biology and the Uniqueness of Man," *Human Ecology* (Frederick Sargent II, Ed.), Amsterdam: North-Holland.

Murdock, Steve H. (1979), "The Potential Role of the Ecological Framework in Impact Analysis," *Rural Sociology*, 44 (3), 543–565.

Sargent, Frederick, II (1974), "Nature and Scope of Human Ecology," *Human Ecology* (Frederick Sargent II, Ed.), Amsterdam: North-Holland.

Wall, Geoffrey, and Ishan Maccum Ali (1977), "The Impact of Tourism in Trinidad and Tobago," *Annals of Tourism Research*, (5) Special Issue, 43–49.

HISTORY

Casson, Lionel (1971), "After 2,000 Years Tours Have Changed but Not Tourists," *Smithsonian*, (2) 6, 53–59.

Hockett, Homer Carey (1949), *Introduction to Research in American History* (2nd Ed.), New York: Macmillan.

King, Doris Elizabeth (1957) "The First-Class Hotel and the Age of the Common Man," *The Journal of Southern History*, (23) 2, 173–188.

Shafer, Robert J. (1969), *A Guide to Historical Method*, Homewood, Illinois: Dorsey Press.

POLITICAL SCIENCE

Gunn, Clare A. (1979), "Public-Private Interface," *Land and Leisure: Concepts and Methods in Outdoor Recreation* (2nd ed.) (Carlton S. Van Doren *et al*, Eds.), Chicago: Maaroufa Press.

Hoover, Kenneth R. (1976), *The Elements of Social Scientific Thinking*, New York: St. Martin's Press.

Jacob, Herbert (1972), "Contact with Government Agencies: A Preliminary Analysis of the Distribution of Government Services," *American Journal of Political Science*, (16) 1, 123–146.

Jenkins, C.L. (1980), "Tourism Policies in Developing Countries: A Critique," *Tourism Management*, (1) 1, 22–29.

Leege, David C., and Wayne L. Francis (1974), *Political Research*, New York: Basic Books.

PLANNING AND DESIGN

Bargur, Jona, and Avner Arbel (1975), "A Comprehensive Approach to the Planning of the Tourism Industry," *Journal of Travel Research*, (14) 2, 10–15.

Deardon, Philip (1980), "A Statistical Technique for the Evaluation of the Visual Quality of the Landscape for Land-Use Planning Purposes," *Journal of Environmental Management*, (10) 51–68.

Gunn, Clare A., *et al.* (1972), *Cultural Benefits from Metropolitan River Recreation—San Antonio Prototype*, Bulletin MP-1046, The Texas Agricultural Experiment Station and Texas Water Resources Institute, College Station, Texas: Texas A&M University.

Proceedings of Our National Landscape: A Conference on

Applied Techniques for Analysis and Management of the Visual Resource (1979), Berkeley, California: Pacific Southwest Forest and Range Experiment Station.

Tuan, Yi-Fu (1974), *Topophilia. A Study of Environmental Perception, Attitudes and Values*, Englewood Cliffs, New Jersey: Prentice–Hall.

Tuckman, Bruce W. (1972), *Conducting Educational Research*, New York: Harcourt, Brace, Jovanovich.

FUTURISM

Cornish, Edward (1977), *The Study of the Future*, Washington, D.C.: The World Future Society.

Kahn, Herman (1979a), "Tourism and the Next Decade," Presentation at the International Symposium: Tourism and the Next Decade, The George Washington University, Washington, D.C., March 11–15, 1979.

Kahn, Herman (1979b), *World Economic Development*, Boulder, Colorado: Westview Press.

Papson, Stephen (1979), "Tourism: World's Biggest Industry in the Twenty-First Century?" *The Futurist*, (13) 4, 249–257.

2

Roles of Research in Tourism Management

J.R. BRENT RITCHIE

The University of Calgary
Calgary, Alberta, Canada

*T*here are many different kinds of tourism research and an even greater number of research methods and techniques. This reality creates two major difficulties for the research professional; it creates confusion among managers as to the true nature of research, and it frequently leads to inappropriate research approaches being used in a given decision-making situation. This chapter attempts to clarify the roles of research as they relate to the field of tourism management. It stresses that to be effective, research strategies must correspond to the nature and level of management decisions.

The concept of research is diffuse and highly abused. While it is generally agreed that the term refers to some systematic form of investigation of a given topic, its true significance is seen to vary with the area of application as well as the perceptions of different individuals within a given field. Archaeological research involving the unearthing of skeletons in remote regions of the world has only a vague conceptual relation to research designed to determine the optimal characteristics of a package tour. This comparison is not meant as a value judgment, in fact, the intention is quite the reverse. Each of these types of research has an important role to play within its proper context. The fact remains, however, that in each case the single word "research" describes a quite different reality. As a result, the term tends to lose its ability to communicate meaning; its significance becomes all too dangerously a function of the individual user rather than being one of objective group consensus.

Even within the more limited field of decision-oriented studies designed to improve the effectiveness of management actions in the field of tourism, the term "research" implies widely varying ideas. The current terminology describing management research abounds with a series of dichotomous expressions derived from a variety of the source disciplines upon which management research methods are based. These include: fundamental and applied, analytical and descriptive, exploratory and causal, empirical and theoretical, cross-sectional and longitudinal, and short term and long term. Such terms—because of their number, interdependence, and generally vague definitions—often are confusing to the manager in his attempts to understand the nature and roles of research within the management process. They hinder his ability to see clearly the potential applications and contributions of research to the improvement of his own effectiveness.

This discussion does not imply that the types of terminology just mentioned are irrelevant or useless. Employed in the proper context, such terms play a useful role in discussing and describing the research process. It remains true, however, that these terms have not always been constructed so as to explain or clarify the nature of various aspects of research as it applies to the management process.

This chapter is concerned with defining the roles and characteristics of the research process as it applies to tourism management decision making. The objective here is to provide a rational basis for classifying and describing different decision-oriented research needs using a framework based on three major dimensions directly related to the management process: the level of management activity; the stage of the management process; and the function of the management activity. The nature of these dimensions will be seen to substantially modify the nature of management information

13

needs required for decision making. Because of these varying needs, it is essential that the appropriate type of research methodology and data collection instrument be employed to satisfy each need.

Based on the proposed framework of research types and an understanding of their roles, limits, and corresponding methodologies, it is hoped that tourism managers will be able to more effectively choose the type of information-gathering process most relevant to each particular decision-making situation.

RESEARCH AS AN INFORMATION SOURCE

Philip Kotler (1981) views the total information system of an organization as consisting of an internal information system composed of management accounting information, an external information system designed to monitor changing conditions in the organization's environment, and a research information system capable of providing in-depth studies pertaining to specific problems or situations. It is important for managers to realize that research should form an integral part of the overall information system related to their decision-making needs, otherwise, the risks of both missing and duplicating information are high.

It should be recognized that the composition of the internal, external, and research information subsystems is in constant evolution as the total system responds to different conditions both outside and within the organization. For example, it might be decided that a specific type of information gathered through a special research project and which has been found particularly useful should be collected on a regular basis and incorporated into either the internal or external information system as the case may be. Similarly, it is possible that information currently collected on a continuous basis (such as the monitoring of tourist attitudes) may be judged too costly in comparison to its contribution to decision making. Data gathering in such instances might become the object of periodic research projects when it is deemed necessary.

In order to classify research functions within the context of management decision making, it is essential to identify the key variables which capture the fundamental nature of the dimensions and which can be considered to characterize the nature of the management process within an organization.

The model presented in this chapter proposes three major dimensions of the management process which it is felt can be usefully employed to define the nature of tourism management information needs and to identify the types of research methodologies most appropriate for satisfying these needs.

The dimensions shown in Fig. 1 are defined as: stages of the management process; levels of management activity within an organization; and functional areas of management activity.

STAGES OF THE MANAGEMENT PROCESS

The number and identity of the stages of the management process are by no means universally agreed upon by scholars in the field. For purposes of the discussion here, four stages (analysis, planning, execution, and control) will be retained as the components of dimension one of the framework.

Analysis represents the initial stage of the management process in which executives are essentially interested in understanding the nature and scope of a given problem. Obviously, by its very nature research has an important role to play in the analysis stage.

Planning, which flows logically from analysis and is often difficult to distinguish from it, may be viewed as the setting of objectives and the evaluation/choice of alternatives for meeting those objectives. Here again formal research has a high potential contribution.

Execution of the selected course of action represents the translation of ideas into reality; the role of research may be considered less important at this stage. Despite this general comment, there are occasions when the collection and monitoring of data during the implementation of a given action may be an essential part of the management information gathering process.

The *control* stage of the management process is that which attempts to measure the extent to which a given activity or action has achieved its original objectives. It is more recently that the potential contribution of research at this stage has been recognized. The contribution involves the returns to be derived from formal research methods in establishing and implementing performance measures which are both reliable and representative of reality. Perhaps more important, such methods provide a mechanism for systematically and objectively exploring the causes or reasons for the successes or failures resulting from management actions.

LEVELS OF MANAGEMENT ACTIVITY

The second dimension of the proposed research classification framework is based on the levels of management activity within an organization, as defined by Robert Anthony (1965). These levels are termed strategic, managerial, and operational. Each deals with a range of activities having distinct characteristics which reflect the nature of the management problems with which they deal.

Strategic activities concern long-term plans and policies that determine or change the character of an organization. The management information needs related to this level of activity can generally be qualified as long-term or broad-scale indicators which measure critical elements of the economic, social, political, and technological environments having a potential impact on the organization. Naisbitt's (1982) review of megatrends affecting societal development is an example of such information.

Managerial or *tactical activities* involve those actions associated with the ongoing administration of the enterprise which are carried on within the limits of objectives and policies defined at the strategic level. As such, the information needs of management at this level usually involve relatively well defined data bearing directly on the solution of a given problem or decision.

Operational activities describe those specific transactions involved in carrying out the tasks required to achieve the variety of objectives defined at the management level. The management information needs related to such tasks tend to be highly structured and recurring in nature.

FUNCTIONAL AREAS OF ACTIVITY

The previous two dimensions of the proposed framework for research classification have applied generally to an organization regardless of the different functional activities which it must execute. It is obvious that the nature of these functions also plays an important role in determining the information and research needs of management. Given this fact, the third dimension of the framework is seen to contain the following components: finance, marketing, production, control, personnel, and the general management function of coordination.

SOME ADDITIONAL DIMENSIONS

There exist a number of additional dimensions or criteria which might be used to classify tourism management information and research needs. For example, the distinction between internal and external information might be employed. Similarly, the difference between fundamental and applied research is often used, and so on. However, the three dimensions which have been retained in the model are felt to be the most relevant and powerful with respect to their ability to capture the essence of the management process insofar as it relates to information and research needs. As such, only the perceived utility of the proposed framework will indicate whether the correct dimensions have been retained.

CLASSIFICATION OF MANAGEMENT RESEARCH

Based on the three previously defined dimensions of the management process, it is possible to identify within the framework five broad categories of research which are used in varying degrees by different management teams. These five categories, shown in Fig. 1, are referred to as operational research, managerial research, policy research, action research, and evaluation research.

Operational research consists primarily of a range of quantitative/analytical techniques designed to formulate and test decision rules which will permit management to optimize relations between the inputs and outputs of a given operational procedure. As such it tends to arrive at programmed models prescribing the actions that are most efficient under a given set of circumstances. Because of the very applied nature of operations research, it tends to integrate all stages of the management process (as shown in Fig. 1). Indeed, built-in feedback loops among different stages are a distinguishing feature of many operational research models. Examples of such research in tourism would include studies to determine the optimal traffic flow within and through a major attraction or to establish decision rules for the setting of overbooking levels in a hotel (Toh, 1985).

Managerial research covers a broad range of research types including those most commonly employed by management. Typically such research deals with an important problem of limited scope for which management has need of additional information on which to base a decision. Examples of such studies include those concerning the market potential for a new attraction, the best approach for the implementation of a new accounting system, or a feasibility study for a new hotel. In general, such research projects have one feature in common: they concern the seeking of solutions as to what should be done to solve a given problem and how to implement this solution. While there are exceptions, there are relatively few studies related to the control aspect of the management process, that is, studies which attempt to evaluate the degree of success of a given marketing activity, accounting system, or investment program. In brief, managerial research tends to be future and present oriented as opposed to taking an interest in the effectiveness of prior actions. This generalization is reflected in Fig. 1.

Action research is the third broad category of approaches suggested by the proposed framework (Whyte and Hamilton, 1964). This form of research involves a continuous gathering and analyzing of research data during the normal ongoing operations of an organization or the execution of a specific management program and the simultaneous feeding of the results into the organization so as to change its model of functioning. As such, it is seen that action research is a continuing, task-oriented form of study designed to provide continuous feedback regarding the performance of a management activity and to improve that performance through direct forms of intervention suggested by the research findings. As shown in Fig. 1, action research is considered to be a part of the tactical level of management activity, and, because of its continuous and recursive nature, it is carried out within both the execution and control stages of the management process.

Strategic research is a more recent phenomenon insofar as its recognition as a formal field of research is concerned. As such, it is less well defined and understood. Despite this situation, two major categories of strategic research can be identified. Policy research relates to the strategic analysis and planning activities of a tourism organization (Fig. 1) on the tourism system as a whole. It appears to be composed of three elements: research which studies how policy formulation occurs with a view to understanding and improving the process; research which is designed to analyze situations at the strategic level and to formulate overall policy proposals; and research which systematically evaluates the priorities to be accorded to conflic-

ting/complementary policy alternatives (Bauer and Gergen, 1968). Methodologies related to actual cases of strategic analysis and policy formulation range from various forms of decision theory to the expert judgment consensus approach commonly referred to as the Delphi Method (see Moeller and Shafer, Chapter 34) and the Nominal Group Technique (see Ritchie, Chapter 37). Approaches to the ordering of the attractiveness of various policy options and studying the trade-offs among them have been referred to as priority analysis (Ritchie, 1985).

The final portion of the conceptual framework pertains to the most recent application of formal research methodology which has been introduced into management research. *Evaluation research* can be viewed as the complement of policy research in which the objectives, strategies, and programs so derived are monitored both during and after their implementation (Fig. 1) in order to determine their degree of success and failure as well as the underlying causes of their impact (Weiss, 1972).

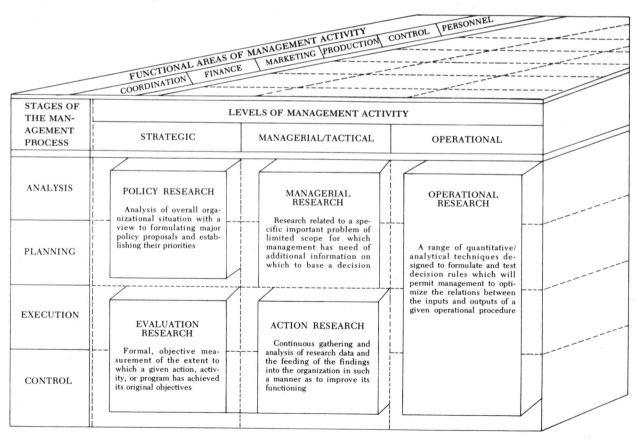

FIGURE 1   Classification of research methodologies according to three dimensions of the management process.

IMPLICATIONS OF THE RESEARCH CLASSIFICATION FRAMEWORK

The remainder of this chapter will compare the five research categories across five important attributes of the research process: the nature of the management situation to which the research methodology applies; the type of information/data required in each situation; the characteristics of the principal data collection instruments used by the research approach; the general nature of the research approach required for obtaining this data; and, finally, the nature of the research output provided to management. This comparison is summarized in Table 1.

NATURE OF THE MANAGEMENT SITUATION

The three different dimensions of the management process give rise to at least five different types of decision-making situations and consequently a category of research appropriate to each situation. Column one of Table 1 is a brief restatement of the conditions defining policy, evaluation, managerial, action, and operational research and as such is intended to provide the logical link between the classification framework (Fig. 1) and its implications concerning the appropriate research characteristic (Table 1).

TYPE OF INFORMATION/DATA REQUIRED

Each of the five research categories has distinctly different data needs. Policy research requires primarily macrolevel data related to the present values and anticipated trends of the major economic, social, technical, and political factors which have a present or potential bearing on tourism as a whole or on the success or failure of the activities of the individual tourism operator. Much of this data is available from government sources, some is available from the private sector, and the remainder must be collected by the organization requiring it.

Evaluation research requires specific data related to the evaluation criteria chosen to represent the objective of a particular facility, activity, or program. As such, there seldom exist readily available data which correspond satisfactorily to the operational definitions of the criteria used to evaluate the program's performance. Therefore, such data must usually be collected within a specially designed project.

Management/tactical research also requires specific data relevant to a particular problem. Such data generally can be placed in one of two categories: descriptive information providing an overall understanding of the key factors involved in a given problem situation or highly precise information used for in-depth analysis of a limited number of variables influencing a particular situation.

Similarly, the data required within the context of a given action research project are directly related to the ongoing situation being studied. Specifically, the type of information needed pertains to both the performance of a given system or organization and the nature of interpersonal/intergroup relations which may affect organizational performance. It will be noted that in some respects there are similarities between the approach and information needs of action research and evaluation research; however, the differences are much more important. Action research strongly deemphasizes evaluative aspects of performance measures and uses them only as guidelines to indicate problem areas and to take immediate corrective action.

Finally, operational research has highly precise information needs related to particular tasks within the organization. Such information must normally be measured using means which provide highly accurate, reliable, and timely data.

CHARACTERISTICS OF DATA COLLECTION METHODOLOGIES/INSTRUMENTS

While it is conceptually easy to distinguish between a data collection methodology and the techniques employed subsequently to extract information from this data, such a distinction becomes less pronounced in the actual practice of research. Accordingly, these two important items (columns three and four of Table 1) and their interactions will be discussed simultaneously.

Policy research employs at least three important types of measures as data sources. While varying widely in their nature, each of these serves as input to analytical techniques which focus on the prediction of future conditions and the implications of these conditions on the activities of the organization.

Longitudinal/time series measures of major indicators form one important source. The level of the data (international, national, regional) depends on the nature of the problem to be studied. Such data can usually be collected only on a continuing basis with respect to economic, social, political, or technical phenomena of interest to a number of sectors of society. As such, they are limited in their ability to provide insight into very specific strategic questions. Thus, to complement such data, researchers in this field often employ the individual judgments of experts having knowledge related to the specific problem of interest. These individual judgments are then combined in a variety of ways in an attempt to reach a consensus opinion across experts. The Delphi Method is one well known version of the consensus approach in which the opinions of experts are obtained iteratively in order to focus on most probable future conditions (see Moeller and Shafer, Chapter 34).

A quite different approach to futures prediction involves large-scale system simulation models designed to test the impact of alternative policy decisions

TABLE 1   Implications of the Classification Framework Concerning Research Methods and Data Collection Frameworks

RESEARCH CATEGORY	NATURE OF THE MANAGEMENT SITUATION	TYPE OF INFORMATIONAL DATA REQUIRED	CHARACTERISTICS OF PRINCIPAL DATA COLLECTION METHODOLOGIES/ INSTRUMENTS	NATURE OF THE APPROPRIATE METHODS AND TECHNIQUES FOR EXTRACTING INFORMATION FROM THE DATA	NATURE OF RESEARCH OUTPUT FROM A MANAGEMENT PERSPECTIVE
Policy Research	Need to provide well defined but broad guidelines which serve to establish priorities to direct the organization's activities.	Macro data related to present values and anticipated trends of major economic, social, technical, and political factors bearing on the organization's activities	Longitudinal/time series measures of major indicators; Expert judgment consensus measures such as those provided by the Delphi methods; Large-scale system stimulation such as that of econometric and industrial dynamics models	Methods which focus on predicting future conditions and their implications for the organization; Methods for establishing priorities and trade-offs among alternative policies	Identification of key dimensions of future organizational priorities; Recommendations concerning the nature of required action along each of these dimensions; Priority levels for alternative actions/ policies
Evaluation Research	Need to know the extent to which completed and continuing programs are performing as projected and to identify the major variables influencing the observed performance levels	Data related to the evaluation criteria chosen to represent the objective of a particular activity or program	Measures of program utilization levels; Measures of program user satisfaction levels; Measures comparing program users to a nonuser control group; Measures of the evolution of performance on evaluation criteria over time through panel methods	Methods for evaluating historical performance with respect to relatively ill-defined and often changing objectives and conditions	Identification of program strengths and weaknesses on an overall basis and within different user groups; Understanding of factors influencing program success with a view towards recommendations for improvement
Management Tactical Research	Need to obtain an in-depth understanding with respect to specific management problems of limited scope. Such problems are often related to a particular functional area	Descriptive information required to understand the key factors involved in a given problem situation; Precise data which will permit in-depth analysis of a limited number of important variables influencing a particular situation	Technical and factual data bearing directly on the problem; Measures of awareness, attitudes, and opinions; Measures of effectiveness/ alternative actions; Measures of behavior	Methods for extracting maximum from secondary data sources; Survey research methods; Experimentation methods for testing of alternatives; Observational methods; Model building	Background document or position paper with respect to the management situation; Precise recommendations for management action to overcome a problem or take advantage of an opportunity

TABLE 1   *(Continued)*

RESEARCH CATEGORY	NATURE OF THE MANAGEMENT SITUATION	TYPE OF INFORMATIONAL DATA REQUIRED	CHARACTERISTICS OF PRINCIPAL DATA COLLECTION METHODOLOGIES/ INSTRUMENTS	NATURE OF THE APPROPRIATE METHODS AND TECHNIQUES FOR EXTRACTING INFORMATION FROM THE DATA	NATURE OF RESEARCH OUTPUT FROM A MANAGEMENT PERSPECTIVE
Action Research	Need to understand the functioning of ongoing operations and programs with a view to modifying the factors affecting these operations. Subsequent monitoring of performance levels leads to repeated intervention so as to continually upgrade system performance.	Continuous information related to the performance of an organization; Behavioral data concerning the nature of interpersonal and intergroup relationships affecting organizational performance and satisfaction.	Measures of organization or program performance; Qualitative and quantitative measures of organizational structure and interpersonal/ intergroup relations	Methods for identifying major organizational problems from performance measures; Methods of intervention in organizational functioning designed to modify behavior or performance as it is occurring	Changes in the work environment; Modification of the reward/punishment system related to performance; Changes in organizational structure
Operational Research	Need to establish decision rules related to repetitive operations in order to reduce required level of management involvement and increase operating efficiency	Highly developed, reliable data pertaining to the performance of a very limited well defined task	Measures indicating level and dispersion of variables describing task performance. Such measures are often obtained through mechanical devices	Construction of analytical/ quantitative models followed by attempts to validate and optimize the models	Decision rules prescribing required operational actions under all probable normal conditions; Precisely defined "management by exception" task performance measures indicating when management is required to take corrective action

on variables important to the organization. At least two important types of models can be identified: econometric models based on input—output approaches to analysis and simulation models which focus on the interdependence (feedback) among the different components of large systems. The limitations of such models concern their ability to capture the complexity of reality, particularly with respect to factors which are more difficult to quantify (see Rovelstad, Chapter 38).

Evaluation research may employ a variety of measures and data collection methods depending on the research objective. In general, it should be kept in mind that the techniques used to analyze these data all have as their primary goal the evaluation of historical performance with respect to a program's or a firm's objectives, however ill-defined or shifting they may be.

The most traditional evaluative measure relates to various aspects of program or facility utilization levels, that is, simply, how many individuals have availed themselves of the service/activity/program in question. More recently there has been a tendency to go beyond this simple accounting approach and to develop measures reflecting the satisfaction levels of users with respect to the entity being evaluated.

To increase the effectiveness of both utilization rate and satisfaction level measures in evaluation research, two additional types of measures are extremely valuable: measures which compare users to a nonuser control group (see Carey, Chapter 22) and measures which trace the evolution of performance over time. Given these additional measures, management is able to judge comparative performance as well as performance with respect to arbitrarily chosen standards.

Management/tactical research involves a range of methodologies designed to provide the information pertinent to a particular decision or problem. These approaches involve, at the simplest level, various aspects of information storage and retrieval designed to permit researchers to extract the maximum information from secondary data sources (see Goeldner, Chapter 15). In parallel, there exist a number of primary data collection approaches which include survey research methods, techniques of laboratory or field experimentation designed to test the effectiveness of alternative courses of action, observational methods which furnish insight into human, organizational, or functional behavior under normal environmental conditions, and the simulation of subsystems of an organization.

The types of measures employed are correspondingly varied and include: technical or factual data bearing directly on the problem; measures of awareness, attitudes, and opinions; measures of effectiveness of and reaction to alternative actions; and measures describing particular aspects of behavior which are relevant to the question at hand. In general, each of these has been the object of significant study and is relatively well understood.

Management action research requires as its basic data inputs a variety of quantitative and qualitative measures related to technical and human levels of performance and satisfaction. The distinguishing feature is the fact that these measures serve directly to define the nature of management intervention which will be made in an attempt to modify the behavior of the system in question. Specific examples of possible types of measures include measures of work flow, job satisfaction, the structure of an organization, the interpersonal/intergroup relations defined by it, and a range of indicators of organizational performance. Such measures need to be gathered within the framework of a continuing, on the site, data collection process which will permit immediate analysis and the rapid identification of major organizational problems. In addition, the analysis must be designed to suggest the immediate interventions necessary to overcome such problems.

Operational research, of course, represents the most limited scope of the research methods, involving primarily the construction, validation, and optimization of analytical/quantitative models describing a particular operational task within the organization. However, it should be noted that operational research is not only "operations research" and may involve other types of studies designed to improve a particular operational procedure. Examples might include personnel administration routines, purchasing practices, and shipping procedures.

Again, the required measures reflect the nature of the research problem and methodology. Such measures usually indicate the level and dispersion of variables describing the performance of a given task, be it by a machine or a human. Such measures must be taken systematically and with a high degree of reliability in order to permit the appropriate type of analysis. As a result, it is common for these measures to be obtained using mechanical devices such as counters, scales, cameras, and timers.

NATURE OF THE RESEARCH OUTPUT

We now turn to the ultimate objective of the research: the information output designed to assist management to more effectively decide or act in a particular situation.

Policy research may be viewed as providing two principal types of output. The first of these can be summarized as the identification of key dimensions underlying future organizational priorities and which are often referred to as policy options. Many policy research studies, because of the nature of their mandate, provide only this first level of output. The second level involves going an important step further and providing recommendations concerning the priorities to be accorded to different policy options and the nature of the action required to implement the selection options.

Evaluation research also results in two possible types of output for management. The traditional output consists of an identification of facility/program strengths and weaknesses according to management selected criteria within the user groups designated by program managers. As a complement to these objective measures of performances, management may also request researchers to provide them with varying degrees of understanding of the major factors which determine program success. Such understanding can serve as the basis of recommendations for program improvement.

Management/tactical research findings can be classified as either exploratory or definitive. Exploratory findings present management with an in-depth description and interpretation of available information related to the decision situation. Such information can be provided relatively quickly and permits management to make a more informed decision concerning whether action can be taken in the light of available knowledge and real world competitive and time constraints. Should the collection of additional information be necessary and feasible, the exploratory research will have clearly specified these in-depth information needs. Definitive findings are the result of such in-depth research and should provide management with a clear understanding of the situation, followed by precise recommendation for actions to overcome the original problem or to take advantage of an opportunity.

Action research is designed to provide suggested courses of action that can be immediately implemented and the results of the implementation followed and studied. As such, the process is continuous and interactive. Types of action suggested by this type of research involve changes in the work environment to improve technical performance or human satisfaction, modification of the reward/punishment system related to performance, and changes in organizational structure designed to increase operating effectiveness.

Operational research provides management with precise answers to precise operational questions. These answers may take the form of explicit decision rules prescribing the required operational actions under all probable conditions. Alternatively, or in parallel, the research findings may be presented as precisely defined "management by exception" task performance measures indicating when management is required to step in and take corrective action. In brief, such results consist of highly detailed instructions concerning "what to do, when to do it, how to do it" in relation to specific tasks within the organization.

CONCLUSION

This chapter, despite its treatment of the theoretical field of research, is not intended as an academic exercise. Rather, it is hoped that the discussion has served to support one very fundamental practical thesis. This thesis asserted that the wide range of problem situations within different levels and functions of an organization, as well as different stages of the management process, implies widely varying information needs for their effective solution. The logical result has been the appearance of different methodological approaches to data collection appropriate to each type of information need. Unfortunately, these fundamental distinctions

have been little appreciated, leading to much confusion on the part of managers as to what research really is, what it can do to improve their effectiveness, and what its limits are as an aid to decision making.

It is hoped that the proposed framework for relating major research approaches to three important dimensions of the process of tourism management has clarified to some extent the question as to the distinction among different categories of research methods and the type of decision situation to which each is most relevant. These distinctions among research and data collection methods should not, however, obscure an important common characteristic and goal of all management research: an ability and desire to provide systematic and objective information for executive decision making which is timely and relevant and which ultimately improves the effectiveness of the organization.

REFERENCES

Anthony, Robert (1965), *Planning and Control Systems: A Framework for Analyses*, Boston, Mass.: Graduate School of Business Administration, Harvard University.

Bauer, A., and Kenneth J. Gergen (1968), *The Study of Policy Formulation*, New York: The Free Press.

Kotler, Philip (1981), *Marketing Management*, 4th ed., Englewood Cliffs, N.J.: Prentice–Hall.

Naisbitt, John (1982), *Megatrends*, New York: Warner Books.

Ritchie, J.R. Brent (1985), "Priority Analysis: A Multiple Input Program Planning Approach," Working Paper, The University of Calgary. Calgary, Canada.

Toh, Rex S. (1985), "An Inventory Depletion Overbooking Model for the Hotel Industry," *Journal of Travel Research*, Vol. 23, No. 4.

Weiss, Carol B. (1972), *Evaluation Research*, Englewood Cliffs, N.J.: Prentice–Hall.

Whyte, William Foote, and Edith Lentz Hamilton (1964), *Action Research for Management*, Homewood, Ill.: Irwin.

3

The Formulation of Tourism Policy— A Managerial Framework

DAVID L. EDGELL

Director,
Office of Policy and Planning
U.S. Travel and Tourism
   Administration
U.S. Department of Commerce
Washington, D.C.

*T*he purpose of this chapter is to present an introductory explanation of the formulation of tourism policy as an aid in the overall planning and management of tourism. The chapter is divided into five sections. The first part gives a simple overview of the need for tourism policy formulation. In the second part descriptions of some of the important tourism policy concerns are summarized under the headings of economic, socio-cultural, and environmental issues. The third part presents some of the key influences on tourism policy-making. In the fourth part an attempt is made to suggest a tourism policy decision-making process.

The tourism industry will be faced with some difficult challenges over the next several years. Managers and executives, faced with making present and future policy decisions on tourism issues, will need a managerial framework for analyzing the various alternatives so that a course of action can be selected. This paper first addresses some of the key tourism policy issues and influences on tourism policy and then presents an introductory explanation of the formulation of tourism policy as a tool to aid in policy decision making.

In its broadest sense, tourism encompasses all expenditures for goods and services by travelers (business as well as pleasure). It includes purchases of transportation, lodging, meals, entertainment, souvenirs, refreshments, travel agency and sightseeing tour services, and personal facilitative services. The full scope of international travel and tourism, therefore, covers the production and output of goods and services of many industries.

Worldwide tourism is an important activity of considerable economic importance and also of great socio-cultural and environmental significance. As a growth industry of increasing importance and complexity, tourism needs policy planning. The 1980s may very well be recorded in future years as the most important decade for formulating policies on tourism. The effects of such policies on the tourism industry will have far-reaching consequences for the many individuals, firms, and other organizations engaged directly or indirectly in tourism activities.

By most forecasts, the future is bright for increased tourism. Worldwide population increases and increases in income and income distribution are making it possible for more people of the world to travel. Changes in work habits and patterns of working conditions are yielding greater leisure time for greater numbers of people to participate in tourism and recreation. As people are becoming better educated and are more exposed to other societies and cultures, they want to visit the places they have read or heard about. Communication and transportation technologies have revolutionized the knowledge and ability to travel. All of these factors suggest that dramatic changes are in store for tourism (Edgell, 1983).

The likelihood of tourism's optimistic growth potential for the future merits and, indeed, requires the focusing of attention on the significance of this activity in overall international policy. The success of the tourism industry will depend heavily on the policies formulated for managing its development, growth, and maturity.

This paper takes a very general approach to tourism policy. It does not reflect a single country's or industry's viewpoint in policy decision making, but rather suggests the key issues for policy determination and important influences in decision making found in most areas of the world. In brief, it seeks the common policy threads which weave through most tourism programs worldwide. My rough definition for tourism policy decision making as I describe it in this paper is as follows: "A policymaker deciding on a present or future action or program based on specific goals and objectives from among alternatives and in light of given conditions."

The first part of this paper gives a simple overview of the need for tourism policy formulation and the direction taken in this paper. In the second part of the paper descriptions of some of the important tourism policy concerns are summarized under the headings of economic, sociocultural, and environmental issues. The third part presents an attempt to determine key influences on tourism policy-making. In the fourth part, taking into consideration the discussions contained in parts two and three, an attempt is made to suggest a tourism policy decision-making process. The final part is a summary and conclusion.

ANALYSIS OF IMPORTANT TOURISM POLICY ISSUES

There are many important tourism policy issues which face today's decision-makers and other issues which will become prominent over the next several years. However, this section will deal with only three such issues: economic, sociocultural, and environmental.

A   ECONOMIC

The increasing significance of tourism as a source of income and employment, and as a major factor in the balance of payments for many countries, has been attracting increasing attention on the part of governments and regional and local authorities, as well as others with an interest in economic development.

Tourism is an important source of income for most of the countries of the world. In 1984, according to estimates by the World Tourism Organization, worldwide international tourism arrivals were about 300 million, with worldwide international tourist receipts of $100 billion. Expenditures for domestic and international tourism taken together in 1984 were estimated at over $750 billion.

Yet, as important as tourism is from an economic point of view, it continues to be relatively neglected as an important international policy issue. The economic benefits of tourism are often discussed but are seldom fully appreciated. Tourism is an important source of income, foreign exchange receipts, and employment for nearly all countries. The construction and maintenance of tourist and travel facilities and the establishment of accompanying services are important stimulants for economic growth and development, especially for those countries with few natural resources and limited industrial capability. However, tourism contains heavy economic costs as well. Especially in developing nations, the negative impact is seen in economic leakages, the low-paying "servantlike" jobs offered the locals, the flight of farmers from agricultural areas to the cities, and the fact that tourists often cause local inflation and a demand for imported goods and services.

B   SOCIOCULTURAL

Sociocultural concerns in tourism range from the inconveniences arising from differences in language, culture, and customs, which act as deterrents to some travelers or as attractions for others, to concerns for protecting local traditions.

Over the past ten years, there has been increasing concern towards culture and national identity. Not all of the interest has centered on positive aspects. In the book *The Golden Hordes*, Ash and Turner discuss not only superficial aspects of tourism's history but also the social and cultural implications surrounding man's increasing need to get away from his home environment and seek pleasure in the world's vacation destinations. They contend that modern-day tourism is a form of cultural imperialism, an unending pursuit of fun, sun, and sex by the golden hordes of pleasure seekers who are damaging local cultures and polluting the world in their quest. In brief, the authors feel that a lot of "tourism" damages the local culture of the host country, perverts the traditional social values, encourages prostitution and hustling among "the natives," and usually results in a proliferation of bastardized, tourist-oriented cultural performances and the sale of cheap souvenirs masquerading as local "arts and crafts" (Ash and Turner, 1976).

In contrast, the potential cultural benefits from tourism, though less obvious than the economic benefits, may be equally significant. A carefully planned, well-organized tourist business can benefit the resident through exposure to a variety of ideas, people, languages, and other culture traits. It can add to the richness of the resident's experience by stimulating an interest in the area's history through restoration and preservation of historical sights. Tourism can serve local craftsmen by providing an audience and market for their art.

C ENVIRONMENTAL

An often overlooked fact is that the increase of tourism also has the potential of destroying or injuring our natural ecosystem. But if we look ahead for a moment, we can see both beneficial and unfortunate aspects of tourism with respect to the ecological balance. With proper planning, reserves can be set aside in the form of national parks, seashores, and forests, both to protect finite scenic resources from overuse or exploitation and to increase travel opportunities for tourists (Edgell, 1978).

In an article entitled "Will There Be Any Nice Places Left?" a number of negative concerns for tourism are cited (Williams, 1980). Polluted beaches, urban blight, eroded landscapes, and sprawling slumlike developments are mentioned as frequent sights in tourism areas. Many tourism developments are overcrowded, noisy, and tasteless. Much of this kind of development in the past has been due to laissez-faire tourism policies and very little national, regional, or local planning.

There has been increasing interest in recent years in the impact of tourism on the environment. More opinions have been expressed on environmental degradation caused by tourism than on positive aspects of tourism. The report of the 1973 European Travel Commission Conference on Tourism and Conservation stated articulately both the positive and negative factors in the interdependent relationship between tourism and the environment:

> First, . . . environment is the indispensable basis, the major attraction for tourism. Without an attractive environment, there would be no tourism. . . .
>
> Second, . . . the interests of tourism demand the protection of the scenic and historic heritage. The offer in the travel brochure must be genuine. . . .
>
> In some countries, tourism . . . is seen by those concerned to protect the environment as their powerful ally. The desire to gain national income from tourism can impel governments to protect monuments or natural areas they might otherwise have neglected.
>
> Third, tourism can directly assist active conservation . . . can prompt men to contribute towards . . . conservation . . . of [famous places such as] Florence and . . . Venice. The entry fees of tourists help to maintain historic structures and parks. . . . Tourist activity may provide new uses for old buildings. . . .
>
> And yet, despite these positive links, many conservationists feel that tourism can present a major threat to the environment, . . . that countless hotels, roads and other facilities provided for the tourists ruin the beauties of the seacoast, disturb the peace of the country, and rob the mountains of their serene grandeur. . . . Streets [become] choked with tourist traffic, and . . . squares and marketplaces [are] turned into parks for visitors. (European Travel Commission, 1974).

The challenge for tourism in the next twenty-five years is to plan and develop it and to invest in tourism facilities to improve rather than degrade the environment.

INFLUENCES ON TOURISM POLICY

There are many influences which cause a policy to shift in one direction or another. These may take the form of government policy whether at the city, state (or other territorial division depending on the country), or federal level. There are in some countries private sector influences which shape national tourism policy. In addition, most countries have laws and regulations which influence policy decisions on tourism. Also of importance are the influences exerted by international tourism organizations.

A GOVERNMENT

There are political interest groups at all levels of government. Some influence only local policies and others affect policies at all levels. Following are some examples at the city, state, and federal levels.

1 City

Historically, cities have functioned as meeting places. They provide airports, convention centers, highways, and other support services and activities for the traveler and they perform important functions as a place to meet and visit as well as servicing tourism (United States Conference of Mayors, 1978). In addition, the managerial resources, financial investment, and the broad spectrum of support services necessary for the growth and maintenance of the tourism industry are located primarily in cities.

Public funds have been used to build coliseums, stadiums, and convention centers. The size and number of these physical resources demonstrate the growth of the cities' commitment to the visitor as a source of income and economic viability.

The direction taken by cities also influences state, regional, and national policies on tourism. Local areas would do well to have carefully prepared tourism policy plans for tourism growth, both for local purposes as well as to link state, regional, and national policies.

2 State (or Other Territorial Division)

It should be noted that while this section is patterned after entities referred to as states, such as, for example, U.S. states, Mexican states, etc., it also generally applies to other territorial divisions within a country.

The decisions of state agencies have an enormous impact on:

- the rate of growth of the tourist sector
- the location of tourist facilities
- the quality of tourist services
- public attitudes towards and treatment of tourists, and
- the seasonality of tourist demand.

State assemblies determine the level of funding of state tourism development divisions and, indirectly, whether their states compete effectively for a share of the domestic and international markets.

State departments of commerce and industry or local industrial development funds determine whether incentives to attract industry are offered to hotels, motels, and resorts.

State departments of education determine whether training for tourism vocations is offered to students enrolled in state institutions of higher learning, and whether students learn about the benefits which tourism bestows upon the state. Course content and textbooks selected by school boards and school officials can affect public attitudes towards tourists, towards travel industry employees, and towards the industry itself. School vacation schedules prescribed by school officials determine, indirectly, when families with children take their vacations, and therefore whether the travel industry prospers throughout the year or only during the summer months.

State and county highway departments determine the quality of roadways in their respective jurisdictions and, indirectly, the volume of tourist traffic entering the state. Well-maintained roads obviously attract more visitors than those which receive indifferent upkeep.

State and local police help determine a state's image—whether it is perceived as a destination offering a hospitable reception or as one gigantic speed trap for out-of-state tourists.

State departments of natural resources and local street or sanitation departments help determine whether public beaches, lakes, and rivers are free from pollutants and safe for tourist use or pose a threat to public health.

Policy objectives which include the above are best met through state and local tourism policies and not necessarily by national policies. Thus, states which regard travel as important to their economy and to their people would benefit from a policy on tourism.

3 Federal

Federal involvement in tourism will vary from country to country. In many countries, the production of travel and tourism services, in fact, is both regulated and operated by the government. The United States is used here as just one example of national tourism policy.

The United States is a latecomer in tourism policy. After many years of study, consultations, and deliberations, the Congress passed the National Tourism Policy Act in 1981. The Act, signed on October 16, 1981, by President Reagan, established a national tourism policy, something that had occurred in most developed nations thirty years earlier. Key policy provisions of the Act include: (1) replacing the United States Travel Service with a new United States Travel and Tourism Administration; (2) broadening the goals and objectives to include greater international policy initiatives; (3) elevating the head of the agency from an Assistant Secretary of Commerce for Tourism to an Under Secretary of Commerce for Travel and Tourism; (4) establishing an interagency committee, the national Tourism Policy Council; and (5) creating a Travel and Tourism Advisory Board.

The basic policy of the new U.S. Travel and Tourism Administration (USTTA) is to promote U.S. inbound tourism as an export. To accomplish this, the USTTA helps the U.S. travel supplier promote and sell his product or service to the foreign travel buyer at the wholesale, retail, and consumer levels. This involves bringing the potential wholesaler/operator or buyer together with the U.S. supplier, often via a travel product inspection visit. On the other hand, USTTA helps make arrangements for U.S. suppliers who wish to go into the foreign marketplace to meet potential buyers at travel trade shows and through travel missions. Whatever the activity, the ultimate goal of USTTA is to act as a catalytic agent in assisting the private sector to increase America's share of the highly competitive international tourism market (Edgell, 1984).

Although, according to Dr. Clare Gunn in an article entitled "U.S. Tourism Policy Development," this promotional element of the policy has become reality, many other policy issues raised over the years may become increasingly important as tourism's national impact becomes more fully realized in the future (Gunn, 1983).

Some of the policy goals of the Act are to optimize economic development of tourism, assure universal travel, encourage educational values, stimulate foreign travel to the U.S., stimulate historic restoration, relate tourism policy to national energy and conservation policy, harmonize public–private development, stimulate competition, upgrade quality of tourism service, and assist in research and planning (Edgell, 1982).

Other broad national interests in tourism policy were identified in the *National Tourism Policy Study: Final Report* (U.S. Senate, 1978) as follows:

- energy conservation
- full employment
- economic growth with minimum inflation
- improved operation of the federal government
- environmental protection
- judicious use of natural resources
- urban revitalization
- preservation of national heritage resources
- consumer protection
- equal opportunities for disadvantaged segments of the population
- improved physical and mental health
- reduced international trade deficits
- equitable taxation
- economic viability of U.S. small businesses
- minimum regulation of private industry
- improved international goodwill, and
- balanced national transportation system.

Whether the Act can be effectively implemented remains to be seen. However, from a purely policy perspective it is important because it recognizes social and environmental issues as well as the importance of tourism to the economy.

B   PRIVATE SECTOR

In many countries of the world the private tourism sector plays a very key role in tourism policy development. In this short discussion only a brief summary will be presented since the private sector involvement encompasses such a large variety of organizations and businesses, and the dividing line for determining which are to be considered as part of the travel industry is somewhat arbitrary. As a result, the policy implications for tourism are broad as well. The travel industry network ranges from concerns for travel volume and flow and travel trends and motivations to destination planning and development and travel sales distribution systems. Transportation policies must coexist with tourism policies to ensure water, land, and air transportation systems. Services include a broad spectrum of components, including accommodations, food and beverage, amusement, recreation and entertainment, and travel arrangements (including travel agencies and tour operators), as well as souvenir shops and foreign exchange establishments.

One way to summarize the private sector impact is through the "linking concept" as presented in the book *The Travel Industry: Concepts and Practices* by Chuck Gee *et al*. He suggests two basic categories for the private sector: direct providers and support services. He describes these categories as follows:

The first category, direct providers, *includes businesses typically associated with travel, such as airlines, hotels, ground transportation, travel agencies, restaurants, and retail shops. These businesses, although not all existing for the sole purpose of servicing travelers (as, for instance, restaurants and retail shops), interface directly with travelers in that they provide services, activities, and products that are consumed and/or purchased directly by the travelers.*

Below the surface lies a large variety of businesses lending support to direct providers. This second category, support services, *includes specialized services, such as tour organizers, travel and trade publications, hotel management firms, and travel research firms. It also includes basic supplies and services, such as contract laundry and contract food services. Businesses providing specialized services, such as those listed above, are dependent upon the travel market for almost all of their businesses. Businesses supplying the basics to direct providers are not solely dependent upon them for their existence, although in an area where travel and tourism are the mainstay of the economy, the bulk of the business for providers of basic supplies and services may come directly from travelers, as in the case of resort areas. (Gee et al., 1984).*

It should be noted that in some instances, a single firm may be involved in directly providing travel services as well as support services.

The private sector may influence tourism policies in several different ways. For the purposes of this paper, two approaches are suggested: the direct and indirect.

The *direct approach* is when a single company, or part of an industry acting in its own self-interest, attempts to influence or make policy decisions. This may take the form of a lobbying effort for specific legislation, seeking special dispensation from regulations, or influencing tourism entities to act in a manner to the benefit of the firm.

The *indirect approach* is usually one which allows for individual or collective policy input through an association or other similar body. The tourism industry for years has had many such organizations acting on behalf of its members. Recently, in 1982, most of the major components of the travel industry came together in the form of one organization. This organization is formally known as the Travel and Tourism Government Affairs Council. The Travel and Tourism Government Affairs Council is now recognized as the major official policy organization representing the travel and tourism industry on government issues. This is an attempt to allow one entity to voice the views and concerns regarding the government activities in tourism.

C   LAWS AND REGULATIONS

Laws and regulations result from the policy decision process and they influence other policies. There are negative and positive aspects of laws and regulations on tourism worldwide. This section will look at the impact of laws and regulations as impediments to the travel and tourism industry. The following comments are based on a draft study entitled *International Travel and Tourism* prepared by the Office of the U.S. Trade Representative, Washington (1983). The results are worldwide in scope.

The impact of laws and regulations as barriers to travel falls on both the individual traveler as well as on travel-related businesses. The Organization for Economic Cooperation and Development has identified 49 specific obstacles to travel.

In summary, the individual traveler may be faced with obstacles such as passport and visa requirements, foreign exchange controls, customs duties, taxes, and other regulations. Depending on the country and regulation, these impediments can have major impacts on the flow of international tourism. For example, excessive passport fees and currency restrictions can have a large bearing on outbound tourism. Visa requirements, like those imposed by the U.S., have a heavy impact on inbound tourism.

Travel-related businesses often face severe burdens. These include such practices by governments as restrictions on foreign remittances, local laws for establishing businesses, requirements regarding the nationality of the employees of the firm, local equity requirements for foreign nationals, and others. Such restrictions inhibit market access and create problems for establishing an office or branch to conduct travel and tourism businesses. This puts some businesses or countries at a competitive disadvantage. For the most part, the information available is inadequate with respect to formulating policies to deal with such negative laws and regulations.

There are some international organizations concerned with impediments to travel. In the next section three such organizations will be mentioned and briefly described. In addition, there are bilateral arrangements among countries which seek to reduce, eliminate, or alleviate the impact of laws and regulations on tourism. The next section will also mention such arrangements in a very general way.

D   INTERGOVERNMENTAL TOURISM POLICY ORGANIZATIONS

There are numerous international and intergovernmental bodies that become involved in worldwide tourism policies. As a point of illustration, this section will describe three such intergovernmental tourism organizations: the Organization of American States (OAS) Tourism Development Program, the Organization for Economic Cooperation and Development (OECD) Tourism Committee, and the World Tourism Organization (WTO). This section will also point out the importance of bilateral tourism agreements for resolving important tourism policies.

The Tourism Development Program of the OAS was formed in 1970 to assist tourism authorities of the member states in developing, promoting, and regulating their respective tourism sectors. It was recently integrated into the Department of Regional Development. An important activity of the OAS tourism program is to provide expertise in the field of tourism training. The program provides tourism training on a wide range of topics at its three regional Inter-American Tourism Training Centers located in Argentina, Barbados, and Mexico.

The OECD has a Tourism Committee concerned with tourism policy and international tourism trends in the member nations. The Tourism Committee prepares a comprehensive yearly publication entitled *Tourism Policy and International Tourism in OECD Member Countries* which contains policy developments and tourism information. An important area of research conducted by the OECD for policy decisions is the efforts made to identify international barriers to trade in tourism.

The only worldwide tourism policy body is the WTO. Inaugurated in 1975, it provides a world clearinghouse for the collection, analysis, and dissemination of technical tourism information. It offers national tourism administrations and organizations the machinery for a multinational approach to international discussion and negotiations on tourism matters. It also provides a mechanism for international conferences, seminars, and other means for focusing on important tourism developmental issues and policies.

Another important avenue for dealing with major policy concerns is through bilateral tourism agreements. Usually such agreements contain provisions for cooperation in facilitation, research, and training. Most also attempt to reduce mutual barriers to travel and some contain provisions calling for joint promotion and marketing.

TOURISM POLICY DECISION-MAKING PROCESS

There has been very little written about the process for making policy decisions in tourism. For most countries, the policy decisions regarding tourism have focused on only two goals: (1) maximizing tourist arrivals and (2) improvement in the balance of payments through international tourism receipts.

One attempt to focus attention on the need for systematic planning for policy decisions in tourism took place during the joint national meeting of the Operations Research Society—The Institute of Management Sciences, Miami Beach, Florida, November 3–6, 1976. In a paper entitled "Public Policy Planning and Operations Research in the Tourism Sector: Never the Twain Shall Meet—Or Shall They?" by Edgell *et al.* (1976), a conceptual representation of the current policy process was presented (Fig. 1). In this same paper a system model was presented (see Fig. 2).

It is necessary to recognize that on any given tourism issue, the policymaker does not make a decision in a vacuum nor always in the same way. The policymaker almost always has certain goals and objectives that guide him or her in the decision-making process. These also vary considerably from country to country. At the same time, there are numerous other considerations which must be accounted for. This is presented visually in Fig. 3.

Another way of looking at the decision-making process is through the use of an equation. In Fig. 4, a basic

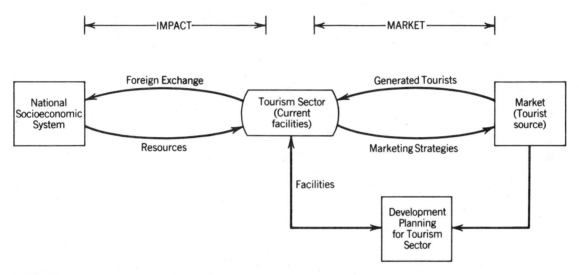

FIGURE 1   Conceptual representation of current process.

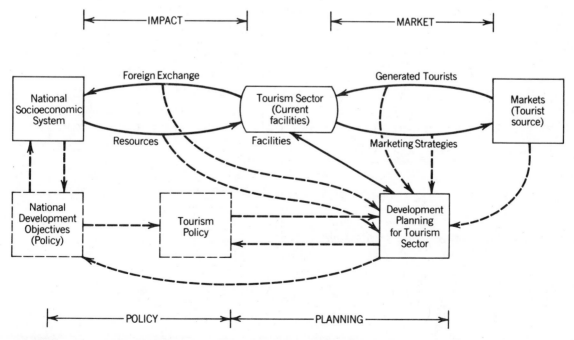

FIGURE 2   Conceptual representation of the system model of the tourism sector.

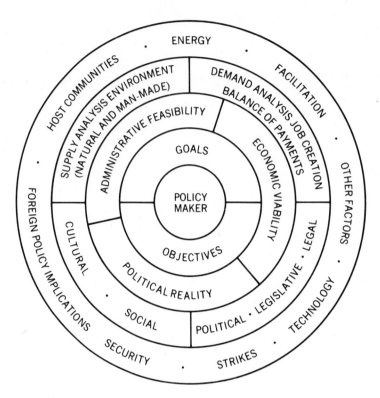

FIGURE 3   Impacts on policymaker in the decision-making process.

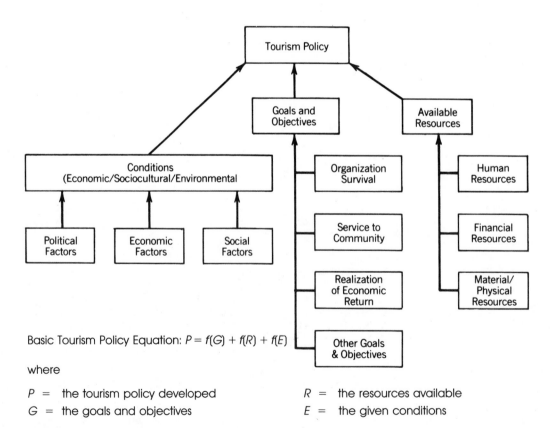

Basic Tourism Policy Equation: $P = f(G) + f(R) + f(E)$

where

P = the tourism policy developed R = the resources available

G = the goals and objectives E = the given conditions

FIGURE 4   The tourism policy development/decision process.

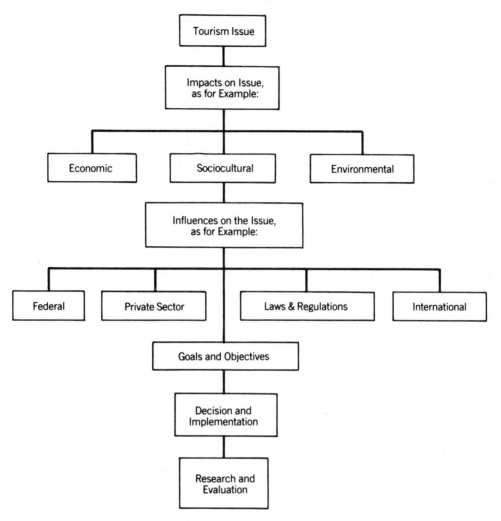

FIGURE 5   International tourism policy formulation: general diagram.

simple equation is shown which summarizes another approach in tourism policy decision making.

Based on numerous observations and experience, a good description of the process can be shown in Fig. 5. This general approach looks at each tourism issue separately. It suggests that tourism issues reflect not only economic considerations but also sociocultural and environmental concerns as well. It points out some of the principal influences on the decision process. Some of these concerns were outlined earlier in this paper.

What hasn't been discussed so far is the need for establishing goals and objectives and then, within these parameters, the making of the decision on the issues at hand. Finally, it is necessary to develop programs to implement the decision and evaluate, through the use of research, the effectiveness of the decision.

A   GOALS AND OBJECTIVES

In terms of describing the tourism decision-making process contained in this paper, the "goal" is the end towards which the effort is directed. There may be one or more goals to provide the policy direction in the decision process. The objectives are the limited choices that pertain to the specific goal. For example, one goal may be to eliminate the travel deficit in the balance of payments. One objective might be the need to provide statistics to facilitate and guide in the planning process towards this goal. Another objective might be reduction of impediments to travel between countries, thus making it easier to reach the goal. Once the goals and objectives are established, it is necessary to develop strategies or plans to obtain the desired end. These may include development of reports or tourism marketing plans, or seeking passage of legislation. Finally, tactics or actions to support a specific strategy or plan must take place. These may include survey research, tourism negotiations, or participation in specific meetings. Whatever the tactic, it must support a specific strategy designed to implement an objective aimed towards a final goal.

B   DECISION AND IMPLEMENTATION

Once the decision is made, based on specific goals and objectives, it is necessary to design programs to implement the decision. These may be short- or long-term programs. The programs will also depend on the resources available to carry them out. Performance measures will need to be established and specific milestones identified.

C   RESEARCH AND EVALUATION

There is a continuous need for research and evaluation in the decision-making process. Research is needed at all phases of the process but particularly in establishing the goals and as part of the evaluation of the decision. Once actions have taken place in implementing programs designed to attain stated goals and objectives, it is necessary to evaluate how well or how much of the goal was accomplished. One quick way to evaluate the progress is to see how many of the milestones were accomplished. This can be expressed through a detailed report of the activities accomplished and resources expanded. Performance measures can be established.

It is also important to conduct research throughout the decision-making process, but particularly in measuring results. This is especially true in most areas of the tourism industry because it is such a dynamic industry.

The research can tell us not only how well we have done, but what else needs to be accomplished. It also helps us to set new policy goals and to design new programs.

Some of the research is of a statistical nature requiring the collection of considerable amounts of data. One approach to presenting an overview of the relationship of tourism statistical data and research information to policy decisions is contained in a paper entitled "Tourism Statistical Information in Relation to Policy Decision Making" by Edgell and Wandner (1977). This paper focuses mainly on the "quantitative" tourism needs for policy decisions. It points out that many of the policy issues facing tourism are relatively new and require new approaches and additional statistical data (Edgell *et al.*, 1976).

The point is that without research and data the decision process is often little more than a guess. With good research information a more intelligent decision can be made. Once the decision is made, additional research needs to be conducted to evaluate the decision and the programs designed to implement the decision.

SUMMARY AND CONCLUSION

The attempt in this paper was to discuss in an introductory way a framework for the policy decision-making process. Tourism policy concerns were introduced and discussed. Some of the influences in the policy-making process were presented. An attempt was made to outline the decision-making process through use of various schematic diagrams.

This paper clearly illustrates the diversity in the field of tourism policy decision making. It suggests that the private sector, states, communities, and government agencies need to be aware of what kinds of social, economic, or political factors are usually associated with policy decisions in tourism. No attempt was made to explain fully how tourism policy decision making is made or what the impact of a policy will be. However, the paper does suggest that policy in tourism can be aided by an integrated management approach that attempts to integrate the various tourism issues.

This paper, while limited, does recognize the need for an organized format for policy planning and decision making. It also points out that the state of the art in tourism managerial systems in policy analysis is in its infancy state.

In conclusion, the tourism policy decision-making process must be guided by carefully planned policies, international in concept and interdisciplinary in its approach and application. It should be developed based not only on economic benefits, but on the ideals and principles of human welfare and the quality of life. The decision maker in tourism must utilize policies which bring economic, sociocultural, and environmental forces together to work for their mutual interests.

BIBLIOGRAPHY

Ash, John, and Louis Turner, *The Golden Hordes: International Tourism and the Pleasure Periphery* (New York: St. Martin's Press, 1976).

Edgell, David L., "International Tourism and Travel" (Chapter 7), *International Business Prospects 1977– 1999*, edited by Howard F. Van Zandt (Indianapolis: Bobbs–Merrill Educational Publishing, 1978). Book is based on "The ITT Key Issues Lecture Series," 1976– 1977, University of Texas.

Edgell, David L., "Recent U.S. Tourism Policy Trends," *Journal of Tourism Management*, June 1982, page 121.

Edgell, David L., "Tourism and the Next 25 Years," *Travel Weekly*, June 1983.

Edgell, David L., "U.S. Government Policy on International Tourism," *Journal of Tourism Management*, March 1984.

Edgell, David L., Charles Gearing, Rodney Stiefbold, and William Swart, "Public Policy Planning and Operations Research in the Tourism Sector," Joint ORSA/TIMS Conference, Miami Beach, Florida, November 3–6, 1976.

Edgell, David L., and Stephen A. Wandner, "Tourism Statistical Information in Relation to Policy Decision Making," Paper presented at the Joint National Meeting of the Operations Research Society—The Institute of Management Sciences, Atlanta, November 9, 1977.

Edwards, Anthony, *International Tourism Development: Forecasts to 1985*, Special Report (London: Economic Intelligence Unit, 1976).

European Travel Commission, *Tourism and Conservation: Working Together* (London, 1974).

Gearing, Charles E., William Swart, and Turgut Var, *Planning for Tourism Development: Quantitative Approaches* (New York: Praeger Publishers, 1976).

Gee, Chuck Y., Dexter J.L. Choy, and James C. Makens, *The Travel Industry* (Westport, Conn.: AVI Publishing Company, Inc., 1984).

Gunn, Clare A., "Industry Fragmentation vs. Tourism Planning" (mimeograph), 1976.

Gunn, Clare A., "U.S. Tourism Policy Development," *Leisure Today*, April 1983.

McIntosh, Robert W., *Tourism Principles, Practices and Philosophies* (Columbus, Ohio: Grid, Inc., 1973).

Office of the United States Trade Representative, *International Travel and Tourism* (Washington, D.C., May 18, 1983).

Sharkansky, Ira, Editor, *Policy Analysis in Political Science* (Chicago: Markham Publishing Company, 1970).

Smith, Valarie L., Editor, *Hosts and Guests: The Anthropology of Tourism* (Philadelphia: University of Pennsylvania Press, 1977).

United States Conference of Mayors, *City Government, Tourism and Economic Development* (Atlanta, Georgia, September 1978).

U.S. Senate, Committee on Commerce, Science and Transportation, *National Tourism Policy Study: Final Report* (Washington, D.C.: U.S. Government Printing Office, 1978.

Williams, Roger M., "Will There Be Any Nice Places Left?" *Next*, September/October 1980.

4

Managing the Research Function for Effective Policy Formulation and Decision Making

JAY BEAMAN
Director

SCOTT MEIS
Manager
Socio-Economic Branch
Parks Canada
Ottawa, Ontario, Canada

This chapter deals with the problems of and solutions to managing applied social and economic research activities to support tourism policy formulation and tourism management activities. A supportive organizational context is identified as an important initial prerequisite. Specific necessary conditions in the organizational environment are discussed. Research management as a distinct activity is defined and two main subactivity components are delineated: research planning and research coupling. For each subactivity, the paper identifies and examines a further series of prescriptions for successful effective applied research management.

It has become fairly commonplace in the applied social science research field generally, and in tourism and recreation research specifically (Capstick and Riley, 1977; Samuels, 1973), to lament the lack of relevant information on planning and implementation decisions regarding facility development and the provision of services. It is also customary to bewail the lack of sufficient resources or time for sophisticated and elaborate studies concerning such complex decision-related issues as social carrying capacity and social and economic impacts. Indeed, several recent reviews have argued that most research and information generated in the field is relatively ineffective or irrelevant to applied decision-making processes (Driver and Knopf, 1981; Rossi *et al.*, 1978; Dimaggio and Useem, 1980). It is much easier for academic observers, who write

most of the critical literature, to identify weaknesses than to suggest possible corrective measures.

The most crucial recent advance in both applied social research and management information systems (MIS) has been the growing understanding of the need for active and careful management of the research and information systems processes (Schwarzbart, 1979; Rossi *et al.*, 1978). If the research process is not carefully managed, many problems arise that compromise the effectiveness and efficiency of the function. Experience has shown that the relevance and expected benefits and impact of most applied research and MIS projects have been greatly overestimated. On the other hand, time, labour requirements, and associated costs for such projects tend to be underestimated. This has led to bad feeling between management and the

35

research and systems development groups, and has also meant that most applied research was ineffective in organizational decision-making processes. In other cases, where researchers have attempted to make their work relevant, it has often been of low professional quality. Although these judgments are leveled at research and information systems development in the social and information sciences in general, an extensive review of the literature or thoughtful reflection is not necessary to realize that they are equally applicable to specific tourism research.

Applied research by its definition involves practical problem solving. The processes, however, by which research projects are defined, initiated, carried out, and successfully integrated into practical problem solving, decision making, and policy formation are not generally well understood. Experience and reviews of the rather diffuse literature indicate that certain series of prescriptions are essential for success. This paper identifies and specifies those prescriptions considered most important by the authors.

It is contended that the generally ineffective state of social research and MIS results from two basic conditions. In most cases, the organizational environment is not conducive to effective applied research. Second, the applied research and information exchange processes are insufficiently or inappropriately managed. In addition, the effective utilization of applied social research in policy formulation and decision making depends on the combination of appropriate organizational conditions and careful management of the interface between the research and principal decision-making functions.

ORGANIZATIONAL PREREQUISITES FOR EFFECTIVE RESEARCH

It is often not recognized that several organizational factors outside a researcher's control are critical to effective research. A supportive organizational environment is one such external prerequisite. An appropriate organizational situation is essential if most of what is suggested is to be relevant to a researcher or research manager.

One can also identify four other important organizational prerequisites essential for the effective use of applied research as a decision-making aid. First, the presence of senior management support is needed to set the tone, style, and criteria for the use of research. Senior management is ultimately accountable for putting organizational structures and processes in place to facilitate research and its use. In other words, senior management must be committed to both specific and general research and recognize their importance in an effective research function leading to informed decision making. Furthermore, this commitment to re-

search must be genuine and not done simply to create the appearance of an informed decision process. In practice, this means that senior management will use research findings, along with other decision inputs, when taking action.

A second organizational prerequisite is that the research function reports to a senior manager of sufficient authority to ensure that research results are considered, where relevant, in a given organizational issue or decision. In a nonsupportive organization the reporting level of the research function is frequently low. As a consequence, the research unit's work has no symbolic authority and research is automatically considered as noninfluential. Ideally, the senior managers responsible for research must understand and, to some degree, approve of the "research" function. In general, they need not have a research background; however, critical senior managers associated with the research function must be able to recognize and explain the strengths and limitations of research to organizational equals and superiors.

Communication between the research function and organization decision-makers at all levels comprises the third organizational prerequisite. If research results are to be relevant and timely, multiple formal and informal direct and open channels of communication must exist between the researchers and the research users involved in decision-making processes. In the nonsupportive organization, formal communication paths between researchers and other functional decision-makers are characteristically nonexistent or of dubious value.

A fourth and final organizational prerequisite for effective tourism research is the management of the research function itself. Someone must be designated to direct the research function and be accountable therefore for the quality and effectiveness of the organization's research activities and its interface with other functions, professional quality and effectiveness. "Research management" is used here to describe that combination of processes, activities, skills, and attributes resulting in rational and efficient research which leads to sound organization decision-making goals and objectives.

These factors have received relatively little concentrated attention in the literature on applied social research, management or management science, with the result that they are not generally well understood. The authors contend that, to be effective, research managers must spend much of their time on two main general activities: research planning and research coupling.

Research planning activities include:

1 Identifying potential areas for research support and establishing needs, rationales, and priorities for supporting these;

2   Selecting appropriate research to support, given finite resources;

3   Selecting the modes and resource levels for supporting such research;

4   Reviewing research activities to see that they are well planned and that they remain "on track" throughout all stages of their execution; and

5   Assessing the successes and failures of research and appropriately modifying project selection, priority criteria, and resourcing.

Research coupling, on the other hand, includes communication and organizational structuring activities directed toward stimulating and facilitating dialogue between researchers and user groups. These communication processes should be two-way, involving users communicating their research and information needs to researchers, and researchers working with the research user to ensure appropriate applications of research results and effective and efficient research designs (Price, 1969).

PLANNING AND RESOURCING PRESCRIPTIONS FOR THE RESEARCH MANAGER

Achieving a good research program involves much more than recognizing a number of "expressed user requirements" and responding to these according to a simple priority plan. Effective and efficient research management depends on substantial attention and importance being given to the process of research selection and planning (Price, 1965; Price, 1969). The selection of research problems can be difficult as there are few guidelines, many choices, high costs, high risks, and slow and uncertain results (Price, 1969; Brooks, 1967). There are far more failures than successes.

It is possible to specify a set of managerial prescriptions for research planning and resourcing processes that can minimize the risks and ensure potential benefits.

A   IDENTIFYING AND SPECIFYING RESEARCH PROBLEMS

Particular care and attention must be given to identifying how the tourism policymaker or decision-maker will use the results of the proposed research (Caplan *et al*., 1975b, p. 10; Berg, 1978, p. 52). At the same time, however, applied research *must* answer the questions of decision-makers or those formulating policy.

While the user's input is critical for defining research problems, this often lacks the logical rigour and specificity necessary to define research needs and, therefore, provide an adequate basis for appropriate research. The importance of this aspect of relevance

was specifically identified by Beaman (1978) as a weakness in early work in tourism research.

It should also be noted that many professionally trained but inexperienced applied researchers are not much better at defining appropriate research problems. Beaman has also identified the need for tourism research programs that train researchers to define problems in terms not limited to (a) meeting vague information requests, (b) investigating "in-vogue" hypotheses, or (c) fitting all problems to a favoured method.

As a consequence of poor research definition, studies of the use of government survey research in general (Rossi *et al*., 1978; Bernstein and Freeman, 1975) and survey research relating to planning and management of arts and cultural activities in particular (Dimaggio and Useem, 1980) have indicated practically no correlation between research results and actual decisions.

The experience of government should serve as a cautionary note to anyone interested in implementing a sound research plan. Almost all surveys of people or businesses, carried out either by or for Canadian and U.S. government departments, are now subject to elaborate front-end research planning and review processes. The major weakness in these government control processes is their emphasis on sophisticated data collection, not on real needs. Whether proposed analyses to achieve applied objectives (i.e., decisions) as part of a research plan are valid is not easily subject to external review, as a client's statements that data are needed to plan or "evaluate" are usually not challenged or adequately verified. In practice, it is questionable if any organization can cope with such management-decision-related formal critiques across organizational units on a continuous basis. This process could probably be better handled through careful internal planning, coupling, and review, or by periodic functional audits.

B   SETTING PRIORITIES

Establishing priorities is probably the second most critical issue for the research manager interested in effective research planning and management. The experienced research manager has no difficulty identifying numerous potential problems for study. As research is a costly, time-consuming, and highly uncertain process, the difficulty lies in deciding on which projects or programs to concentrate resources. A sustained focus on certain specific directions, programs, and projects is essential.

Determining research priorities is seldom simple. Initially, of course, some indications of appropriate priorities are given by senior management or through extrainstitutional direction regarding program needs. The research manager must then integrate projects with these needs. To do this, linkages between the current major program needs must be specified, the problems determined, and, finally, those research programs and projects that can address those problems with a reasonable probability of success arrived at (Ledley *et al.*, 1967).

While such a process will provide a general set of priorities, it alone is insufficient for determining the specific priorities of any given time, program, or project. This requires that the manager also assess a number of other, "softer" judgmental considerations. In the rest of this discussion some of these other criteria are considered as independent prerequisites for effective research planning and resourcing. All, however, play an additional role as the secondary criteria in the manager's prioritization decisions.

C SEARCHING FOR STANDARD RESPONSE MODES TO STRUCTURED PROBLEMS

The efficient research manager constantly searches for ways to attain more control over the work load by identifying standard problems and converting their solutions from expensive one-time research to more cost-efficient activities. Such activities may use existing data, established administrative routines, automated systems, or other management science tools.

The important consideration in managing the research work load in terms of this objective is the extent to which decision-making needs are highly structured (Keen and Scott-Morton, 1978). Simon (1960) used the terms "programmed" and "non-programmed" to differentiate between tasks having set rules or decision procedures and tasks that are one-time or require changing criteria with each recurrence. The point made by the authors cited is that highly structured problems can be routinized or automated while semi-structured problems are not easily answered by routine research solutions. Unstructured problems can only be supported by new research activity, and then only partially at best (Keen and Scott-Morton, 1978, p. 11).

Based on analysis of various decision support systems (DSS), the appropriate research response can vary from developing clerical processes (Keen and Scott-Morton, 1978) to developing a data base and associated analysis systems. DSS analysis may point to systematic solutions as alternatives to existing research approaches. Certainly, if analysis shows that structured decision making can be supported by cost-effective developments, these will have high priority for implementation.

While consistently attempting to convert decision support responses from costly one-time research projects to routine information systems, the research manager must review routinized and automated "research" or MIS functions for their cost effectiveness. Since they are part of structured decision making, they require virtually fixed commitments of resources. Accordingly, the relevance of such work and the percentage of a budget committed to such activity should never be taken for granted.

D TAILORING RESEARCH SCALE AND SCOPE TO USERS' DECISION REQUIREMENTS

In addition to considering the mode of research activity, the research manager must frequently determine the scope and scale for the research activity which will adequately satisfy the decision-makers' needs. As noted earlier, the successful tourism research and information system manager has no shortage of problems and, in fact, is often besieged with requests, problems, and proposals. To make the most of resources, the research manager must be conscious of, and skilled at, determining the scale, scope, and precision of projects and selecting the appropriate mode of response to each request.

The user's budget should not be the sole criterion dictating the elaborateness or precision of the research design. The level of aggregation, scope, and the degree of accuracy of the required research results should also be included. These variables are frequently other aspects of the user's request. Three other attributes are the size of the user's organization, the level of decision making being addressed, and the stage of the decision process concerned (Ritchie, 1980, pp. 338–339).

Anthony (1965) and Ritchie (1980) have pointed out that the management level of users influences the level of decision making and thus the nature of the research or information systems required. In large organizations, top management generally has a strong interest in strategic planning which involves setting organizational objectives and formulating overall policies. Management control and tactical planning, largely carried out by middle management, is concerned with issues such as facility location, product development, and budget preparation. Operational planning and control focus on the use of existing facilities and resources to carry out activities effectively (Ritchie, 1980). Information requirements differ at each of these levels of activity. Ritchie (1980, p. 341) cites these differences as follows: "In general, strategic planning requires more outside information, less accuracy, and more summarization than tactical planning. Management control and planning tends to require more accurate, precise (problem-focused), and current data than strategic planning. Operations activities tend to use data in a less aggregate form than management control." These are only some of the more striking differences in the characteristics of information required by the different decision-making levels.

In a somewhat similar manner, the stage of the client's decision-making process affects the degree of rigour and precision required in the research response. Ritchie (1980), in discussing the developing of tourism information systems, cites an elaboration (Davis, 1974) of Simon's (1960) three-stage decision-making model. The stages of the decision-making process are claimed to be (1) intelligence (problem recognition), (2) design (solution identification and analysis); and (3) choice (choice, implementation and feedback).

Without careful management of these stages of the decision-making process research resources can be wasted or communication failure can occur. Generally, the collected data have a level of detail not needed by the management involved or the level of detail is such that further analysis by management is required to discern what is relevant and what is trivial.

One example of an inefficient decision-making process occurs frequently. Data collected for use as a basis for long-range forecasts or long-range market estimates often have a level of statistical accuracy that is irrelevant. Long-range futures estimated from these data are wasted as estimates with confidence limits of $\pm 25\%$, $\pm 50\%$, or even $\pm 100\%$ would be acceptable. Although this is only one example of ineffective, inefficient, or inept practices, it illustrates that an important key to effective and efficient research involves intelligently tailoring research activity to the client's needs.

E   MAINTAINING PROJECT FLEXIBILITY

While it is crucial to tailor research projects to satisfy the decision-maker's specific requirements, it is nevertheless also desirable to strike a balance between obtaining information of specific relevance and that which is likely to be generally useful or useful in the longer run. In this way, the manager can continue to support a project should there be changes in the specific focus of the client's interest or the decision-maker's needs during the life cycle of the project.

A balance of this sort can be struck if one first designs and rationalizes studies in terms of certain primary objectives relating to the specific needs of specific organizational clients. Then, at the same time, the studies are planned to satisfy certain secondary information objectives relating to less specific, less clearly defined, or possible future needs. By mixing specific and general objectives the work will remain relevant to some needs even if, by the time the research is completed, the client or the decision problem has changed.

F   MAINTAINING A WORK LOAD MIX OF BOTH BROAD- AND NARROW-SCOPE PROJECTS

In addition to those project-specific planning actions described previously, the effective research manager must exercise care and judgment to ensure a mix of projects in the overall program of research activities.

As part of this planning process, special consideration must often be given to the mix of broad phenomena, such as mass leisure trends, and the specific focal points within those fields. While an agency's research program should have a "centre of gravity of interest" (Price, 1966) which meets the needs of the agency it supports, at the same time the distribution of projects must not be restricted by too narrow a definition of relevance. It should be recognized that areas of research, such as tourism and outdoor recreation behaviour, may have special importance to several "mission-oriented" organizations and that support of these areas by more than one organization or business can be important not only to assure adequate research support in these vital areas but also to provide an added basis for communication within the field (Price, 1966, p. 46). A mix of work of both broad and narrow scope is also justifiable, given the uncertainties in our knowledge of tourism phenomena. Providing this mix ensures that the results of any particular study remain relevant even when new alternatives for projects are being considered or needs have changed in other ways.

G   MAINTAINING A MIX OF BOTH BASIC AND APPLIED RESEARCH

For research management to be effective in the long run, tourism research managers must understand and successfully manage the interface between applied and basic social science research (Price, 1966; Rossi et al., 1978). While the dividing line between these two types of research is by no means always clear, they can be differentiated by the purposes for which they are conducted. Applied research aids in the solution of "real world" problems while basic research enhances our knowledge of a phenomenon. In Coleman's words (1973), applied research is "decision" oriented and basic research is "phenomena" or "discipline" oriented. In other words, one is technology and the other is science.

The common conceptual model has assumed a linear relationship between these two areas of science and technology. But a number of recent studies have shown that the relationship between these two areas of endeavour is fundamentally interactive: each field facilitates but does not produce developments in the other. More specifically, new science sustains further scientific development in the context of a permissive, ambient technology while technological developments lead to still further technology in the context of a permissive, ambient science.

Phenomena-oriented research usually does not result directly in new and unexpected technological opportunities. Experience in observation of the effects of research results does not support the conventional model in which unique scientific events are followed in an orderly manner by applied research developments or new technology leads directly to new theory and conceptual development. Both need separate attention (Price, 1967, p. 42).

An example illustrates this point: When designing a tourist agency's research program, it would be a mistake to allocate the entire research budget to projects which support specific applied technological goals. Such a commitment would assume that the scientific- or phenomena-oriented concerns would look after themselves or would follow directly from the applied studies. Any tourist organization that does only statistical analysis, survey design, and demand model research would end up with a mass of applied technology but little general knowledge and conceptual development. Some researchers, in fact, feel that this state of affairs characterizes tourism and outdoor recreation studies in general (Coleman, 1979; Stankey, 1980). The unbalanced allocation of resources has three weaknesses: first, a broad continuous flow of information is absent; second, there is little opportunity to develop an increasingly sophisticated general field-wide handling of technological problems; and third, there is no development or elaboration of conceptual frameworks which integrate research findings and applications (Stankey, 1980).

H   THE DECISION TO MAKE OR BUY RESEARCH

The successful and efficient tourism research manager must also control the mix between in-house research and that contracted out. Problems frequently occur that demand skills or expertise that are unavailable or that one cannot afford to keep on strength.

Appropriate decisions in this realm are important for several reasons. Well-chosen and judiciously applied contract research increases the manager's leverage on the work load. It can also reduce the risk associated with particularly tricky projects. Contracting is frequently the best approach when some of the following conditions apply.

1   Short-term needs for specialized knowledge and skill are beyond in-house capabilities.

2   There is a need for greater objectivity and a fresh view of problem identification and specification of research.

3   An assignment has to be performed promptly and on schedule to be relevant to the management decision-making process, but staff size or previous commitments limit the internal capability to respond in a timely fashion.

4   An independent researcher is able to state something that cannot be said by organization personnel because of policy, credibility or political considerations.

5   Cost-saving advantages are possible by buying into syndicated research programs (Heit, 1978).

6   Contracting allows field work and analysis to be managed efficiently at peak and slack work periods, thereby preventing project backlogs (Forman and Bailey, 1969).

7   The financial responsibility for the research needs to be shifted to the user from the in-house research unit (Forman and Bailey, 1969). (This may allow the client to determine if the research is worth what it costs.)

8   Contract staff can compensate for the organization's inability to recruit competent in-house researchers because of some larger organizational problem such as a nonresponsive staffing function (Forman and Bailey, 1969).

9   Theoretical, conceptual, or methodological development work is needed that cannot be justified as a priority for an in-house applied research unit, but can be funded (resourced) at a low level by contract (e.g., with universities).

While the research manager gains certain strategic or political advantages from contract research, it too has limitations. Among these are the following.

1   The problem at hand can require a period of extensive in-house education and orientation which makes an external approach inefficient (Forman and Bailey, 1969).

2   The problem may be relatively unstructured and subject to many changes over the course of the project life cycle which makes it incompatible with an agency's relatively rigid contracting procedures (Forman and Bailey, 1969).

3   The problem may be sufficiently conducive to the development of programmed solutions that the tourism agency prefers to conduct the work, thereby gaining any educational benefits, in-house expertise, or standard solutions to the problem which may result from the research (Forman and Bailey, 1969).

4   Buying research requires a set of skills and allocation of effort different from that required for conducting research itself. The skills and resources for this operation may be unavailable within the research unit at any given time (Heit, 1978).

RESEARCH COUPLING PRESCRIPTIONS

As mentioned earlier, research coupling activities are done by the research manager to bridge the gap between the researcher and the client. Considerable general scientific literature now exists on this subject. In a review of this literature, Seidel (1982) observed that most of the prescriptions in this area can be subsumed under three different theories for effective information and technology transfer activities. He refers to these as (1) communication theories, (2) linkage theories, and (3) collaboration theories.

A COMMUNICATION

Training for employee presentations, language use, and other communications aids are frequently mentioned as appropriate to the improved communication of research information. A number of writers, including Glaser *et al*. (NIMH, 1971), Caplan and Barton (1976), Berg (1978), Glaser and Taylor (1973), Paisley (1968), and Rosenblatt (1968), have commented on particular aspects of the report-packaging problem as a means of increasing the effectiveness of research results. Important aspects include simple language (NIMH, 1971), good graphics (NIMH, 1971), effective translation (Caplan and Barton, 1976), targeting (Glaser *et al*., NIMH, 1971, p. 9; Rosenblatt, 1968; and Paisley, 1968), and personal contact (Glaser and Taylor, 1973). In the final analysis, however, authors reviewing "packaging" or formatting of social science presentation usually concluded that presentation is not the critical factor in effective research use (Korobkin, 1975, pp. 13–23). The crucial factor is linkage.

B LINKAGE

While the general applied science literature suggests that collaborative approaches are best for coupling with the research user, other linkage strategies appear to be most effective for allowing the research manager to maintain productive relations with researchers in the academic scientific community. In the field of tourism research and management there are at least three distinctly different interest groups: researchers, users, and managers. The three interest groups are further separated by communities of cultures. Despite their differences, information can be passed back and forth if appropriate linkage structures are created. Such linkage structures include middlemen, advisory committees, opinion leaders, information-transfer specialists, conferences, travel symposia, and other information-transfer events.

Special events, symposia, advisory committees, and opinion leaders seem partially successful in bringing phenomena-oriented information problems to the attention of potential researchers. They do not, however, seem particularly successful with applied users (Seidel, 1982). For them, the linkage theorists suggest the use of information transfer specialists. It has been noted by several commentators that this is easier said than done. It is difficult to find people who can bridge the gap who are not producers or users themselves (Dror, 1971; Frankel, 1969, p. 57).

C THE COLLABORATIVE MODEL

The literature on coupling suggests that a collaborative approach remains the most important key to the effective application of research and technical information to decision processes (Seidel, 1982; Driver and Knopf, 1981). This approach involves structuring problem-solving situations so that research information producers and users can work together to produce appropriate information plans, decisions, and actions. One important condition for such collaboration is that the policymaker or decision-maker has to know what the problem is and what information should influence decisions on it and has to understand that the formulation of a problem is essential to its solution because how it is defined determines what is done about it (Seidel, 1982; Caplan *et al*., 1975a).

Other conditions are also essential for successful collaboration. The policymaker and the researcher must have an understanding of the problems, policy issues, and required knowledge (Caplan *et al*., 1975a). Finally, the researcher, in particular, must understand the limitations of his or her scientific contribution to the decision problem. This involves recognizing what contribution science or data-based knowledge will make as opposed to less objective non-research-based knowledge or intuition (Caplan *et al*., 1975a).

This broad-based mutual understanding cannot be taken for granted. In fact, several observers have noted specifically that managers and researchers generally do not share this understanding initially. For example, Duncan (1974, p. 1160) comments that they often possess different values, particularly on their criteria of a good theory or finished product.

> *Both researchers and managers place considerable importance on practicality, usefulness, and applicability to specific problems in evaluating what is and what is not acceptable theory. However researchers display more concern for empirical validity while managers place considerable importance on profitability or the likelihood of payoffs in research efforts.*

Furthermore, Driver and Knopf (1981) suggest that the two professions attract different personality types. Individuals attracted to research tend to be stimulated by mental games, like to work with abstract things, have a high degree of tolerance for uncertainty (unpredictability and ambiguity), and are not greatly bothered by the time required to solve a problem. Research reports often reflect these characteristics. Individuals attracted to the managerial profession, on the other hand, tend to be more "down to earth" and prefer to deal with more tangible matters. As a rule, they have less interest in things that are uncertain, unpredictable, and abstract and need a clear cut and familiar environment. For them, the solution to problems must usually be evident, and they tend to want immediate results from their efforts. Managers are described by researchers as not liking to read research reports or hear what researchers have to say. While this can be the case in some instances, it could be that they require a certain manner of presentation. Certainly, managers don't want "iffy" statements or the conditional "maybe" and "perhaps" of many researchers. They are not interested in heavily qualified material. Instead, managers want clear-cut answers or specific, tangible steps which they can take to resolve the problems they face on a daily basis.

It should also be stated that managers, under the constraints of time and daily pressures, frequently do not have the time to sufficiently study problems at hand. While their understanding can be intuitively sound, it is frequently quite difficult for them to articulate clearly what their managerial objectives are in a specific problem situation (Driver and Knopf, 1981). In this regard, Driver and Knopf (1981) again argue that managers and researchers respond to markedly different professional recognition reward structures.

Collaboration has been proven to break down barriers. It also allows researchers and users to clarify their responsibilities and goals. Seidel (1982, p. 22) writes:

> Examining the results of over twenty studies supporting the collaboration theories, Glaser et al. (NIMH, 1971, p. 17) noted that increased relevance of information, mutual trust and education, and greater commitment to research results were products of collaboration between the researcher and the user.

But what, then, are the keys to good collaboration? There appear to be four: commitment, involvement, competence and recognition of the other party's requirements (Seidel, 1982). Both parties must meet the first three qualifications. In the case of the fourth, the manager must recognize the importance of specifying the problem in a manner that can be researched. In turn, the researcher must recognize that the user will make a decision with or without his or her help. In the end, the tourism manager must draw conclusions or take a position with respect to the decision problems in question. The researcher will rarely have the luxury of waiting until all the evidence is in before he or she speaks.

SUMMARY AND CONCLUSION

The premise of this paper is that several factors can be identified to explain why tourism research has generally not been effectively applied. First, appropriate organizational conditions are usually not present. Prerequisites for successful research operations include senior management support, sufficient reporting levels, direct channels of communication, and defined functional accountability.

Following these conditions, the research manager has to successfully master and manipulate two areas of activity: research planning and resourcing, and research coupling. A series of specific prescriptions have been offered for successful research planning and implementation: specifying the problem, priorization, standardizing solutions, scaling research to requirements, maintaining flexibility, mixing projects of different scope, mixing basic and applied work, and maintaining a mix of in-house and contractual research.

In the area of research coupling the need for attention to three coupling activities was emphasized. These are communication techniques, linkage strategies, and collaboration.

Endeavouring to satisfy the organizational and planning conditions described will help achieve the goal of improved research for more effective policy formulation and decision making in tourism.

BIBLIOGRAPHY

Anthony, Robert N., *Planning and Control Systems: A Framework for Analysis.* Boston: Division of Research, Graduate School of Business Administration, Harvard University. 1965.

Beaman, J., "Leisure Research and Its Lack of Relevance to Planning Management and Policy Formulation: A Problem of Major Proportions," *Recreation Research Review*, Vol. 6(3), pp. 18–25. 1978.

Beaman, J., *Education for Tourism Research for The 1980's.* Ottawa, Ontario: Socio-Economic Division, Program Co-ordination Branch, Parks Canada. 1980.

Berg, M.R., *The Use of Technology Assessment Studies in Policy-Making*, Ann Arbor: Center for Research on Utilization of Scientific Knowledge, Institute for Social Research, University of Michigan. 1978.

Bernstein, I.N., and Freeman, H.F., *Academic and Entrepreneurial Research.* New York: Russell Sage. 1975.

Brooks, H., "Science and the Allocation of Resources," *American Psychologist*, Vol. 22(3). March, 1967.

Brooks, H., "Applied Research: Definitions, Concept, Themes," *Applied Science and Technological Progress*, pp. 21–55. A report to the Committee on Science and Astronautics, U.S. House of Representatives, by the National Academy of Sciences. Washington, D.C.: U.S. Government Printing Office. June, 1967.

Caplan, N., and Barton, E., *Social Indicators 1973: A Study of the Relationship between the Power of Information and Utilization by Federal Executives.* Ann Arbor: Center for Research on Utilization of Scientific Knowledge, University of Michigan. 1976.

Caplan, Nathan S., Morrison, Andrea, and Stambaugh, Russell J., *The Use of Social Science Knowledge in Policy*

Decisions at the National Level: A Report to Respondents. Ann Arbor: Institute for Social Research, University of Michigan. 1975a.

Caplan, Nathan S., *et al.*, *A Minimal Set of Conditions Necessary for the Utilization of Social Science Knowledge in Policy Formulation at the National Level.* Prepared for the Conference on Social Values and Social Engineering, International Sociological Association. Ann Arbor: University of Michigan. April, 1975b.

Capstick, Margaret and Riley, Stuart, "Problems of Implementing Tourism Policy to Achieve Optimum Economic Impact," *Tourism as a Tool for Regional Development.* Edinburgh: Leisure Studies Association Conference. 1977.

Cohen, E., "Rethinking the Sociology of Tourism," *Annals of Tourism Research*, Vol. 6(1), pp. 18–35. 1979.

Coleman, E., "Rethinking the Sociology of Tourism," *Journal of Tourism Research*, Vol. 6(1), pp. 18–35. January–March 1979.

Coleman, J.S., "Problems on Conceptualization and Measurement in Studying Policy Impacts," *Public Policy Evaluation*, pp. 19–40. Beverly Hills: Sage. 1973.

Davis, Gordon B., *Management Information Systems: Conceptual Foundations, Structure and Development.* New York: McGraw–Hill. 1974.

Dimaggio, P., and Useem, M., "Small-Scale Policy Research in the Arts," *Policy Analysis*, Vol. 6(2), pp. 187–209. 1980.

Driver, B.L., and Knopf, R.C., "Some Thoughts on the Quality of Outdoor Recreation Research and Other Constraints on Its Application," *Social Research in National Parks and Wilderness Areas*, pp. 85–99. Atlanta: USDI, National Park Service, Southeast Regional Office. 1981.

Dror, Y., "Applied Social Science and Systems Analysis," *The Use and Abuse of Social Science.* New Brunswick, N.J.: Transaction Books. 1971.

Duncan, W.J., "The Researcher and the Manager—Comparative View of the Need for Mutual Understanding," *Management Science*, Vol. 20(8), pp. 1157–1163. 1974.

Forman, Lewis W., and Bailey, Earl L., *The Role and Organization of Marketing Research: A Survey.* New York. Conference Board. 1969.

Frankel, C., "Being In and Being Out," *The Public Interest*, Vol. 17, pp. 44–59. 1969.

Glaser, Edward M., and Taylor, Samuel H., "Factors Influencing the Success of Applied Research," *American Psychologist*, Vol. 28(2), pp. 140–146. February, 1973.

Heit, M.J. and Farrell, R.P., "The Consultant–Client Process: Toward More Effective Research," *Recreation Research Review*, Vol. 6(3) October 1978.

Keen, Peter F. and Scott-Morton, Michael S., *Decision Support Systems: An Organization Perspective.* Reading, Mass.: Addison–Wesley. 1978.

Korobkin, Barry J., *Images for Design: Communicating Social Science Research to Architects.* Cambridge, Mass.: Cambridge Architecture Research Office, Harvard University. 1975.

Kotler, Philip, *Marketing Management: Analysis, Planning and Control* (3rd edition). Englewood Cliffs, N.J.: Prentice–Hall. 1976.

Ledley, R.S., Shaller, H.I., Rotolo, L.S., and Wilson, J.B., "Methodology to Aid Research Planning," *I.E.E.E. Transactions on Engineering Management.* June, 1967.

McFarlan, Franklin W., Nolan, Richard L., and Norton, David P., *Information Systems Administration*, New York: Holt, Rinehart & Winston. 1973.

Morton, J.A., "A Model of The Innovation Process," *Proceedings of a Conference on Technology Transfer and Innovation, 1966.* Washington, D.C.: National Science Foundation. 1967.

National Institute of Mental Health (NIMH), *Planning for Creative Change in Mental Health Services: A Distillation of Principles on Research Utilization*, Vols. I and II. DHEW Publication No. (HMS) 73-9148. Washington D.C.: Department of Health, Education and Welfare and NIMH. 1971.

National Institute of Mental Health, *Planning for Creative Change in Mental Health Services.* Rockville, Md.: U.S. Government Printing Office. 1972.

Paisley, W.J., "Information Needs and Uses," *Annual Review of Information Science and Technology*, Vol. 3, pp. 1–30. New York: Wiley– Interscience. 1968.

Piore, E.R., "Science and Technology in Industry," *Interaction of Science and Technology.* Urbana, Ill.: University of Illinois Press. 1969.

Price, D., "Is Technology Historically Independent of Science? A Study in Statistical Historiography," *Technology and Culture*, Vol. 6(4), pp. 553–568. Fall 1965.

Price, W.J., "Concerning the Interaction between Science and Technology," *OAR Research Review*, Vol. 5(10). December 1966.

Price, W.J., "Planning Phenomena-Oriented Research in AFOSR," *Planning Phenomena-Oriented Research in a Mission Oriented Organization.* 12th Institute on Research Administration. April 24–27, 1967. Washington, D.C.: The American University Center for Technology and Administration. 1967.

Price, W.J., "The Key Role of a Mission-Oriented Agency's Scientific Research Activities," *The Interaction of Science and Technology.* Urbana, Ill.: University of Illinois Press. 1969.

Quinn, James B., and Cavanaugh, R.M., "Fundamental Research Can Be Planned: Excerpts from Studies," *Harvard Business Review*, Vol. 42, pp. 111–123. January 1964.

Ritchie, J.R.B., "Marketing and Marketing Research in Tourism Management," *Management Problems in the Sphere of Tourism.* 26th Congress of Association internationale d'experts Scientifiques du tourisme. Bern, Switzerland: Editions Gurten. 1976.

Ritchie, J.R. Brent, "Tourism Management Information Systems—Conceptual and Operational Issues," *Tourism Marketing and Management Issues*, Donald E. Hawkins et al. Eds., pp. 337–355. Washington, D.C.: George Washington University. 1980.

Rosenblatt, A., "The Practitioner's Use and Evaluation of Research," *Social Work*, Vol. 13, pp. 57–59. 1968.

Rossi, Peter H., Wright, James D., and Wright, Sonia R., "The Theory and Practice of Applied Social Research," *Evaluation Quarterly*, Vol. 2(2), pp. 171–191. 1978.

Rubenstein, A.A., and Haberstroh, C.J. (Eds.), *Some Theories of Organization*. Homewood, Ill.: Irwin. 1965.

Samuels, J.A., "Research to Help Plan the Future of a Seaside Resort," *The Marketing of Tourism and Other Services: Proceedings of the 12th Marketing Theory Seminar*. Lancaster, England: University of Lancaster. 1973.

Schwarzbart, G., "Recent Advances and Trends in the Design and Implementation of Management Information Systems," International Symposium on Information Systems, Terminology and Controlled Vocabularies, 1979, Hamburg, Germany/IUFRO Subject Group 6.03 Information Systems and Terminology. pp. 87–94.

Hamburg: Kommissionsverlag, Buchhandlung M. Wiedebusch. 1979.

Sherwin, C.W., and Isenson, R.S., "Project Hindsight," *Science*, Vol. 156(3782), pp. 1571-1577. June 23, 1967.

Seidel, Andrew D., "Usable EBR: What Can We Learn from Other Fields?" *Knowledge for Design: Proceedings of the Thirteenth Conference of EDRA*. pp. 16–25. College Park, Md.: Environmental Design Research Association. 1982.

Simon, Herbert A., *The New Science of Management Decisions*. New York: Harper & Brothers. 1960.

Stankey, G.H., "Integrating Wildland Recreation Research into Decision Making: Pitfalls and Promises," *Symposium Proceedings: Applied Research for Parks and Recreation in the 1980's, March 22, 1980*, Victoria, British Columbia: Department of Geography, University of Victoria. 1980.

PART TWO

FUNDAMENTALS OF TOURISM RESEARCH

This second part of the Handbook contains five chapters dealing with topics considered to be of fundamental importance to an understanding of research in the field of travel, tourism and hospitality. The initial chapter has been authored by a leader in the field of tourism statistics, Robin Chadwick. Its purpose is to provide a comprehensive and insightful review of the issues which need to be resolved to bring order to a complex and sometimes confused field of study. Formally entitled "Concepts, Definitions, and Measures used in Travel and Tourism Research," this chapter reviews alternative approaches which have been used both over time and within different geographical regions. More important, the chapter uses this review to delineate a comprehensive framework for standardizing the concepts and definitions used by managers and researchers in the field.

In Chapter 6, Abraham Pizam (University of Central Florida) provides a comprehensive and rigorous overview of the steps involved in the planning and execution of research intended to provide management with valid, reliable, and cost-effective results. The reader will note that the author has made a very conscious attempt to provide a very practical framework for the planning of tourism research while at the same time ensuring that the need for rigor and attention to detail is not overlooked. In terms of content, the chapter identifies seven sequential steps into which a tourism research investigation may be divided. While these seven steps are applicable to research in many fields, the manner in which Dr. Pizam relates it to the field of tourism should make this chapter one which is referred to frequently by both managers and beginning researchers.

Chapter 7 has been prepared by another of the leading experts in the field of tourism. In this chapter, Brian Archer (University of Surrey) presents an insightful discussion concerning demand forecasting and estimation, a topic of considerable interest to virtually all individuals involved in either the management or the research aspects of the tourism industry. The chapter has been written in a manner designed to make it of value to even nontechnical readers. Its contents focus on criteria to be kept in mind when attempting to choose an appropriate forecasting method in relation to a particular information need. Discussion subsequently focuses upon the various quantitative forecasting techniques which are available and describes their individual characteristics and normal areas of application. The chapter concludes with a review of more qualitative approaches to forecasting which are frequently employed when the quality of data or the available time does not permit the development of more rigorous quantitative forecasting models.

The fourth chapter included in this section on fundamentals of travel, tourism and hospitality research deals with the critical area of scaling and attitude measurement. Readers will be well aware that the field of travel, tourism, and hospitality research draws heavily upon survey methods which in turn rely extensively on the use of various scaling techniques to measure respondent perceptions and views concerning a broad range of topics. Chapter 8, authored by Gordon McDougall and Hugh Munro (Wilfrid Laurier University), first provides a concise yet thorough review of the literature related to attitudes and their characteristics. It then examines a number of theoretical considerations related to scaling and discusses how these considerations are reflected in the development of specific types of scales commonly used in the field of travel, tourism, and hospitality research. The scales discussed include the Thurstone scale, the Lickert scale, and the Semantic Differential as well as others. Following this conceptual discussion, the authors provide practical suggestions concerning the choice of an appropriate scale for a given research situation. This discussion is followed by a set of guidelines designed to assist individuals who find it necessary to undertake the construction of an attitude scale. Finally, the authors review several alternative approaches to attitude measurement and outline a number of special problems or issues that may arise in conducting attitude research in the travel, tourism and hospitality area.

The final chapter in Part Two is entitled "Issues in Sampling and Sample Design—A Managerial Perspective." As the title implies, this chapter, authored by John Cannon (U.S. Bureau of the Census), is intended to provide readers with a fundamental understanding of sampling in general as well as particular issues in sampling which pertain to the field of travel, tourism, and hospitality research. The initial section of the chapter includes a brief description of four basic sampling approaches and their advantages and disadvantages. Throughout the discussion, the author reminds the reader that nonsampling as well as sampling errors must be kept constantly in mind when assessing the value of different approaches to data collection. Following this conceptual part of the chapter, the focus of the discussion shifts towards the application of the various sampling methods discussed. The applications in question involve the National Travel Survey conducted by the U.S. Bureau of the Census and the Canadian Travel Survey conducted by Statistics Canada. It should be emphasized that in being asked to prepare this chapter, the author was requested to provide examples of broad scale national surveys (such as those referred to above) since these form a common reference point and are extensively used by virtually all persons in the travel, tourism, and hospitality industry. At the same time, readers should keep in mind that the basic concepts of sampling which are discussed are applicable to much smaller surveys as well.

5

Concepts, Definitions and Measures Used in Travel and Tourism Research[1]

ROBIN A. CHADWICK

Statistics Canada
Ottawa, Ontario, Canada

This chapter is a serious attempt to offer some leadership in consolidating the growing consensus regarding both the terminology and fundamental definitions of the area of human activity, business and research known as travel and tourism. Without the adoption of common standards and definitions, the discipline of travel and tourism cannot develop as a united body of thought. Furthermore, it cannot be expected to acquire credibility amongst the research community if it is unable to explain itself clearly and consistently.

Various concepts of tourism are discussed; alternative terminologies and definitions for travellers and tourists are examined; a comprehensive classification of travellers is proposed; the idea of a travel and tourism industry is considered; broader aspects of tourism are noted; some aspects of trip characteristics are presented; and measures used in travel and tourism research are explained.

TRAVEL AND TOURISM

The term "travel and tourism" is used in this book to describe the field of research on human and business activities associated with one or more aspects of the temporary movement of persons away from their immediate home communities and daily work environments for business, pleasure and personal reasons.

The "travel and tourism" approach represents a compromise between those who favor the use of one word over the other. Some current usage of these fundamental terms is given in Exhibit 1. In the 1980s a trend toward greater acceptance of the word "tourism" rather than "travel" has been identified.

It is common practice to use the two words "travel" or "tourism" either singly or in combination to describe three types of concepts:

A The movement of people

B A sector of the economy or an industry

C A broad system of interacting relationships of people, their needs to travel outside their communities, and services which attempt to respond to these needs.

EXHIBIT 1 Travel and Tourism Choosing the Term and Definition

Everyday usage:	'Tourist' and 'tourism' mean pleasure travel.
Frechtling (1976):	"The term 'tourist' has two strikes against it: it is too exclusive and pejorative in common parlance. 'Travel' has one strike against it: it includes extraneous activity. On balance . . . I believe the term traveler is best for representing one who takes a trip."
Arthur D. Little, Inc. (1978) National Tourism Policy Study:	'Travel' and 'tourism' treated as synonyms.

International Organizations:	Use the term 'tourism' not 'travel.' Examples: Tourism Committee of the Organization for Economic Co-operation and Development (OECD); The World Tourism Organization (WTO); formerly International Union of Official Travel Organisations (IUOTO).
Britain:	The term 'tourism' is becoming more popular. Example: name change from British Travel Association to British Tourist Authority in 1969 (Eagers 1979).
United States:	In the 1970s preferred the term 'travel.' Example: United States Travel Data Center. In the 1980s more acceptance for the word 'tourism.' Example: United States Travel Service 1977 study indicated "the public sector of the tourism industry" preferred the term 'travel' to 'tourism.' A 1981 study indicated 33 states used 'tourism' or 'tourist' in their titles while only 20 states used 'travel'. In 1981 the National Tourism Policy Act established the United States Travel and Tourism Administration, replacing the U.S. Travel Service (Wynegar 1984).
Canada:	In all 12 provinces and territories departments responsible for travel and tourism research and promotion were using the word 'tourism' in their title by 1982. In 1978 the Travel Industry Association of Canada became the Tourism Industry Association of Canada.

THE MOVEMENT OF PEOPLE

The chapter now looks at the concept of the movement of people and the terminology and definitions applied by international agencies and by each of the United States, Canada, the United Kingdom, and Australia. A comprehensive classification of travellers endeavors to reflect a consensus of current thought and practice.

INTERNATIONAL AGENCIES

The basic international approach was established by the Committee of Statistical Experts of the League of Nations in 1937, when a "tourist" was defined as: "Any person visiting a place for a period of at least 24 hours." This definition included those travelling for business reasons as well as those travelling for pleasure, for family reasons, or for health. It excluded persons travelling to establish a residence or to take up an occupation, students travelling to an educational establishment, and commuters going to work. Persons arriving for less than 24 hours were classified as "excursionists."

Following proposals made at the 1963 United Nations Conference in Rome on International Travel and Tourism, an Expert Statistical Group on International Travel Statistics, reporting in 1967, recommended the use of the term "visitor" to cover both "tourists" and "excursionists" and to provide a breakdown of data on the two groups whenever possible (OECD Tourism Committee 1980).

In classifying travellers for inclusion in international travel statistics, the World Tourism Organization (WTO) (1978a) pointed out that the main distinction to be made is between residents and nonresidents. Updated definitions were published by WTO in 1983.

Residents are described as persons returning from visits abroad (including foreign nationals having their usual place of residence in the country) while *nonresidents* are visitors from abroad (including nationals having their usual place of residence abroad). Nonresidents who come to visit are the basic category of travellers referred to as visitors.

International visitors are defined as any persons visiting a country other than that in which they have a usual place of residence, for not more than one year, and whose main purpose of visit is other than following an occupation remunerated from within the country visited. The category of international visitors is subdivided into *international tourists* and *international excursionists.*

International tourists are international visitors staying at least 24 hours but not more than one year in the country visited and the purpose of whose trip may be classified under one of the following headings:

A Pleasure, recreation, holiday, sport
B Business, visiting friends and relatives, mission, meeting, conference, health, studies, religion.

The international tourist category is regarded as including crew members who visit or stop over in the country visited and use its accommodation facilities.

International excursionists are international visitors staying less than 24 hours in the country visited. Also treated as a subset within international excursionists are visiting crew members who do not use the country's accommodation facilities.

Domestic travel was not a subject of much interest to the international agencies until the late seventies. WTO put forward some tentative definitions in its first publication on Domestic Tourism Statistics (1978b). These were subsequently updated and approved in 1983 as follows: *Domestic visitors* are any persons, regardless of nationality, resident of a country and who travel to a place within the same country for not more than one year and whose main purpose of visit is other than following an occupation remunerated from within the place visited. The category of domestic visitors is subdivided into *domestic tourists* and *domestic excursionists.*

Domestic tourists are domestic visitors staying at least 24 hours, but not more than one year, in the place visited and the purpose of whose trip can be classified under one of the following headings:

A Pleasure, recreation, holiday, sport
B Business, visiting friends and relatives, mission, meeting, conference, health, studies, religion.

Domestic excursionists are domestic visitors staying less than 24 hours in the place visited.

WTO observes that one other element not included in this definition, but usually employed in national definitions of domestic tourism, is a minimum distance criterion, such as 25, 50, or 100 miles (40, 80, or 160 kilometers). This is required primarily for practical reasons in data collection to identify a reasonable cutoff to eliminate purely local travel and other short trips which would be difficult for the respondent to recall and which are less likely to be of interest to users of tourism statistics.

UNITED STATES

The Western Council for Travel Research (1963) employed the term "visitor" and defined a "visit" as occurring every time a visitor entered the area under study. The United States Department of Commerce (Little 1969) suggested the use of the concept "promotable tourist" when the motive behind a study is to determine a state's promotion budget.

The definition of tourist used by the National Tourism Resources Review Commission (1973) was: "A tourist is one who travels away from home for a distance of at least 50 miles (one way) for business, pleasure, personal affairs, or any other purpose except to commute to work, whether he stays overnight or returns the same day." A subsequent report, the *National Tourism Policy Study* (Little 1978), treated "travel" and "tourism" as synonyms and defined both terms as: "The action and activities of people taking trips (to a place(s) outside of their home communities) for any purpose except daily commuting to and from work."

The National Travel Surveys of the United States Bureau of the Census (1979) and the United States Travel Data Center (1984) report on all round-trips with a one-way route mileage of 100 miles or more. These household surveys include these trips whether or not a night was spent away from home and regardless of purpose, excluding only crews, students, military personnel on active duty, and commuters.

CANADA

In the series of quarterly household sample surveys, known as the Canadian Travel Survey, which commenced in 1978, trips qualifying for inclusion are similar to those covered in the National Travel Survey in the United States. The main difference is that in the Canadian survey, the lower limit for the one-way distance is 50 miles (80 km) instead of 100 miles (Statistics Canada 1980a). The 50 mile figure was a compromise satisfying concerns about problems of recalling shorter trips and about the possibility of the inclusion of trips completed entirely within the boundaries of a large metropolitan area such as Toronto.

The determination of which length of trip to include in surveys of domestic travel has varied according to the purpose of the survey and the survey methodology employed. Whereas there was general agreement that commuting journeys and one-way trips should be excluded, qualifying distances, when used, varied between 25 miles and 100 miles. Two provinces had no mileage qualification for trips and included in their surveys all trips involving either a one-way distance of 25 miles or one or more nights away (Statistics Canada 1979a, pp. 88–89).

Canada and the United States have a cooperative arrangement to collect statistics on travel between their countries. The primary groups of travellers identified are nonresident travellers, resident travellers, and other travellers. Both nonresident and resident travellers include both same-day and business travellers. Commuters are included and are not distinguished from other same-day business travellers. Other travellers consist of immigrants, former residents, military personnel, and crews (Statistics Canada 1979b).

UNITED KINGDOM

Heeley (1980) observed that the British statistics on travel and tourism included business trips and excluded most trips without overnight stays. On the other hand, he favored excluding business trips and including same-day trips. Heeley noted: "Tourism should be defined conceptually as those aspects of leisure-time behavior and their consequences which occur as a result of temporary trips away from the home environment and which are motivated exclusively by a concern for recreational matters."

The concept of a tourist trip in Britain seems to be best reflected in the definition employed by the British Tourist Authority (1980) in the British Home Tourism Survey: "A stay of one or more nights from home for holidays, visits to friends or relatives, business, conferences or any other purposes except such things as boarding education or semipermanent employment." The English Tourist Board, however, was sufficiently interested in same-day travel to institute a Survey of Leisure Day Trips in the months of July to September in 1981 and 1982 (English Tourist Board 1983).

AUSTRALIA

The Bureau of Industry Economics (1979) placed length of stay and distance travelled constraints in its definition of tourists as follows: "A person visiting a location at least 40 km from his usual place of residence, for a period of at least 24 hours and not exceeding twelve months."

Leiper (1979) also distinguished tourists from other types of travellers generally, by claiming that their activities represent a discretionary use of time and monetary resources. The Leiper definition of a tourist is: "A person making a discretionary temporary tour which involves at least one overnight stay away from the normal place of work, excepting tours made for the primary purpose of earning remuneration from the points en route."

A COMPREHENSIVE CLASSIFICATION OF TRAVELLERS

The main types of travellers are indicated in Fig. 1. It recognizes the fundamental distinction between residents and visitors and the interest of travel and tourism practitioners in the characteristics of nontravellers as well as of travellers. It also reflects the apparent consensus that business and same-day travel are both within the scope of travel and tourism, despite the reservations of writers such as Heeley and Leiper. Some discussion of the topic appeared in the Canadian Geographer (Britton 1979, Mieczkowski 1981, Chadwick 1981).

Placed to one side are some other types of travellers generally regarded as being outside the area of inter-

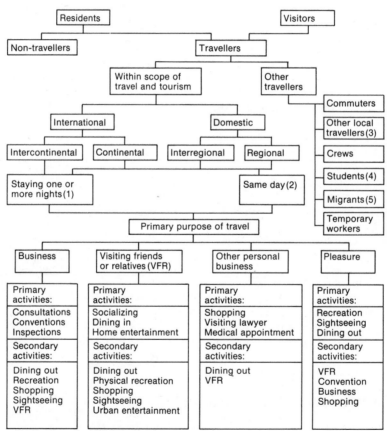

(1) "Tourists" in international technical definitions.
(2) "Excursionists" in international technical definitions.
(3) Travellers whose trips are shorter than those which qualify for travel and tourism, e.g. under 50 miles (80 km) from home.
(4) Students travelling between home and school only — other travel of students is within scope of travel and tourism.
(5) All persons moving to a new place of residence including all one way travellers such as emigrants, immigrants, refugees, domestic migrants and nomads.

FIGURE 1 *Classification of travellers.*

est, although included in some travel surveys. Foremost amongst these exclusions are commuters which, it seems to be unanimously agreed, fall outside the area of interest of the travel and tourism community. Other travellers generally excluded from studies on travel and tourism are those who undertake trips within the community, which for convenience are arbitrarily described as trips involving less than a specific one-way distance, such as 50 miles (80 km).

The broad class of travellers categorized as migrants, both international and domestic, is also commonly excluded from tourism or travel research. They are excluded on the grounds that their movement is not temporary, although they use the same facilities as other travellers, albeit in one direction, and frequently require temporary accommodation on reaching their destination. The real significance of migration to travel and tourism, however, is not in the one-way trip in itself, but the long-run implications of a transplanted demand for travel and the creation of new travel destinations for separated friends and relatives. Dunstan (1980) spoke of the significance of immigration on travel in Australia and the Canadian Government Office of Tourism (1980a) highlighted the importance of visiting friends or relatives as a motivation for vacation travel by Canadians both inside and outside Canada. The influence of migration on travel is a subject discussed in terms of a "churn rate" (the rate of gross interprovincial and international migration per 1000 population) by Statistics Canada (1984a).

Other groups of travellers are commonly excluded from travel and tourism studies because their travel is not affected by travel promotion, although they tend to compete for the same type of facilities and services. Students and temporary workers travelling purely for reasons of education or temporary employment are two leading examples and they are included in the international definitions (WTO 1983b). Another frequently excluded group consists of crews, although they can be regarded as special subsets of tourists and excursionists (WTO 1978a).

Of those travellers directly within the scope of travel and tourism, basic distinctions are made between those whose trips under study involve international travel and those whose trips are solely domestic and between those whose trips demand overnight accommodation and those whose trips are completed within one day. An additional meaningful division may also be made between those international travellers whose travel is between continents and those whose international trip is confined to countries in the same continent. In the case of the United States, the distinction is between trips to or from the neighboring countries of Canada and Mexico or elsewhere in the Americas and trips made to or from countries in Europe or other continents. The six WTO regions are the Americas, Africa, Europe, Middle East, South Asia, and the Pacific (WTO 1981).

The same type of distinction may be made in domestic travel between interregional and regional. In the United States there are eight travel regions. Travel between them would be regarded as interregional and within them as regional. In Canada, five major regions may be identified: Atlantic, Central, Prairies, West, and North. In practice, travel studies in Canada tend to show interprovincial data because of the large size of some provinces and the research and planning needs of each provincial department of tourism.

The purposes of travel identified in Fig. 1 go beyond those traditionally accepted because of the growing evidence that "visits to friends and relatives" (VFR) is a basic travel motivation and a distinctive factor in marketing, accounting for a major proportion of travel. In any event, "primary purpose" is an arbitrary concept because many journeys are undertaken for a combination of reasons, including activities such as those indicated in Fig. 1.

TRIP CHARACTERISTICS

Surveys of travel and tourism are undertaken for a variety of reasons. The types of information they collect fall into four main categories: socioeconomic data on travellers; opinions and attitudes of travellers; geographic facts regarding origins, destinations, and places visited; and information about the characteristics of trips.

Trip characteristics are the most fundamental findings of travel surveys. They provide basic information on the "Why, When, What, and How" of travel, as distinct from the "Who and Where" covered by socioeconomic and geographical questions. Leading examples of trip characteristics are purpose of trip, mode of transportation, type of accommodation used, and activities engaged in.

The primary purposes for travel listed in Fig. 1 may be subdivided. The United States National Travel Surveys identify more specific purposes such as conventions, as a subset under business, and outdoor recreation or sightseeing, under the heading of pleasure. British statistics record "holiday inclusive tours" (i.e., package tours) separately from other pleasure travel described as "holiday independent visits" (Economist Intelligence Unit 1983).

Mode of transportation can lead to a complex classification, although the main modes of general interest in North America are primarily commercial airplane and private automobile, with lesser interest shown in bus, rail, and water transportation. A further breakdown of commercial air travel of value to the travel trade and travel, tourism and transportation planners may be made between charter flight and scheduled flight. Depending upon the use to which the data can be put, automobile trips can be distinguished to identify the use of rental vehicles or vehicles equipped for camping as was done in the 1977 National Travel Survey (U.S. Bureau of the Census 1979).

Overnight accommodation types exist in considerable variety, with regional and national variations. Despite pronounced differences between the types of accommodation found in different parts of the world, the OECD Tourism Committee distinction between main and supplementary types may be applied universally. The main types of commercial accommodation in North America are the hotels and motels including specialized variations such as motor inns, motor hotels, resort hotels, and lodges. This basic accommodation stock is supplemented by campgrounds and trailer parks, rented condominiums and vacation homes, commercial cottages and cabins, and hostels. Most travel surveys also record nights spent by travellers in private accommodation facilities, including homes of friends or relatives and personally owned vacation homes.

"Activities engaged in" is an important trip characteristic but a difficult one on which to collect meaningful information because the frequency and duration of involvement cannot be readily assessed. Nevertheless, the 1977 National Travel Survey (U.S. Bureau of the Census 1979) collected, compiled, and published information on attendance at six different types of events and attractions and participation in eleven specific recreational activities. The Canadian Travel Survey instituted an activity question in 1982 which identified ten different events and attractions and five specific outdoor recreational or sports activities (Statistics Canada 1984a).

UNITS OF MEASUREMENT IN SURVEYS OF TRAVEL AND TOURISM

The units of measurement are a function of the type of survey method or source that is selected. There are fundamentally only three different types of surveys used to collect information on the volume of travel and tourism:

- Household surveys collect information on the travel experience of individuals over a given recall period.
- Location surveys obtain counts of visitors or information from them about their current visitor trip.
- Business surveys, which provide general information on travel and tourism business operations, sometimes also collect traveller or visitor—customer information.

HOUSEHOLD SURVEY MEASURES

From a household survey it is possible to determine whether or not a person, or the members of a household, travelled over a given period of time. It is also possible to produce a count of *persons*, distinguishing between those who did not travel (*nontravellers*) and those who did travel (*travellers*), according to the definitions of travel employed in the survey. For the travellers, it is also possible to determine their *frequency of travel* and, thereby, produce counts of those who travelled once, twice, or more often during the survey period.

The survey period, to which the frequency of travel applies, depends upon the methodology of the survey. It may be impossible to produce data on frequency of travel over one whole calendar year, when the survey recall period is only three months. In the 1977 National Travel Surveys (U.S. Bureau of the Census 1979), that problem was addressed by attempting to retain the same sample for each quarter of the calendar year. In the Canadian Travel Survey, the sample of households changes for every quarterly survey. Therefore, measures of frequency of travel are not available on an annual basis (Statistics Canada 1984b).

To measure the volume of travel, it is necessary to collect information in such a way that it may be organized in units such as person-trips, household-trips, person- (or household-) nights, and person- (or household-) days. The basic unit, the *person-trip*, represents the travel from home and return of one person. In order to determine the volume of travel originating from households, the term *household-trip* is employed. When one person from a household travels alone, both one person-trip and one household-trip are scored; but if two persons from the household travel together the score is two person-trips and one household trip. Sometimes the term *trip* is used alone, but it can be ambiguous if not defined.

The same type of ambiguity can arise when the term *vacation trip* is used. It is necessary to distinguish between vacation trips taken by individuals, i.e., vacation person-trips, and those which reflect the participation of members of a household, i.e., vacation household-trips (Canadian Government Office of Tourism 1980a).

Care must also be taken to understand the definition of the word *vacation* when it is applied to trips of any type. In the National Travel Surveys (U.S. Travel Data Center 1984), the respondent is asked for every trip reported, "Was this a vacation trip?" On the other hand, in the surveys of Vacation Travel by Canadians, which are concerned only with vacation trips, respondents are requested to omit reporting on trips made exclusively on weekends or on long weekends. In the United States surveys there is tabulation flexibility that allows weekend trips to be either included or excluded, depending upon user need.

Possibly the clearest definition of vacation trip is the one employed by the Tourism Committee of OECD (1980). It recommends that *holidays* (vacation trips) should be taken to mean "a stay outside the place of residence for health and recreational purposes and including at least four consecutive nights." This definition has the disadvantage of excluding many so-called *minivacations.*" However, in a general travel survey such minivacations could be identified as "stay outside the place of residence for pleasure purposes for 1 to 3 nights."

The concept of *party-trip* is less easily applied in household surveys. Party-trips include persons from two or more households travelling together. The concept has been effectively employed in a report on Vacation Travel by Canadians (Canadian Government Office of Tourism 1980b) but is more readily used in exit or in-flight surveys such as the Survey of International Air Travelers (USTTA 1984).

Person-trips, household-trips, or party-trips are basic measures of travel volume, giving no indication of length or duration of stay or of likely impact upon the economy. A favored means of refining trip measurement is to take account of the length of time away in order to produce person-day or person-night measures. *Person-nights* are achieved simply by multiplying number of travellers by number of nights away. This is not necessarily fully reflected in the use of commercial accommodation because the majority of domestic tourists and many international tourists stay in the homes of friends or relatives. For international comparisons, OECD (1980) and WTO (1983a) data on person-nights (overnight stays) of tourists in different countries are footnoted with a variety of definitions pertaining to the types of overnight accommodation that they include.

Person-days are similar to person-nights and are arrived at by multiplying the number of travellers by the number of days away. For any one person-trip there is generally regarded to be one more person-day than person-night, although Frechtling (1978) favors equating person-days with person-nights. For same-day trips the number of person-nights tally zero and, therefore, person-night data can be misleading for researchers who want to include same-day travel in their studies. On the other hand, person-day data can be equally misleading for users interested only in travel involving overnight accommodation.

In addition to units of duration there are units of distance. They are arrived at simply by multiplying the number of travellers by the number of units of distance each travels to produce *person-miles* or *person-kilometres*. Users should determine if such data are one-way or round-trip and straight-line or actual. Straight-line distances can be calculated from a computer program adjusted to trip distance as in the National Travel Surveys (U.S. Travel Data Center 1984) or simply derived from respondent estimates as in the Canadian Travel Survey.

Perhaps the most useful travel survey measurements, but also possibly the most difficult to record, are *expenditure data.* They can be estimated directly by respondents as in the national household travel surveys of the U.S. Bureau of the Census and Statistics Canada or developed from expenditure formulae applied to person-trip estimates as calculated by the United States Travel Data Center. Information may be collected for each aspect of tourism service purchased, e.g., transportation, accommodation, food, recreation, entertainment, retail goods. In practice it is not easy for travellers to recall their expenditures or to itemize them, particularly in the case of packaged tours or business travel (United States Bureau of the Census 1979).

There are also a variety of conceptual questions to be raised when expenditure information is either included in travel surveys or estimated in respect of travel. These include such questions as: inclusion or not of travel-related expenditures incurred in anticipation of a trip, such as sports equipment, language lessons, and guidebooks; provision or not for a portion of the depreciation cost of major consumer durables used on the trip, such as a new automobile, a motor home, or a boat; the relevant calculation for the true cost of automobile usage on a trip, over and above fuel consumption; the appropriate geographical allocation of transportation expenses represented by fares paid to carriers; and the handling of certain day-to-day living costs which would have been incurred in the home locality if the trip had not been taken. These types of questions are dealt with in the expenditures studies of the United States Travel Data Center (1979).

LOCATION SURVEY MEASURES

Surveys taken at locations may be related to attendance at an event or attraction, to a count of passing travellers, or to users of a transportation facility. This family of survey types includes visitor surveys, entry and exit surveys, in-flight surveys, and highway counts. The information can all be collected at one point in time or it can include a questionnaire to be returned later, as in the case of some surveys on travel between the United States and Canada (Statistics Canada 1979b).

The basic units are different from those in household surveys because the information collected is normally related only to the one visit and may not even cover a whole trip. The resulting data, therefore, are recorded as *visits* which are only approximately equal to person-trips. Using the example of travel across the United States—Canada border, it is quite possible for two or more visits to be made in the course of one trip. In fact it is regular practice for United States residents travelling between the states of Michigan and New York State to travel via southwestern Ontario in both directions on one trip. Likewise automobile travellers from central Canada to both western and eastern provinces have the option of choosing between the Trans-Canada Highway and interstate highways or other routes in the United States.

For overseas (intercontinental) travel, counts of returning residents are very similar to overseas person-trip counts because multiple reentries from overseas on the same trip are unlikely. On the other hand, a distinction has to be made between counts of reentries of residents and numbers of visits of residents to overseas countries. This is because it is common for tourists to visit more than one country in the course of a trip. In the case of Canadian residents, for example, information is collected and published not only on reentry from the United States and other countries, but also on numbers of visits to selected states of the United States and selected countries (Statistics Canada 1984c).

A time element may be applied to location surveys. An example is the National Parks Service of the United States Department of the Interior (1980), which, in maintaining records of usage, employs a unit of time that may be readily used in other location or visitor surveys. This is the *visitor-hour*, which is described as "the presence of one or more persons in a park for continuous, intermittent or simultaneous periods of time aggregating one hour."

Location surveys are also a means of collecting expenditure data. In some respects, this source of expenditure data might be expected to give more accurate results than household surveys, because of the elimination of much of the recall problem. However, information collected from travellers is liable to be incomplete if they have to supply their answers under time pressures or in connection with customs declarations. In this respect, care is also required in distinguishing between expenditures made outside the country and expenditures made within it and whether or not both are reported in a survey. Care should also be taken to determine whether transportation expenditures relate to both domestic and foreign carriers.

BUSINESS SURVEY MEASURES

Surveys of businesses typically relate to a full financial year of operation, although more limited information may be available on a monthly basis. Examples of such businesses include hotels, restaurants, travel agents, passenger transportation companies, and recreational attractions. Information collected from these sources normally consists primarily of receipts. It is frequently difficult to distinguish between receipts from travellers and from local residents. However, operators of businesses can be asked to give informed estimates of the breakdown of the sources of

their receipts between local residents and visitors, between business travellers and pleasure travellers, and between visitors from other parts of Canada, from the United States, and from other countries. Other information can sometimes be obtained from businesses on such matters as their employees, their facilities, and even certain characteristics of their clients.

In North America, campgrounds and certain other accommodation establishments such as youth hostels may keep records in terms of numbers of visitors, person-nights, or party-nights. Campground data have to be particularly carefully scrutinized to determine the type of visitor units employed, the method of counting, and the definitions used. *Visitors* may be recorded in person-days or person-nights, or without regard to length of stay in terms of visits, number in party, or campsite registrations.

It is common practice for accommodation establishments in Europe to maintain a record of visitors according to their country of permanent residence and the number of nights that they stay. This type of information is not available in North America, although some information is produced on occupancy rates, without regard to country of residence of visitors. Occupancy data in Europe tend to be based on beds occupied (OECD Tourism Committee 1980), whereas in North America, rooms or other units of accommodation are used.

Managers of events and attractions commonly count or estimate numbers of visits or visitors and sometimes arrange for special surveys to be conducted to determine the socioeconomic and geographical origin of their visitors. Examples of published data on these types of counts are to be found in reports of the United States Travel Data Center (1980) and of the English Tourist Board (1979).

In North America, the passenger transportation companies producing the most complete origin and destination passenger data are the airlines, which have been required through the Civil Aeronautics Board (1980) in the United States and the Canadian Transport Commission to supply this information from samples of used flight coupons from passengers on scheduled flights (Statistics Canada 1984d). A serious limitation of this type of ticket-based data is that it relates only to flows of passengers, with no identification of place of residence or even place of ticket purchase, and with no demographic, social, or economic information whatsoever. The airport origin information is not even an indicator of residence, because origin may be either airport of commencement of outward segment of trip or airport of commencement of return segment of trip. For these data, the unit is the passenger or one-way trip. This means that it takes approximately two one-way airline trips, assuming air is used in both directions, to equate with one person-trip from a household survey.

Particular care needs to be taken of the use of the term "trip" in airline and airport activity statistics. It is sometimes used interchangeably with "leg" or "enplanement." In this case if a person flies from New York to Los Angeles, but changes planes in Chicago, there are four trips, compared to one person-trip in household surveys. In terms of airport arrivals and destinations, this same single person-trip might in fact acquire the status of eight trips if each airport arrival and departure is counted.

More complete information is available on the origin and destination of passengers on charter flights, both international and domestic (Statistics Canada 1979b). However, for charter airline passenger data the unit of measurement is also the passenger or the one-way trip.

TRAVEL AND TOURISM INDUSTRY

The degree of acceptance given to the idea of a travel and tourism industry depends upon the nature of the definition of the word "industry" that is used. Macroeconomists who look at the overall picture of national economies are inclined to argue that tourism and travel do not comprise an industry because there is no distinct product or service that can be described. Furthermore, they argue that any attempt to account for travel and tourism is liable to lead to double counting, because activities of all establishments are already allocated to existing industries. On the other hand, the very existence of the national trade associations, the Travel Industry Association of America and the Tourism Industry Association of Canada, clearly indicates that there is a sector of North American business which identifies itself as a travel or tourism industry.

Government is less inclined to refer to tourism and travel as an industry. Nevertheless, the *Report of the Tourism Sector Consultative Task Force* (Powell 1978) stated that:

> *Tourism is both an industry and a response to a social need: society's adoption of travel as part of a lifestyle. The industry does not have a discrete image like other industry sectors, partly because of its heterogeneity and because many of its components are largely composed of small businesses, but it is pervasive across Canada. Its product includes all the elements that combine to form the tourism consumer's experience and exists to service his needs and expectations.*

The definition used in the National Tourism Policy Study (U.S. Senate Committee on Commerce 1976) reads as follows:

> *The interrelated amalgamation of businesses and agencies which totally or in part provide the means of transport, goods, services, accommodations, and other facilities, programs, and resources for travel out of the home community for any purpose not related to local day-to-day activity.*

A more concise definition is to be found in Leiper (1979):

> *The tourist industry consists of all those firms, organizations and facilities which are intended to serve the specific needs and wants of tourists.*

Leiper identified the main components of the industry as transportation, accommodation, food, and related services.

One of the clearest definitions coming from an international agency is to be found in a publication of the United Nations (UNCTAD 1971):

> *The 'tourist sector' or 'tourist industry' . . . can be broadly conceived as representing the sum of those industrial and commercial activities producing goods and services wholly or mainly consumed by foreign visitors or by domestic tourists.*

This United Nations source identified seven industrial areas which could be regarded as belonging in different degrees to the tourist sector, although for the most part not concerned exclusively with tourism. These were accommodation, travel agents and tour operators, restaurants, passenger transport enterprises, manufacturers of handicrafts and souvenirs designed for visitors and related outlets, establishments providing facilities for recreation and entertainment of visitors, and government agencies concerned with tourism. Of these seven, the United Nations source identified three areas which it considered were practical for the development of statistical series: accommodation, travel agents, and passenger transport enterprises.

THE STANDARD INDUSTRIAL CLASSIFICATION

Most countries classify their industries in terms of those areas of production of goods and services which form a statistically meaningful and identifiable portion of their economies. Various attempts have been made to utilize these classifications to identify those segments applicable to tourism and travel.

Reference was made in the United Nations study of 1971 to the use of the international standard industrial classification (SIC) in order to identify some branches of tourist activity. It pointed out, however, the impracticality of using the SIC to define the tourist industry, because typically only part of the output of a SIC industry is sold to tourists. Similar conclusions have been reached in studies made in Australia (Bureau of

Industry Economics 1979), in Canada (Kates, Peat, Marwick and Company 1969, The Laurentian Institute 1974, and McCloy 1975), and in the United States (Little 1969, Kahn 1975, and Frechtling 1976, 1977). Furthermore, there are no guarantees that statistics are available on industries identified in the SIC structure (The Laurentian Institute 1974).

Despite the limitations of the SIC as an aid in measuring the significance of the travel and tourism industry, it is a fundamental basis for industry identification. The main elements of the SICs are grouped in Appendix 2 in three degrees of association following the precedents of the United Nations, Frechtling, and Kahn. The primary group consists of accommodation, transportation, travel trade, and government. Even with this group, identifications of travel and tourism elements may not be easy. Information on those elements of government departments responsible for travel and tourism activities may not be readily disaggregated. Passenger transportation figures may be difficult to access because of the problems of isolating intercity and passenger data from reports of establishments which are involved also in local or freight transportation.

At other levels of association, identification of data meaningful to travel and tourism is even more difficult, with the necessity of adopting arbitrary percentage allocations. Quite often it takes a combination of traveller and local resident demand to support a major cultural attraction. Gadbois (1975) has referred to the internationally renowned zoological gardens in San Diego as an example of an amenity strongly supported by both visitors and residents, while Jafari (1982) describes the dual role of restaurants serving both tourists and residents.

TRAVEL AND TOURISM SYSTEMS

Systematic approaches to the study of travel and tourism have been developed by a number of researchers. One of these is the tourism process of Chau (1977) in which he described the tourist as the demand, the travel industry as the supply, and attractions as the tourist product and summarized the interrelated process as the subject, means, and object of tourism. Gunn, in his book *Tourism Planning* (1979), referred to a "tourism functional system" involving five components: tourists, transportation, attractions, services—facilities, and information—direction. Leiper (1979) had a slightly different approach in his system involving five basic elements: tourists, generating regions, transit routes, destination regions, and a tourist industry operating within physical, cultural, social, economic, political, and technological environments.

The travel and tourism system proposed in Fig. 2 illustrates the concept of *people* requiring *services* in order to achieve certain *objectives*. When these *objectives* are located outside their community, of necessity they become *travellers* and require *services* available to those who travel. Thus if residents of a northern community have the objective of a winter vacation in warm southern sunshine, they must travel outside their community using transportation services, possibly a travel agent, and certainly accommodations, food, recreation, and entertainment services at their destination. Likewise, residents of a location with a warm dry winter location would require a similar package of services if their *objective* was a snow-skiing vacation.

Figure 2 indicates that some *travellers* qualify neither as *residents* travelling outside the community nor as *visitors* from other communities and are, therefore, designated as unrelated to *travel* and *tourism*. It also refers to those persons (*non-travellers*) who are not motivated to travel during the study period. Recognition is given to the main segments of the service industries relating to travel and tourism, pointing out that significant portions of each industry provide services unrelated to travel and tourism. It also recognizes that the four primary objectives of travellers can at times be fulfilled without indulging in travel. Most personal activity is accomplished within the home community. It can also be the location of many pleasurable activities, the place to socialize with those friends and relatives who live locally, and the venue for much business activity.

CONCLUSION

This chapter illustrates the trend toward the greater use of the word "tourism," either alone or in combination with "travel," to describe the area of program administration or research concerned with travel outside the community of residence. The conclusion is that to minimize confusion, the area should be described as "travel and tourism."

The consensus of international and North American opinion seems to be that, despite certain arguments to the contrary, both same-day and business travel should be considered part of "travel and tourism," while commuting and local travel of under 50 miles from home should be excluded. There seems to be general acceptance of the idea that crews, students, migrants, and temporary workers do not belong in the study of travel and tourism, although, like nontravelling residents, they do compete for use of certain travel and tourism facilities.

A classification of travellers and accompanying definitions is presented (Fig. 1). Reference is made also to the classification of leading trip characteristics, such as purpose of trip, mode of transportation, type of accommodation, and activities. Units of measurement

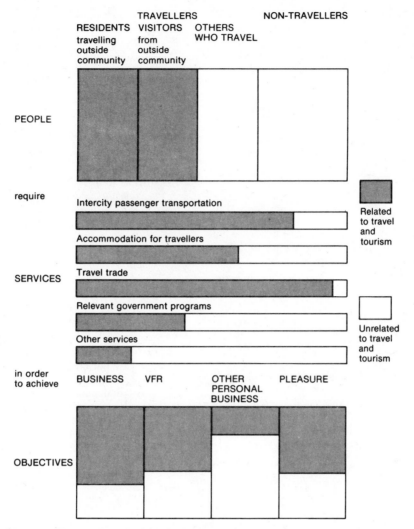

FIGURE 2   A systematic approach to travel and tourism.

are discussed in terms of household, location, and business surveys.

Household surveys are shown to have a special ability to distinguish the characteristics of travellers from nontravellers, the frequency of trips taken, and in determining aggregate volumes of travel in terms of person-trips, household-trips, and person-nights.

It is explained how the volume data collected in location surveys use the concept of the visit, which corresponds only roughly to the person-trip in household surveys. Business surveys are separately distinguished as sources for traveller statistics recorded in terms of visitors, passengers and receipts, but typically cannot provide information on socioeconomic characteristics of travellers or of the overall characteristics of their trips.

It is concluded that there is growing acceptance of travel and tourism as an industry or sector of the econ-

omy, although macroeconomists point out that the recognition of tourism as an industry can lead to double counting because standard industrial classifications fully account for all elements of the economy without finding it necessary or appropriate to recognize tourism. Nevertheless, there is a consensus that there is a tourism sector of the economy that includes accommodation, travel agents and tour operators (the travel trade), intercity passenger transport enterprises, government agencies responsible for tourism programs and tourism facilities, and major elements of other businesses in the food service, entertainment, and recreational fields.

Reference is made to a variety of proposed tourism systems and a fundamental conceptual approach is offered linking together *people* who require *services* outside their community of residence in order to achieve certain *objectives*.

APPENDIX 1 Definitions for Travellers

TRAVELLERS are any persons who travel. For the purpose of any one study, the within scope traveller has to be more precisely defined according to the objectives of the study, the reference period, the geographical area of interest, and the practical restraints of the methodology employed.

VISITORS are travellers entering or travelling in the area under study, but resident outside the area under study.

RESIDENTS are persons living permanently (a term in itself subject to interpretation) within the boundaries of the study area, such as a city, region, province, country, or group of countries. A study may exclude Residents, deal with them exclusively or take into account their travel only within the study area. In any event it is normal if they are included to look at their travel separately from that of other Visitors.

NONTRAVELLERS are those residents of an area who, over the reference period of a study, took no trip which qualified as travel.

TRAVELLERS WITHIN SCOPE OF TRAVEL AND TOURISM are visitors or residents who travel for business, pleasure, and personal reasons beyond the limits of their local community and return to it.

DOMESTIC TRAVELLERS are persons travelling within their country of residence.

INTERNATIONAL TRAVELLERS are persons travelling outside their country of residence, including residents in the process of leaving their country of residence or in the process of returning from other countries.

SAME-DAY TRAVELLERS are persons who travel without spending a night away from home. They are similar to, but not necessarily identical to, EXCURSIONISTS in the definitions of the international agencies, who are visitors to a particular area and stay there less than 24 hours.

ONE OR MORE NIGHTS TRAVELLERS are persons who travel and stay one or more nights away from home. They are similar to, but not necessarily identical to, TOURISTS in the definitions of the international agencies, who are visitors to a particular area and stay for 24 hours or more.

OTHER TRAVELLERS outside the scope of travel and tourism are as follows:

COMMUTERS are persons travelling to a regular place of work or education provided that they do not stay overnight.

OTHER LOCAL TRAVELLERS are persons travelling within or close to the community in which they reside on trips which fall outside the distance, geographical boundary, or time duration limits of the study, but who do not qualify as Commuters.

STUDENTS are persons travelling in order to attend or to return from an educational establishment as students for a full academic year or more.

CREWS are persons operating or providing service on a passenger or freight transportation vehicle, e.g., truck drivers and air crew, including airline attendants.

MIGRANTS are persons on one-way journeys, changing their place of residence, including those without a home address, emigrants, immigrants, refugees and nomads, and others planning to stay away for more than one year, but excluding seasonal migrants such as retired persons moving to a warm climate for the winter season.

TEMPORARY WORKERS are persons travelling to engage in temporary seasonal work, such as fruit picking.

APPENDIX 2

Standard Industrial Classifications Related to Travel and Tourism

	STATISTICS CANADA (1980)		APPROXIMATE EQUIVALENTS	
			UNITED STATES (1972)	UNITED NATIONS (1971)

Primary Classifications—all or some establishments primarily concerned with tourism

Accommodation	9111-4	Hotels, motels, tourist courts, tourist homes	7011/21	6320*
	9131	Camping grounds and travel trailer parks	7033	6320*
	9141/9	Outfitters, other recreation camps	7032	6320*
Transportation	4511/2	Air	4511/2	7131
	4572	Interurban and rural transit	4131	7112*
	4574	Charter and sightseeing bus services	4142/4119*	7116*
	4531	Railway transport	4011	7111

APPENDIX 2   *(Continued)*

	STATISTICS CANADA (1980)		APPROXIMATE EQUIVALENTS	
			UNITED STATES (1972)	UNITED NATIONS (1971)
	9921	Automobile and truck rental	7512	7116*
	4541/2/9	Water transport	441-5	7121-3
Travel Trade	9961-2	Travel agencies, tour wholesalers and operators	4722*	7191*
Government Departments	8172/8272/ 8372	Resource conservation and industrial development	9512	9100*

Secondary Classifications—some establishments derive much of business from tourism

Food Service	9211-13	Restaurants, take-outs	5812	6310*
	9221	Taverns, bars, nightclubs	5813	6310*
Retail Trade	6331	Gasoline service stations	5541	6200*
	6322	Boat, etc. dealers	5551	6200*
	6321	Motor home and travel trailer dealers	5561	6200*
Recreation	9651	Golf courses	7992	9490*
	9653	Skiing facilities	7999*	9490*
	9654	Boat rentals and marinas	4469	9490*
Culture/Entertainment	8551	Museums and archives	8411	9420*
	9696	Botanical and zoological gardens	8421	9420*
	9631/9	Theatre and entertainment	7922/9	9414
	9641	Professional sports clubs	7941	9490*
	9643/4	Race tracks	7948	9490*
	9692	Amusement parks	7996	9490*

Tertiary Classifications—some establishments have significant tourism business

	4575/81	Limousines and taxis	4111*/21	7113*
	7122	Credit card companies	6153*	8102*
	7741	Advertising agencies	7311	8325
	9723	Self-service laundries/dry cleaners	7215	9520*
	6351	Garages (general repairs)	7358	9531
	6571	Camera and photographic supply stores	5946	6200*
	6582	Gift, novelty, and souvenir stores	5947	6200*

[1]Industry classification more general than in Canadian SIC.

REFERENCES

British Tourist Authority (1980), *British Home Tourism Survey 1978*, London: English Tourist Board.

Britton, R. (1979), "Some Notes on the Geography of Tourism," *The Canadian Geographer*, 23 (Fall), 276–282.

Bureau of Industry Economics (1979), *Economic Significance of Tourism in Australia*, Canberra: Australian Government Publishing Service.

Canadian Government Office of Tourism (1980a), *Vacation Travel by Canadians in 1979*, Ottawa: Canadian Government Office of Tourism.

Canadian Government Office of Tourism (1980b), *Party Size of Canadian Vacation Trips*, Ottawa: Canadian Government Office of Tourism.

Chadwick, Robin A. (1981), "Some Notes on the Geography of Tourism: Comments," *The Canadian Geographer*, 25 (Summer).

Chau, P. (1977), "Unification of Tourism Measurement Criteria," discussion paper, The World Tourism Organization Seminar on Tourism Statistics, Caracas.

Civil Aeronautics Board (1980), *Airport Activity Statistics of Certificated Route Air Carriers*, Washington D.C.: U.S. Government Printing Office.

Dunstan, P.J. (1980), "Tourism in Australia," *World Tourism*, 154, 43-44.

Eagers, Derek (1979), "Development of Policies for Tourism and the Organization Structure," *British Tourism, Diagnosis and Prognosis, Conference Proceedings*, Farnborough: The Tourism Society, 23-26.

Economist Intelligence Unit (1983), *The U.S.A. and the U.K. on Holiday*, London: The Economist.

English Tourist Board (1979), *Sightseeing in 1978*, London: English Tourist Board.

English Tourist Board (1983), *Leisure Day Trip in Great Britain Summer 1981 and 1982*, London: English Tourist Board.

Frechtling, Douglas C. (1976), "Proposed Standard Definitions and Classifications for Travel Research," *Marketing Travel and Tourism, Seventh Annual Conference Proceedings*, Boca Raton: The Travel Research Association, 59-74.

Frechtling, Douglas C. (1977), "Travel as an Employer in the State Economy," *Journal of Travel Research*, 15 (Spring), 8-12.

Frechtling, Douglas C. (1978), "A Brief Treatise on Days and Nights," *Journal of Travel Research*, 17 (Fall), 18-19.

Gadbois, R.N. (1975), "Tourism in San Diego: Developments and Overview," *The Impact of Tourism, Sixth Annual Conference Proceedings*, San Diego: The Travel Research Association, 25-27.

Gunn, Clare A. (1979), *Tourism Planning*, New York: Crane Russak and Company.

Heeley, John (1980), "The Definition of Tourism in Great Britain: Does Terminological Confusion Have to Rule?" *Tourism Review*, 2 (1980), 11-14.

Jafari, Jafar (1982), "Paratourism and Its Contribution to the Hospitality Industry," *The Practice of Holiday Management*, Westport, Conn.: AVI Publishing Company.

Kahn, Terry D. (1975), "Estimating Tourist Industry Employment: The Primary Data Approach," *The Impact of Tourism, Sixth Annual Conference Proceedings*, San Diego: The Travel Research Association, 167-175.

Kates, Peat, Marwick and Company (1969), *The Economic Significance of Travel in Canada (Summary Report)*, Toronto: Canadian Tourism Association.

Laurentian Institute, The (1974), *The Standard Industrial Classification: Its Application to the Travel Sector*, Ottawa: Canadian Government Office of Tourism.

Leiper, Neil (1979), "The Framework of Tourism: Towards a Definition of Tourism and the Tourist Industry," *Annals of Tourism Research*, 6(4), 390-407.

Little, Arthur D., Inc. (1969), *Tourism and Recreation, A State-of-the-Art Study*, Washington, D.C.; U.S. Government Printing Office.

Little, Arthur D., (1978), *National Tourism Policy Study, Final Report*, Washington, D.C.: United States Congress.

McCloy, D.B. (1975), "Employment Research in the Canadian Travel Industry," *The Impact of Tourism, Sixth Annual Conference Proceedings*, San Diego: The Travel Research Association, 49-51.

Mieczkowski, Z.T. (1981), "Some Notes on the Geography of Tourism: Comments," *The Canadian Geographer*, 25 (Summer).

National Park Service (1980), *National Park Statistical Abstract, 1979*, Denver: Statistical Office, National Park Service.

National Tourism Resources Review Commission (1973), *Destination U.S.A., Volume 2, Domestic Tourism*, Washington, D.C.: U.S. Government Printing Office.

OECD Tourism Committee (1980), *Tourism Policy and International Tourism in OECD Member Countries*, Paris: Organisation for Economic Cooperation and Development.

Powell, John A. (1978), *Report of the Tourism Sector Consultative Task Force*, Ottawa: Department of Industry, Trade and Commerce.

Statistics Canada (1979a), *Travel, Tourism and Outdoor Recreation—A Statistical Digest*, Ottawa: Publications Distribution, Statistics Canada.

Statistics Canada (1979b), *Data Collection and Dissemination Methods for International Travel Statistics in Canada*, Ottawa: International Travel Section, Statistics Canada.

Statistics Canada (1980), *Standard Industrial Classification Manual*, Ottawa: Statistics Canada.

Statistics Canada (1984a), *Tourism and Recreation*, Ottawa: Statistics Canada.

Statistics Canada (1984b), *Canadian Travel Survey, Canadians Travelling in Canada*, Ottawa: Statistics Canada.

Statistics Canada (1984c), *Travel between Canada and Other Countries*, Ottawa: Statistics Canada.

Statistics Canada (1984d), *Air Passenger Origin and Destination, Domestic and Canada–United States* (2 reports), Ottawa: Publications Distribution, Statistics Canada.

United Nations Conference on Trade and Development (1971), "A Note on the 'Tourist Sector,'" *Guidelines for Tourism Statistics*, New York: United Nations, 30.

United Nations, Statistical Office of the (1971), *Indexes to the International Standard Industrial Classification of All Economic Activities*, New York: United Nations.

United States Bureau of the Census (1979), *National Travel Survey, Travel During 1977*, Washington, D.C.: U.S. Government Printing Office.

United States, Executive Office of the President (1972), *Standard Industrial Classification Manual*, Washington, D.C.: U.S. Government Printing Office.

United States Senate Committee on Commerce (1976), *A Conceptual Basis for the National Tourism Policy Study*, Washington, D.C.: U.S. Government Printing Office.

United States Travel Data Center (1979), *National Travel Expenditure Study Summary Report*, Washington, D.C.: United States Travel Data Center.

United States Travel Data Center (1980), *1979 Quarterly Travel Trends, Fourth Quarter*, Washington, D.C.: United States Travel Data Center.

United States Travel Data Center (1984), *1983 National Travel Survey, Full Year Report*, Washington, D.C.: United States Travel Data Center.

United States Travel Service (1977), *Analysis of Travel Definitions, Terminology and Research Needs Among States and Cities*, Washington, D.C.: U.S. Department of Commerce.

Western Council for Travel Research (1963), "Chapter II, Information Needed," *Standards for Traveler Studies*, Salt Lake City: University of Utah.

World Tourism Organization (1978a), *Methodological Supplement to World Travel Statistics*, Madrid: World Tourism Organization.

World Tourism Organization (1978b), *Domestic Tourism Statistics*, Madrid: World Tourism Organization.

World Tourism Organization (1981), *Development of Intra-regional and Interregional Tourism in the Six WTO Regions*, Madrid: World Tourism Organization.

World Tourism Organization (1983a), *Domestic Tourism Statistics*, 1981–1982, Madrid: World Tourism Organization.

World Tourism Organization (1983b), *Definitions Concerning Tourism Statistics*, Madrid: World Tourism Organization.

World Tourism Organization (1983c), *Determination of the Importance of Tourism as an Economic Activity within the Framework of the National Accounting System*, Madrid: World Tourism Organization.

Wynegar, Don (1984), "USTTA Research: New Tools for International Tourism Marketing," *Travel Research: The Catalyst for Worldwide Tourism Planning, Fifteenth Annual Conference Proceedings*, Philadelphia: Travel and Tourism Research Association, 183–200.

6

Planning a Tourism Research Investigation

ABRAHAM PIZAM

University of Central Florida
Orlando, Florida

*T*his chapter outlines the sequential steps which are involved in carrying out a tourism research investigation. The emphasis is upon the need for careful planning throughout the process in order to ensure valid, reliable, and cost-effective results.

RESEARCH PLANNING—FOR WHAT PURPOSES?

The objective of tourism research is to provide information that will assist tourism managers in making decisions. Tourism research is an investigative process that can be distinguished from other forms of investigations by three unique requirements: objectivity, reproducibility, and systematisation (Brown 1980).

Objectivity requires an approach that is independent of the researcher's personal view with respect to the answers to the problems under investigation. Reproducibility is a procedure that ensures other researchers could duplicate the research and obtain the same results. Finally, systematisation in research investigation is the most important of the three requirements. A systematic approach requires each step to be planned so that it will yield that which is necessary at the next step. Systematisation organizes the research process into sequential and interdependent steps that have to be specified and planned in advance. In other words *systematisation* in research is synonymous with *planning of research*. Therefore no investigation can fulfill the three requirements of a research investigation unless it is properly planned in advance.

Many inexperienced researchers have logged hundreds of man-hours and thousands of dollars in the actual collection of data, only to find later that the data were not in the appropriate form for data analysis nor were the variables and concepts operationally defined. This would not have happened had those researchers systemized their investigation by planning each step in advance.

Investigators divide the research process into a series of steps. While the number of such steps and their names vary from one individual to another, the recognition of a sequence is universal.

As can be seen from Fig. 1, we prefer to divide the tourism research investigation into the following seven sequential steps:

A   Formulation of research problem.
B   Review of related research.
C   Definition of concepts, variables, and hypotheses.
D   Selection of research design.
E   Selection of data collection technique.
F   Selection of subjects.
G   Planning of data processing and analysis.

A   FORMULATION OF THE RESEARCH PROBLEM

Every research investigation starts with the identification and selection of a research topic. The general topic of a study may be suggested by some *practical* concern or by some *scientific* or *intellectual* interest.

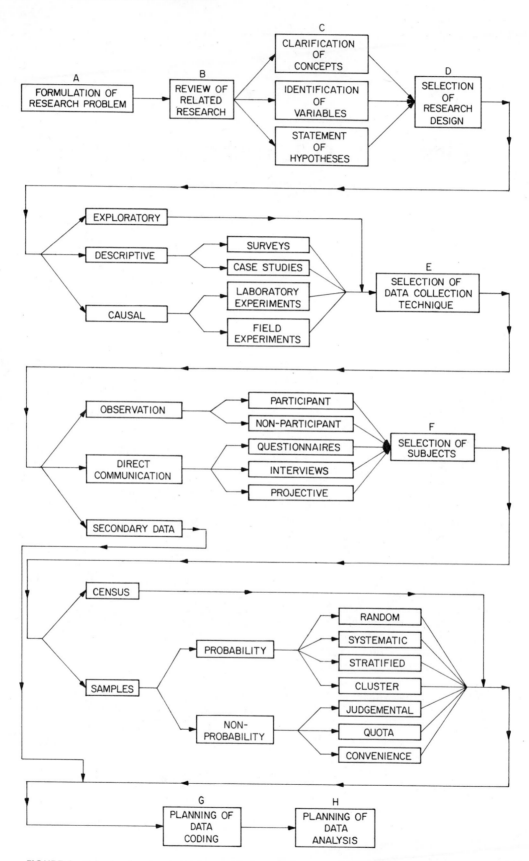

FIGURE 1 Steps in planning a tourism research investigation.

In tourism a wide variety of *practical* concerns may present topics for research. Basically, these can be divided into three categories:

1 Provision of information for decision making on the need for some new or enlarged facilities or services. Included in this category are: feasibility studies (hotels, restaurants), marketing studies for new tourism products or services, physical and land resources studies, and the like.

2 Provision of information concerning the probable consequences of various courses of action for deciding among proposed alternatives. For example, an airline may need to know which promotional fare would be more popular and profitable: an APEX or a back-to-back charter?

3 Prediction of some future course of events in order to plan appropriate action. For example, what would be the impact of gasoline rationing on tourism expenditures in the city of Boston?

Scientific or *intellectual* interests may suggest an equally wide range of topics for research. Here, the selection of the topic may arise from a concern with (a) some social problem (tourist-related environmental pollution, tourist-induced inflation, tourist-inspired cultural change, etc.), (b) from an interest in some general theme or area of behavior (tourist motivation, destination attitudes change, expenditure patterns, etc.), or (c) from some body of theory (economic theory, psychoanalytic theory, etc.).

The major difference between topics suggested by *practical concern* and those dictated by *scientific interests* is that the latter are less likely to involve the study of a specific situation primarily for the sake of knowledge about that particular situation (Selltiz, Wrightsman, and Cook 1976, pp. 26–27).

The topic selected should be of such scope that not all aspects of the problem should be investigated simultaneously. Too often, novice investigators select a topic that is too vast or too vague to study meaningfully. If the magnitude of the topic is such that it cannot be handled in one single study, the topic should be divided into a number of subtopics that can be dealt with in separate studies.

Before the investigator can select data collection and data analysis procedures, he or she needs to formulate *a specific problem* which can be investigated. A scientific *problem* is an interrogative sentence or statement that asks what relation exists between two or more variables. The answer is what is being sought in the research (Kerlinger 1973, p. 17). For example, what is the relation between disposable income and propensity to travel internationally among North American residents? As has been said by Albert Einstein and L. Infeld (1938), "The formulation of a problem is far more often essential than its solution. . . ."

Therefore, the second step in the planning of a tourism research investigation is to discover a problem in need of solution. "A problem well defined is a problem half solved" says an old maxim. Only when the problem has been clearly defined and the objectives of the research precisely stated can the planning of research investigation move to the next phase. In the statement of the problem the investigator has to describe what it is he or she plans to investigate. For example, an investigator might be interested in: What is the relation between socioeconomic characteristics of a given population and its expenditures on touristic products? The general goals of this study would be to determine the relative importance of such socioeconomic characteristics as: income, education, occupation, and geographic location on annual touristic expenditures.

Unfortunately, it is not always possible for a researcher to formulate his problem simply, clearly, and completely. He may often have only a rather vague or diffused notion of the problem. This difficulty, however, should not affect the necessity of formulating his problem nor be used as a rationalization to avoid it.

In the process of problem formulation, the investigator has to undertake several personal, social, and methodological considerations, such as the ones listed in Table 1.

B REVIEW OF RELATED RESEARCH

Science is a systematically cumulative body of knowledge. Theories interrelate individual findings, making their implications more general and permitting generalization and transfer to new situations. No study starts *de novo*. In general, each study rests on earlier ones and provides a basis for future ones. Investigators that build their studies upon work that has already been done have a better chance of contributing to knowledge than those who start anew. The more links that can be established between a given study and other studies on a body of theory, the greater the scientific contribution.

There are two main reasons for reviewing the general and research literature related to the research problem (Kerlinger 1973, p. 696):

1 To explain and clarify the theoretical rationale of the problem.

2 Tell the reader what research has and has not been done on the problem.

In addition, the search for related literature may serve as one of the quickest and most economical ways to discover hypotheses.

Unfortunately, being human, investigators want their ideas to be considered as original and unrelated to what others have done. Therefore, one often sees

TABLE 1 Social, Personal, and Methodological Considerations in the Process of Problem Formulation

Social
1 Contribution to the knowledge in the tourism field.
2 Practical value to practitioners and scientists in the tourism field.
3 Originality—the investigation should not be a duplicate of another work that has been adequately done by someone else (Van Dalen and Meyer 1966, Chap. 7).

Personal
1 A genuine interest in the problem coupled with a lack of biases in it.
2 Possession of the necessary skills, abilities, and background knowledge to study the problem.
3 Access to the tools, equipment, and subjects necessary to conduct the investigation.
4 Possession of time and financial resources to complete the investigation.
5 Access to adequate data.
6 Ability to muster administrative support, guidance, and cooperation for the conduct of the study.

Methodological
1 The problem should express a relation between two or more variables.
2 The problem should be stated clearly and unambiguously in question form.
3 The problem should be such as to imply possibilities of empirical testing.

investigators "rediscovering America" or "reinventing the wheel" because they neglected to do the proper background research.

If the proposed study has a theoretical base, the investigator must be sure to relate it to the theory by formulating the research problem at a level sufficiently abstract. This will enable one to relate the findings of the present study to findings of other studies concerned with the same concept.

Even investigators who plan to conduct studies that arise from the need to answer practical questions are neither exempt from the need to search for background research nor from relating their study to others on a sufficiently abstract level. For example, suppose that an investigator is interested in a typical practical problem: Why is room occupancy at hotel X down? Doing the proper background research by analyzing published data and trade literature in both the tourism industry and others will quickly and clearly indicate whether the problem is hotel X's, the destination in which hotel X is located, the tourism industry as a whole, or the national economy.

In planning this section, the investigator should search and select those studies which provide a foundation for the proposed project and discuss these studies in sufficient detail to understand their relevance. The search may involve conceptual literature, trade literature, or published statistics.

Since this search is usually slow and time-consuming, valuable tools have been developed to assist the investigator in the search for relevant literature. These tools fall into three general categories: indices, abstracts, and bibliographies. For listings of available re-

source materials see Chapter 15, "Data Sources for Travel and Tourism Research" by C. Goeldner.

Lately a new development in the application of computers has made literature search faster, more accurate, and more comprehensive. Nowadays most university libraries as well as research institutions have a Computer Assisted Literature Search where for a certain fee one can get a complete listing of published works accompanied by abstracts of each entry for a given defined subject. The searches are done through a console terminal hooked up to the vendor via telephone lines. Currently there are three major vendors: Lockheed Dialogue System, Bibliographic Retrieval System (BRS), and System Development Corporation (SDC). Each of these offers access to a multitude of data bases. Unfortunately, most of the major tourism periodicals are not included in any of the existing data bases. Nevertheless, the tourism investigator could still get significant assistance from tourism articles published in nontourism periodicals.

This author has found the following data bases to contain some tourism-related research literature:

ABI−Inform
Management Contents
PREDICAST (Statistical Data Base)
Psychological Abstracts
Sociological Abstracts
Social Science Research
Dissertation Abstracts
EIS−PLANTS (a directory of companies with specific information on manufacturing firms)

EIS—NON MAN (a directory of companies with specific information on nonmanufacturing firms)

Most of the above data bases are restricted to the last ten years. However, since citations of current works refer to past ones, the significant past literature has rapidly become well mapped.

In the process of literature search, it is advisable, if possible, to include studies currently under way which are likely to overlap the proposed project. In the U.S., the Science Information Exchange of the Smithsonian Institution in Washington, D.C., maintains a record of all projects currently funded through the U.S. federal branches of the government and the larger foundations. Since this service is computerized, custom searches can be made on request for a fee.

C   CONCEPTS, VARIABLES, AND HYPOTHESES

Once the review of the relevant research literature has been completed, the next logical step in the design of a research project is to develop and define concepts, variables, and hypotheses. As can be seen in Fig. 2, concepts, variables, and hypotheses are the linking pins between theory and empirical tests.

Concepts

The basic components of theory are concepts and variables, which are related in propositions called postulates, theorems, or hypotheses. Sets of propositions in turn may be interrelated to form theories. Concepts are terms that refer to the characteristics of events, situations, groups, and individuals that we study (Selltiz, Wrightsman, and Cook 1976, p. 16).

Concepts may be impossible to observe directly, such as justice or love, or they may have referents that are readily observable, such as a tree or a table (Bailey 1978, p. 33).

The explication of theory involves the use of concepts which are nominally defined. Nominal definitions of concepts are those definitions frequently found in dictionaries. For example, the nominal definition of the concept "wealthy" is "having large possessions of lands, goods, money, or securities" (Webster 1963, p. 2589).

To test a theory or proposition, the nominally defined terms must be put to an empirical test. This requires their operational definition. Operational definitions are nothing more than nominal definitions quantified (Black and Champion 1976, pp. 182–183). For example, the operational definition of "wealthy" is "people having assets in excess of $1,000,000," etc.

Operational definitions enable us to identify the presence or absence of a given concept in a person, group, or event. For instance, if we wish to know whether or not a concept such as "well traveled tourist" is a characteristic of a given person, we must first define what the empirical characteristics of our concept "well traveled tourist" are. We may, therefore, operationally define a "well traveled tourist" as "a person who has traveled for the last five years at least once a year to a destination 500 miles or more away from his permanent residence."

Variables

Concepts that have been operationally defined become variables. Variables can be defined as relational units of analysis that can assume any one of a number of designated sets of values (Black and Champion 1976, p. 34) or as properties that take on different values—a symbol to which numerals or values are assigned (Kerlinger 1973, pp. 29–30). Examples of variables used in tourism research are age, sex, income, education, trip expenditure, miles driven on vacation, etc.

Variables have several qualities central to any scientific explanation:

1   They represent features that are changeable.
2   They can assume any one of a designated set of values.
3   They can be arranged in a certain time order with respect to each other, enhancing the prospects

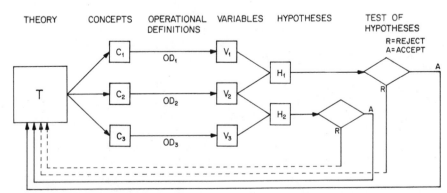

FIGURE 2   The relationship between theory, concepts, variables, and hypotheses.

for asserting cause–effect relations among them (Black and Champion 1976, p. 14).

Variables can be classified in at least three possible ways: (a) according to their relationships with each other, (b) according to the research design, and (c) according to their level of measurement.

A   Relationship with each other   Under this category variables can be divided into four types: independent, dependent, intervening, and control.

- *Independent variables* are so called because they are "independent" of the outcome itself; instead they are presumed to effect or influence the outcome. Sometimes they are referred to as *predictor* variables.
- *Dependent variables* are so called because they are "dependent" on the independent variables. They are presumed to be the effect of the independent variables. Dependent variables sometimes are referred to as *criterion* variables.
- *Intervening variables* are variables that come between the independent and the dependent variables. Intervening variables are sometimes referred to as *moderating* variables.
- *Control variables* are so called because they need to be held constant, or randomized, so that their effects are neutralized or compensated.

B   Research design   In experimental design the variables that are manipulated are called *active* variables (i.e., exposure to media), and the variables that are measured are called *attribute* variables (i.e., selection of tourist destination for yearly vacation).

C   Level of measurement   Under this category variables can be categorized as either *discrete* or *continuous*.

- *Discrete* or *categorical* variables are those variables which have a set of finite or fixed values. In such variables there are two or more subsets of the set of objects being measured. All the members of the subset are considered the same and all are assigned the same name and the same value. When a value is assigned to such a variable, it serves merely as a label or means of identification. Examples of such variables are religion (Protestant, Catholic, Jew, Muslim, Other), occupation (Physician, Lawyer, Dentist, etc.), sex (Male, Female), etc. These variables are sometimes referred to as *nominal* or *polytomies*.
- *Continuous* variables have no separate and distinct categories; rather, there is a continuum that represents gradually greater and greater amounts of the characteristic or quality. On such variables subjects can differ among themselves by very large amounts or by infinitely small degrees. To provide descriptions of subjects we arbitrarily "mark off" intervals along a scale, the intervals representing equal amounts or degree of the property. For instance, height is one such variable which can be marked off in inches or centimeters. In actual practice the quantitative description assigned to a subject is never precise, but rather an approximation. If the measuring device is crude the intervals may be few and broad. If the measuring device is more refined it may divide the continuum into a large number of narrow intervals, thereby providing much more precise descriptions. As the categories increase in number and become narrower and narrower, we approach a true continuum (Ghiselli, Campbell, and Zedeck 1981, pp. 25–26).

The specified relations between variables are expressed hypotheses.

Hypotheses

A hypothesis is a proposition that is stated in testable form and that predicts a particular relation between two or more variables. It is a tentative statement about things that the investigator wishes to support or refute. Consider, for example, a possible relationship between age and preferred touristic activity. If we assume that some relationship exists between these two variables, then we have to state its form. For example, H_a—"The older the tourist is, the less inactive will be his preferred touristic activities."

As stated earlier, hypotheses are important, indispensable, and powerful tools of scientific research. They are powerful because they appear in the form of predictions: If X, then Y. Even when hypotheses are not confirmed, they have power. Negative findings are sometimes as important as positive ones, since they cut down the total universe of ignorance and sometimes point out fruitful further hypotheses and lines of investigation (Kerlinger 1973, p. 26).

Hypotheses can express relationships between variables in three different ways: *univariate*, *bivariate*, and *multivariate*. A *univariate* hypothesis is one that discusses a single variable. For example: "Tourism expenditures for the U.S. will increase between 1980 and 2000." A *bivariate* hypothesis is one that expresses the relationship between two variables—usually one dependent and one independent. For example: "The higher the number of English-speaking residents in a generating country, the higher is their propensity to travel to the U.S." Finally, a hypothesis relating more than two variables is called *multivariate*. For example: "The higher the proportion of English-speaking residents in a generating country (X_1) and the higher their disposable income (X_2), the higher will be their propensity to travel to the U.S. (Y_1)."

Hypotheses are usually stated in two forms: *null* hypotheses and *research* hypotheses. The *null* hypothesis (H_0) is the hypothesis of "no relationship" or "no difference"; it is the one actually tested statistically. It is set up for possible rejection and is an arbitrary convention, hypothesizing that any relation or difference in the findings is due to chance or sampling error (Isaac and Michael 1971, p. 142).

The *research* hypothesis (H_a) states the expectations of the investigator in positive terms. The probability that one dependent variable has multiple causes (independent variables) is always greater than the probability that it is caused by a single independent variable. For example, the dependent variable tourist expenditures (Y_1) is likely to be influenced not only by his disposable income (X_1) but also by occupation (X_2), education (X_3), exposure to media (X_4), etc. Following this, if a hypothesis—X_1—was disproved (in other words, we failed to reject the X_1 null hypothesis), it would be discarded in favor of other rival hypotheses—X_2, X_3, X_4—predicting the dependent variable Y_1. From this point of view the task of scientific research is not confirming research hypotheses. Rather it is rejecting the null hypotheses. Even when one has rejected a null hypothesis, the corresponding research hypothesis has not been *fully* confirmed yet. All that it means is that the corresponding research hypothesis has *possibly* been supported. It cannot be fully supported as long as there are rival hypotheses that have not been disconfirmed. This logic leads one to the conclusion that hypotheses can only be discarded (Blalock and Blalock 1968, p. 390).

D RESEARCH DESIGN

Once the concepts, variables, and hypotheses have been formulated and stated, investigators need to consider their research design. A research design is a form of a carefully developed and controlled plan to carry the research investigation. It indicates what steps will be taken and in what sequence. A research design's major purpose is to ensure that the study will (1) be relevant to the problem and (2) employ economic procedures (Churchill 1979, p. 46).

Types of Research Designs

Research designs can be categorized into three main types: exploratory, descriptive, and causal.

A Exploratory designs Exploratory designs serve primarily to acquaint the investigator with the characteristics of his research problem. Studies using this design can have one or more of the following purposes (Selltiz, Wrightsman, and Cook 1976, p. 90):

1 Formulation of problem for more precise investigation at a later date.
2 Generation of hypotheses for further study.
3 Familiarization with the problem.
4 Clarification of concepts, etc.

As can be seen from the above, the common denominator for all of these purposes is discovery of ideas and insights. Therefore, exploratory studies are usually flexible enough to permit consideration of all aspects of the research problem. It is important to point out that exploratory designs, in comparison with descriptive or causal designs, "seek relations" rather than "predict relations."

Consider, for example, the question of "Future Energy Impact on the Tourism Industry in the U.S." Since the problem is too vague to be stated in hypotheses and statistically tested, one needs to conduct first an exploratory study which will clarify the concepts, define them, and generate specific hypotheses. More specifically, it is necessary to define and analyze the types of impacts (perceived or objective, economic or social), the individual or units impacted (tourists of types $I_1 - I_n$, tourist enterprises of types $K_1 - K_n$, destinations of types $J_1 - J_n$, etc.), the manifestation of the impact and its measurement, and so on. An exploratory study concerned with this problem could probably be based on the 1979 summer gasoline shortage in the U.S., which will help to formulate the problem for a more precise investigation at a later stage.

B Descriptive designs Descriptive designs are used when the objective is systematic description of facts and characteristics of a given population or area of interest factually and accurately. In such designs the investigator measures the subjects of interest as they exist naturally. Descriptive designs are used for one or more of the following purposes (Churchill 1979, pp. 53–54):

1 To describe the characteristics of certain groups (i.e., The Sociodemographic Characteristics of Big Spenders in U.S. Tourism vs. Little Spenders).
2 To estimate the proportion of people in a specified population who behave in a certain way.
3 To make specific predictions or discover relations and interactions among variables (i.e., disposable income is positively associated with annual tourist expenditures).

Descriptive designs include all forms of research except experimental and historical, and they are not limited to any one method of data collection. Such designs cannot be used to establish causality. They can, however, provide investigators with a vast amount of information that will enable them to construct experimental designs that will permit determination of causality. Kerlinger (1973, p. 379) refers to this type of design as Ex-Post Facto design and defines it as "systematic empirical inquiry in which the scientist does not have direct control of independent variables because their manifestations have already occurred or because they are inherently not manipulable." Descriptive designs have several major weaknesses (Kerlinger 1973, p. 390): (1) the inability to manipulate independent variables; (2) the lack of power to randomize; and (3) the risk of improper interpretation. In other words, it lacks rigid control measures. Despite its weaknesses, the majority of tourism research is conducted using this design. This is because in tourism, like in most other social sciences, the problems do not lend themselves to experimental design.

The two major types of descriptive studies are surveys and case studies.

Surveys are studies of large and small populations by selecting and studying samples from the population to discover the relative incidence, distribution, and interrelations of variables (Kerlinger 1973, p. 410). Sample surveys are conducted when the study of the population is impossible, difficult or costly. Surveys have the following advantages compared to other designs:

1 Flexibility in choosing data collection techniques (i.e., mail questionnaire, interview, telephone interviews, etc.).
2 Generalization to the whole population and other similar populations is possible.
3 Relative low cost per subject or unit of analysis.
4 Enables the collection of large amounts of information.
5 High accuracy of results.

On the other hand, surveys have some serious weaknesses, such as shallow penetration, time-consuming, no control over individual responses (misconceptions, misunderstandings, etc.), and, in the case of attitudinal surveys, unstable reflections of the attitudes (attitudes may change very frequently and may be affected by many exogenous variables).

Survey samples studies are very commonly used in the tourism industry. Two well known examples of such surveys in the U.S. are the National Travel Survey conducted by the Bureau of the Census as a part of the Census Transportation and the Consumer Expenditures Survey also conducted by the Bureau of the Census.

Case studies are thorough examinations of specific social settings or particular aspects of social settings (Black and Champion 1976, p. 90). They constitute in-depth investigations of a given social unit resulting in a complete, well organized picture of that unit (Isaac and Michael 1971, p. 20).

The major characteristic of case studies is that they usually examine a small number of units (sometimes even one) across a large number of variables, for example, a study of the personnel practices in one airline.

Case studies have the following advantages over other types of research designs (Black and Champion 1976, p. 91):

1 They are flexible with respect to data collection methods used.
2 They may be conducted in practically any kind of social setting.
3 They are inexpensive.

In addition, they can be useful for obtaining background information for planning major investigations and serve as hypotheses generators. In other words, they can be used as economical substitutes to exploratory studies.

On the other hand, case studies have the following grave limitations: limited generalizability, time consuming, and vulnerable to subjective biases. In tourism, case studies have been used primarily by anthropologists who favor this method over any other.

C Causal designs In the social sciences, as in natural sciences, the only viable way to determine causality among variables is by using an experimental design. Experimental design is a highly controlled method of attempting to demonstrate the existence of causal relationship between one or more independent variables and one or more dependent variables. In experimental design, the investigator has complete control over introduction of independent variables. In addition, he has control over the environment in which the experiment is conducted, and over the composition of the experimental and control groups by random assignment of subjects. The experimental design offers the following advantages over any other research design: (1) establishes causality; (2) offers the best opportunity in control; and (3) provides the opportunity for studying change over time. Conversely, its greatest weaknesses are that it takes place in an artificial environment and that the experimenter's expectations can affect the results of the experiment (Bailey 1978, pp. 192–194). Experiments can be divided into two major types: laboratory and field.

A *laboratory experiment* is a research study in which the variance of all possible influential independent variables not pertinent to the immediate problem of investigation is kept at a minimum. This is done by isolating the research in a physical situation apart from the routine of ordinary living, and by manipulating one or more independent variables under rigorously specified, operationalized, and controlled situations (Kerlinger 1973, p. 398). Consider, for example, the following hypothetical laboratory experimental design set up for the purpose of determining the causal relationship between exposure to certain information and choice of tourist destination: A test facility resembling a travel agency is set up in which various similar destinations are displayed. The experimenter selects a group of subjects and randomly assigns them to two different groups: one exposed to information (experimental group) and one which is not (control). Each subject is then given a free coupon to select a travel of their choice. Given the proper handling of the control over the destination selection and subjects' assignment, this design can determine the causal effect of information exposure over destination selection.

In *field experiments*, the behavior under examination takes place in its natural setting. The researcher exerts experimental control through matching rather than by physical means (Cox 1979, pp. 154–155). In addition, the experimenter can compare a situation in which the causal variable is present with another in which it is not and from this infer causality. For example: consider the hypothetical question of determining the impact of different packaging on destination selection using a field experiment design. The experimenter selects three travel agencies with clientele that has been statistically matched, each one offering a different package for the same destination while holding control (matching) over exogenous variables such as cost, number of days, season of the year, etc. Any statistically significant difference in selection between the three agencies could be attributed (caused by) to the packaging.

In tourism, experimentation in both lab and field is most often avoided in the belief that subjects do not behave naturally under analysis. Except for a small group of tourism marketing researchers, all others— sociologists, psychologists, economists, recreationists, geographers, anthropologists, etc.—have neglected the experimental design. As Blalock and Blalock (1968, p. 333) suggest, this is a grave error undertaken by most social scientists, for the experimental method can be a necessary and valuable tool in the study of social phenomena.

E   DATA COLLECTION TECHNIQUES

The purpose of the various data collection techniques is to produce trustworthy evidence that is relevant to the research question being asked (Selltiz, Wrightsman, and Cook 1976, p. 161). The instruments used to collect the data are usually acceptable definitions of the important variables and have proper measurement characteristics.

Essentially, there are three means of collecting data. First, data can be obtained by the investigator observing the phenomena. Second, data can be obtained by the investigator or his agents communicating directly with the subjects. Third, data can be obtained from other sources who have collected it for another purpose. Each of these three categories can be further broken down in specific techniques. The remainder of this section will discuss the specific techniques within each category and analyze their appropriate use.

Observation

Observation can be defined as the process of watching and listening to other persons' behavior over time without controlling or manipulating it and recording findings in ways that permit some degree of analytical interpretation (Black and Champion 1976, p. 330). Observation is a primary technique for collecting data on nonverbal behavior, and it is used when it is important to understand dynamic behavioral processes in natural settings. This technique is not concerned with what a respondent places on paper or what he says in an interview, but deals with the behavior of persons (Pelegrino 1979). Observational methods are used for the following purposes (Selltiz, Wrightsman, and Cook 1976, p. 255):

1   When there is a need to describe behavioral patterns (i.e., tourists' behavior in a disco).

2   When the research phenomenon cannot be investigated in the laboratory (i.e., mass behavior).

3   When there is a need to describe ongoing behavior as it occurs (i.e., dining in a restaurant).

Observational methods have the following advantages over other data collection techniques: they (a) are superior to any other data collection method for the study of nonverbal behavior; (b) take place in a natural setting; and (c) enable the study of phenomena or subjects over a much longer time period than other methods.

On the other hand, they have some disadvantages too, such as: (a) lack of control over the environment and possible extraneous contamination; (b) difficult to quantify; (c) usually restricted to small samples which makes generalization very difficult; and (d) may arouse objections and lack of cooperation from subjects due to lack of anonymity (Bailey 1978, pp. 217–218).

There are two major types of observational methods: participant observation and non-participant observation. In the *participant observation* the investigator is a part of the natural setting in which the observation is being made but his role as a researcher is not known to other participants. For example: an investigator joins a Caribbean cruise as a tourist and while on board observes tourists' behavior. In the *nonparticipant observation*, the investigator observes the behavior of others in a natural setting but is not an actual participant in the behavior being examined. His role as outside member and investigator is known to all participants. For example: an investigator fully dressed observes and records tourists' behavior on a beach.

In the tourism research field the observation method is not very popular and is mostly used by anthropologists who study either tourists' behavior or the local residents' reaction to the tourism phenomenon.

Techniques for Direct Communication with Subjects

Within this category, three specific techniques will be analyzed: the questionnaire, the interview, and projective methods.

A Questionnaires The questionnaire is a pencil and paper measurement instrument used when data are collected by means of self-reporting techniques (Cox 1979, p. 192). Questionnaires are either mailed or handed face-to-face to the respondents and filled by them without any help from the investigator. In questionnaires, the information obtained is limited to the written responses of respondents to prearranged questions (Selltiz, Wrightsman, and Cook 1976, p. 294). All questionnaires perform at least two functions: (1) description of individual or group characteristics and (2) measurement of individual and/or group variables such as values, attitudes, opinions, etc. (Black and Champion 1976, p. 380). The most important goal of a questionnaire, however, is to provide complete, valid, and reliable information from respondents (Bailey 1978, p. 132). Questionnaires may be classified according to (1) type of response required and (2) type of questionnaire administration (Black and Champion 1976, pp. 383–389).

Type of response required Responses to questionnaires may be (a) fixed, (b) open-ended, or (c) a combination of fixed and open-ended. The following is an example of one question asked in an open-ended format and fixed format.

Open ended—Please state below the major reason for your visit at this destination. _____

Fixed—What is the major reason for your visit to this destination? Please select one category only.

1 Visit friends and relatives.
2 Recreation.
3 Business.

4 Sightseeing.
5 Health.
6 Other (please specify _____).

Type of questionnaire administration Questionnaires can be administered in two ways: (a) by mail and (b) in person.

A Mailed questionnaires consist of mailing a form to designated subjects with instructions for completing it, a cover letter explaining the purpose of the study, and a self-addressed, stamped return envelope provided.

B In person questionnaires are handed by an investigator or his agents to the respondents and asked to be completed in the investigator's presence.

Questionnaires have the following advantages over other data collection techniques:

1 Relatively inexpensive.
2 Requires almost no skills to administer.
3 Assures respondents' anonymity (if properly designed).
4 Can be administered to a large number of respondents simultaneously.
5 Can be sent through the mail.
6 Eliminates interviewer bias.
7 Enables standardization and uniformity.

On the other hand, questionnaires have some disadvantages too, the major ones being:

1 Low response rate (with mailed questionnaires it is not unusual to have a response rate as low as 20%).
2 Restricted to verbal behavior.
3 Lack control over the research setting (Bailey 1978, p. 156; Selltiz, Wrightsman, and Cook 1976, p. 296).

B Interviews A research interview is a face-to-face interpersonal role situation in which one person, the interviewer, asks a person being interviewed, the respondent, questions designed to obtain answers pertinent to the research problem (Kerlinger 1973, p. 481).

In research, interviews are used either as the major means of data collection or as a supplement for other methods. In addition, it can be used as an exploratory device to help identify variables and relations and generate hypotheses.

Interviews can be classified into two major types according to the degree to which they are structured: unstructured and structured.

Unstructured interviews are a free form of conversation in which the interviewer probes the general nature of the problem he is interested in, and asks the interviewee questions about it. It is a flexible form in which the content of the questions, their sequence, and their wording are left to the discretion of the interviewer.

Structured interviews, on the other hand, are more uniform and rigid. In this type of interview the questions, their sequence, and the wording are fixed. The interviewer usually reads the questions from interview schedules that have been previously prepared (Black and Champion 1976, pp. 364–368; Kerlinger 1973, p. 481).

The interview has the following advantages over other data collection techniques:

1 Permits greater depth and probing.
2 Often has a higher response rate than questionnaires.
3 Provides information on nonverbal behavior.
4 Enables control over the environment in which it is conducted.
5 Enables spontaneity.
6 Provides greater sensitivity to misunderstanding by respondents.
7 More appropriate for revealing information about feelings and emotions regarding different subjects.

On the other hand, it also has the following disadvantages:

1 Very costly.
2 Time-consuming.
3 Prone to interviewer personal bias.
4 Anonymity is usually not provided.
5 Inconvenient.
6 Contaminated by the eagerness of the respondent to please the interviewer (Bailey 1978, pp. 157–159; Selltiz, Wrightsman, and Cook 1976, pp. 296–297; Isaac and Michael 1971, p. 96).

The interview technique is used extensively in tourism research.

C Projective methods Projective methods are any one of a number of specific tests wherein a subject is presented with a visual or audio stimulus and is asked to respond. In this situation, the subject's response is not taken at face value but is viewed as a clue to his private interpretation of himself, the stimulus, or his world. This is an indirect data collection technique since it avoids direct questions about the topic of interest and even disguises it.

Implicit in the use of projective methods is the assumption that the way an individual organizes a relatively unstructured stimulus (i.e., interprets a picture) reflects the basic trends in his or her perceptions of the world and his or her response to it (Selltiz, Wrightsman, and Cook 1976, p. 333).

Projective methods are used in cases where subjects may be unwilling or unable to discuss controversial topics, to reveal intimate information about themselves, or to express their undesirable attitudes and opinions.

One of the most frequently used projective techniques is the Rorschach Inkblot Test consisting of a series of inkblots. The subject is asked to describe what he sees in each inkblot. Another technique is the Thematic Apperception Test (TAT), where the subject is confronted with a series of pictures and asked to tell a story on each. Other tests include word association, sentence completion, figure drawing, etc.

The use of projective techniques in tourism research is relatively scarce and restricted to psychologists and some marketing researchers. This is quite unfortunate since the technique has a valuable potential in the field of tourism motivation. The present author demonstrates in class the utility of projective methods by use of the following experiential exercises. Students are shown pictures of two destinations, one, Daytona Beach, Florida (or Club Mediterranean in Martinique), and the other, Miami Beach (or the Catskills, New York), and asked to describe the type of tourist who goes to each. The Daytona Beach (or Martinique) tourist is usually described as a young, well-to-do, educated, energetic, and creative individual, while the Miami (or Catskills) tourist is described as an elderly, New York resident, lazy, insecure, unintelligent, and boring individual. These findings can be used to interpret the image college students have of these destinations.

Secondary Data

Secondary data are data gathered not for the immediate study at hand but for some other purpose. Secondary data can be obtained from either private sources or public sources.

Private sources of secondary data include both personal documents and published materials of various companies, voluntary organizations, research organizations, and other societies.

Public sources include data archives (e.g., Social Science Data Archives) and governmental data (e.g., U.S. Census, Census of Transportation, Consumer Expenditures Survey). Many of the above listed sources, especially the public ones, contain statistical data on socioeconomic demographic characteristics of samples and populations and are readily available for public use. For more information on this topic, see Chapter 15, "Travel and Tourism Information Sources."

The use of already collected data has the advantage of being low in cost (many times it is free) and does not require any time to collect. On the other hand, it may not fit perfectly for the research problem as defined and in many cases it is out of date (Churchill 1979, pp. 128–129).

No matter which of the data collection techniques is used, an investigator has the responsibility to analyze the validity, reliability, and sensitivity of his instruments before using them. *Validity* is the degree to which the instrument predicts a criterion. For example, suppose we develop a questionnaire the purpose of which is to measure residents' attitudes towards tourism. Validity in this case will be the extent to which people's score on this questionnaire will correspond to their "true" attitude towards tourism. This type of validity is referred to as criterion-related validity and is the most important of all validities. Other types of validity include content validity, construct validity, and face validity. *Reliability* is the extent to which a measure gives consistent results. It is the accuracy of precision of a measuring instrument. A reliable instrument will tend to elicit the same results each time it is applied under the same circumstances. For example, a reliable test intended to measure "touristic innovativeness" should produce similar results when admitted repeatedly to the same group of subjects and the conditions have not changed. *Sensitivity* is the extent to which an instrument is capable of making distinctions fine enough for the purpose it serves. For instance, an instrument intended to measure a tourist's satisfaction with a destination should be sensitive enough to measure not only the direction—satisfied or dissatisfied—but also the degree of satisfaction or dissatisfaction (i.e., a five-point scale, 1 indicating complete dissatisfaction, 5 complete satisfaction, and 3 as the neutral point).

F   SELECTION OF SUBJECTS

Once the data collection techniques have been selected, the next step in the research process is to select those elements from which the information will be collected. One way of doing this would be by studying all elements within the population (a census); another way would be to collect information from a portion of the population by taking a sample of it. The term population as it is used in this context does not refer only to individuals. It refers to entire groups having some common characteristics. These groups may be objects, materials, individuals, organizations, states, countries, etc. The sum total of all the groups (or units of analysis) is a population (Bailey 1978, p. 69).

Ideally, one would want to study the entire population. Often, however, it is impossible or infeasible to do this and, therefore, one must settle for a sample. A sample is a portion of elements taken from a population (Black and Champion 1976, p. 265). It is a proportion of the population which *is considered* to be representative of that population (Kerlinger 1973, p. 118). A sample is always viewed as an approximation of the whole (population) rather than as a whole in itself.

There are four major advantages of using samples rather than populations (Pelegrino 1979, p. 74):

1 Less expensive.
2 Enables speedier processing of data and presentation of results.
3 Can secure more information per dollar from one investigation.
4 Enables accuracy with known precision which may be specified in advance and calculated from the sample itself.

Types of Sampling Procedures

Sampling procedures can be divided into two major types: probability and nonprobability.

A   Probability sampling   In probability sampling each element of the population has a known nonzero chance of being included in the sample (Churchill 1979, p. 299). Probability samples can be subdivided into four specific techniques: simple random sampling; systematic sampling; stratified sampling; and cluster sampling.

- *Simple random sampling* is the best known form of probability sampling. It is a method of drawing a sample of a population so that each element of the population will have an equal chance of being included (Kerlinger 1973, p. 118).
- *Systematic sampling* is a probability sampling procedure involving the selection of successive sampling units at a specified interval throughout the sample (Cox 1979, p. 272). Systematic sampling is one of the most convenient forms of probability sampling, certainly the most popular, and often a good approximation of random sampling.
- *Stratified sampling* is a probability sampling technique that is distinguished by the following two-step procedure (Churchill 1979, p. 317):

  1 The population is divided into mutually exclusive and exhaustive subsets.
  2 A random sample of elements is chosen from each subset.

Stratified sampling can be done by using two or more variables simultaneously (i.e., Male/Female or Male College Educated/Female College Educated; Male High School/Female High School; Male Elementary School/Female Elementary School).

Stratified samples can be either proportionate or disproportionate. Proportionate stratified samples have specified characteristics in exact proportion to the way in which those same characteristics are distributed in the population (e.g., 50% males, 50% females). In disproportionate samples the substrata are not necessarily distributed according to the proportionate distribution in the population from which they were drawn (e.g., 30% males, 70% females).

- *Cluster sampling* is a simple random sample in which each sampling unit is a collection or cluster of elements (Bailey 1978, p. 80). In this type of sample, individuals are not selected at random. Rather the sampling unit is a "bunch" or cluster of elements (Pelegrino 1979, p. 326). Cluster sampling involves the following steps (Churchill 1978, p. 326):

1 The population is divided into mutually exclusive and exhaustive subsets.

2 A random sample of the subsets is selected.

3 All the population elements in the selected subsets are used in the sample.

Cluster samples can be single-stage or multistage, in which case steps 1 and 2 are repeated as many times as is necessary and then step 3 is performed.

B Nonprobability sampling Nonprobability samples are those samples that provide no basis for estimating how closely the sample characteristics approximate the population's characteristics from which the sample was obtained (Black and Champion 1976, p. 267). Since nonprobability sampling does not depend upon chance as a selection procedure, the researcher cannot properly control the probability of a unit being included in the sample, and, therefore, cannot claim representativeness of the population. This is a serious and major weakness of this sampling type. However, as stated by Kerlinger (1973, p. 129), this weakness can be to some extent mitigated by using knowledge, expertise, and care in selecting samples.

Nonprobability samples can be divided into three major techniques: judgmental sampling; quota sampling; and convenience sampling.

- *Judgmental sampling* or purposive sampling is a sampling procedure in which the representativeness of the sample is based on an evaluation by the researcher or some other "expert" (Cox 1979, p. 269). In this case, the researcher uses "expert" judgment as to which respondents to choose, and

picks only those who meet the purpose of the study. This judgment is a deliberate effort to obtain representativeness by including "presumably typical" population elements in the sample (Kerlinger 1973, p. 129).

- *Quota sampling* is an attempt to ensure that the sample is representative by selecting elements in such a way that the proportion of the sample elements possessing a certain characteristic is approximately the same as the proportion in the population (Churchill 1978, p. 303). Quota sampling derives its name from the practice of assigning quotas, or proportion of sample units for interviewers (Kerlinger 1973, p. 129).

- *Convenience sampling* is a procedure in which representativeness of the sample is sacrificed for the sake of ease in obtaining it (Cox 1979, p. 268). In this sampling method the investigator chooses the closest units as respondents.

Convenience sampling is undoubtedly the weakest form of sampling but, unfortunately, the most frequently used. The basic problem with this technique is that certain elements have a very high probability of being included in the sample, while others have none. Thus, the sample becomes unrepresentative, inconsistent, and biased (Cox 1979, p. 268).

For more information on samples and sampling techniques, see the Chapter 9, "Issues in Sampling and Sample Design—A Managerial Perspective."

G DATA PROCESSING AND INFORMATION ANALYSIS

The last two steps in a tourism research investigation that need to be planned before the actual execution of the study are data processing and information analysis.

Data processing is an operation on data to achieve a desired result. It involves the conversion or reduction of information that is collected into a form that will permit statistical tabulation, ease of storage, and access for future use (Selltiz, Wrightsman, and Cook 1976, p. 434). Data processing can be done either manually or with the aid of the computer.

To prepare the data for proper processing, the investigator needs to code the data. The process of coding involves the translation of the data into symbolic form by using numbers to represent the information. Coding is performed at the conclusion of the data collection. However, the planning and development of the coding scheme is done at the time the research instrument is developed. The coding scheme or coding manual is an outline that describes what is coded and how it is to be coded.

If the processing is to be done by computer, then the investigator needs to plan and develop not only a coding scheme but also a means of converting the data that permits it to be analyzed, stored, and retrieved by the computer (i.e., cards, magnetic tapes, disks).

The purpose of *information analysis* is to summarize the completed data collected in such a manner that it yields answers to the research questions. Like data processing, information analysis is conducted after the information has been collected; however, the planning for analysis should be done in the earlier stage of the investigation. This planning scheme should specify the various forms of tabulation anticipated and the kind of statistical analysis of data that is to be performed.

Once the data processing and information analysis plans have been completed, the process of planning a tourism research investigation is terminated. What remains to do is the actual collection of data, its processing and analysis, and the interpretation and inferences to be drawn.

In summary, what we have attempted to achieve in this chapter is a presentation of the sequential steps in the conduct of a tourism research investigation. These steps, as stated previously, need to be planned well in advance of their execution to assure valid, reliable, and cost-effective results.

Those readers who would be interested to learn more about social science research methodology are advised to look into some of the publications and manuals mentioned in the references.

REFERENCES

Bailey, Kenneth D. (1978), *Methods of Social Research*, New York: Free Press.

Black, James A., and Dean J. Champion (1976), *Methods and Issues in Social Research*, New York: Wiley.

Blalock, Hubert M.J., and Ann B. Blalock (1968), *Methodology in Social Research*, New York: McGraw–Hill.

Brown, Francis E. (1980), *Marketing Research: A Structure for Decision Making*, Reading, Mass.: Addison–Wesley.

Churchill, Gilbert A., Jr. (1979), *Marketing Research*, 2nd ed., Hinsdale, Ill.: Dryden Press.

Cox, Eli P., III (1979), *Marketing Research—Information for Decision Making*, New York: Harper & Row.

Einstein, Albert, and L. Infeld (1938), *The Evolution of Physics*. New York: Simon & Schuster.

Ferber, Robert, Ed. (1978), *Readings in Survey Research*, Chicago: American Marketing Association.

Galtung, Johan (1967), *Theory and Methods of Social Research*, New York: Columbia University Press.

Ghiselli, Edwin E., John P. Campbell, and Sheldon Zedeck (1981), *Measurement Theory for the Behavioral Sciences*, San Francisco: W.H. Freeman & Co.

Isaac, Stephen, and William B. Michael (1971), *Handbook in Research and Evaluation*, San Diego: Edits Publishers.

Kerlinger, Fred N. (1973), *Foundations of Behavioral Research*, 2nd ed., New York: Holt, Rinehart & Winston.

Miller, Delbert C. (1970), *Handbook of Research Design and Social Measurement*, 2nd ed., New York: David McKay Co.

Pelegrino, Donald A. (1979), *Research Methods for Recreation and Leisure*, Dubuque, Iowa: William C. Brown Co.

Selltiz, Claire, Lawrence S. Wrightsman, and Stuart W. Cook (1976), *Research Methods for Social Relations*, 3rd ed., New York: Holt, Rinehart & Winston.

Van Dalen, D.B., and W.J. Meyer (1966), *Understanding Educational Research*, New York: McGraw–Hill.

Webster, Noah (1963), *Webster's Third New International Dictionary*, Springfield, Mass.: G & C Merriam Publishing Co.

7

Demand Forecasting and Estimation

BRIAN ARCHER

Department of Management Studies for
Tourism and Hotel Industries
University of Surrey
Guildford, Surrey, England

In economic terms demand *can be defined as the quantity of a product or service which people are willing and able to buy during a given period of time. In consequence,* demand forecasting *is the art of predicting the level of demand which might occur at some future point or period of time. This chapter describes the strengths, weaknesses, and limitations of the principal forecasting methods and their applicability in the field of tourism and travel. Sections of the chapter deal with the need for forecasting, the problems faced by forecasters and forecasting as an aid to management decision making.*

THE NEED FOR FORECASTING

Since the future is not predetermined, no forecast can guarantee complete accuracy. The aim of demand forecasting, therefore, is to predict the *most probable* level of demand that is likely to occur in the light of known circumstances or, when alternative policies are proposed, to show what different levels of demand may be achieved.

Forecasting should be an essential element in the process of management. No manager can avoid the need for some form of forecasting: a manager must plan for the future in order to minimize the risk of failure or, more optimistically, to maximize the possibilities of success. In order to plan, he must use forecasts. Forecasts will always be made, whether by guesswork, teamwork, or the use of complex models, and the accuracy of the forecasts will affect the quality of the management decision.

Forecasts are needed for marketing, production, and financial planning. Top management needs demand forecasts for implementing long-term objectives; lower echelons of management require forecasts to plan their activities over a more limited horizon. In the tourism industry, in common with most other service sectors, the need to forecast accurately is especially acute because of the perishable nature of the product. Unfilled airline seats and unused hotel rooms cannot be stockpiled and demand must be anticipated and even manipulated.

CHOICE OF METHOD

The question that should be asked is not whether but how to forecast. The method chosen, the amount of detail provided, the frequency of the need for forecasts, and the time horizon of the forecasts vary according to the differing requirements of managers in different parts of the industry. In every case, however, it is essential that a forecast should:

- provide the information required by managers;
- cover the specified time periods for which the forecast is needed;
- be of sufficient quality for its purpose.

Within these constraints several factors govern the approach adopted and influence the choice of model or combination of models employed.

FACTORS GOVERNING THE CHOICE OF METHOD

The Purpose of the Forecast

The objectives of forecasts vary widely and, in order to select a suitable method, forecasters need to know the amount of detail required by managers and in what form it is useful, e.g., tourism demand can be forecast by market area, by market segment, by region, by month, by season, or by some combination of these.

The Time Period for Which the Forecast Is Required and the Degree of Accuracy Which Is Needed

Different techniques are used to make short-, medium-, and long-term forecasts and, in order to choose an appropriate method, forecasters need to know the time horizon required by policymakers and planners.

Short-term demand forecasts (up to two or three years) are normally built up from the available detail, but in the longer run the emphasis is often placed on forecasting overall levels of demand and then breaking these down into their main segments. The former approach is called "bottom-up" forecasting and the latter "top-down."

Other things being equal, the more distant the forecast's time horizon, the lower is the degree of accuracy attainable. Even so the accuracy of long-term forecasts can be much improved if appropriate methods are used.

The Availability of Information

The choice of appropriate forecasting techniques is constrained by the reliability and accuracy of the information available as well as the time horizon of the forecast. However rigorous the forecasting technique, the results are unlikely to be accurate if the basic data are suspect or contain biases which cannot be removed. In such cases and also where insufficient data are obtainable, mathematical and econometric forecasting techniques should give way to more qualitative approaches.

The Forecasting Environment

The multivariate nature of the factors affecting tourism demand makes analysis very difficult and renders forecasts liable to various forms of error. This is particularly true in the case of long-term forecasts and in such cases it is important that the approach adopted should take into account the many economic, social, political, technological, and competitive factors which may affect future demand.

The Cost of Producing Forecasts

The costs of establishing and operating different forecasting methods vary widely. For some purposes the simplest and cheapest methods can provide adequate results. To meet other needs highly sophisticated computer models with an exhaustive appetite for expensively acquired data are essential. In general terms forecasters should choose the simplest, least expensive model which is capable of providing all the information needed by managers.

FORECASTING METHODS

Either mathematical, econometric, or other quantitative techniques can be used to analyze and generate data, or the qualitative opinions of experts can be used to predict future demand. Perhaps the most successful approaches are those which involve both quantitative and qualitative analyses. Rarely, however, is such a comprehensive approach adopted, although the forecasting techniques used by some of the more progressive airlines and national tourist boards go some way towards meeting this ideal.

QUANTITATIVE TECHNIQUES

Three types of quantitative techniques are available—time series, causal, and systems models—although some of the more sophisticated models incorporate elements of each. Time series models are based upon the premise that what has happened in the past has some relevance for the future. They ignore the determinants of demand per se and assume that the effects of causal factors are already implicit in the past data of the variable to be forecast. Forecasts are obtained by analyzing trends in the data and extrapolating these forward into the future. In consequence, although they may provide accurate forecasts, they give no reasons for the predictions. Causal models, on the other hand, take into account the principal factors influencing demand and analyze their separate effects upon the variable under consideration. Forecasts are made by calculating the impact on demand of predicted changes in causal factors such as income levels, relative prices, and the cost of travel. Systems models describe the operation of systems and/or economies and can be used to assess the effects of changes in demand on their operation.

TIME SERIES MODELS

All of the approaches described in this section are *univariate*, i.e., they are concerned solely with the statistical analysis of past data for the variable to be forecast. Such models are available in varying degrees of sophistication from simple trend extrapolation to highly complex mathematical algorithms, involving the analysis and projection of individual components of the data.

Simple Trend Projection

In cases where the data exhibit great regularity, forecasts can be obtained merely be extrapolating the principal trends. The most common relationships are linear, exponential, and cyclical and the objective is to project these curves forward into the future. Since it is unrealistic to expect these relationships to hold for more than a limited period, simple trend projection is suitable only for very short term forecasting.

One variant of trend projection, however, known because of its shape as an S-Curve, is used in some industries for long-run forecasting. This technique is used to analyze past demand over a period of several years and, on the basis of the mathematical relationship disclosed, to forecast by making various assumptions about the future growth path of demand. Because of the heroic nature of the assumptions which have to be made, the technique should be regarded as no more than a useful aid to forecasting and its results in isolation should be treated with extreme caution. It can be used, however, as an adjunct to several of the qualitative approaches described later in this chapter.

Arithmetic Moving Averages

Another naive technique which can produce usable results is to base the forecast on an arithmetic moving average of previous data. In essence, the data for previous years, months, or seasons are added together and divided by the number of observations to give an average figure. When the next observation becomes available, the oldest in the sequence is dropped, the new one is included, and a new average is calculated. Unfortunately, the presence of linear or cyclical trends in the data causes the moving average to lag behind the movement of the data. Although methods exist to ameliorate the effects of such lags, the technique in its simplest forms is not accurate enough to produce reliable forecasts.

Decomposition Analysis

A more sophisticated use of moving averages is to break down (decompose) the main components in the time series and to analyze each of these mathematically. The task is to identify each of the principal components—seasonal variations, secular trends, and irregular fluctuations—and to produce formulae which describe their interrelationships. Forecasts are produced by applying moving averages, where relevant, to each of the data series. The forecasts are updated by including new data as soon as they become available. This approach can be used with any tourism data which exhibit sufficient regularity.

Perhaps the most successful application of this technique in the field of tourism is the work of Baron (1975) in Israel who forecast tourist arrivals, foreign currency earnings from tourists, the demand for bed-nights in hotels, and the numbers of residents departing.

Because moving averages inevitably lag behind movements of the data, however, decomposition analysis is not an appropriate technique to use when substantial changes are taking place in the data.

Exponential Smoothing

Moving averages, however, can be estimated exponentially as well as arithmetically. In such cases the object is to produce a weighted moving average of past data with the weights assigned in geometric progression so that the heaviest weights are given to the most recent data and past data are discounted more heavily. As in the case of arithmetic moving averages, the data are then extrapolated into the future to produce a forecast. Largely because of the assumptions of compound growth inherent in geometric progressions, exponential smoothing is not suitable for medium- or long-term forecasting. Although in isolation it is infrequently used as a forecasting technique, it forms an intrinsic element in the Box—Jenkins approach described below.

Box—Jenkins Method I

The time series approach developed by George Box and Gwilym Jenkins (1970) is a highly sophisticated technique which is relatively inexpensive to use.

Basically the approach is (1) to identify the form of model which expresses relatively well the relationships between the values of a series of data through time and then (2) to use the model to calculate numerical values for these relationships. Unlike other mathematical forecasting techniques, therefore, the model is purpose-built to fit the data. In addition, a systematic process is used to allow identification, estimation, and diagnostic checking.

The technique can provide short- and medium-term forecasts as accurately as most causal approaches. An interesting example of the degree of accuracy attainable with this method can be seen in a study of tourism in Hawaii (Guerts and Ibrahim 1975, Guerts, Ibrahim and Buchanan 1976). Their 24-month forecast of tourist arrivals in the state was shown to have an average forecast error of only 3.5 percent—a level of accuracy which would be very acceptable for any causal model.

In its simplest forms the Box—Jenkins method is univariate, i.e., it is concerned with the extrapolation of a time series of data based on its own movements through time. It can be used to predict when but not why demand may change and in consequence it cannot be used to assess the impact of changes in any of the factors which influence demand. Yet Box and Jenkins themselves (1970, pp. 337—420) showed how the model can be adapted to take some causal factors into account (see Box—Jenkins Method II below). It is in this latter form that the technique provides a bridge between simple univariate time series analysis and the causal approaches described below.

CAUSAL APPROACHES

Causal models involve the analysis of data for other variables considered to be related to the one under consideration and the use of these to forecast demand for the one of interest. The approaches vary in sophistication from the use of simple indicators and surveys to the application of complex mathematical and econometric techniques.

Indicators

A simplistic causal approach is to study an individual or a combination of time series data for other economic activities to forecast tourist arrivals without using a modeling approach. If it were possible to identify one or more time series which always gave correct indications of tourism demand, there would be no need to use more sophisticated forecasting techniques. Unfortunately, the factors governing tourism demand are very complex and it would be unusual if all indicators (or barometers) gave the same signal at the same time. Hence although indicators are a useful aid to forecasting for predicting the direction of changes and turnabouts in activity, alone they cannot achieve the degree of accuracy attainable by using more rigorous approaches.

Box—Jenkins Method II

Although normally used in its univariate form, more sophisticated versions of the Box—Jenkins method involve the use of a transfer function, which takes into account the movement through time of another variable or variables thought to affect the one of concern.

Thus, for example, forecasts can be made of tourist arrivals at a particular destination country by relating visitor arrivals to movements in real incomes per capita in the tourists' countries of origin (it may prove necessary, however, to use time lags to allow the effect of the changes in income to be reflected in the arrivals data).

An interesting application of this technique is a study of tourist arrivals in Puerto Rico (Wandner and Van Erden 1979), where forecasts were obtained by relating the time series data for tourist arrivals to changing levels of unemployment in New York, the principal origin area.

It is in its transfer function form that the Box—Jenkins technique offers its most effective medium-term alternative to econometric model building.

Market Analysis

Surveys—of tourists, potential tourists, or business establishments—are perhaps the most popular form of market analysis. Although not strictly a quantitative method, surveys can provide valuable data and useful insights into potential demand. Unfortunately, surveys aimed at discovering the future intentions of tourists are rarely accurate: apart from the normal difficulties of obtaining a representative sample when the potential tourists are numerous and difficult to locate, tourists rarely plan their holidays more than one year ahead and for most the planning horizon, at least as far as a particular destination is concerned, is even shorter.

Nevertheless, for very short term forecasts, surveys can yield valuable information. The Austrian National Tourist Office (Schulmeister 1973), for example, carries out surveys of tourism managers and hotel owners in selected areas of the country at the beginning of winter and summer to discover their expectations for the coming season. The results are then grossed-up to give representative figures for the whole of the country.

Because of the inherent weaknesses and limitations of survey techniques, however, it is unrealistic to use the results of such surveys for medium- or long-term forecasts. There are, however, three other forms of market analysis. One of these, Sales Force Estimates, is considered later as a qualitative technique. The other two are described below.

A Market study The first of these, used by the Port Authority of New York and New Jersey, is a method of relating the travel patterns of various sectors of the population to their principal socioeconomic characteristics. Basically the population of the area under consideration is divided into cells classified by age, education, occupation, and income. Demand forecasts are made by first estimating population growth in each of these cells and then calculating the resultant number of trips (by multiplying the number of people in each cell by the percentage of those who take holidays). The estimates for each cell are then summed and adjusted for any elements not covered in the survey to produce totals for future years.

The main weakness of this approach, however, is that it cannot take into account the effects of changes in the principal variables that affect demand, e.g., an increase or decrease in fares. Nevertheless, it is a useful method of identifying the segments of the market which generate most travel.

B Market share analysis Market share analysis is particularly useful in forecasting tourism demand for a new destination or facility for which no past data are available. The approach is (1) to forecast the growth for the whole of the sector of demand for which the new destination is competing and then (2) to assess the destination's future share in the market.

The first stage is to identify the past and present proportions of total travel from the principal origin areas to the types of destination which are likely to compete with the new area (in terms of the nature of its attractions, distance, and price). Second, quantitative techniques, such as trend projections, regression, etc., are used to forecast the growth of the identified market segment. Third, the new destination's market share is measured. This can be assessed by dividing the market between the competing destinations on the basis of various subjective assumptions. A more realistic approach, however, is to develop a Market Potential Ranking Index. First, each destination is compared in terms of its cost, attractions, facilities, ease of access, and image. A points system is allotted for each factor and the scores are weighted according to the relative importance of each element in attracting or repelling holidaymakers. Once suitable adjustments have been applied to allow for the relative maturity of each of the competing destinations and for their possible competitive reactions to the entry of the new destination area, a trend curve can be drawn to show the new area's movement towards maturity.

Despite its popularity, however, the approach is unlikely to achieve a high degree of accuracy and needs the support of other forecasting methods.

The Clawson Technique

In its basic form the Clawson approach is a mechanistic method of calculating future demand for a facility based upon past usage. The approach, developed by Marion Clawson (1966) from earlier work by Hotelling, involves the construction of a demand curve which shows the number of visitors in relation to increases in the price charged.

In its simplest form the approach contains some weaknesses and limitations, but later refinements have included the addition of further explanatory variables. More sophisticated versions of the model involve the use of multivariable regression analysis and bear little resemblance to the original model.

Multivariable Regression Demand Analysis

Multivariable regression analysis is the most popular causal technique used for demand forecasting. A survey of business establishments in Britain (Turner 1974), for example, showed that the approach is used widely in the manufacturing and service sectors. In the field of tourism and travel, regression analysis is used regularly by airlines, aircraft companies, and tourism researchers.

The essence of the approach is the formulation and testing of a hypothesis. Typically, the basic model states that the demand for tourism to a particular area is a function of factors such as the levels of income of the tourists, the costs of travel from the tourists' homes to the destination, relative price levels in the two countries or regions and in alternative destinations, and, in the case of international tourism, the currency exchange rates.

Data for each of these variables are fed into a computerized model to calculate the part played by each of the explanatory factors in influencing demand. Forecasts are obtained by estimating the expected future values of each of the explanatory variables and running these into the regression model to produce a predicted future level of demand.

The approach is most suitable for short- and medium-term forecasting. Beyond about four years ahead, it is no longer realistic to assume that the existing relationships between variables will remain constant and the use of other techniques should yield more accurate forecasts.

Spatial Models

Spatial models postulate some basic relationships to explain the flow of traffic between specified places. In their simplest form—gravity models—the movement of traffic is stated to be directly proportional to the population of each region and inversely proportional to the distance apart of the origins and destinations.

More complex models incorporate a number of additional variables to explain the movement of traffic. Some of these variables relate to the propensity of an area to generate travel; others are concerned with the factors which attract visitors to the particular destination. Thus, for example, the variables which generate travel from an origin area, in addition to the size of its population, are likely to include the level and distribution of income and the age composition, education levels, social structure, etc., of the population. The factors which attract visitors to a particular destination, in addition to the size of its population, include the physical attractiveness of the area compared with alternatives, as well as its climate, historical heritage, cultural factors, etc. The travel constraints imposed by distance are often more appropriately expressed in terms of the costs and/or time involved in travel.

A distinction is sometimes drawn between trip generation models, which explain the propensity of an area or several areas to generate travel, and trip distribution models, which explain the flow of visitors to a particular destination or several destinations. In practice, more accurate demand forecasts can be achieved by constructing a model specifically for the type of forecast required. If, for example, the aim is to forecast tourist demand to a particular region, the model should include variables to explain the propensity of each origin area to generate travel plus variables to describe the "attractiveness" of the particular destination area in relation to its competitors. Travel time and/or the cost of travel should be included as a constraint.

Such models closely resemble multivariable demand models and estimates are often computed by the same technique—least squares.

Spatial models have a wide application and have been used by tourism researchers to predict the future spatial demand for international tourism, to analyze the flow of tourists between particular countries and regions, to estimate the future demand for recreational and tourist facilities, and to examine how the demand for tourism is affected by highway improvements, increases in fares, etc. The principal difference between spatial models and multivariable demand models lies more in their initial formulation than in their application.

Growth Scenario Model

A growth scenario model was used by the Bureau of Management Consulting to provide long-term forecasts for the Canadian Government Office of Tourism (Bureau of Management Consulting 1975a). The technique concentrates on the implications of growth trends rather than on providing an exact explanation of particular behavior patterns. The aim is to quantify and project the variables thought to affect tourism and, in the process, to determine which socioeconomic variables are most important in altering tourism demand.

When data are inadequate for regression analysis the technique offers a relatively efficient and inexpensive alternative.

SYSTEMS MODELS

Systems Dynamics

Systems dynamics involves the construction of large-scale computerized mathematical models to simulate the behavior of a system in response to internal and external changes. In common with most other complex mathematical techniques, the approach is useful for forecasting only as long as the relationships expressed in the formulae remain constant. Once these alter, the forecast loses its accuracy.

Input—Output Analysis

Input—output analysis is a matrix technique used to analyze the structure of an economic system and to assess the impact of changes. Although not a suitable technique to use for tourism demand forecasting, it provides a useful method of assessing the economic effects of changes in demand.

QUALITATIVE TECHNIQUES

There are three situations in which qualitative methods are preferable to quantitative techniques. These are when:

- data are insufficient or known to be unreliable;
- it is not possible to construct a suitable numerical model;
- time is insufficient to initiate and operate a quantitative analysis.

Qualitative methods range from hunches and managerial inspiration at one end of the scale to carefully structured attempts to gather and amalgamate the opinions of many experts at the other. Qualitative forecasts are particularly suitable for long-term forecasting when changes of a large and unprecedented nature may be expected.

SIMPLISTIC APPROACHES

Executive Opinion

"Seat of the pants" forecasting, based upon a lengthy practical experience of the tourism business, is still widely used in the private sector. Indeed, at the microlevel, e.g., in deciding whether or not to construct a new restaurant at a particular location, entrepreneurial flair can sometimes forecast demand as accurately as, or even more accurately than, the most rigorous econometric techniques.

Even so it is more usual nowadays for chief executives to seek the views of other members of their organizations in order to broaden the base of the forecast and to reduce its subjectivity. Unless such discussions are structured, however, the process can deteriorate into a guessing game.

Sales Force Estimates

One of the most popular methods of demand forecasting in many industries is to analyze and then amalgamate the forecasts of salesmen and sales managers. In the tourism and travel industry the equivalent method is to bring together the predictions of travel agents, tour operators, and others.

Whilst such forecasts benefit from the specialized knowledge and experience of those involved in selling the service, they merely shift the onus for forecasting onto people with insufficient knowledge or understanding of the factors involved in demand forecasting. Such forecasts are unlikely to be very accurate for more than a season ahead.

TECHNOLOGICAL FORECASTING

Technological forecasting does not necessarily imply forecasts of technological changes. The term is used to define the prediction of the feasible and/or desirable characteristics of demand performance in the light of long-term changes, especially future technologies. Such approaches attempt to show what is possible, what is expected, and what is desirable.

Such forecasts can be exploratory or normative. Exploratory forecasts attempt either to generate new information about future structures and levels of demand or to simulate the outcome of expected events. Essentially they are used to broaden management's knowledge of what levels of future demand may be expected. The most frequently used exploratory forecasts include Delphi Studies, Morphological Analysis, Scenario Writing, and Cross-Impact Analysis, in addition to S-Curve Analysis mentioned earlier in this chapter.

Normative forecasts are concerned also with generating new information or simulating the outcome of events, but such forecasts are made within the context of achieving certain objectives. Usually the aim of such forecasts is to identify critical turning points and linkages and to show what steps can be taken to achieve the desired objectives. In addition to the exploratory techniques already mentioned, normative methods include Relevance Trees and Decision Analysis.

Delphi Studies

Details of this method can be found elsewhere in this Handbook and in the principal literature (Linstone and Turoff 1975). The Delphi Technique is gaining in popularity in the tourism and travel industry and in recent years studies have been made by airframe manufacturers and trade associations (IATA 1977), tourist boards (D'Amore 1976), and various other research organizations (Dyck and Emery 1970, Shafer, Moeller and Getty 1974).

Morphological Analysis

The aim of morphological analysis is to structure the existing information in an orderly manner in order to identify the possible outcome of events. To forecast demand the first stage is to identify the most important variables. This is normally carried out intuitively. Second, each of the variables is considered in turn to assess its possible magnitude and effects. Third, each of them is placed in a multidimensional matrix (called a morphological box) to assess its interactions on demand. This process provides an indication of various attainable levels of demand under varying assumptions about the performance of each variable. Last, an estimation is made of the most desirable level of demand in relation to the variables at work and an assessment is made of how this level might be achieved. In common with most qualitative approaches, morphological analysis lacks rigor unless it is supported by numerical analysis, but it can form a valuable input into group forecasting discussions such as the Delphi approach.

Scenarios

A scenario is an outline of a situation which could develop given the known facts and trends. A hypothetical sequence of events is described showing how demand is likely to be affected by various causal factors. The account focuses attention both on the variables which affect demand and on the decision points which occur, in order to indicate what action can be taken to influence the level of demand at each stage. By such means a number of scenarios can provide a series of alternative strategies for achieving, modifying, or altering the forecast.

Scenario writing is not so much a forecasting technique as a method of clarifying the issues involved. As such it can form a valuable input to group forecasting approaches such as Delphi.

Cross-Impact Analysis

Cross-impact analysis is a method of studying the interdependence of the factors which affect forecasting. The methodology is based upon an analysis of the probabilities attached to the occurrence and magnitude of each of a number of interdependent events and their relationships to each other. A matrix is constructed to show these relationships and to indicate the direction and strength of the impact that one occurrence would have upon the probability of others taking place.

The data are obtained by asking panelists to place scaled ratings on the likely occurrence of each event and its impact on others under various circumstances.

The technique is not a forecasting method per se but a way of examining the issues involved. It gives managers an insight into the sensitivities and interrelationships between different policy options.

Relevance Trees

This is another method of plotting and comparing alternative paths to a goal and at the same time identifying areas where more research is needed. Basically, the approach is to construct a matrix which shows the alternative means by which a goal can be achieved matched against the criteria which affect its realization. Numerical weightings are applied subjectively to both the alternatives and the criteria in order to decide the most suitable path to take.

Although the technique has been used in other areas of forecasting, it has not yet found wide acceptance in tourism circles.

PROBLEMS IN TOURISM AND TRAVEL FORECASTING

The level of accuracy tolerable in any forecast depends upon:

- the use to which the forecast will be put and the nature of any decisions which have to be made;
- the nature of the product being forecasted—tourism demand is more variable in some parts of the world than in others;
- the length of the forecast horizon—the degree of uncertainty is greater in long-term forecasting;
- the coverage of the forecast—greater accuracy can normally be achieved in predicting demand for an entire sector than for a particular subgroup.

Inaccuracies in a forecast can result from any one or combination of six different factors:

- an inappropriate model may have been used;
- a valid model may have been used incorrectly;
- errors may exist in the calculation of the relationships within the model;
- errors may exist in the forecasts of the explanatory variables;
- significant variables affecting demand may have been omitted from consideration;
- the data used to produce the prediction may be inadequate or inappropriate for the type of forecast required.

There are several tests available to evaluate both the data and the model, one of which is Theil's U Statistic (Theil 1965), which can be used among other things to compare the past performance of the model during the estimation period with the observed changes during that period.

Like many other social science phenomena, the determinants of tourism and travel demand are often difficult to identify and quantify. In the first place, the motives governing individuals' decisions to travel are very complex and often subjective and irrational. In recent years a number of researchers have devoted considerable effort to the analysis of such motivations (see, for example, Woodside, Ronkainen, and Reid 1977).

Among the principal factors affecting tourism demand, though not in any order of importance, are changes in (1) income levels and income distribution, (2) the quantity of leisure time and its distribution, (3) educational levels, acting through consumer tastes and travel preferences, (4) the size of population in the origin areas, (5) the level of urbanization in the origin areas, (6) travel costs, (7) the relative price levels in competing destinations, (8) exchange rates, (9) the relative prices of other goods and services which compete for the tourist dollar, (10) communication networks and the speed of travel, and (11) other socioeconomic factors, including the age and occupational distributions of the populations in the origin areas.

Fortunately many of these determinants change relatively slowly through time and for short- and medium-term forecasting their effects can be largely ignored. In the long run, however, their influence may be important and should be taken into account when making forecasts.

The demand for tourist services is subject also to many external factors which can cause major shifts in demand from one destination to another. Perhaps the most potent of these are political and social unrest in the destination countries, although temporary problems can be caused by supply constraints or travel bottlenecks. The long-term effects of such factors are often difficult to forecast.

The difficulties inherent in forecasting tourism demand are compounded by the lack of adequate data. Tourism data are in general much inferior to those for other sectors. Despite the efforts made by several international bodies, no unifying data system exists and data from different countries and regions are difficult to compare. In consequence, forecasters are often compelled to carry out expensive surveys to gather data to feed into their models. In such cases, it is essential that sufficient funds are made available to support the necessary data collection.

FORECASTING AND MANAGEMENT DECISIONS

Forecasting should be an essential element in the process of management.

National Tourist Organizations

National Tourist Organizations (NTOs) need short- and medium-term forecasts to plan their marketing strategy and to take other measures to reduce potential peaking and improve all-year occupancy rates. Such forecasts can also alert NTOs to likely shifts in the type of visitor and so enable plans to be made in time to cope with changes in the type of tourist services required and also to shape demand through promotion and marketing.

Long-term forecasts are required to plan in detail for the long-run development of the tourism industry. Such forecasts can be used to identify future infrastructure needs (new airport facilities, roads, utilities, etc.), to estimate future accommodation needs and related requirements and their mix, and to calculate future labor requirements and training needs.

In addition, long-term demand forecasts enable estimates to be made of future foreign exchange earnings, the contribution which tourism might make to national income, and the social and cultural impact which tourism might have on the country.

Tourist and Travel Operators

Airlines, tour operators, hotel companies, and other business organizations require forecasts to plan their strategy and operations. Short-term forecasts of traffic flows, occupancy rates, and visitor spending are important ingredients in the planning of marketing strategies, pricing policy, revenue targets, cash flow positions, stock requirements, and labor force needs. Medium-term forecasts provide essential data for the timing of new operations and services, the planning of future budgets, and the assessment of manpower and training needs.

Long-term forecasts are needed to determine the future direction and strategy of the organization and to plan capital expenditure in the light of any major market or supply changes revealed by the forecast or to be initiated after a study of alternative possibilities.

British Airways, for example, uses weekly forecasts to compare the prevailing situation with previous target figures, quarterly forecasts to relate traffic flows to the prevailing economic environment, fiscal (or budgetary) forecasts to enable aircraft and marketing resources to be allocated in an optimum manner, development forecasts (from two to seven years ahead) to examine the overall market situation, in order to plan routes and the size of its fleet most effectively, and speculative forecasts (over seven years ahead) to examine new products and market areas.

REFERENCES

Archer, Brian H. (1976), *Demand Forecasting in Tourism*, Cardiff: University of Wales Press.

Archer, Brian H. (1980), "Forecasting Demand: Quantitative and Intuitive Techniques," *Tourism Management*, 1 (March), pp. 5–12.

Baron, Raymond R. (1975), *Seasonality in Tourism*, London: Economist Intelligence Unit Ltd.

Box, George E.P., and Gwilym M. Jenkins (1970), *Time Series Analysis: Forecasting and Control*, San Francisco: Holden–Day.

Bureau of Management Consulting (1975a), *Methodology for Long-Range Projections of Tourism Demand*, Ottawa: Department of Supply and Services.

Bureau of Management Consulting (1975b), *Tourism Impact Model*, Ottawa: Canadian Government Office of Tourism.

Canadian Government Office of Tourism (1977), *Methodology for Short Term Forecasts of Tourism Flows*, Ottawa: Economic Research Section, Policy Planning and Industry Relations Branch.

Clawson, Marion (1966), *Economics of Outdoor Recreation*, Baltimore: Johns Hopkins Press.

D'Amore, L.J. (1976), "The Significance of Tourism to Canada," *The Business Quarterly*, 3 (Autumn), pp. 27–35.

Dyck, H.J., and G.J. Emery (1970), *Social Future of Alberta 1970–2005*, Edmonton, Alberta: Human Resources Research Council of Alberta.

Guerts, Michael D., and I.B. Ibrahim (1975), "Comparing the Box–Jenkins Approach with the Exponentially Smoothed Forecasting Model Application to Hawaii Tourists," *Journal of Marketing Research*, 12 (May), pp. 182–188.

Guerts, Michael D., I.B. Ibrahim, and T.A. Buchanan (1976), "Use of the Box–Jenkins Approach to Forecast Tourist Arrivals," *Journal of Travel Research*, 14 (Winter), pp. 5–8.

International Air Transport Association (1977), *IATA Regional Passenger Traffic Forecasts 1976–1982 Scheduled International Services*, Geneva, Switzerland: International Research Division.

Linstone, Harold A., and Murray Turoff, Eds. (1975), *The Delphi Technique*, Reading, Mass.: Addison–Wesley.

Makindakis, Spyros, and Steven C. Wheelwright (1978), *Forecasting Methods and Applications*, New York: Wiley.

Ostergaard, P. (1974), *A Geographically-Oriented Marketing Model of Automobile Tourist Flows from the United States to Canada*, Ottawa: Canadian Government Office of Tourism.

Schulmeister, Stephen (1973), *Erhebung zur kurzfristigen Prognose des Fremdenverkehrs in Osterreich*, Vienna: Osterreichisches Institut fur Wirtschaftsforschung.

Schulmeister, Stephen (1979), *Tourism and the Business Cycle*, Vienna: Austrian Institute for Economic Research.

Shafer, E.L., G.H. Moeller, and R.E. Getty (1974), *Future Leisure Environments*, Upper Darby, Penn.: USDA Forest Service.

Taylor, Gordon D., and Peter H. Chan (1976), "An Approach to Forecasting Tourism Future," in *Forecasting in Tourism and Outdoor Recreation*, TTRA Canada, Art Chapter National Conference, Montreal, Quebec: L.J. D'Amore and Associates Ltd.

Theil, H. (1965), *Economic Forecasts and Policies*, Amsterdam: North-Holland.

Turner, John (1974), *Forecasting Practices in British Industry*, Leighton Buzzard: Surrey University Press.

Wandner, Stephen A., and James D. Van Erden (1979), "Estimating the Demand for International Tourism Using Time Series Analysis," a paper presented at the International Symposium: Tourism in the Next Decade, Washington, D.C., 13 March 1979.

Wanhill, Stephen R.C. (1980), "Methods of Forecasting Demand," in *Managerial Economics for Hotel Operation*, Richard Kotas, Ed., London: Surrey University Press.

Woodside, Arch D., Ilkka Ronkainen, and David M. Reid (1977), "Measurement and Utilization of the Evoked Set as a Travel Marketing Variable," in *The 80's. Its Impact on Travel and Tourism Marketing*, TTRA Eighth Annual Conference Proceedings, Salt Lake City: Bureau of Economic and Business Research, University of Utah.

8

Scaling and Attitude Measurement in Tourism and Travel Research

GORDON H.G. MCDOUGALL

HUGH MUNRO

Wilfrid Laurier University
Waterloo, Ontario, Canada

*T*he purpose of this chapter is to provide a review of the basic scaling and attitude measurement techniques and their potential in tourism and travel research. The review first discusses attitudes, their components, and their characteristics. Next, the main scaling/attitude measurement techniques are outlined and the advantages and disadvantages of each technique are considered. Subsequently, some of the unique aspects of measuring attitudes in the tourism/travel domain are presented and examples of attitude measurement in tourism management decisions discussed. Finally, some conclusions concerning attitudes and travel research are drawn.

A primary reason for measuring attitudes is to gain an understanding of the reasons *why* people behave the way they do. Knowledge of people's feelings and beliefs, what they consider important in making choice decisions, the major benefits they are seeking when they select one alternative over another, all of these facts can aid managers in the design and implementation of effective marketing programs. To illustrate, attitude measurement has been used to:

- shed useful light on the attitudes of tourists towards National Parks as vacation destinations (Mayo, 1975);
- identify the perceptions held by potential visitors about various tourist-recreation regions (Hunt, 1975);
- provide, through vacation lifestyle dimensions, a better understanding of the major vacation orientations which different households assume (Perreault, Darden, and Darden, 1977).

This type of information can help in selecting target markets for promotional campaigns and in the posi-

tioning of resort areas. Clearly, attitude research has a wide range of applications because of the insights offered into people's behavior.

ATTITUDES

While attitudes have been defined in a variety of ways, most definitions contain some reference to an enduring predisposition towards a particular aspect of one's environment. This predisposition can be reflected in the way one thinks, feels, and behaves with respect to that aspect. One's attitude towards foreign travel would be reflected in one's beliefs, feelings, and behavioral orientations with respect to foreign travel. In this section the discussion focuses on the structure of attitudes, some of their important characteristics, and the attitude–behavior relationship.

COMPONENTS OF AN ATTITUDE

In an attempt to capture the multifaceted nature of attitudes many researchers have conceptualized attitudes as being structured along three dimensions: (1) a

87

cognitive component, (2) an affective component, and (3) a behavioral component. Each of these components and their interrelationships are discussed below.

Cognitive Component

The cognitive component consists of the individual's beliefs and knowledge about a particular object or the manner in which the object is perceived. For any object of interest, it is likely that an individual will possess a number of beliefs or perceptions. For example, an individual might perceive a particular tourist resort as (1) being relatively inexpensive, (2) offering a number of entertainment options, (3) having a variety of lodging and dining facilities, and (4) being extremely popular among the younger tourists. Each of these beliefs may be viewed as representing the individual's current knowledge of a characteristic or attribute of the particular tourist facility. Collectively, these beliefs or perceptions constitute the cognitive component of the individual's attitude towards that resort.

It is conceivable that an individual could possess certain beliefs about a particular tourist area without ever having visited the resort. The beliefs or perceptions could have been formulated through reading about the facility and/or through discussions with friends. As an individual gains more knowledge about a particular object or place and, in particular, when that knowledge has been acquired through personal experience (e.g., the individual actually visits the area), the structure of beliefs becomes more established and organized. In addition, certain beliefs about the characteristics of a particular object or place are likely to assume more importance than others. Some conceptualizations of attitudes explicitly incorporate the differences in importance that individuals place on the various beliefs they hold (Ajzen and Fishbein, 1980). The issues surrounding importance measures are addressed in a subsequent section of the chapter.

Affective Component

An individual's feelings of like or dislike for a particular object or place constitutes the affective component of an attitude. An individual may state that he or she dislikes a particular tourist facility which tends to reflect his or her overall evaluation of the facility. It is likely that if the individual was to elaborate, evaluations of specific characteristics associated with the facility would surface. The individual might state that the lodging and dining facilities were too expensive and/or that the facility was too crowded for his or her liking. Collectively, the evaluation of specific characteristics associated with a particular object or place will contribute to an overall evaluation (i.e., like or dislike) of that object or place. Traditionally, a measure of this overall evaluation has served as a surrogate for one's attitude.

Behavioral Component

The behavioral component of an attitude reflects the action taken or the expressed intent to act with respect to a particular object or place. Continuing with the example of a tourist facility, an individual's actual visit to the facility or an expressed intent to vacation there would constitute the behavioral component of that individual's attitude. In most instances the behavioral dimension is oriented towards the overall object or place as opposed to being specific to a particular characteristic or attribute. It is highly likely that the multifaceted nature of many travel and tourism related activities would contribute to situations in which an individual could exhibit behavior related to specific aspects of a facility.

The three components of an attitude are expected to be related in a consistent manner. An individual's beliefs about or perceptions of a particular attitude object should be consistent with his or her evaluation of that object. The behavior exhibited towards that object should also be congruent with the other elements of the attitude structure. It is this latter relationship that has created much of the controversy surrounding the utility of attitude measurement. This issue is given special attention in a subsequent discussion on the attitude–behavior relationship.

Not all researchers are proponents of conceptualizing an attitude along three dimensions. Some theorists feel that the dispositional characteristics of attitudes are captured in measures of belief (Fishbein and Ajzen, 1975) and/or belief and affect (Heberlein, 1973). Others perceive little utility in differentiating among any of the attitude components (McGuire, 1969). Despite these alternative positions sufficient support and interest exists in examining all three components of an attitude (Bagozzi, 1978).

SOME IMPORTANT CHARACTERISTICS OF ATTITUDES

The complex nature of individuals contributes to their possessing many attitudes related to various aspects of their environment. As such, it is useful for both managerial decision making and research purposes to distinguish the types of attitudes that an individual can possess. The following discussion highlights some of the more important characteristics of attitudes.

The first important distinction with respect to attitudes is their level of specificity. Attitudes can range from being very general or global in nature to being very specific to a particular object, place or event. This distinction has important implications for the approach adopted for attitude measurement. Measurement of an individual's general attitude towards leisure would likely have to incorporate a wide variety of related beliefs, feelings, and behaviors. Support for this is found in the work of Neulinger and Breit (1971), who identified five relatively independent dimensions in the leisure domain that they feel capture a person's general attitude towards leisure. The items used to generate the five dimensions were similar in nature to the psychographic measures employed by Perreault *et al.* (1977) in their classification of vacation lifestyles. However, in measuring an individual's attitude towards a particular event, the domain is more clearly defined and the items can be tied to specific beliefs, feelings, and behaviors related to that event. An example of such an approach is provided in Crompton's study of Mexico as a vacation destination (1979).

It is quite common for researchers to employ measures of general attitudes, interests, and opinions (i.e., lifestyle items like those of Wells, 1974) in conjunction with demographic factors in an attempt to profile those with specific attitudes towards a particular object, event or situation. Woodside and Pitts (1976) have used this technique in the tourism and travel domain.

Another important consideration is how closely the attitudes are linked to a person's underlying value system. The connection between an individual's personal values and attitudes is referred to as centrality. A strong link between a positive attitude towards foreign travel and personal values on being independent, broad-minded, and imaginative would contribute to a fairly central attitude. Researchers have found that since values are relatively stable, the more central the attitude the more difficult it is to change (Eagley and Himmelfarb, 1978).

The last distinction relates to the intensity of the attitude or how strongly the individual feels. The intensity of an individual's feelings is determined by the affective component of an attitude. Like centrality, the more intense (i.e., strongly held) an attitude the more difficult it is to change. Researchers and managers can gain valuable insights into the potential for attitude change by assessing the centrality and intensity of an attitude.

THE ATTITUDE–BEHAVIOR RELATIONSHIP

A key factor underlying the widespread use of the attitude construct is the assumption that there exists a consistent relationship between attitudes and behavior and that an understanding of a person's attitudes will permit an understanding and accurate prediction of his or her behavior.[1] Although the validity of this assumption has been questioned (Calder and Ross, 1973), there is empirical evidence that does demonstrate a strong relationship between attitudes and be-

behavior (Kelman, 1974). Further support for this relationship with respect to the cognitive, affective, and behavioral components of attitudes towards leisure is provided in the work by Ragheb and Beard (1982). The apparent consensus among researchers is that attitudes are generally good predictors of behavior but that factors exist which can affect the strength of this relationship.

> *The question facing researchers is, therefore, no longer whether an individual's attitudes can be used to predict his overt behavior, but when. The task is to specify those variables which determine whether an observed attitude behavior relationship will be relatively strong or weak. (Regan and Fazio, 1977, p. 30)*

The following are some of the major factors that have been found to influence the attitude–behavior relationship:

1 The degree of correspondence in the measures of attitude and behavior entities (Ajzen and Fishbein, 1977);

2 The extent to which behavior is influenced by situational factors (Belk, 1975);

3 The importance an individual places on complying with the norms established by relevant others (Snyder and Tanke, 1976);

4 The relevance or importance of an attitude (Houston and Rothschild, 1978); and

5 The manner in which an attitude is formed (Regan and Fazio, 1977; Olson and Mitchell, 1975).

The above findings suggest that researchers and practitioners should be concerned with more than simply measuring attitudes and should attempt to explore their derivation, their many dimensions, and their importance to those who hold them. In addition, to fully understand the relative role of attitudes in shaping behavior it would be useful to incorporate some of the relevant situational factors. This is likely to be particularly insightful in the travel and tourism domain where such forces are known to be operant.

PROPERTIES OF SCALES

Prior to the discussion of attitude measurement techniques, a brief review of the properties of scales will be outlined. It is important to understand the scale properties attained with any survey instrument as both statistical techniques and interpretation are dependent upon the level of measurement.

Measurement, in its broadest sense, is the assignment of numerals to objects, according to some specified rule (Garner and Creelman, 1970). The numerals

---

[1]The sequence in the relationship among beliefs, feelings, and behavior can also be reversed. Behavior may lead to changes in the affective and cognitive components of attitude as a result of learning (Olson and Mitchell, 1975) and self-perception or dissonance effects (Scott, 1978; Cummings and Venkatesan, 1976).

represent a particular kind of scale and care is required in determining which scale properties are applicable. The issue is to determine the properties of the attribute itself, and then ensure that the numerals are assigned so that they properly reflect the properties of the attributes. Further, good measurement occurs when the properties of the scale employed are consistent with the phenomenon being measured. The four major properties of scales, referred to as levels of measurement, are briefly reviewed in this section.

NOMINAL SCALES

At the lowest level numbers are used to classify objects, people, or characteristics. People are classified as males or females, and areas are classified as countries, states, or cities. The formal property of nominal scales is that classes or groups are assigned to a set of mutually exclusive subclasses. The only relationship involved is that of equivalence; members of any one subclass must be identified on the property being scaled. Statistics that may be used to describe, summarize, or understand nominal data include the mode, frequency, and in most cases, chi-square. The appropriate statistical tests are nonparametric (Seigal, 1956).

ORDINAL SCALES

An ordinal scale requires objects in one category to be described in relation to those in another category, that is, one category relative to another category can be described as being more popular, greater than, or more difficult. Ranking of vacation destinations in terms of choice (first, second, third) provides an ordinal scale. In this case statistics such as the median and percentiles can be used to determine the most popular vacation destination. What cannot be determined is how much more or less popular a particular destination is in comparison to other measured destinations. While the appropriate statistical tests for ordinal scales are nonparametric, in practice this constraint is often violated.

INTERVAL SCALES

When the distances between any two numbers on the scale are of known size, then an interval scale has been achieved. Interval scales have a constant unit of measurement although the units as well as the zero point on the scale are arbitrary. If people are asked to what extent they agree or disagree with a particular attitude statement (e.g., "Westerners are very friendly people") and seven response categories are provided (e.g., strongly agree to strongly disagree), it is frequently assumed that the level of agreement can be measured in intervals. In this example, it would be assumed that the interval between strongly agree and slightly agree can be measured. The most important aspect of obtain-

ing interval scale data is that parametric statistical tests can be used which are more powerful than nonparametric tests. All of the "traditional" statistics, such as the mean, standard deviation, and product-moment correlations, can be used with interval scales.

RATIO SCALES

Scales that have a zero point as their origin are ratio scales. In a ratio scale, the ratio of any two scale points is independent of the unit of measure. Thus, a ratio scale can determine that one unit is twice as large as another unit. Examples of ratio scales are sales, income, and age. Attitude measurement techniques seldom, if ever, achieve a ratio scale.

THE ISSUES

The importance of determining the level of measurement of a scale is that the appropriate statistical techniques must be *matched* to the measurement level. In simple terms, parametric tests cannot be used on nominal or ordinal scales whereas both parametric and nonparametric tests can be used with interval and ratio scales. This issue is particularly relevant in the field of attitude measurement because it is frequently assumed that the measures have interval properties, an assumption that may be incorrect (Seigal, 1956, p. 26). The use of inappropriate statistical techniques and the resultant misinterpretation of the analysis and incorrect conclusions have been well documented (Adams et al., 1965; Aaker and Day, 1983). Unfortunately, reasonable and clear-cut guidelines for addressing these issues have not been established.

ATTITUDE MEASUREMENT SCALES

Assuming the decision has been made to identify consumer attitudes towards some particular object (e.g., vacation destination) or activity (e.g., leisure), the researcher must decide what type of attitude measurement technique to use. This section of the paper will briefly review the major scales used to measure attitudes. Then some of the issues raised in terms of attitude measurement will be discussed.

In selecting a particular attitude scale, it should be noted that each has strengths and weaknesses and most techniques can be adapted to measurement of the attitude components. What follows is a brief description of the well-known attitude measurement techniques. An illustration of each scale is provided in Table 1.

THURSTONE SCALE

The Thurstone scale, also referred to as the "equal-appearing interval" scale, is designed to obtain a score which will identify a person's position on a scale reflecting a particular attitude. The scale is developed in two stages (Thurstone, 1970). The first step requires the collection of a large pool of statements (up to 100) related to the attitude under consideration. This pool is given to a sample of judges who sort each item into one of eleven categories that they consider to be at equal intervals ranging from extremely unfavorable through neutral to extremely favorable. The median or average value of the item (statement) is determined by its position in the category. Items for which judges exhibit little agreement as to their position are discarded. The final scale contains between 10 and 20 items whose scale values are more or less equally spaced along the scale in terms of favorability and it has the properties of an interval scale. The scale is then administered to respondents by asking each individual to check those statements with which he or she agrees and the attitude score is obtained by calculating the median or mean scale value of the items checked. For example, a person who agreed with four statements whose scale values were 1.4, 2.3, 3.6, and 4.2 would have a mean attitude score of 2.9.

Because the Thurstone scale requires a two-stage process which can be time-consuming and expensive, its use in attitude measurement has been limited. However, once the scale has been constructed, it is easy to administer and requires a minimum of instruction. An interesting application of a modified Thurstone scale (Case V) dealt with the touristic benefits sought by a group of international travellers (Good-

TABLE 1   Example of Scales

Thurston Scale

	Agree	Disagree
The primary purpose of a vacation should be rest and relaxation.	———	———
Any vacation spot I visit will have a quiet beach.	———	———

Likert Scale

	Strongly Agree	Agree	Neither Agree Nor Disagree	Disagree	Strongly Disagree
I like to relax when I am on vacation.	———	———	———	———	———
I look for a quiet beach when I'm on vacation.	———	———	———	———	———

Semantic Differential Scale
The "vacation site" is: relaxing: ___ ___ ___ ___ ___ ___ ___ :not relaxing
quiet: ___ ___ ___ ___ ___ ___ ___ :noisy

Stapel Scale
The "vacation site" is:

	+3		+3
	+2		+2
	+1		+1
Relaxing	−1	Quiet	−1
	−2		−2
	−3		−3

Comparative Scale
Compared to "vacation site A", "vacation site B" is:

Very Quiet	Neither Quiet Nor Noisy	Very Noisy
▢	▢	▢

Constant-Sum Scale
Please divide 100 points among the following characteristics so that the division reflects the relative importance to you in the selection of a vacation site.

Relaxing	———
Quiet	———
Sporting activities	———
Nightlife	———

rich, 1977a). The eleven benefits were ranked on seven-point importance scales and the results provided the opportunity to compare the relative importance or preference ordering of a set of stimuli (in this case, the benefits).

LIKERT SCALE

The Likert scale, also referred to as the "summated ratings" scale, requires respondents to indicate a degree of agreement or disagreement with a set of statements (items) concerning a particular attitude object. Frequently, respondents are asked to check the extent to which they agree or disagree with each item in terms of a five-point scale, defined by the labels agree strongly, agree, undecided, disagree, and disagree strongly (Likert, 1970). The items to be included in the scale are selected from a large pool which is usually generated by the researcher. This pool is administered to a sample of respondents representative of the population under study. The next step is to perform an item analysis to determine if each item discriminates between people with positive and negative attitudes. The respondents can be divided into two groups (frequently defined as the 25 percent of respondents with the most favorable total score and the 25 percent with the most unfavorable score) and a "good" item is one for which the mean scores for the two groups are very different. Simply put, item analysis is to select from a pool of statements the ones that discriminate between groups.

The final set of 10 to 20 statements are then administered to a sample of the population under investigation. The score for an individual is the sum or average of the statement scores where "1" can represent "strongly agree" and "5" can represent "strongly disagree." An individual who "strongly agreed" with all statements on a five statement scale would receive a total score of 5 or mean score of 1.

This scale is popular for measuring attitudes because it is relatively easy to construct and administer. Its drawbacks include a concern that the scale does not have interval properties. Likert scales, or variations of the scale, have been widely used in tourism and travel research to identify such things as the psychographic correlates of national parks' attractiveness (Mayo, 1975), the important psychographic dimensions of vacation lifestyles (Perreault, Darden and Darden, 1977), and the relationship between leisure activities and need satisfaction (Tinsley and Kass, 1978). Two of these studies provide a reasonable amount of detail on the methods used to construct the scale (Perreault, Darden, and Darden, 1977; Tinsley and Kass, 1978).[2]

The Likert scale has been frequently used in a modified fashion to collect information on a wide range of

attitude dimensions including psychographics (Wells, 1974) and activities—interests—opinions (Wells and Tigert, 1971). In fact, the proliferation of Likert-type scales has sometimes created some confusion as to what constitutes a Likert scale. Researchers have taken considerable latitude with these scales and the reliability of some scales has been questioned (Wells, 1975; Mehorta and Wells, 1977).

SEMANTIC DIFFERENTIAL

The semantic differential consists of a set of bipolar adjectives such as good—bad and strong—weak that can be used to measure respondents' attitudes towards organizations, brands, stores, activities, vacation destinations, or a wide variety of objects. Normally, respondents are asked to rate an attitude object on a series of five- or seven-point scales anchored at each end by bipolar adjectives or phrases (Osgood *et al.*, 1957).

In using this technique, care must be given to ensure that the adjectives or phrases used are meaningful and important to the respondents. Further, the negative (positive) poles should be rotated between the right and left sides to avoid a response tendency or the "halo effect." This effect may occur when all favorable (or unfavorable) poles are on one side and the respondent simply checks off one side of the scale. The main drawback to the semantic differential scale is that it may not have interval properties although researchers often assume that it has interval properties when in many instances it does not.

Semantic differentials have been widely used because of their ease of construction and descriptive capabilities. In the travel and tourism area, semantic differentials have been used to measure the images potential visitors have of various tourist-recreation regions (Hunt, 1975), the role attitudes in recreationists' choice decision (Murphy, 1975), and as a partial validation of the wilderness scale (Heberlein, 1973). Examples of how semantic differential scales and Likert scales could be used to measure the attitude components are provided in Table 2. Some concern has been expressed with the use of semantic differentials in image measurement of tourist-recreation areas because it limits respondents' answers to given dimensions and comparisons of several tourist-attracting regions though the use of many semantic differential scales may be a cumbersome task (Goodrich, 1977b).

OTHER ATTITUDE MEASUREMENT SCALES

A number of other scales exist for the measurement of attitudes, many of which are modifications of the above-mentioned scales. The Stapel scale is a simplified version of the semantic differential scale (Stapel, 1968) and the itemized-category scale is a modification of the Likert scale as is the comparative scale (Aaker and

---

[2]For a comparison of the Likert scale and the Thurstone scale see Seiler and Hough (1970).

TABLE 2   Examples of Scales to Measure Attitude Components

Examples of True or Modified Semantic Differential Scales

Knowledge
• Attribute beliefs—This vacation site is:
    very relaxing: ___ ___ ___ ___ ___ ___ ___ :not relaxing at all
Affect or liking
• Overall preference—I would consider this vacation site as:
    not appealing: ___ ___ ___ ___ ___ ___ ___ :ideal destination
• Specific attributes—In choosing a vacation site, relaxation is:
    very important: ___ ___ ___ ___ ___ ___ ___ :not important at all

Examples of True or Modified Likert Scales

Knowledge
• Attribute beliefs—

	SA	A	NA ND	D	SD
This vacation site is very relaxing:	___	___	___	___	___

Affect or liking
• Overall preference—
  I think this vacation site is an
  ideal destination: ___   ___   ___   ___   ___
• Specific attributes
  Relaxation is an important
  consideration in the vacation site
  I choose: ___   ___   ___   ___   ___
Action
• Intentions—
  I will definitely take my vacation
  at Site A this year: ___   ___   ___   ___   ___

Day, 1983). A comparison of the semantic differential scale, the Stapel scale, and the Likert scale concluded that there were no marked differences with respect to measure validation (Menezes and Elbert, 1979). The Guttman scale was designed to determine whether a set of beliefs or intentions can be ordered along a single dimension (Guttman, 1970). Rank order scales are designed to determine if a set of objects can be arranged with regard to a common criterion (Aaker and Day, 1983).

CHOOSING A SCALE

Researchers have a range of choices regarding which scale they could select to measure attitudes. In deciding on a particular scale a number of criteria must be considered including the properties of the scale, which was discussed in an earlier section. A second criterion is the number of items/statements to be used in the scale. Generally speaking, the Likert scale and the semantic differential scale are suitable for relatively large numbers of items/statements. A third criterion is the importance of reliability and validity. These items will be discussed in the next section. A final criterion is the method of interviewing (e.g., telephone, mail, personal interview), which will influence the type of scale used.

There are also some technical considerations, including the extent of the category description, treatment of respondent uncertainty or ignorance, balance of favorable and unfavorable categories, and whether comparison judgment is required. These considerations as well as some guidelines in choosing a scale (Table 3) are discussed by Aaker and Day (1983).

CONSTRUCTING A SCALE

There are three basic approaches to constructing an attitude scale. The first, and easiest, is to select a scale that has been previously developed and tested by others. This approach has the obvious advantages of using a scale that is reliable and valid. Further, the results can be compared to prior research with the potential of generalizing the results to large settings. The major drawback is that, depending on the purpose of the research, there may be no scale that "fits" the present situation. A number of scales have been developed in the tourism and travel area, including psychographic or activities—interests—opinions scales (Mayo, 1975; Perreault, Darden, and Darden, 1977), wilderness scales (Heberlein, 1973), attitude towards leisure scales (Neulinger and Breit, 1971), leisure activity scales (Ritchie, 1975), and traveller's attitude scales (Thompson and Troncalli, 1974). A review of these

TABLE 3   Appropriate Applications of Various Attitude Scales

Attitude Component	Type of Scale				
	Itemized-Category	Rank Order	Constant-Sum	Likert	Semantic Differential
Knowledge					
awareness	··				
attribute beliefs	··	·	·	·	··
attribute importance	··	·	··	·	
Affect or liking					
overall preferences	··	·	··	·	·
specific attributes	··	·	·	·	··
Action					
intentions	··	·	··	·	

·· = very appropriate.   · = sometimes appropriate. *Source:* Aaker and Day (1983).

TABLE 4   Procedure for Developing Better Scales

Step	Recommended Coefficients or Techniques
1 Specify domain of construct	Literature search
2 Generate sample of items	Literature search Experience survey Insight-stimulating examples Critical incidents Focus groups
3 Collect data	
4 Purify measure	Coefficient alpha Factor analysis
5 Collect data	
6 Assess reliability	Coefficient alpha Split-half reliability
7 Assess validity	Multitrait—multimethod matrix Criterion validity
8 Develop norms	Average and other statistics summarizing distribution of scores

Source: Churchill (1979).

related studies can provide an inventory of existing attitude scales.

The second approach is to develop a scale by either modifying an existing scale or introducing a new set of items. This approach is appropriate when the research objective is relatively simple and straightforward, when further research in the area is unlikely, and when there are time pressures to complete the study. In this type of situation, selecting one of the basic measurement techniques, designing the scale items, and conducting a pretest to determine the usefulness of each item in providing a distribution of responses should be sufficient in developing the scale.

The third approach is to develop a new scale that is valid and reliable. In this situation, the research objective would likely entail some long-term strategy. The approach offered here has been developed by Ragheb and Beard (1982), Churchill (1979), Antil and Bennett (1979), and Peter (1979). It involves eight steps and is appropriate when designing a scale using multiple items. The eight steps, illustrated in Table 4, will be discussed in turn.

Specify Domain of Construct

The first step requires a relatively precise definition of the construct (i.e., attitude) which states what is to be included *and* excluded. In establishing the domain, there is no substitute for a thorough literature search. The end product of the literature search should be an operational definition of the construct. Unfortunately, few examples of well-defined, operational constructs are available in the tourism and travel area. One exception is the leisure attitude construct developed by Ragheb and Beard (1982).

Generate Sample of Items

The purpose of this stage is to generate items which measure the defined attitude/construct. The available techniques include literature searches, experience surveys, insight stimulating examples, critical incidents, and focus groups (Selltiz *et al.*, 1976). The literature search should offer some existing scales that can be used as a starting point. Focus group or open-ended interviews with some experienced subjects (e.g., campers, frequent travellers) can lead to further ideas and items (Hollender, 1977). An interesting example of item generation was reported by Abbey (1979) in preparing a lifestyle scale in a study of the design of package travel tours. In this case the researcher reviewed the literature to identify vacation lifestyle dimensions that were consistent with the theoretical framework employed. Then the research literature that employed lifestyle variables was reviewed. Third, discussions were held with travel agents and tour organizers to gain some practical insights. Finally, tour specialists were asked to review the proposed instrument in terms of appropriate questions.

After a large number of items have been generated, item editing should occur. Items that are redundant, ambiguous, or not clearly positive or negative should be either rephrased or eliminated. The remaining items can then be pretested.

Collect Data

A convenience sample can be used in the pretest as long as the attitude/construct has some relevancy for the respondent. Because the purpose of this stage is to develop the scale, most sampling issues (e.g., representative) are not relevant.

Purify Measure

Two analytic techniques are useful in establishing acceptable levels of reliability and validity (Antil and Bennett, 1979). Factor analysis can be used to identify those items which are highly correlated with one another on any single dimension and also to divide the data into a number of dimensions. The investigator may be more certain of what underlying dimensions the scale is actually measuring. Because of the number of "garbage items" at this stage, factor analysis should probably not be used in a confirmatory fashion (Churchill, 1979).

Item analysis is used to determine the internal consistency of a set of items, thereby increasing the reliability of the scale. The measure, coefficient alpha (Cronbach, 1951), is the most commonly accepted formula for assessing the reliability of a measurement scale with multipoint items (Peter, 1979). Of interest is to obtain a "high" alpha (Nunnally, 1967) for the scale *and* to ensure that the item-to-total correlations are also high. Item reduction can be accomplished by eliminating items with low item-to-total correlations (Antil and Bennett, 1979) and recalculating alpha.

A fair amount of iteration is likely to occur in this stage, depending on the results obtained (Churchill, 1979). In the best case, a satisfactory alpha is obtained and further testing of the scale can occur. In the worst case, an unsatisfactory alpha is obtained and the researcher must return to steps 1 and 2 and repeat the process.

Collect New Data and Assess Reliability

Assuming a satisfactory alpha is obtained, the revised scale is tested with a new sample of respondents. The item analysis procedure is repeated, and at this time factor analysis can aid in "purifying" the scale. During this phase, the researcher is also interested in reducing the number of items in the scale without reducing the reliability. Shorter scales are normally preferred because they reduce respondent fatigue and allow for the inclusion of other measures in the questionnaire.

Further pretesting of the reduced, revised scale may also be appropriate. In this case, the data should be collected from a representative sample or a sample of the target population. Of interest here is ensuring that the reliability of the scale remains high. As well as testing for internal consistency, two other measures of reliability can be used, test–retest and alternative forms (Peter, 1979), although some questions have been raised about the use of test–retest in this context (Churchill, 1979).

Assess Validity

The prior steps should result in a measure which has content or face validity and is reliable. At issue is whether the measure has construct validity, that is, to validate the theory underlying the measure or scale (Bohrnstedt, 1970). To establish the construct validity of measure, one must determine (1) the extent to which the measure correlates with other measures designed to measure the same thing and (2) whether the measure behaves as expected (Churchill, 1979). The recommended approach in dealing with correlations with other measures is through the multitrait–multimethod matrix (Campbell and Fiske, 1970). One reasonable approach in dealing with the expected behavior is to compare the results obtained on the scale from a sample of "normal" respondents and an "interest" group. A wilderness scale could be validated by comparing the results for "average" people with a group who belong to the Sierra Club.

Develop Norms

In some cases it may be desirable to develop norms for scales (Churchill, 1979). This stage requires obtaining measures on relatively large numbers of representative respondents and can only be justified if the scale is to be widely used (e.g., personality measures, intelligence tests).

Summary

It is apparent that the development of a "good" scale requires considerable effort and expertise. While individual researchers may wish to avoid or eliminate some of the stages, it should be recognized that the emerging attitude measurement literature in the travel and tourism area will only progress through the development of reliable, valid scales. To quote, "this body of knowledge . . . about travel behavior that allows us a clear view of its structure and consequences . . . can only be developed through the painstaking process of building on the research of others in examining behavior and attitudes" (Frechtling, 1979, p. 2).

ALTERNATIVE APPROACHES TO ATTITUDE MEASUREMENT

Multidimensional Scaling

The techniques discussed thus far involve the explicit specification of attributes or characteristics about an attitude object. It is assumed that the information provided by having respondents evaluate alternatives on these prespecific characteristics (i.e., assessing their beliefs) will provide valuable insights into their attitudes towards those alternatives. One concern in using this approach is the extent to which the characteristics specified accurately reflect the evaluative dimensions that the respondents would employ if the choice was theirs. A technique which alleviates this problem is multidimensional scaling.[3] Individuals are asked to rate alternatives on the basis of perceived similarity to one another. They are not told which criteria to use to determine similarity. A multidimensional scaling computer program converts the similarity data into distances on a map with a small number of dimensions so that similar alternatives are close together. An example of a map generated via multidimensional scaling is provided in Fig. 1.

The program determines the underlying dimension-

[3]For a more detailed discussion of multidimensional scaling see Shephard, Romney, and Nerlove (1972).

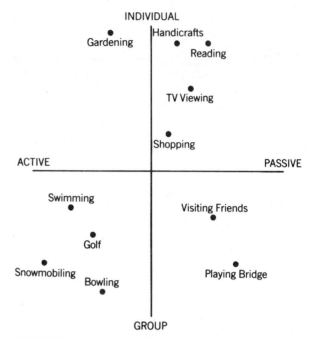

FIGURE 1   An example of a perceptual map generated by multidimensional scaling. Source: This illustration is adapted from J.R.B. Ritchie (1975), "On the Derivation of Leisure Activity Types: A Perceptual Mapping Approach," *Journal of Leisure Research*, 7, 2, 128–140.

ality to individuals' similarity judgments and the position of alternatives on each of those dimensions. The interpretation of the resulting dimensions is based on an understanding of the characteristics of those alternatives that are located close together on the map. For example, in Fig. 1 the activities gardening, handicrafts, and reading are located very close to one another on the top end of the vertical dimension. Similarly, playing bridge, bowling, and snowmobiling are located close to one another but on the opposite end of the vertical dimension. The author, based on the positioning of the various activities, subjectively labelled this vertical dimension as reflecting the extent to which an activity is an individual or group event.

The technique also lends itself to assessing individuals' preferences. This is accomplished by having individuals include an "ideal" alternative and rate its similarity to the other alternatives. The distance between each alternative and the ideal alternative is then used to generate preferences. The results can be generated on an aggregate basis or for one individual.

The major advantages of such an approach are that it provides an overall structure of the various alternatives as the individuals perceive them (i.e., a perceptual map) and it eliminates the risk of specifying evaluative characteristics for individuals which may not be relevant. One limitation is that researchers must interpret the dimensions generated, although this could be facilitated with the collection of additional data on the characteristics (i.e., attributes) of the alternatives.

CONSTANT SUM SCALE

The importance that individuals place on certain characteristics when evaluating alternatives poses another issue for attitude measurement. As previously discussed, the importance of certain beliefs or characteristics can be assessed directly via a rating or ranking procedure. Another variation is to employ the constant sum scale (briefly discussed earlier), which asks respondents to allocate a fixed number of points (e.g., 100) to each characteristic in proportion to their relative importance. One difficulty with many approaches is their failure to indicate those characteristics which are determinant in consumers' evaluation processes. For example, an attribute or characteristic can be considered important by consumers but the alternatives may not be perceived as being different with respect to that characteristic. That characteristic is likely to be given less weight in the evaluation process than those that are not only perceived to be important but also can be used to differentiate among alternatives (i.e., determinant). These determinant characteristics are more relevant in that they provide greater insights into consumers' evaluations and choice processes.

An additional limitation in assessing importance through rating approaches is that the characteristics are considered independently. This tends to contribute to respondents rating many characteristics as being important and reduces the ability to distinguish among those that are considered more important than others. This weakness is alleviated to some extent when the constant sum scale is employed.

CONJOINT ANALYSIS

Conjoint analysis, an indirect approach to assessing attribute importance, offers a means for addressing the limitations discussed above. The technique involves the trade-off of alternatives having characteristics which are varied in systematic ways. Based on respondents' preferences for the various alternative profiles inferences are made about the underlying value systems or importance of characteristics. A detailed discussion of conjoint analysis is contained in this book and those interested are referred to Chapter 39. (Claxton, 1986).

SPECIAL CONSIDERATIONS

There are a number of problems/issues that may arise in conducting attitude research in the travel and tourism area. The researcher might review these concerns to see if they are applicable for a particular situation. Five issues are worthy of mention.

THE MULTIFACETED AND MULTIATTRIBUTE DIMENSIONS OF VACATIONS

Unlike even relatively complex products that usually have a known and definable set of dimensions, vacation destinations can offer a large number of possible dimensions that may be difficult for the researcher to identify. While respondents' attitudes towards the benefits of various vacation destinations can be measured, the motivations for a particular site may range from esoteric (e.g., escape from realism) to mundane (e.g., visit an aunt) and the perceptions of a site may vary depending on the distance the respondent is from that site (Scott, Schewe, and Frederick, 1978). Further, the variations in these motivations may lead to subject responses that are not comparable. Researchers in the travel/leisure area must take care to construct scenarios that are factually explicit to ensure that measured differences in attitudes are referring to the same rather than different concepts (Ritchie, 1975). Simply put, when one measures attitudes towards products usually the important factors/dimensions can be identified through a consumer-based approach. When one measures attitudes towards vacation destinations even a consumer-based approach may lead to an incomplete list or a large list that may be unmanageable in a survey.

THE HIGH-INVOLVEMENT JOINT DECISION

The vacation decision can typically be described as one where active information search occurs, the process is fairly long, and it involves, to some degree, all members of the household (Ritchie and Filiatrault, 1980). This type of decision process implies that attitudes towards various vacation destinations may be well structured and may be easily measured but they also may change as additional information is obtained. Further, the measurement problem is complicated because it is likely to be a joint decision and it may be necessary to interview both the male and female heads of households (Ritchie, 1975).

TIME BETWEEN PURCHASES

For most consumers, vacations are an annual event. This infrequent decision (as opposed to repetitive decisions) can create some problems. For example, a weak relationship between attitudes and behavior may surface unless this time element is reflected in the measures employed.

THE REPEAT-PURCHASE DISCONTINUITY

When consumers purchase a product, then experience it through use, they will tend to purchase the same brand again if satisfaction levels are acceptable. High satisfaction with a particular vacation may not lead to a repeat purchase of that vacation site. Because many consumers want similar but *new* experiences with vacations, the destinations vary each year. The problem with respect to attitude measurement is that while consumers may be highly satisfied and have very favorable images of the destination they visited last year, they will not visit it again. Consequently, the attitude–behavior intention link is not present. Researchers need to be cognizant of this fact.

PERCEIVED RISK AND TRAVEL

It appears likely that because a vacation choice may be a high perceived risk decision, risk may operate as a moderating variable between attitudes and intended behavior, that is, consumers with a tolerance for risk are more likely to "go where their attitudes take them," whereas those with a low tolerance for risk are likely to return to familiar spots, even if another, new destination is preferred.

ATTITUDE RESEARCH AND TOURISM MANAGEMENT

The primary reasons for using attitude research in tourism management are to gain an understanding of *why* and *how* people make travel decisions. This understanding enables managers to more effectively market their particular transportation or destination modes. The following examples illustrate how attitude research can lead to more effective marketing.

IDENTIFYING CONSUMER BENEFITS

The foundation of any successful marketing campaign, be it for soap or sailing, is a thorough understanding of the consumer benefits that can be satisfied by the offered product or service. Knowledge of these benefits assists in segmentation, positioning, and strategy. A service or facility can be successfully positioned in the marketplace by offering benefits that are important to a particular customer group and yet different from those benefits offered by competitors. With respect to vacation destinations, because they frequently can satisfy a multitude of needs, attitude measurement can help determine the importance or rank order of the benefits for various segments. An interesting illustration of the determination of benefits (e.g., sightseeing opportunities, camping opportunities) through the use of factor analysis is provided by Crask (1981).

Establishing Segments and Target Selection

A critical aspect of any marketing plan is the identification of various segments and the selection of some of these segments for a focused marketing strategy. Psychographic or lifestyle research has been particularly useful in identifying segments such as the "bud-

get vacationers" and the "adventurers" (Perreault, Darden, and Darden, 1977). It is likely that a particular tourist facility will not be able to effectively service the desires of all customers. However, a clear understanding of the attitudes of the various customer groups will assist in identifying viable market segments in terms of potential revenue or heavy use and permit an effective channeling of resources in appealing to those segments.

DESIGNING MARKETING STRATEGIES

The essence of marketing strategy is the matching of the firm's product/service offering with some target segments. In this context, vacation destinations can be matched to selected consumer travel segments. A strategy is then designed to cement this match. For example, a tourist service or facility may be developed or modified such that it offers those characteristics desired by a particular group of customers. Research has shown that tour travellers prefer tours designed with vacation lifestyle, as opposed to demographic information, and this data can be used to design strategies which are compatible with the motivations, attitudes, and opinions of tour travellers (Abbey, 1979).

IMPLEMENTING THE MARKETING MIX

The final step in the marketing process is to design a specific marketing program (e.g., advertising, etc.) to encourage the selected segments to visit/vacation at a particular destination. In the tourism domain the major component of the mix is usually advertising and attitude research can be useful in identifying the salient attributes (to the consumer) of the program. Promotional efforts can then be directed at reinforcing favorable attitudes or altering consumers' perceptions such that more favorable attitudes will be formed. Examples of the various advertising strategies that can stem from a knowledge of consumers' attitudes are offered in a framework provided by Boyd, Ray, and Strong (1972). A practical illustration of the implementation of a promotional strategy is the decision of the Michigan Travel Bureau to increase advertising in high potential geographic markets based on vacation preference types (Bryant and Morrison, 1980).

CONCLUSIONS

An important aspect of understanding and predicting human behavior is the study of attitudes: the knowledge, feelings, and behavioral components individuals have with respect to some object or activity. With this understanding, the probability of designing effective marketing programs is greatly enhanced. This is particularly true in the travel and tourism domain, where knowledge of consumers' attitudes towards leisure, travel, and vacation destinations can assist in preparing successful strategies.

The measurement of attitudes requires an understanding of what constitutes an attitude and what possible relationships may exist between attitudes and behavior in various situations. Further, it is important to appreciate what attitude measurement technique is appropriate given a particular research project. Within the travel and tourism domain these issues can be addressed by ensuring that the attitude constructs under consideration are well defined and the possible linkages between attitudes and behavior have been carefully documented. While some unique problems exist in measuring attitudes in the tourism/travel domain, they can be overcome. The major requirements are expertise and a knowledge of the field of investigation and the attitudes to be studied.

In completing this review it became apparent that attitude measurement in the tourism/travel area has offered and continues to offer considerable potential. As a maturing field it is now appropriate to spend more effort on the construction of reliable and valid attitudes scales, an objective which this chapter has attempted to accomplish.

REFERENCES

Aaker, D.A., and Day, G.S. (1983), *Marketing Research: Private and Public Sector Decisions* (2nd ed.), Wiley, Toronto, Chapter 8.

Abbey, J.R. (1979), "Does Life-Style Profiling Work?" *Journal of Travel Research*, 17, 3 (Summer), 8−14.

Adams, E.W., Fagot, R.F., and Robinson, R.E. (1965), "A Theory of Appropriate Statistics," *Psychometrika*, 30, 99−127.

Ajzen, I., and Fishbein, M. (1977), "Attitude−Behavior Relations: A Theoretical Analysis and Review of Empirical Research," *Psychological Bulletin*, 84, 5, 888−918.

Ajzen, I., and Fishbein, M. (1980), *Understanding Attitudes and Prediction Social Behavior*, Prentice−Hall, Englewood Cliffs, N.J.

Antil, J.H., and Bennett, P.D. (1979), "Construction and Validation of a Scale to Measure Socially Responsible Consumption Behavior," in *The Conserver Society*, K.E. Henion and T.C. Kinnear, Eds., American Marketing Association, Chicago, pp. 51−68.

Bagozzi, R.P. (1978), "The Construct Validity of the Affective, Behavioral, and Cognitive Components of Attitudes by Analysis of Co-variance Structures," *Multivariate Behavioral Research*, 13, 9−31.

Belk, R.W. (1975), "Situational Variables and Consumer Behavior," *Journal of Consumer Research*, 1, 2 (December), 157−164.

Bohrnstedt, G.W. (1970), "Reliability and Validity Assessment in Attitude Measurement," in *Attitude Measurement*, G.F. Summers, Ed., Rand McNally & Company, Chicago, pp. 80−99.

Boyd, H.W., Ray, M.L., and Strong, E.C. (1972), "An Attitudinal Framework for Advertising Strategy," *Journal of Marketing*, 36, 27−33.

Bryant, B.E., and Morrison, A.J. (1980), "Travel Market Segmentation and the Implementation of Market Strategies," *Journal of Travel Research*, 18 (Winter), 2−7.

Calder, B.J., and Ross, M. (1973), *Attitudes and Behavior*, Learning Press, Morristown, N.J.

Campbell, D.T., and Fiske, D.W. (1970), "Convergent and Discriminant Validation by the Multitrait−Multimethod Matrix," in *Attitude Measurement*, G.F. Summers, Ed., Rand McNally & Company, Chicago, pp. 100−124.

Churchill, G.A., Jr. (1979), "A Paradigm for Developing Better Measures of Marketing Constructs," *Journal of Marketing Research*, 16 (February), 64−73.

Claxton, J.D. (1986), "Conjoint Analysis in Travel Research: A Manager's Guide," in *Travel, Tourism, and Hospitality Research—A Handbook for Managers and Researchers*, C.R. Goeldner and J.R.B. Ritchie, Eds., Wiley, New York, Chapter 39.

Crask, M.R. (1981), "Segmenting the Vacationer Market: Identifying the Vacation Preferences, Demographics, and Magazine Readership of Each Group," *Journal of Travel Research*, 19 (Fall), 29−34.

Crompton, J.L. (1979), "An Assessment of the Image of Mexico as a Vacation Destination and the Influence of Geographical Location upon That Image," *Journal of Travel Research*, 17, 4 (Spring), 18−23.

Cronbach, L.J. (1951), "Coefficient Alpha and the Internal Structure of Tests," *Psychometrika*, 16 (September), 297−334.

Cummings, W.H., and Vankatesan, M. (1976), "Cognitive Dissonance and Consumer Behavior: A Review of the Evidence," *Journal of Marketing Research*, 13, 3, 303−308.

Eagley, A.H., and Himmelfarb, S. (1978), "Attitudes and Opinions," *Annual Review of Psychology*, 517−554.

Fishbein, M., and Ajzen, I. (1975), *Belief, Attitude, Intention and Behavior: An Introduction to Theory and Research*, Addison−Wesley, Reading, Mass.

Frechtling, D.C. (1979), "What's Wrong with Travel Research," in *The Travel Research Association Proceedings*, University of Utah, Salt Lake City, pp. 1−3.

Garner, W.R., and Creelman, C.D. (1970), "Problems and Methods of Psychological Scaling," in *Attitude Measurement*, G.F. Summers, Ed., Rand McNally & Company, Chicago, pp. 42−79.

Goodrich, J.N. (1977a), "Benefit Bundle Analysis: An Empirical Study of International Travelers," *Journal of Travel Research*, 16, 2 (Fall), 6−9.

Goodrich, J.N. (1977b), "Differences in Perceived Similarity of Tourism Regions: A Spatial Analysis," *Journal of Travel Research*, 16, 1 (Summer), 10−13.

Guttman, L. (1970), "A Basis for Scaling Qualitative Data," in *Attitude Measurement*, G.F. Summers, Ed., Rand McNally & Company, Chicago, pp. 187−202.

Heberlein, T.A. (1973), "Social Psychological Assumptions of User Attitude Surveys: The Case of the Wilderness

Scale," *Journal of Leisure Research*, 5 (Summer), 18–33.

Hollender, J.W. (1977), "Motivational Dimensions of the Camping Experience," *Journal of Leisure Research*, 9, 2, 133–141.

Houston, M.J., and Rothschild, M.L. (1978), "Conceptual and Methodological Perspectives on Involvement," in *Research Frontiers in Marketing: Dialogues and Directions*, S.C. Jain, Ed., American Marketing Association Educators Proceedings, Chicago.

Hunt, J.D. (1975), "Image as a Factor on Tourism Development," *Journal of Travel Research*, 13, 8 (Winter), 1–7.

Kelman, H.C. (1974), "Attitudes Are Alive and Well and Gainfully Employed in the Sphere of Action," *American Psychologist*, 29, 310–324.

Likert, R. (1970), "A Technique for the Measurement of Attitudes," in *Attitude Measurement*, G.F. Summers, Ed., Rand McNally & Company, Chicago, pp. 149–158.

Mayo, E. (1975), "Tourism and the National Parks: A Psychographic and Attitudinal Study," *Journal of Travel Research*, 14, 1 (Summer), 14–18.

McGuire, W.J. (1969), "The Nature of Attitudes and Attitude Change," in *The Handbook of Social Psychology*, *Vol. III* (2nd ed.), G. Lindsey and E. Aronson, Eds., Addison–Wesley, Reading, Mass., pp. 136–171.

Mehorta, S., and Wells, W.D. (1977), "Psychographics and Buyer Behavior: Theory and Recent Empirical Findings," in *Consumer and Industrial Buying Behavior*, A.G. Woodside *et al.*, Eds., North–Holland, New York, pp. 49-65.

Menezes, D., and Elbert, N.F. (1979), "Alternative Semantic Scaling Formats for Measuring Store Image: An Evaluation," *Journal of Marketing Research*, 16 (February), 80–87.

Murphy, P.E. (1975), "The Role of Attitude in the Choice Decisions of Recreational Boaters," *Journal of Leisure Research*, 7, 3, 216–224.

Neulinger, J., and Breit, M. (1971), "Attitude Dimensions of Leisure: A Replication Study," *Journal of Leisure Research*, 3 (Fall), 108-115.

Nunnally, J.C. (1967), *Psychometric Theory*, McGraw–Hill, New York.

Olson, J.C., and Mitchell, A.A. (1975), "The Process of Attitude Acquisition: The Value of a Developmental Approach to Consumer Attitude Research," in *Advances in Consumer Research: Vol. II*, Mary J. Schlinger, Ed., Association for Consumer Research, Chicago, pp. 249–264.

Osgood, C.E., Suci, G., and Tannenbaum, P. (1957), *The Measurement of Meaning*, University of Illinois Press, Urbana.

Perreault, W.D., Darden, D.K. and Darden, W.R. (1977), "A Psychographic Classification of Vacation Life Styles," *Journal of Leisure Research*, 8, 3, 208–224.

Peter, J.P. (1979), "Reliability: A Review of Psychometric Basics and Recent Marketing Practices," *Journal of Marketing Research*, 16 (February), 6–17.

Ragheb, M.J., and Beard, J.G. (1982), "Measuring Leisure Attitudes," *Journal of Leisure Research*, 14, 2, 155–167.

Regan, D.T., and Fazio, R.H. (1977), "On the Consistency between Attitudes and Behavior: Look to the Method of Attitude Formation," *Journal of Experimental Social Psychology*, 13, 28–45.

Ritchie, J.R.B. (1975), "On the Derivation of Leisure Activity Types: A Perceptual Mapping Approach," *Journal of Leisure Research*, 13 (Spring), 1–10.

Ritchie, J.R.B., and Filiatrault, P. (1980), "Family Vacation Decision-making—A Replication and Extension," *Journal of Travel Research*, 18, 4 (Spring), 3–14.

Scott, C.A. (1978), "Self-perception Processes in Consumer Behavior: Interpreting One's Own Experiences," in *Advances in Consumer Research, Vol. V*, H. Keith Hunt, Ed., Association for Consumer Research. Ann Arbor, Mich.

Scott, D.R., Schewe, C.D., and Frederick, D.G. (1978), "A Multi-Brand/Multi-Attribute Model of Tourist State Choice," *Journal of Travel Research*, 16 (Summer), 23–29.

Seigal, S. (1956), *Nonparametric Statistics for the Behavioral Sciences*, McGraw–Hill, New York.

Seiler, L.H. and Hough, R.L. (1970), "Empirical Comparisons of the Thurstone and Likert Techniques," in *Attitude Measurement*, G.F. Summers, Ed., Rand McNally & Company, Chicago, pp. 159–173.

Selltiz, C., Wrightsman, L.S., and Cook, S.W. (1976), *Research Methods in Social Relations* (3rd ed.), Holt, Rinehart & Winston, New York.

Shephard, R.N., Romney, K.A., and Nerlove, S.B. (1972), *Multidimensional Scaling: Theory and Applications in the Behavioral Sciences, Vols. I and II*, Seminar Press, New York.

Snyder, M., and Tanke, E.D. (1976), "Behavior and Attitude: Some People Are More Consistent than Others," *Journal of Personality*, 44, 501–517.

Stapel, J. (1968), "Predictive Attitudes," in *Attitude Research on the Rocks*, L. Adler and I. Crespi, Eds., American Marketing Association, Chicago, pp. 96–115.

Thompson, J.R. and Troncalli, M.T. (1974), "A Psychographic Study of Tennessee Welcome Centre Visitors," in *The Travel Research Association Proceedings*, Salt Lake City, pp. 46–51.

Thurstone, L.L. (1970), "Attitudes Can Be Measured," in *Attitude Measurement*, G.F. Summers, Ed., Rand McNally & Company, Chicago, pp. 127–141.

Tinsley, H.E.A., and Kass, R.A. (1978), "Leisure Activities and Need Satisfaction: A Replication and Extension," *Journal of Leisure Research*, 10, 3, 191–202.

Wells, W.D., and Tigert, D.J. (1971), "Activities, Interests, and Opinions," *Journal of Advertising Research*, 11 (August), 79–85.

Wells, W.D. (1974), *Life Styles and Psychographics*, American Marketing Association, Chicago.

Wells, W.D. (1975), "Psychographics: A Critical Review," *Journal of Marketing Research*, 12 (May), 196–213.

Woodside, A.G., and Pitts, R.E. (1976), "Effects of Consumer Life Styles, Demographics, and Travel Activities on Foreign and Domestic Travel Behavior," *Journal of Travel Research*, 14, 13–15.

9

Issues in Sampling and Sample Design— A Managerial Perspective

JOHN C. CANNON[1]

Chief, Housing Surveys Branch
Demographic Surveys Division
Bureau of the Census
Washington, D.C.

*T*his chapter briefly describes four basic samples and their advantages and disadvantages. Also included is a summary of sampling and nonsampling errors and issues a manager should consider in selecting a sample design. The chapter ends with illustrations on bringing these variables together to select a sample plan.

The development of sampling theory and the acceptance of sample survey results have made it possible for persons who make decisions to have the ability to collect information relatively quickly and inexpensively and to use that information in their decision making. Managers and government officials involved in the travel and tourism industry are among those taking advantage of this. Service industries such as airlines and hotel/motel chains conduct surveys to learn about their customers and how they can improve their service. State and local government agencies use data from surveys to determine the impact of tourism on their economy and how best to use their advertising dollar. The Federal Government uses survey data to measure the levels of travel and the tourism economy at different intervals of time. Such information is used to help in planning to meet current and future needs in these and related areas, such as transportation. Indeed, taking surveys has become a relatively common practice and may, in some instances, be the standard response when information is needed.

IS A SURVEY NECESSARY?

Surveys are a good way of obtaining accurate information quickly and relatively inexpensively. However, there may be other alternatives that are cheaper, quicker, and more accurate. In many cases the information needed may already be available. There is a great deal of information that has been published or is otherwise accessible to the public. Before undertaking the expense of a survey a cost conscious manager should make the effort to see if someone else, perhaps even someone inside their own organization, has already acquired the information. In other cases, a business or organization's administrative or sales records may provide the data required. A summary of these records, or even a sample of the records, could provide the manager with the quick, reliable data that are needed at little or no cost.

In those instances when the information needed is not available from other sources or administrative records, a manager should ask whether the data needed are important enough to justify the expense of conducting a survey to collect it. Can the manager make do with the information that is available or rely on common sense to come up with the answer he is seeking? If the decision is that a survey is necessary then there are several decisions left to be made. The re-

[1]The author gratefully acknowledges the assistance of Dennis J. Schwanz, Chief, Longitudinal Surveys Branch, Statistical Methods Division, Bureau of the Census in preparing the technical sections of this paper.

maining part of this chapter will focus on some basic issues in sampling and sample design.

TYPES OF SAMPLES

Basically, sampling describes the activity of selecting a few from the total and using characteristics of the few to estimate the characteristics of the whole. How the selection of the few is done largely determines the accuracy of the estimates derived from the sample. There are several different types of sampling and various options that can be employed to enhance the quality of each. Books have been written describing various sampling methods, the mathematical proof of the theory and their advantages and disadvantages. What will be attempted in the next few pages is to briefly summarize the major types of samples and their good and bad points so that the manager will at least have a starting point in considering what type of sample and sample design is needed. An attempt will be made to do this simply and without being overly technical. Those interested in a detailed, technical explanation of sampling should refer to any of the several complete books written by experts in this field. Four such books are mentioned at the end of this chapter.

A SIMPLE RANDOM SAMPLING AND SYSTEMATIC SAMPLING

Simple random sampling is basically a sampling method where each possible combination of persons/establishments/houses or whatever that exist in the area of interest (the universe for the study) has the same chance or probability of being selected as every other combination. It is the base on which some other types of sampling are built. A sample using this method is selected by assigning a number serially to every unit in the universe and then choosing the sample by drawing numbers out of a hat or fishbowl or using a random number table.

Simple random sampling is one of the purest forms of selecting a sample. Sometimes the size of the universe, and sample, makes sample selection using this method an overly burdensome task. An alternative is systematic sampling. Using this method requires that first a list of all units in the universe be created. Once the list is completed, the sample is drawn by selecting one out of every so many on the list in a predetermined systematic fashion. The selection is made by dividing the number of units in the universe by the sample size. The result of this calculation provides the interval between units that are selected. For example, if the number of units in the universe is 100 and the sample size is 10, the sample is selected by taking one out of every 10 units on the list. The proper procedure, continuing with this sample, would be to randomly select a number between 1 and 10 as a random start and then select every tenth unit on the list.

Systematic sampling may sometimes be confused with simple random sampling. The difference between the two methods is that while in simple random sampling every possible combination of units in the universe is possible, using systematic sampling only certain combinations are possible. If a sample of two units out of a universe of four (A, B, C, D) was needed, under systematic sampling only the combinations of A and C or B and D would be possible (start with the first or second on the list and take every second unit). In simple random sampling, a token to represent each unit is placed in a hat and two are selected as the sample. In this fashion, every combination is possible (A-B, A-C, A-D, B-C, B-D, C-D).

For systematic sampling to be an acceptable alternative to simple random sampling, the list must be arranged in a nearly random order. If there is a suspicion of any regularity in the sequence of the listing which could conform to the sampling interval, systematic sampling should be avoided. For example, suppose the manager of a 100-unit hotel wanted to select a sample of 10 units and interview the occupants of those units to learn more about the characteristics of the hotel guests. The manager selected the sample by listing all the rooms in the hotel in room number order and then drew a 1 in 10 sample. In many cases, this would be no problem. In this case, however, all the room numbers ending in "0" are luxury suites which rent for very much higher rates while all the room numbers ending with "5" are very small, inexpensive rooms that can sleep only one person. Depending on what the random start was, the manager could have a sample of all luxury suites, a sample of all one-person rooms, or a sample which included neither. Although using a simple random sampling method could have a similar result, in this situation systematic sampling guarantees that the sample will not be representative as long as the list is arranged by room number.

As long as the list is arranged properly, systematic sampling is a simple, straightforward way of scientifically selecting an approximately random sample. If a list is readily available or can be made up with little effort and there is nothing unique about certain elements within the universe which would affect the objectives of the surveys, systematic sampling would be the cheapest and the easiest. There are disadvantages in addition to the one regarding the arrangement of the list. One possible disadvantage is the development of a complete list of elements in the universe. The effort required to develop a complete list of attendees at a travel conference that didn't require registration or other similar means of check-in would probably be quite great and in all likelihood be more effort than that required to do the survey once the list was made. Another disadvantage would be if the uniqueness of a few elements within the universe had a direct impact on the objectives of the study. Using a travel conference as an example, suppose the objective of the study was to estimate the amount of money participants expended to attend the conference. In this example, most of the attendees come from the surrounding area and therefore spend little for transportation or lodging while a relative few travel long distances and therefore spent large amounts to attend the conference. Depending on the luck of the draw, the estimate might be too low (if the sample includes too many "locals") or too high (if the sample contains a disproportionate share of the "big spenders"). Although this can happen with any type of sample, there are ways of controlling this using some form of stratification which will be discussed later.

Another disadvantage to systematic sampling occurs if the universe is widely dispersed, either geographically or over a period of time. The disadvantage here is mainly one of expense rather than survey quality. To list all persons or addresses in a large geographic area or record all occurrences (such as arrivals at bus stations) throughout a long period of time in order to develop a sample universe can be very time-consuming and costly. Cost is also a problem if personal interviews are required and the sample is spread evenly throughout the entire geographic area. The use of mail and telephone surveys makes geographic dispersion a less serious problem.

B STRATIFIED RANDOM SAMPLING

This form of sampling is similar to systematic sampling and overcomes one of the disadvantages while introducing another possible disadvantage. Stratification means dividing the units of the universe into smaller groups in which the units within each group have similar characteristics, making each of the groups as dissimilar as possible and placing the units within each group together on the list before selecting the sample. Again using the attendees at the travel conference as an example, by placing all the "big spenders" together on the list and all the "locals" together on the list, a systematic sample method would then provide a relatively proportionate sample from each of the two groups in attendance. Stratification overcomes the problem of uniqueness of certain elements within the universe but does require a prior knowledge of key characteristics of the elements. It would be hard to implement a stratification if knowledge about the elements in the universe was unavailable to the sampler. Another disadvantage in using stratification is that if the interest is in several somewhat unrelated characteristics, stratifying using just one or two of the characteristics might damage the study of the unstratified characteristics. The problem may be that by stratifying on one characteristic the randomness of the distribution of another characteristic on the list is destroyed.

C CLUSTER SAMPLING

Cluster sampling is used to overcome the cost problems of geographic dispersion or to reduce the size of the list one needs to develop or work with in selecting a sample. In cluster sampling the universe is divided into distinct geographic areas such as census enumeration districts, townships, or counties. In the case of mail or telephone surveys the area might be zip code boundaries or telephone area codes or exchanges. By first selecting a sample of areas and then selecting a sample of elements within the sample areas, the number of areas that must be contacted are reduced and the number of sample cases are concentrated in fewer geographic areas. This is also known as two-stage sampling. At each stage the sample is selected randomly or systematically.

The method has cost advantages if the universe to be covered is households, businesses, or persons that are scattered throughout a large geographic area, particularly if the area must first be canvassed to create a list of eligible elements, such as addresses. In the case where lists exist, such as commercial address lists, telephone directories, or generating telephone numbers randomly, clustering would reduce the size of the list to more manageable, and efficient, proportions. While cost is the major advantage to cluster sampling, it also usually produces a larger sampling error, that is, the estimate obtained is not likely to be as reliable. The reliability of a cluster sample is affected by the composition of the clusters. If the members within clusters are very similar in respect to the characteristic of interest, then the cluster sample would have a larger sampling error or be less reliable than a simple random sample of the same size. Conversely, if the members within clusters are relatively dissimilar in respect to this characteristic, then the cluster sample would be as reliable or more reliable than a simple random sample of the same size. In other words, the situations that result in an efficient stratified sample make for inefficient cluster sampling. The more alike units are within a cluster, the better the results will be if the cluster is used as a group in stratified sampling and the worse the results will be if it is used in a cluster sample.

Nonetheless, for a fixed budget, use of cluster sampling may increase the sample size above the number the same budget would allow for simple random sampling. If the increase in sample size more than compensates for the increase in sampling error resulting from the use of a cluster sample, then there will be a net gain in the reliability of the data.

D QUOTA SAMPLING

This method of sampling requires the enumerators to interview a fixed number of elements with certain characteristics, i.e., a quota is established for the number and type of elements to be selected. Selecting a sample in this fashion is simple, ensures that elements with selected characteristics are represented, and in certain instances may be the only way that a sample of the population can be drawn. The quota is usually established based on known characteristics of the universe. Using the travel conference again as an example, if the purpose of the study is to determine the amount of money spent to attend the conference, and the length of travel required to attend the conference for each of the attendees is known, the attendees could be divided into groups based on length of travel. The interviewers would then be given a list of names in each group and instructed to interview a set number of persons in each group so that a representative sample is selected. The interviewers, armed with their lists, would then proceed to interview those persons on the list that were cooperative and easiest to contact. Those persons that refuse to be interviewed or are consistently moving about are less likely to be included in the universe.

The major disadvantage of quota sampling is that the selection of the persons to be interviewed is not based on a random or systematic selection but on the accessibility and cooperativeness of those responding. For this reason, the chances that the sample is truly representative are less. Continuing with the travel conference example, if the people who were interviewed were easy to contact because they were spending their evenings in their room reading a book and eating a sandwich while those persons who were difficult to contact were spending their evenings out dining, bar hopping, and attending shows, the estimate of expenditures derived from the sample would not be accurate.

There are times when using a quota is the only reasonable way to select a sample. This is particularly true when it is extremely difficult, if not impossible, to list and identify all the potential elements in the universe. A resort might want to brag about the size of fish available in its fishing area. Since most people would not go to the trouble of catching all the fish in the water to select a sample of fish to weigh, a quota sample would permit a catch of a selected number of the different types of fish available to serve as the sample for estimating average size.

APPLYING THESE METHODS

Up to this point, each of the sample types has been discussed individually. In large surveys, two or more of these methods may be used in combination to select the sample. Three such surveys selected as examples are:

1 The 1977 National Travel Survey (NTS) conducted by the U.S. Bureau of the Census.
2 The Canadian Travel Survey (CTS) conducted by Statistics Canada.

3 The 1980 U.S. Travel Data Center National Travel Survey (NTS).

THE 1977 NTS

The sample used for the 1977 NTS was addresses that had previously been in the Census Bureau's Current Population Survey (CPS) or in the Bureau's Quarterly Household Survey (QHS). Since the cost of selecting a large national sample of addresses is extremely high, many surveys done by the Census Bureau use samples of addresses that were included in earlier surveys, or combine surveys so they are conducted during the same visit to an address. Both the CPS and the QHS samples are selected using the same methodology.

The CPS design and methodology are described in detail in Technical Paper 40, which is mentioned in the list of references at the end of this chapter. A brief overview of the CPS design shows that first the United States was divided into Primary Sampling Units (PSUs) which are, for the most part, made up of one or more counties within the same census region. Certain guidelines are imposed to provide minimum population and maximum land area limits.

Once this was done, the next step was to group the PSUs into several strata (stratification). This grouping (stratification) was carried out in such a way that PSUs with similar demographic and economic characteristics were put together to form many homogeneous strata of approximately the same population size. The number of strata were determined by variance and cost considerations. One PSU was selected from each stratum to be in the sample. This was done by ordering the PSUs by population, selecting a random number between 1 and the total population size of the stratum, and then finding in which PSU that number falls on the list (systematic sampling). Those PSUs with the largest populations (the major metropolitan areas) were each put into their own stratum so that they would be included in the sample with certainty.

After the sample PSU within the strata is selected, sample areas within the PSU are selected. The land area in each PSU is divided into several enumeration districts (EDs). The EDs are listed in a prescribed manner based on land use and geographic proximity. A measure of size is calculated for each ED. A random start is selected and a systematic sample of EDs is drawn using the measure of size. Within the EDs, one or more groups of four addresses (cluster sampling) are selected to be interviewed.

THE CTS

The Canadian Travel Survey is really a series of quarterly surveys that are done in conjunction with the Canadian Labour Force Survey (LFS). A detailed description of the methodology used in selecting the sample for the LSF has been published and is included in the list of reference materials at the end of this chapter.

In the LFS, each of the ten provinces included in the survey is divided into economic regions (ERs) which consist of geographically contiguous areas of similar economic structure. These ERs are the primary strata (stratification) from which a sample is drawn. Each of the ERs is then further divided (stratified) into two major groups—self-representing units (SRUs) which primarily consist of cities and other large concentrations of population and non-self-representing units (NSRUs) which consist of areas outside SRUs. Further stratification was done within the SRUs and NSRUs. The last strata was made up of one or more groups of households called clusters. A sample of clusters was selected from each group. This was done by randomly arranging the clusters on a list with a value assigned to each cluster reflecting the number of households in the cluster. Clusters were then selected based on the assigned values using systematic sampling principles. A sample of households was selected from each cluster using systematic sampling.

In the CTS, a further sampling was done to select only one person in the household to interview. This selection was made using simple random sampling.

THE 1980 NTS

Although the sample selected for the 1980 NTS conducted for the U.S. Travel Data Center consisted of telephone numbers instead of addresses, the sample methodology is still similar to those of the 1977 NTS and the CTS. Essentially the sample for the 1980 NTS was selected by first dividing (stratifying) the United States into the eight travel regions. Counties in each of the eight regions were then placed into one of two groups, Standard Metropolitan Statistical Areas (SMSA) and non-SMSA areas. The SMSAs in each region are assigned on a list in order of population. A systematic sample of SMSAs was selected in each of the eight travel regions. In the non-SMSA strata, the states, and counties within the states, are arranged in a prescribed manner and a systematic sample of counties was drawn. In both the SMSA and non-SMSA strata, systematic sampling was used to select Minor Civil Divisions (MCDs) within the selected SMSAs or non-SMSA counties. Systematic sampling was then used to select telephone numbers from the largest telephone book containing the MCD. The numbers selected were the base for the survey sample with adjustments made to represent nonlisted telephone numbers in the sample. A more complete description of the sample methodology is included in the Technical Description of the survey which is referenced in the list of materials at the end of this chapter.

SAMPLING AND NONSAMPLING ERRORS

There are two basic types of errors in any sample survey. One type of error is associated with the fact that the sample used was only one of a large number of possible samples of the same size that could have been selected. Each sample selected would give a different estimate of the characteristics being measured. The variability of the estimates among all the possible samples is called the sampling error. The measure of this sampling error is commonly referred to as the standard error. When the results of a survey are announced and the estimate is given with a modifying statement like "This estimate is subject to a 3 percent error either way," the 3 percent is the calculated standard error on the estimate. This is a measure of the statistical reliability of survey estimates. The estimates of the standard error should be provided along with the results of any survey. Formulae for calculating standard errors are presented in the Appendix.

The sample estimate and its estimated standard error enable one to construct interval estimates such that the interval includes the average result of all possible samples with a known probability. For example, if all possible samples were selected, and each of these samples was surveyed under essentially the same general conditions and an estimate and its estimated standard error were calculated for each sample, then:

1 Approximately 68 percent of the intervals from one standard error below the estimate to one standard error above the estimate would include the average result of all possible samples.

2 Approximately 90 percent of the intervals from 1.6 standard errors below the estimate to 1.6 standard errors above the estimate would include the average result of all possible samples.

3 Approximately 95 percent of the intervals from two standard errors below the estimate to two standard errors above the estimate would include the average result of all possible samples.

The average result of all possible samples either is or is not contained in any particular computed interval. However, for a particular sample one can say with specified confidence that the average result of all possible samples is included in the constructed interval.

In some cases, the standard error may be just as important to the manager as the survey estimate itself. An estimate which has a great deal of variability, or error, associated with it should be used with much caution, particularly if a modest change in the estimate could affect the future of the business. Two major factors which determine the size of the sampling error are the sample size and the proportion of the universe which has the characteristic being measured. Usually the larger the sample size the smaller the sampling error. As can be seen by reviewing the standard error formulae in the Appendix, however, because the standard error is a function of a square root, doubling the sample size does not result in a comparable decrease in the sample error. The proportional representation of a characteristic in the universe affects the size of the error in relation to the size of the estimate. A characteristic with a small proportion of the population will usually have a smaller absolute range of error than a characteristic with a large proportion. The characteristic with the large proportion will, however, have a relatively narrower margin of sampling error and, therefore, theoretically be a better estimate.

To illustrate, a characteristic is estimated to take place in 5,000 cases in a universe of 100,000 and the sampling error is 2,500, or 50 percent of the estimate. If the characteristic took place in 50,000 cases in the universe of 100,000, the sampling error could be 5,000, which in absolute terms is larger than the 2,500 but in relative terms is only 10 percent and, therefore, much smaller.

The second type of error is nonsampling error. There are many possible sources of nonsampling error including those created by poorly worded questions, not obtaining interviews for every sample unit, inadequate coverage of the universe in selecting a sample, and errors made in the processing of the data. Regardless of how well a sample is selected, the results of the survey are not going to be accurate if the questions are not properly phrased. Perhaps one of the most common phrasing problems is designing questions that assume a prior fact. The question "Have you stopped beating your spouse?" assumes the respondent did beat his spouse. If the only answers allowed to this question are "Yes" and "No," the respondent who never beat his spouse is unable to answer. Likewise, if a representative sample of 100 is drawn but only 50 interviews are obtained and the 50 that were not interviewed had different characteristics than the interviewed 50, the results are not representative of the entire universe because only a portion of the sample was interviewed. While it is nearly impossible to interview every unit selected, the higher the percentage of noninterviews, the more likely it is that the results will not be truly representative of the universe.

Selecting a sample from an inadequate or incomplete sample list can also create problems. Most everyone is aware that to select a sample of an area by using a telephone book would exclude those units without telephones and those units with unlisted telephone numbers. When situations like this occur, the sample is said to have a bias, that is, some elements in the universe have no chance of selection and therefore the

estimate is not based on a sample that would be expected to reflect accurately the population in the universe.

ISSUES TO BE CONSIDERED IN SELECTING A SAMPLE DESIGN

The first part of the chapter briefly discussed the basic types of sample selection methodologies. This section will briefly discuss what issues should be considered in selecting the appropriate sample method.

In deciding on a sampling plan the first thing a manager should consider is the type of information needed, i.e., what is the major reason a survey is being considered. As mentioned earlier, in some cases the information needed can only be obtained by conducting a survey; the next question to answer then is who to interview. Depending on the information needed there may be many different sources from which a sample can be selected. These sources are referred to as sample frames. Examples of sample frames include:

1 All households or persons living in a defined geographic area such as a city, county, or state;
2 All business establishments in a defined geographic area;
3 Membership lists of organizations; or
4 Persons using a specific facility or service, such as guests registered at a hotel, persons in an airplane, or persons visiting an amusement park.

In choosing the best, or most efficient, sample frame several points must be considered.

A THE TYPE OF INFORMATION NEEDED

This is the major factor in making any decisions regarding survey or sample design. There have been too many instances when the primary goal of the survey got lost when side issues were introduced. When this occurred, too often the result was an unsatisfactory performance in achieving what really was the purpose of the survey.

In selecting a sample frame the individuals or businesses in the frame must have the information being sought. It would do little good to survey a group of hotel owners to find out how many times rental cars were used. Hotel owners could, by reviewing their records, tell how many nights people spent in their establishments and possibly where the people came from. Surveying hotel owners could also report how many hotel owners use rental cars. However, except in rare situations, hotel owners do not have information on the number of times rental cars were used.

In cases where several possible sample frames could

provide the key information, secondary information needs should be considered. Returning to the example on use of rental cars, suppose there is also a need for information about the number of times a rental car user rents a car during the course of a year. Among the possible sample frames for determining rental car usage would be (1) a sample of rental car agencies or (2) a sample of the general population. By surveying rental car agencies an estimate could be obtained on the use of rental cars. However, unless the rental car agencies would release the names and addresses of their customers, it would probably be very difficult, if not impossible, to determine the number of times each rental car user rented a car during a year. All other things being equal, a survey of the general population would seem to be the best way to get an estimate on the number of times rental cars were used *and* the number of times a rental car user rents a car during the course of a year.

When reviewing the information required, a related point that should be considered is whether the sample design and collection plan chosen will provide the information needed. In some cases it may not. Continuing with the rental car example, assume the purpose of the survey is to provide an estimate on the number of persons who rent cars and the number of times they rent cars during the course of a year. This is no problem in a general population survey if the reference period for the question is 1 year, i.e., "Did you rent a car at any time in the past year?" However, in many cases, surveys have a much shorter reference period, such as 1 month or 3 months, so that events, such as trips, are still relatively fresh in the respondent's mind.

Combining or linking the results of monthly or quarterly surveys to provide estimates for a longer time period such as a year is usually a simple matter of adding the results together until the time period desired is obtained. However, this approach does not work when the purpose is to determine participation rates or the frequency with which people participate unless the same people are interviewed throughout the time period. To estimate how many different persons rented a car during a year, a participation rate, by adding the results of four quarterly surveys will result in an overestimate because it is possible that at least some of the people who rented a car in the first quarter also rented a car in one or more of the subsequent quarters. If exactly the same people are interviewed for each of the four quarters, the car rental participation rate can be determined by matching each person's report for the four quarters, summing the persons who reported renting a car at least once, and comparing that to the total number of persons in the sample.

The information in Table 1 below helps illustrate this point. The sample consists of four persons, A, B,

TABLE 1   Persons Who Rented Cars by Interview Period

PERSON	INTERVIEW PERIOD			
	1ST QTR	2ND QTR	3RD QTR	4TH QTR
A	Y	Y	Y	Y
B	N	N	Y	N
C	N	Y	N	N
D	N	N	N	N
Quarterly participation rate	25%	50%	50%	25%

C, and D. They were interviewed quarterly and asked to report whether they used a rental car on a trip taken during the quarter. Their responses were as follows: The sum of the four quarterly participation rates is 150 percent, an obviously incorrect number. The true participation rate is 75 percent since three out of the four people in the sample rented a car at least once during the four quarters. A similar method would be used to estimate how many times during a year a rental car user rents a car, or the frequency of use.

If the sample changes from quarter to quarter, an accurate estimate of participation and frequency over a time period longer than the survey reference period cannot be obtained because a person's past and/or future behavior can change. Determining a person's behavior for an entire year based on 3 months' experience can be subject to a great deal of error. Likewise estimates obtained by other means such as matching persons with similar characteristics would only be as good as the extent to which the matching characteristics determine participation and frequency.

B   THE STATISTICAL RELIABILITY (OR QUALITY) OF THE DATA NEEDED

The major point or question here is how reliable do the data need to be. How much confidence in the data does the manager need to make a decision based on the results? As was stated previously, any type of sample survey has a margin of sampling error associated with it. The error is there because only a sample of the population was surveyed instead of everyone. By adjusting the size and the way in which the sample is selected, the desired statistical reliability of the data can be approximately determined before interviewing begins. Formulae are given in the Appendix for determining the sample size needed to achieve a specific level of reliability. Here again it is important to remember the major reason the survey is being conducted. If the main data need is an estimate on the number of times rental cars were used, then the type of sample and sample size should be designed to provide this estimate at the desired level of precision. It is a waste of resources to develop a sample design and require a sample size to provide an estimate on the number of times blue carpet was requested when renting a car if that is not one of the key data items required in the survey.

In deciding on the quality needed from a survey, a manager must keep in mind what the data are needed for. Some surveys are taken so that the results may be used as a promotional tool. For example, the manager of Smith Island may take a survey to determine the number of guests on his or her island and the other neighboring (competing) islands. If the results show that there are more guests on his/her island then the next promotional literature may headline the fact that a survey indicated "More people come to Smith Island than any other island along the coast. There must be a reason." A survey of this type does not really need to have a large sample or a small degree of sampling error in the estimate. All it needs is the right results and some foundation in acceptable survey practices so that no one can seriously question the manager's integrity. In situations such as this, the statistical reliability of the data should not be much of a deciding factor.

Another use made of survey results is for marketing purposes. When an individual or organization is planning to introduce a new product or service, a marketing study (survey) is sometimes conducted to determine how this new product or service will be received. The statistical reliability of the data for these purposes would probably strongly depend on the amount of money being invested.

If the manager of the Jones Hotel on Smith Island notices that many of his/her guests were eating dinner at other establishments, he/she may decide that the problem is that his/her restaurant does not have a salad bar. To verify that the addition of a salad bar would increase his/her restaurant business, the manager may decide to take a "survey" of the hotel guests. Assuming the cost of establishing and maintaining a salad bar is not prohibitively expensive, the owner may do no more than ask (survey) a few of the guests to determine if the addition of a salad bar would entice these people to eat dinner at the hotel restaurant. If the guests say "yes" the manager builds the salad bar. If they say "no" he/she thinks of something else, or decides the sample was no good and builds the salad bar anyway. In this example, obviously the statistical reliability was not a factor. Of course, the manager could have conducted the survey more scientifically by preselecting the occupants of certain rooms during certain days during certain months and reviewing the results before making the decision. This manager, probably correctly, figured that it wasn't worth the effort and could find out what he/she wanted to know by asking a few of the guests.

A decision by the Jones Hotel to buy the adjoining swamp land and build a championship golf course would (should) be based on a much more sophisticated approach. The manager would need to develop an estimate of the additional business the golf course would produce and then determine whether the additional business would cover the cost of developing and maintaining the course and providing a satisfactory profit. It would seem that precision of the estimate would have to be fairly good. A decision based on an estimate which could be off 50 percent could mean financial disaster. If the manager's decision on investing funds for the golf course is to be based in part on the survey results, then the statistical reliability, or quality of the data, needs to be high.

A third reason for taking a survey is to gather information for general planning or policy-making. In these situations the quality requirements of the survey are usually rather high since estimates which are off by 50 percent have little practical value and common sense will usually reach the same conclusions at a fraction of the cost. Because of the general purpose of such a survey they are rather large in scope and serve many uses. Such surveys are usually conducted periodically to measure trends or changes and in some instances to see if a change in policy or practice had the desired impact. To measure all but the most radical changes requires a fairly reliable estimate. Many businesses can measure change by reviewing records or measuring sales. General planning surveys are usually undertaken by government agencies or private organizations who need to study or service a wide range of activities or interests.

C RESOURCES REQUIRED OR AVAILABLE

Once it has been determined what information is needed and what degree of statistical reliability (quality) is required, the next step is to develop an estimate of the resources required to complete the job. Included as "resources" are money, staff, and time.

If the type of information required at an acceptable level of statistical reliability can only be obtained at a cost way beyond the money available, other alternatives have to be explored including increased funding, reducing the reliability requirements, collecting the information from another, or existing, source, or deciding that the information was not really needed anyway. A manager should be aware of the options available if funds are not adequate. There are also instances where funds are secured first and then the planning begins involving the goal of the survey and the quality required. This approach can be very inefficient. A manager should also be on the lookout for situations in which the objectives of the survey can be met without spending all the money available. Why spend more money than is necessary just so better statistical reliability and/or additional information can be collected even though there is no need for the better reliability or no plans for using the data?

The availability of staff must also be considered. If it is decided to undertake a survey the staff should have both the time and the skills necessary to complete the survey or the manager must be willing to pay someone else to do part or all of the work. Staff time is not only a consideration in conducting a survey but also in analyzing and using the results. A survey that produces a great deal of valuable information really is of little use if no one has the time to make use of it.

Time is another resource that is important. If the data needed at the quality level determined won't be available until two years after it is needed then the data will not be of use. Likewise, if it will take four months to prepare the materials necessary to begin the survey but the time period or situation to be surveyed is only one month away, the manager must decide if the preparation time can be shortened, the time period rescheduled, or whether the survey should be conducted. In many cases surveys which require a high degree of sophistication and/or a high level of quality can't be successfully conducted by arbitrarily reducing the preparation time. Inevitably, a key factor is overlooked or done incorrectly which delays completion of the survey or makes the results less useful. The situation illustrated by the phrase "Do you want it right or do you want it Tuesday?" is not unique. Every manager has had to make this decision. If it appears that the manager will be faced with this sort of decision after reviewing the timing for the survey operation and the answer would be "Tuesday," the manager should consider other survey alternatives including the possibility of cancelling the survey.

SELECTING A SAMPLE—AN ILLUSTRATION

The remaining part of the chapter will provide an illustration of selecting a sample plan and determining the sample size. The manager of the Smith Island Hotel will be used as an example.

A SELECTING A SAMPLE PLAN

Suppose that the manager wants to learn more about the guests' satisfaction with the hotel and future plans for visiting Smith Island so that improvements in hotel services and marketing plans can be determined. Since the hotel's records do not have this information, a survey seems to be the only way.

Who should the manager interview? He/she could take a sample of households in the United States plus a sample of tourists visiting the United States from other countries and ask questions of those that stayed at the hotel. This obviously is very expensive and inefficient when a sample could be drawn from the hotel records. After some thought, the manager decides that the sample should consist of persons who have stayed at the hotel during the past year. Persons who last stayed at the hotel more than 1 year ago may not be aware of the changes that were made during that period. The manager also decides not to select the sample from current or future guests because that will lengthen the time needed to collect the data (waiting for future guests) and the manager wants the people surveyed to have time to reflect on their experience.

The next step is to decide which of the four basic sample types to use. Using simple random or systematic sampling would mean compiling a list and then selecting one out of every so many. A possible problem with this approach is that the manager wants the sample to adequately represent the out-of-state tourists. A simple random or systematic sample might underestimate this relatively small but important segment of the hotel's business.

A stratified random sample would ensure that the out-of-state tourist segment was adequately represented. The manager could stratify on these characteristics because the registration cards provide home address and purpose of trip but this would require extra effort and time in preparing the list.

Because the manager has decided to conduct the survey by mail, the advantages of cluster sampling do not apply. The manager has decided that the cost of mailing to addresses spread throughout the world is not prohibitive enough to warrant the extra effort involved to select the sample and to adjust for the somewhat higher sampling error that is associated with cluster sampling.

The manager also considered quota sampling but decided against it because he/she did not have enough demographic information about the guests to adequately control the sample to the point where there would be confidence in the results.

B CHOOSING THE SAMPLE

The manager has decided to use systematic random sampling to select the sample. The list is compiled in the order in which their cards were found in the files. This did not result in any unusual ordering of the list. The final list of all guests in the past year contained 15,000 names. The major goal of the survey is to determine whether the guest was satisfied with the hotel during his/her last visit. Because no earlier surveys or studies on this subject were done before, the manager uses formula 1.B in the Appendix to calculate the sample size. To use this formula the manager must approximate the number of people on the list that would be dissatisfied and how reliable an estimate is needed. Although the manager believes (hopes) the number of dissatisfied guests is very small, he/she decides to take no chances and assumes that half (7,500) were dissatisfied. A 50–50 split would provide for the maximum sample size. The manager also wants to have enough confidence in the survey results so that the final survey estimate would be, according to sampling theory, within a range of 10 percent of the true measure 68 times out of 100. A range of 10 percent on a survey estimate of 7,500 translates into a standard error of 750. Using these numbers, the manager determines that a sample size of 100 is needed:

$$\frac{(7,500)(7,500)}{(750)^2} = \frac{56,250,000}{562,500} = 100$$

Since there are 15,000 names on the list, the manager will select a sample of 1 in every 150. Using a random number table, the manager picks a number between 1 and 150 as a starting point and then selects every 150th person on the list for inclusion in the sample.

C STANDARD ERROR CALCULATION

To illustrate the calculation of a standard error from the survey results, assume the manager has collected the information for all 100 sample persons. The results showed that 96 out of the 100 in the sample were satisfied. The manager determines that X' (the number of satisfied guests if a complete census of the 15,000 were taken) is 14,400:

$$X' = \frac{N}{n} X = X' = \frac{15,000}{100} 96 \; X' = 14,400$$

This is included as part of the formula for determining the standard error specified in formula 3 in the Appendix. To determine how reliable that estimate is, the manager computes the standard error using formula 3 and finds it to be 294.

Standard error of
$$X' = \sqrt{(15,000)^2 \, (0.9933) \left(\frac{3.84}{9,900}\right)} = 294.428$$

This means that the 68 percent confidence interval would be from 14,106 to 14,694 (i.e., $14,400 \pm 294$) and that the 95 percent confidence interval would be from 13,812 to 14,988 (i.e., $14,400 \pm 588$). Thus the manager concludes that the average estimate derived from all possible samples of satisfied guests lies within the interval from 13,812 to 14,988 with 95 percent confidence.

APPENDIX Formulae

FORMULAE FOR DETERMINING THE SAMPLE SIZE NEEDED TO ACHIEVE A SPECIFIC LEVEL OF RELIABILITY

1 Simple Random Sampling and Systematic Sampling

A If a sample survey was previously conducted for which a standard error estimate is available for the characteristic of interest in your survey, then the formula for determining the sample size needed to achieve a specific level of reliability for this characteristic of interest is as follows:

let:

x = the characteristic of interest

σ_x = the standard error for the characteristic of interest as calculated from the previously conducted sample survey

n = the sample size of the previously conducted survey

σ'_x = the standard error for the characteristic of interest that you hope to achieve in your survey (i.e., the specific level of reliability)

n' = the sample size needed for your survey to achieve the specific level of reliability

$$= \left(\frac{\sigma_x}{\sigma'_x}\right)^2 n.$$

Note that this formula assumes that both surveys (i.e., the previously conducted survey and your planned survey) utilized simple random samples or systematic samples selected from randomized orderings of the universe (i.e., approximately simple random samples). If the sample size n' calculated using the above formula is large relative to the universe size, the sample size that should actually be used is

n'' = the sample size that should actually be used

$$= \frac{n'}{1 + \dfrac{n'}{N}}$$

B If a standard error estimate of your characteristic of interest is *not* available from a previously conducted survey, then the formula for determining the sample size needed to achieve a specific level of reliability for the characteristic of interest is as follows:

let:

X = your characteristic of interest

N = the size of the universe

σ_X = the standard error for the characteristic of interest that you hope to achieve in your survey (i.e., the specific level of reliability)

n = the sample size needed for your survey to achieve the specific level of reliability

$$= \frac{X(N-X)}{\sigma_X{}^2} .$$

Note that this formula assumes that your planned survey will employ a simple random sample or a systematic sample selected from a randomized ordering of the universe (i.e., an approximate simple random sample) and that the characteristic of interest is a type of characteristic that can be expressed as a proportion of the universe. If your characteristic of interest is a proportion of the universe then the sample size formula would be

$$n = \frac{p(1-p)}{\sigma_p{}^2}$$

where

$p = \dfrac{X}{N}$ = the proportion which is your characteristic of interest.

If the sample size, n, calculated using the above formulae is large relative to the universe size, then the sample that should actually be used is

n^1 = the sample size that should actually be used

$$= \frac{n}{1 + \dfrac{n}{N}}$$

2 Stratified Random Sampling

A Proportional allocation Using proportional allocation, the sample is allocated to each strata using the formula

$$n_h = \frac{N_h}{N} n$$

where

N = the universe size

N_h = the universe size in the hth stratum

n = the sample size

n_h = the sample size in the hth stratum.

If you plan to use proportional allocation, then the formula for determining the sample size needed to achieve a specific level of reliability for the characteristic of interest is

$$n = \frac{N \sum\limits_{h=1}^{L} N_h S_{hx}^2}{\sigma_x{}^2}$$

where

X = the characteristic of interest

L = the number of strata

N = the universe size

N_h = the universe size for the hth stratum

n = the sample size

σ_x = the standard error for the characteristic of interest that you hope to achieve in your survey (i.e., the specific level of reliability)

S_{hx}^2 = *the within-strata variation in the hth* stratum for the characteristic of interest

$$= \frac{\sum\limits_{i=1}^{N_h} \left(X_{hi} - \dfrac{X_h}{N_h} \right)^2}{N_h - 1} .$$

If data are not available from which an estimate of S_{hx}^2 can be made, then it can be approximated by

$$S_{h_x}^2 = X_h (N_h - X_h)$$

If the sample size, n, calculated using the above formula is large relative to the universe size, then the sample size that should actually be used is

n^1 = the sample size that should actually be used

$$= \frac{n}{1 + \dfrac{n}{N}}$$

B Optimum allocation Using optimum allocation, the sample is allocated to each strata using the formula

$$n_h = \frac{N_h S_{hx}}{\sum\limits_{h=1}^{L} N_h S_{hx}} n$$

where

X = the characteristic of interest

L = the number of strata

n = the sample size

n_h = the sample size in the hth stratum

S_{hx} = the square root of the within-strata variation in the hth stratum for the characteristic of interest

$$= \sqrt{\frac{\sum_{i=1}^{N_h}\left(X_{hi} - \frac{X_h}{N_h}\right)^2}{N_h - 1}}.$$

If you plan to use optimum allocation, then the formula for determining the sample size needed to achieve a specific level of reliability for the characteristic of interest is

$$n = \frac{\left(\sum_{h=1}^{L} N_h \, S_{hx}\right)^2}{\sigma_x^2}$$

where:

σ_x = the standard error for the characteristic of interest that you hope to achieve in your survey (i.e., the specific level of reliability)

If data are not available from which an estimate of S_{hx} can be made, then it can be approximated by

$$S_{hx} = \sqrt{X_h \, (N_h - X_h)}$$

If the sample size, n, calculated using the above formula is large relative to the universe size, then the sample size that should actually be used is

n^1 = the sample size that should actually be used

$$= \frac{n}{1 + \dfrac{\left(\sum\limits_{h=1}^{L} N_h \, S_{hx}^2\right)}{\sigma_x^2}}$$

FORMULAE FOR CALCULATING STANDARD ERRORS OF SAMPLE ESTIMATES

3 Systematic Sample

Notation:

n = the sample size

N = the universe size

X_i = the estimate of characteristic X for the ith sample case

$X = \sum_{i=1}^{n} X_i$ = the sum of the estimates of characteristic X for the n sample cases

$X' = \dfrac{N}{n} X$ = the sample estimate of characteristic X for the universe.

Standard Error of $X' = \sqrt{\dfrac{N^2\left(1 - \dfrac{n}{N}\right)\sum\limits_{i=1}^{n}\left(X_i - \dfrac{X}{n}\right)^2}{n(n-1)}}$

(This formula assumes that the systematic sample was selected from an ordering of the universe which was essentially random with respect to the items being measured.)

4 Stratified Simple Random Sample

Notation:

L = the number of strata

N = the universe size

N_h = the universe size in the hth stratum

n = the sample size

n_h = the sample size in the hth stratum

X_{hi} = the estimate of characteristic X for the ith sample case in the hth stratum

$X_h = \sum_{i=1}^{n_h} X_{hi}$ = the sum of the estimates of characteristic X for the n_h sample cases in the hth stratum

$X' = \sum_{h=1}^{L} \dfrac{N_h}{n_h} X_h$ = the sample estimate of characteristic X for the universe.

Standard Error of

$$X' = \sqrt{\sum_{h=1}^{L} N_h^2\left(1 - \frac{n_h}{N_h}\right)\frac{\sum\limits_{i=1}^{n_h}\left(X_{hi} - \dfrac{X_h}{n_h}\right)^2}{n_h(n_h-1)}}$$

5 Cluster Sample

Notation

N = the universe size

n = the sample size

m = the number of clusters in the sample

X_i = the estimate of characteristic X for the ith sample cluster

$X = \sum_{i=1}^{m} X_i$ = the sum of the estimates of characteristic X for the m sample clusters

$X' = \dfrac{N}{n} X$ = the sample estimate of characteristic X for the universe.

Standard Error of

$$X' = \sqrt{N^2\left(1 - \frac{n}{N}\right)\sum_{i=1}^{m}\frac{m\left(X_i - \dfrac{X}{m}\right)^2}{(n^2)(m-1)}}$$

This formula is only appropriate if each of the n sample cases has the same probability of being in the sample.

6   Quota Sample

A quota sample is basically a stratified sample with a nonrandom selection of the sample within the strata. Consequently, standard error formulae cannot readily be applied with confidence to the results of quota samples.

REFERENCES

The purpose of this chapter was to discuss briefly and simply basic issues in sampling and sample design. There are several books that contain one or more chapters which discuss those points in greater detail without going too deeply into sampling theory. Although certainly not a complete listing, among the books that may be referenced are:

Bowen, Earl K. (1960), *Statistics with Applications in Management and Economics*, Homewood, Illinois: Irwin.

Cochran, William G. (1953), *Sampling Techniques*, New York: Wiley.

Hansen, Morris H., William W. Hurwitz, and William G. Madow (1953), *Sample Survey Methods and Theory—Volume I, Methods and Applications*, New York: Wiley.

Yates, Frank (1960), *Sampling Methods for Censuses and Surveys*, New York: Hafner.

These books should be available in most of the larger public and university libraries.

For more complete information on the methodology used by the U.S. Bureau of the Census, Statistics Canada, and the U.S. Travel Data Center in their surveys, refer to:

Methodology of the Canadian Labour Force Survey (1977), Catalogue 71-526 Occasional, Statistics Canada.

1980 National Travel Survey Monthly Report, (1980), Technical Description, A-1, U.S. Travel Data Center.

The Current Population Survey—Design and Methodology (1978), Technical Paper 40, U.S. Bureau of the Census.

Finding references to articles and other types of publications which describe specific sample designs used in travel and tourism surveys is much harder. Most articles discuss the results and uses made of the surveys and devote little, if any, space to describing the sample design. TTRA members and others who have access to the *Journal of Travel Research* and/or the materials in the Travel Reference Center in the Business Research Division at the University of Colorado in Boulder, Colorado should find references to survey sample designs as part of articles in results of surveys and survey methodology.

A review of the proceedings of past TTRA annual conferences indicate a wide range of papers which had some discussion on sample plans. Among the papers were:

Ditmars, Earl E., and William H. Troxel (1978), "Usage of Consumer Sentiment Indices," *The Travel Research Association—Ninth Annual Conference Proceedings*, pp. 9-12.

Fredericks, Alan (1976), "Marketing through Travel Agents," *The Travel Research Association—Seventh Annual Conference Proceedings*, pp. 27–30.

Funk, Deborah (1978), "National Tourism Policy Study: A Description of the Survey Research Components," *The Travel Research Association—Ninth Annual Conference Proceedings*, pp. 197–204.

Gilbert, Hamlin M. (1978), "Focus on Travel," *The Travel Research Association—Ninth Annual Conference Proceedings*, pp. 71–75.

Gilbert, Sandy (1977), "The Car Rental Market in the '80's," *The Travel Research Association—Eighth Annual Conference Proceedings*, pp. 53–56.

Goodrich, Jonathan N. (1978), "Qualitative Travel Research: A Study with American Express," *The Travel Research Association—Ninth Annual Conference Proceedings*, pp. 87–93.

Hogenauer, Alan K. (1978), "The Research and Marketing Jigsaw Puzzle: Making the Pieces Fit," *The Travel Research Association—Ninth Annual Conference Proceedings* pp. 197–204.

Marzella, Dennis A., Samuel S. Shapiro, and George R. Conrade (1977), "How to Develop a Marketing Information Subsystem for a Tourist Destination," *The Travel Research Association—Seventh Annual Conference Proceedings*, pp. 91–98.

Standish, Theodore C. (1978), "How the Computer Views the Family Vacation Travel Market," *The Travel Research Association—Ninth Annual Conference Proceedings*, pp. 77–80.

Woodside, Arch G., William H. Motes, and David Reid (1978), "Profiling Inquirers from Magazine Advertising and Its Implication for Value Assessment: An Initial Evaluation," *The Travel Research Association—Ninth Annual Conference Proceedings*, pp. 81–83.

PART THREE

NATIONAL, REGIONAL, AND MUNICIPAL PERSPECTIVES

This third part of the Handbook provides an overview of the manner in which travel and tourism research is viewed by the national, regional, and municipal organizations responsible for tourism at each of these levels. It also includes a chapter summarizing the various sources of information available on the field of travel, tourism, and hospitality largely from governmental sources.

Chapter 10 by Gordon Taylor of Tourism Canada examines the role of research within a National Tourist Organization (NTO). Mr. Taylor has extensive experience as a researcher in government and the contents of his chapter clearly emphasize that NTO research must be planned and managed in relation to the major functions of the organization. In doing so, he emphasizes that the tourism system, and thus tourism research, operates within more general economic, cultural, political, and social environments to which it must be related—and that the kind of research conducted by an NTO must reflect this fact. Having made this point, Mr. Taylor goes on to describe the various types of research which are commonly conducted by a National Tourist Organization and how these research outputs are used for program planning, market development, and the monitoring of tourism industry operations. Finally, Mr. Taylor briefly considers various alternative organizational arrangements that are possible within an NTO for the conduct of research.

As a complement to Chapter 10, we have included in this section another perspective on the nature and role of research in National Tourist Organizations. In Chapter 11, Martinus Kosters (Netherlands Institute of Tourism and Leisure Studies) provides an overview of the kinds of research conducted within NTOs in major European countries with a particular emphasis on the kinds of difficulties encountered when several countries are jointly involved in the collection and use of tourism data for planning purposes. In terms of its specific contents, the chapter by Kosters first reviews the major activities pursued by various National Tourist Organizations, particularly those in a position to have offices in foreign countries. He then examines the forces which lead NTOs to undertake research as well as those factors which determine the manner in which that research is conducted. The major emphasis is upon reviewing the various kinds of research approaches which are available and their relative costs in relation to the information needs of the NTO and the resources which are available to it. The chapter concludes by providing readers with considerable insight into the manner in which the European Travel Commission was created as a means of facilitating collaborative research and marketing among various countries in Europe. It is particularly interesting to note Kosters' comment that "although to a certain extent the NTOs are competitors, cooperation appears to be possible and even necessary."

Chapter 12, authored by Peter Shackleford of the World Tourism Organization, provides yet another complementary perspective on research within National Tourist Organizations. In this case, interest focuses upon the research needs of developing regions and the extent to which such needs are currently being met in various countries. The chapter starts off by reviewing and characterizing the research needs of emerging nations with a particular emphasis on demonstrating the difficulties they face. Having identified these difficulties, the author goes on to provide statistics describing the extent to which resources are being allocated to tourism research as derived from the best available data. While the figures indicate, perhaps not surprisingly, that the research efforts of developing countries are insufficient, they also show that the amounts spent compare favorably (in proportional terms) with those of more industrialized nations of comparable size. In the second half of the chapter, Mr. Shackleford reviews the nature of planning and programs in tourism in developing countries and discusses the kind of research information that is required by such countries for tourism development. He emphasizes in this regard that three specific areas are of critical importance, namely, tourism supply, manpower and infrastructure development. The discussion subsequently focuses on the difficulties involved in the gathering and analysis of statistics in developing countries related to each of these three areas. The author emphasizes that such statistics are critical if meaningful feasibility studies on which to base development and to assess the potential impacts of tourism are to be carried out. Mr. Shackleford concludes the chapter with a brief discussion of the particular role of research as a vehicle for avoiding foreign stereotyping of a country and a review of some of the factors that need to be considered when choosing personnel for a tourism research department in a developing country.

In Chapter 13, Suzanne Cook of the U.S. Travel Data Center provides an overview of research programs conducted by state and provincial travel offices. In the discussion, Ms. Cook provides information concerning the current level of state and provincial involvement in tourism as reflected by overall budgets as well as direct expenditures on research. The chapter then examines the research needs of state and provincial tourism organizations and provides specific examples of the types of research conducted by state and provincial travel offices. The chapter concludes by examining the major factors which need to be considered when establishing a comprehensive travel research program at the state and provincial level.

A frequently neglected level of research, namely, the municipal level, is the object of review and discussion in Chapter 14. This chapter, which is authored by Uel Blank and Michael Petkovich of the University of Minnesota, acknowledges that urban tourism research is among the most misunderstood and underestimated of all tourism types. The purpose of this chapter, then, is to clarify the nature of urban tourism research and to provide some insights into the very detailed kinds of research activities that are required at the municipal level. In examining this chapter, readers will become aware that while the type of research conducted in urban areas may be conceptually similar to that carried out at the state or provincial level, it often differs substantially with respect to the level of funding available, the degree of sophistication involved, the attitudes towards research which surround it, and the availability of qualified personnel to execute it. With this in mind, the authors go on to identify the specific kinds of information that must be gathered at the municipal level and discuss a number of issues related to the data collection process. Finally, they emphasize the need to put the research information which has been assembled into use and provide some suggestions for bringing this about.

The final chapter in Part Three has been prepared by Charles R. Goeldner of the University of Colorado and deals with sources of secondary information which are available in the field of tourism, travel, and recreation. This chapter has been included here to reflect the fact that much of the available information in tourism has been assembled and is disseminated by various government organizations at the international, national, state/provincial, and municipal levels. While the chapter makes reference to all available sources in a very comprehensive manner, it explicitly recognizes that no group collects more information on the tourism industry than government agencies. While the contents of Chapter 15 are constantly subject to decay over time (and indeed start becoming outdated at the point of publication), it was felt important to provide readers with a general, yet comprehensive overview of the various kinds and sources of travel and tourism research information that are available. Thus, while certain of the specific references may not be totally current, they are still quite indicative of available information and should serve as a useful starting point for interested researchers.

10

Research in National Tourist Organizations

GORDON D. TAYLOR

Manager
External Liaison Research Program
Tourism Canada
Ottawa, Ontario, Canada

*R*esearch must be related to the basic roles of an organization and it must provide analysis and interpretation of analysis keyed to the main functions of the agency. The research must be grounded on a comprehensive data bank that develops out of periodic and consistent data gathering processes.

The objective of this chapter is to develop a basic outline for operation of a research function within national tourist organizations. While the emphasis throughout the paper will be on national tourist organizations, the principles would apply equally well to agencies with related functions at the state, provincial, regional, county, and local government levels. As the functions and responsibilities of individual national tourism organizations will vary from country to country, the approach that has been developed in this chapter is conceptual. The adaptation of the concept to any individual agency will depend, of course, upon the specific responsibilities of that agency and the role that it occupies within a particular governmental structure. Some specific examples of the response within Tourism Canada are given as an illustration of a direct application of the principles involved.

FUNCTIONS OF A NATIONAL TOURIST ORGANIZATION

Two basic roles are generally assigned to National Tourist Organizations:

A A responsibility for the development of tourism markets.
B A responsibility for the development of tourism products.

These two elements of tourism cannot be seen as distinct entities conceptually as one is dependent upon the other, although in many organizations they are separated for administrative purposes. If the basic elements of the marketing mix are price, product, promotion, and place, the rationale for treating the two elements as a single entity should be clear. Thus, there is little logic in developing a research activity that reflects such a dichotomy, hence in thinking through the

research needs of a National Tourist Organization, it would appear that there are four functions of the agency that can be articulated:

A Strategic and policy planning.
B Program planning for marketing and development.
C Market and product analysis.
D Special projects.

It is around these functions that research must be developed.

Consequently, the research needs of each of these functions will be outlined in succeeding sections. It must be recognized that the needs of each of these functions cannot be placed in discrete compartments; there will be areas of overlap between them. The broad thrust of interest for each one, however, should be clear. An attempt will be made to outline the information needs of each of these functions and to propose a system for determining the research activities that will be required as responses to these needs. In addition, a structural outline for a research organization will be suggested.

The research carried out in a National Tourist Organization must be viewed as applied. Studies must be designed, conducted, and interpreted to meet the ongoing planning and operational needs of the organization. These studies, in addition, constitute a resource that should be used for more basic and academic research. While individual researchers within an NTO may extend their interest beyond the very applied environment of the work place, the theoretical research so needed in tourism must come primarily from other researchers. A key responsibility of the National Tourist Organization is to make access to its data files relatively easy in order to foster other legitimate research interests.

RESEARCH OBJECTIVES

The research activity must be planned and managed in relation to the major functions of the organization. A basic set of guidelines has been developed to assist in the determination of the needs and for the design of the responsive activities.

These guidelines are:

A Establish an information base to be anchored on periodic and consistent surveys that will supply tourism intelligence on a regular basis.
B Provide projectable information on tourism needs for marketing and development planning.
C Develop the analytical capacity required to interpret research findings for decision-making purposes.
D Develop a research capability to deal with specific problems that are not of a recurring nature.

All of the research activity should be based on the intent of these guidelines.

STRATEGIC AND POLICY PLANNING

The needs of strategic and policy planning will be evident in all of the research areas that will be specified. There are, however, some broadly based specific requirements that can be identified. These broad subjects relate to the total environment in which tourism operates and to the significance and importance of tourism in the country concerned.

THE ENVIRONMENT

Tourism operates within an environment that has a great deal of effect upon it, but over which tourism has little or no control, although it does have impacts upon the environment. First-level research needs must be directed towards understanding the relationships that exist between tourism and the environment within which it operates. The nature of the relationships is shown in Fig. 1.

Thus, tourism operates within an economic, physical and cultural, political, and social environment that strongly influences it, but over which it exerts little or no control. Tourism also impacts, to a greater or lesser degree, upon the elements.

Economic

There is no doubt that the state of the economy in the country concerned (and in the countries seen as major markets for its tourism products) has a profound influence on tourism. This influence is particularly important to the flow of travelers into and out of the country as well as within, and upon the development of the tourism plant. Economic conditions in all countries are measured, documented, and analyzed by many public and private agencies. The National Tourist Organization needs to ensure a consistent receipt of the pertinent studies and documentation that are provided by the appropriate agencies.

The economic data that will need to be analyzed should include such facts as disposable income, gross national product, unemployment rates, exchange rates, Travel and Consumer Price Indices, interest rates, taxes, and so on. The analytical role is to determine how each of the elements taken individually and in combination influences tourism and to establish trends so that these influences can be monitored over time. The key to this activity is a regular reporting system that transmits the analytical results to management.

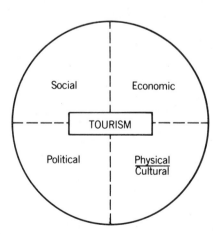

FIGURE 1   The environment.

Physical and Cultural

The physical and cultural resources of a country provide its prime tourism assets. Tourism's concern must be with the preservation of the quality of the physical and cultural environment and with the monitoring of the effects of tourism development upon that environment. Research's role should be concentrated in the conceptualization, verification, and institution of appropriate monitoring devices, so that any existing or potential deterioration in the environment can be quickly identified and remedial action proposed and carried out. It must also be concerned with the identification and assessment of these elements as prime tourism attractions.

Political

Tourism operates within a political system and it will be influenced by a variety of political decisions made from time to time. The role of the National Tourist Organization in this area should be to develop estimates of the probable outcome of the effects on tourism of political decisions and to attempt to influence the decisions in order to optimize tourism benefits to its nationals. It should also prepare recommendations for policy changes in order to ensure orderly growth of tourism within the national economy. Research must be one of the prime sources of the data and analytical techniques required for policy work.

Social

A wide range of social elements influence the development and performance of tourism. Such factors as population growth, population distribution, aging, urbanization, migration, social attitudes, and values can be taken as illustrative of the many items that could be listed. The analysis of these data must be directed towards determining the influence each factor taken individually or in combination has on tourism.

Most social factors are measured, documented, and analyzed by a variety of public and private agencies. As with the economic sector, the ongoing receipt of surveys and reports prepared by other agencies is essential. The critical research role is the interpretation of the findings into touristic terms, and the onward transmission of the analytical results to management.

Thus, one of the key elements of a research plan must be to ensure that receipt of data pertaining to the economic, physical, political, and social environment of the country and the countries that now and in the future will constitute the major markets for its tourism. The data received must be analyzed and interpreted in order to assist in the understanding of the environment in which tourism must operate. The research role in this area is primarily analysis and interpretation and not data collection per se.

SIGNIFICANCE AND IMPORTANCE OF TOURISM

Tourism impacts the environment and the dynamics of these impacts are of concern to strategic and policy planners. Examples of the research needs in this area are described in the following paragraphs.

Impacts of Tourism

Tourism, through the movement of people, the concentration of these people in popular tourist areas, and the expenditures related to this movement and concentration, has important impacts upon the economic, social, physical and cultural, and political environments. Some of the key economic impacts are employment, income generation, tax generation, and induced investment. The research role is to determine what these impacts are and to analyze changes in the impacts over time. Another research task is to determine the share of business for which tourism is responsible in a wide variety of business establishments. This latter role is vital if the true impacts of tourism are to be measured and if the industry is to be defined in a satisfactory manner. Very few business establishments receive all of their revenue from tourism. The proportion that tourism contributes will depend upon the type of business and its location.

The introduction of tourists into an area can have both positive and negative social effects. It is necessary to understand what these impacts are, both upon the visitors and upon the residents and upon the social relationships between the two groups. In the case of positive impacts, it is necessary to know what they are and how to reinforce them. It is also necessary to understand the causes of negative impact and how to recognize that they are occurring in order to develop plans for ameliorization or elimination.

The concentration of tourists in particular places can lead to detrimental physical and cultural environmental effects. The research interest must be in what the effects are, how they are caused, and what corrective action can be proposed, and to monitor the results of any such action. Too severe negative impacts in any of the above areas can also have profound political effects.

Tourism's Role in the National Economy

While tourism's role in the national economy is closely related to any study of economic impacts, it does present a separate macroeconomic case. In the total economy, there must be an understanding of tourism's contribution to, or share of, the gross domestic product, tourism's role in the international balance of payments, and its importance as an earner of foreign exchange.

The performance and competitiveness of the tourism industry at both the micro- and macroeconomic levels must be studied. In essence, it is important to examine the profitability of the individual enterprises. There must also be concern for the output of the tourism industry relative to the traditional inputs of land, labor, and capital and of comparing these outputs with those of other economic sectors and with the tourism industry in countries known to be competitive in the tourism market place.

Trends

Trends and the implications of them in terms of the numbers of tourists and in the tourism products available need to be developed over time. Trend data play an important role in understanding what has happened and in developing forecasts for the future.

Market Share

A constant monitoring of market share both domestically and internationally should be instituted. Particular concern must be directed towards the country's share of total world tourism, and how the market share is moving in relation to those countries seen as major competitors. The same concern must lead to tracking the share obtained from each of the major tourist origin countries and, where possible, of the major market segments within those countries.

PROGRAM PLANNING

The tourism industry should have two major ongoing program planning activities based upon medium- and short-term time frames:

A Market development plans for appropriate markets.
B Industry development plans.

There must be a strong research activity relating to the specific tourism information requirements of these two functions. Although the emphasis will differ, both activities have needs for information relative to:

A Travel, travelers, and potential travelers.
B The tourism plant.
C The linkages between them.

There are research needs relative to each and there is a requirement for the development of an analytical framework to provide the essential relationships between the three data sets.

The relationship between the market needs and the available product, for example, is essential for market and development planning. In this type of analysis it will be necessary to develop a technique that will describe how well the market needs are met by the product available in various geographic areas. The market, for this analysis, will be described in terms of the facilities required by all relevant segments to achieve the tourism experience sought. The product will be described in terms of geographic areas. The basic approach is outlined in Fig. 2.

The specific techniques that will be used will have to be developed but the necessity of this type of analysis must be kept in mind when determining data needs for both the market and product.

MARKET AND PRODUCT ANALYSIS

In addition to the broad needs outlined under strategic, policy, and program planning, there are specific needs for information related to the market and the product.

Geographic Areas / Market Segments	A	B	C	D	E	F	G
1							
2							
3							
4							

FIGURE 2 Market/product analysis.

MARKET

In the market area there is a need for analysis and information on the traveler, on travel, and on the dynamics of the market. Within the traveler and travel data sets, information is required for each market and potential markets of interest to the country on the following subjects:

1. who	4. what	7. expenditures
2. when	5. how	
3. where	6. why	

The outlines of the data set can be shown diagrammatically, see Fig. 3.

The research needs relative to the dynamics of the market would include such topics as:

1 Trends, forecasts.
2 Growth segments.
3 Attitudes and motivations to travel and to travel to the country.
4 Consumer satisfaction.
5 Leisure time: changes in activity preferences.

PRODUCT

On the product side, data and analysis are required on each of the following six main sectors of the national tourism industry:

1 Transportation.
2 Accommodation.
3 Food and beverage.
4 Recreation, entertainment, sports and cultural facilities.
5 Tourism-related retail trade.
6 Scenic and historic attractions.

Data \ Market	Domestic	International A	International B
Who			
When			
Where			
What			
How			
Why			
Expenditure			

FIGURE 3   Data elements for tourism markets.

The information needs relative to each sector of the plant would include:

1 Type.
2 Quantity.
3 Location.
4 Quality.
5 Utilization.
6 Trends, forecasts.
7 Potential.

The relationship between the two sets of data required about the product can be illustrated. Fig. 4 indicates that for each of the industry sectors, all of the items in the above list would be needed.

In addition to defining the specific items that will be required in this data collection process, a number of related problems must be solved. For all of the sectors of the tourism plant except transportation, the elements have a fixed location in geographic space. Transportation is both spatial and linear in nature. Terminal facilities such as airports, railway and bus stations, and ship terminals are fixed in space; the transportation network linking them is linear. It is also subject to frequent, often seasonal, changes in frequency and capacity.

To meet the spatial requirements of this type of inventory, a geographical designation system will be required. The key to establishing such a system will be the smallest geographic area for which data will be required.

ACTIVITY SPECIFIC

The results of the proposed periodic and consistent surveys cannot be expected to meet all of the research needs of the organization. Special problems that require specific solutions will arise from time to time. The research capability to deal with these problems must be developed. In addition, certain activities will have their special needs for study from time to time.

The types of activities covered by this topic would include:

A Advertising pre- and posttest of creative concepts and communication themes.
B Special market studies, such as the ski market, weekend market.
C Local market data in terms of a specific origin or destination.
D Site location, for tourism development.
E Feasibility of specific marketing, development, and data collection projects.

Sector \ Details	Type	Quantity	Location	Quality	Utilization	Trends	Forecasts	Potential
Transportation								
Accommodation								
Food Service								
Beverage Service								
Recreation								
Entertainment								
Sports								
Cultural								
Retail Trade								
Parks								
Scenic Areas								
Historical								

FIGURE 4   Data elements for tourism plant.

Many other topics that would be of particular interest to an individual organization could be added. The main concern in this paper is with information that is a common requirement to many agencies. Hence, specific and special needs are really beyond its purview, but the necessity of recognizing these needs and of developing the capability to deal with them is important.

Each study in this section would have to be designed, executed, and analyzed to meet the specific objective established at the time it was required. This situation would apply to cases A, B, and C above. Insofar as D and E are concerned, attention must be paid to collecting and collating data in such a way that they can be used as inputs to specific studies that will usually be carried out by other divisions or outside agencies.

TOURISM DATA BASE

The review of the data needs that have been outlined in the past four sections leads to the conclusion that the requirements can be encompassed within the framework of a comprehensive tourism data base. This data base would constitute an element, albeit a major one, of an overall tourism information base.

A description of such an information base is beyond the scope of this paper. The concern of a research group is restricted to the data portion of such a system. Three different types of data are required to meet the needs of the functions discussed above. These data, which are described in detail below, should be thought of as constituting the fundamental inputs to a tourism data base. They can be grouped into three broad classes:

A   Data relative to travel and travelers.
B   Data relative to the operation of the tourism industry.
C   Data relative to the physical facilities available for tourism.

The more precise requirements under each of these headings will be spelled out in the course of this section.

DATA RELATIVE TO TRAVEL AND TRAVELERS

More specific details about the general requirements for data relative to travel and travelers are outlined in this section along with an outline of an assessment technique for reviewing the availability of data for any market.

Basic information on the "market" would consist of the following data sets:

who:

- demographic characteristics such as age, income, education, occupation, marital status, sex, place and type of residence, etc.

when:

- the time that the trip actually takes place based on either start or end date, usually expressed in terms of month or quarter
- the length of time that a trip actually lasts, usually expressed in nights

where:

- the destination of the trip; may be expressed in terms of a locality, region, province, country or continent
- the origin of the trip; may be expressed in the same terms as above
- the trip routing may also be collected

what:

- the purpose of trip
- the activities during a trip
- the use of specific tourism services

how:

- the mode of transportation
- the type of accommodation
- the use of travel agents and packages

why:

- benefits sought from and gained through travel
- travel as part of lifestyle
- attitudes and motivations to travel
- attitudes and perceptions to the tourism product offered and/or experienced

expenditure:

- expenditures by purpose incurred while traveling, i.e., transportation, accommodation, food and beverage, entertainment and recreation, other

These seven main elements constitute the key market parts of a tourism information base. For each of the items listed, a specific definition is required.

When the main data elements are identified and defined, the next step is to determine, by means of a careful analysis of existing data, how well the data needs are being met. This review will identify the existing data and the source of those data and will highlight the need for any additional data. Revisions of existing data collection procedures or the development of new ones are then possible.

The basic layout for the review procedure is outlined in Fig. 5.

In actual practice, the process will be more complicated than Fig. 5 might indicate. Each of the sub-elements under a main element would need to be outlined in detail, and the extent of data availability carefully worked out. On the basis of this type of review, the adequacy of existing data can be judged, and new or modified data collection procedures can be instituted to fill the gaps. The detailed review sheet is shown in Fig. 6.

DATA RELATIVE TO THE OPERATION OF THE TOURISM INDUSTRY

Central Statistical Agencies usually collect and disseminate a great deal of data directly relative to the operation of the tourism industry. The basic problem in the use of these data is the lack of a clearly defined tourism industry within Standard Industrial Classifications (see Chapter 5).

The types of data that should be available from the Central Statistical Agency are the essential operational ones, e.g., labor utilization and/or employment and economic and financial. These data are necessary for such analyses as cost/price competitiveness, capital growth, manpower utilization, profitability, financial solvency, economic impact, and interindustry comparisons. It is necessary with regard to these data to determine how tourism is treated within the Standard Industrial Classification and to work out, ideally, a clearly defined tourism sector.

DATA RELATIVE TO THE PHYSICAL FACILITIES AVAILABLE FOR TOURISM

The operational data sets described above do not constitute an inventory of the tourism plant, but they do provide essential data. The definition and establishment of a complete tourism plant inventory that would be useful for development, planning, marketing, and policy decisions is a very complex problem. Experience elsewhere with comprehensive inventories is that they are expensive in terms of personnel and money and too frequently the output does not justify the expense.

The broad data requirements for a tourism plant inventory were outlined in Fig. 4. The plant inventory requirement should be spelled out in the same detail as that established for market data. If a plant inventory

Data Element		Availability of Data		
		Markets of Interest		
		Domestic	Country A	Country B
Who:	(a)			
When:	(a)			
	(b)			
Where:	(a)			
	(b)			
	(c)			
What:	(a)			
	(b)			
	(c)			
How:	(a)			
	(b)			
	(c)			
Why:	(a)			
	(b)			
	(c)			
	(d)			
Expenditure:	(a)			

FIGURE 5 General market data review.

Data Subelement	Markets of Interest		
	Domestic	Country A	Country B
Who			
Demographic Characteristics			
Age			
Income			
Education			
Occupation			
Market Status			
Sex			
Type of Community			
Ownership of			
recreational			
artifacts			

FIGURE 6 Specific market data review.

does not exist, there are several key steps that should be undertaken before such a data collection procedure is contemplated. The first, and most important, step is to determine who the users of the inventory will be and to what uses will the data be put. Until these two facts are known, it is not possible to proceed to the next two steps: determine the basic data elements and the level of detail to be included in such an inventory and define the level of areal disaggregation needed.

In addition to an inventory of the physical plant available, it is also necessary to inventory the physical resource base available. A procedure similar to that outlined for the plant inventory would need to be followed.

RESEARCH RESPONSE

In this section attention will focus upon some of the market research activities that have been developed within Tourism Canada as a result of a review of data needs and availability.

Canada, in common with most developed countries at least, is in the position where the mainstay of its tourism industry is domestic travel. An analysis of existing data revealed that very little information existed on all of the components of this type of travel. The problem in connection with domestic tourism could be stated clearly as one of measuring the value, volume, and characteristics of travel by Canadians within Canada. There was a management stipulation that the study or studies required be carried out by the most cost-efficient method possible. There was also a requirement that the work be done in conjunction with the central statistical agency, Statistics Canada. It is important to note that in many cases the research activity is governed by requirements and conditions laid down by management and/or central agencies of government.

The first step was to determine what the specific data requirements were. Given the stated problem three areas of data deficiencies were readily apparent:

A   *Value* An expenditure element was inherent and there were no existing comprehensive data on this topic.

B   *Volume* The capacity to develop origin–destination estimates on a person-trip and person-night basis for travel within a province and between provinces was essential, and again there was a paucity of existing information.

C   *Characteristics* The characteristics were clarified as demographic characteristics of travelers and nontravelers, trip information on purpose, mode, accommodation, distance, and duration, and basic attitudes and motivations to travel and to awareness of Canada and satisfaction with the variety of tourism products. These data were also not available from existing sources.

In examining the problem the first circumstance to emerge was that a household survey would be required. Statistics Canada operates a monthly household survey, the Labor Force Survey, that consists of six samples of approximately 10,000 households each. Government departments may purchase supplementary questions to the main survey in units of 10,000 households. After some experimentation it was decided that one survey unit would be the minimum sample that would provide reliable data on Canadian travel although three units or one-half of the sample would provide better data. Interprovincial travel could be handled with one survey unit and intraprovincial travel was better served with three. The decision made by Tourism Canada was to provide four surveys of one unit each year, each survey covering travel in the preceding three months. If more reliable results were required in any quarter other government departments and/or provinces could purchase additional sample units. Surveys have now been conducted for 11 consecutive quarters; from October 1978 to April 1981, for the summer of 1981, and for all of 1982 and 1984. An evaluation of the results obtained prior to 1981 indicated that the reliability of the results and the stability of travel patterns were such that surveys every quarter every year were not necessary. As a result the survey was continued on a biennial basis starting in 1982. In many cases where there is little change from survey to survey the need for annual surveys is difficult to justify.

The survey did not yield results on attitudes and motivations to travel in general and to travel in Canada in particular, nor did it measure any degree of satisfaction with travel. These data, therefore, have been collected by a separate survey conducted in 1983.

Another type of domestic travel survey has been conducted annually in Canada since 1966. The Vacation Pattern Study, as it is called, is based on a commercial omnibus survey and deals exclusively with vacation travel. Hence only part of domestic travel was surveyed and this survey could not produce all of the data required or met by the Canadian Travel Survey. It is also used for some specific awareness questions each year and it is for this flexibility to address current topics that this particular survey has its greatest value.

Canada's international markets are divided into two main groups: the United States of America and the rest of the world. This latter group, or the overseas markets, is further divided into three categories: primary, secondary, and emerging. These markets are differentiated as follows:

A   *Primary* Those countries that have consistently produced a large visitor volume and that have shown significant growth rates in the past decade; United Kingdom, France, Netherlands, West Germany, Japan, Australia, and Mexico.

B   *Secondary* Those countries that have produced fewer visitors than the primary markets but have shown consistent growth in the past decade: Belgium, Switzerland, Sweden, Denmark, Austria, Hong Kong, Brazil, and Venezuela, for example.

C   *Emerging* Those countries that by virtue of economic conditions and/or external travel patterns seem to indicate that a market potential for Canada could be developed.

In the overseas markets four specific research activities are conducted on a regular and planned basis. The first of these is a special analysis based on the detailed results of questionnaires completed voluntarily by visitors and compiled initially by Statistics Canada for the purposes of balance of payments information. Detailed data for up to 18 countries are made available annually for Tourism Canada purposes. The number of countries for which this analysis can be done are dependent upon the volume of responses to the questionnaire and may vary from year to year.

Two specific Tourism Canada research activities are also carried out. Every two years, in each of the seven primary markets, a market probe consisting of from seven to nine questions on a national omnibus study with a minimum base sample of 2,000 households is conducted. This type of study is designed to provide share of market, basic sociodemographic characteristics of the long-haul market and of a prime Canadian market, and some measures of the awareness of Canada. The questions are consistent over time and between countries. This method provides usable results quickly and at relatively low cost. It also constitutes a basis for the establishment of trends.

Similar studies are carried out on secondary and emerging markets as needed to provide some preliminary market data. In these studies the number of questions used can range from three to eight.

At longer intervals, every four to five years, detailed personal interviews on the attitudes of residents of other countries towards Canada as a holiday destination are commissioned in primary markets. The sample is drawn from adults who have traveled or who plan to travel interregionally within a specific time period. Again, consistency over time and between countries is maintained as far as possible.

Two of the key factors in these detailed studies are the determination of the importance of a list of criteria related to the selection of a holiday destination and the development of a comparative rating on how Canada ranks with a member of competitive destinations on each of the items. In addition, a good deal of data can be collected on travel patterns, habits, activities, use of travel agents and packages, media habits, and so on. Also, a great deal of travel market information produced by individual countries is reviewed and pertinent data are included in our country market reports. The importance of secondary data sources cannot be overemphasized.

The research activity in the United States is moving towards the same basic structure as the overseas markets although in that country the emphasis will be on regional and state or city market data rather than on national data. In addition, Tourism Canada participates on a regular basis in syndicated research studies that provide national data on travel and market conditions.

RESEARCH ORGANIZATION

There are two factors that must be considered with regard to the organization that is needed to carry out the research functions that have been described. The first of these factors relates to the location of the research group within the total organization and the second deals with the internal structure of the group.

Research is clearly a staff function and as such should not be located within a line branch. The head of research should have direct access to the senior decision-makers and should report to the senior officer of the organization. In this way the research needs of the whole organization can be handled by a single research unit, and the implications of results from a study done, say, for marketing can be brought to the attention of development. As a result the research can be done more effectively and more efficiently.

Within the research unit itself there are a number of options for internal organization. The unit can be organized along functional lines, i.e., research management, data collection, data analysis and interpretation, and information dissemination. The advantage of this structure is that it permits the development of specialists in the different research functions; the disadvantage is that an individual researcher is never involved in a study from beginning to end. As a result there is probably a lack of pride in the completion of a finished product as the study will have passed from one officer to another as the need for specialization changes during the life of a study.

A second option is to structure the research unit along the same lines as the total organization, i.e., a market research unit, a development research unit, and so on. While this structure allows the development of specialization along specific subject matter lines, it can lead to a myopic view of research and a real tendency to miss the relevancy of findings from market research for development, and from both for the policy planning.

A preferred structure would be to use a project team approach. Under this system a project team would be set up for each study and the team would remain in existence for the life of the project. Project teams would vary in size and duration depending upon the scope of the particular research study. At any one time a single research officer could be involved in several teams.

The type of research organization that will best suit the needs of any specific National Tourist Organization will depend upon the size of the research budget and the number of person-years available. In a small research unit an informal structure on a project basis would probably be used and in a larger organization a more formal structure would be needed, but within this formal setting a project system of operation would still offer the best approach to carrying out the research function.

CONCLUSION

The research needs of a National Tourist Organization are complex and interrelated. A basic criterion in the establishment and operation of a research activity within an NTO must be that the needs of the user are paramount. Total data needs and the appropriate analysis of those data should be identified clearly at the outset. Each research activity should then be judged on its contribution to the total needs. The second criterion is that the research studies should be both consistent and periodic. Priority in the assignment of resources should be to studies that fulfill the second criterion. A third key consideration is that emphasis should be placed on analysis and interpretation rather than on data collection. Restraint must be exercised to collect only those data that are essential.

It is also a responsibility of the research group to ensure that the analyzed and interpreted data are presented to the users in a clear, understandable manner. When several studies are used as sources of information, the results should be integrated before presentation to avoid any confusion by the recipients.

11

Tourism Research in European National Tourist Organizations

MARTINUS JAN KOSTERS

Deputy Director and Lecturer of Tourism of
the Netherlands Institute of Tourist and
Leisure Studies (NWIT)
Breda, the Netherlands

*T*his chapter deals with the current, general research of National Tourist Organizations (NTOs) in Europe. There are many differences between the various countries and their respective NTOs. Various types of research are being conducted, from a simple desk research to the more sophisticated and expensive types of field research. There is a significant collaboration of 23 NTOs in the European Travel Commission.

When we speak of Europe we have to bear in mind that Europe is not a political unity. It comprises over 30 sovereign nations. There is no tourism policy covering the entire region. Indeed, several countries do not even have a specific, national tourism policy. When a country does have a policy in the form of a written manual, then it is, generally speaking, more a platform for practical operations than a thorough philosophy with short- and long-term priorities.

Every country has its own National Tourist Organization (NTO). Each of the 23 Western European countries has an NTO either in the form of a private organization with some government influence, like Austria, the Netherlands, West Germany, Switzerland, and the United Kingdom, or as a part of the government system itself, like Belgium, France, and Spain. In either case every NTO has the statutory obligation to stimulate tourism to the NTO's country in favour of the private tourist industry involved. In the eight Eastern European countries, NTOs are always part of both the national government systems and the tourist industry in their countries. In this case, the NTO promotes only the packages for its own organization. Traveling for pleasure in these countries is often restricted or forbidden in some areas.

As the political structure of every nation varies, the statutory task and the organization of every NTO vary from country to country as well. There is no uniform structural framework within which the NTO fits; it may be a section of a ministry, commissariat, or commission, or a board or council, or even part of a corporation. However, we can identify some main elements in the different packages of the many NTOs and we shall attempt to outline these common activities before focusing our attention on the research field.

WHAT IS AN NTO?

A National Tourist Organization is the official body of a country which is responsible for the development of promotion, research, and marketing of tourism of its country. Every NTO has a complete inventory of the country's tourist attractions and facilities at its disposal. It develops marketing plans for selected tourist markets abroad in cooperation with, or sometimes without, the interested private travel and accommodation industry and organizations. The same applies to domestic tourism but, within this context, that is of minor importance. The NTO is preeminently the organization that should attempt to coordinate the tourism promotion plans of the country. For a good and alert policy the NTO needs offices in the foreign markets. Such offices form an extension of the NTO in a specific market.

Here, an important observation should be made before discussing certain issues in detail. When a marketing organization makes proposals to adapt or to reshape a given tourist product, it is not self-evident that the industry will follow this advice. The NTO and the industry are different bodies (except in the Eastern European countries) and, consequently, the views of the partners may differ. When the process of the producing, marketing, and selling of services is in the hands of one agency, there should be at least a good internal discussion why the advice of the marketing department is ignored.

Dependent on the national policy in tourism every country formulates its own goals for the NTO. As a result organization structures of NTOs differ. To illustrate this, two organization charts of two NTOs are presented here as examples. Figure 1 is of the Austrian Oesterreichische Fremdenverkehrswerbung (OFVW) at Vienna and Fig. 2 is of the Dutch National Bureau voor Toerisme (NBT) at The Hague. Both NTOs promote their respective countries, but as modern NTOs they also favour research. In addition the Dutch NTO has a task for product development. Only in the Neth-

erlands and in Ireland is this particular aspect a main role of the NTO.

THE CHANGING PACKAGES OF ACTIVITIES OF NTOs

In all Western European countries tourism is not completely left to the initiative of the private sector, not even in countries with a relatively free economy. While the degree of state intervention varies from country to country, the respective governments do intervene in the activities of their NTOs to stimulate incoming tourism (and also domestic tourism).

Basically, two types of NTO activities are well known: (a) tourist information and (b) tourist promotion. Both activities are directed straight at the consumer, e.g., the foreign tourist. Until the seventies these functions were the main activities. Subsequently, the more progressive NTOs started to organize campaigns to influence travel organizations and carriers to encourage tours to the country involved or to increase the number of tours. This is a more direct approach to the consumer because the travel organization develops its own consumer-oriented promotion campaigns for its travel program. When a certain country receives considerable attention in such a program, the NTO has succeeded in obtaining free publicity

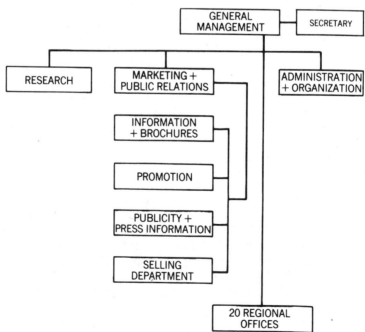

FIGURE 1 Organizational structure of the Austrian NTO OFVW (Dec. 1981).

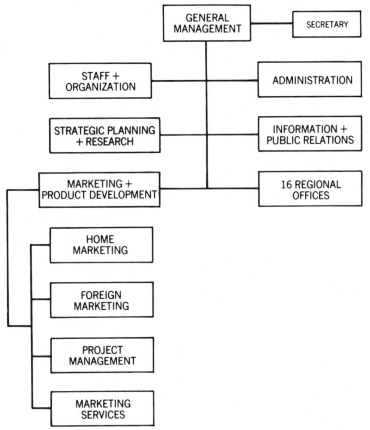

FIGURE 2   Organizational structure of the Dutch NTO NBT (1982).

using the travel organization. In certain cases the NTO agrees to pay the travel organizations for the promotional support provided.

PROMOTIONAL ACTIVITIES AIMED AT FOREIGN CONSUMERS

Broadly speaking, for a very passive NTO a postbox and a telephone number in the home country are enough to help a consumer with information about tourism. But for potential tourists it is clearly not a desirable situation to phone to another country, especially when they do not speak the language. Besides, it is a rather expensive way of communication. As a result, the majority of active NTOs establish offices in the capitals or big cities of those countries which represent potential tourist markets. Sometimes they have more than one office in a particular market. It is obvious that the decisions to establish operating offices abroad are primarily influenced by budgetary concerns.

When an NTO decides to establish an office in a foreign country they have to decide on the city and its location in that city. In the past the European NTOs have always sought to occupy street level premises in the main streets of the capitals and big cities. Such an office was seen as a suitable point of distribution for tourist literature to the public in the main shopping areas. Some NTOs, however, have recognized that this is an expensive formula, and question its effectiveness. These NTOs have realized that their main purpose is to service the providers of tourist services—for that part of their job they do not require an office in a busy street. Consequently, they have gradually moved to other locations in the same town. However, this decision remains an important concern; whether to go for the prestigious, expensive street level premises downtown or select more modest off-street premises.

CONSUMER-ORIENTED ACTIVITIES

The main objective of these activities is to inform the public about the NTO's home country. By mail, this is a time-consuming and expensive operation, but it is hardly to be expected that nobody will write. For many people it is a problem to write at all, but in a foreign language it is very difficult. Therefore, the NTO needs staff who have command of the languages of the prime tourist markets. Much the same holds for clients' inquiries by telephone, but it is somewhat easier to help them and, generally, more effective. Consequently, it is important to have an office in the target market. If there is an office it will always be possible to respond to potential clients. Besides, a wide range of printed matter should be available, as well as multi-dimensional presentations. The NTO office can offer all these services irrespective of its location.

Depending on the promoting country and on the market, each NTO office should be supplied with tourist literature: general and specialized brochures about the country, information bulletins about the various accommodation facilities, food and drinks, museums and tourist attractions, maps and communications, and specialized information about towns, provinces, and regions and about sporting facilities like yachting, boating, fishing, and swimming.

Today, more and more tourism fairs or exhibitions for tourists are organized in Western Europe. The biggest exhibition in the world is the "Internationale Tourist Borse" (ITB) in West Berlin, where more than 80 countries present themselves to the tourist trade and to hundreds of thousands of consumers. In diverse countries several of these exhibitions are regularly organized. NTOs are expected to participate in them, even when an NTO runs an office in the same town. The NTOs could attract other market segments at an exhibition. So, many NTOs have changed their priorities in favour of tourism exhibitions.

In conjunction with other bodies an NTO sometimes organizes a special week in a city, e.g., a Dutch week in New York. Depending on the budget allocated for such an occasion and the collaboration of various organizations, shops might offer Dutch products and establish window display units about Holland. Newspapers, magazines, radio, and television stations might provide information about Holland (not only tourist information) and restaurants might serve Dutch food on their menus and pubs might offer Dutch drinks. There might be concerts by Dutch orchestras and performances by Dutch groups, and exhibitions of Dutch folklore and art and of Dutch products in general. In other words, for a few days a Dutch atmosphere would be created in the city, so that everyone will experience it. Although this is not pure tourism promotion, it may result in a strong impact on tourism from New York to Holland in the near future.

The NTOs also play an important role in the dissemination of information to authors, journalists, and producers of tourist programs on radio and TV. NTOs seek to provide these people with regular issues of press releases, the bulletins containing topical information, photographic material, slides and films, documentation, and assistance during visits. They may even organize trips for VIPs to the home country.

On special festive occasions every NTO officer is prepared to assist in presenting food and drinks from the home country or to place some typical gifts or presents at the disposal of organizers of public events, so that the attention of many people can be focused on the country. NTOs always have colorful posters at their disposal. NTOs may offer special familiarization trips to their country if this provides much free publicity.

Every NTO is always engaged in advertising campaigns. While such campaigns take a substantial part of the budget, NTOs recognize the need to inform large segments of the population about the existence of their country with the goal of creating an increase in tourism demand. Very often NTOs invite the readers to ask for more free information by filling out coupons.

TRADE-ORIENTED ACTIVITIES

The following activities are more or less part of the trade-oriented tasks of European NTOs.

1   Visits to the travel trade in the target markets with concrete offers for package tours, suggestions for travel destinations, excursions, facilities, or joint promotional campaigns. However, one must be aware that wholesalers and carriers may attempt to play off NTOs against each other.

2   The most progressive NTOs organize workshops for the representatives of the travel trade in a particular country and for the representatives of the incoming tourist industry in their own country. The NTO invites participants and provides the opportunity for bringing them together to do business face-to-face.

3   The NTO organizes study tours for managers of the interested travel trade, either to open up new markets or to acquaint the tour operator's sales staff with the various aspects of the product.

4   Seminars where the various representatives of the travel trade in a particular market meet the staff of the NTO and its related organizations provide a suitable platform for the exchange of information about the many products, services, (potential) markets, and prices. The goal is to discuss how to improve the results for the next season or for the next year.

5   Every NTO attempts to inform its business contacts through current information and travel data. Most of the NTOs publish a special magazine or newsletter, often in the form of a monthly bulletin.

6   In addition, NTOs undertake direct mailings of up-to-date tourism literature to the managers of the travel industry.

7   On special occasions NTOs organize cocktail parties or banquets for their most important business friends.

8 NTO offices stage information meetings for the sales staff of travel agencies where slides, films, or multimedia presentations are used to familiarize them with the tourist product of the NTO's country. They also present awards to the top sellers of tours to their country.

9 The travel trade in every country now has its own trade press. So, NTOs are more inclined to advertise in its magazines and journals. It is easily understandable that the information in the travel press should be different from the information in the advertising campaigns directed at the consumers.

10 Some NTOs take a very active part in attracting incentive travel to their country. Sometimes they attract the entire staff of companies or factories for a tour. Much the same holds for persuading international or national organizations to hold a congress or an exhibition in the NTO's country.

RELATIONS BETWEEN THE HEADQUARTERS AND THE OFFICE ABROAD

It is clear that there should be a good understanding between the headquarters in the home country and the offices in foreign markets. Strictly speaking, the office abroad is no more than an extension of the home office in a foreign market. In all cases the offices abroad carry out many of the tasks mentioned before. In addition, they form important antennae for monitoring developments in the market in order to devise (with or without the home office) marketing strategies for the coming season or year. The headquarters in the home country should coordinate the activities of the offices abroad. Some NTOs maintain only a few offices. However, the bigger NTOs, such as Austria, Great Britain, France, and West Germany, have over 20.

The office abroad should provide the home base with market information. Conversely, the home office has to supply the office abroad with up-to-date tourist information and literature in the various languages. Every three to five years a progressive NTO should formulate both a long-term program and yearly a marketing plan in a dialogue with the managers of the offices abroad.

RESEARCH

In nearly every type of industry and in individual enterprises research is considered of vital importance but, oddly enough, not in tourism. However, the situation is now improving. The better tourism businesses have now incorporated research as a regular part of their operations. So do some NTOs, but there exist appreciable differences among a number of European NTOs. Only a few countries carry out very comprehensive research programs. For others it is still a matter of either implementing a different management philosophy or providing a bigger budget before research can be carried out.

It is by no means necessary for the NTO to undertake its own research. An NTO may collaborate in a research project with one or more interested private companies. It is obvious that research cooperation between the NTO and the flag carrier(s) should be feasible. On the other hand, it is also possible that several NTOs can combine their research activities. More will be said about this in the section on the European Travel Commission.

In the following sections we shall analyze various types of research done by European NTOs. So far the techniques and results of research have been very modest, with a few notable exceptions. Nearly all countries, however, possess professional research teams in the form of the national bureaus of statistics or distinguished tourism research specialists. So there exist possibilities for an NTO to farm out research to these specialists when the specialists required are not on the NTO's staff.

DESK RESEARCH

The least demanding type of research an organization like an NTO can carry out is some desk research. This implies that an NTO should have at least one or two specialist staff members at the headquarters who gather information and collect data on tourism research carried out by others. These data can be obtained in the first instance from the national bureau of statistics and from private companies offering research results.

In addition to information from its own country, every NTO should collect relevant information from other countries. Within this context, it is interesting to mention that only a few countries such as Great Britain, the Netherlands, West Germany, France, Sweden, Switzerland, and Austria, yearly provide data on the tourist behavior of both their inhabitants (i.e., on domestic and outgoing tourism) and incoming tourists. In these countries the official bodies undertake very accurate research into the holiday patterns and holiday behaviors of their population through questionnaires administered to people selected by a representative, random sample of the whole population. In these questionnaires the respondents are asked to provide information about the number of holidays made in a particular year; the destinations inside and outside the country; the means of transport, type of accommodation, and duration of each holiday trip; the period of the year; the expenditure; the booking period; and the type of holidays. In addition, there are questions about personal characteristics such as sex, age, marital status, family composition, income, profession, education, and place of residence and about personal belongings such as car, travel trailer, second home, yacht, or boat.

It is regretful that such research is not done systematically in every European country, although a few countries, such as Belgium, France, Sweden, Norway, and Denmark, do it periodically. Some countries, such as Britain, the Netherlands, and West Germany, have typologies of holidaymakers at their disposal, and sometimes of non-holidaymakers too.

An important difference between Europe and North America regarding this type of research is the fact that in Europe *holidays are defined in terms of nights away from home* and in North America the emphasis is on *geographical displacement*, which makes it completely impossible to compare between the two continents. In Europe, a holiday is defined as a period of at least five consecutive days spent for recreational reasons outside the place where one normally lives and works. It is clear that, for their own desk research, NTOs are very interested in the results of the above-mentioned form of research of the other European countries.

Nearly all countries gather data about tourism as evidenced by the annual reports published by the Organization for Economic Cooperation and Development (OECD, Paris) and the World Tourism Organization (WTO, Madrid). In doing so, most countries collect the following types of statistical information:

A   Volume statistics: counting arrivals at the borders, arrivals in the various forms of accommodation, the number of bed-nights, and the number of visits.

B   Expenditure statistics: measuring the expenditures at the destination of the journey and the exchange of money by the banks.

C   Tourism characteristics: providing information on the profile and behavior of holidaymakers, participants in short duration trips and daytrippers.

In fact, Great Britain is the only European country with a complete range of statistics on an annual basis. In this respect, the insular character of the country is important. For instance, the officials can count every visitor because the number of the country's points of entry are limited. No other European country possesses anything like the Home Office Immigration Statistics. Besides, each year Britain carries out the International Passenger Survey, a sample survey designed to obtain information about travel to and from Britain.

Very few Western European countries have such reliable frontier information. The Benelux countries do not have such statistics at all. These examples show that an NTO desk researcher has to gather several statistics, which very often measure different things, so that making comparisons is a rather laborious task. This lack of a universal research methodology in Europe and the completely different systems used in North America make desk research complicated, but not impossible.

The NTO researcher has to combine the above-mentioned relevant statistical information with the information gathered from incidental research, from the offices abroad, from articles in newspapers and magazines, and from statements made by tourism managers, and so on. In this way the European NTOs can do at least some research. The more dynamic and progressive NTOs present the information they gather in annual publications for the travel trade in the home country. With the help of the results of this desk research, an NTO can formulate its promotional campaign. For instance, it might increase its promotional activities aimed at countries from which the number of tourists are decreasing. Conversely, it could decrease its activities in markets which keep generating massive tourism flows to the NTO's country. However, if the results of the desk research are not sufficient to develop policies, field research is needed.

FIELD RESEARCH

Since field research is very expensive, the average NTO only rarely has the opportunity to commission a comprehensive research in a given country. Conversely, every NTO likes to get periodically up-to-date information about every one of its important markets. This implies that each year several studies are needed. It may be worthwhile for an NTO to combine its research on a specific market with another interested NTO so that they can share the costs. We shall discuss later what the European NTOs are currently doing in this area.

In what type of field research might an NTO be interested? To answer this question, it is useful to distinguish between quantitative and qualitative research. Although a clear distinction cannot be made, quantitative research may be viewed as research that is mainly interested in describing a market with respect to such features as the number of visitors, their origin and destination, the amount of money spent, and so on. Qualitative research can be described as research that is mainly interested in such factors as motives, attitudes, and images which form the basis of human behavior.

Quantitative Research

As has already been mentioned, every NTO needs quantitative information on the target markets, but it is often difficult to gather this information. In every country, however, there are now research agencies specializing in quantitative research through so-called "omnibus surveys." These agencies use groups of consumers which are representative of the population in a country (the so-called panels). At weekly, monthly, or bimonthly intervals the members of these panels answer a list of questions on a broad range of topics. The agency tries to interest various industries, sellers, suppliers, and advertisers who cannot afford separate research for their products under certain circumstances. For each client the agency includes a few questions about his "problem" in a questionnaire which is filled out by the panels. Thus, each participant in the omnibus survey can ask some questions depending on their budget and problem.

Of course, the entire survey in a particular week may be carried out for a single principal. It is very attractive for an NTO, especially for the NTO offices abroad, to participate in such an omnibus survey. It is cheap and very fast. Within a few weeks it is possible to have the information required. On the other hand, since the research is based on a few questions, the scope of the answers provided is limited. Thus, an NTO should be very clear about its objectives and the questions included in the omnibus survey phrased very precisely and unambiguously.

An omnibus survey is not the only way to gather quantitative information. We have dealt with it because this approach is well known and very popular. In fact, all the above types of desk and field research provide quantitative information, but they tend to be much more expensive and require more preparation.

Market Research

Currently, the European NTOs recognize the importance of their marketing function. Thus, it is worthwhile to consider which market segments in a particular country should be covered and how. Through image research the NTO obtains general information for its campaigns. With the aid of field research among special target groups, like car owners, anglers, teenagers, families with preschool-age children, families with postschool-age children, elderly people, owners of travel trailers, rail travelers, amateur photographers, and the like, the NTO can gain in-depth information on how to approach each market segment.

The type of research that an NTO wants to carry out is determined by the information that is needed. If the NTO has a good team of researchers, it is not impossible for the NTO to carry out the field research under its own direction with the help of interviewers. But that is more an exception than a rule. In general, it is advisable to employ a local research agency in the target market. If necessary, there is always the possibility that the specialized research agency carries out the field work with the NTO staff evaluating the results and drawing the conclusions.

What is needed for this type of field research is a random sample of the target group. If the group is organized, e.g., members of unions or associations, it will not be so difficult to obtain the addresses for the sample. However, if the target group is not organized, it may be much more difficult to do a field research.

Depending on the situation, a choice has to be made regarding the approach of the target group, through a home interview, a mailed questionnaire, or a telephone interview. Each of these techniques has its advantages and disadvantages. It is the task of the NTO's research department to determine how many respondents are needed with regard to the accuracy required and to formulate the projects. When the data of the field research have been compiled, it is again the task of the NTO researchers to interpret the results and to identify their implications for the design of marketing campaigns.

Effectiveness of Campaigns

It is clear from the foregoing that an NTO in Europe has to perform many tasks. Not every task is difficult, but as the task becomes more important or more complicated, the NTO should undertake to design and evaluate its own campaigns and efforts. A commercial company either within or outside the field of tourism can measure the effects of specific extra efforts in the short term. However, for a promotion organization this is much more complex. It is nearly impossible to measure the real effect of a campaign because it is spread among thousands of companies.

Even when there are positive results for a specific firm, it is extremely difficult to ascribe them to the NTO's campaign. Consequently, every NTO has serious problems with the feedback from its own industry. The NTO would like to hear that its campaigns are successful, but the industry often states that the results, if any, are only of marginal importance. Therefore, the NTO's research department should do follow-up studies of the results of its promotional efforts.

As a rule, an NTO does not possess the funds for carrying out such research. It could be done by the NTO itself, but it would be better to employ a specialized research agency as described above. When the NTO does not properly monitor its own activities, it is unlikely that it will optimize its results with its relatively small and limited budget. Again, this is a matter of priorities. Reliable advertising agencies always include research on the results of a campaign as part of its services. Why should an NTO not do so? In the past much money has been wasted through a lack of critical assessment of an NTO's own activities.

Coupon Research

A relatively easy and inexpensive type of research is the information an NTO can obtain from coupons included in advertisements in journals and magazines. Consumers are invited to return the coupons in order to receive information on topics mentioned in the advertisement. Through codes on the coupons the NTO can check which journal or magazine provides a good return. It should be noted that the NTO can farm out the servicing of returns to specialized agencies.

If the NTO wants to obtain specific information through a coupon reply system, a few additional questions may be inserted besides those asking for name, address, and place of residence. This is important for those managers of the offices abroad who have to step up their campaigns in their respective countries. Mostly they cannot afford a full-time research professional on their staff. When the NTO engages an ongoing coupon reply system, it can gather quite a lot of useful information and improve the effects of its campaigns.

QUALITATIVE RESEARCH

Besides quantitative information, every organization needs qualitative information about the market. Image research is a good example of qualitative information.

Through the research agency an NTO can have at its disposal focus groups of 5–12 people, representative of a specific market segment, who will discuss special topics with the help of experts of the research firm. For example, a country like Spain is heavily dependent on charter flights with tourists from the Northern European countries and Great Britain. As a result of steadily increasing fuel prices, the prices of package tours to Spain have increased considerably since the beginning of the eighties. So, the authorities in Spain will be worried about the future. Will the tourists keep coming despite the price increases? Will they opt for other modes of transportation and other destinations? Will they travel to foreign destinations each year? These are basic questions you can discuss with focus groups. The members of the group can react to each other. When different groups, independently from each other, have discussed the same items, the experts can analyze the responses. The findings of such research may be insufficient or contradictory. In the latter case, the principal can do hardly anything with the information received. However, a target group interview may also serve as a starting point for a more comprehensive research with a random sample of the population and questionnaires.

Image Research

For each NTO it is important to know how to approach a particular market. Although a good local manager of the office abroad will be generally aware of consumer attitudes within his market, he and his advisers may only have knowledge of several segments of the total market. Field research among a cross section of the population on the basis of a questionnaire is without any doubt a suitable means to diminish these risks. With this information an NTO can learn how people perceive its country; what they like and dislike and why; whether they want to go there or not; how long and where they prefer to stay and what they want to visit; how much time and how much money they are willing to spend; the way they like to travel, etc.

It is very important to know how a foreigner perceives your country. For example, in West Germany, the Netherlands (as a small but leading industrial country in the world) still has the image of being an agricultural country of cattle and tulips. Although these factors are correct, the Dutch prefer to emphasize different aspects. The same applies to other results of the above image survey: the Dutch population is very tolerant and open-minded, business-oriented, and many-sided. The Germans criticize Dutch cleanliness and traffic behavior. These opinions were mainly based on the experiences of German users of Dutch camping grounds, summer houses and pensions, but not on the experiences of hotel guests. So the Dutch NTO concluded that Holland attracts mainly the lower-paid segments of the German tourist market. The well-to-do tourists prefer destinations farther away from home. Average holiday duration was 20 days and average expenditure per head per holiday was substantially lower than the average amount spent by Germans in other European destinations.

The Dutch tourism authorities were slightly surprised that the sandy beaches along the North Sea coast and the many small, old towns with their outstanding architectural beauty were hardly mentioned. In other words, the German consumers were attracted by attractions other than those the Dutch tourist industry in Holland has emphasized in its promotional campaigns.

On the basis of the findings of such (expensive) market research, it is possible to incorporate different items in promotion campaigns. Clearly, it still remains important to "sell" the tulip fields and the windmills, although many a Dutchman believes that this is not the right picture of his country. Many are even reluctant to continue to promote tourism by focusing on these traditional images. However, they ignore the fact that potential consumers search for information in which they are interested, and not always that which experts believe is good for them.

When a country has carried out an image survey in diverse countries, it is very interesting to notice how the impressions of the country involved as perceived by tourists from these countries will differ. A country should then emphasize different aspects in its campaigns in the respective markets.

OTHER TYPES OF RESEARCH

The NTO has to do research in each market in which it is going to conduct a campaign. As the European NTOs organize several forms of campaigns in different markets, an NTO has to engage in several forms of research. We have discussed the most important types of research, but we have not finished yet. So we shall outline some other relevant types of research.

Participation

When an NTO wants to test new posters or designs for campaigns, it is useful to submit them to a couple of panels in collaboration with the staff of a particular NTO office. They can observe which design appeals most to people and why. In the same way the NTO can learn how tourists behave and feel in a specific situation, or on a certain location. Through observation and participation much can be learned regarding the approach of people in such a situation, or how to lure people to a tourist attraction.

Photographs and Pictures

When an NTO is interested in the behavior of groups of tourists, pictures of a situation may be a great help in analyzing a situation.

Letters

Every NTO receives letters with questions or complaints. Although it is a special group of people that writes letters, the NTO can learn from the remarks or complaints. Together with the information obtained during seminars and the evaluation of business contacts, the research department can process this information for the marketing department.

Various Research Possibilities

Every NTO has incidental possibilities for research because of cooperation with private companies intending to do research in a particular market. A less important, but quite interesting, type of research is that done by students of a university or institute of higher education. They may study a special problem in which the NTO is interested (e.g., in the form of a thesis). For the students it is very stimulating to do research for the benefit of an organization like an NTO. For the NTO it is an inexpensive form of research, although some of its experts have to spend some time supervising the students. Also, since students are not experienced researchers, there is always the risk of failure.

To conclude, it should be emphasized that research is not a goal in itself, but it is a cornerstone (and not the only one) of a successful NTO policy. Broadly speaking, we must conclude that in Europe some NTO management teams are less and others more research oriented.

THE EUROPEAN TRAVEL COMMISSION

As was indicated before, cooperation between NTOs in research and marketing, and also an exchange of distinct information, can be a great help and save costs. In 1948 the European NTOs founded the European Travel Commission (ETC), of which there are 23 members now. For a complete list of the members with their respective addresses, see the Appendix. The ETC is a nonprofit organization which derives its direct support solely from the funds supplied by its members. In the ETC the NTOs join their forces in research and marketing related to overseas markets, notably, the United States, Japan, and Canada. The ETC fulfills several other functions as well, but they will not be discussed here.

The current objectives of the ETC are:

- To promote greater visitor traffic in and to Europe, particularly from the United States, Canada, and Japan.
- To foster international tourism cooperation in Europe.
- To facilitate among members the exchange of information on tourism development projects and marketing techniques.
- To undertake or to commission appropriate travel research.

For these purposes the ETC has a small executive unit for coordination, support, and initiation of actions not otherwise covered. The full commission is composed of the chief executives of the member NTOs. They have set up a steering committee and several specialist committees, e.g., for marketing, research, and environment. The ETC has operation groups established in the United States (New York) and Japan (Tokyo).

THE ROLE OF THE RESEARCH COMMITTEE

Given the goals of this Handbook, the role of the research committee is important. Its functions are:

- To outline a research strategy in accordance with the Commission's policy and marketing needs.
- To undertake and/or to commission research as requested by the Marketing Committee.
- To recommend and, where approved, to undertake and/or to commission other research.
- To gather information on relevant research projects undertaken by other organizations and to update ETC research material.

- To monitor the use of research undertaken by or on behalf of the Commission.

Several interesting research studies have been published in the more than 30 years of existence of the ETC. Some of the studies published after 1975 are given in Table 1.

TABLE 1   Selected Studies of the European Travel Commission (since 1975)

- Use of Travel Brochures by the German Travel Trade, 1976.
- Distribution and Utilization of Tourist Office Literature in the U.S.A., 1976.
- The North Atlantic "Apex" Traveller, 1976.
- Industry Interviews on the OCT Fares, 1976.
- American Attitudes to Pleasure Travel in Europe— Change or Continuity? 1977.
- Conferences, Meetings, and Incentive Travel—A Pilot Investigation, 1977.
- Collective Promotion Effectiveness, 1977.
- A Pilot Investigation of Industry Attitudes to the New Promotional Fares, 1977.
- Japan, Travel Market for Europe, 1977.
- Europe's New Tourism—Report of the Zurich Conference, 1978.
- Quarterly Intelligence Bulletin
- A Pilot Study for Tourism Prospects in Europe in the Eighties, 1978.
- A Pilot Study of New Promotional Fares: Super Apex, Budget, Standby, Skytrain, 1978.
- Canadians' Awareness of and Attitudes towards Europe as a Vacation Destination, 1978.
- European Tourism Future Prospects, 1980.

It should be clear that an active ETC is currently of vital interest to the European NTOs, perhaps more than in the past, now that research and marketing form the basis for the policies of the modern European NTOs. Although to a certain extent the NTOs are competitors, cooperation appears to be possible and even necessary!

SUMMARY

In this chapter we have attempted to highlight the important functions of the European NTOs with regard to research. The Eastern European NTOs are mentioned pro memoria because of their different tasks and their political involvement.

We have seen that the Western European NTOs have focused on two types of activities: consumer promotion and trade-oriented promotion. Both approaches contain many small scale activities. To operate successfully, the NTO should effectively monitor its operations. Consequently, research is a cornerstone, especially now as tourism professionals in Europe begin to recognize the importance of research and marketing techniques.

This chapter has briefly indicated which types of research are done, or can be done, by NTOs. As NTOs are competitors in several markets, there appears to be no urgent need for cooperation. Nevertheless, the 23 Western European NTOs cooperate harmoniously in the ETC. The weak financial position of the majority of the NTOs has forced them to do so and made the ETC a real success in terms of collaboration and research activities in the overseas markets.

APPENDIX   List of Members of the European Travel Commission (ETC)

Secretariat ETC: Confederation House, Kildare Street, Dublin 2, Ireland.

COUNTRY	NAME OF ORGANIZATION	ADDRESS
Austria	Oesterreichische Fremdenver-kehrswerbung	Margaretenstrasse 1 A-1040 Wien IV
Belgium	Commissariaat-Generaal voor Toerisme	Grasmarkt 61 1000 Brussel
Cyprus	Cyprus Tourism Organization	Th.Theorodou Strasse 18, Zena Building P.O. Box 4535 Nicosia
Denmark	Danmarks Turistrad	Vesterbrogade 6D 1620 Copenhagen V

APPENDIX *(Continued)*

COUNTRY	NAME OF ORGANIZATION	ADDRESS
Finland	Finnish Tourist Board	Asemapaallikontatu 12B, P.O. Box 53 SF. 00521 Helsinki
France	Ministere de la Jeunesse des Sports et des Loisirs	17 Rue de l'Ingenieur Keller 75740 Paris Cedex 15
Germany	Deutsche Zentrale für Tourismus	Beethovenstrasse 69, D-6000 Frankfurt (Main)1
Greece	National Tourist Organization of Greece	2 Amerikis Street Athens 133
Iceland	Iceland Tourist Board	Laugavegur 3 101 Reykjavik
Ireland	Bord Failte Eireann	Baggott Street Bridge, Dublin 2
Italy	Ministero de Turismo e dello Spettacolo	Via Della Ferratella Roma 00184
Luxembourg	Office National du Tourisme	Boite postale 1001 77 Rue d'Anvers Luxembourg
Malta	National Tourist Organization— Malta	Harper Lane Floriana
Monaco	Department des Finances et de l'Economie Principaute de Monaco	Bd. des Moulins 2a Monte Carlo
The Netherlands (Holland)	Nederlands Bureau voor Toerism	Vlietweg 15 2266KA Leidschendam
Norway	Norwegian Tourist Board	H.Heyerdahlsgt 1, 0160 Oslo 1
Portugal	Portuguese National Tourist Office	Avenue Antonio Augusto de Aguiar 86-6, Apartado 1929 1004 Lisboa Codex
Spain	Secretaria de Estado de Turismo	Calle de Maria de Molina Madrid 6
Sweden	Swedish Tourist Board	Box 7473, Hamngaten 27 2-10392 Stockholm
Switzerland	Office National Suisse du Tourisme	Bellariastrasse 38 CH 8027 Zürich
Turkey	Turizm ve Tanitma Bakanligi Tanitma Genel Mudurlugu	Ataturk Bulvari No33 Ankara
United Kingdom	British Tourist Authority	24 Grosvenor Gardens London SW1W ODU
Yugoslavia	Federal Secretariat for the Market and General Economic Affairs, Sector of Tourism	Bulevar AVNOJ-a 104, 11070 New Belgrade

SELECTED BIBLIOGRAPHY

Burkart, John, and S. Medlik (1974), *Tourism, Past, Present and Future*, London: Heinemann.

ETC Secretariat (1979), *The European Travel Commission Handbook*, Dublin: ETC.

International Tourism Quarterly, No. 3, 1976, "The Role and Functions of a National Tourist Office"; No. 3, 1983, "National Tourist Offices, the Role and Functions of an NTO Abroad," London.

Kosters, Martinus (1979), "Holland and Tourism in the Next Decade," International Symposium on Tourism in the Next Decade, George Washington University, Washington, D.C.

Kosters, Martinus (1981), *Focus op Toerisme*, Den Haag: Vuga.

Organization for Economic Cooperation and Development (1984), *Tourism Policy and International Tourism in OECD Member Countries 1979−1983*, Paris: OECD.

Wahab, Salah, Jack Crampon, and Louis Rothfield (1976), *Tourism Marketing*, London: Tourism International Press.

World Tourism Organization (1983), *World Tourism Statistics*, Madrid: WTO.

World Tourism Organization, (1980), *Budgets of National Tourism Administrations 1977−1979*, Madrid: WTO.

World Tourism Organization, (1980), *Role and Structure of National Tourism Administrations*, Madrid: WTO.

12

Research Needs of Developing Countries

PETER SHACKLEFORD[1]

Chief of Studies
World Tourism Organization
Madrid, Spain

Developing countries have special research needs. Distance from generating markets, fragile human environment and ecology, and tricky calculation of economic benefits are major reasons. But analysis of developing countries' NTA research efforts shows them to be proportionally low compared with total budget, although absolute totals are sometimes higher than those of comparable industrial market economies. Bearing in mind that resources of developing country NTAs are not unlimited, the author sets forth priority tasks of their research departments, formulates practical suggestions for staffing, and proposes new research themes to reflect states' growing responsibilities in the field to tourism.

WHAT ARE THE NEEDS?

There are a number of reasons for believing that the tourism research needs of the developing countries are especially strong. These include the following.

DISTANCES FROM GENERATING COUNTRIES

Unlike tourism-receiving countries located in the industrialized regions, the developing countries receive their international visitors from generating markets situated at great distances—often many thousands of miles. Accordingly, a finely tuned statistical apparatus is needed to evaluate incoming tourism and identify trends.

[1]The author gratefully acknowledges the consent of the Secretary-General of the World Tourism Organization, Mr. Robert C. Lonati, for preparation of this chapter. He also acknowledges the secretarial assistance of Ms. Rosamond Deming. Though material of the World Tourism Organization has been employed in compiling this chapter, it remains a personal contribution to the Handbook and is not to be interpreted as necessarily reflecting the views of the Secretary-General of the World Tourism Organization nor of its Member States.

HIGHLY SEGMENTED MARKETS

Generally, visitors come from particular socioeconomic layers of the populations of industrialized and capital-surplus, oil-exporting countries. It requires relatively sophisticated market research to identify and analyze the profiles and preferences of these visitors (Burkart and Medlik 1981, Parts III and VII).

LACK OF MEANS OF DOMESTIC TOURISTS

Although in most developing countries a prosperous minority exists that is capable of undertaking domestic tourism, many inhabitants lack the income and wherewithal to travel. Accordingly, research must focus not only on measurement of domestic tourism but on ways and means of improving access of underprivileged layers of the population to holidays and travel, and on devising economical, but adequate, means of supply (accommodation and transportation) to achieve this aim.

COMPLEXITY OF ECONOMIC IMPACT

The need to import goods and services to supply the tourism sector and the prominent role played by non-resident (frequently transnational) enterprise and expatriate staff make evaluation of tourism's economic impact more difficult for the developing country. Scarcity of foreign exchange in many developing countries makes it a priority to measure accurately tourism's foreign exchange contribution to the economy (WTO 1980b).

CULTURE AND LIFESTYLE DIFFERENCES

The disparities of culture, attitudes, and lifestyles existing between developing countries and industrialized nations require more attention to be paid through research to tourism's sociocultural effects (WTO 1981d).

FRAGILE ENVIRONMENT

The delicate environments of many developing countries (especially in the tropics) make it more urgent to undertake impact studies and research into carrying capacity to determine the optimum number of visitors a destination can receive.[2]

HIGH PROJECT COSTS—SCARCE INVESTMENT FUNDS

Costs of tourism investment for a developing country are likely to be higher relative to the size of capital markets than in industrialized countries. Too often projects will compete for scarce investment funds. Accordingly, research needs to focus on practical and effective project appraisal techniques.

If developing countries have great research needs, what are they and how should they be met? This chapter will attempt to answer that question. It therefore has both an analytic and a prescriptive aim. First, available data concerning the research efforts deployed by national tourism administrations (NTAs) of developing countries will be analyzed in broad quantitative terms, i.e., budgets and human resources. Second, suggestions will be formulated regarding developing countries' tourism research needs, bearing in mind in particular the new responsibilities incumbent upon States as a result of their adherence to the principles of equal access to holiday expressed in the Manila Declaration of 1980 (WTO 1980).

Analysis of NTA budgets is not quite a precise indication of total tourism research effort ongoing in developing countries. Apart from the NTA, tourism development corporations exist in some countries as well as research and teaching establishments such as Utalii College (Kenya) or the Asian Institute for Tourism (Philippines). Also, at any time, sectoral support or technical cooperation missions to developing countries may be under way through multilateral assistance.

[2]*Workshop on Environmental Aspects of Tourism* (1984), organized jointly by WTO and the United Nations Environment Programme (UNEP) at Madrid from 5 to 8 July 1983, Madrid: WTO.

However, while the achievements of individual institutions or particular research missions should not be neglected, it will be necessary for the purposes of this analysis to disregard them since they are essentially temporary or sporadic and not concerted or permanent.

Published research budgets of developing countries, taken from the most recent edition of WTO's *Budgets of National Tourism Administrations*, were analyzed (WTO 1982c). This produced data for thirty middle-income countries (using the World Bank classification) and seven low-income countries (Table 1). Under the heading of middle income, 1980 GNP ranges from $420 per capita in the case of Ghana to $5820 per capita in the case of Czechoslovakia, $4930 for Singapore, and $4380 for Greece, so the spread is quite great and a number of quite industrialized tourist-receiving countries are included (World Bank 1982). Low-income countries appeared to be underrepresented which would tentatively lead to the conclusion that they do not enjoy abundant research opportunities due to constrained financial circumstances. While accepting this as a working hypothesis, an attempt was made to correct for underreporting by having recourse to a previous survey carried out in 1975 when NTAs were asked to describe their research activities in detail. Though not recent, this survey could be taken to be indicative of research efforts and details are reproduced in Table 2 since the situation is unlikely to have changed significantly since that year (WTO/IUOTO 1975).

In *Budgets of National Tourism Administrations* (WTO 1982c), NTAs are asked to classify their research activities under three headings: research into tourism development; collecting and compiling tourism statistics; and drawing up plans and sectoral programs for national tourism development. Most countries indicate that their research activities fall under all three headings.

Taken together, the three headings comprise data gathering, data analysis, and formulating propositions of future action based on the conclusions of analysis. This fairly broad definition of "research" will be employed hereafter unless otherwise indicated by the context.

Before analyzing the figures some preliminary comments are necessary. The overall budgets of NTAs conventionally include the following main headings: promotion, investment, research, training, and administration. With the exception of those NTAs which invest significantly in tourist plant, "promotion" is generally the most important budgetary item. The NTA is unlikely to be alone in engaging in promotional activities. Airlines, hotels, tour operators, and regional and local tourism bodies are also active. Accordingly, in 1980, for every dollar spent by the NTA on promotion a "return" in the form of international tour-

TABLE 1 **Research Staff and Budget of Middle- and Low-Income Countries—1981**

COUNTRY	GNP PER CAPITA 1980 IN U.S. $	RESEARCH BUDGET OF NTA IN U.S. $ (THOUSANDS)	AS PERCENTAGE OF TOTAL NTA BUDGET	NO. OF STAFF
Middle-Income Countries				
Argentina	2390			
Bahamas	na[a]	244 (1980)	1.3	26
Bermuda	na	133	1.5	26
Brazil	2050	2594	16.0	35
Colombia	1180	273	1.5	na
Congo	900	152	25.3	5
Cyprus	na	35	1.1	9
Czechoslovakia	5820	739	0.5	32
Ecuador	1270	24	0.4	54
Ghana	420	55	0.8	11[b]
Greece	4380	3	0.01	14
Hong Kong	4240	107	1.0	15
Hungary	4180	288	3.7	8
Indonesia	430	192	0.2	42
Iran	1648	290 (1979)	0.9	20
Jamaica	1030	114	0.8	12
Kenya	420	22	1.1	na
Malaysia	1620	250	2.5	na
Morocco	900	281 (1980)	4.2	16
Papua New Guinea	780	15	3.3	5
Paraguay	1300	5	0.6	na
Peru	1285	900	4.5	na
Korea, Rep.	1520	201	0.6	32
Senegal	450	73	2.1	15
Singapore	4430	48	0.2	23
Syrian Arab Rep.	1340	1500	10.8	18
Thailand	670	263	5.0	85
Venezuela	3630	1000	3.3	na
Yemen	430	24	2.9	3
Yugoslavia	2620	62	1.0	4
Low-Income Countries				
Sierra Leone	280	12	1.8	3
Sri Lanka	270	4	0.1	na
United Rep. of Cameroon	670	31	1.1	15[c]
Madagascar	350			2
Togo	410			4
Burkina Faso	210			3

Source: WTO, *Budgets of National Tourism Administrations 1978–1981.*

[a]na = not available.

[b]includes investment staff.

[c]includes training staff.

TABLE 2   Tourism Research Effort in 1975

COUNTRY	FUNCTION OF THE RESEARCH UNIT OF THE NATIONAL TOURISM ADMINISTRATION	NO. OF STAFF	1975 RESEARCH BUDGET (U.S. $)
Middle-Income Countries			
Bolivia	Tourism planning and development. Preparation of statistics.	6	na[a]
Brazil	Compilation, exchange, and publication of information and studies on every aspect of tourism.	40	na
Egypt	Studies of every aspect of tourism.	10	na
El Salvador	Studies of and plans for the development of domestic and international tourism.	15	na
Ghana	In-depth studies of economic and social trends of tourism in Ghana. Appraisal of the tourist industry. Preinvestment studies. Execution and monitoring of projects of the tourist board.	7	na
Hong Kong	Research and statistics to implement an effective marketing policy. Collection and quantification of information on tourist products and markets and their correlation with market trends and socioeconomic factors.	11	90,167
Israel	Organization of the system of tourism statistics. Research and publication of its results. Analysis and forecasts for the master tourism development plan and other objectives. Preparation and monitoring of research contracts awarded to outside firms.	4	na
Jamaica	Research on every aspect of tourism.	14	na
Jordan	a) Studies and research section: Project evaluation and studies of tourist movements. b) Economic studies section: Economic appraisal of tourist projects.	2	na
Malaysia	Collection processing and analysis of tourism information and its dissemination to other divisions within the NTA, government department, and the public.		
Mexico	Tourism planning, statistics, projects, and catalogue. Research, appraisals, feasibility studies, and forecasts.	78	na
Morocco	Collection, analysis, and dissemination of tourism statistics. Tourism planning.	4	na
Nigeria	Research on tourism supply and demand.	na	na
Philippines	Collection of monthly tourism statistics.	30	na
Singapore	Collection and publication of monthly and annual statistics on tourist arrivals and accommodation. Market survey and studies to promote the marketing of Singapore as a tourist destination.	18	na
Spain	Research, technical assistance, and planning in the field of tourism.	20	360,000
Thailand	Collection and analysis of tourism statistics, surveys on tourist expenditures; studies of and research on all aspects of tourism.	3	na
Tunisia	Research on and studies of the various aspects of tourism to determine overall guidelines and objectives of tourism policy.	3	325,000
Turkey	Social and economic studies for tourism development under the program.	6	315,531
Venezuela	Preparation of plans and programs for submission to the President.	30	na
Zambia	Investment studies for the tourist board and the national hotels corporation. Market research. Tourism and hotel statistics for the hotel's board and the Ministry of lands, natural resources, and tourism. Consultancy services. Itinerary design and costing for the tourist board.	2	na
Low-Income Countries			
Bangladesh	Social and economic research, statistics, general tourism research, and publication of findings.	10	na

(continued)

TABLE 2   *(Continued)*

COUNTRY	FUNCTION OF THE RESEARCH UNIT OF THE NATIONAL TOURISM ADMINISTRATION	NO. OF STAFF	1975 RESEARCH BUDGET (U.S. $)
Burundi	na	na	na
Central African Republic	Tourism and accommodation statistics	1	na
India	Collection and dissemination of tourism statistics.	24	na
Indonesia	Research on every aspect of tourism for the development of domestic and international tourism.	11	na
Pakistan	Collection, tabulation, and analysis of tourism statistics. Market research.	9	na
Senegal	Studies of tourism projects, economical and statistical research, and co-operation in the planning and monitoring of tourism development.	7	na
Sri Lanka	Carrying out research and statistical studies on tourism. Collection of basic tourism statistics, market research, and in-depth studies of visitor motivations.	8	7,273
Sudan	Collection and tabulation of tourism statistics. Studies of current and future tourism projects. Participation in drawing up of development programs. Preliminary study of tourist agreements. Information.	9	2,940
Zaire	Preparation of the five-year tourism development plan. Regional studies of the need for hotel accommodation. Feasibility studies. Statistical reports. Hotel classification and inspection.	9	na

Source: WTO, 1975. Middle- and low-income countries as characterized by the World Bank classification.

Note: According to WTO in 1975, the following research budgets were reported by other national tourism organization administrations, whether or not a specialized research unit existed: Bahamas $98,765; Belgium $127,194; Canada $281,000; Chile $74,074; Cyprus $4,201; Denmark $32,840; Finland $98,300; Iran $73,684; Ireland $472,585; Japan $48,500; Netherlands $53,700; Panama $585,000; Syrian Arab Republic $108,108; United Kingdom $58,333; U.S.A. $641,000; Vietnam $64,685.

[a]na = Not available

ist receipts of $570 was earned. Put another way, for every $100 earned in receipts, the average NTA ploughs back only 17.5 cents in promotional expenditure. Even when the existence of other tourism promotion bodies is borne in mind, this is a remarkably low ratio and conventional wisdom has suggested that NTAs should aim to reinvest at least 1% and preferably closer to 3% of international tourist receipts. The fact that promotional budgets are relatively small will place firmly in perspective the following conclusions about the size of NTA research budgets quoted from *Budgets of National Tourism Administrations, 1982 edition*:

Research budget ranks the lowest in NTA budgets. At times, this item is not even budgeted and rarely does it exceed 2 percent, except in Australia (3.7 percent in 1981), Canada (3.1 percent in 1981), Chile (4.5 percent in 1981), Colombia (3.3 percent in 1980 but 1.5 percent in 1981), Ghana (5.8 percent in 1980 but 0.8 percent in 1981), Italy (3.2 percent in 1981), Malaysia (2.6 percent and 2.5 percent in 1980 and 1981), Morocco (4.2 percent in 1980), Peru (4.5 percent in 1981), Turkey (2.5 percent in 1980) and Yemen (2.5 percent in 1980 and 2.9 percent in 1981). There are two exceptions, viz. Brazil, where the research budget ranges from 6 to 16 percent and in Thailand where it

exceeded 9 percent in 1979 and 1980 (as opposed to 5 percent in 1981). (WTO 1982c, pp. 22–23)

Table 1 gives full details of the research budgets of middle- and low-income country NTAs and it will be seen that 20 out of the total of 37 possess research budgets equal to less than 2% of the total budget, and in some cases significantly less.

It is easy to conclude on the basis of these figures that the research effort of developing countries is insufficient. But the conclusion requires amplification if it is to lead to useful recommendations. The following questions might be asked. How do developing countries' research budgets compare with those of industrialized countries? What should be the priorities? How can research assist in meeting future responsibilities? The reply to the first question seems to be that most developing countries spend much the same proportion of their total budget on research as industrialized countries but that absolute amounts spent on research by individual developing countries often exceed those of industrialized countries of comparable market size. These conclusions may be drawn by comparing figures in Table 1 with those of Table 3, which shows research budgets of eight industrial market economies (according to the World Bank classification) (World Bank

TABLE 3 Research Staff and Budget of Industrial Market Economies—1981

COUNTRY	GNP PER CAPITA 1980 IN US $	RESEARCH BUDGET OF NTA IN US $ (THOUSANDS)	AS PERCENTAGE OF TOTAL NTA BUDGET	NO. OF STAFF
Australia	9,820	383	3.4	4
Canada	10,130	907	3.1	26
Finland	9,720	111	0.6	6
France	11,730	176	0.6	na[a]
Germany, Federal Republic of	13,590	100	0.6	5
Italy	6,480	667	3.2	17
Netherlands	11,470	128	0.9	3
Spain	5,400	770	1.3	na

Source: WTO, *Budgets of National Tourism Administrations 1979–1981.*
[a]na = not available.

1982). Thus, among major industrialized countries whose research budgets do not exceed 2% of the total NTA budget are Finland 1.3%, Federal Republic of Germany 0.6%, Netherlands 0.9%, and Spain 1.3% (perhaps surprising given its preeminent tourist-receiving situation). By way of comparison, in 1981 Venezuela spent U.S. $1 million on research compared with Spain's U.S. $770 thousand; Peru spent U.S. $900,000 compared with Italy's US $667,000; Syrian Arab Republic spent U.S. $1.5 million compared with France's U.S. $176,000; and Brazil spent no less than U.S. $2.6 million compared with Federal Republic of Germany's U.S. $100,000. Naturally, these figures should be compared with caution as a number of industrialized market economies possess independent research institutions whose activities are not reflected in Table 3. Still, the comparison does seem indicative of a trend.

The replies to the second and third questions constitute the watershed of this chapter and mark the transition from the analytical to the prescriptive. Before proceeding it would be well to underline that the research needs of particular countries will vary according to the degree of development of tourism. Thus, a country which is embarking on tourism development will give more emphasis to project appraisal and planning. A country with a significantly developed market may be more concerned with improving market research and impact analysis. A country with an undeveloped domestic tourism market will be more concerned with ways of ensuring equal access to tourism.

Therefore, while the areas "Planning and Programs," "Statistics," and "Development" should be germane to the needs of all countries, each country will need to give slightly differing emphasis to the different aspects and to vary deployment of human and financial resources accordingly.

PLANNING AND PROGRAMS

The planning function enables the research unit to contribute to policy formulation and avoids the danger of its activities being carried out *in vacuo*. Lately, tourism planning has become appreciably more sophisticated with the technique known as integrated planning gaining in importance. Simply defined, integrated planning is a technique which takes account systematically of alternative forms of development to the one being considered and of the repercussions of planning decisions in the area concerned beyond the limits of the sector being developed, in the case of tourism. Naturally, integrated planning techniques have come to be closely identified with a more immediate concern for the sociocultural impact of tourism and its impact on the natural environment. (Lawson and Baud-Bovy 1977, WTO 1978, Pearce 1981).

But a key role of planning in the developing countries will be in the formulation of the immediate goals of tourism policy. These can conveniently be placed under three headings:

- goals for domestic tourism.
- goals for regional tourism.
- goals for intercontinental tourism.

It is important to confront policymakers with these three goals since otherwise attention may focus only on international tourism at the expense of other market sectors. A close link should also exist between the tourism planning function and the overall national planning process. While this is implicit in the concept of integrated planning, it does mean, for example, that regional development aims should be borne in mind when planning for tourism. This technique should frequently bring the planners of the NTA research department into contact with the formulation of overall national policy goals such as whether to develop an area for tourism or for farming. The use of an integrated approach should be especially helpful in identifying linkages and synergy effects. For example, tourism generally gives impetus to the handicraft industry though not all artifacts produced will be sold directly to tourists but will be exported to industrialized countries for sale to consumers. Likewise, a more intensive pattern of air transport for tourism purposes frequently improves prospects for merchandise trade. So flights to industrialized tourism-generating markets may create opportunities for air-freighting high-value, perishable goods such as tropical fruit and flowers. Given high levels of unemployment in developing countries, particular emphasis in planning should be placed on the creation of small- and medium-sized, often family-run, enterprises and on providing the necessary practical training opportunities. Opportunities may exist in the tourism sector itself, or in export industries such as those described above, or again in the field of import substitution, whereby goods intended for use and consumption by tourists can be produced domestically rather than brought in from abroad. A manager of a transnational hotel chain has claimed to this writer to have virtually created a local market for fruit juice served in hotels while local production of furniture and decorations for hotels (often in authentic local style) is an established feature of much tourism development.

Three specific areas should receive the attention of planners: tourism supply, manpower, and infrastructure. Supply planning will be concerned fundamentally with accommodation to be offered to international and domestic tourists. Work by WTO has shown (WTO 1981a) that import content in hotel construction need not be too high, while there is an urgent need for the developing of new models of supply for domestic tourism consistent with income levels and possibilities of domestic tourists. Manpower planning should concentrate on staff numbers and skills and on identification of training needs—the last being a constant concern for most developing countries. Finally, in the field of infrastructure, the tourism planner will need to be alert to the possibilities that exist for joint use of resources (i.e., for tourism and other purposes). Evident possibilities are offered by projects such as construction of roads and airports or provision of water supplies which benefit not only tourists but also local populations.

STATISTICS

Statistics may be considered in two parts: the gathering of statistics and the analysis of statistics. It is apparent from the 1975 WTO survey that some research units cover both these aspects, while others are concerned only with the analyzed final results (see Table

2). Naturally, when a research unit is responsible for the gathering of statistics the effect upon manpower is significant. Possibly, the research unit will be responsible too for the conduct or commissioning of market research based on the need for additional information about tourists' motivations or their socioeconomic profile. In this case, it is more likely that the research will be commissioned out-of-house with consequent budgetary appropriations being set aside for this purpose. While the need for market research should not be belittled, it is evident that the undertaking of meaningful market research by a developing country may involve considerable expense since it is basically interested in the profiles and attitudes of a small segment of the population in the industrialized or energy-surplus countries often situated at considerable distances. Accordingly, given the generally lower intensity of tourist flows to the developing countries, the lesser pressures of facilitation, and the opportunity for eliciting more statistical information from tourists at both the beginning and the end of their stay, it is suggested that before market research is undertaken the possibility of obtaining additional relevant information from tourists actually visiting the country should be seriously considered. Departure surveys, concentrating on attitudes, socioeconomic profiles, and expenditure patterns, are likely to be particularly worthwhile since international tourists preparing to undertake relatively long-distance journeys generally arrive at the point of departure *in good time* and can be relied upon to recall fairly accurately the details of their expenditure on their trip as well as giving impressions of their stay and other matters. Again, it is strongly recommended that a data base be compiled covering the three sectors

- domestic tourism.
- regional tourism.
- long-distance intercontinental tourism (WTO 1981c).

Another possibility of keeping market research expenditure to a reasonable level was suggested at the World Tourism Conference, Manila, 1980. The Conference drew attention to the frequent duplication of effort existing in the obtention of market information on tourism and called upon WTO "to continue its efforts to facilitate the exchange of technical tourist information, specifically by considering the possibility of establishing a worldwide tourist information system . . . so as to increase the capacity of all countries and especially developing countries, for action and management and thus to strengthen their technological economy by means where appropriate of advanced technologies such as data tele-processing" (WTO 1980a). Finally, the possibility exists of a number of countries within the same region undertaking joint market research within the generating markets and sharing the expenses. In this context it may be noted that a similar policy is pursued by the industrialized countries themselves through bodies such as the European Travel Commission.

DEVELOPMENT

The third principal area of research for which NTAs assume responsibility is that of feasibility analysis (from the economic, cultural, political, and social standpoints) of tourism development. Evidently such activity gives a useful practical orientation to the NTA research unit since it involves close contact with tourism enterprises (hotels, etc.) and with techniques for calculating the financial and other returns of the tourism sector. In the field of project appraisal two needs are strongly felt. They are, first, access to the methodology of appraisal employed by major international financing institutions (the World Bank, regional development banks, etc.), and, second, the elimination of manual calculations and the introduction of computer techniques for project analysis. As a result of this, not only can the whole process be speeded up but also a greater degree of sensitivity analysis can be conducted, aimed at identifying the fate of the project under a wider series of assumptions. In this connection, inexpensive but versatile microcomputers are becoming more widely available, while data teleprocessing through the use of terminals installed in developing countries offers the possibility of feeding input data into a central computer located, perhaps, in another continent, so as to obtain relevant output data rapidly and economically for project appraisal purposes. Interest is also being shown in the models employed by the major hotel chains for project analysis and the possibility of applying these models to projects put forward by hotel development corporations and similar semipublic bodies established within the developing countries to promote the development of tourism particularly in the regions lacking in supply facilities (WTO 1980b).

The study of impacts is one of the most interesting and challenging tasks facing the research unit of the NTA in any developing country. Social, cultural, and environmental as well as economic impacts should receive attention and a whole series of techniques and models must be brought to bear upon the task confronting the researchers. This may, therefore, require the use of a large number of techniques by a relatively small group of individuals comprising the research unit. Again, the need is felt for the ready availability of a number of models which can be employed to analyze situations prevailing in different countries using input data compiled by the research unit. So far as economic impact models are concerned, while the development of a single universally applicable impact model is no easy task, it does appear, nonetheless, that within the next few years certain basic impact models should be available to subscribers in developing countries through the data teleprocessing network. Other areas of impact involve so many subjective factors that the use of mathematical models may not always be appropriate. Possibly the greatest area of difficulty in relation to, for example, social and cultural impact models has been that researchers coming from developed market economy or socialist countries have interacted insufficiently. Their reports, considered the work of outsiders, have (as might be expected) come to be treated somewhat at arm's length and the impact upon the planning process has not always been of significance. In tackling this urgent and frequently delicate problem in the future, a greater degree of preparation would be desirable, involving both the technician and researcher, possibly from the third country, but also a counterpart from the developing country and representatives of travel trade partners such as tour operators and the management of transnational hotel chains. Clearly this approach is more likely to yield results which command a consensus and can lead to timely action to reduce unfavorable impacts and strengthen favorable ones.

RESEARCH AND NEW RESPONSIBILITIES

The three main areas of responsibility described above are those which, conventionally and historically, have been entrusted to research departments of national tourism administrations. Accordingly, they fulfill the classical research needs of NTAs. However, they are not a sufficient nor a complete statement of needs since they fail to reflect the dynamics of tourism research and especially the requirements which will increasingly arise as a result of the new responsibilities incumbent upon States as a result of their adherence to the Manila Declaration on World Tourism of 1980. In this part of the chapter some attention will accordingly be devoted to this subject (WTO 1980a).

The Manila Declaration on World Tourism laid the foundations for a much broader conception of tourism than hitherto accepted with noteworthy emphasis being placed on social, cultural, and educational aspects of travel. Also, the right of underprivileged layers of the population to gain access to vacations was emphasized, as was the need to give proper weight to domestic vis-à-vis international travel.

The practical effect of the Manila Declaration is to place new responsibilities before States and their tourism administrations. Some will evidently be entrusted to research departments. In Table 4 possible research topics suggested by the operative paragraphs of the Manila Declaration are listed. This list is of course only indicative since the Manila Declaration is a rich source of projects and activities for the research departments of developing and, indeed, industrialized countries.

TABLE 4   Research Topics Suggested by the Manila Declaration

PARAGRAPH NUMBER OF THE MANILA DECLARATION AND SUBJECT MATTER	POSSIBLE RESEARCH TOPIC
1 Tourism's direct effects on social, cultural, and economic sectors of national societies.	Classification of different effects and assessment of their importance.
1 Enjoyment of freedom to travel and identification of facilitation.	Study of economic, social, and administrative barriers to travel measures to be adopted.
4 Best practical, effective, and nondiscriminatory access to travel and tourism.	Study of ways of ensuring equal access to tourism.
6 Tourism's contribution to national economic activity and international transactions.	Continuing analysis of tourism's economic impact and significance. Study of role of transnational corporations in tourism.
7 Domestic tourism.	Research into ways of expanding domestic tourist movements, *interalia*, through encouragement of small- and medium-sized, often family-run, enterprises.
8 Tourism as an opportunity for the citizen to get to know his environment and to gain deeper awareness of national identity.	Research into tourism's effects in promoting greater knowledge of one's own country and awareness of national heritage and identity.
10 Social tourism.	Research into ways of ensuring that less privileged citizens can exercise their right to rest and recreation through travel.
11 Tourism's effect on physical and mental health of individuals.	Study of tourism's effect on individual and community working capacity and health.
12 Tourism as a source of new employment and of training needs.	Study of direct and indirect employment creation through tourism. Development of new, practical training schemes for tourism and travel personnel.
13 International relations and quest for peace.	Study of tourism's effects on the international understanding and attitudes. Study of significance of tourism in resolution of conflict situations.
14 Avoidance of distortions brought about by economic factors.	Formulation of guidelines for public and private investments.
15 Travel for the young, the elderly, and the disabled.	Study of ways of improving access to tourism for these groups of the community.
16 Establishment of a New International Economic Order.	Study of transfers of technology and know-how in tourism and development of recommended practices for conditions under which such transfers take place.
17 Conditions of employment for tourism workers.	Study of status of tourism professions.
18 Nature and environmental conservation.	Study of conservation needs of developing countries.
22 Preparation of the individual for travel.	Development of suitable educational programs.
Increased attention to development of tourism.	Incorporation of tourism in national development plans and programs and furnishing necessary data and research inputs for this purpose.

THE ROLE OF RESEARCH IN AVOIDING STEREOTYPING

Two final points might be made. A number of developing countries, particularly in Africa, are showing evident signs of frustration as they contemplate a development process which—in their view—seeks to impose alien cultures and modes of life. Development of international tourism is not free from such criticisms. In such a situation, it may be asserted that those countries who opt for a sizable tourism research effort choose rightly because of the capability that a research unit possesses of operating as a "think tank" for the whole national tourism administration. Not only figures but ideas too may be expected to flow from a properly functioning research team and some of those ideas may germinate to become the policy guidelines of tomorrow, expressing the distinctive personality of the country concerned and avoiding stereotyping.

Second, it is implicit in this chapter that other travel trade partners, such as transporters, hoteliers, and tour and travel agencies, should cooperate with the national tourism administration in a coherent program of research. The research needs of developing countries are too great for fragmentation of the research effort to be tolerable.

CHOICE OF PERSONNEL

Staffing an NTA research department is no easy matter since qualified researchers are unlikely to be more readily available in a developing country than in their industrialized counterparts. Faced with scarce resources, both human and financial, what should be the response of an NTA? Staff should, naturally, reflect the basic skills demanded by the three areas: planning, statistics, and analysis, which would suggest a planner, a statistician, and an economist. Better still, a combination of skills could be deployed so as to achieve a degree of multidisciplinary interaction, e.g., a planner with some sociological/cultural background, an economist with experience of financial/project analysis, and a statistician with understanding of market research/household techniques. As previously emphasized, communication of results is vital. So at least one member of the team should have the ability and the personality to communicate the findings of research to management and to outline their significance for policy. It is not to be expected that all relevant disciplines will be represented in a research unit. This would be uneconomical as input of certain branches of skill and knowledge will be required only on a part-time or short-term basis. Therefore, recourse will frequently be had to outside consultants, experts, and firms. Here a further skill is required which may be reflected either in management or in the research team itself: the ability to buy-in research, to brief consultants, and to integrate the results of their contributions into the overall research effort. For this purpose, a broad general culture and education, a practical common-sense approach to problems, and a reluctance to engage in academic speculation or theoretical argument are necessary.

CONCLUSIONS

This chapter has asserted that the research needs of the developing countries are greater than those of the industrialized countries for the following reasons: (a) distance from generating countries; (b) highly segmented markets; (c) lack of means of domestic tourists; (d) complexity of economic impact; (e) culture and lifestyle differences; (f) fragile environment; and (g) high project costs—scarce investment funds.

Analysis of resources attributed in 1981 to the research departments of NTAs of both medium- and low-income countries revealed that these were low in relative terms (i.e., compared to total budget), although in absolute terms there was some clear evidence of their being substantially higher than those of the industrialized countries (WTO 1982c). Analysis of figures published subsequently by WTO revealed that, under the effects of the world recession, there was little change in resources devoted to research during the period 1982–1984. However, due to the strength of the U.S. dollar and the weakness of the currencies of certain developing countries, especially in Latin America, the gap which had earlier been apparent between absolute resources devoted to research by industrialized and developing countries narrowed.

Functions of research departments were deduced from a detailed WTO 1975 survey (WTO/IUOTO 1975) supported by the information contained in WTO's 1981 *Budgets of National Tourism Administrations*. Needs of developing countries were seen to focus on three specific areas: planning, statistics, and development. But emphasis placed on each area was seen to vary according to the stage of development of tourism in the country concerned. In planning, the value of an integrated approach was recognized. Statistics were seen to fall under two headings: gathering and analysis. The somewhat less urgent pressures of facilitation in developing countries were seen to justify the use of administrative checks for gathering statistics. Scope was seen for joint market research and a centralized data bank accessible to all less developed countries. Under development could be grouped activities of project appraisal and impact analysis. The need was seen here for developing countries to become more familiar with project appraisal methodologies employed by major financial institutions, without the results just being "handed down."

Analysis of new responsibilities was carried out by reference to the Manila Declaration on World Tourism of 1980 to which the vast majority of developing countries throughout the world have subscribed. A primary focus of this analysis was on the need for study of ways and means of ensuring more equal access to tourism and vacations. Research into possibilities of domestic travel and tourism development, focusing on small-and medium-sized, often family-run, enterprises, was seen to be a key activity too (WTO 1980a and 1985).

Finally, the personnel requirements of tourism research in developing countries were analyzed. On balance, it seemed to be worthwhile to cultivate a reasonable range of specializations within the research department while recognizing that it will not be possible to include all relevant disciplines. Emphasis was placed on research personnel having the ability to communicate the findings of research to management and to outline their significance for policy. Not only figures but ideas were seen to flow from a properly functioning research department, helping the developing country to express its own distinctive personality and to adopt its own individual approach to the development of tourism.

REFERENCES

Burkart, A.J., and S. Medlik (1981), *Tourism Past, Present and Future*, London: Heinemann.

Lawson, F., and M. Baud-Bovy (1977), *Tourism and Recreation Development*, London: Architectural Press.

Pearce, D. (1981), *Tourist Development*, London: Longman.

World Bank (International Bank for Reconstruction and Development) (1982), *World Development Report 1982*, New York: Oxford University Press.

World Tourism Organization and International Union of Official Travel Organizations (1975), *The Structure of Research Units of National Tourist Organizations*, Geneva: IUOTO unpublished report.

World Tourism Organization (1978), *Integrated Tourism Planning*, Madrid: WTO.

World Tourism Organization (1980a), *Manila Declaration on World Tourism*, Madrid: WTO.

World Tourism Organization (1980b), *Evaluating Tourist Projects*, Madrid: WTO.

World Tourism Organization (1980c), *Report on Physical Planning and Area Development for Tourism in the Six WTO Regions*, Madrid: WTO.

World Tourism Organization (1981a), *Guidelines for Using National Resources in the Construction and Maintenance of Tourist Plant*, Madrid: WTO.

World Tourism Organization (1981b), *Guidelines for Collection and Presentation of Domestic Tourism Statistics*, Madrid: WTO.

World Tourism Organization (1981c), *Guidelines for Collection and Presentation of International Tourism Statistics*, Madrid: WTO.

World Tourism Organization (1981d), *Social and Cultural Impact of Tourist Movements*, Madrid: WTO.

World Tourism Organization (1982a), *Acapulco Document*, (adopted by the World Tourism Organization), Madrid: WTO.

World Tourism Organization (1982b), *Economic Review of World Tourism*, Madrid: WTO.

World Tourism Organization (1982c and 1984), *Budgets of National Tourism Administrations*, Madrid: WTO.

World Tourism Organization (1985), International Conference on the Adaptation of Training for Tourism and Travel Personnel: Final Act, Madrid: WTO.

13

Research in State and Provincial Travel Offices

SUZANNE D. COOK

Assistant Director
U.S. Travel Data Center
Washington, D.C.

As an overview of research programs conducted by state and provincial travel offices, this chapter provides summaries and analysis of research needs and objectives of travel offices, as well as the major research techniques used. It is designed to explore the range of current research activities, rather than to provide detailed descriptions of any particular type of research.

STATE AND PROVINCIAL ROLE IN TRAVEL PROMOTION AND DEVELOPMENT

Each state, province, and territory in the United States and Canada has an agency for travel promotion and development. All of these, with the exception of one in the U.S., are part of the state/provincial government.

The breadth of responsibilities and perspectives encompassed by state and provincial travel offices is unmatched by the private sector and provides a vital supplement to private promotion efforts. Travel office budgets for travel promotion and development directly contribute to economic expansion by increasing traveler expenditures, which in turn produce new jobs, personal income, and tax receipts for all levels of government. Further, they play a unique and vital role in affecting the terms of this growth by encouraging cooperation between industry sectors, providing assistance to the private sector in terms of travel marketing and development, and attending to planning and quality control. In addition, travel offices represent the views of both travel-related businesses and consumers in discussions of policies or regulations which might affect the industry. Finally, state/provincial travel offices provide important informational services to the traveling consumer, unavailable anywhere else.

CURRENT LEVELS OF STATE AND PROVINCIAL INVOLVEMENT

OVERALL PROGRAMS AND BUDGETS

In fiscal year 1984–1985, travel office budgets in the U.S. totaled $189 million, or approximately $3.8 million per state. Budgets vary widely, however, and range from a high of $14.4 million to a low of $560,000 (U.S. Travel Data Center 1985b). Provincial travel office budgets tend to be significantly larger than those in the United States.

Travel offices conduct a variety of programs including advertising, promotion, operation of highway welcome/information centers, participation in travel shows, package tour development, education and training, and research. In most cases, advertising and other promotional activities represent the largest portion of the travel office budget.

RESEARCH PROGRAMS

Research tends to enjoy a somewhat higher priority among provincial travel offices than among those in the U.S. Reflecting generally higher total budgets, travel offices in Canada tend to have substantially higher research budgets and larger research staffs than offices in the U.S.

153

In a special survey conducted by the U.S. Travel Data Center (1980) among state/provincial travel offices, respondents were asked to rate the importance of research in formulating travel promotion and development programs. In both countries, nearly 90 percent of all respondents indicated that research plays a very or fairly important role.

Research should be an important part of the travel office program. While funding for such programs tends to be limited, particularly in the U.S., most travel officials recognize its value and attempt to maximize their research efforts by cooperating with other groups and making use of techniques which generate the greatest amount of accurate data in the most cost-effective way. The remainder of this chapter discusses the research activities of state and provincial travel offices in detail.

RESEARCH NEEDS AT THE STATE AND PROVINCIAL LEVEL

The size and sophistication of research programs vary considerably among travel offices in the U.S. and Canada, and depend significantly on monetary and other resources available.

Establishment of research priorities should be based on a thorough analysis of the research needs of the particular state or provincial travel office and of the citizens and private sector which it serves. Such an analysis should take into consideration the following types of factors.

EXISTING DATA

A careful review of research conducted in the past by the travel office and other existing data sources should be one of the first steps in defining research needs. Travel/tourism research is conducted by a variety of public and private organizations. Agencies of the federal government conduct major research efforts related to travel and tourism, the results of which are available to the public. Examples include the United States Travel and Tourism Administration (formerly U.S. Travel Service), the United States Bureau of the Census, Tourism Canada, and Statistics Canada. The annual *Program Report of the U.S. Travel and Tourism Administration* (1984) and the semiannual *Canadian Travel Research Notes* (Tourism Canada 1985a) are just two of the regular publications which describe travel research programs at the federal level.

The U.S. Travel Data Center (1978) has published the *Travel Data Locator Index*, a cross-indexed catalog of more than 1,000 statistical series available to the general public.

Finally, travel research is frequently conducted by colleges and universities, private consulting firms, and travel-related companies. Goeldner and Dicke's (1980) comprehensive nine-volume bibliography is an excellent place for any state/provincial research department to start its review of existing data.

MAJOR USERS

Knowledge of the most important users of research is also vital in determining research needs and in setting priorities. Based on potential users' requirements, the travel office can more effectively establish acceptable definitions, define the types of data to be collected, and design specific research projects to provide the necessary information.

IMPORTANCE OF TRAVEL AND TOURISM TO THE ECONOMY

The importance of the travel industry to the overall economy varies widely among different areas in the U.S. and Canada. Areas highly dependent on the travel industry as a source of jobs, for example, may consider economic impact studies and market research, designed to provide information useful in maintaining or increasing their market share, to be most important. Areas with less developed travel industries may place a higher priority on research designed to document current levels of investment in the industry, to compile inventories of travel/tourism resources, and to identify geographic areas having potential for growth and new target markets for travel promotion.

Related to this factor is the level of support for the travel industry among the citizens and legislature of the state or province.

LEVEL OF CITIZEN AND LEGISLATIVE SUPPORT

It has been shown that states having active citizen, executive, and legislative support are most likely to succeed in their travel promotion programs. Further, there is evidence that states using economic impact research as justification for larger promotional budgets have been most successful in gaining such support (The Council of State Governments 1979).

The present level of support for tourism in a particular state or province is, therefore, likely to be seriously considered when determining needs and priorities. Areas suffering from a lack of citizen and legislative support might be wise to direct at least part of their resources to the documentation of travel/tourism's importance through economic impact research.

THE IMPORTANCE OF VARIOUS TYPES OF TRAVEL

The types of travel viewed by officials to be the most important to their state/province will in large part determine the content covered by research and the definitions used.

A survey conducted by the U.S. Travel Service

(1977) (now USTTA) among 46 states and 130 U.S. cities indicates that nonresident motor vehicle travel is judged to be the most important type of travel by the majority of those responding. Respondents also agree that they have the greatest need for research in this area and tend to limit their definitions of travel and to design their research programs accordingly.

OTHER CONSIDERATIONS

There are a number of other factors which should be considered in determining research needs and priorities. Every state or province has a different product to market, problems to identify and resolve, and opportunities for growth and development.

Travel offices currently share a number of common problems such as the depressing effects of favorable exchange rates in foreign destinations on domestic travel activity. Other problems, however, may be more unique. Smaller or more isolated states and provinces often suffer from inadequate investments in travel-related businesses and underdeveloped infrastructure. A larger, more tourism-dependent state or province, on the other hand, may experience the opposite type of problem, that of overdevelopment, and may need to deal with reconciling continued growth with the needs of its citizens. Research projects should be designed to address those problems of most critical concern.

Finally, to be most effective, a research program should be developed in conjunction with other major programs conducted by the state or provincial travel office. The typical travel office has a variety of responsibilities, the most important of which is the marketing and promotion of the state or province as a travel destination. Research is not its primary function, and is not an end result. Research is important only to the extent that it provides data to help plan more effective marketing strategies.

To be most effective, research must be based on a thorough assessment of the needs of the particular state or province. This assessment should consider the types of factors discussed above. Once research needs are determined and available resources are considered, objectives may be determined and specific research projects designed.

TYPES OF RESEARCH CONDUCTED BY STATE AND PROVINCIAL TRAVEL OFFICES

In early 1980, the U.S. Travel Data Center conducted a survey among all state and provincial travel offices to collect information on their research programs. Forty states and territories in the U.S. and seven provinces and territories in Canada responded.

Respondents were asked to indicate the frequency with which they conduct a variety of types of research. Table 1 summarizes the results.

This table shows that research programs in the U.S. emphasize somewhat different projects than those conducted by Canadian provinces. State travel offices tend to stress research on the economic benefits of travel/tourism development, as well as studies of current and potential markets and evaluation research.

Among offices in both the U.S. and Canada, market and evaluation research provides the basis for a system of monitoring travel activity over time. In addition, nearly 90 percent of the travel offices responding to the survey indicated having, at one time or another, conducted special studies in response to particular difficulties, such as gasoline shortages. Forecasting studies are conducted somewhat more frequently in the U.S. than in Canada. The least frequently conducted types of research include psychological, environmental, and societal impact studies.

Market and evaluation research are also popular among Canadian travel offices, but impact studies are conducted much less frequently than in the U.S. Canadian programs are more likely to include research to identify travel/tourism resources, reflecting the current concern with development in many of the provinces.

The results of this survey, supplemented by information from a number of other sources, suggest that the types of research most often conducted by travel offices fall into the following major categories:

1 Impact analysis.
2 Market analysis.
3 Evaluation research.
4 Identification of travel/tourism resources.
5 Monitoring travel activity over time.

IMPACT ANALYSIS

Impact analysis refers to the broad category of research designed to measure the positive and negative economic, psychological, environmental, and social effects of travel and tourism activity (The Ontario Research Council on Leisure 1977, pp. 93–108).

Sources of data most frequently used by U.S. and Canadian travel offices in conducting economic impact research are:

1 State/provincial and national data on travel-related businesses.
2 Surveys of travel-related businesses.
3 Estimates from expenditure and economic impact models.
4 Expenditure surveys with travelers.

TABLE 1   Types of Research Conducted

	UNITED STATES			CANADA	
TYPE	PERCENTAGE OF STATES CONDUCTING	PERCENTAGE OF STATES CONDUCTING ANNUALLY	TYPE	PERCENTAGE OF PROVINCES CONDUCTING	PERCENTAGE OF PROVINCES CONDUCTING ANNUALLY
1 Impact analysis— benefits	95	69	1 Market research— current markets	100	71
2 Market research— current markets	90	55	2 Evaluation research	100	57
3 Market research— potential markets	90	33	3 Identification of travel/ tourism resources	100	43
4 Evaluation research	87	55	4 Research of the international visitors	100	29
5 Identification of travel/ tourism resources	87	42	5 Impact analysis— benefits	100	14
6 Research on effects of situational factors	87	26	6 Psychological studies of travel motivation and behavior	86	0
7 Forecasting studies	67	21	7 Research on effects of situational factors	86	0
8 Psychological studies of travel motivation and behavior	66	18	8 Market research— potential markets	71	14
9 Research on the international visitors	58	21	9 Forecasting studies	57	14
10 Impact analysis—costs	44	25	10 Impact analysis—costs	14	0

n = 40 U.S. states/territories and 7 Canadian provinces/territories.
Source: U.S. Travel Data Center

Travel offices in both the U.S. and Canada rely heavily on data generated by other state/provincial government agencies, the federal government, and other national organizations. State/provincial revenue departments are a major source of sales, receipts, and tax revenue data for travel-related industries at the retail level. Employment and wage/salary data for the same industries may be obtained from state/provincial employment security offices. On the federal level, economic censuses conducted in the U.S. by the Bureau of the Census and in Canada by Statistics Canada provide national data on sales and receipts of individual industries, available on a state/province and county or regional basis.

Many states and provinces also rely on data produced by national expenditure and economic impact models. The National Travel Expenditure Model and the Travel Economic Impact Model, developed by the U.S. Travel Data Center (1975), provide annual estimates of travel expenditures and travel-generated employment, payroll, and federal, state, and local tax receipts for each of the 50 states and the District of Columbia, as well as a large number of individual counties. The Tourism Expenditure Model (1975a) and Tourism Impact Model (1975b), developed by the Canadian Bureau of Management Consulting, produce similar data for provinces and provincial regions.

In addition to the prevalent use of secondary data, many travel offices also conduct primary research, usually involving survey research. Some travel offices survey travel-related businesses directly to collect the economic data described above. Surveys are also frequently conducted with the traveling consumer, often to collect information on expenditure patterns.

Expenditure surveys may be conducted in a variety of ways. Most common in Canada is the use of exit surveys, employing personal interviews with travelers as they leave the province. U.S. travel offices also frequently conduct surveys at various locations in the state, such as highway welcome/information centers, or survey travelers by mail or telephone after they have returned home. These latter techniques are employed less frequently by provincial travel offices.

The major problem with the types of expenditure surveys discussed above is one of recall. An alternative method involves the use of self-administered, mail-back expenditure diaries distributed to travelers as they enter the area. The most significant problem with this method is the relatively low response rate achieved and the resulting problem of nonresponse bias (Belden Associates 1978, p. 13). For a more detailed review of economic impact research, see Douglas Frechtling's discussion of the topic in Chapter 28.

Other types of impact analysis are conducted much less frequently. Among these, psychological impact research tends to be the most popular. Psychological impact research covers a wide variety of phenomena concerning human values. Most often, it addresses the effect of the travel experience on the emotional well-being of individuals and estimates the degree of satisfaction derived by travelers within the state/province. Also included in this type of research are studies of the attitudes of residents toward visitors, as well as evaluation of how the presence of visitors in the community may both positively and negatively affect residents of that community. An excellent example of this type of research is Pizam's (1978) study of the social costs of travel and tourism development in Cape Cod, Massachusetts.

The other two major types of research in this category include environmental and societal impact research. Environmental impact studies assess the effects of travel industry development on the natural system of the state/province. While infrequently conducted by travel offices, such studies are useful in selecting appropriate sites for development of particular facilities and in determining which of a number of types of development would be least detrimental to the environment of a particular area. Research on societal impacts assess the influence of travel and tourism upon the society as a whole. It may include the evaluation of economic, psychological, and environmental impacts, as well as the interrelationship among all three.

MARKET ANALYSIS

The second major objective of state and provincial travel office research is to identify and describe current and potential markets. It provides guidance for the development of new facilities and markets, creates a foundation on which to base attractive and effective marketing and promotional programs, and is necessary for evaluating the success of such programs. Data produced through market analysis are also often used in other research projects, such as economic impact analysis.

Market research studies collect information concerning the number of travelers in the state/province, as well as data on major traveler characteristics, such as origin and socioeconomic characteristics, and trip characteristics, such as mode of transportation, duration of stay, and overnight accommodations used.

Sources of data most frequently used by travel offices when conducting marketing research are:

1 State/provincial and national data on travel-related activities.
2 National/regional travel surveys.
3 Counts of visitors at public/private parks, attractions, welcome/information centers, and exit/entry points.
4 Surveys conducted with travelers at home.
5 State/provincial and national data on demographic and socioeconomic characteristics of current and potential markets.

Most travel offices make extensive use of secondary data produced by governmental agencies, associations, and private organizations to measure current levels of travel-related activities within their jurisdiction. Information on travel markets is also produced through consumer surveys conducted by agencies of the federal government and other national organizations.

In Canada, for example, a Canadian Travel Survey has been conducted quarterly since the third quarter of 1978 by Statistics Canada for Tourism Canada and Transport Canada. The survey provides detailed information on travel by Canadians available at the provincial and, in some cases, subprovincial or "tourist region" level. Summaries of the results from each wave are released in a series of publications entitled *Canadian Travel Survey Research Bulletins* (1985b). A *Canadian Vacation Patterns Survey* (1984) is also conducted annually by Traveldata Ltd. for Tourism Canada which provides information on vacation travel by province. A number of international market studies are also conducted each year.

In the U.S., the United States Travel and Tourism Administration (USTTA) conducts a basic research program to collect and publish data on international tourism in terms of travel volume, receipts, and expenditures. In 1982, the USTTA implemented a quarterly *Survey of International Air Travelers* (1984a) to and from the United States. Extensive market segmentation analyses include breakdowns by U.S. regions visited. States and cities may contract for profiles of their visitors. Data from this survey have also been used in the U.S. Travel Data Center's Travel Economic Impact Model (1985a) to estimate foreign visitor expenditures and the payroll income, employment, and tax revenue generated for each state during 1983.

Since 1979, the U.S. Travel Data Center has been conducting a monthly National Travel Survey (1985c). Quarterly and annual summaries of the data collected, tabulated on a regional basis, are used by many travel offices to supplement other secondary data and primary research efforts. In addition, some states receive custom tabulations of the data, while others use the survey as a vehicle for collecting additional information of use in their marketing and promotion programs.

The majority of states and provinces also conduct original research to estimate the size and characteristics of their markets. Most commonly, counting procedures are employed at areas such as welcome/information centers and attractions to obtain estimates of levels of usage. In many cases, visitors are asked to complete registration forms which ask for information on origin, demographics, trip characteristics, expenditures, and, in some cases, attitudinal data as well. Respondents are frequently asked for their names and addresses, thus producing a list of actual travelers in the state or province who may then be contacted in follow-up surveys. While such an approach is cost-effective and relatively easy to administer, there is always the concern that visitors to particular areas or facilities may be different in a number of ways from those who do not visit and thus may not be representative of the total market. A recent study by Cadez and Hunt (1978), for example, found significant differences between visitor center stoppers and nonstoppers, particularly with regard to expenditures, duration, and purpose of trip.

Exit surveys are another popular way to collect market data. Most states and provinces conduct exit surveys periodically, usually on main highways or in air, bus, or rail terminals, but very few do so on an annual basis. Personal interviews are generally conducted, although in some cases mail-back questionnaires are distributed to be completed and returned later by respondents. A variation of this approach, the in-flight survey, is used rarely, although it is popular in states like Hawaii which are highly dependent on air arrivals. Major airlines utilize this approach extensively and in some cases may share data with states or provinces. Air Canada, for example, surveys most long-haul and a sampling of short-haul flights on a quarterly basis, and provides some of the resulting data to the provinces.

Other types of survey research, for example, mail or telephone surveys with travelers at home, are conducted less frequently. Studies of this type usually focus on nonresident travel, although a few of the provinces have in recent years conducted domestic travel surveys of their residents. An example of this type of study is the *Ontario Travel Survey* (Ministry of Tourism 1984). *Identifying Traveler Markets: Research Methodologies* contains useful guidelines and suggestions for conducting survey research (Belden Associates 1978).

The research methodologies described above provide the following types of data: counts of travelers which may be used to estimate total demand; descriptive data on trip characteristics, such as duration, mode of transportation, purpose of trip, accommodations used, and expenditures; and information on traveler characteristics, such as origin and socioeconomic characteristics. From these data, traveler profiles are compiled.

Although less common, traveler profiles may also include other types of information, such as psychographic data. Psychographic research attempts to identify characteristics of consumers that may affect their response to various products, advertising, and promotional efforts. The variables most frequently investigated include psychological characteristics, such as self-concept, lifestyle data which deal with time and monetary allocations of individual consumers, and measures of attitudes, interests, and opinions (often known as AIOs). *Lifestyle and Psychographics*, published by the American Marketing Association, provides a number of examples of the use of this type of analysis in marketing research (Wells 1974).

Other types of psychologically oriented market research include investigations of the informational needs of travelers and assessments of the usefulness of informational materials currently produced by the travel office, user evaluations of facilities and services, and studies of how visitors view the state/province as a travel destination. Less frequently conducted are studies designed to study psychological processes such as motivation, how travel decisions are made, and constraints on travel.

Federal offices in both the United States and Canada conduct psychologically oriented travel research. The USTTA has recently conducted surveys in Australia, France, Japan, Mexico, the United Kingdom, and West Germany to determine the U.S. market share of travelers from each of these countries. The surveys also identified sources of information and levels of awareness of specific U.S. destinations among respondents. Further, the relative importance of various touristic attributes and the relative ratings of the U.S. against competing destinations for each attribute were measured (USTTA 1985).

Tourism Canada has undertaken an extensive motivational study, but one focused on its own residents. The study, *Canadian Tourism Attitude and Motivation Study* (1985c), identified and described the size, travel characteristics, and attitudinal and demographic characteristics of pleasure travel markets within Canada. The study also investigated basic pleasure travel motivations, including lifestyle, vacation style, benefit segments, and product/activity needs in Canada. A similar study of U.S. residents, *U.S. Pleasure Travel Study*, has also recently been completed by The Longwoods Research Group for Tourism Canada (1986).

Many travel researchers believe that states and provinces, in their leadership role, should be conducting more basic research, thus helping to advance the state of research technology. It has been argued that if travel research is to advance beyond its present level of development, a shift from collecting only macrolevel, descriptive data to one in which microlevel and more psychologically oriented research is included as well is essential (Ritchie 1975).

The types of research discussed above are all used to determine primary travel markets for the state or province. Market analysis also involves identification of new markets and estimation of their potential. As in analysis of existing markets, potential markets are frequently segmented by geographic area. Information on residents of those areas is then collected through the use of secondary data, such as that produced by the U.S. Bureau of the Census or Statistics Canada, and special household surveys. The demographic, psychographic, and travel characteristics of present and potential markets may then be compared in an attempt to identify those markets having the most potential for producing travel to the state or province.

PROGRAM EVALUATION

The research projects previously discussed all become part of the travel office's evaluation research program. Continuing data on the volume and characteristics of travelers to the state/province or to particular facilities and areas provide information useful in monitoring the effectiveness of various marketing strategies over time and suggest ways to increase market share. Impact analysis allows travel officials to demonstrate in meaningful and understandable terms the importance of their programs and provide quantitative measures of the success of various programs. Psychological studies provide information useful in evaluating current information programs, such as distribution of literature to consumers.

A major component of many evaluation research programs is advertising research. Advertising typically represents one of the largest items in the travel office budget. It is not surprising, therefore, that travel offices place advertising evaluation among their top research priorities.

Advertising research is conducted for a variety of purposes. These include investigation of the need for advertising, identification of specific ads and media most likely to be successful, and measurement of the effectiveness of advertising campaigns, in terms of changes in consumer awareness, visitor volume, and/or travel-related sales.

Types of advertising evaluation research most frequently conducted by state and provincial travel offices are:

1 Coupon conversion studies.

2 Pre- and postadvertising studies to measure impact of advertising on awareness and attitudes.

3 Pretests of alternative advertisements, media, and/or exposure time.

The most common type of advertising research utilized in the United States is the coupon conversion study, conducted annually by nearly half of all state travel offices. Advertisements are often directed toward stimulating inquiries and, when placed in magazines or newspapers, contain a coupon for readers to return requesting additional information on the advertised destination. A coupon conversion study can range from the single counting of the number of coupons returned by origin to surveying, usually by mail, those returning coupons to determine their attitudes and behavior since requesting the information. While the actual methodology used to conduct coupon conversion studies varies widely among travel offices, the primary measure of interest is the "conversion rate," an estimate of the number of people who saw the ad and converted this perception into an actual visit (Muha 1976).

Conversion rate estimates can be used in conjunction with information on the cost of particular advertising campaigns to determine the cost per conversion, a measure useful in comparing the relative effectiveness of different advertisements and use of different media.

Additional data collected through coupon conversion studies include demographic and trip characteristics, and in some cases expenditure data, useful in comparing the effectiveness of an advertising campaign across various market segments. These data are also frequently used in some general market analysis.

It should be noted that coupon conversion studies conducted by mail may produce biased results. Experience has shown that coupon returners who subsequently visited the state/province advertised have a higher propensity to respond to a survey than those who did not visit. This can result in a highly inflated conversion rate. It has been recommended that to minimize this problem telephone surveys or mail surveys, with several follow-up mailings and increasing incentives, be used whenever possible (Hunt and Dalton 1983).

A type of advertising research most popular in Canada, but also conducted at least occasionally by many states, is impact evaluation surveys. This approach is designed to measure changes in attitudes toward, or awareness of, the destination being promoted. Generally conducted by telephone, a sample of people in the target market is interviewed before and after placement of the ad and their responses to the pre- and postadvertising studies can then be compared to measure change.

Finally, prior to introducing an advertising campaign, some travel offices conduct research to measure the relative effectiveness of a number of different ads, different media, and a number of other variables such as exposure times. Travel-related companies with large budgets use this method continuously to design the most effective adertising programs possible. Among Canadian offices, more than half conduct such research at least annually, while the incidence is much lower in state travel offices.

IDENTIFICATION OF TRAVEL AND TOURISM RESOURCES

Another major objective of research is to describe the travel/tourism product by compiling an inventory of travel-related business establishments, natural, scenic, and cultural attractions, and special events within the state or province.

Nearly all states and provinces have, at some point, compiled such inventories and more than half of all offices in both countries do so on an annual basis. An example of an inventory of travel/tourism resources is contained in the *Delaware Tourism Policy Study* (U.S. Travel Data Center and Fothergill/Beekuis Associates 1979). Guidelines for preparing such an inventory are provided in Part II of Volume II of the series of publications entitled *Tourism USA* (University of Missouri 1978, pp. 31–41).

From a travel/tourism resource inventory, geographic and industry areas suffering from lack of investment may be identified. Areas heavily involved in planning and development, particularly in Canada, are active in this area of research and conduct a number of studies to identify investment opportunities, assess development potential, and examine the feasibility of various development programs.

Research on the travel/tourism plant is crucial to the formulation of comprehensive development plans, to securing further investment and locating geographic and industry areas suffering from lack of investment, and to identifying travel industry sectors which might benefit most from cooperative advertising and promotional efforts.

MONITORING TRAVEL ACTIVITY OVER TIME

A final objective of state/provincial travel research is to continually monitor travel activity in an effort to determine how the travel product and markets, economic and other impacts of travel on the state or province, and effectiveness of travel office programs change over time.

In some respects, the monitoring objective is similar to evaluation research, in both purpose and data requirements. Much of the information collected through a travel office's market research program may be used in conjunction with other readily available information to analyze the effects of a number of situational and transient factors, such as adverse weather conditions and gasoline shortages, on travel demand. In some cases, however, additional research, designed to address previously unresearched areas, may be needed.

Some other types of research most frequently conducted by travel offices to monitor travel activity over time are:

1 Studies of seasonal variation in travel demand.
2 Studies of effects of external factors, such as gasoline shortages, inflation, and weather conditions.
3 Forecasting studies.

Studies of seasonal variation in travel demand are popular in both the U.S. and Canada and may be readily conducted by analyzing existing data from market research studies. The information generated is valuable in identifying peak seasons and in suggesting ways to increase demand during shoulder periods.

Investigations of the effects of gasoline shortages or higher prices have been conducted by a majority of travel offices in recent years. Studies of other situational factors such as inflation, increased travel costs, and adverse weather conditions, while less common, have been conducted by travel offices as needed.

Forecasting studies are another type of research falling most logically within this group. Research of this type attempts to project what the future holds for travel and tourism in the state or province based on a number of different scenarios. Generally uncommon in state and provincial research programs, forecasting research has been conducted by a number of government, industry, and academic groups, as evidenced by the substantial number of studies listed in the report entitled *Forecasting Travel and Tourism: An Annotated Bibliography* (Green and Nichols 1979).

Most simply, time series, trend, and regression analysis may be used to project future demand based on current travel trends. Travel office researchers, however, often go beyond this and use secondary population and other types of data, as well as research on the effects of various factors, to produce different assumptions upon which forecasts may be made. The most sophisticated approach in this area is the development of large-scale econometric models which take into account all major international, national, state/provincial, and local factors affecting travel.

One last approach receiving some attention, particularly in the academic community, is the Delphi Technique (Hawkins, Shafer, and Rovelstad 1980). This technique is discussed in more detail in Chapter 34.

A travel monitoring system should be, therefore, the basic goal of a travel office's research department. Through creative use of data produced through other projects, in addition to studies designed to meet special needs, a travel office can develop such a system which will help ensure the success of its marketing and promotion programs.

DEVELOPMENT OF A COMPREHENSIVE TRAVEL RESEARCH PROGRAM

This chapter has focused on the research needs and objectives of state and provincial travel offices, and on the major techniques used to conduct research. To summarize the major points, this section reviews major steps to be taken and issues to be considered in establishing a comprehensive travel research program.

ASSESS RESEARCH NEEDS

Before implementing any changes in an existing research program or establishing a new one, the research needs of the particular state or province should be reviewed and discussed with other members of the travel office staff, as well as all potential users of the data to be produced. Two major elements to be considered in such an analysis include the requirements of other data users and the present level and usefulness of research conducted by the travel office. A thorough review of available data sources, many of which are discussed in this chapter, as well as discussions with officials from other travel offices, should also be part of this assessment process. Other factors, such as the current contribution of the travel industry to the state/provincial economy and the level of support given the industry by citizens and legislators, should also be considered.

CONSIDER LIMITATIONS

State and provincial travel offices currently face a number of difficulties in developing a comprehensive travel research program. The U.S. Travel Data Center survey of travel office research activities asked respondents to rate the seriousness of a number of obstacles facing travel officials in developing such a program. The most serious problems according to respondents were:

- budget constraints
- limited staff/time
- complexity of factors affecting travel industry today
- lack of research training among staff members
- lack of reliable travel research methods
- lack of a workable data collection system

Among travel offices in both the United States and Canada, the most serious problem perceived by officials involves limited resources, both in terms of funding and staff. In the U.S., for example, research budgets averaged $85,000 per state during fiscal year 1984–1985. Further, only about one-third of all state travel offices have a full-time researcher on staff.

If money is available to conduct research but staff members are not, the travel office might consider contracting with an outside organization, such as a university, research center, or consulting firm with known expertise in the field of travel and tourism research.

Travel officials also concur that the complexity of factors affecting the travel industry today makes it difficult to design a comprehensive program. Situations such as gasoline shortages, which are a major deterrent to travel one year, may be replaced the next year by some other problem requiring specialized research.

Respondents appear to be less concerned with the research methodologies and data sources available today, although most reported minor problems and suggested that there is room for improvement. Most officials, however, indicated that they have the computer technology and facilities needed to conduct research and that they have experienced little problem with lack of cooperation from other segments of the travel industry in their states or provinces.

When designing a research program, such limitations should be seriously considered. The needs analysis will help determine which research projects should be conducted, while a review of available resources for such projects will suggest how much research can realistically be undertaken.

ESTABLISH PRIORITIES

A comprehensive program of continuing travel research is necessarily an ambitious project. The ultimate goal should be the development, over time, of a research program which includes the five types of research discussed in this chapter, conducted on a continuing and consistent basis. Most importantly, the program should be designed to complement and to provide data necessary to the effective implementation of other travel office programs.

It is doubtful that any state or provincial travel office can implement all elements of such a program immediately, given current research budgets. By considering available resources in conjunction with a thorough needs assessment, travel officials should be able to determine priorities for the various types of research discussed.

Further, as each research project is being designed, those involved should consider methods of collecting data which will be useful to other types of analyses and continue to look for opportunities to expand their research activities.

INVESTIGATE ALTERNATIVES

Cooperation and creative use of research are two important ways that travel offices can expand their research programs substantially without incurring additional expenditures. Many travel offices cooperate with other organizations, such as universities, regional travel councils, tourism associations, and other state/provincial agencies, as well as companies in the private sector, on travel research programs. This is particularly true in the United States, where research budgets tend to be substantially smaller than among provincial travel offices.

Hawaii, for example, has an excellent research program, focusing particularly on market research. The program includes monthly counts of visitors by origin, plus sophisticated analyses of origin/destination, purpose, expenditure, and socioeconomic characteristics data. The program is made possible in large part through cooperation among the Hawaii Visitors' Bureau and a number of travel-related firms such as transportation carriers, banks, travel agencies, and hotels, as well as the University of Hawaii.

A somewhat different type of success story, but equally instructive, is the case of the state of Michigan. Recently, the travel office implemented a research program designed to better define current and potential market segments, to determine the economic impact of tourism on the economy at that time, and to evaluate present advertising and promotional programs. The results of the multipart program helped identify untapped markets with high potential for growth, demonstrated where advertisements should be increased or introduced, provided useful information for new product development, and, perhaps most importantly, impressed Michigan legislators sufficiently to boost the travel office budget from $1.8 million in 1976 to $2.3 million in 1977 and $3.7 million in 1979. Its budget for 1984–1985 was $9.1 million, the sixth largest in the U.S. With increased funding, the travel office has established monitoring and tracking systems to collect necessary travel and tourism data. An article in the *Journal of Travel Research* describes the Michigan program in more detail (Bryant and Morrison 1980).

MONITOR RESEARCH PROGRAMS

Finally, if possible, at least one staff member should be assigned to research as a full-time responsibility. This individual would be responsible for monitoring the program, reviewing the quality of the information being produced, and assessing its usefulness to others in both the travel office and travel industry in marketing the state or province effectively as a travel destination.

It is also recommended that a research advisory committee, made up of major users of the research conducted by the travel office, be established to meet once a year to set program priorities for the following year. While new projects may be proposed to address newly emerging problems of opportunities, it is important that the basic types of research discussed in this chapter continue to be conducted regularly to provide a data base of market, economic impact, and other types of information necessary to the effective operations of the travel office.

Research in state and provincial travel offices has often been a neglected part of the overall program. This chapter has attempted to provide an overview of the current levels of research at the state and provincial level, to suggest those areas most important for inclusion in a comprehensive travel research program, and to offer some guidelines in the establishment of such a program.

It is hoped that as travel officials learn more about the research activities of other offices and become increasingly aware of the value of a continuing and consistent research program, such programs will grow and increase in sophistication in the future.

REFERENCES

Belden Associates (1978), *Identifying Traveler Markets: Research Methodologies*, Washington, D.C.: U.S. Government Printing Office.

Bryant, Barbara E., and Andrew J. Morrison (1980), "Travel Market Segmentation and the Implementation of Market Strategies," *Journal of Travel Research*, 18 (Winter), 2–8.

Bureau of Management Consulting, Canadian (1975a), *Tourism Expenditure Model, a Functional Planning and Policy Making Tool*, Ottawa: Department of Supply and Services.

Bureau of Management Consulting, Canadian (1975b), *Tourism Impact Model*, Ottawa: Department of Supply and Services.

Cadez, Gary, and John D. Hunt (1978), *A Comparison between Port-of-Entry Visitor Center Users and Nonusers*, Logan, Utah: Institute for Outdoor Recreation and Tourism, Utah State University.

Council of State Governments, The (1979), *Tourism: State Structure, Organization and Support: A Technical Study*, Washington, D.C.: U.S. Government Printing Office.

Goeldner, C.R., and Karen Dicke (1980), *Bibliography of Tourism and Travel Research Studies Reports and Articles*, Boulder: University of Colorado and The Travel Research Association.

Green, Susan, and Jan L. Nichols (1979), *Forecasting Travel and Tourism: An Annotated Bibliography*, Washington, D.C.: U.S. Travel Data Center.

Hawkins, Donald E., Elwood L. Shafer, and James M. Rovelstad, Eds. (1980), *Summary of Recommendations: International Symposium of Tourism and the Next Decade*, Washington, D.C.: The George Washington University.

Hunt, J., and M. Dalton (1983), "Comparing Mail and Telephone for Conducting Coupon Conversion Studies," *Journal of Travel Research*, 21 (Winter), 16–18.

Longwoods Research Group, The (1986), *U.S. Pleasure Travel Study*, Ottawa, Tourism Canada.

Ministry of Tourism, Ontario (1984), *Ontario Travel Survey*, Toronto: Ontario Ministry of Tourism.

Muha, Steve (1976), *Evaluating Travel Advertising: A Survey of Existing Studies*, Washington, D.C.: U.S. Travel Data Center.

Ontario Research Council on Leisure, The (1977), *Analysis, Methods and Techniques for Recreation and Leisure Studies*, Ottawa: Environment Canada.

Pizam, Abraham (1978), "Tourism's Impact: The Social Costs to the Destination Community as Perceived by Its Residents," *Journal of Travel Research*, 16 (Spring), 8—12.

Ritchie, J.R. Brent (1975), "Some Critical Aspects of Measurement Theory and Practice in Research," *Journal of Travel Research*, 14 (Spring), 1—10.

Statistics Canada (1980), *Canadian Travel Survey: Canadians Traveling in Canada*, Ottawa: Statistics Canada.

Tourism Canada (1985a), *Canadian Travel Research Notes*, Ottawa: Tourism Canada.

Tourism Canada (1985b), *Canadian Travel Survey Research Bulletins*, Ottawa: Tourism Canada.

Tourism Canada (1985c), *Canadian Tourism Attitude and Motivation Study*, Ottawa: Tourism Canada.

Traveldata Ltd. (1984), *Canadian Vacation Patterns Survey*, Ottawa: Tourism Canada.

Travel Data Center, U.S. (1975), *Travel Economic Impact Model, Volume I, Final Economic Analysis Methodology*, Washington, D.C.: U.S. Travel Data Center.

Travel Data Center, U.S. (1978), *Travel Data Locator Index, Second Edition*, Washington, D.C.: U.S. Travel Data Center.

Travel Data Center, U.S. and Fothergill/Beekhuis Associates (1979), *Delaware Tourism Policy Study*, Dover: Delaware State Travel Service.

Travel Data Center, U.S. (1980), *Survey of State/Provincial Travel Office Research Programs*, unpublished study, Washington, D.C.: U.S. Travel Data Center.

Travel Data Center, U.S. (1985a), *Impact of Foreign Visitors on State Economies. 1983*, prepared for the U.S. Travel and Tourism Administration, Washington, D.C.: U.S. Travel Data Center.

Travel Data Center, U.S. (1985b), *1984—85 Survey of State Travel Offices*, Washington, D.C.: U.S. Travel Data Center.

Travel Data Center, U.S. (1985c), *1984 National Travel Survey Full Year Report*, Washington, D.C.: U.S. Travel Data Center.

Travel and Tourism Administration, U.S. (1984a), *Survey of International Air Travelers*, Washington, D.C.: U.S. Travel Data Center.

Travel and Tourism Administration, U.S. (1984b), *Twenty-eighth Program Report: 1983*, Washington, D.C.: U.S. Government Printing Office.

Travel and Tourism Administration, U.S. (1985), *USTTA Travel Market Surveys: Consumer Surveys of Six Individual Country Markets*, Washington, D.C.: U.S. Travel and Tourism Administration.

Travel Service, U.S. (1977), *Analysis of Travel Definitions, Terminology and Research Needs among States and Cities*, Washington, D.C.: U.S. Travel Service.

University of Missouri (1978), *Tourism USA*, Washington, D.C.: U.S. Government Printing Office.

Wells, William D., Ed. (1974), *Lifestyle and Psychographics*, Chicago: American Marketing Association.

14

Research on Urban Tourism Destinations

UEL BLANK

Professor

MICHAEL D. PETKOVICH

Research Assistant
University of Minnesota
Minneapolis, Minnesota

This chapter treats the pros, cons, and techniques of conducting urban area tourism research. Objectives that can be achieved with each type of research are discussed. The most detailed treatment is given to overall impact studies as a means toward improved understanding of urban tourism.

The discussion provides information about researching the tourism industry of an urban area. The reader is assumed to have interest in the subject. But researching your city's tourism is something that you cannot do alone; you need a great amount of support. For that reason the chapter begins by supplying some of the "whys" and "whats" of urban tourism research. It moves from there to overall responsibilities of a sponsor in such an effort. The bulk of the chapter is then devoted to pros, cons, and techniques of urban research methodologies.

THE URBAN AREA AS A SUBJECT OF TRAVEL RESEARCH

Urban places are major tourism destination areas. Despite this, urban tourism is almost certainly among the most misunderstood and underestimated of all tourism types. It suffers from underestimation—sometimes even unrecognition—by some who are major beneficiaries. How, in the present day, when economic segments appear to be carefully analyzed, can such oversights occur?

- Tourism is often defined in so restrictive a manner that major urban tourism segments fail to be counted as tourism. Examples of frequently omitted segments include those visiting friends and relatives, nonconvention business travelers, and individuals traveling on personal business.
- Urban economic sectors are ordinarily defined,

and their data displayed, such that most of tourism's economic impact is hidden. Standard Industrial Classifications (SICs) of the U.S. Census of Business show very few sectors that are recognized as tourism. Instead urban tourism is the sum of parts from a large number of the different SICs. Nearly every sector offering services or goods at retail participates directly in tourism sales.

- The diverse and heterogeneous nature of urban tourism makes it difficult to measure comprehensively and accurately.

The above are in addition, and partly related, to the long-standing problem that services sectors such as tourism have in being recognized as an industry. Services suffer particularly in contrast to manufacturing operations that produce a tangible, physical product. For this reason it is worth reviewing urban tourism's nature and its outputs to the community.

THE NATURE AND CONTRIBUTION OF URBAN TOURISM

The first and most important fact about urban tourism is that *every* city has a tourism industry. Tourism is or can be an important generator of profits, employment, rents, and tax in the same manner as other economic activities. Systematic attention to tourism development can pay off in terms of these economic benefits.

Tourism, for most urban areas, diverges markedly from popularly held concepts of tourism. Tourism is commonly thought of in simple terms as vacation travel. This restricted view of tourism limits it to recreation travel such as to the gambling casinos of Las Vegas, to relax in a fun-in-the-sun spot in Florida or Arizona, or to relive the nation's history at Williamsburg, Virginia. Most urban tourism, in contrast, is complex and heterogeneous.

Why this complexity? Because cities are concentration points for human interaction, part of which occurs between the city and its tourists. As indicated in Table 1, the nature of visitor interaction—their purpose for coming—differs greatly from one city to another.

Adding to this complexity are the following factors:

- Cities are, by definition, areas of high population density. Thus travel to "visit friends and relatives" ranks relatively high in many cities. These "visitors," because of their sheer numbers, exert a major impact upon the destination city.

- Most cities are major travel nodes. Nearly all owe their establishment and growth to an initial travel advantage. Because cities are the focal point of highways, railroads, and air and water routes, most who travel any distance must go to a city whether they wish to or not.

- Cities are the focal point for commerce, industry, and finance. For example, the Minneapolis–St. Paul SMSA has 40 percent of Minnesota's popula-

tion. But it has 53 percent of the value of retail trade, 73 percent of the value of wholesale trade, and 67 percent of the Minnesota "value added in manufacturing." All of these commerce and industry activities require a flow of travel and people interaction. An adequate set of hospitality businesses is needed to service this travel. Thus the tourism plant is essential to all components of the SMSA's economy.

- Just as commerce and industry concentrate in cities, so do all manner of people services. These include health care, education, government, and headquarters for religious, industry, other special interest groups, and associations. Concentration of these services in cities often creates the critical mass that allows a higher level of quality to be offered. Travel from a distance is attracted to take advantage of this superior quality of services.

- Cities offer a wide variety of cultural, artistic, and recreational experiences. These vary from opera performances to major sports, from art exhibits to nightclubs, and from historical interpretation to zoos. These are available not only to residents but also attract tourists. Tourists' purchases of these services often make possible facilities and programs of a quality that the resident population could not otherwise afford.

Because of the rich variety of activities and attractions offered by the city, most travel to cities is multipurpose. That is, most travelers undertake more than one activity while there (Blank and Petkovich, 1980). They usually have a major purpose, such as to make sales contacts, but they may also attend a theatre performance in the evening. Studies in the Minneapolis–St. Paul SMSA have shown that those whose purpose for coming is to "visit friends" also generate a large volume of retail purchases in addition to participating in

TABLE 1 Tourists to Selected SMSAs by Purpose for Travel (Percentage of Person-Trips) 1977

PURPOSE	ORLANDO FLA.	INDIANAPOLIS IND.	WILMINGTON N.C.	PORTLAND OREG.
Visit friends and relatives	18	38	27	29
Business/convention	12	30	10	30
Outdoor recreation	6	3	47	3
Entertainment/sightsee	53	8	10	13
Personal	5	13	2	17
Shopping	1	0	0	3
Other	5	8	4	5
	100	100	100	100

Source: 1977 U.S. Census of Travel.

many other activities. Thirty-three percent of 1977 travelers to Washington, D.C., reported "work or convention" purposes for travel, but it may be hypothesized that a high proportion of these also went to the theatre and/or sightseeing in the nation's capital. Each city will have its own distinctive mix of visitor activities and socioeconomic market types.

Patterns of overnight lodging will vary widely depending on the urban area. In some cases, and for some purposes, tourists staying in hotels and motels may adequately define the tourist population. Usually, however, the tourist definition will need to be wider. In many cities the person-nights spent by tourists in the homes of friends and relatives will substantially outnumber nights in commercial lodging. For many purposes tourists not staying overnight represent a component that, in the interests of defining the city's ability to attract travel, cannot be overlooked. Such segmentation of tourists according to lodging patterns can add depth to understanding a given city's tourism.

Finally, as already partially noted, for most cities travelers may come by a wide variety of travel modes. This, again, is in contrast to some recreational destinations where one mode of travel may predominate. Cities grow because of travel access which usually includes nearly all modes. Island locations such as Honolulu and Hong Kong are exceptions.

Urban tourism will be seen as complexly varied, with each city having a unique set of amenity attractions, hospitality services, geography, and travel systems. These factors add to the difficulty of research in urban tourism. But proper investigation will reveal the rich tapestry of social and economic interaction of which your city's tourism consists.

SPONSORING GROUP RESPONSIBILITIES IN RESEARCHING YOUR CITY'S TOURISM

This section reviews briefly the overall responsibilities of the sponsoring organization for your city's tourism. These points are covered in detail in other sections of this Handbook. They are summarized here for the convenience of those primarily interested in urban tourism.

The first and most important task of the sponsoring group is to answer this question—"What do we want to know about our city's tourism?" In all probability a problem arose that made you think of conducting tourism research. What is this problem? Who brought it up?

A first response to the above key question may be "we need to know everything." Such a response is useless; no research or research series can yield all knowledge. The problem must be sharply defined and priorities established: What is the *most important* information need?

Closely related to problem refinement is the definition of "tourism" and "tourists." Only the sponsoring group can define a tourist, because it must fit their research purposes. Beware of too narrow a definition. To avoid this, it is suggested that you think first of *all nonresidents who enter your city as tourists.* Then systematically eliminate those in each group who are *not* to be included. For most purposes commuters are excluded. Will you exclude all travelers living within 50 miles? 100 miles? Will you exclude those not staying overnight in commercial lodging? In many cities this would amount to excluding 70 to 95 percent of the visitor person-trips. Will you exclude those traveling on business? If you make this exclusion what will you do with those business travelers who stay an extra day and attend a football game, or attend a theatrical performance in the evening, or whose spouses accompany them? In any event, be sure that you have thought the matter through thoroughly.

You, the sponsor, must define the scope and scale of the research. These in turn will be dictated by the purposes, resources available, and time limits. Resources include money, but they also include ready availability of reliable research advice, existing data about your city and its tourism, and the sponsor's capability to conduct the work or oversee it adequately. Time limits come into play if data are needed within, for example, six months. In this situation it will not be possible to collect data over a 12-month period. All of these factors have a bearing on the nature of the research that is done.

The sponsor is responsible for the accuracy of the research results. This may come as a surprise—but there is no way to avoid final responsibility for findings produced. This is true even if you hire a professional to conduct the actual research. It underscores the need to be familiar with other sections of this Handbook. You need not necessarily know a lot about statistical methods and statistical probabilities, but you must be sure that these are known and applied by whoever designs the research. You must be able to evaluate procedures, oversee them, and be certain that they accomplish established research objectives.

Finally, and most importantly, the payoff! You must put the research to work: Make it widely available and use it to stimulate and help direct the development of your urban area's tourism. For detailed suggestions, see the section of this chapter "Getting Mileage out of the Research."

RESEARCH PROCEDURES— ARE PRIMARY DATA NEEDED?

A key procedural question concerns whether "secondary data" can be used for your city's research. These are data collected and published by others. The alternative is to collect data yourself. This is called "primary data." Primary data collection is expensive and time-consuming.

You may wish to refer to the following chapter for a discussion of secondary data sources of travel and tourism. What data are already available for your city that fit your purposes?

Most research projects require the use of both primary and secondary data. Despite its costs there are at least four major reasons for gathering primary data about tourists to your city.

- Your city, every city, is unique. If you wish to know about tourists to your city it is often necessary to study them specifically. Table 1 illustrates the great variety among cities' tourism patterns.

- Primary data can be gathered that fits your specific purposes. Every secondary data set has within it an implicit definition of the industry or population that it describes. Seldom will this definition fit your purposes exactly.

- If you need data about travelers to your city the best information can usually be achieved by questioning these travelers specifically about their trip to your city. Few secondary data sources of this kind are available.

- If your overall purpose is tourism industry development, the conduct of a major tourism study may be an efficient early step to this end. Such a study should involve many individuals and agencies who are thus alerted to the research and sensitized to tourism. This participation is essential in order that they understand, believe, and take part in follow-up activities.

These factors can assist your thinking as you study the next section and formulate your overall research strategy.

TOURISM RESEARCH TYPES FOR URBAN AREAS

Table 2 summarizes examples of major tourism types that are applicable to urban areas. The list in this table can be helpful in thinking through your own research priorities. None of these types applies exclusively to urban areas and nowhere else. Therefore most are treated in other chapters. However, whatever type or types of research are employed it must be adapted to the purposes and nature of the given city. Each type is discussed briefly below.

URBAN TOURISM IMPACT RESEARCH

Impact research is used to assess the scale, economic returns, overall markets, and economic segments involved in tourism. When repeated it may be used to monitor progress. It may be of two kinds: the assess-

ment of a single event or the assessment of a certain tourist type, such as convention travel studies done by the International Association of Convention and Visitors Bureaus (IACVB). It may be an overall measurement of impacts and markets for the entire metropolitan area. Because overall studies of urban tourism are relatively rare up until this time, detailed treatment is given to procedures for this latter research in the next separate section.

URBAN MARKETING RESEARCH

Specialized market research can be used to estimate market potential for given facilities and services, or as a guide to kinds of facilities and services needed. It can help answer questions such as: Are transportation facilities adequate? What is the profit potential for added lodging? Can a major sports stadium, recreational park, or art museum attract sufficient paying users?

In another form, marketing research can determine the effectiveness of specific promotional efforts. It can also measure response to educational awareness programs for residents. The reader is referred to other chapters of the Handbook for further marketing research details.

TOURISM FACILITY MANAGEMENT AND PERSONNEL TRAINING NEEDS RESEARCH

Visitor image research can be helpful in guiding the management and development of facilities and services and/or to measure need for service personnel training. Visitors are asked to report their satisfactions (and dissatisfactions) with facilities, services, and treatment by personnel. Usually qualitative results are sufficient, that is, the responses need not be aggregated into an accurate overall total, as long as reasonable care is taken to get responses from a random group of travelers. This greatly simplifies the operation. On the other hand, a high degree of sophistication is required in design and administration of the questionnaire.

RESEARCHING CITY ATTITUDES TOWARD TOURISM

Urban tourism is a community affair, that is, a wide segment of the businesses and citizens is involved in it. It may be useful to determine the extent of citizen, employee, and business manager understanding of tourism. Questions may be treated ranging from knowledge of tourism's economic role in the economy and/or in their own businesses, feelings toward visitors, and family use of city amenities to their personal role in hosting visitors—family, business, international, etc.

THE CITY'S TOURISM PLANT

Assessing the nature of your tourism facilities, services, and attractions could be viewed more as simple

TABLE 2   Types of Urban Tourism Research

TYPE	OBJECTIVES TO:	PROCEDURAL EXAMPLES AND SUGGESTIONS
I Impact		
Overall Impact and Markets Dollars; Visitors	—Assess scale and value of city's tourism —Measure market types —Monitor progress	—Include all tourism segments and all relevant industries —Cover a 12-month period —Multiple procedures required
Single Event or Traveler Segment	—Assess scale or value of event or segment —Measure market types —Monitor progress	—Tally "registrations" where applicable —Contact a random sample of travelers during the event
II Marketing		
Advertising Effectiveness	—Determine results from a specific marketing/promotional effort	—Track responses to ad —Household surveys of target areas (mail, telephone)
Market Potential	—Determine target audience for marketing efforts —Provide guide to scale of market	—Household surveys of target areas (mail, telephone) —Survey predetermined travel types while in city, at home, or at business
III Development/Training Needs		
Visitor Image	—Guide development of facilities and services —Guide training programs for personnel	—Question, in person, a random sample of visitors using target services —Survey a sample who register at a given service (mail, telephone) —Marketing research procedure may be adapted to this use
IV Resident		
Citizens	—Determine citizen attitudes toward the tourism industry —Determine activities of residents in support of tourism	—Survey resident households (in person, mail, telephone)
Business Managers/Employees	—Determine understanding and attitudes toward tourism —Determine positive attitudes toward tourism —Determine positive actions in support of tourism	—Survey business managers —Survey employees in selected business types
V Tourism Plant		
Facilities/Services	—Prepare a definitive list of services available to tourists —Determine the physical scale and geographical distribution of tourism services —Determine the qualitative range of the tourism plant	—Gather by geographic jurisdictions; use telephone directories, association lists, brainstorming by knowledgeable people —Gather by industry classes

inventorying than as research. But in another view this operation is the complement to market research: What is there to attract and serve the visitor? The variety and volume of the urban tourism plant are astonishing. A Minneapolis–St. Paul investigation conducted in 1969 found over 8,000 different operations, sites, and organizations. These were distributed through 270 catego-ries (Blank and Numerich, 1969). The definitions, classifications, and search procedures required for this effort demand systematic knowledge of tourism as well as considerable ingenuity. Systematic knowledge about the urban tourism plant serves as one measure of impact, provides a basis for contact with managers having direct interest in tourism, is necessary data in judgments about tourism service development, and is a needed input into information systems that answer travelers' questions.

RESEARCHING OVERALL IMPACT AND MARKETS

Research of overall tourism impact on urban areas is treated here in detail as a sequel to the opening thesis of this chapter: most urban tourism studies investigate only parts of the traveler pattern. Hence there is widespread underestimation and misunderstanding of urban tourism. As a serious consequence, many urban leaders give tourism less support than if its true role were more clearly defined. Further, market studies, which must often be limited in scope, are best undertaken in full knowledge of the total market. This knowledge can only be obtained by means of an overall study.

Researching the full scope of your city's tourism impact usually means conducting a coordinated set of research investigations. This is dictated by the complex nature of urban tourism. Information from secondary sources must often be complemented and qualified by primary data which are gathered to define specific tourism segments.

Usually a number of different questionnaires must be designed. Air travelers may require a different approach than automobile travelers. A questionnaire designed for hotel establishments will usually not fit a major sports stadium.

Consider "boxing in" your estimate of tourist segments using all data sources that are available. For example, suppose that you are estimating total expenditures for lodging using data from a sample of travelers. Are there also estimates of city lodging revenues generated by sales tax collections and/or the Census of Business? These should be investigated and compared. Estimates from your research may be different. But, if this is the case, you must be able to explain *why* your estimate differs.

A similar test of the reasonableness of tourism estimates should be made whenever possible, even for those items where tourist expenditures represent only a fraction of total sales. For example, gasoline sales to tourists at filling stations may be only 10 to 15 percent of the total. Interviews with knowledgeable petroleum dealers may be helpful. Total gallons of gasoline sold in the area may be available from an agency licensing such sales. Restaurant and theatre sales to tourists may be similarly checked. The procedure can sometimes help avoid major errors. One added caveat is in order: secondary sources of data may also be subject to error, sometimes large error. Again, data of a given activity from two different sources may not agree but there should be an explanation for the disagreement.

INDUSTRY APPROACH TO OVERALL IMPACT

The most commonly used approach to overall impact measurement of urban area tourism is by industries. The procedure makes use of data of the Standard Industrial Classifications (SIC) of businesses that make sales to tourists. The percentage of sales to tourists in each SIC group is multiplied by total sales and the results from all of the groups summed to determine total dollar impact.

The principal SIC classes used for this purpose are:

SIC 70 —Lodging.
SIC 58 —Food and beverage.
SIC 55 and 75—Automobile transportation.
SIC 78 and 79—Entertainment.
SIC 53 and 59—Retail purchases.

A review of all SIC classes will reveal others that may be important tourist sales generators in a given urban setting. Included may be a wide range of retail sales operations, health services, legal services, museums, etc.

The method has the advantage of yielding a total impact estimate quickly and inexpensively. This assumes that satisfactory percentage breakdowns of tourist sales by SIC groups are available from other studies. Disadvantages include problems of inaccuracy if SIC tourist sales percentages from other studies are used. Each city has a unique tourism pattern and it will be inadequately shown using this method. This disadvantage can be overcome by surveys in representative types of operations by SIC groupings to determine the actual percentage of sales made to tourists. Full accuracy requires actual checks of a sample of purchasers at the time of purchase. It also requires that it be conducted throughout the year.

Retail sales groups may be particularly subject to error. Studies have found this to be the major metro tourism expenditure (Blank and Petkovich, 1979a). But since tourists' purchases are only 10 to 20 percent of total sales of these types of operations, exact measures using random checks of sales are subject to problems of statistical variation.

Another limitation of the industry approach is the lack of data about the market: Who are the tourists? What are their characteristics? Data from the U.S. Census of Travel that are available for certain SMSAs can be used to provide some of this market information. Further, if direct studies of purchases are conducted, as discussed in the preceding paragraph, market data can also be gathered by the same means.

HOUSEHOLD APPROACH TO OVERALL IMPACT

U.S. Census of Travel estimates are made from interviews of households. Impact data for selected large SMSAs are available from this source. Some proprietary research groups have also employed this method. Given the present state of the art, the method appears to be useful for general measures or limited specific information. Thus far, fully comprehensive studies of a given city's tourism impact have not been conducted using a household survey as the primary method.

A TRAVELER APPROACH TO OVERALL IMPACT

This approach, in its most comprehensive form, consists of interviewing travelers while they are in the act of traveling. It offers potential for yielding the most complete data obtainable from one study about tourism dollars, activity impact, and market characteristics. But the method is difficult and expensive to use and because of its complexities easily subject to errors.

This section treats the gathering of primary and secondary data about urban tourists by specific travel modes. These include air, bus, train, water, and auto/truck. In some cities with controlled means of access

this procedure may be relatively easily used. Heartland cities, which are freely accessible by automobile, will find its application more difficult. But, because of the comprehensive understanding of tourism thus obtained, it merits serious attention by any urban area wishing to emphasize development of its tourism industry.

Table 3 lists the several travel modes. It gives suggestions for secondary data sources and primary data gathering procedures. The accompanying discussion expands on the outline in Table 3. Since most cities operate as year-round tourist attractors, observations taken through a 12-month period will be most accurate and yield the most information.

Scheduled air flights Scheduled air flights are perhaps the easiest type of transportation mode about which to collect primary and secondary data. The Federal Aviation Agency requires airports to keep records on the number of passengers arriving and departing each day, and this information can be of great value.

TABLE 3 Urban Travel Modes

TRAVEL MODE	EXAMPLES OF SECONDARY DATA	EXAMPLES OF PRIMARY DATA METHODS
Scheduled Air	Data of passenger arrivals and departures from airport management	—Interview passengers in boarding areas —Give mail-back diary on arrival while in baggage area
Charter Air	Data of passenger arrivals and departures from airport management	—Interview passengers in boarding area (note: permission may be difficult to obtain)
Private Air (General Aviation)	Takeoffs and landings from airport management	—Interview pilots (note: lack of schedule makes this difficult)
Scheduled Bus	Bus arrivals and departures from bus company	—Interview passengers in the boarding area
Charter Bus	Data from U.S. Tour Operators Association and related groups	—Questionnaire to hotel sales managers —Questionnaire to tour operators
School Bus	Limited useful data available	—Mail questionnaire to schools in travel range
Train	Data of passenger arrivals and departures from Amtrak	—Interview passengers in boarding area —Give mail-back diary on arrival
Water	Data from port authority; Operational data from locks	—Questionnaire to commercial operations —Interview sample of water travelers at exit points
Auto	Traffic origin–destination studies of Dept. of Transportation; Traffic counter data and route volume estimates; Data of check-in points, customs, toll systems, and agricultural checks	—Stop a random sample of in-bound travelers and give a mail-back diary —Exit interviews of random sample of travelers —Interviews of auto travelers at gasoline stations
Truck	Same as auto Licenses, trucking operations data, Dept. of Transportation	—Same as auto —Mail questionnaire to trucking firms
Commercial Transportation Crews		—Questionnaire to sample of crew members —Questionnaire to transportation firms

One must remember that this data does not include information about passenger origin and destination or whether the passenger is in the airport only to change airplanes. Sometimes this information can be supplemented with surveys done by the local airport commission or by airlines.

Primary data are easy to collect because departing passengers must pass through the boarding gate and most have free time before boarding to complete questionnaires. This requires involving the local airport commission at the beginning of the study; they can contact all of the airlines to get permission to interview passengers. Interviewers can easily survey three to four flights in 2 to 3½ hours in a preselected random pattern. Experience suggests avoidance of three procedures: Do not put interviewers on the airplane; do not ask cabin attendants to distribute or collect questionnaires; and avoid mail-back problems by having interviewers complete the questionnaire on the spot.

Charter air flights Charter air secondary data are similar to scheduled air data and have the same shortcomings. Primary data collection, while also similar to scheduled air, is more difficult because corporations and institutions charter aircraft. Airlines are reluctant to give permission for interviewing unless the group renting the aircraft has also given permission.

Private air flights Of all the transportation modes, private air (general aviation) presents the most difficulty in collection of primary or secondary data. Information collected by the Federal Aviation Administration is limited to total takeoffs and landings with no data on total passengers. But occasionally nation-wide private air surveys are done by the federal government that can give useful estimates on local traffic. When no control tower is present at an airport, the total takeoffs and landings may be estimated by traffic counts from other airports.

Primary data collection is expensive per questionnaire because of the nature of private air travel. Unscheduled flying times and small numbers per flight make the use of paid personnel difficult. A box of self-administered questionnaires for pilots works in part. An alternative is to use other surveys, such as those done by the FAA, and extrapolate the results to the local region.

Scheduled buses Primary and secondary scheduled bus data are similar to scheduled air. Data on the number of bus arrivals and departures are held by the bus companies, and the interviewing of passengers is facilitated because of a common boarding area. One major problem is that there are remote passenger pickups located in suburbs, and these passengers should be included in the survey. Adjustment can be made by examination of the number of remote stops and the percentage of tickets taken there.

Charter buses Charter buses present difficulties. Data are kept on the number of charter buses stopping at central terminals, but there is usually no prior notice of the stop. More serious, some buses do not stop at the terminal, and there is no central record of their visit in the city. Two alternatives are suggested: a survey of local hotel sales managers asking data of patrons arriving by tour bus and surveys of firms chartering buses into the city.

School buses Many cities serving as the trading, cultural, and/or governmental center for a large hinterland will have a large number of visits by young people transported in school buses. Excellent response has been received to a one-page mail questionnaire to superintendents of school districts asking for this information.

Trains Trains are much like scheduled air flights and buses. Records on total passenger arrivals and departures are kept, all passengers must go through a boarding gate, and departure times are fixed. There are typically far fewer departing train passengers and fewer departure times than for airplanes or buses.

Autos In most cities auto travelers do not "check in" at any one point. This characteristic makes auto travelers difficult to interview. For this reason considerably more attention is given here to gathering primary data about auto/truck tourists than to other travel modes. Furthermore, auto/truck tourists are overwhelmingly the most important tourist by mode of travel for most cities; they commonly make up 80 to 95 percent of all tourist person-days. Auto travel is complex and there is limited experience in comprehensive measurement of city auto visitors. But it is possible to design a procedure for your city, and the wealth of information obtained on automobile tourists will make the effort worthwhile.

Estimates of total traffic flow on all highways into and out of the city are usually available from transportation authorities. The problem is to classify this traffic flow and obtain information from a representative sample of those who are classed as tourists.

The theoretically most accurate means of researching auto travelers is to interview a randomly selected sample of them just as they leave the border of the metropolitan area. The procedure is similar to that of highway department origin−destination (O−D) studies which are conducted each year in most states and provinces. There are differences: surveys should be repeated on selected routes throughout the year— many O−D surveys are operated for only one day; only departing travelers are interviewed; and the questionnaire is changed to gather information about the traveler's stop in the destination area. The questionnaire must be short. Many O−D surveys have a goal of holding motorists for only three minutes. Any city contemplating a tourism study should discuss with the highway agency the existing highway data and the feasibility of gathering new data by O−D survey means.

Origin−destination-type studies have serious drawbacks which may prevent complete reliance upon them for auto/truck data. Among the difficulties are:

- O-D surveys are relatively expensive.
- Weather causes problems; cold and snow in some cases, rain and heat in others.
- Highway safety may be one of the most serious difficulties with O−D sampling. Most traffic departs cities on high-speed freeways. In times of high traffic flow stopping a sample may be imprudent, and this could lead to serious gaps in the data.
- Limitations on the length of time that motorists can be held pose a problem in gathering detailed information. Only minimal, basic questions can be asked.
- Exit interviews have memory bias problems with expenditure reporting. Careful questionnaire construction and interviewer training can reduce this problem.

Are there alternatives?—Yes, partially. But some O−D studies at the area's border are almost essential. Most importantly, they serve as guides. Further, there is no other way to get information about vehicular traffic that enters the area, passes through, and leaves without stopping at all. Precise data about this group are probably not important but a comprehensive understanding of an area's tourism must include at least a quantitative estimate of those who are physically there but who do not feel that there is a sufficient attraction to make any kind of stop.

Substitutes, supplements, and/or complements to complete reliance upon O−D-type procedures include:

- Traffic departing many cities is regularly stopped: at toll bridges, toll tunnels, highway toll gates, and customs and quarantine stations. These may serve even better than an O−D traffic station.
- Moving traffic surveys can sometimes pick up much of the information needed. In this procedure traffic is classified from a visual vantage point without stopping it or making oral contact. Data thus obtained can sometimes be refined by operating an O−D station part of the time to learn the relationship between classifications made by "eyeballing"

traffic compared to its actual measured composition. License plates can often be used to identify residents compared to nonresidents. Some studies have recorded license plate numbers and sent mail questionnaires to owners of the vehicles.

- Highway vehicles do "check in" at one place—the gasoline stations. If the study area is sufficiently large so that motorists are likely to need to refuel within its boundary, questionnaires can be administered at the stations. This procedure has been successfully used in a large SMSA. But there is one major problem: the resulting sample is a sample of vehicles that *stopped for gasoline*. It is not a sample of *all* vehicles. Adjustment must be made for this fact.
- Time limitations in holding traffic at O−D stations have been partly solved by giving the motorist an additional longer questionnaire to be completed and mailed back. Because of low rates of return this procedure may be unreliable except to get qualitative information.
- Diaries are sometimes used to get further activity detail and to reduce memory problems in exit interviews. In this procedure a sample of *incoming* traffic is stopped and given a diary to record activities and expenditures while in the destination area and then mail back. In common with many procedures requiring mail-back, it suffers from the problem of low completion rate. Low response rates from mail-back questionnaires and diaries can be partly adjusted with the use of data gathered when the sample is contacted in person.

Trucks Truckers are also tourists. They use hospitality services and participate in many recreational activities. Data can be gathered from them in the same manner as for other motorists when using O−D-type procedures. Fuel station data of heavy trucks may be unreliable because trucks fill at base terminals. Mailing addresses of companies licensed to ship into an area can often be obtained from the Department of Transportation. Good response has been obtained with a short questionnaire mailed to a sample of these trucking firms.

Transportation crews While they are not a separate travel mode, crews of commercial transportation systems can be included as part of tourism's impact. Data about their numbers can be obtained from the several carrier firms. Individual crew members can be interviewed in the process of contacting passengers in the transportation terminals.

Water Most cities in the world owe their initial location to access by water. Technological development in travel has reduced water travel to a minor factor in many cities. In cities served by commercial water travel, tourists using this travel mode may be measured in a manner similar to those used by bus and train, working in cooperation with the port director and the travel company. Cities located on rivers where locks are used can often get needed information through the Army Corps of Engineers. A survey of public and private docking facilities may be needed to complement data from the above sources.

GETTING MILEAGE OUT OF THE RESEARCH

The possible uses of tourism data about your city have been indicated in the foregoing. By way of summary they are:

- To "sell" the value of tourism—so there is a wider base of ongoing support for tourism programs.
- To manage the marketing of tourism: gain insights into the range of your city's market segments and their relative importance; provide guidelines for marketing of specific urban tourism facilities and/ or experiences; and guide the provision of information services to travelers.
- To manage the development of tourism services and facilities: develop needed tourist-serving facilities; indicate training needs for service personnel who contact travelers; and upgrade "hosting" of guests by city residents.

At least two things must take place in order that the product of tourism research may be put to its best use:

- The information gathered must be relevant to intended purposes and accurate, and data treatment and display must be appropriate.
- The research findings must be disseminated to those who need it and can make use of it.

USE OF THE DATA DEPENDS UPON ITS USEFULNESS

The data must first be reliable. Second, the more specifically research findings meet needs of users the greater will be its usefulness. For example: data concerning retail purchases by tourists will have specific value to retail merchants; characteristics of tourists who travel by bus will be more useful to bus firms than overall traveler characteristics; and theatres want to know which tourists attend cultural offerings.

The above paragraph places the responsibility upon research design for relevance. The tourists interviewed and questions asked must accurately gather the needed information. Analysis of this data must follow through so that relevant questions are answered:

- What is the overall impact?
- How do seasonal patterns vary?
- What are the segments of tourists according to activity patterns (reasons for coming, specific activities, lodging, travel patterns, expenditures, etc.)?
- What are our tourist market segments according to demographic, socioeconomic, and/or other characteristics?

These and many other questions make research findings usable and hence increase their use.

SPREADING THE WORD

The first step toward spreading the word about your tourism research begins at the start of the research. Don't do the research job yourself, that is, involve as many others in the research process as possible. This is especially true of those agencies and persons having need for the findings. Opportunities for this involvement vary. An advisory committee can be established consisting of people who can contribute to and gain from the proposed research. Most research projects require cooperative action on the part of a variety of agencies and facility operators. These actions range from sharing of data to assisting with data collection on premises.

Those involved in research will be more likely to support and use the findings.

If the project requires a long period of time—for example, you are collecting data for an entire 12-month period—a short periodical newsletter reporting progress will help to sustain interest, and help prospective users prepare to utilize the new information.

PLAN A SPECIFIC PROGRAM FOR SPREADING THE WORD

Research findings that gather dust on the shelf do no good. Nor can these findings be used by any agency or firm that does not know about them. Some methods of spreading the word that have been used include:

- Hold a workshop with the steering committee or advisory group. This can include a thorough review of findings and a probe of the meanings and implications for action. This procedure can not only inform the group but take advantage of their insights and experience. Consider having separate workshops with each of the agencies or kinds of firms that has representation on the advisory committee.
- Publish the findings in a report or in a series of reports. One may be a summary report. Another may provide detailed information. Other reports

might be written for special interest groups, such as those interested in tourists who use commercial lodging, the purchases at retail, or visitors attending artistic/cultural facilities. These printed reports provide ready reference for ongoing use.

- Consider a media event or press release at the time when the findings are first available. Plan this to attract community-wide attention to tourism's impact.
- Follow up the major media event with news stories drawn from the research findings which are regularly released. If these cannot be presented as news acceptable by the media, they may be used in Chamber of Commerce and similar publications.
- Develop a series of media shorts, each highlighting a specific finding. Offer them to radio and/or television for public service spots.
- Develop a speakers bureau that is available to clubs, council groups, etc., on the subject of tourism for your city. Provide a video tape, slide show, or automated slide-tape that highlights research findings for use by clubs and other groups seeking program materials and who can put this information to work.

The net result sought is to put information gained to work in the management of your city's tourism industry. The goal is to realize payoff in terms of profits, employment, and tax base, and/or in terms of living amenities for urban and regional residents.

UPDATING AND FOLLOW-UP

Don't stop with one research effort. A major "use" of research is to raise many added, necessary questions about your city's tourism industry. The better it is, the more you distribute the information, the more questions it should raise. What more do you need to know about marketing to specific tourist segments? What are the results from a given advertising program effort? Has our employee training program improved our hosting abilities? What is the visitor's image of our new downtown mall? or waterfront? or airport?

Yesterday's research findings quickly become outdated due to the dynamic nature of most cities' tourism. How will you update them? An annual updating can be done using secondary data series. Ongoing data series such as air and auto traffic figures and retail sales can be used to index year-to-year growth. But structural changes also occur: in the ratio of auto to air travelers, the distribution of dollars spent, the patterns of overnight lodging, and other variables. This means that each five to ten years all or parts of the impact study should be repeated.

EXAMPLES OF URBAN TOURISM RESEARCH

Listed here with short descriptions are examples of urban tourism research conducted in the past decade. These provide readers with suggestions about the range in research approaches and methods.

All examples given use basically valid procedures. But note that the part of the tourism spectrum defined by each study varies greatly. The range is from the IACVB studies, which include only those who attend major conventions, to studies which attempt a fully comprehensive measurement. It should also be noted that the quality of results may vary depending upon the care used in applying the given procedure and the availability of data that are specific to the given geographic area and the given tourism segment.

1977 National Travel Survey Data for specific SMSAs have been prepared by the United States Travel Service. This data is based upon household surveys of a national probability sample of about 24,000 households. All travel of 100 or more miles one way is included. The census is conducted every five years.

Las Vegas Visitor Profile Studies These studies are ongoing quarterly. Their purpose is to profile the commercially significant visitor. The procedure is to interview visitors in three categories: at hotels and motels, at the airport, and at the bus depot. It would thus appear to understate automobile visitors who stay with friends and relatives or who do not stay overnight.

Minneapolis–St. Paul's Travel Tourism This year-long survey was done for the period July 1977 to June 1978. It measures travelers using personal interviews by all traffic modes while they were within the SMSA. A number of special-purpose studies were used to gather data about travel segments not sampled adequately by the primary procedures; these included tour buses, heavy trucks, school buses, and private aviation.

Profile: San Diego's Visitor Industry in 1982 This study projects 1975 data ahead to 1982. It is based primarily upon convention visitors and data of visitors to primary attraction points such as the San Diego Zoo and Sea World. But data from other visitor studies, demographic data, and hospitality industry data are also employed.

A Market Analysis of the Lodging Industry in the Twin Cities (Minnesota) Metropolitan Area This 1971 study is based upon a sampling of the lodging industry folios in which all available registration information is utilized. It is thus a study of lodging industry guests only. The SMSA's lodging industry is subdivided into six categories by location and class of service.

Spokane: 1979 Visitor and Convention Study

This study makes use of secondary data to estimate visitor numbers and dollar impact. Major reliance is upon census of travel data and patterns of expenditure estimates made by the U.S. Travel Data Center. Local primary tax data and hotel guest data are also used.

Duluth (Minnesota) Travel Industry   This is the

only study to place primary reliance upon highway origin–destination procedures. A highway cordon line was maintained for two summer weeks. The relatively small size (about 130,000) of the community made this procedure workable. An independently conducted airport study in the same year (1972) made it possible to estimate both auto and air tourists.

Convention Delegate Expenditures   These are

studies conducted periodically in the United States and Canada by the International Association of Convention and Visitors Bureaus (IACVB). They gather data by sampling guests at major conventions. The primary purpose is to determine the dollar impact of these convention visitors.

BIBLIOGRAPHY

Ballman, Gary, and Uel Blank (1982), *What Does Tourism Mean to Ely?* Minneapolis: University of Minnesota.

Blank, Uel (1976), "Metropolitan Travel/Tourism Markets—Are Current Measures Misleading?" *Marketing Travel and Tourism, Proceedings*, TTRA, pp. 151–158.

Blank, Uel (1982a), *Duluth–Superior's Travel–Tourism Economy*, Staff Paper P82-14, Minneapolis: Department of Agricultural and Applied Economics, University of Minnesota.

Blank, Uel (1982b), *Life Style Tourism Interrelationships of Minneapolis–St. Paul Residents*, Staff Paper P82-9, Minneapolis: Department of Agricultural and Applied Economics, University of Minnesota.

Blank, Uel, and Elizabeth Numerich (1969), "Recreational Services and Facilities of the Twin Cities Metropolitan Area," unpublished paper prepared for the Minneapolis–St. Paul Metropolitan Tourist Council.

Blank, Uel, and Michael Petkovich (1979a), *Minneapolis–St. Paul's Travel Tourism, Executive Summary*, Minneapolis: University of Minnesota.

Blank, Uel, and Michael Petkovich (1979b), "The Metropolitan Area Tourist: A Comprehensive Analysis," *A Decade of Achievement, Proceedings* TTRA, pp. 227–236.

Blank, Uel, and Michael Petkovich (1980), "The Metropolitan Area: A Multifaceted Travel Destination Complex," in *Tourism Planning and Development Issues*, D.E. Hawkins, E.L. Shafer, and J.M. Rovelstad, Eds., Washington, D.C.: George Washington University, pp. 393–405.

Brazlau, David (1975), *The Socio-Economic Role of Aviation in Duluth, Minnesota*, Minneapolis: Minnesota Department of Aeronautics.

British Tourist Authority (1980), *Survey Among Overseas Visitors to London, Summer, 1980*, London: British Tourist Authority.

Chang, Semoon (1981), "Measuring Economic Impact of the Mobile Municipal Auditorium upon Alabama," *Journal of Travel Research*, Vol. 19, No. 4, 12–15.

Dandurand, Laurence (1980), *Las Vegas Profile Study—1979*, Las Vegas: Las Vegas Convention and Visitors Authority.

Dunn, Diana R. (1980), "Urban Recreation Research: An Overview," *Leisure Sciences*, Vol. 3, No. 1, 25–57.

Hooker, Raymond W., and Kenneth R. Potter (1970), *An Input–Output Analysis of the Economic Impact of I-80 on Evanston, Wyoming*, Laramie: Division of Business and Economic Research, University of Wyoming.

Johnson, Dennis (1973), "A Market Analysis of the Lodging Industry in the Twin Cities Metropolitan Area," unpublished M.S. thesis, Minneapolis: Department of Agricultural and Applied Economics, University of Minnesota.

Learning, George F. (1967), "Recreational Tourism: Its Impact on Tucson and Nogales," *Arizona Review*, Vol. 16, No. 10.

Learning, George F., and Nat de Gennaro (1973), "Phoenix Winter Air Travelers: Who, Where, Why," *Arizona Review*, Vol. 22, No. 1.

Learning, George F., and Michael J. Shirley (1970), "Tucson's Air Travelers: Who, Where, Why," *Arizona Review*, Vol. 19, No. 11.

New Orleans Tourist and Convention Commission (1970), *Ten Year Report, New Orleans Tourist and Convention Commission, 1960–1970*.

Niagara Resort and Tourist Association (1978), *Niagara Falls Market Research Study*, Niagara Falls, Ontario.

Peterson, Jerrold M. (1979), *Duluth Tourist Survey 1978*, Duluth: Bureau of Business and Economic Research, University of Minnesota at Duluth.

Peterson, Jerrold M., and William Benson (1979), *Duluth Convention Visitors Survey*, Duluth: Bureau of Business and Economic Research, University of Minnesota at Duluth.

Rose, Warren (1981), "The Measurement of Economic Impact of Tourism on Galveston, Texas: A Case Study," *Journal of Travel Research*, Vol. 19, No. 4, 3–11.

Safavi, F. (1971), "A Cost Benefit Model for Convention Centers," *Annals of Regional Science*, Vol. 2, No. 2, 221–237.

Sciullo, Henry A., and Laurence Dandurand (1977), *The Economic Impact of McCarran International Airport*, Las Vegas: Las Vegas Convention and Visitors Authority.

Sciullo, Henry A., and Laurence Dandurand (1978), *Las Vegas Composite Visitor Profile, 1967–77*, Las Vegas: Las Vegas Convention and Visitors Authority.

Somersan, Ayse (1979), *Spokane Economic Impact*, Madison: Recreation Resources Center, University of Wisconsin.

Somersan, Ayse, and William Pinkovtz (1980), *Milwaukee Visitor Economic Impact—1980*, Madison: Recreation Resources Center, University of Wisconsin.

U.S. Travel Data Center (1981), *Analytical Report on the 1978–79 IACVB Convention Income Survey*, Washington, D.C.: U.S. Travel Data Center.

Waldo and Edwards, Inc. (1971), *The Economic Impact of Los Angeles International Airport*, Las Vegas: Las Vegas Convention and Visitors Authority.

Zlatkovich, Charles P. (1973), *Visitor Economic Impact: The Austin Texas Example*, Austin: Bureau of Business Research, University of Texas.

15

Travel and Tourism Information Sources

CHARLES R. GOELDNER
Director, Business Research Division
University of Colorado
Boulder, Colorado

*T*his chapter presents a comprehensive list of sources of information available on tourism, travel, and recreation. It is divided into eight sections: indexing services, bibliographies and finding guides, periodicals, trade and professional associations, government, yearbooks, annuals, and handbooks, data bases, and some final suggestions. A summary of the type of information available in each source is also provided.

The sources of secondary information available on tourism, travel, and recreation continue to grow. In the rapidly expanding, dynamic world of tourism, practitioners must know what is available and where to find it. Information gathering requires a great deal of the tourism executive's time; yet little exists to guide them to the best sources of data for their particular concerns. Thus, this chapter provides a comprehensive list of the numerous sources along with a summary of the type of information available in each.

The chapter is organized into eight main categories: (1) Indexing Services, (2) Bibliographies and Finding Guides, (3) Periodicals, (4) Trade and Professional Associations, (5) Government, (6) Yearbooks, Annuals, Handbooks, etc., (7) Data bases, and (8) Some Final Suggestions. The sources are arranged alphabetically within each heading.

Considerable effort has been made to make the list up-to-date and give enough information to enable users who cannot find the information in their own library or the public library to send requests to the sources indicated. Readers should be aware that names, addresses, and prices change frequently.

One of the biggest mistakes in travel and tourism research is to rush out and collect primary data without exhausting secondary source information. Only later do researchers discover they have duplicated previous research. Often existing sources could have provided information to solve the problem for a fraction of the cost. Therefore, users should exhaust secondary sources before turning to primary research for additional data.

In selecting sources of information, efforts have been made to (1) emphasize prime data, (2) list sources which can be used to locate more detailed data, and (3) keep the list brief enough to be actually read and used rather than just filed. Effective utilization can save money and hours of time and provide useful information that might otherwise be missed.

1 INDEXING SERVICES

Unfortunately, there is no one convenient heading where you can look and automatically find travel research information listed. Travel research studies may be found under many headings. The most important subject heading in the indexes is tourist trade. Examples of other headings that contain useful information are: travel, travel agents, vacations, transportation, tourist camps, motels, hotels, recreation, and national parks.

Business Periodicals Index (New York: H.W. Wilson, monthly, except August). A cumulative subject index covering periodicals in the fields of accounting, marketing, finance, advertising, banking, etc.

Predicasts F & S Europe (Cleveland, Ohio: Predicasts,

Inc., monthly). Devoted exclusively to Europe. Covers the Common Market, Iberia, Scandinavia, Eastern Europe, the Soviet Union, and other European countries.

Predicasts F & S Index International (Cleveland, Ohio: Predicasts, Inc., monthly). Indexes articles from foreign publications, information arranged by (1) industry and product, (2) country, and (3) company. Covers Canada, Latin America, Africa, Middle East, Oceania, Japan, and other Asian countries.

Predicasts F & S Index United States (Cleveland, Ohio: Predicasts, Inc., weekly). Indexes articles from the United States and from foreign sources that may affect U.S. business.

Public Affairs Information Service Bulletin (New York: Public Affairs Information Service, semimonthly). A selective list of the latest books, pamphlets, government publications, reports of public and private agencies, and periodicals relating to economic and social conditions, public administration, and international relations.

Reader's Guide to Periodical Literature (New York: H.W. Wilson, semimonthly). An index of the contents of the nation's general magazines.

2   BIBLIOGRAPHIES AND FINDING GUIDES

Baretje, R. *Bibliographie Touristique* (Aix-en-Provence, France: Centre d'Etudes du Tourisme, Fondation Vasarely 1, Avenue Marcel Pagnol 13090). Contains an exhaustive inventory of the world literature in tourism. The Centre has been publishing since 1964 in the collection *Etudes et Memoires*, which is a reference book of all studies in tourism. Over 25 volumes have been issued to date and have recorded over 36,500 documents classified according to subjects, countries, and authors. These books are published once or twice each year.

Baretje, R. *Tourist Analysis Review* (Aix-en-Provence, France: Centre des Hautes Etudes Touristiques, Fondation Vasarely 1, Avenue Marcel Pagnol 13090). Published every three months, this review printed on 40 heavy-duty pages gives complete references of studies and a short synopsis of their contents. Each issue analyzes 160 books or articles dealing with tourism.

Bibliography of Theses and Dissertations in Recreation, Parks, Camping and Outdoor Education (Alexandria, Virginia: National Recreation and Park Association, 1970), 555 pp., $7.50. A compilation and annotation of nearly 4,000 theses and dissertations in the recreation field.

Bibliography of Theses and Dissertations in Recreation and Parks (Alexandria, Virginia: National Recreation and Park Association, 1979), unpaged, $15.00. A compilation and annotation of 2,798 theses and dissertations in the recreation field. This volume updates the 1970 edition.

Book Catalogue of Tourism Research Studies (Ottawa, Ontario: Tourism Research and Data Centre, Tourism Canada, 235 Queen Street, K1A 0H6, annual). This is a listing of publications produced primarily by Canadian sources, categorized by annuals, Statistics Canada publications, list of descriptions, and a subject index.

Goeldner, C.R., and Karen Dicke. *Bibliography of Tourism and Travel Research Studies, Reports and Articles* (Boulder, Colorado: Business Research Division, College of Business, University of Colorado, 1980), 9 vols., 762 pp., complete set $60.00. This nine-volume bibliography is a research resource on travel, recreation, and tourism. Volume I, *Information Sources*, covers bibliographies, classics, books, directories, proceedings, list of travel and tourism trade and professional publications, list of U.S. travel and tourism associations, list of universities involved in travel and tourism research, list of U.S. travel contacts, selected list of Canadian travel contacts, and list of world travel contacts. Volume II, *Economics*, covers general, analysis, balance of payments, development, employment, expenditures, feasibility studies, impact, indicators and barometers, international, and multipliers. Volume III, *International Tourism*, covers general; Africa; Asia and the Pacific; Canada; Central, Latin, and South America; Europe (excluding the United Kingdom); Middle East; and the United Kingdom. Volume IV, *Lodging*, covers general, financial aspects, innovations, management, marketing and market research, statistics, and second home development. Volume V, *Recreation*, covers general, boating, camping, carrying capacity, demand, economics, forecasts, forests, hiking, hunting and fishing, land development, management, parks, planning, public input, research and research methodology, rural, skiing, snowmobiling, sports, statistics, urban, user studies, and water. Volume VI, *Transportation*, includes transportation—general and forecasts; air—general, costs, commuters, deregulation, economics, fares, forecasts, international, passengers, planning, and statistics; highways and roads—bus, auto, and recreational vehicles; rail; water; and other. Volume VII, *Advertising—Planning*, covers advertising and promotion, attitudes, business travel, clubs, conferences and conventions, education, energy, environmental impact, food service, forecasts, gambling, handicapped traveler, hospitality, leisure, management, and planning. Volume VIII, *Statistics—Visitors*, includes statistics, tourism research, travel agents, travel research methodology, vacations, and visitors. Volume IX,

Index, includes several indices to the material in Volumes I—VIII.

Jafari, Jafar, "Tourism and the Social Sciences: A Bibliography," *Annals of Tourism Research* (Menomonie, Wisconsin: Department of Habitational Resources, University of Wisconsin—Stout), Vol. 6, No. 2 (April—June 1979), pp. 149—194, $4.00. The purpose of this bibliography is to bring together a selection of publications dealing with the study of tourism. This list of bibliographies is from 1970—1978.

Leisure, Recreation and Tourism Abstracts (formerly *Rural Recreation and Tourism Abstracts*) (Oxford, U.K.: Commonwealth Agricultural Bureaux, quarterly), annual subscription rate is $100.00. The abstracts, arranged by subject, provide short informative summaries of publications with full bibliographical details and often a symbol for locating the original documents.

Oaksford, Margaret J. *Bibliography of Hotel and Restaurant Administration* (Ithaca, New York: *The Cornell Quarterly*, School of Hotel Administration, 327 Statler Hall, Cornell University, annual), $15.00. This publication lists references from the hospitality and tourism press, books, and includes names and addresses of publishers.

PATA Research Library Bibliography (San Francisco: Pacific Area Travel Association, April 1977), 12 pp. The library of the PATA Research Department contains more than 1,000 volumes relating to tourism and tourism research. In addition, records of visitor arrivals at all of the PATA member countries are maintained. The volumes selected for the bibliography are either recently published, published in previous years but not updated, or are frequently used for their historical value. Listings include PATA call numbers and an annotation of the report.

Pisarski, Alan. *An Inventory of Federal Travel and Tourism Related Information Sources* (Boulder, Colorado: Business Research Division, University of Colorado, 1985), 107 pp., $25.00. This inventory of existing Federal data programs relevant to travel and tourism provides a comprehensive listing and description of pertinent government sources.

Tourism: A Guide to Sources of Information (Edinburgh, U.K.: Capital Planning Information Ltd., 6 Castle Street, Edinburgh EH2 3AT, Scotland, 1981), 73 pp. This publication gives a selected and evaluative listing of tourism literature primarily about the United Kingdom; however, it also includes some international sources.

Tourism and Vacation Travel: State and Local Government Planning (Springfield, Virginia: National Technical Information Service, U.S. Department of Commerce, February 1985), 96 pp., $40.00. Economic and socioeconomic aspects of vacation travel and tourism in various localities of the United States are documented. Most of these studies deal with the use of tourism for the economic development of local communities. Special attention is given to wilderness, coastal zone, lake, waterway, and Indian reservation areas. This updated bibliography covers the period 1970 to February 1985 and provides 181 citations.

"The Travel Research Bookshelf," *Journal of Travel Research* (Boulder, Colorado: Business Research Division, College of Business, University of Colorado). A regular feature of the quarterly *Journal of Travel Research*. "The Travel Research Bookshelf" is an annotated bibliography of current travel research materials. Sources and availability of materials are shown for each entry.

University Research in Business and Economics (Morgantown, West Virginia: Bureau of Business Research, College of Business and Economics, West Virginia University, for the Association for University Business and Economic Research (AUBER), annual), $25.00. This bibliography covers the publications of members of AUBER and member schools of the American Assembly of Collegiate Schools of Business for the calendar year. Subject classifications 531, 615, 635, 721, and 941 cover travel and tourism subject matter.

3 PERIODICALS

The following illustrate periodicals that contain travel research information:

Annals of Tourism Research (Elmsford, New York: Pergamon Press, quarterly), $65.00.

ASTA Travel News (New York: Communications International, monthly), United States and Canada, $10.00 a year; single copy $1.00; $12.00 elsewhere, single copy $1.20.

Canadian Travel News (Don Mills, Ontario: Southam Communications, biweekly), $33.00 per year in Canada, $41.50 per year in the United States, $64.00 elsewhere, single copy $3.00.

The Cornell Hotel and Restaurant Administration Quarterly (Ithaca, New York: School of Hotel Administration, Cornell University, quarterly), $25.00 a year in the United States, $35.00 Canadian in Canada, $55.00 elsewhere; single copies $7.50.

Courier (Lexington, Kentucky: National Tour Association, monthly), $36.00 a year.

Hotel and Motel Management (Cleveland, Ohio: Harcourt Brace Jovanovich, monthly), $20.00 a year in the United States, $25.00 in Canada, $50.00 elsewhere; single copies $2.00 in the United States, $4.50 elsewhere.

Hotels & Restaurants International (Boston: Cahners, 10 times a year), $30.00 per year in the United States, $40.00 in Canada and Mexico, elsewhere $75.00 (air mail) and $65.00 (surface); single copy $5.00 U.S., $6.00 Canada and Mexico, $7.00 elsewhere.

ICTA Journal (Wellesley, Massachusetts; Institute of Certified Travel Agents, twice a year).

International Journal of Hospitality Management (Oxford, U.K.: Pergamon Press, quarterly), $85.00 a year.

International Tourism Quarterly (London: The Economist Publications, 40 Duke Street, London, W1A 1DW, quarterly), $180.00 a year.

Journal of Leisure Research (Alexandria, Virginia: National Recreation and Park Association, quarterly), United States, $17.00 a year; foreign, $20.00 nonmember rates.

Journal of Travel Research (Boulder, Colorado: Business Research Division, College of Business, University of Colorado, quarterly), free to members of the Travel and Tourism Research Association, nonmembers $65.00 a year in the United States, $70.00 Canada and Mexico, $80.00 elsewhere.

Leisure Sciences (New York: Crane, Russak, quarterly), $48.00 a year, single copies $13.00.

Leisure Studies (London: E & F.N. Spon, three issues a year), individual subscription rates are $72.50 in the United States and Canada, single copies $30.00.

Lodging (New York: American Hotel Association Directory Corporation, monthly except August), $35.00 a year.

Meetings and Conventions (New York: News Group Publications, monthly), $30.00 a year in the United States, $40.00 elsewhere, single copies $3.00 U.S., $4.00 elsewhere.

Resort & Hotel Management (San Diego: Western Specialty Publications, monthly), $25.00 a year in the United States, $60.00 elsewhere, single copies $5.00.

Revue de Tourism—The Tourist Review—Zeitschrift fur Fremdenverkehr (St. Gallen, Switerland: AIEST, Varnbuelstrasse 19, CH-9000 St. Gallen, quarterly), 47 Sfr.

Tourism Management (Guildford, U.K.: Butterworth Scientific, quarterly), $153.00 a year in the United States, single copies $45.00.

Tourism Recreation Research (Indira Nagar, Lucknow, India: Centre for Tourism Research, semiannually), $25.00 a year.

The Travel Agent (New York: American Traveler Division, Capital Cities Media, twice weekly), $12.00 a year, single copies 50¢.

Travel Printout (Washington, D.C.: U.S. Travel Data Center, monthly), $49.00 a year United States, Canada, and Mexico, $59.00 elsewhere.

Travel Trade (New York: Travel Trade Publications, weekly), $8.00 a year in the United States, $10.00 in Canada, $20.00 elsewhere.

Travel Weekly (New York: News Group Publications, twice weekly), $24.00 a year in the United States, Canada, and Mexico, $44.00 elsewhere, single copies $1.00.

World Travel (Madrid: World Tourism Organization, published every second month), $14.00 a year.

There are also many other periodicals and journals dealing with the travel field. The sources for locating these are:

Business Publications Rates and Data (Skokie, Illinois: Standard Rate and Data Service, monthly). A listing of more than 3,800 U.S. business, trade, and technical publications and about 200 international.

Ulrich's International Periodicals Directory (New York: R.R. Bowker, annual). Includes entries for over 65,000 in-print periodicals published throughout the world.

4 TRADE AND PROFESSIONAL ASSOCIATIONS

Many trade and professional associations publish valuable data on the travel industry. Examples are:

Association Internationale d'Experts Scientifiques du Tourisme (AIEST), Varnbuelstrasse 19, CH-9000, St. Gallen, Switzerland. AIEST is composed primarily of academicians interested in tourism research and teaching. It publishes the *Tourist Review* and annual proceedings of its meetings.

Pacific Area Travel Association (PATA), 228 Grant Avenue, San Francisco, California 94108, publishes the *PATA Annual Statistical Report* and other publications and holds research seminars.

Travel and Tourism Research Association (TTRA), P.O. Box 8066, Foothill Station, Salt Lake City, Utah 84108, publishes the *Journal of Travel Research*, proceedings, bibliographies, and operates the Travel Reference Center.

Travel Industry Association of America, 1899 L Street, N.W., Washington, D.C. 20036, has a publication program that includes special reports and newsletters.

The World Tourism Organization (WTO), Capitan Haya, 42, Madrid, 20/Spain. One of the main tasks of the WTO is to give members continuing information on tourism and its incidence on the social, economic, and cultural life of nations. It offers a number of publications and educational programs. A publications list can be received by writing the organization.

Some other associations are:

The Tourism Industry Association of Canada, 130 Albert Street, Ottawa, Ontario, Canada K1P 5G4; Air Transport Association of America, 1709 New York Avenue, N.W., Washington, D.C. 20006; International Air Transport Association, 26, Chemin de Joinville, P.O. Box 160, 1216 Cointrin Geneva 15, Switzerland; American Hotel and Motel Association, 888 Seventh Avenue, New York, New York 10019; International Association of Amusement Parks and Attractions, 115 E. Commercial, P.O. Box 776, Wood Dale, Illinois 60191; International Association of Convention and Visitors Bureaus, 702 Bloomington Road, Champaign, Illinois 61820; Association of Travel Marketing Executives, 804 D Street, N.E., Washington, D.C. 20002; American Society of Travel Agents, 4400 MacArthur Boulevard, Washington, D.C. 20007; National Tour Association, 120 Kentucky Avenue, Lexington, Kentucky 40502; Institute of Certified Travel Agents, 148 Linden Street, Wellesley, Massachusetts 02181; National Recreation and Park Association, 3101 Park Center Drive, Alexandria, Virginia 22302.

If you are in doubt about trade associations in the field, check:

Encyclopedia of Associations: 1985, 19th ed. (Detroit: Gale Research, 1984), Volume I, *National Organizations of the United States*, 2,023 pp., Volume 2, *Geographic and Executive Indexes*, 1,090 pp., Volume 3, *New Associations and Projects*.

5   GOVERNMENT

Probably no group collects more information on the tourism industry than government agencies. The government agencies vary according to the objectives of the particular country and in most cases to the degree of importance of the tourism sector. Generally, the following public agencies are involved in tourism and travel research activities: (1) ministries of tourism; (2) undersecretarial or underministerial tourism organizations; (3) specific governmental organizations for tourism and travel; (4) statistical agencies for collection, analysis, and publication of data related to tourism and travel, such as Statistics Canada and the U.S. Census Bureau; and (5) state or provincial tourism organizations.

Most government travel organizations are members of the World Tourism Organization (WTO), Capitan Haya, 42, E-Madrid, 20/Spain. Researchers can write for a list of members and associate members or purchase a copy of their publication, *Tourism Compendium*, as it contains this information. Another source of government agencies involved in tourism is *World Travel Directory*, published annually (News Group Publications, One Park Avenue, New York, New York 10016), $85.00.

The major U.S. government tourism development organization is the U.S. Travel and Tourism Administration, Department of Commerce, Washington, D.C. 20230. An inventory of Federal agencies by Pisarski is listed in Section 2: Bibliographies and Finding Guides.

Selected examples of useful government publications in the travel field include:

Canadian Travel Survey: 1984 (Ottawa: Statistics Canada, Travel, Tourism and Recreation Section, 1985), 72 pp., $32.00 in Canada, $33.00 elsewhere. This report provides statistics on travel by Canadians on trips of 80 kilometers or more with destinations in Canada. Information is provided on who the travelers are, why they traveled, when they traveled, how they traveled, where they stayed, how much they spent, and what they did. A general summary of the travel situation in Canada is given and the importance of domestic travel is demonstrated.

A Conceptual Basis for the National Tourism Policy Study (Washington, D.C.: Committee on Commerce and National Tourism Policy Study, U.S. Senate, October 1976), 70 pp., 85¢. This report identifies the federal programs and policies that significantly impact tourism research, planning, development, and promotion. It also contains an overview of legislation that directly and indirectly affects one or another aspect of tourism; a discussion of the national interests in tourism and other interacting interests; a discussion of the definitional problem with tourism, and how the term is defined for purposes of the report; and a review of federal tourism and tourism-related legislation. Order from the Superintendent of Documents, U.S. Government Printing Office, Washington, D.C. 20402.

"International Travel and Passenger Fares, 1984," *Survey of Current Business* (Washington, D.C.: Bureau of Economic Analysis, U.S. Department of Commerce, May 1985), $30.00 a year in the United States, $37.50 elsewhere; single copy $4.75 in the United States, $5.95 elsewhere. This article reviews development affecting the travel accounts that appear in the U.S. balance of international payments. Total spending by U.S. residents traveling abroad, spending by foreign visitors to the

United States, and data on passenger fares for transoceanic transportation are covered.

The United States Travel and Tourism Administration's *In-flight Survey of International Air Travelers* (Washington, D.C.: U.S. Department of Commerce, United States Travel and Tourism Administration, quarterly), $100.00 per quarter, $400.00 per year. The in-flight survey provides a comprehensive consumer marketing data base on international travel to and from the United States. Some 25,000 foreign visitors and 35,000 U.S. residents traveling abroad respond to the survey annually. One series analyzes inbound travel to the United States and another focuses on travel from the United States. Tables profile international travelers by residency, trip characteristics, and regional destinations.

National Tourism Policy Study—Ascertainment Phase—Report on the Ascertained Needs of the State and Local Government and Private Sectors of the Tourism and Travel Industry (Washington, D.C.: Committee on Commerce, Science and Transportation, U.S. Senate, June 1977), 217 pp. This report represents extensive input from the public and private sectors of the travel and tourism industry. It details the issues and problems confronting the industry in general, and their more specific relationships to Federal agencies and programs. The findings of the report are based on the views and recommendations expressed by participants at the six regional meetings and seven national meetings of the *National Tourism Policy Study*. A follow-up questionnaire was sent to meeting participants. The report is organized into chapters dealing with the issues confronting the tourism and travel industry, broad programmatic needs at the Federal level identified by participants at the regional and national meetings, specific recommendations for programmatic change organized by major issue, specific recommendations for change organized by Federal agencies, and summary of the results of the NTPS questionnaire survey.

National Tourism Policy Study—Final Report (Washington, D.C.: Committee on Commerce, Science and Transportation, U.S. Senate, 1978), 361 pp. This report by Arthur D. Little, Inc. presents the findings of the final phase of the *National Tourism Policy Study*. It was designed to develop a proposed national tourism policy for the United States; to define appropriate roles for the Federal government, the states, cities, private industry, and consumers in carrying out, supporting, and contributing to the national tourism policy; and to recommend organizational, programmatic, and legislative strategies for implementing the proposed national tourism policy.

Summary of Passport Statistics (Washington, D.C.: Bureau of Consular Affairs, U.S. Department of State, annual), free. Statistics are detailed by sex and age groups, occupation, length of stay, first-area destination, countries to be visited, and object of travel. Monthly reports are also available.

Tourism in Japan (Tokyo: Japan National Tourist Organization). This annual report is divided into two parts. The first part explains travel trends in and around Japan. It covers modes of transportation, types of accommodations, travel agency business, and the protection and development of tourist resources that have been undertaken by various ministries. The second part explains the functions of the organization for the past fiscal year. The activities of promotion, research, and the use of statistics are described.

Travel between Canada and Other Countries (Ottawa: Statistics Canada, quarterly and annually), $8.40 in Canada, $8.90 elsewhere; quarterly reports $31.80 a year in Canada, $38.15 elsewhere. A statistical report on travelers between Canada and other countries that provides estimates of international travel expenditures arising from all types of movements across the frontiers. Many of the movements are short term and local in nature due to close interrelationships of communities lying near the border; therefore, the data do not coincide with the movements and expenditures relevant for the "tourist" industry.

Travel, Tourism and Outdoor Recreation, A Statistical Digest, 1980 and 1981 (Ottawa: Statistics Canada, 1983), $10.60 in Canada, $12.70 elsewhere. This report brings together in one document related data on travel, tourism, and outdoor recreation that are to be found in a wide variety of publications and also some of the unpublished material of several divisions of Statistics Canada.

U.S. International Air Travel Statistics (Cambridge, Massachusetts: Transportation Systems Center, U.S. Department of Transportation, monthly). The report is compiled using data collected by the U.S. Immigration and Naturalization Service. It contains world area travel statistical data and is available as a subscription service to anyone who wishes to acquire the information.

6 YEARBOOKS, ANNUALS, HANDBOOKS, ETC.

Air Transport 1985 (Washington, D.C.: Air Transport Association of America, annual), 21 pp., free. The official annual report to the U.S. scheduled airline industry containing historical and current statistical data on the industry.

Budgets of National Tourism Administrations, 1981–1982–1983 (Madrid: World Tourism Organization, 1984), various paging. This document presents a summary and analysis of national tourism organization budgets drawn up under the main expenditure items—promotion, capital expenditure, research, and administration.

Caribbean Tourism Statistical Report, 1983 (Christ Church, Barbados: Caribbean Tourism Research and Development Centre, 1983), 87 pp. Report provides a single source of key statistics on tourism in the Caribbean, focusing on tourist arrivals, seasonality, cruise passengers, and accommodation capacity.

Economic Analysis of North American Ski Areas, 1984–85 (Boulder, Colorado: Business Research Division, University of Colorado, annual), 139 pp., $50.00. The major objective of this survey of ski operations for the 1984–1985 operating season was to provide ski area characteristics and financial figures in understandable tabulations so ski area operators and others could assess the characteristics and the economic health of the ski industry.

The 1984–85 Economic Review of Travel in America (Washington, D.C.: U.S. Travel Data Center, annual), $45.00. This annual report on the role of travel and tourism in the American economy reviews the economic contributions of travel away from home, developments in the travel industry, and the effects of economic changes on travel and tourism.

National Travel Survey (Washington, D.C.: U.S. Travel Data Center, quarterly and annual). In March 1979, the U.S. Travel Data Center began conducting a monthly *National Travel Survey*. Since that time, quarterly and annual summaries of the results have been published to provide researchers with timely, consistent, and relevant data on major trends in U.S. travel activity.

PATA Annual Statistical Report, 1983 (San Francisco: Pacific Area Travel Association, 1984), 107 pp. $40.00 members, $65.00 nonmembers. Report presents the visitor arrival statistics and other relevant data reported by PATA member governments. The report gives visitor arrival data for the individual countries by nationality of residence and mode of travel. Selected market sources of visitors to the Pacific area are given, along with data on accommodations, length of stay, visitor expenditures, and national tourist organization budgets.

Tourism Compendium (Madrid: World Tourism Organization), approximately 300 pp., $35.00. This book provides quantitative and qualitative data covering many aspects of domestic and international tourism. It contains major statistical series relating to levels and trends in tourist movements by countries, by regions, and worldwide, and assessments of tourism's economic effect on both generating and receiving countries. A list of national and international organizations in the field of tourism and a bibliography is included.

Tourism Policy and International Tourism in OECD Member Countries (Paris: The Organisation for Economic Co-operation and Development, annual). Annual report on tourism statistics in Australia, Austria, Belgium, Canada, Denmark, Finland, France, Federal Republic of Germany, Greece, Iceland, Ireland, Italy, Japan, Luxembourg, the Netherlands, New Zealand, Norway, Portugal, Spain, Sweden, Switzerland, Turkey, the United Kingdom, and the United States.

Travel Industry World Yearbook: The Big Picture (New York: Child and Waters, annual), 136 pp., $52.00 in the United States, $55.00 foreign airmail. This annual issue presents a compact up-to-date review of the latest happenings in the world of tourism.

Travel Trends in the United States and Canada (Boulder, Colorado: Business Research Division, University of Colorado, 1984), 262 pp., $45.00. This document is published every three years and provides statistics on visits to recreation areas, number of tourists, tourist expenditures, length of stay and size of party, economic impact of tourism, tourism-related employment, mode of transportation used, tourism advertising, passport statistics, international travel, foreign visitor arrivals, travel costs, and highlights from national travel surveys. Data have been compiled from 260 sources.

Trends in the Hotel Industry, International Edition (Houston: Pannell Kerr Forster, annual), $50.00. A statistical review incorporating operational and financial data on hotels. Data included represent voluntary contributions by 500 establishments located outside the United States.

Trends in the Hotel Industry, USA Edition (Houston: Pannell Kerr Forster, annual), $50.00. Statistical highlights are analyzed and data are provided on operating results as measuring guides for hotel and motel operators. The data included represent voluntary contributions by 1,000 establishments. Current trends are compared with previous years and graphs and charts illuminate the statistics.

U.S. Lodging Industry (Philadelphia: Laventhol and Horwath, annual), $50.00. This annual report on the lodging industry covers comments from around the country, market data, the trends of business, percentages of occupancy, hotel earnings, payrolls, taxes, restaurant operations, credit and collection data, balance sheet statistics, and statements of income.

World Air Transport Statistics (Geneva: International Air Transport Association, annual), $40.00. This is an annual compilation of facts and figures illustrated with numerous graphs and charts, representing the most up-to-date and complete source of data on the air transport industry.

World Tourism Statistics (Madrid: World Tourism Organization, annual). This work gives detailed breakdowns of international tourist arrivals and nights by country of residence and nationality and of average foreign tourist expenditure.

World Wide Lodging Industry (New York: Horwath and Horwath International, annual), $50.00. This annual edition provides information on market data, performance measures, sales, occupancy, length of stay, payroll, income, operating expenses, and restaurant operations.

7 DATA BASES

In this era of the computer we would be remiss if we did not mention data bases. Several data bases containing travel and tourism information are available now. One of the quickest ways of finding information is to conduct a computer search of these data bases. Some data bases available are:

CENTRE DES HAUTES ETUDES TOURIST-IQUES, Fondation Vasarely 1, Avenue Marcel Pagnol, 13090, Aix-en-Provence, France. This center maintains a comprehensive collection of the world literature on tourism which has now been computerized. The Centre has been publishing since 1964 in the collection *Etudes et Memoires*, which is a reference book of all studies in tourism. The 25 volumes issued to date have recorded over 36,500 documents. The Centre also publishes *Tourist Analysis Review* every quarter. Rene Baretje heads the Centre and requests everyone send him complimentary copies of their tourism studies.

DIALOG, Information Services, Inc., 3460 Hillview Avenue, Palo Alto, California 94304, (415) 858-2700. Included in Dialog is the CAB Abstracts, a comprehensive file of the 26 journals published by Commonwealth Agricultural Bureaux in England. CAB Abstracts include a subfile entitled Leisure, Recreation and Tourism Abstracts. Subject areas covered in LRTA are leisure, recreation, and tourism; natural resources; tourism; recreation activities and facilities; culture and entertainment; and home and neighborhood activities.

IATA Statistical Information System (ISIS), P.O. Box 160, 1216 Cointrin-Geneva, Switzerland, 022-983366. IATA's computerized information service on airline traffic, capacity, revenue, and costs is now available to member airlines and affiliated interests. It provides timely, easily accessible statistics on commercial air transport. ISIS consists of a centralized data base and a number of easy to use programs enabling retrieval, processing, analysis, and display of information compiled by IATA.

INS—U.S. INTERNATIONAL AIR TRAVEL STATISTICS, U.S. Department of Transportation, 400 Seventh Street, S.W., Washington, D.C. 20590, (202) 426-4000. Maintains monthly time series showing the number of passengers flying between the United States and other ports. Data are broken down according to passenger citizenship, flight type, and the nationality of the carrier.

TOURISM REFERENCE AND DATA CENTRE (TRDC), 3rd Floor West, 235 Queen Street, Ottawa, Ontario K1A 0H6, Canada, (613) 995-2754. The Centre maintains the most comprehensive computerized collection of tourism-related information in Canada. The holdings of more than 5,000 books and documents include research papers, statistics, surveys, analyses, journals, conference proceedings, speeches, proposals, feasibility studies, legislation, guidebooks, bibliographies, and more. Information on this material is held in a data bank that can be accessed by TRDC staff or by the users of remote terminals in other parts of the country. The computer system at TRDC is a bilingual, bibliographic information storage and retrieval system that allows users to search the holdings using 1,500 key words or "descriptors." Information is classified into eight major sectors: transportation, accommodation, conventions, hospitality services, events and attractions, recreational activities and facilities, education, and tourist-related enterprises. The descriptors can be used singly or in combination to produce the information required. Searches can be undertaken, for instance, by subject, author, sponsor, date, document type, geography, or various combinations of these. The information has been compiled to assist the industry and officers of Tourism Canada; however, it is also available to the general public.

TRAVEL REFERENCE CENTER, Business Research Division, Campus Box 420, University of Colorado, Boulder, Colorado 80309, (303) 492-8227. The reference center was established in 1969 to assist the travel industry in finding information sources and provide a facility to house a comprehensive collection of travel studies. The center is a joint venture of the Travel and Tourism Research Association (TTRA) and the Business Research Division, University of Colorado, Boulder, Colorado. Services of the Center are available to TTRA members without charge and to nonmembers for $50.00 an hour. The Center now comprises the largest collection of travel, tourism, and recreation research studies available at any one place in the United States. The present collection numbers over 8,000 documents and is growing daily. The collection was computerized in 1985 and the Center can do literature searches using over 900 descriptors.

8   SOME FINAL SUGGESTIONS

This section provides information on the U.S. Travel Data Center and identifies some well-known books and reports on travel research.

U.S. Travel Data Center, 1899 L Street, N.W., Washington, D.C. 20036, was organized early in 1973 as an independent, nonprofit corporation dedicated to serving the travel research needs of the industry and nation. Today, the Data Center is the focal point of a multitude of efforts to measure and understand the travel activities of Americans and of foreign visitors to this country. In some instances, the Data Center gathers, analyzes, and disseminates statistical data published by other recognized research organizations. In other cases, the Data Center collects original data for analysis and publication. Selected programs of the Data Center are (1) National Travel Survey, (2) Impact of Travel on State Economies, (3) Survey of State Travel Offices, (4) Travel Price Index, and (5) annual travel outlook forum. A catalog of its publications is available and can be obtained by writing them.

Bosselman, Fred P., *In the Wake of the Tourist* (Washington, D.C.: The Conservation Foundation, 1978), 278 pp. This book examines experiences in Israel, Mexico, France, Australia, the Netherlands, England, West Germany, and Japan, ranging from the planning development of Cancun on the Yucatan Peninsula to the unplanned proliferation of hotels in Jerusalem and London, from consideration of the sophisticated planning systems of the Netherlands and England to the impact of citizen activism in the German city of Westerland and the Mexican village of Zihuatanejo. The author concludes that tourism can be most beneficial if it makes the tourist more aware of the special qualities of places.

Burkart, A.J., and S. Medlik, *Tourism: Past, Present and Future* (London: Heinemann, 1981), 366 pp. This book is an excellent reference for those interested in the world tourist picture and especially tourism in Britain. The book contains numerous statistical tables and a number of appendices.

The Character and Volume of the U.S. Travel Agency Market, 1983 (New York: Travel Weekly, 1984), 191 pp. This report was prepared by Louis Harris and Associates, Inc., and presents the findings of the seventh comprehensive study of the travel agency business. It updates information obtained in previous studies on the dimensions and scope of the travel agency market and on the sources and components of agency business. Like the 1976, 1978, and 1981 studies, this study also describes the importance of various criteria influencing travel agents' choices of air carriers, hotels, cruise ships, car rental agencies, and package tours for their clients. In addition this survey analyzes the impact of airline deregulation; satisfaction with hotels, car rental companies, and cruise lines; the booking of motorcoach tours; and use of on-line automated reservation systems. The data presented were derived from personal interviews with executives of 721 conference-appointed travel agencies. The June 1984 issue of *Travel Weekly* (Vol. 43, No. 57) is the Louis Harris study issue and contains the entire study plus *Travel Weekly* commentary and analysis.

Destination USA, Volume I, *Summary Report*, National Tourism Resources Review Commission (Washington, D.C.: Government Printing Office, June 1973), 108 pp., $2.00. This report discusses the travel needs and resources of the United States and addresses the part tourism plays in reducing the balance-of-payments deficit. This volume presents a summary of the commission's findings and lists their recommendations.

Gee, Chuck Y., Dexter J.L. Choy, and James C. Makens, *The Travel Industry* (Westport, Connecticut: AVI, 1984), 283 pp. $26.50. The emphasis in this text is on introducing concepts about travel as an industry. It provides a basic understanding of travel and tourism and provides insights into the development and operations of the various components of the travel industry.

Gunn, Clare A., *Tourism Planning* (New York: Crane Russak, 1979), 328 pp. This text takes a human ecology approach and describes opportunities for greater expansion of tourism on the state and regional scale, without damage to our delicate natural resources. The book provides a unique framework for understanding and regrouping the complicated elements that make up tourism. By relating planning to tourism, constructive guides for the future are offered.

Lawson, Fred, and Manuel Baud-Bovy, *Tourism and Recreation Development* (London: Architectural Press, 1977), 210 pp. This book is primarily concerned with physical planning for tourism and leisure, providing a factual basis of quantitative and qualitative norms and standards, as well as a detailed methodological approach to planning.

Lundberg, Donald E., *The Tourist Business* (Boston: Cahners, 1980), 334 pp. This book explores the travel industry and covers travel modes, the role of travel agents, why tourists travel, the economic and social impacts of tourism, tourist destination development, and travel research.

Lundberg, Donald, *International Travel and Tourism* (New York: Wiley, 1985), 254 pp., $23.95. The perspective of this book is American—why Americans go abroad, something about where they go, how they get there, and how they get around once they have arrived. Only the highlights of international travel are included. The amount of information presented about particular destinations varies according to their popularity for American travelers. It was written as a textbook for international travel.

McIntosh, Robert W., and Charles R. Goeldner, *Tourism: Principles, Practices, Philosophies* (New York: Wiley, 1986), 562 pp., $29.95. The fifth edition of this classic introduction to tourism provides a broad global perspective with emphasis on planning and developing tourism. It investigates the cultural, economic, sociological, and psychological aspects of tourism. The book is divided into five parts: Understanding Tourism: Its Nature, History, and Organization; Motivation for Travel and Choosing Travel Products; Tourism Supply, Demand, Economics, and Development; Essentials of Tourism Marketing and Research; and Tourism Practices and Prospects.

Mill, Robert C., and Alastair M. Morrison, *The Tourism System* (Englewood Cliffs, New Jersey: Prentice—Hall, 1985), 457 pp. A book presenting a comprehensive systems view of tourism stressing the interrelationships and interdependencies of its various elements. The authors cover all aspects from a marketing point of view and describe how tourism works.

Powers, Thomas F., *Introduction to Management in the Hospitality Industry* (New York: Wiley, 1984), 469 pp. This book covers the hospitality industry. It discusses the management problems of institutions that offer shelter or food or both to people away from their homes.

Rosenow, John E., and Gerreld L. Pulsipher, *Tourism: The Good, the Bad, and the Ugly* (Westport, Connecticut: AVI, 1979), paperback, $12.95. This book is about travel in America, but with an orientation toward tourism's role in helping to preserve the diversity of our nation and helping to make our communities better places in which to live.

Tourism's Top Twenty (Boulder, Colorado: Business Research Division, University of Colorado, 1984), 109 pp., $25.00. This book, compiled in cooperation with the U.S. Travel Data Center, Washington, D.C., provides facts and figures on travel, tourism, recreation, and leisure. Information is presented primarily for the United States; however, some coverage is provided on world tourism. It provides fast facts on a wide array of tourism-related subjects, including advertising, airlines, attractions, expenditures, hotels and resorts, recreation, world travel, and travel statistics. Sources are given for each table and complete addresses for the sources are provided in an appendix. A subject index is also included for ease in locating information.

Young, George, *Tourism: Blessing or Blight?* (Baltimore, Maryland: Penguin Books, 1973), 191 pp. This book describes tourism, identifies what the important issues are, and indicates possible solutions. It is aimed at the layperson, rather than at the tourism expert, as it is the former who should make the vital decisions about the role tourism should play in the life of his or her country. The book shows how tourism has grown and describes in broad terms the nature of the tourist phenomenon. It also takes a look at mistakes of others and the lessons that can be learned from the past and gives solutions that appear to be most favorable to the countries involved.

PART FOUR

SOME DISCIPLINARY PERSPECTIVES

This part of the Handbook is intended to emphasize the fact that tourism is a multidisciplinary field of study. As such, it is essential that we be aware of and utilize the rich resource base available to us from the various basic disciplines. Because of the number of these disciplines from which tourism research draws, it was not possible in this single publication to include chapters covering all possible fields. However, the four chapters which are included represent some of the most important areas, in terms of both past development of tourism thought as well as some new and evolving directions.

Chapter 16, which has been authored by Lisle Mitchell of the University of South Carolina, reviews research in tourism as viewed from the discipline of geography. In opening the chapter, Professor Mitchell clearly points out that the geographer's bias is towards research which involves the study of place and space—he or she is interested in the factors, forces, and processes that explain why a phenomenon is located where it is or why certain phenomena are distributed in a particular pattern in a specific region. Having defined this orientation, the author then presents a number of conceptual considerations pertaining to tourism research and certain fundamental constructs drawn from the field of geography. Following this discussion, Professor Mitchell provides several examples in which general concepts from geography have been applied to the study of specific tourism situations. In providing these examples, particular importance is attributed to the concept of "linkage" as the concept necessary for the understanding of travel to and from and participation in a recreational activity. Subsequently, the author moves from reported examples of previous research to a discussion of other possible applications, particularly those having a managerial perspective.

The second chapter in Part Four is rooted in the field of psychology. This chapter, entitled "Understanding Psychographics in Tourism Research," was authored by Stanley Plog, who is widely recognized as one of the most insightful consultants in the travel, tourism, and hospitality field. In this chapter, Dr. Plog focuses on personality research as it applies to tourism and attempts to show how the underlying principles of personality/psychographic research can be effectively utilized in achieving a better understanding of tourists. The initial part of the chapter examines the need for psychographic research in tourism and discusses its relationship to the field. It is emphasized that the purpose of psychographic research is to enable segmentation of the market into groups of people having different sets of motives and behaviors so that unique appeals can be developed for each of the separate groups. Having shown the relevance of psychographic research in tourism, the author subsequently provides a review of previous applications of psychometrics in the field of travel, tourism, and hospitality. This brief section is followed by a much more extensive discussion on how to carry out psychographic research. Throughout, the emphasis is on presenting the concepts in a clear, understandable, and usable manner. At the same time, the author ensures that the reader remains aware of the psychological origin of the concepts discussed. The latter part of the chapter summarizes some of the common dimensions of psychographic findings which have been found to be of particular relevance to the field of tourism.

Chapter 18 focuses upon a discipline which until recently has received relatively little attention as a contributor to tourism thought. The discipline in question is that of political science. In Chapter 18, Linda Richter of Kansas State University provides a framework for examining some of the major political issues which increasingly affect tourism. Discussion in the chapter is presented from three main perspectives. The first is that of the host country which must be concerned with balancing the positive and negative impacts of tourism. In the discussion related to this topic, Professor Richter provides a thorough review of the broad range of political considerations which must be assessed in relation to tourism. The second political perspective addressed by the chapter is that of the country of origin of tourists. While the issues involved here are perhaps less substantial in terms of their potential repercussions on all segments of the population, they nevertheless represent an important range of political considerations which need to be evaluated by a country which permits its citizens to travel freely throughout the world. Finally, the chapter examines tourism from a number of international perspectives which have a political dimension to them. In particular, emphasis is placed on the role of the international corporation. While many of the issues involved go well beyond the field of tourism as such, the discussion nevertheless brings clearly into focus how international organizations function at the interface between host countries and countries which generate large numbers of tourists.

The final chapter in Part Four represents a second contribution by Clare Gunn entitled "Environmental Design and Land Use," a comparatively new area of research. In this case, the disciplinary origin of the field is less well defined and, in fact, is still emerging. As such, Dr. Gunn's contribution to this Handbook will undoubtedly receive considerable attention as the field develops. The chapter first reviews why the field of environmental studies in tourism has achieved prominence. Dr. Gunn notes that while initial motivations may have been related to overcoming negative impacts, there is increasingly a recognition of the positive contributions from tourism development when carried out in an environmentally sensitive manner. The second major topic addressed by this chapter is the nature of the major criteria employed in environmental design. In all, seven such criteria are identified and discussed. These include functional design and planning, market acceptance, owner rewards, relevance to transportation, resource protection, local community goals, and environmental decision-makers. Having identified the design criteria that must be satisfied, Dr. Gunn then turns to an examination of the processes that must be put in place for effective environmental research and planning. In line with Dr. Gunn's previous writings, the emphasis is upon planning at the regional level with an emphasis on such fundamental concepts as clustering, environmental capacity, and landscape development. The chapter concludes with a brief discussion of examples of legislation that have been passed in various jurisdictions to ensure that tourism development is undertaken in an environmentally sound manner.

16

Research on the Geography of Tourism

LISLE S. MITCHELL

Professor of Geography
University of South Carolina
Columbia, South Carolina

This chapter has a sixfold purpose. First, to discuss the interrelationships between the geographer and the manager. Second, to distinguish between the approach of the geographer and other scientists. Third, to provide a definition of the geography of tourism. Fourth, to outline some basic conceptual considerations of the discipline of geography. Fifth, to illustrate a theoretical frame-of-reference by presenting examples of research endeavors. Sixth, to offer some possible solutions of geographic research to management problems.

Tourism or traveling for pleasure consists of two parts, one static and the other dynamic (Fig. 1A) (Matley, 1976, p. 2). The static aspect is a recreation experience that occurs at a desired site. The dynamic aspect is travel to and from a destination. This view of tourism is based on the relationship existing between population and environment (Fig. 1B). Population, or a selected segment of the population (i.e., tourists), interacts with physical and cultural environments during both phases of the tourism process. The travel phase is characterized by interaction along and through various landscapes (i.e., natural environment) utilizing appropriate technological modes such as the automobile, airplane, or cruise ship (i.e., cultural environment) and in a particular social setting such as relatives, friends, or neighbors (i.e., cultural environment). Interaction also occurs at recreation sites that are user oriented (i.e., cultural environment), resource oriented (i.e., physical environment), or have an intermediate orientation (i.e., both environments) (Clawson and Knetsch, 1966). This interaction may lead to beneficial results such as satisfaction of hosts' and guests' desires, improvement of travel routes, construction of accommodation and entertainment facilities, and increased employment opportunities; or it may lead to harmful results such as traffic congestion, air and water pollution, crime, utility shortages, and carrying capacity problems.

It is the totality of the beneficial and harmful results of the interaction between population (i.e., hosts and guests) and the environment (i.e., physical and cultural) that creates the context within which managers and geographers operate (Fig. 1C). The manager of an individual establishment is charged with the task of supervising the population–environment interaction. He is responsible for the planning and construction of facilities, for formulating recreation programs and activities, for the care and maintenance of facilities, for the safety of the patron, for transport and parking, for wise land use practices, and for the security of life and property. The geographer has the task of understanding the population–environment interaction and developing conceptual models and tools to enable the manager to supervise more effectively and efficiently. The primary tasks of the manager and geographer, therefore, are to supervise and examine the interaction between population and environment.

The differences between managers and geographers are important, but the correspondence of needs is the rationale behind this chapter. A significant interrelationship exists between the two groups and it is the purpose of this chapter to clarify the fundamental nature of geography. The procedures followed to achieve this goal are: first, to distinguish between the approach of the geographer and other social scientists to the study of tourism; second, to provide a definition of the

(1A)

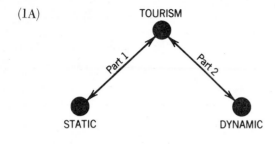

(1B)

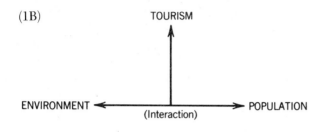

(1C)

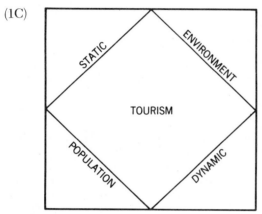

FIGURE 1 The geography of tourism.

geography of tourism and to outline some conceptual considerations; third, to present some research examples that illustrate the conceptual frames of reference; and fourth, to discuss some possible applications of geographic research to management problems.

THE GEOGRAPHIC APPROACH

The geographer and other disciplinary specialists who investigate tourism all study the same phenomena and collect data from the same sources. The difference between the approaches of the various disciplines is explained by the unique perspectives out of which they operate. A discussion of nongeographic points of view is beyond the scope of this chapter but special issues of the *Annals of Tourism Research* have extended explanations and examples of these perspectives (e.g., Sociology, Vol. 6, Nos. 1 and 2, 1979; Anthropology, Vol. 7, No. 1, 1980, and Vol. 10, No. 1,

1983; Management, Vol. 7, No. 3, 1980; Tourism Education, Vol. 8, No. 1, 1981; Economics, Vol. 9, No. 1, 1982, and Vol. 13, No. 1, 1986; Planning, Vol. 9, No. 3, 1982; Political Science, Vol. 10, No. 3, 1983; Social Psychology, Vol. 11, No. 1, 1984; Anthropology and Sociology, Vol. 11, No. 3, 1984, and Vol. 12, No. 1, 1985; and History and Geography, Vol. 12, No. 3, 1985).

The geographer's bias is toward place and space. His fundamental question is—Where? He is interested in the factors, forces, or processes that explain why a phenomenon is located where it is or why certain phenomena are distributed in a particular pattern in a specific region on the earth's surface. The tool that separates the geographer from other scientists is the map. Archival searches, computer applications, field investigations, inductive and deductive approaches, library research, and quantitative techniques are methodologies that are used by all investigators. Geographers, however, believe that an appropriate map or series of maps provides insights into subject matter that can be gained in no other way. Therefore, maps, various cartographic devices (i.e., spatial models), and the application of qualitative and quantitative methods to those maps and models along with a spatial perspective are the characteristics that distinguish the geographer from other scientists.

CONCEPTUAL CONSIDERATIONS

DEFINITION

In a special issue of the *Annals of Tourism Research* tourism geography was defined as being "concerned essentially . . . with the spatial expression of . . . the relationships and phenomena arising out of the journeys and temporary stays of people traveling primarily for leisure or recreational purposes" (Pearce, 1979, p. 248). This definition consists of five separate parts: (1) space or place; (2) relationships; (3) phenomena or facilities and activities; (4) travel; and (5) leisure or recreation. The geographer, therefore, views tourism within a spatial or place context. In other words, the geographer's bias pertains to specific site and general situational characteristics of a particular area or region. In addition, the relationships of distinct activities and facilities are emphasized. The travel aspect of tourism implies the journey to a given location and the pleasurable experience engaged in at the destination and the return trip. Both phases, travel and activity, take place during leisure time and are of a recreational nature. It may be concluded that tourism geography is concerned with patterns of the use of leisure and travel as it occurs in space. Tourism geographers observe, analyze, and explain the relationships of specific activities and facilities that are located in particular areas or regions. The geographer's view of the tourism land-scape may be examined through two simple models.

MODEL ONE

The first model consists of three basic ideas: demand, supply, and linkages (Ullman, 1956, pp. 867–871). These ideas are analyzed from two perspectives: spatial and aspatial. Tourism demand is defined as an expressed but unattained desire to travel to some other place and to participate in some recreation activity or activities. Demand is a result of the complex interrelationships between personality, cultural values, and socioeconomic class of an individual or individuals. Comprehension of demand is difficult because the knowledge and perspective of potential tourists are subject to wide variation. Demand does not occur in a vacuum but rather exists in space. Individuals who demand tourist experiences reside at specific locations and if these locations are known then it is possible to describe and analyze their spatial distribution. An understanding of demand and places of demand is necessary to the comprehension of the tourism landscape.

Supply of tourist experiences is based on two principles: one is to provide a service (e.g., camping space or water and electricity) to the general public at little or no cost and the other is to earn a profit from providing goods (e.g., a meal or a motel room) or services (e.g., automobile repair or entertainment). Service and profit motives are the main reasons for the provision of tourism opportunities. Establishments which attempt to satisfy the needs and wants of the traveling consumer tend to locate in one of three places. The first is to select a position as close to the potential consumers as possible. The second is to choose a site on or near a physical resource (i.e., a body of water, scenic vista, or other natural feature) which serves as a magnet to attract customers. The third is to locate at a position between places of demand and supply, usually along transportation routes and especially at major intersections.

Linkages are the connections between places of demand and supply. The most important association between those two places is complementarity. In other words, the desires of the potential tourist should be satisfied by a place of supply, and the purposes of the place of supply should be achieved by the demander's use of the facilities provided. Consumption or attendance rates are a valid measure of complementarity. Consumption, however, cannot take place unless the places of demand and supply are linked by communication and transportation networks. Communications are necessary to provide potential tourists with information required to overcome the distance separating the places. Consumption, communication, and transportation patterns are the vital links between demand

and supply and between places of demand and supply. The tourism landscape has no meaning and no unity unless there are physical linkages between places.

MODEL TWO

The second model utilized by geographers to view the tourism landscape consists of three concepts: purpose, structure, and location. This model assumes that there is a fundamental purpose or rationale behind the decisions and actions of tourists and members of the tourism industry. It is believed, therefore, that the spatial and aspatial aspects of purpose, structure, and location provide valuable insights into tourism (Lovingood and Mitchell, 1978, pp. 33–34).

Purpose is defined to include an understanding of the reasons why an individual or group is interested in participating in a specific tourism experience or in providing tourism opportunities for others. In other words, the purpose of a tourism activity may be explained by physical, emotional, economic, or social wants and needs, and these factors are fundamental to the ideological and/or value systems which are the basis of rational decision making and planning.

Structure consists of two components: stratification and categorization. Stratification refers to formal and informal institutions, such as socioeconomic classes, which segregate individuals during the normal course of tourist events. Categorization refers to the classification of tourist facilities and activities into either functions (e.g., seaside resort as different from mountain skiing village) or a hierarchy of activities which differ more in degree than in kind (e.g., hotels of varying quality and cost). Structure, therefore, is concerned with the organization of individuals and/or groups of tourists on the basis of some socioeconomic or other criteria in order to match their characteristics with the most appropriate facility or activity. It should be noted that structure and its components logically follow and are based on the value systems which are rudimentary to the idea of purpose.

The location of tourism sites and facilities may be described using several spatial measures. First, tourist attractions may be oriented toward (1) the residence of tourists, (2) the site of natural or cultural resources which are modified for tourist consumption, or (3) a position which is intermediate between tourist and resource locations (Clawson and Knetsch, 1966, pp. 36–40). Second, tourist establishments may be distributed in a concentrated, random, or uniform pattern. All tourist units have individual site and situational characteristics and those spatial attributes reflect the unique purposes and structures of the units. For example, hotels and motels are user oriented. The vast majority are located in or adjacent to metropolitan centers because potential consumers tend to agglomerate in such places. On the other hand, some hotels and motels are found at sites of physical resources (e.g., Mammoth Cave) or cultural resources (e.g., Las Vegas). Finally, some hotels and motels select locations along major transport routes or at principal intersections and/or interchanges to take advantage of the traveling public's need for accommodation. These sites are selected to attract the largest possible clientele and to maximize profits, which is a basic purpose of management. This purpose influences the cost of rooms and other services, and costs stratify potential consumers into various groups to match the large number of classes of hotels and motels. In summary, the location of hotels and motels or any other tourist unit is largely determined by its purpose and the logically associated structure. Therefore, the concepts of purpose, structure, and location are inextricably interlocked and interrelated.

CONCEPTUAL MATRIX

These models may be used in a variety of ways as both provide interesting insights into tourism. Examples of applications of these schema will not be presented as they are beyond the scope of this chapter. The models may, however, be placed in a three-by-three matrix to serve as a guide to the geography of tourism (Fig. 2). The placement of the elements of each scheme in this position results in some interesting associations. Each of the cells numbered 1 through 9 may be thought of as the intersection of two concepts, for example:

Cell 1: Purpose—Place of Demand
Cell 2: Purpose—Place of Supply
Cell 3: Purpose—Linkage
Cell 4: Structure—Place of Demand
Cell 5: Structure—Place of Supply
Cell 6: Structure—Linkage
Cell 7: Location—Place of Demand
Cell 8: Location—Place of Supply
Cell 9: Location—Linkage

The connecting of the ideas of purpose and place of demand in Cell 1 might raise such questions as: What is the purpose of demand for a tourist experience? or What are the causes of demand for tourism? or What are the socioeconomic characteristics of potential tourists? These questions and others like them suggest the limits of the cell. Each cell could be considered in the same manner.

The framework is logical and flexible enough to be used as a description of the present state of the geography of tourism, a tool for the classification of geographic literature, and as a device for the formulation of research questions or the focusing of research efforts. While individual cells serve as a research concentration, it is also possible to view combinations of rows or columns at a second level of application (Fig. 2). The row entitled "Purpose," including Cells 1, 2, and 3, is concerned with human values; the row "Structure," or Cells 4, 5, and 6, pertains to activities, facilities, and institutions; and the row "Location," Cells 7, 8, and 9, has a regional bias. The column labeled "Demand," including Cells 1, 4, and 7, has a behavioral thrust; the column "Supply," or Cells 2, 5, and 8, centers on management or physical and cultural environmental impacts; and the "Linkage" column, Cells 3, 6, and 9, concentrates on transportation, com-

	DEMAND	SUPPLY	LINKAGE	
PURPOSE	1	2	3	Ideology Values
STRUCTURE	4	5	6	Institutions Facilities Activities
LOCATION	7	8	9	Physical Distribution Geometry
	Behavior	Management Impact Environment	Transportation Interaction Participation	

FIGURE 2 Tourism research frame-of-reference.

munication, interaction, and participation. The analysis of the matrix by row or column, rather than by cell, produces a general combination of four interrelated ideas although one of these—the row or column title—is of primary concern. These procedures add to the versatility and utility of the matrix and broaden its scope beyond the apparent narrowness of the nine cells.

In summary, the ideas contained in the two models form the basic elements of the matrix. The matrix, in turn, is utilized as a geographer's guide to the investigation of tourism. In the remainder of this chapter relevant research examples and possible applications will be organized with the matrix serving as a principal frame of reference.

RESEARCH EXAMPLES

Examples of geographic research will be presented by examining the columns of the matrix and focusing on the concepts of demand, supply, and linkage. The concepts of purpose, structure, and location will be incorporated in the discussion of each column. This organizational structure has been selected because the conceptual and factual findings in the literature are more easily arranged following this general approach.

DEMAND AND PLACE OF DEMAND

Demand and consumption are often assumed to be the same but they are, in fact, opposites. Demand is an individually felt want, or desire, while consumption is an act of acquiring, participating, or utilizing (Mercer, 1973). Demand, therefore, is a feeling, emotion, or belief, but consumption is an activity. The participation in a tourism experience (i.e., consumption) may satisfy an individual's tourism desire (i.e., need) but consumption of tourism activities is not the same as need for tourism activities. The significance of the distinction between demand and consumption will become clearer in the discussion of linkage.

Even though demand is an emotion, it exists in space like any other fact and geographers have attempted to identify the factors that seem to explain demand for tourist experiences. According to Wolfe (1951) demand is influenced by physical factors, such as distance and access, and these factors have been verified by Laber (1969), Malamud (1973), and Gurgel (1976). Wolfe (1951) also notes the significance of sociological factors as predictors of demand. These factors are expanded upon by Mercer (1973) to include population size, age, income, mobility, and available leisure time. Yu (1981) points to the importance of social status and its impact on tourist demand. The supply of tourist activities stimulates demand and according to Demars (1979) the attractivity of tourist centers and market

conditions are prominent explanatory variables. The quantity and quality of tourist resorts or complexes is important in understanding the rationale of tourist desires (Stanfield, 1971). Market conditions, such as inflation, interest rates, employment, amount of expendable income, and available leisure time, have a significant effect on tourist needs.

Decisions pertaining to touring and recreation experiences are based on individual needs and values, and a logical attempt is made to maximize satisfaction and to minimize monetary and time costs (Stutz, 1977). The decision-making process involves not only personal characteristics but the sources of information and degree of knowledge about alternative attractions and transportation facilities (Murphey, 1979). Information and knowledge are collected from a number of sources that may be as simple and direct as word-of-mouth advertising or as complicated, indirect, and impersonal as a radio or television commercial. No matter what the source, an individual must decide between competing tourist establishments and alternative transportation modes. Not all tourist facilities are equally attractive and those that project the best image have an obvious advantage (Murphey and Rosenbloom, 1974). Likewise not all sites have equal access and such factors as physical and cultural barriers, transportation networks, and physical and psychological distance are important in explaining the selection of one tourist unit over another.

Demand for and decision processes pertaining to tourism are made at some place, usually the residence of the individual involved. It is well known that tourists and thus tourist demand are concentrated like the general population in central cities and surrounding suburbs (Wolfe, 1951; Fussell, 1965; Bell, 1977; Wolfe, 1978; and Van Doren, 1981). The locational pattern of demand from activity to activity and from facility to facility is illustrated for beach activities by Fussell (1965), state parks by Enger and Guest (1968), second homes by Ragatz (1979), camping facilities by Taylor and Knudson (1973), ski resorts by Ewing and Kulka (1979), and urban cultural facilities by Wall and Sinnott (1980). Nevertheless, the spatial distribution of demand in both general and specific instances may be better understood if factors of demand (i.e., purpose) and decision-making processes (i.e., structure) as well as location are considered.

SUPPLY AND PLACE OF SUPPLY

The purpose of supply is seldom examined in the geographical literature because it is assumed that the provision of tourism services is the function of governmental agencies and the earning of profit is the goal of tourism corporations. Lovingood and Mitchell (1978), however, investigated the differences between public and private recreation units in Columbia, South Carolina. It was discovered that public agencies provide general recreation activities to the lower to middle classes as close and accessible to their residences as possible. Private concerns, on the other hand, offer relatively specialized facilities to the middle and upper economic classes at locations which are intermediate or resource oriented. Thus the public and private tourism sectors tend to be complementary to each other and there is relatively little duplication of recreation opportunities.

Places of supply (i.e., structure) have been classified by Wolfe, Fussell, and Gunn. The major summer resorts of the province of Ontario, Canada, are grouped into three classes (Wolfe, 1951). Three hundred and seventy-nine resorts are included in 43 resort areas, 22 resort regions, and 10 recreational divisions. The classification scheme is based on contiguous regions with physical and cultural factors used to delineate boundaries. The South Carolina coastal area is categorized by Fussell (1965) using a modified version of a system utilized by the Outdoor Recreation Resources Review Commission. Seven self-explanatory groups are listed: (1) high-density recreation areas, (2) general outdoor recreation areas, (3) natural environment areas, (4) unique natural areas, (5) primitive areas, (6) historic and cultural sites, and (7) low-density and high-cost recreation areas. Tourist regions or community-attraction complexes are divided into five basic elements by Gunn (1972). The elements are: a transport system linking a region or complex with its market (i.e., external transportation), an entrance point or points where information and directions are dispensed (i.e., gateway), an urban settlement that provides goods, services, facilities, and recreation attractions (i.e., community), sites and facilities providing a wide variety of recreation opportunities (i.e., recreation clusters), and a transit network connecting the gateway, community, and recreation clusters (i.e., internal circulation). These three classification schemes, spatial, descriptive, and functional, are methodologically simple and relatively easy to apply to a managerial problem. However, a great deal of research needs to be conducted on the classification of tourist regions.

The best known and most widely used system to explain the locational pattern of tourism enterprises is by a nongeographer, Marion Clawson (Clawson and Knetsch, 1966). This scheme is based on the tendency of places of tourism supply to be oriented toward users, resources, or positions intermediate between population and resources. According to Christaller (1964) tourism is a peripheral activity and most geographic studies tend to concentrate on resorts that focus on natural or cultural resources. Most of the studies cited in this chapter center on resource-oriented locations: wilderness cottages (Wolfe, 1951), the shoreline (Fussell, 1965), coal mines (Deasy and Griess, 1966), and

caves (Wall, 1978). However, urban studies have been conducted on user-oriented sites such as Vancouver by Murphey (1979), on Canadian cities by Rajotte (1975), on recreation business districts by Stanfield and Rickert (1970), and on recreational boating by Heatwole and West (1982). The only article found specifically related to intermediate tourist places was by Eiselen (1945).

The investigation of supply and places of supply of tourism experiences is technically simple. Inventories of tourism activities, facilities, programs, and policies are conducted continuously but the examination of the rationale of establishments, the classification of enterprises and their influence on consumption, and the location patterns of places and supply are seldom examined. Tourism attractions studied in a context that excludes spatial considerations are missing an important dimension that can provide valuable insights into serious operational problems.

LINKAGE

Marion Clawson (Clawson and Knetsch, 1966) has identified five phases of a tourism experience: planning, travel to the site, participating in a recreation experience, the return trip, and the recollection of the total experience. The planning or decision-making phase was discussed earlier and the recollection or recall phase is beyond the scope of this chapter. However, travel to and from, and participation in, a recreation activity is basic to the idea of linkage.

Connections between places of demand and supply are not made unless there is some degree of complementarity. In other words, a place of supply must provide some recreation good (i.e., a drink, meal, or novelty), or services (i.e., a room, activity, or program), that is desired by a tourist. The trip to a tourist attraction, engaging in recreation experiences, and the return trip are identified as consumption. Consumption is the satisfaction, at least to some extent, of a tourist demand (i.e., purpose). The examination of linkage from a geographic perspective is, therefore, concerned with complementarity and the consumption of tourism goods and services and related concepts (Gunn, 1972).

Wall (1978) compared the consumption patterns of a National and State Park in Kentucky. The National Park had approximately twice the attendance of the State Park: 1,739,957 vs. 926,750. The National Park was larger in size, had more recreation and travel facilities, and had a more central and accessible location than the State Park, thus the greater attractivity of the National Park explains its larger attendance. To further explain the consumption pattern, Wall noted that the average distance traveled to the National Park was greater than that to the State Park, 302 vs. 108 miles, and that the percentage of visitors from out-of-state was higher at the Federal park, 73.8 vs. 61.6 percent. This study demonstrates three spatial principles. First, consumption or attendance is positively correlated with attractivity, or the more attractive tourist establishment is more likely to have greater attendance than less attractive facilities. Second, tourist sites may be classified on the basis of their attractivity. Third, tourists are willing to travel relatively long distances to visit tourist sites that are highly attractive.

Two classes of visitors to Wasaga Beach were identified: cottagers and transients (Wolfe, 1952). The cottagers were middle-class individuals and families from the suburbs of metropolitan Canada, who were escaping the urban environment to the more rural atmosphere of the beach area. The transients were blue-collar workers from the congested central cities of Canada, who were escaping their crowded conditions but enjoying the urban amenities of the Wasaga Beach Village. It may be concluded that different groups of people from the same general environment are attracted to tourist regions for completely different motives. The use of similar tourist environments for different reasons by different groups of people demonstrates the significance of the concept of the structure of linkages.

The hinterlands of two tourist attractions in Pennsylvania were identified and demarcated by Deasy and Griess (1966). The criterion used to determine the area was the ratio of registered visitors to the total population of all source counties. This resulted in hinterlands of different shapes and sizes. One had a skewed circular shape and the other was an east to west shaped rectangle. The authors had hypothesized that the service areas would have circular shapes. They offered six reasons why the hypothesized shapes did not occur: one, invalid data; two, differences in access to the sites; three, intervening opportunity or competition from other tourist attractions; four, regional orientation of the population in Pennsylvania and surrounding states; five, the degree of familiarity of the population with the two establishments; and six, advertising.

While all of the factors played some role in influencing hinterland shapes the authors noted three as being more important. Access as related to the distance–decay concept seemed significant. In general, the rate of attendance decreased as distance from the site increased although not at a uniform rate or in all directions. The rate of decrease was slower in those sectors that were more urban in nature, and thus reinforcing the notion that tourists tend to be concentrated in heavily populated areas. The population's familiarity with the attractions was also an important factor: both enterprises used a similar advertising focus but stressed different aspects of the theme. The sections of the hinterlands that generated more than their expected share of attendance had logical reasons for being aware of the differences between the attractions,

and thus familiarity explains a significant portion of hinterland size and shape.

The factor the authors believed to be most important was advertising. They stated that advertising appears to be a key element in producing major modifications in the shapes of the hinterlands under study. The correlation between newspaper advertising and counties included in the hinterland was extremely high. The authors conclude that "if it were necessary to make a case for the effectiveness of advertising in promoting tourist enterprises, one would need search no further for convincing evidence" (Deasy and Griess, 1966, p. 303).

The linkages that directly bind place of demand to place of supply are communications and transportation networks. Indirect connections are related to the concept of complementarity (i.e., purpose) and are observed in consumption patterns; classes of tourists (i.e., structure); hinterland sizes and shapes; minimum, mean, and maximum distances traveled; and explanatory factors like access, familiarity, and advertising (i.e., location).

POSSIBLE APPLICATIONS

The research needs of managers of tourism facilities are large, complex, and specific. Nevertheless, it is believed that the general geographic concepts and examples presented have value. It is assumed that managers who are responsible for the successful operation of a place or places of supply have a direct interest in the structure and location of places of demand and the linkages between places of demand and supply. Furthermore, it is assumed that managers rationalize their decision-making processes and therefore are aware of the significance of their formal programs, activities, policies, and location characteristics.

This portion of the chapter will be organized around a manager's view of the conceptual framework and the research examples presented above. A manager must first consider the supply of tourism goods and the place of supply (i.e., the actual tourism establishment under consideration). In turn, demand, place of demand, and linkages are examined (Fig. 3). A series of questions about supply, demand, and linkage considerations will be stated with regard to purpose, structure, and location in order to illustrate the implications of geographic research for the tourism manager.

SUPPLY AND PLACE OF SUPPLY

Table 1 contains examples of the kinds of questions a manager might ask about the purpose, structure, and locational characteristics of supply as related to his establishment. From a geographic perspective the ability to provide goods and services to the traveling public centers on location. The location type, site, and

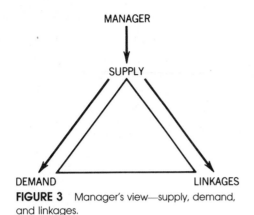

FIGURE 3 Manager's view—supply, demand, and linkages.

situation within the local landscape, and position in relationship to potential patrons are fundamental to the purpose and the place of the establishment in the structure of the tourist-scape. The economic viability (i.e., the minimum number of patrons needed to earn a profit) of a business is directly related to location. Associated with location and the economics of operation are the type of individual, family, or group to be served and the number and quality of the attractions developed to entice potential patrons. Once the purpose is rationalized, concern for facilities and programs to suit customers, the complementary and/or competitive nature of surrounding enterprises, and the existence of beneficial external institutions must be investigated.

Possible applications of geographic research to the questions of supply are fourfold. First, an analysis of the site would be useful to determine the most advantageous positioning of facilities and buildings, and to ensure convenience and safe entrance and exit to the establishment. Second, an investigation into the situational relationship between the site and the potential market area is necessary to come to an understanding of the source regions of tourists. Third, a study of the functional association between the establishment and both complementary and competitive businesses is helpful to the comprehension of how the establishment fits into the tourist attractions surrounding the site. Fourth, an examination of the activities and facilities of an establishment is important to understand the class of tourist served.

DEMAND AND PLACE OF DEMAND

Examples of general questions pertaining to the purpose, structure, and locational aspects of demand are found in Table 2. Implications from geographic research suggest the following applications. First, an analysis of the spatial distribution of tourists can provide information about residential patterns. Tourist positions can be classified as being distributed in a concentrated, uniform, or random fashion, and each locational form needs to be approached utilizing different management strategies and tactics. Second, once the locational characteristics are known a study of socioeconomic characteristics and personality profiles can result in a better understanding of tourist wants and needs. Finally, after the basic motives and values of tourists are discovered then it is possible to develop methods to inform and attract them to a tourism attraction. All three of these approaches are closely interrelated and must be considered simultaneously, although systematically, to be effective.

TABLE 1 Questions about Supply

Purpose

1. What is the minimum patronage needed to cover capital and operating costs?
2. What quantity and quality of facilities, activities, programs, policies, and promotions will attract the minimum patronage?
3. The market for this particular enterprise consists of what socioeconomic level?

Structure

1. What level of attraction is provided by this enterprise?
2. How does this enterprise fit into the surrounding businesses?
3. What surrounding businesses are complementary and/or competitive?

Location

1. What type of location does this establishment have: user, intermediate, or resource oriented?
2. Does this site have any locational advantages and/or liabilities?
3. What are the situational characteristics of this establishment in the local tourism landscape?

TABLE 2   Questions about Demand

Purpose

1. What are the needs, motives, and values of potential patrons? What do they want and what do they want to do?
2. How can tourists be attracted to this establishment?
3. How familiar are tourists with this establishment?

Structure

1. What are the socioeconomic characteristics of tourists who might be attracted to this establishment?
2. What is the personality profile of a typical touring individual or family?
3. What type of attraction is desired by potential patrons?

Location

1. Where do potential patrons reside?
2. Are there spatial concentrations of potential patrons?
3. Are there spatial voids of potential patrons?

TABLE 3   Questions about Linkages

Purpose

1. How many patrons have been attracted in the past?
2. What are the possibilities of increasing consumption?
3. How do the economy and the fuel situation affect consumption?

Structure

1. What are the facility needs and skill abilities of the patrons?
2. What goods and services do patrons consume?
3. What individual or family types utilize the facility?

Location

1. What is the size and shape of the market area?
2. What transportation modes and routes are used to reach this establishment?
3. What is the minimum, maximum, and average distance traveled to this establishment?

LINKAGE

Questions about the linkages connecting places of supply and places of demand are found in Table 3. Geographically, the first concern is with the size and shape of the market area, the transportation networks utilized, and various distance measures of tourist travel. Therefore, the delimiting and demarcating of the market area and the analysis of related spatial concerns are of foremost importance. Second, but related to the first, is the examination of attendance records. Studies of past consumption are a key to understanding present and future trends. This is especially true when the

records are viewed in the context of the state of the economy and when variables like fuel costs and/or availability are considered. In this light an investigation of attendance in relation to the market area can be a valuable management tool. Third, and last, the onsite experiences of tourists should be evaluated. The socioeconomic class level and skill abilities of the tourist to a large extent determine the kind of goods and services that are demanded and the type of consumption that will take place. Thus, an activity and facility analysis of tourist participation can be helpful in making management decisions.

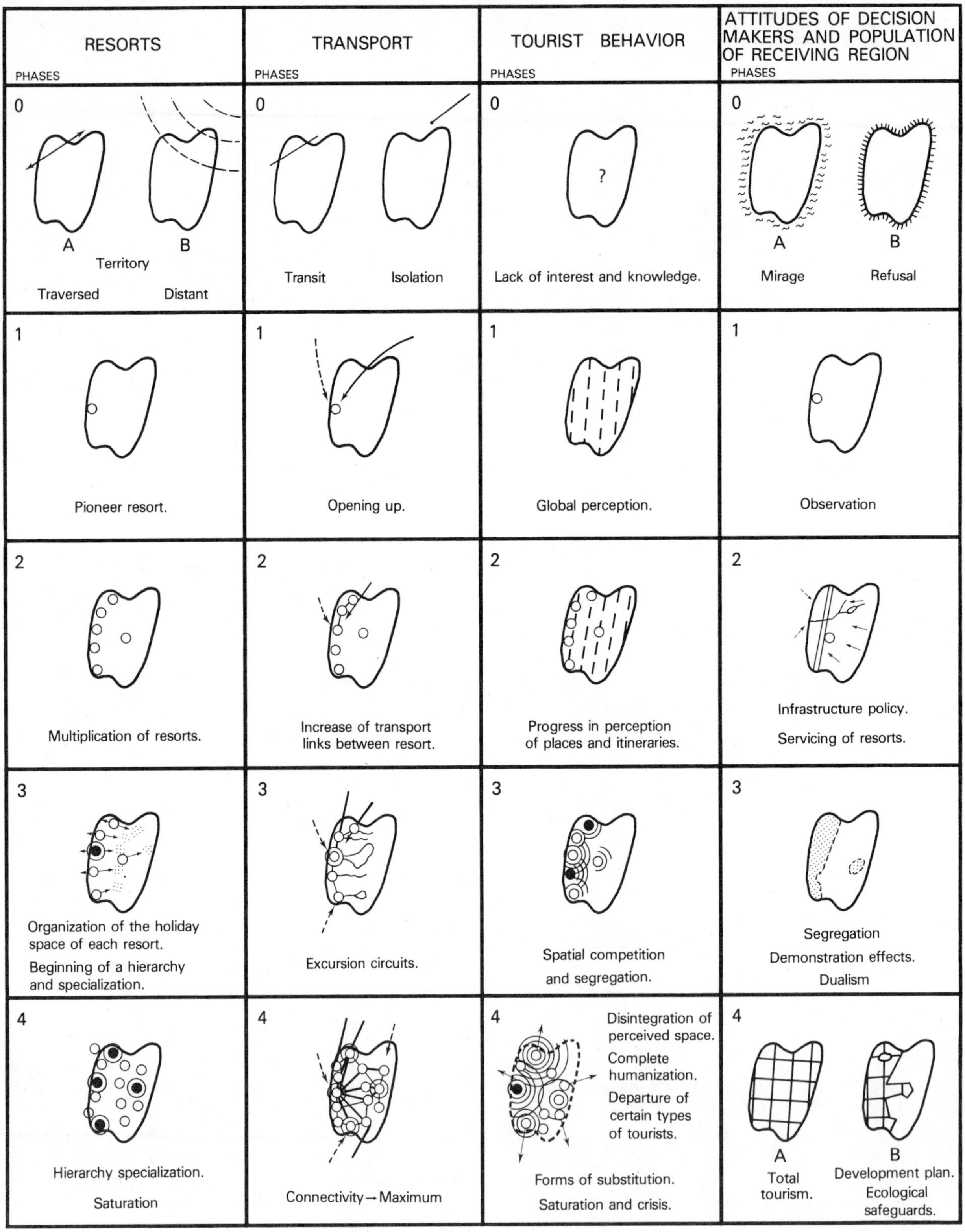

FIGURE 4 A model of tourist space. Source: Miossec J.M., (1976), "Elements pour une Theorie de l'Espace Touristique," *Les Cahiers du Tourisme*, C-36, CHET, Aix-en-Provence.

SUMMARY

The geographer's bias toward space and place is reflected in the types of research carried out and the possible applications of methods and findings to the problems of tourism managers. The spatial connections between places of supply and places of demand are fundamental to the geographer. The study of consumption reflects the complementarity that exists between supply (i.e., managers) and demand (i.e., tourists) and demonstrates that distance and other physical and cultural barriers to travel have been overcome. The classification of attractions and the stratification of visitors illustrate the structure of the tourism system. The size and shape of the market area are directly related to both purpose and structure and are a product of the interconnecting transportation systems and the distances traveled by tourists.

A model of tourist space developed by Miossec (1976) synthesizes many of the concepts discussed in this chapter. The original article, unfortunately not formally translated into English at this date, considers four basic elements: resorts (i.e., supply), transportation networks (i.e., linkages), the behavior of tourists (i.e., demand), and the attitudes of local decision-makers and population (i.e., purpose). The spatial model (Fig. 4) incorporates the concepts of structure and location. Thus, this prototype with its emphasis on space and place and the use of maps provides imaginative insights into the developmental phases of the tourist-scape. Geographic research that is comprehensive, internally consistent, and logical, like this example, is of value to managers in the solution of problems of market segmentation, classification schemes, carrying capacity, and spatial orientation (i.e., supply); the distribution of tourists, decision-making processes, and matching the wants and needs of tourists with goods and services of tourist establishments (i.e., demand); and to locate and determine the size and shape of the market area, to discover the major modes and routes of travel and estimate the minimum, mean, and maximum distances traveled, and to define the spatial thrust of advertising efforts (i.e., linkage).

CONCLUSION

Geographic investigations of tourism attractions do not have to be large or expensive. It is possible with the use of probability theory to draw a relatively small sample of data that is either readily available or easily obtained to produce findings of significant value to managers. Rigorous research design based on fundamental managerial objectives, carefully collected data, and effective utilization of research methodology can result in useful spatial generalizations that are normally overlooked by the tourism industry.

REFERENCES

Annals of Tourism Research, various vols. and nos. (1979–1986).

Bell, Michael (1977), "The Spatial Distribution of Second Homes: A Modified Gravity Model," *Journal of Leisure Research*, Vol. 9, No. 3, pp. 225–233.

Christaller, Walter (1964), "Some Considerations of Tourism Location in Europe," *Papers, Regional Science Association*, pp. 95–105.

Clawson, Marion, and Jack L. Knetsch (1966), *Economics of Outdoor Recreation*, Baltimore: Johns Hopkins Press.

Deasy, George F., and Phyllis R. Griess (1966), "The Impact of a Tourist Facility on Its Hinterland," *Annals of the Association of American Geographers*, Vol. 56, No. 2, pp 290–306.

Demars, Stanford (1979), "British Contribution to American Seaside Resorts," *Annals of Tourism Research*, Vol. 6, No. 3, pp. 285–293.

Eiselen, Elizabeth (1945), "The Tourist Industry of a Modern Highway, US 16 in South Dakota," *Economic Geography*, Vol. 21, No. 3, pp. 221–230.

Enger, Bruce M., and B. Ross Guest (1968), "The Response of a State Park to Demand for Recreation," *Professional Geographer*, Vol. 20, No. 3, pp. 171–176.

Ewing, Gordon O., and Terrence Kulka (1979), "Revealed and Stated Preference Analysis of Ski Resort Attractiveness," *Journal of Leisure Sciences*, Vol. 2, Nos. 3 and 4, pp. 249–275.

Fussell, James R. (1965), "Recreation and the South Carolina Coast," *Southeastern Geographer*, Vol. 5, pp. 48–56.

Gunn, Clare A. (1972), *Vacationscape: Designing Tourist Regions*, Austin: Bureau of Business Research, The University of Texas.

Gurgel, Klaus D. (1976), "Travel Patterns of Canadian Visitors to the Mormon Cultural Hearth," *Canadian Geographer*, Vol. 20, No. 4, pp. 405–418.

Heatwole, Charles A., and Niels C. West (1982), "Recreational-Boating Patterns and Water Surface Zoning," *Geographical Review*, Vol. 72, pp. 304–311.

Laber, Gene (1969), "Determinants of International Travel between Canada and the United States," *Geographical Analysis*, Vol. 1, No. 4, pp. 329–336.

Lovingood, Paul E., Jr., and Lisle S. Mitchell (1978), "The Structure of Public and Private Recreation Systems: Columbia, South Carolina," *Journal of Leisure Research*, Vol. 10, No. 1, pp. 21–36.

Malamud, Bernard (1973), "Gravity Model Calibration of Tourist Travel to Las Vegas," *Journal of Leisure Research*, Vol. 5, No. 4, pp. 23–33.

Matley, Ian M. (1976), *The Geography of International Tourism*, Washington, D.C.: Association of American Geographers, Resource Papers No. 76-1.

Mercer, David C. (1973), "The Concept of Recreation Need," *Journal of Leisure Research*, Vol. 5, No. 1, pp. 37–50.

Mercer, David C. (1979), "The Geography of Leisure—A Contemporary Growth Point," *Geography*, Vol. 55, No. 3, pp. 261–273.

Miossec, J.M. (1976), "Elements pour une Theorie de l'Espace Touristique," *Les Cahiers du Tourisme*, C-36, CHET, Aix-en-Provence.

Murphey, Peter E. (1979), "Tourism in British Columbia: Metropolitan and Camping Visitors," *Annals of Tourism Research*, Vol. 6, No. 3, pp. 294–306.

Murphey, Peter E., and Lorne Rosenbloom (1974), "Tourism: An Exercise in Spatial Search," *Canadian Geographer*, Vol. 18, No. 3, pp. 201–210.

Pearce, Douglas (1979), "Towards a Geography of Tourism," *Annals of Tourism Research*, Vol. 6, No. 3, pp. 245–272.

Ragatz, Richard Lee (1979), "Vacation Homes in the Northeastern United States: Seasonality in Population Distribution," *Annals of the Association of American Geographers*, Vol. 60, No. 3, pp. 447–455.

Rajotte, Freda (1975), "The Different Travel Patterns and Spatial Framework of Recreation and Tourism," *Tourism as a Factor in National and Regional Development*, Peterborough, Canada: Trent University, Department of Geography, Occasional Paper 4, pp. 43–52.

Stanfield, Charles A., Jr. (1971), "The Geography of Resorts: Problems and Potentials," *Professional Geographer*, Vol. 23, No. 2, pp. 164–166.

Stanfield, Charles A., and John E. Rickert (1970), "The Recreational Business District," *Journal of Leisure Research*, Vol. 2, No. 3, pp. 213–225.

Stutz, Frederick P. (1977), "A Descriptive Model of Non-work Travel," *Yearbook Association of Pacific Geographers*, Vol. 39, pp. 89–103.

Taylor, Charles E., and Douglas M. Knudson (1973), "Area Preferences of Midwestern Campers," *Journal of Leisure Research*, Vol. 5, No. 2, pp. 39–48.

Ullman, Edward L. (1956), "The Role of Transportation and the Basis for Interaction," *Man's Role in Changing the Face of the Earth*, William L. Thomas, Jr., *et al.*, Eds., Chicago: The Chicago University Press, pp. 862–880.

Van Doren, Carlton S. (1981), "Outdoor Recreation Trends in the 1980's: Implications for Society," *Journal of Travel Research*, Vol. 19, pp. 3–10.

Wall, Geoffrey (1978), "Competition and Complementarity: A Study in Park Visitation," *International Journal of Environmental Studies*, Vol. 13, pp. 35–41.

Wall, Geoffrey, and J. Sinnott (1980), "Urban Recreational and Cultural Facilities and Tourism Attractions," *Canadian Geographer*, Vol. 24, pp. 50–59.

Wolfe, Roy I. (1951), "Summer Cottages in Ontario," *Economic Geography*, Vol. 27, No. 1, pp. 10–32.

Wolfe, Roy I. (1952), "The Wasaga Beach: The Divorce from the Geographic Environment," *Canadian Geographer*, Vol. 1, No. 2, pp. 57–65.

Wolfe, Roy I. (1978), "Vacation Homes as Social Indicators: Observation from Canadian Census Data," *Journal of Leisure Sciences*, Vol. 1, No. 4, pp. 327–343.

Yu, Jih-Min (1981), "A Leisure Demand Projection Model," *Journal of Leisure Sciences*, Vol. 4, No. 2, pp. 127–142.

17

Understanding Psychographics in Tourism Research

STANLEY C. PLOG

Plog Research, Inc.
Reseda (Los Angeles),
California

*D*emographics, although useful in travel research, does not explain underlying motivations for travel. Psychographics, in contrast, answers many important questions about the how, what, and why of travel, allowing travel marketers and developers to become more focused and effective in their efforts. This chapter describes the historical antecedents of contemporary psychographic research, offers examples of how it can be used effectively, and provides a framework for interested researchers to develop their own psychographic systems.

In the art of building, an intelligent and expert carpenter is entitled to the foremost place, or first degree of eminence. . . . His profession depends on the practical application of the most plain, simple, and unerring principles; and more pleasure results from the view, as well as more comfort from the use, of a neat well-constructed common house, than from the most superb but ill contrived palace. (From the Preface to The Carpenter's Pocket Directory *by William Pain, published in Philadelphia, 1797.)*

The beauty of colonial architecture is founded on these clear and direct words—to follow the "unerring principles" of simplicity, plainness, and commonness. There is no attempt to adorn beyond what is necessary, no need to add gimmickry or gingerbread detail to attract the eye, and no attempt to divert the attention of a beholder from the central purpose of the structure. And yet colonial architecture—simple and direct—continues to be elegant and beautiful, even in our contemporary times.

Our topic is research—personality research as it applies to tourism. Our problem is that it tends *not to* be plain, common, and simple. Rather, it is often complex and confusing and the underlying logic may be often convoluted. The end result is not a structure of common beauty but a research edifice which is intelligible only to its developer. Who knows how many buried psychographic and lifestyle studies lie unused in the files of travel and tourism companies because the results were incomprehensible or unusable? The researchers forgot the common dictum of the KISS philosophy—Keep It Simple, Stupid!

Simplicity does not mean we use a simplistic research design or elementary statistics. We choose and use the methods appropriate to the task. But, we come prepared to seek clarity at every stage of effort and commit ourselves to avoid trying to dazzle others when simpler explanations will do.

In this paper, we will attempt to present the underlying principles of good personality/psychographic research as it applies to travel and tourism topics. We have some inherent biases about how it should be done—and what goes wrong in many studies—but we will make these clear so that the reader can pass final judgment.

THE USES AND DEMANDS FOR PSYCHOGRAPHIC RESEARCH

Survey research grew up on demographics. From the time of its early beginnings, during the late 1920s and early 1930s, slicing the population into various categories by age, sex, income, occupation, area of residence, etc., was common. It was an easy thing to do, quite useful for interpretation, and readily understood by all readers. This tendency has been so prevalent that it is intertwined in all research and marketing concepts to the point that we now buy print and broadcast media primarily on the basis of audience demographics.

Psychographics is a newer field and, as a result, has not had the time to make the same impact in research and marketing circles. Unless there is standardization in some manner, it probably never will.

But, psychographic/personality-based research is still useful for many of the research needs in travel and leisure. The reason is that demographic categories are far less predictive than they used to be. And, when we really want to "get inside the skin" of travelers to understand why they do what they do and how we can fulfill their needs, we have to look beyond the standard tools of the research industry.

There are many uses for psychographic research. Ideas occur almost spontaneously to anyone involved in the travel industry because they relate to critically important marketing questions such as, "I wonder what kind of person my customer really is?"; "Why did he or she not buy my product (service)?"; "What motives should I appeal to in my advertising?"; "What kinds of media fit the lifestyle(s) of my target markets?"

Examples of psychographically relevant topics in travel/leisure research include:

- Destination development—clarifying the concept of a new resort to be developed, the markets to be served, the services and amenities to be provided to visitors, etc.

- Product positioning—focusing a product or service to a greater degree on the needs and psychology of its primary users. Much like an automobile, or a food product company, travel/leisure companies must position their products and services to appeal to specific market segments.

- Development of supporting services—determining which services are essential and which are optional for a travel-related company. Essential services must be included, while optional services should be considered only if they are not very costly or they add to the overall marketability of the product.

- Advertising and promotion—focusing the message on the appropriate group of travelers. Their psychology, personal whims, motivations, and basic needs can be appealed to through messages that are highly targeted.

- Packaging—making certain that you not only have the right products and services, but that you have also packaged them appropriately. It is possible that a destination area may have all of the amenities, facilities, and activities desired by a group of travelers, but not be identified as such. Advertising can get the message out, but the concept must be presented (packaged) in such a way that it fits the customer's *perceived* needs.

- Master planning—developing a master plan which protects the inherent beauty and attractiveness of a destination, while still meeting the needs of travelers. This requirement is fundamental to all groups concerned with travel and tourism, such as visitors' associations, developers, hotels, airlines, and cruise ship companies.

DOES PERSONALITY RESEARCH RELATE TO TRAVEL AND TOURISM?

Since demographics, as a research tool, has held sway for so long—and it continues to be useful—the obvious question has to be answered. Is it necessary to know anything about personality, lifestyle, or other psychological variables to understand the growth and development of travel and tourism throughout the world? The answer is simple: you need to know basic demographics about tourist populations. But, in today's world, you can't say much about people who travel after you have defined their income, age, and marital status.

The fact is that the butcher, the baker, and the candlestick maker—and the doctor, lawyer, and Indian chief—may all make rather good income these days. They may live in the same neighborhood, shop at the same stores, go to the same church or temple, and have the same amount of money left over to take vacations. But there the similarity ends since they choose different destinations for vacations, different modes of transportation to get there, and they participate in different activities after they arrive. The only way to find out about why they choose different vacation lifestyles is to get inside their heads to determine what makes them tick. By definition, that means examining their psyches.

This task has come to be called psychographics—the measurement of personality dimensions through a questionnaire instrument. It has developed a somewhat tarnished name in recent years because the proselytizers of the field have often overpromised and underdelivered. Excessive claims about wondrous benefits of one psychographic system vs. another have only proved that lots of researchers will jump on any bandwagon, if it seems to be moving.

In spite of these problems, a need exists to understand why different types of people travel (psychographics) and *what* they want to do when they get there (lifestyle). At Plog Research, we believe in it and we also are committed to the idea that it *can* be done. Personality can be measured on dimensions that predict

- which segments of the population will travel;
- what motives can be tapped to increase their interest in travel;
- what types of destinations or resorts they want to visit;
- what they want to do when they get there;
- what types of experiences and/or facilities will make them want to return;
- how advertising can focus more effectively on their important motives and needs.

To accomplish these tasks, it is obvious that *psychographic research requires segmenting the market into groups of people with different sets of motives and behaviors so that unique appeals can be developed for each of the separate groups.*

A quick example will demonstrate the utility of psychographic research. As part of a major resort development, the owners of the property were planning to construct an integrated sports clubhouse and facilities for golf and tennis. Costs of construction would be less and, more important, it would allow them to emphasize the size of their recreational facilities in their promotional materials. On the surface, golfers and tennis players who travel are demographically very much alike. Incomes are high, occupational categories include a heavy representation of professionals and business executives, age categories are similar, and they stay at destinations for about the same length of time. But, the research pointed out major differences in personality structures. In fact, there is an underlying hostility between the two groups of sports enthusiasts:

- Golfers play the game because of their social needs. The betting, constant ribbing, and 19th hole camaraderie are all demonstrations of the heavy need for friendship (need for affiliation). Tennis players, however, attempt to prove to themselves that they are winners and the game becomes a true competitive struggle (need for achievement). Conversation between points is restricted, compliments are given out less often and frequently in an off-hand manner, arguments over calls can develop, and after-match socializing and drinking are limited.
- Golfers like the good life. They eat more, drink more, stay up for shows at night, most often ride around the course in a golf cart, and generally spend more to have a good time at a destination. Tennis players, on the other hand, are more Spartan personality types. They eat less, skip much of the nighttime entertainment, go to bed earlier, utilize fewer of the amenities at a facility, and generally spend less while they are there. In short, golfers are much more desirable as guests at a resort location because they are the bigger spenders.

The group of developers followed the advice and golfers and tennis enthusiasts now coexist at the resort—with separate but equal facilities—but otherwise they have limited contact with each other.

The utility of personality-based research becomes even more obvious when you examine the larger pieces that make up the tourism jigsaw puzzle. Different destination areas of the world attract different types of personalities. There is a whale of a difference in the psychology of someone whose preferred next trip is to China vs. someone who wants to go to the French Riviera, and Miami attracts a very different set of travelers than individuals who want to explore the Oregon coastline.

Understanding the basis of travel personalities, then, sets the stage for successful development of travel destinations—a critical task in a world in which there is an ever increasing number of travel possibilities and a more finite number of travelers. Travel planners must target in on specific market segments and provide them with the experiences they want. And the framework for understanding must be plain, common, and simple, or the results will be impossible to implement.

PSYCHOGRAPHIC RESEARCH: A FOCUSED REVIEW

The antecedents of psychographic research are diverse, but meaningful. The field draws on a background deriving from personality research, sociology, marketing research, and segmentation statistics.

The contributions of sociology and marketing research are self-obvious and are not the subject of this chapter. Basically, the method for developing psychographic profiles must rely on questionnaire instruments. The skill of the researcher in designing well-constructed instruments that are easy to administer and provide focused and meaningful data will determine the ultimate usefulness of the psychographic scale. Questionnaire construction continues to be an art, not a science, although there are some general rules which can be followed.

Segmentation statistics are also utilized in most

psychographic research projects. While techniques may vary, the typical approach is to:

- employ factor analysis to determine the primary factors (psychographic types);
- clarify the cutting points between these factors, by means of cluster analysis and/or discriminant function analysis;
- utilize regression statistics to determine which consumer behaviors can be predicted by each psychographic personality characteristic, and to what degree.

Somewhat different orderings of the above sequence, and different statistics, are employed by various researchers (including the present author), depending upon the needs of the moment.

The more important field, for our present purposes, relates to personality research and its historical antecedents.

Although it is possible to follow the chain of psychographic investigations back to the foundations of scientific psychology, in the laboratory of Helmholtz, the most important early contributions relate to the works and writings of Sigmund Freud. His psychoanalytic concepts were systematic and explained a wide range of motives and behaviors (especially those which were unconscious). The influence of Freud extended far beyond psychoanalysis. All of the social sciences and much of popular literature were impacted by his conclusions, and market research followed suit. Motivational psychology was the latter-day result, which was prevalent as recently as the 1970s. Unfortunately, the concepts of the id, ego, and superego, and the dynamic interplay between the various psychosexual stages of development do not lend themselves to measurement through personality tests, let alone by means of questionnaires.

The real impetus to psychographics came from psychologists who developed basic, and still useful, personality tests. Their fundamental assertion, a necessary precondition for all psychographic research, is that self-report (answering questions) can be reliable and predictive of behavior. For example, the Allport–Vernon Study of Values is still a useful conceptual tool for market researchers. The field was given an even greater lift, however, by Raymond B. Cattell, who used systematic research techniques and sophisticated statistics to develop his Trait Factor Theory of Personality and the Cattell Personality Scale to support his conclusions. Other powerful instruments followed, such as the Minnesota Multiphasic Personality Inventory (MMPI), the most widely used diagnostic test employed by clinicians, and the California Psychological Inventory (CPI), a more general measure of personality.

There are other instruments, some of which will be mentioned later in this chapter, but the important point is that these researchers set the stage for psychographic research. Not only did they show that personality factors can be measured reliably (test/retest reliability is very high for some of these instruments), but the method of test development set the stage for how psychographic instruments would be formulated.

Psychographic measurement, i.e., using personality items to develop profiles of consumer types, is a young field. It has grown up approximately in the last 20 years. Except for a few early marketing books which did not rely on data, such as Pierre Martineau's *Motivation in Advertising* (1957), the general focus has been to become research centered. The early studies tended to use standardized instruments to determine relationships between personality variables and buying behavior, such as the MMPI, CPI, and Allport–Vernon scales, and various measures of persuasability and other more recent concepts, such as "yea saying" and "nay saying" (identified by Couch and Kenniston 1960) and dogmatism (Rokeach Scale). Most of these studies offered very few correlations (limited predictability to consumer choice for products) because the standardized instruments were developed for basic research purposes rather than for the more focused and limited needs of a market researcher. The discouragement was such that it led a veteran psychographic researcher to conclude, "To summarize, then, I would say that the environment is so important in determining consumer behavior, and the problems of measuring personality traits are so difficult to handle in consumer studies that personality traits may never have much value in consumer work" (Wells 1966, pp. 187–188). A few years later, however, his views had mellowed and he now believes that personality/consumer behavior research shows utility in several areas (1975).

This early discouragement leading to more focused and tentative acceptance has been typical of other researchers (Yankelovich 1964, for example). The primary reason is that researchers are now developing scales which are more specific to the needs at hand. Thus, there is a greater likelihood that the personality characteristics measured will have some meaningful relationship to consumer behavior.

There are several authors whose works are useful to review by interested persons (the complete references are at the end of this chapter). These include:

- Elayn K. Bernay
- Joseph T. Plummer
- William D. Wells
- Douglas J. Tigert
- Ruth Ziff
- Harold H. Kassarjian
- Daniel Yankelovich
- William R. Darden

In addition, the American Marketing Association has

supported the development of two useful reference documents, one on personality research in marketing (Bibliography Series No. 23) and the other on market segmentation (Bibliography Series No. 28). It must be remembered, however, that psychographics is still a young field and the concepts employed are often conceptually elusive. As a result, demographics still dominates most advertising and marketing research. It's not that demographics predicts behavior very well (it doesn't!), but psychographics, by definition, has taken on a heavy assignment. Its fundamental task is to predict behavior, reliably and with utility, in areas where demographics has failed.

HOW TO DO PSYCHOGRAPHIC RESEARCH

Over the doorway to an entrance hall at Annapolis, through which naval cadets pass on a daily basis, is the inscription:

"A turtle never gets anyplace unless it sticks its neck out."

And so it is with personality research. A lot of effort can be devoted to developing a new personality-based classification system, but if it doesn't pan out your research neck gets chopped off. To forestall this uncomfortable possibility, a considerable amount of work must take place at several important stages.

Unlike demographic questions, there are no standard, commonly available psychographic approaches to tourism research . . . or consumer goods research . . . or automobile research . . . or . . . whatever. The common tests of personality produced by social science publishing houses possess little direct relevance to travel and tourism, and these are almost impossible to use in a research setting because they are too time-consuming, too personal, or have prohibitions from being employed in all but psychiatric or counseling settings. The end result is that you will probably have to use a system developed by a researcher (or company) or devise one yourself. Since we cannot adequately describe the detailed features of many of the systems on the market (which also tend to be proprietary), we'll give you some principles for a "do-it-yourself" program. Even if you don't attempt this task yourself, perhaps you will be in a better position to evaluate the research provided to you by others. And, we will also try to keep the explanations plain, common, and simple.

There are two basic approaches to developing measures of personality—inductive and deductive. The inductive method, stated simply, consists of noticing that two groups of people seem to differ in their behavior—travel behavior, as an example. The researcher develops a large list of questions and items and administers them to each of these groups. Those items that are answered differently by the two groups are retained; those that are not are discarded. It is pure empiricism because a firm data base has been utilized to produce the personality dimensions.

The method works! The MMPI was developed this way. Thousands of questions were administered to thousands of people who were diagnosed as exhibiting specific psychiatric symptoms. The discriminating items were assembled into a final instrument that measures symptomatologies and personality defense mechanisms in normal and not-so-normal people.

The MMPI is enormously successful in psychiatric settings, but it has a fundamental flaw that is characteristic of almost all empirically derived instruments when applied to survey research projects (beyond the fact that we customarily are not concerned about the *psychiatric diagnosis* of tourist populations). It contains nearly 500 items and requires 45 minutes to an hour and 15 minutes to complete. The respondent is not likely to be very cooperative when he or she is asked to answer additional questions about travel behavior. Empirically derived instruments also demonstrate a secondary flaw: many of the questions often seem to be unrelated to the topic of discussion (travel) or are too sensitive ("Did you play spin the bottle as a child?").

There are additional problems of empirically derived tests which, although not as important in scope, contribute to the difficulty of using them in travel research settings. The potpourri of ill-selected and seemingly unrelated items that distinguish between different personality types frequently does not provide a way to interpret the multivariate-based personality dimensions which grow out of the research. How do you interpret dimensions that might be based on the fact that a given personality type likes to brush his teeth after every meal, hates exercise machines, and never allows a parking attendant to park his car? It is difficult to understand the personality "glue" that holds those items together, let alone relate them to other behaviors (as the propensity to take pleasure trips). The story is told, whether true or not, that Macy's department store in New York City developed a screening test to help them select better Christmas help. They finally discarded the instrument because wearing glasses was a negative indicator (poor risk) and liking brown shoes was a positive indicator.

The second approach to developing personality/psychographic dimensions is *deductive*. Ideas about personality are postulated and questions are written which test the postulates. If the answers to the items are in directions that are predicted from the personality/psychographic theory, then the theory is supported by the data. If not, then scratch the takeoff and build a new launch pad. The question, then, is how strongly do the data have to fall in predicted directions. Although there are no hard or fast rules, you should expect to develop correlations of .25 or better for *each* item, with levels of .40 and above being much more acceptable. The total predictability and utility of your scale is higher, however, because the individual items contribute collectively to greater statistical power.

A number of personality tests have been developed this way. A theory of personality is translated into a relatively large number of questions on the basis of deducing how a given personality type would probably act or think in specific situations. Question items are retained or eliminated on the basis of how well they discriminate between groups *and* whether the discrimination is in the *predicted* direction.

The pitfalls of deductively derived psychographic dimensions in travel research center around the difficulty of being able to hypothesize or derive a relevant travel/tourism theory. You can waste enormous sums of research dollars testing out concepts which prove to be either invalid or, more likely, difficult to measure. Besides, if you really understand the psychology of travel so well that you can easily develop a discriminating test, then perhaps you don't need research after all. Just follow your hunches! Many resort developers and tour operators do, and they are quite successful. But, in a rapidly changing world, the question is whether their footwork will be fast enough to stay ahead of the variable needs of new traveling populations.

THE INDUCTIVE/DEDUCTIVE METHOD

There is an alternative. It grows out of the sound research practices and approaches that are followed, to some degree, by many companies. It combines both inductive and deductive approaches to research. It is efficient, cost-effective, and able to be contained within the framework of the constraints of most projects—for both budget and time. The heavier emphasis is on the deductive side of the equation, but empirical/inductive reasoning is also a strong contributor to the final result.

The inductive portion of developing psychographic (personality) characteristics of travelers is dependent upon good qualitative research. A short example will help. In this case, we must talk about research we conducted because it follows our example. We are not attempting to convince anyone of the validity of what we have done, however. It's just that we have used this approach a number of times for travel studies and in consumer product research.

We were given the task by 16 airline/travel companies to determine what could be done to broaden the base of the travel market, i.e., to turn more nonflyers into flyers. Our early search of the literature pointed out that there was a hard core of the population which refused to fly, even when disposable income was sufficient and there were compelling reasons to fly. Obviously, the personal psychology of these people kept them from participating in experiences that others were enjoying, in spite of the fact that they are often severely inconvenienced by their unwillingness to travel by air. It could be fear of flying, unfamiliarity with flight, maintenance of old habits, etc. Whatever the reason, we became convinced that there was a strong emotional core to the problem and personality-based exploratory research was necessary.

We opted for in-depth, one-on-one, two-hour, psychologically based interviews with nonflyers who had median incomes above the national average. We structured an interview that looked at their current explanations for nonflying, the amount of traveling they do currently (and had done in the past), their early family experiences, and important life events.

During the interviews, the standard reason these nonflyers gave for not flying was, "I simply have not had any reason to fly." It was obvious that this innocuous statement covered over more important reasons.

Analyzing the transcripts of these interviews, we noticed a common pattern among nonflyers that included:

- "Territory boundness"—a tendency for these people to have traveled less throughout their lifetimes. They came from families which were not very venturesome, and this very conservative, cautious approach continued until today.

- "Generalized anxieties"—a strong feeling of insecurity in daily life, about one's job, regarding one's relationship to others, about personal skills and abilities, etc. In short, these people were very uncertain of themselves and they demonstrated a tendency to "wear their anxiety on their sleeves."

- A "sense of powerlessness"—a feeling that they have very little control over the fortunes and misfortunes which are likely to strike them during their lifetimes, and that they are likely to be victims of much of what is bad that can happen in life.

Because of the common tendency for these characteristics to appear in each nonflyer, we gave it a name—Psychocentrism. It refers to a person whose center of attention is focused on self-doubts and anxieties, rather than using this energy to venture out into the world to explore it.

At this point, the task became relatively easy. Some of these dimensions had the ring to them of the characteristics described by David Riesman *et al.* in *The Lonely Crowd* (inner-directed vs. other-directed individuals) and by Julian Rotter in his Internal/External scale. The internalizer is an individual who is more self-confident, comfortable, and likely to do things his way. The externalizer looks for support and comfort from others, and is much more cautious. Not all aspects of this dimension were covered in the ideas of Riesman and Rotter, and questions were written which focused more clearly on generalized anxieties and territory boundness.

The end result? It requires a maximum of eight questions to separate people on a continuum into different travel personality groups, ranging from Psychocentric to Allocentric (a dimension developed to extend the scale to its polar opposite), leaving the vast majority of the questionnaire free to explore other topics necessary for travel studies. And, surprisingly, the dimension distributes along a bell-shaped curve rather well (Fig. 1). We call these self-inhibited and anxious personality types "Psychocentrics." Their more venturesome and self-assured counterparts have been labeled "Allocentrics."

The question is, then, does it work? If you fully understand the psychology of your travelers, then there is no reason why it should not.

Based on this project, *Reader's Digest* put together a two-year advertising campaign of eight-page inserts in the *Digest* (sponsored by a select group of the original study sponsors). It focused on the psychology of these nontravelers to induce them to fly. By focusing on their fears and concerns and using testimony of "experts" to provide the reasons why they should travel (for health, for job advancement, for a better marriage, for educational broadening, etc.), the needs and fears of these nontravelers were addressed. In a memorandum dated July 2, 1970 from Rene Isaac, Director of Advertising Research for *Reader's Digest*, to all U.S. sales staff, he reported on an analysis of the Starch readership scores for the ad series, and indicated:

> *"The readership scores, all of which are long test (multipage) ads are at least twice the average for the travel and resort category."*

The *Digest* was also given the "Discover America Award" for the best magazine travel promotion.

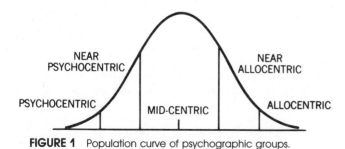

FIGURE 1   Population curve of psychographic groups.

THE SOURCES OF PSYCHOGRAPHIC AND LIFESTYLE DIMENSIONS

The source for dimensions may come from the use of qualitatively based research methods (in-depth interviews or focus groups), as was described earlier in this chapter, but this does not mean that all of the ideas have to be generated by the researcher. There is a rich source of personality theories in the literature, concepts that have taken a lifetime to develop by their promulgators. The concepts and ideas they expound may not be directly related to travel, but there may be sufficient relevance to make further examination and development quite fruitful. These researchers may have developed tests that divide people into different personality types. Test items *cannot* be used in survey instruments, without the express permission of the author (which normally will not be given), but the theoretic framework on which they are based is open for additional development by interested researchers.

As was indicated earlier, it is our experience that the psychoanalytic-based theories of Freud and most of his disciples have proved to be of very little value in data-based research. Not only are the concepts loose and hard to pin down for research purposes, but the dimensions cannot be tied directly into advertising or promotional programs.

The concepts of the basic "needs" developed by Henry A. Murray, however, show much greater utility. These "needs" tend to show low intercorrelations, suggesting that they are relatively independent of each other, and they cover some psychological characteristics of people that are important in day-to-day social interactions (15 of the dimensions have been pulled together by Allen Edwards into a well-standardized test).

Listed below are some of Murray's needs, a few of which are admittedly obscure in their meaning, but others are very relevant.

LIST OF MURRAY'S NEEDS

Abasement	Harm avoidance
Achievement	Intraception
Affiliation	Nurturance
Aggression	Order
Autonomy	Play
Counteraction	Rejection
Defendance	Sentience
Deference	Sex
Dominance	Succorance
Exhibition	Understanding

An example of the utility of some of these dimensions is:

- *Need for achievement* The desire to get ahead and be successful, especially to be competitive. It measures higher in persons who participate in competitive sports vacations (tennis, hunting clubs, sailing regattas, handball, racquetball) or who are serious about jogging, distance running, skiing, and other high-exercise activities which also demand skill coordination. A tennis-oriented resort facility should organize tournaments with prizes which clearly indicate that superb effort and achievement were necessary to win one of the trophies.

- *Need for affiliation* The desire for friendship with others and to be with others in sociable settings. This dimension tends to be higher among golfers and others who like an easier and relaxed time on vacations, including heavy use of entertainment facilities, dining and restaurant facilities, etc. Also, there is a preference for warm climates for vacations with the availability of a broader array of leisure time activities and pursuits. The awards and prizes for a golf tournament can be more humorous and "off beat," and it is useful to have photos taken of all of the winners together to emphasize the camaraderie.

- *Need for intraception* This dimension relates to an interest in understanding others, communicating with them, having empathy for their problems, their position in life, etc. This type of individual tends more to be inclined towards intellectual/historical/cultural trips which tour places to meet "native" people or to view and understand the significance of historical settings. Brochure material about these destinations should emphasize the common bond of all cultural groups, with a special emphasis on how we can learn more about ourselves by interacting with different cultures.

- *Need for succorance* A desire to be cared for, entertained, provided for by others. Obviously, the dimension relates closely to types of vacations and destinations which provide more total care. Complete tour packages, with all ground arrangements provided, are reflective of the types of choices made by these people, as are cruise packages in warm water areas such as the Caribbean, the Greek Islands, Mexico, etc.

These are just a few examples of the utility of some of the dimensions that can come from the Murray system of needs.

Other systems are around also which can provide some useful help at various times. The depth psychology of Carl Gustav Jung has been translated into a very easy to administer test—the Myers–Briggs. The test requires so little time that it can be administered in a survey research setting, and it is not obnoxious to respondents. The respondent indicates a preference between groups of words that are related to:

- Introversion
- Extraversion
- Sensing
- Intuition
- Thinking
- Feeling
- Judgment
- Perception

The interpretation of these dimensions is a little more sensitive, requiring the analyst to have a strong background in personality theory and clinical research. This is not as difficult a task as it may seem since qualified people are available as consultants. The dimensions are useful for determining the types of people who are attracted to specific kinds of advertising, or who like to participate in selected activities at destinations, or generally in situations which require greater understanding of the psychology of travelers.

An excellent resource for still more general and special-purpose psychological tests is the most recent edition of the *Mental Measurements Yearbook* edited by O.K. Buros.

THE COMMON DIMENSIONS OF PSYCHOGRAPHIC/PERSONALITY-RELATED TRAVEL RESEARCH

Unlike demographics, there are no standard psychographic categories or ways of defining people. Rather, it is up to creative insight, or the whimsical fantasy, of the researcher to develop the dimensions, and even if the questionnaire items contributing to the personality dimensions appear to be similar in two different survey instruments, the multivariate statistics involved may have been manipulated in somewhat different ways by the two researchers. Further, researchers may actually come up with fairly similar dimensions but may label them differently.

As it turns out, there probably are a very limited number of psychographic/personality dimensions which have been discussed in travel research. These dimensions may be more clearly defined, or recombined in various ways, but they are covered by about eight broad categories. These are listed below and, in each case, there typically is an opposite character type at the other end of the spectrum from the dimension.

- Venturesomeness—called by a variety of titles, it relates primarily to the type of individual who is more seeking and exploring. In terms of travel destinations, new products, or new marketing concepts, it is this individual who tends to be the first user.

- Pleasure-seeking—the type of person who desires a considerable amount of luxury and comfort in all aspects of travel, transportation carrier services, hotel services, entertainment and other activities, etc.

- Impulsivity—the tendency to want to do something now. Very low on the ability to delay gratification, persons who measure high in this characteristic are more apt to live more for the moment and will be high spenders. Trip decisions are made quickly, at the last moment, and without much planning.

- Self-confidence—a characteristic growing out of some of the other variables, self-confidence is closely related to the willingness to do unique and very different things, such as selecting the unusual in tour destinations or activities at these destinations.

- Planfulness—an obvious reference to very systematic, planful characteristics in people. Individuals who are strong on this dimension not only will think about and plan their trip well in advance, but will typically look more for bargains and prepackaged tour programs.

- Masculinity—this dimension is sometimes called "the outdoorsman." It is the action-oriented man whose primary goal is to seek the outdoors in the very traditional sense (fishing, camping, hunting, field and stream pursuits). This type of person is more likely to travel by car and take many things with him. Wives are often forced into going along with these interests or they are left at home.

- Intellectualism—this characteristic refers to that type of individual who not only possesses high-brow interests (goes to plays, museums, and other cultural activities), but has a heavy orientation towards historical touring. Old historic cities, cultural events, and exploring the undiscovered antecedents of present-day societies are of prime interest to persons dominated by this characteristic.

- People orientation—this is a desire to get close to people through travel and to experience the many cultures of the world. The dimension includes some combination of sociability, lack of organization (frequently bordering on disorganization), unique venturesomeness, and some degree of impulsivity.

To summarize, dimensions and labels may look different than those described above, but they are likely to be reflective of many of these patterns.

THE QUESTION OF VALIDITY

Standardized tests that are commonly available through publishers have typically gone through a rigorous series of trials designed to measure their statistical reliability and validity. These measures of their quality and "power" are defined in the manuals that accompany each test.

The authors of these personality instruments have a luxury which is not available to the travel researcher. It may have required years of effort to develop the final standardized test instruments, but that amount of time and accompanying costs are beyond the freedoms allowed most travel researchers. As a result, psychographic tests typically are devoid of research related to statistical reliability, and only the most cursory questions about statistical validity can be answered.

The ultimate dream in designing tests is to determine whether the instrument measures well on statistical tests of criterion validity. Job performance tests are good examples of criterion validity since the instrument can take a sample of the behaviors required in a job situation (a typing test is a good measure of on-the-job performance for typists). Since personality is usually defined on the basis of a conceptual framework of a researcher, however, there is no possibility of developing a measure of criterion validity. Only two more indirect measures of validity are feasible.

- Face validity—do the items that measure each psychographic dimension appear to have some relationship to the dimension (i.e., on the "face of it" does it make sense)? When a researcher develops a questionnaire for a study, that person accepts it at the level of *face validity*, since there is no way to know whether each item is measuring the population in the way that it should.

- Construct validity—this concept refers to the idea that, when someone has developed a theory, it should be possible to predict, in advance, how different types of persons defined by the theory will answer questions related to their personality interests. Do travelers answer questions in the direction you predict, nontravelers in the direction you predict, etc.? Correlational statistics will also let you know about the interrelatedness of the items contributing to the different personality types. Construct validity is a well accepted method for validating personality instruments, and it can and should be used in travel/leisure research. The big point is that it is not difficult to conduct construct validity tests of psychographic dimensions.

PUTTING IT ALL TOGETHER

The ultimate and most important question to ask after a study has been completed is whether the results have been used. The task, at this point, is to communicate with persons who will have to implement the results—marketing executives, advertising directors, and creative types at ad agencies. At this point, we are back to raising questions about how effective the research is in communicating findings to others and how willing the user is to learn everything possible about the new concept(s). A couple of examples will help to clarify the point.

Our most useful and predictive psychographic dimension continues to be Allocentrism vs. Psychocentrism, described earlier. It can be applied to a variety of product and service categories. Since Allocentrics are the early adopters of new products, one of our beverage clients consistently introduces new brands to the Allocentric audience. Advertising is focused on these types of persons' basic motivational structure, their subtle but quick forms of humor, and their ability to absorb great amounts of information at a glance.

The advertising strategy assumes that these early adopters will introduce the products to the near Allocentrics and then the near Allocentrics will "pass" the products on to the mid-Centrics, each group becoming a "mover and shaker" for the personality type that is a little more conservative in its consumer behavior than the group which "passed" the product on. As the product moves towards the great population bulge in the center of the bell-shaped curve, the humor becomes less sophisticated and the message much simpler. It may be duller advertising, but it is oriented appropriately towards its audience. This is a common market introduction for a new consumer product.

The approach can also work in reverse. Boise Cascade, the developers of Waikoloa on the big island of Hawaii, felt that the resort was missing something. Although it was very luxurious, it lacked a positive appeal and focal point which would capture more of its prime target audience—the near Allocentrics. They wanted to attract persons who would return time and again, lead others to come, and, in the process, buy property. To accomplish their task, they set aside more acreage as natural preserves, held back on commercial development, and developed some of the finest promotional materials available for any resort. As an example, the Waikoloa brochure gently persuades its audience with words which evoke images of the past, along with visions from the present.

Waikoloa was crown land which ruling chieftains reserved for themselves as a place of resort. The Ali'i (Hawaiian royalty) selected Waikoloa Beach to escape from the duties of their court and from the tension of long, exacting rituals performed to preserve rapport with their gods.

This royal land was protected from unwarranted intrusion by lava fields, which themselves hold historic re-cords of early visitors—petroglyphs, enigmatic symbols scratched into the lava, burial caves protected by a kapu (taboo) against vandalism and the King's Trail, an arrowlike footpath used for centuries by commoners and warriors.

Waikoloa is a sanctuary of the present in the Hawaii of the past where you may join the new pioneers who are following the footsteps of the old nobility—play the emerald golf course which is carved into the dramatic landscape like a giant modern petroglyph—ride the same rugged rangeland of the legendary Hawaiian cowboys or break the sand of the Gold Beach where only the footprints of royalty were once allowed—swim in the same gentle bay that welcomed the first brave polynesians who had sailed across a trackless Pacific and live in harmony with the land, with nature and with yourself.

In a changing world the spirit of this land remains. (Brochure in possession of author.)

The big task is to ensure that the marketing department wants to follow through on the results. This can be best achieved by working closely with the end-user groups from start to finish. Involve them in the formulation of the research, provide periodic progress reports, discuss problems as they arise, and be willing to work at selling your ideas after the project has been completed.

IN CLOSING

Psychographic research is not new. It is simply that it has become more sophisticated in recent years. Travel and leisure groups are attempting to become more adept at positioning their product and segmenting their markets to appeal to the right kinds of travelers. The *National Geographic*, that great magazine with a long history of stimulating interest in travel and unique leisure pursuits, carried the tag line for many years after World War I (printed on each page of its advertising), "Mention the Geographic—it identifies you." The class and quality of the magazine, by implication, carry over to the person who reads it. That, too, is the message of much of today's travel advertising. Mention where you've been, how you got there, or what you did while you were there, and you have given others a mental picture of the kind of individual you are. You've presented a word picture of your own psychographic personality.

REFERENCES

Allport, Gordon W., Philip E. Vernon, and Gardner Lindzey (1960), *Study of Values* (3rd edition), Boston, Mass.: Houghton—Mifflin.

Bernay, Elayn K. (1971), "Life Style Analysis as a Basis for Media Selection," in *Attitude Research Reaches New Heights*, C. King and D. Tigert, Eds., Chicago: American Marketing Association, pp. 189−195.

Buros, Oscar K. (1978), *The Eighth Mental Measurements Yearbook, Volume II*, Highland Park, N.J.: The Gryphon Press.

California Psychological Inventory, Harrison G. Gough, Consulting Psychologists Press, Inc., 577 College Avenue, Palo Alto, California 94306.

Cattell, R.B. (1950), *Personality: A Systematic Theoretical and Factual Study*, New York: McGraw−Hill.

Couch, A., and K. Kenniston (1960), "Yeasayers and Naysayers: Agreeing Response Set as a Personality Variable," *Journal of Abnormal Social Psychology*, 60 (March), 171−174.

Dahlstrom, Leon E. (1972), *An MMPI Handbook, Revised Edition: Volume I*, clinical interpretation, Minneapolis: University of Minneapolis Press.

Darden, William R. (1974), "Backward Profiling of Male Innovators," *Journal of Market Research*, 11 (February), 79−85.

Darden, William R., and Fred D. Reynolds (1972), "Predicting Opinion Leadership for Men's Apparel Fashions," *Journal of Market Research*, 9 (August), 324−328.

Edwards, A.L. (1967), *Edwards Personality Inventory Manual*, Chicago: Science Research Associates.

Freud, S. (1938), *The Basic Writings of Sigmund Freud*, A.A. Brill, Ed., New York: Modern Library.

Isaac, Rene, "Memo to U.S. Sales Staff," *Reader's Digest*, July 2, 1970. Information provided to author by Anthony L. Antin, Vice-President, *Reader's Digest*.

Jung, C.G. (1968), *The Archetypes and the Collective Unconscious* (2nd edition), translated by R.F.C. Hull, Bollingen Series XX, Princeton, N.J.: Princeton University Press.

Kassarjian, Harold H. (1971), "Personality and Consumer Behavior: A Review," *Journal of Market Research*, 8 (November), 409−418.

Martineau, Pierre (1957), *Motivation in Advertising*, New York: McGraw−Hill.

Minnesota Multiphasic Personality Inventory, Starke R. Hathaway and J. Charnley McKinley, Psychological Corporation, 304 East 45th Street, New York, New York 10017.

Murray, Henry A. (1938), *Explorations in Personality*, New York: John Wiley & Sons.

Myers−Briggs Type Indicator, Isabel B. Myers and Katharine C. Briggs, Educational Testing Service, Suite 100, 17 Executive Park Drive, Atlanta, Georgia 30329.

Myers, Isabel B. (1962), *Manual for the Myers−Briggs Type Indicator*, Princeton, N.J.: Educational Testing Service.

Plummer, Joseph T. (1971), "Life Style and Advertising: Case Studies," in *American Marketing Association Proceedings*, pp. 290−295.

Plummer, Joseph T. (1975), "Psychographics: What Can Go Right?" in *1974 Combined Proceedings*, R. Curhan, Ed., Chicago: American Marketing Association, pp. 41−44.

Riesman, David, with Revel Denney and Nathan Glazer (1950), *The Lonely Crowd*, New Haven: Yale University Press.

Rokeach, M. (1968), *Beliefs, Attitudes, and Values*, San Francisco: Jossey−Bass.

Rotter, J. (1966), "Generalized Expectancies for Internal versus External Control of Reinforcement," *Psychological Monographs*, 80 (1, Whole No. 609).

Tigert, Douglas J. (1974), "Life Style Analysis as a Basis for Media Selection," in *Life Style and Psychographics*, W.D. Wells, Ed., Chicago: American Marketing Association, pp. 173−201.

Wells, William D. (1966), "General Personality Tests and Consumer Behavior," in *On Knowing the Consumer*, J.W. Newman, Ed., New York: John Wiley & Sons, pp. 187-189.

Wells, William D. (1974), *Life Style and Psychographics*, Chicago: American Marketing Association.

Wells, William D. (1975), "Psychographics: A Critical Review," *Journal of Market Research*, 12 (May), 196−312.

Wells, William D., and Arthur D. Beard (1973), "Personality and Consumer Behavior," in *Consumer Behavior: Theoretical Sources*, S. Ward and T.S. Robertson, Eds., Englewood Cliffs, N.J.: Prentice−Hall, pp. 141−199.

Yankelovich, Daniel (1964), "New Criteria for Market Segmentation," *Harvard Business Review* (March/April), 83−90.

Ziff, Ruth (1971), "Psychographics for Market Segmentation," *Journal of Advertising Research*, 11(2), pp. 3−9.

18

The Political Dimensions of Tourism

LINDA K. RICHTER

Department of Political Science
Kansas State University
Manhattan, Kansas 66502

*T*his chapter examines some of the major political issues affecting decision making on tourism at the international, national, and subnational levels. Special attention is given to those issues affecting developing nations. Because political science has neglected the study of tourism, the chapter also identifies where more research is particularly needed.

The numerous facets of political and legal decision making about tourism constitute an enormous topic. Directed as they are at so many nations and other political units, it requires some conceptual simplification. The focus in this article is on the political aspects of tourism from the vantage points of key decision-makers at the local, national, and international levels. The goal in this essay is to enable those in the industry and within policy-making circles to encourage the type of tourism likely to be politically and economically successful for both the entrepreneur and the "host" environment. This analysis sees tourism as *potentially* compatible with the public and the private interests. To make that potential real and not just myth, both the industry specialist and those involved in broader questions of community, regional, and national planning have to appreciate the political and legal constraints upon one another.

The chapter is divided into three parts addressing the political issues as seen from (a) the *host country*, (b) the *country of tourist origin*, and (c) the *international arena*. Because of the immense variety that exists in political conditions globally this chapter attempts only to suggest avenues of inquiry and to make suggestions for the reader's further research.

HOST COUNTRY PERSPECTIVES

Decision-makers can expect governmental interest in tourism to be most uneven globally. It appears, however, to be a function of general patterns of industrial and commercial development (Young 1977; DeKadt 1979, pp. 32–33). If the government has been generally content to leave business development to the private sector as in the United States, interest in the political and legal implications of tourism is likely to follow the industry's lead. This has led in the United States and elsewhere to rather haphazard and often conflicting regulations and direction. The efforts needed to secure a national tourism policy for the U.S. reflects both government's and industry's belated recognition of the confusion that has evolved (National Tourism Policy Study 1978; Creal 1980).

If government is committed to elaborate national planning as in India and Mexico then tourism planning will be a part of that strategy (Richter and Richter 1985a). For those governments centrally directed and where private ownership is severely restricted, such as in socialist states, tourism will be under state control and presumably reflect only national priorities in its pace and shape of development (McIntosh 1972). Extensive political interest and regulation may also be dictated by the sudden emergence of the tourism industry as central to the nation's economy, as in Spain, or as the result of particular political needs unrelated to tourism per se, as in the Philippines (Richter 1980a; Pi-Sunyer 1979).

For those interested in the encouragement of national policies favoring tourism and travel generally, it is critical to recognize those *political* advantages and disadvantages national government decision-makers need to weigh.

POLITICAL USES OF TOURISM

Prestige and Political Legitimacy

Tourist arrivals are a barometer not only of a nation's currency relative to other currencies but also of the reputation of the nation. Since tourism is critically dependent on law and order, tourist arrivals then are a commentary on the political stability of the society and its desirability as a destination. Similarly, boycotts or restrictions on travel are one of the most obvious indicators of political disapproval, as in the case of the efforts by the U. States to discourage travel to the Moscow Summer Olympics in 1980 and to Libya in 1981, or the USSR's boycott of the 1984 U.S. Summer Olympics (Richter 1983a).

Specific propaganda objectives underlie many tourism programs in capitalist and communist nations alike. The Soviet Union, Cuba, and China have historically designed tourism programs to attract clienteles targeted more for their influence than their pocketbooks (Schuchat 1979). Other tours cater to educators and students at bargain rates while admitting only those foreign individual travelers willing to pay handsomely for the trip (Richter 1983b).

Tourism development can be politically useful in countries attempting to overcome a vague or indifferent national image, to change political directions, or to overcome a "bad press" internationally. Pakistan is a country that seized upon tourism as a priority vehicle in 1972 for all three of these reasons (Richter 1984a). The Philippines also sought to use tourism to legitimize martial law with specific promotions designed to defuse criticism of martial law, as with the slogan "Where Asia Wears A Smile" (Richter 1982).

Aid

Though one might quarrel with specific tourism decisions taken, the evidence suggests that rapid expansion of tourism under priority incentives has paid off as a *political* strategy in most developing nations. Countries with active tourism programs seem to attract more foreign aid, for example, than comparable countries without such programs (Young 1973). This relationship probably reflects the fact that most international tourists are from the major aid-giving nations.

Tourism destinations may also benefit disproportionately from international investment, but at this juncture existing research does not establish a distinct causal link between amount of tourism and amount of foreign investment. A probable explanation is that the investment and aid are a likely result of the political stability and government receptivity to foreign influence that also permit tourism to flourish. Such a political climate also encourages international lending institutions like the World Bank and UNESCO to become involved in tourism support.

There is, however, increasing evidence of a waning of enthusiasm for such projects in international lending institutions. The World Bank, which provided nearly a half billion dollars in development aid over the seventies, decided in 1979 to disband its tourism department. The Bank's affiliates, such as the International Finance Corporation, will, however, continue to invest in tourism (Sturken 1980).

Immigration

Tourism has a largely unnoticed political potential for spurring immigration from other countries. Obviously the tourist industry prefers the regular visitor, but it is a powerful inducement to some nations contemplating expanded tourism programs to think in terms of permanently enlarged tax bases from affluent and/or young skilled immigrants. Israel has been particularly adept in utilizing tourism planning for the promotion of immigration (Stock 1977). Mexico is another country that has benefitted from an influx of resident aliens who came originally as tourists, but have opted to retire there.

It should be noted, however, that immigration as a result of tourism is not an unmixed blessing. Often such individuals tend to be more affluent than the rest of the population. This may give them a disproportionate political and economic influence which it is well for decision-makers to anticipate. Fear of impoverished individuals using tourism as a pretext for immigration has also encouraged countries like the United States to maintain stringent tourist visa requirements.

Foreign concentrations can also lead to separatist activities as in the independence bid by the Abacos Islanders from the Bahamas. Possible problems may also arise from parent government concerns such as the British government's fears for its citizens permanently based in Cyprus following the Turkish invasion of the island (Turner 1976).

Political and Cultural Support

Host country governments appreciate tourism as a policy offering broad political discretion. Conditions of admission, duration of visits, rates of currency exchange, degree of freedom to travel internally, and often the conditions of accreditation for lodgings, restaurants, and tour and travel agencies are under the jurisdiction of some governmental level.

Not only can the government manipulate the entry, movement, and facilities of tourists, but even the most laissez-faire governments have great leverage in influencing the selective development of tourism. At one governmental level or another they can determine the ground rules for most of the supportive infrastructure for the industry such as airports, roads, port facilities, water and electric power, and often the timing and terms under which hotels, casinos, and transport are developed.

Government tourism policy represents an opportunity to selectively assist depressed or politically troubled areas or areas of highest political priority (Richter 1980a; Clarke 1981). Tourism may also help weakly integrated areas identify its interests more strongly with the national government.

The successful entrepreneur must be ready to demonstrate to those in government making such decisions how the industry can assist the government in rewarding areas (and individuals) of highest political priority through incentives for industry development with or without local involvement.

Getting information about the political regulations governing tourism usually varies in difficulty in inverse proportion to the ease with which private entrepreneurs can become involved. For example, it may be easier to determine which level, department, office, and individuals make decisions about the tourism sector in a centrally controlled system, but it may require higher levels of executive commitment to get the original access or approval for tourism projects.

Even in countries where tourism is primarily privately owned and promoted, tourism can be profoundly influenced by government policy. Just as the industry can be affected by government policy, a well-developed tourism industry can be a powerful political ally to a government intent on expanding transportation and communication linkages, attracting new businesses and cultural attractions, or launching a major campaign for crime control. The foreign exchange and domestic revenues from tourism will be important, but if it is an organized sector of the economy, its political "clout" may also add needed assistance to the government's policy proposals.

Governments have discovered that tourism may encourage secular and cosmopolitan attitudes, while paradoxically providing a support base for the restoration and preservation of the most unique features of the traditional culture (Richter 1980b; McKean 1978; Gamper 1981; Swain 1978). Tourism may also help to make feasible expensive commitments to beautification, to pollution control, and to the arts (Stock 1977).

For many countries tourism represents an entree to international politics and regional cooperation. Southeast Asian nations, through the Association of South-

east Asian Nations (ASEAN), and countries like Switzerland, Iceland, Fiji, Spain, and Bermuda are only a few of the many nations that have found it possible to build political strength from a tourist base.

POLITICAL PROBLEMS OF TOURISM

The political disadvantages of tourism are becoming increasingly salient to governments and travel specialists alike. The recognition of certain political problems is an entirely healthy development, however, entirely consistent with the long-range interests of the industry. Fortunately, with some care many of the political liabilities can be anticipated and the problems correspondingly reduced.

Much of what follows may seem common sense to those interested in tourism. Yet it is seldom as obvious in concrete development proposals of the industry. Tourism, ironically, can do more damage to the industry and the societies in which it flourishes through myopic and thoughtless expansion than by lackluster and sluggish development (Richter 1980b; OECD 1980; Holden 1984a).

Too Narrow a Base

One of the foremost political disadvantages can result from an industry dependent on too narrow an economic clientele or too few countries of origin. Affluent tourists, for example, are notoriously fickle, and some of the more exotic and remote resorts are ill-suited to a switch to mass tourism. Countries may also discover belatedly that promotion efforts and geography may have resulted in a tourist industry perilously dependent on very few nations. Frequently Country A may discover to its chagrin that over one-third of its tourists are from Country B. Nor is this dependence reciprocal. Country B's tourists may have a huge impact on Country A, yet outward tourist flow to Country A may represent only a tiny fraction of its outward-bound travelers. Asymmetrical vulnerability and commitment are common to tourism (Hivik and Heiberg 1980).

Nations like Sri Lanka, Thailand, and the Philippines have realized dramatic slumps in tourism as a result of shifts in the advice tourist-generating countries give to its citizens going abroad. The political frictions such situations engender between host country and country of origin have their own "multiplier effect" within the host country. The local travel industry feels abandoned by the government, and the government feels betrayed by those who "sold" tourism incentives, tax holidays, and major government involvement with the argument that tourism was a "sure thing." Diversification of facilities, attractions, and clienteles which could reduce such political problems is paid lip service, but often is neglected in the actual planning and implementation stages (Richter 1985b).

Land Use Controversies

Of course success is not without its share of political headaches even when diversification is assured. Land use disputes may be severe, especially in nations where land is scarce and land pressure from tourism is great. Typically, islands have the most intense land use struggles. In many instances the disputes pitting industry, conservationists, the travel industry, and residential interests can be anticipated in detailed planning. Often, as a result, tourist design can mitigate power, water, pollution, and multiple-use disputes (Fukenaga 1976).

Inflation

Where tourism has increased rapidly and massively, there may be political fallout from the resultant inflation, including spiraling land prices, increased transport, housing, and food costs, and the boom—bust cycle of the construction industry. Case studies of the Philippines and the Seychelles illustrate the social and political havoc that can ensue (Richter 1980a; Franda 1979; Wilson 1979). By contrast, countries or regions developing gradually, as did Bermuda and India, are able to "digest" tourism growth much more easily (Richter and Richter 1985a).

Urbanization

Tourism can also result in the problem of too much migration to some regions, as in parts of Hawaii, California, and the Pacific Northwest of the United States. In other societies, it is the movement of people from the countryside into the cities for jobs in tourism that creates political problems. Such migration to the cities may offset the gains made in using tourism for regional development.

Poor Advice

It may appear obvious that the government and the industry consider some of the issues discussed above, but unfortunately many such political problems are never openly considered at all. The industry has erred in emphasizing marketing almost exclusively. Just as the industry may betray the tourist through misleading promotional materials, the industry frequently underestimates the problems that must be considered in its eagerness to sell potential destinations on the advantages of tourism development.

Many governments, especially in developing nations, either by ignorance, neglect, or inexperience, lack planning, personnel or data independent of marketing biases (Richter 1985a,b). Relatively few have staff or skills to monitor more than very crude tourism indices like arrivals, bed-nights, surveys of tourist expenditures, and gross receipts (Richter 1983b). Rarely do governments, developed or developing, attempt

net receipt figures, social impact studies, or systematic independent appraisals of market needs (Richter 1984b, 1985c). Surprisingly the host country almost never attempts to assess the expectations or reactions of its own citizens (Hivik and Heiberg 1980) to what has been described as "the most successful agents of change (short of political or military agents) active in the contemporary world" (Nunez 1978). Much more research attention needs to be directed here (Belisle and Hoy 1980).

Political Opposition

It should not be surprising then that increasingly both local and national governments are discovering that their "high profile" tourist industry, chosen for its economic and political promise some years earlier, has become a rallying point for the politically disgruntled in societies as varied as Hawaii, Iran, Barbados, and Pakistan.

Sometimes the tourist industry is controversial as in the Philippines, because there much of the tourism is owned or controlled by those close to the ruling elite, thus causing resentment about the disproportionate attention given to tourism. In this country a rash of arson and bombing attacks has been directed at the hotels. Efforts also have been made to embarrass the regime and disrupt tourism by threats and bombs directed at international tourism conclaves. Though the Philippine government moves swiftly to contain the political damage by offering travel agents and those affected free hospitality and travel, the political and economic costs are immense (Richter 1982, 1985d). Sniping incidents in Hawaii have been directed at tourists, who in some minds symbolize the ravishing of Oahu with unsightly overconstruction and relentless inflation (Kent 1983; Governor's Conference on Tourism 1984).

Political opposition may also be a reaction to inadequate consideration of the type of tourism introduced and the prevailing cultural mores (O'Grady 1981; Holden 1984b). Some nations like Singapore are modern, strong, and geographically compact enough to restrict entry to the conventional tourist the government wants. However, in other countries traditional religious values are strong, whether Muslim, Christian, or Hindu, and the presence of leisured, often scantily clad tourists is a persistent affront to local sensibilities. That such cultural irritations have political import is abundantly clear in the political resurgence of conservative Christian and militant Islamic movements (Matthews 1978).

Entrepreneurs in Iran, Pakistan, and elsewhere have noted too late the change in political climate and as a consequence have found themselves without any leverage when the political order changes. In this way enormous investments by government and local and international bodies have been wasted as prejudice against future tourism has been fanned (Richter 1983a; Laurie n.d.).

Failure to anticipate potential negative consequences of certain types of tourism in given societies leaves the government and the entire industry vulnerable to sabotage and tourism is astoundingly easy to destroy. The tourist has so many other alternative destinations that neither he nor the marketing agent is likely to plot a trip anywhere that has a hint of insecurity about it.

Tourism is also vulnerable to the general political climate within the country and in nearby destinations. For example, violence in Sri Lanka in 1984–1985 and in Jamaica in 1976–1977 crippled tourism despite the calm in tourist areas. Similarly, political upheavals in Uganda took a heavy toll in tourist trade from neighboring Kenya in the early 1970s and again in 1985.

Sabotage of tourism efforts may also take place from outside the host country. Disputes between important marketing agents and the government or local industry personnel may leave the host government with little leverage over the fate of international tourism to its own country (Turner 1976; Richter 1983a).

SUB-NATIONAL POLITICAL DIMENSIONS OF TOURISM

It is extremely difficult to generalize about research at the subnational level. Most has concentrated on the usefulness or problems associated with using tourism as a tool for regional or local development. The perspective in such instances has been national. Studies of tourism from a regional or local perspective have been primarily case studies and have been investigated primarily by anthropologists and sociologists rather than by political scientists (Belisle and Hoy 1980; Papson 1981). As a consequence the issues raised have not usually focused on such political issues as power, control, legitimacy, support, and authority. Recent attempts to investigate the public sector dimensions of subnational tourism in the U.S. suggest that this is an important level of analysis for future research (Richter 1984b, 1985c).

The following categories are by no means exhaustive but do suggest some political categories in which research has been and needs to be done to provide those in tourism management with some guidance at this level.

Level and Source of Political Support

Tourism, while ranking as one of the top three sources of revenue in 46 of the 50 states of the United States, is still erratically funded and almost whimsically developed in most parts of the U.S. State governments heavily dependent on tourism may, as Hawaii did until 1981, consider tourism simply as something to be con-

trolled rather than aggressively fostered. However, increasingly *all* states are taking tourism promotion seriously. States with far fewer natural attractions may need to spend disproportionately more for tourism development and may have initially fewer political choices about the nature and type of tourism to attract.

Political leadership is also an uncertain variable at the local level. Gubernatorial and mayoral candidates differ widely in their commitment to tourism and they can be decisive in shaping legislative responses to the industry (Richter 1984b, 1985e).

Pace and Control of Tourism Development

The pace of development and the nature of its control is another dimension of the local political support for tourism. Little research has been conducted on these issues. What has been done suggests that tourism's development and impact have cyclical tendencies which cause the least disruption to community values when political power is dispersed fairly evenly (Peck and Lepie 1978).

Case studies of the 1982 World's Fair in Knoxville confirm that as with world fairs in general, such fairs characteristically represent a narrow elite initiative that can create severe political problems. These occur because of the speed with which a tourism infrastructure is developed, its typically short duration, and the havoc it entails for those caught in the housing squeeze and the inflationary spiral such sudden and massive development creates. Other research suggests that the political traumas are likely to be greater the smaller and less diversified the city (Loukissas 1978).

Tourism Promotion and Planning

Regional multistate and intrastate organizations may also constitute political allies for the tourism industry. In some areas these are wholly sponsored by the private sector while in others economic development agencies of several states develop together regional promotion. Such collaboration often acts as a spur to states to compete even as they cooperate for the tourist dollar.

Research on regional and multistate tourism development is scant indeed and is, as noted earlier, focused on the impact of tourism on the *region* rather than on the impact of regional politics and planning on *tourism*.

How important the latter can be has been demonstrated by the National Organization of Women's boycott of states that did not ratify the Equal Rights Amendment. A significant percentage of the more than 200 professional organizations that supported the ERA refused to hold national or regional meetings in such major convention centers as Chicago, St. Louis, Kansas City, and Miami from 1977 to 1982. Losses of convention revenue have been in the hundreds of millions of dollars to these tourism centers even as other regions have enjoyed expanded convention bookings as a result. Since this strategem has been upheld by the courts as not an illegal restraint of trade, the way is open for tourism revenue to be used as a political ploy in future political battles.

Characteristic Political Issues Involving Tourism

Many political conflicts are generated over the type of tourism. For example, several states have debated whether casinos, state lotteries, racing, and other gambling would attract enough tourism revenue to offset the potential increase in crime or social problems. Other states like Kansas, seeking to develop convention centers in Kansas City, Kansas, and Wichita, have had heated political controversies over liquor-by-the-drink. Hotel and airport taxes have been other political battlegrounds (Governor's Conference on Tourism 1984).

In other communities the political tension has not been over how to develop or what type of tourism market should be targeted but over whether tourism represents an industry compatible with certain rural or traditional lifestyles. Often the very hospitality of a community is perceived as threatened by tourism, the "hospitality industry."

Subnational research on the integration of tourism is critically needed. Most of what is available is focused on Hawaii, where traditional rural values have collided abruptly in the last generation with mass tourism (Fukenaga 1975; Chow 1980; Kent 1983). These studies document the relatively modest "trickle down" effect of either political or economic power—a chronic problem area sure to make tourism increasingly controversial in communities throughout the world. Studies on this topic include such settings as Catalan, coastal development in France, and Canadian provincial government (Clarke 1981; Papson 1981).

India, Canada, and other countries with fairly decentralized tourism programs have found that the advantages of federalism allow for flexible and varied responses to tourism locally, but the diffusion of political debate is certainly no political panacea as U.S. tourism illustrates.

HOST COUNTRY PERSPECTIVES OF THE DEVELOPING NATIONS

"International tourism is simultaneously the most promising, complex, and understudied industry impinging on the Third World" (Turner 1976, p. 253). The 120-plus developing nations in the world experience most of the advantages and disadvantages of tourism development common throughout the world, but they also experience some political aspects that are peculiar to their underdevelopment.

Tourism receipts have been increasing rapidly among many nations in excess of other development sectors and at a rate that far exceeds tourism growth in developed countries. Such advances throughout the 1970s, in the face of soaring fuel costs and economic uncertainties globally, made tourism look unusually attractive. Asia is a case in point. There, tourism receipts have grown 13 percent at a time when overall growth in the area has been 2 percent (Dannhorn 1979). But the picture may be misleading. Political conditions in Cambodia, Uganda, Kenya, Barbados, Jamaica, Haiti, Iran, Afghanistan, Grenada, and Sri Lanka, for example, threatened tourism in those developing societies. Elsewhere, other developing nations most enamoured with tourism had experienced it in mass form for less than a decade.

PROBLEMS OF PERCEIVED NEOCOLONIALISM

Neocolonial appearances may enrage nationalists and threaten a tourism backlash. For example, there may be a genuine sense of "relative deprivation" when nationals see leisured tourists spend in hours what may take them several months to earn (Blanton 1981). Moreover, such a "demonstration effect" by affluent tourists may spur political anger or unrealistic consumption demands that are costly in the very foreign exchange tourism is supposed to generate (Karunatilake 1978; O'Grady 1981; Holden 1984a, b).

Aggravating tensions is the very real likelihood that, in most parts of the developing world, the most frequent tourists will be from a new nation's former colonial master (Hivik and Heiberg 1980). The superior wealth and power of the tourist relative to the citizens who will service his needs are made still more politically sensitive by the racial dimension. Most tourists are white; most of the developing world isn't.

Neoimperialistic economic ownership and/or control of tourism facilities may also raise political issues for the government and its foreign investors (Centre on Transnational Corporations 1982). In some small countries, the foreign tourism establishment may be the most powerful political force in the country. In Gambia, for example, there is no economic or political counterweight to the foreign-controlled hotels (Harrell-Bond 1978). Before the Seychelles even recognized the political dimensions of tourism, much of the land was in foreign hands (Franda 1979).

The degree of dependence a nation may experience has been suggested before in terms of the general importance of conservative political stability, accord with international marketing agents, etc. All nations face such constraints, but the developing nation which has opted for tourism development is especially vulnerable. Such countries lack clout when by intent or indifference decisions are taken internationally that affect them. Consider, for example, Pan Am's decision to cut service to Antigua shortly before the peak winter season in 1975-1976 (Britton 1980). Decisions to cancel large conventions or change itineraries for large tour operators may have similarly disastrous consequences for weak undiversified economies. The collapse of Britain's largest tour operator, Court Line, led to the closure in 1974 of 180 hotels in Majorca alone (Turner 1976).

HIRING

Colonial and/or racist patterns may also seem apparent in the filling of top industry positions with foreigners, while recruiting local people for primarily menial jobs. In some countries, particularly for international standard tourism, such decisions may be inevitable; in others it is clearly the result of habit and convenience (Richter 1982b). Though the political elite may not pressure entrepreneurs on this issue of local hiring, it is clearly in the long-term political interest of government and investor to integrate personnel at the top levels as soon as possible. By doing so, opposition to the industry can be defused on this issue, which by the nature of the typically large numbers of unemployed can be explosive. One apparently successful approach to this issue has been in Cyprus, where the legislature mandated the employment of local personnel in the tourist industry (DeKadt 1979).

Another response is also possible: bypass international standard tourism for more modest industry development. The *net* economic and political gains, not to mention the reduced likelihood of social and cultural problems, may easily offset the gains from more lavish approaches. Careful studies of Indonesian tourism development challenge the profitability of international standard tourism on several socioeconomic dimensions (Rodenburg 1980; Noronha 1979) and substantiate the results of other critics of international tourism elsewhere (Turner 1976; Matthews 1978; Wood 1984).

INTEGRATED OR ENCLAVE TOURISM

Though tourism is rarely a policy assumed under duress, this does not mean it is always chosen freely. For some nations, e.g. Nepal or Burma, the decision to permit tourism was less enthusiasm for the industry than the absence of other more attractive development options. In such countries as well as others where local traditions are both an attraction for tourists and a potential basis for misunderstanding, and where tourist dollars are needed desperately but their impact on society feared, the government decision-makers must make some particularly important political decisions. Through failure to specifically target desirable clienteles, the government can lose control over a powerful social phenomenon and greatly reduce the industry's ability to contribute to the society.

Ideally, the government should either insist that whatever elements are promoting the country design their promotions to attract clientele unlikely to be intrusive or stipulate that facilities for tourists be well removed from the general population. Either decision has important political consequences. The integrated option generally means a very gradual development of tourism paced to the overall development of the country, where tourism's relationship to the society evolves with increased interaction. Particularly well-suited may be religious or cultural tourism, where either the visitors share the nation's religious traditions or the visiting groups are small and relatively unobtrusive. They may be affluent but their motivations for travel are more cultural than comfort oriented.

The enclave option as found in the numerous "Club Med" resorts or in the large-scale developments in Tanzania, Indonesia, and the Maldives, reduces the social impact of the tourist and its political consequences, but greatly restricts the diffusion of industry profits. Moreover, the elaborate infrastructure created for such developments can be used only by the tourists and actually reduces the amount of capital available for public facilities and transport (Enloe 1975; Richter and Richter 1985a).

Despite the desirability of local participation in tourism and the advantage of gradual expansion of the industry with maximum diffusion, some governments may lack the luxury of options on this issue. Where major infrastructure like a new airport is required, "only rapid and large-scale development will earn a reasonable rate of return on the airport. Rather than choosing between slower and faster or dispersed and concentrated tourism the choice may have to be between tourism and no tourism" (DeKadt 1979, p. 27).

THE COUNTRY OF ORIGIN
POLITICAL ADVANTAGES OF OUTBOUND TRAVEL

Though countries prefer to keep their wealth at home, there are numerous advantages to national policies that permit orderly travel abroad and do so without unduly restricting destinations.

Public Relations

The propaganda advantages are perhaps the clearest benefit that accrues from nationals going abroad. This was articulated most forcefully in the 1984 slogan of the first U.S. National Tourism Week, "Travel: The Perfect Freedom." It is difficult to argue the desirability of one's political system while curtailing the exit of one's citizens. Freedom of travel was in fact one of the most revealing controversies during the negotiation of the Helsinki Accords in 1975. The Soviet Union was most reluctant to agree to such a provision, and has subsequently interpreted it narrowly. More common than outright bans on foreign travel are the stipulations that travelers take only limited amounts of currency for foreign exchange.

The United States restricts somewhat the travel abroad of resident aliens seeking naturalization and prohibits citizens from going to specific countries. The U.S., like many other countries, expands and contracts permission to travel to certain countries as a signal of normalization or worsening political relations. In general, however, countries permit as much travel as they believe is politically and economically feasible because of the negative connotation of restrictions.

Tourists abroad may have a positive "demonstration effect." Their presence and behavior reflect their country's prosperity, culture, and values. The increase, for example, in Japanese tourism in the 1970s parallels the economic strength of the country. As a consequence, the travel industry as a whole has adjusted to the needs and tastes of this important clientele group.

In catering to the desires of powerful tourist clienteles their home countries may benefit from expanded trade designed to import abroad products familiar to major tourist groups. Moreover, Country A's businesses may be more welcome in Country B if there is a flourishing tourist trade from A to B.

International Cooperation

Tourism is also an arena for regional and international cooperation which may facilitate constructive exchanges on other thornier issues. Normalization of travel is often the very early issue in the repair of political relationships, and it can also be a base for multilateral efforts as the ASEAN and other regional political associations have demonstrated.

DISADVANTAGES OF OUTBOUND TRAVEL
Currency Flight

Currency flight is a major disadvantage of out-bound tourism. Strict customs regulations and limits on currency taken out of the country and a requirement that the national carrier be used may help, but effective controls require more repression than most governments want to enforce. While currency flight is at root an economic issue, the decision of whether or how to confront it is political in nature.

Political Opposition

Societies that have the most lenient travel policies will occasionally find dissidents have been able to leave the country posing as tourists, only to harass the government from some sanctuary abroad. However, there appears to be an inverse relationship between government policies allowing for easy exit and their abuse by critics. Countries restricting travel like the USSR, Cuba, and the Philippines seem to have more such problems.

Citizens in Trouble

A more serious problem is the danger that tourists will get involved in incidents abroad that may embarrass their own country (drug traffic, arms sales, prostitution) or endanger their lives, as in the kidnapping of Japanese tourists in the southern Philippines in the mid-1970s or the sporadic violence that has involved tourists primarily in Europe and the Middle East.

Political instability abroad may threaten lives or simple fraud in the sale of charters may provoke demands for government action on behalf of stranded travelers. Consulates have limited authority and funds to help nationals overseas.

WHAT TO DO: A MINI—MAX STRATEGY

From the home country's perspective several steps are important for minimizing the political risks and maximizing the political advantages of nationals touring abroad.

It is important to monitor political developments in "tourist belt" areas and encourage travel agencies and airlines to have tour leaders or individual travelers check with their embassies if local conditions are unsettled. Travel agencies are often reluctant to say anything that might discourage travelers, but it is shortsighted for the industry to behave irresponsibly in this regard.

Tourists should also be informed of countries on their itinerary where their reading material may be confiscated or their customs check prolonged by their nationality or dress. For example, *Playboy* and other "girlie" magazines are contraband in many, particularly non-Western, countries. Bibles, critical literary works, and even several pairs of jeans may be suspect in the USSR. Stiff sentences under grim conditions are the norm in many countries for individuals found with even personal quantities of illicit drugs. Travelers in general should be urged to be especially careful if venturing to countries without consular treaties with their home country.

Female travelers should be advised that Muslim nations, particularly in the Middle East and North Africa, have become increasingly conservative about dress, and there are many countries where local custom does not permit unescorted women access to points of historical, religious, or touristic interest. (One unobtrusive measure of the expectation that women will not be out in public is the almost total absence of restrooms in restaurants, hotels, government offices, and at tourist sites.) Both sexes should be aware that severe punishment is likely for those indulging in extramarital relations. Briefings and orientation sessions common to student tours may also be desirable in some form for charter groups, convention travelers, and standard business and government travel (Holden 1984a).

The country of origin's best approach to reducing the negative political impact of external travel is to launch and encourage domestic tourism appropriate to the level and pattern of discretionary spending of the society. A developed country may offer a wide variety of facilities, where a developing country may prefer to focus on hostels or low-cost accommodations near religious shrines as a means of providing for economy mass travel (*Eastern Economist* 1978, p. 930). Domestic tourists may also be allowed preferential rates or certain exemptions from local bed or hotel taxes that foreigners must pay. Such steps encourage local tourism, improve profitability of establishments, and keep facilities from becoming dominated by outsiders. Hawaii's "kamaaina" rates are but one example.

To mitigate the economic impact of outbound travel, tourism promotion overseas is a must. Special tour packages like "Discover America," Eurail Pass, and their equivalents in the British Isles, India, and elsewhere are especially important for their ability to tap long-distance clienteles and to diffuse such tourists' expenditures. Too often long-haul travel may leave only 10 percent of the tourist dollar at the destination (Turner 1976). Touring packages within the country or region improve the rate of return. Such promotions as "Holland on the House," which discounted travel and lodging for one day, also may be a successful means of attracting tourists for longer visits to countries often overlooked on grand tours.

Targeted nostalgia tours like "Balikbayan" and "Reunion for Peace" in the Philippines and similar promotions in Korea may also combine economic and political objectives to increase in-bound tourism (Richter 1980a).

The most predictable though blunt approach to reducing outbound tourism and increasing arrivals almost overnight is the government decision to devalue the currency (Turner 1976). Whether it is a wise political or economic decision hinges particularly on the country's need to import items from abroad for tourism and other policy sectors.

INTERNATIONAL PERSPECTIVES

There is a scarcity of research on the politics of tourism generally and international politics in particular. Much of what has been done is not readily available. In this section, therefore, there will be a brief survey of the political issues that need to be addressed by various participants in the field of international tourism with suggestions for further research.

INTERNATIONAL CORPORATE PERSPECTIVE

Corporations have proved unusually adaptable in working with governments of every political persuasion in the development of tourism. Ideology has played surprisingly little role in initial access of a corporation to a country. French and Swedish firms have built hotels in the USSR; the Austrians, Americans, and French have been active in Pakistan; Filipinos and Americans have been active in Chinese tourism; while Japanese firms have supplied both transport and hotel expertise in Hawaii and the Philippines.

Ownership, leasing arrangements, and overall planning are, however, likely to reflect national attitudes toward external capital and expertise. It is hard to generalize about such matters because local sensibilities differ from area to area and regime to regime.

Outside of limited contractual agreements for noninvestment relationships like consulting advice, market surveys, and tourism planning, corporations will want to consider carefully the likely political consequences of investment outside the "home base." The following represent a general and by no means exhaustive checklist of some of the political factors to be considered from the corporate perspective.

Political Stability

Political stability is of the foremost importance to any investment, but it is of special consequence to tourism because of what is being sold: serenity, leisure, fun, comfort. These can only be marketed under stable conditions. No destination has a monopoly on desirability that would encourage risk-taking common to other investments.

To evaluate political stability is not easy, especially when one is dealing with national leaders interested in tourism and willing to offer liberal terms for investment. There are, however, a few techniques one may use. First, in the United States, there are a few consulting firms that specialize in political forecasting and crisis investing.

The subject of risk analysis is a large and relatively unrefined one for the international tourism entrepreneur. Broad studies focusing on the political forecast for a specific nation may not be very helpful for an investor concentrating on one segment of the market. Situations like agrarian unrest constituting hazards for Del Monte or United Fruit may create genuine opportunities for tourism as the government searches for new avenues for garnering foreign exchanges (La Palombara 1982; Kobrin 1979; Laurie n.d.).

A second approach is to attempt to predict the security of an investment in terms of the pattern of outside capital flowing into a nation. If there is growth in investment, some travel industries conclude, the political situation is stable for tourism. No statistics are available that either confirm or refute that relationship. But such figures have been notoriously unreliable on occasion as a basis for prediction, as in Cuba before the takeover by Fidel Castro set Cuban tourism back thirty years or as in Iran in 1979. This approach also does not take into consideration the possibility that tourism itself may be the focus of political strife as in Hawaii or the Philippines in recent years (Kent 1983; Richter 1982).

A third barometer of political stability is the country's credit record. Heavy World Bank or International Monetary Fund loans are sometimes looked upon as an indicator of the country's overall political stability and credit worthiness. This indicator is, however, flawed by the fact that credit is just as easily a measure of political compatibility with the major creditor powers as it is a measure of de facto fiscal responsibility and political stability (Payer 1982).

Executive Commitment

Sophisticated political preplanning should employ more care. That it rarely does so is a serious defect. It is crucial to have a detailed understanding of the current leadership's commitment to tourism and any caveats it may have about the industry. For example, in several countries profitability and initial investments in luxury hotels were premised on the assumption that there would be casinos and supper clubs. A change in regimes in Pakistan and a misreading of executive sentiments in the Philippines changed all that leaving the hotels in dire financial straits (Richter 1982, 1984a).

It is also important to consult with likely leaders of the political opposition regarding their attitudes toward tourism. Their relative strength and their sentiments toward the tourist industry may influence the timing of investments, bargaining terms, or even the decision to invest at all. Jamaica, Grenada, and Nicaragua are three nations where just such sleuthing might have saved the industry considerable grief.

Government History toward Foreign Investment

Other political cum economic considerations include the government's political history toward outside capital. Indian hotel magnate Oberoi learned to his chagrin that Pakistan had expropriated five of his luxury hotels following the 1965 Indo-Pakistani war (*Asiaweek* 1980). Nationalization of tourist establishments in China, Cuba, and Vietnam is the exception, but in numerous other countries there have been policies of expropriating key industries. If tourism became central to such economies, they too might become targets for nationalization. In fact, investors are now recommended to anticipate such nationalization in the initial contracts drawn, thereby providing that "in the event of a dispute regarding compensation, recourse to international arbitration or other previously agreed upon dispute settlement facilities may be had at the request of either party" (OECD Policy Statement 1981).

Government Conditions of Investment and Access

The availability of local or national capital and/or investment incentives is another area deserving intense political scrutiny. Even the poorest countries have concessions that can be made to encourage investment. Finding the most appropriate ones consistent with corporate and national objectives is important. Studies suggest that the countries rather than the corporations are likely to be poor bargainers (Britton 1980; Centre on Transnational Corporations 1982), but that does not mean that the corporation automatically gains in the long run from lopsided agreements. Developing terms of mutual interest may in fact mean more predictable gains from the venture than the shrewd corporate deal that soon leaves the host country disenchanted.

Leasing rather than buying land, for example, may be more advantageous to both sides than outright foreign ownership. For the corporation it minimizes the commitment of locked-up capital and reduces the degree of vulnerability to the country's long-range political fortunes and/or changes in tourist tastes. At the same time, leasing can defuse national concerns about the extent of foreign ownership in the society, a factor of concern to nations as disparate as the United States and Fiji. Despite that logic, disputes between multinationals and host developing countries have generally been more severe where the corporations have no equity involved (Centre on Transnational Corporations 1982).

Foreign airlines seeking routes or other agreements on air travel will need to negotiate with both the host country and the country of origin. Scheduling, the degree of reciprocity sought for the host country's national carrier, and other issues may involve not only economic issues but the relations between the host country, the country of origin, and often several other countries that may be involved in the routing.

In the United States, for example, despite deregulation airlines need to deal with both houses of Congress, the Department of State, and even the President when, as in 1985, the latter attempted to reduce tax deductions for business travel. In some less pluralistic countries, like the Philippines under President Marcos, certain key individuals may have almost total discretion about such matters, i.e. the Minister of Tourism.

Having specific contractual agreements does not prevent their abrogation of course in times of political tension. Many airlines will refuse to fly into countries at war or involved in great civil strife. In other instances curtailment of flights between nations displeased with each other is a favorite government weapon. In late 1981, for example, President Reagan suspended Aeroflot flights to New York as a signal of his displeasure with Soviet influence in Poland, and other Western European countries followed suit after the USSR shot down a Korean civilian plane in 1983.

Much of the discussion above has focused on bilateral political negotiating by entrepreneur and national government. However, that does not include the usually inevitable regulations of the National Tourist Organization (NTO) with rules governing other levels of planning and negotiation with state, province, or city governments. Consulates or embassies are the best preliminary sources of legal and trade information. They will have addresses and titles of specific agencies charged with tourism information for investors.

POLITICAL LINKAGES

The entrepreneur and the host government are themselves "politicking" in the midst of a much larger web of political decisionmaking that may make critical decisions for the industry in which their own participation may be peripheral at best. Consider, for example, the disastrous impact of world energy prices on tourism costs in the 1970s and the subsequent pressure for deregulation of transportation that was accepted by several of the nations most active in tourism.

In the United States linkages between tourism and environmental, energy, tax, and employment policies are becoming especially salient as the government struggles to implement the broad objectives of its national tourism policy. To date, the federal response can be most charitably labeled indecisive (Borcover 1985).

Though the tourist industry prefers to see the government's commitment as proportionate to the industry's importance to the national economy, other scenarios are also reasonable. Is the responsibility for promotion in the face of lucrative returns on promotion necessarily the government's? Is there some optimal ratio of private to state to federal involvement? Do those lucrative returns from promotion constitute a subsidized bonanza for the tourist industry or does the national balance of trade, tax revenues, and increased employment constitute a significant national interest that government should foster?

Moreover, is the stimulation of tourism consistent with the government's energy needs, and what modifications are appropriate to fairly meet national goals vis-à-vis tourism and energy? Though specific national needs differ, the United States' effort to formulate a national tourism policy suggests a few of the most obvious political issues which the tourist industry and the government must continually negotiate. Even in less pluralistic countries, the political balance of tourism and other policies continues to be difficult.

INTERGOVERNMENTAL ORGANIZATIONS

Increasingly international organizations have become involved in the planning, regulation, and pressure group activities central to tourism politics. Also, what little monitoring of the industry has taken place has been done typically by a few academics and such international bodies as the World Bank, UNESCO, UNCTAD, and the International Civic Aviation Organization (ICAO). Regional groups like OECD, the OAS, ASEAN, and RCD countries have also begun

tentative efforts to facilitate and improve tourism, though the latter have focused primarily on promotional and marketing concerns.

International tourism organizations are quite naturally preoccupied with the politics of tourism (with politics within the organizations sometimes almost as time-consuming as tourism issues per se). Of these, the World Tourism Organization (WTO) is the newest and most important of the hospitality-centered organizations. Formed in 1975 in response to increased governmental interest in tourism, it supplants its predecessor, the International Union of Official Travel Organizations. Unlike the IUOTO, which was nongovernmental, the WTO is intergovernmental in nature. Members include sovereign states, associate memberships of territories or groups of territories, and affiliate members which are international bodies involved in tourism.

The WTO is designed to be an operative rather than deliberative body helping members maximize benefits from tourism. It intends to function as a sort of global data bank—identifying markets, assisting in tourism planning, and identifying funding possibilities for a wide range of tourism enterprises (Henson 1979, pp. 194–196). It is primarily an informed cheerleader for the industry and for governments interested in tourism. It is an unlikely critic, though at its 1980 conference it did consider a variety of quasi-political issues (Gunn and Jafari 1980, pp. 478–487).

Regional tourism organizations like the Pacific Area Travel Association (PATA) or the Caribbean Tourism Association are also important in tourism politics. Like the American Society of Travel Agents (ASTA), these organizations are primarily interested in group or charter travel. Their perspective tends to weigh the interests of consumers more heavily than the impact on host communities, as in the revealing theme of one PATA convention, "The Consumer: The Only One that Really Matters!"

In the transportation sector of the industry, the most important international group is the International Air Transport Association (IATA), which regulates ticketing and fares of member airlines on a nongovernmental basis. Membership is voluntary with the outstanding holdout being Icelandic Airlines.

CONCLUSION

The complexity of political and legal dimensions of tourism should not dismay or discourage decisionmakers. By anticipating them in the preplanning, consultation, and contractual agreements the potential for positive results from tourism are enhanced for all participants. Tourism *can* succeed if the political issues are directly confronted. As one journalist observed: "Tourism is like fire. It can cook your food or burn your house down" (Fox 1976, p. 44).

It is beyond the scope of this short chapter to do much more than suggest the participants and the parameters of typical political issues that are emerging in the realm of tourism, but it can be expected that international organizations of global or regional scope will increasingly play important planning and lobbying functions in the shaping of tourism in various countries.

REFERENCES

Asiaweek, October 24, 1980.

Belisle, Francois J., and Don R. Hoy (1980), "The Perceived Impact of Tourism by Residents: A Case Study in Santa Marta, Colombia," *Annals of Tourism Research*, 7 (1), 83–101.

Blanton, David (1981), "Tourism Training in Developing Countries: The Social and Cultural Dimension," *Annals of Tourism Research*, 8 (1), 116–131.

Borcover, Alfred (1985), "Funding Cuts Imperil U.S. Tourism Agency at Inopportune Time," *The Atlanta Constitution*, May 12, 3-F.

Centre on Transnational Corporations (1982), *Transnational Corporations in International Tourism*, New York: United Nations.

Chow, Willard T. (1980), "Integrating Tourism with Regional Development," *Annals of Tourism Research*, 7 (4), 584–607.

Clarke, Alan (1981), "Coastal Development in France: Tourism as a Tool for Regional Development," *Annals of Tourism Research*, 8 (3), 447–479.

Creal, James (1980), "A National Tourism Policy: Good Business for America," *National Journal*, 10 (40), 1981.

Dannhorn, Robin (1979), "Asia's Tourism Catalyst," *Far Eastern Economic Review*, (January 21), 36–37.

DeKadt, Emanuel (1979), *Tourism: Passport to Development?*, New York: Oxford University Press.

Enloe, Cynthia (1975), *The Politics of Pollution in a Comparative Perspective*, New York: McKay.

"Facilities for the Small Budget Tourist" (1978), *Eastern Economist*, 70 (May 12), 930.

Fox, Morris (1976), "The Social Impact of Tourism: A Challenge to Researchers and Planners," in *A New Kind of Sugar*, Ben Finney and Karen Ann Watson, Eds., Honolulu: East–West Center Press, p. 44.

Franda, Marcus (1979), "Quiet Turbulence in the Seychelles. Part 1. Tourism and Development," *American Universities Field Staff Reports*, No. 10.

Fukenaga, Lawrence (1976), "A New Sun in North Kohala: The Socioeconomic Impact of Tourism and Resort Development on a Rural Community in Hawaii," in *A New Kind of Sugar*, Ben Finney and Karen Ann Watson, Eds., Honolulu: East–West Center Press.

Gamper, Josef (1981), "Tourism in Austria: A Case Study of the Influence of Tourism on Ethnic Relations," *Annals of Tourism Research*, 8 (3), 432–446.

Governor's Conference on Tourism (1984), Honolulu, Hawaii, December, 11–12, 1984.

Gunn, Clare A., and Jafar Jafari, (1980), "World Tourism Conference: An Intergovernmental Tourism Landmark," *Annals of Tourism Research*, 7 (3), 478–487.

Harrell-Bond, Barbara (1978), "A Window on an Outside World: Tourism as Development in the Gambia," *American Universities Field Staff Reports*, No. 19.

Henson, Edda (1979), "World Tourism Organization in Asia and the Pacific," *Fookien Times Yearbook*, Manila: Fookien Times Yearbook Co.

Hivik, Tord, and Turid Heiberg (1980), "Centre–Periphery Tourism and Self-reliance," *International Social Science Journal*, 32 (November), 69–98.

Holden, Peter, Ed. (1984a), *Alternative Tourism with a Focus on Asia*, Bangkok: Coalition on Third World Tourism.

Holden, Peter, Ed. (1984b), *Contours*, Volume 1, Bangkok: Coalition on Third World Tourism.

Karunatilake, H.N.S. (1978), "Foreign Exchange Earnings from Tourism," in *The Role of Tourism in the Social and Economic Development of Sri Lanka*, no author given, Colombo: Social Science Research Centre.

Kent, Noel (1983), *Hawaii: Islands under the Influence*, New York: Monthly Review.

Kobrin, Stephen J. (1979), "Political Risk: A Review and Reconsideration," *Journal of International Business Studies*, (Spring/Summer), 67–80.

La Palombara, Joseph (1982), "Assessing the Political Environment for Business: A New Role for Political Scientists," *PS*, (Spring), 180–187.

Laurie, Donald, "International Risk . . . Six Questions for the Concerned Executive," no publishing information.

Loukissas, Philippo J. (1978), "Tourism and Environment in Conflict: The Case of the Greek Island of Myconos," in *Tourism and Economic Change*, Valene L. Smith, Ed., Williamsburg, Virginia: College of William and Mary.

McIntosh, Robert W. (1972), *Tourism, Principles, Practices and Philosophies*, Cleveland, Ohio: GRID, Inc.

McKean, P.F. (1978), "Towards a Theoretical Analysis of Tourism: Economic Dualism and Cultural Innovation in Bali," in *Hosts and Guests*, Valene L. Smith, Ed., Oxford, England: Basil Blackwell.

Matthews, Harry (1978), *International Tourism: A Political and Social Analysis*, Cambridge: Schenkman.

Nash, Dennison (1978), "Tourism as a Form of Imperialism," in *Hosts and Guests*, Valene L. Smith, Ed., Oxford, England: Basil Blackwell.

National Tourism Policy Study Final Report (1978) (April 21), Washington, D.C.: United States Government Printing Office.

Noronha, Raymond (1979), "Paradise Reviews: Tourism in Bali," in *Tourism: Passport to Development?* Emanuel DeKadt, Ed., New York: Oxford University Press.

Nunez, Theron (1978), "Touristic Studies in Anthropological Perspective," in *Hosts and Guests*, Valene L. Smith, Ed., Oxford, England: Basil Blackwell.

O'Grady, Ronald (1981), *Third World Stopover*, Geneva: World Council of Churches.

Organisation for Economic Cooperation and Development

(1980), *The Impact of Tourism on the Environment*, Paris: OECD.

Organisation for Economic Cooperation and Development (1981), *Tourism Policy Statement*, Paris: OECD.

Papson, Stephen (1981), "Spuriousness and Tourism: Politics of Two Canadian Provincial Governments," *Annals of Tourism Research*, 8 (2), 220–235.

Payer, Cheryl (1982), *The World Bank: A Critical Analysis*, *Monthly Review*.

Peck, J.G., and A.S. Lepie (1978), "Tourism and Development in Three North Carolina Coastal Towns," in *Hosts and Guests*, Valene L. Smith, Ed., Oxford, England: Basil Blackwell.

Pi-Sunyer, Oriol (1979), "The Politics of Tourism in Catalonia," *Mediterranean Studies*, 1(2), 46–69.

Research and Policy Committee of the Committee for Economic Development (1981), "New Policies for a Changing World Economy," in *Transnational Corporations and Developing Countries*, New York: Centre on Transnational Corporations.

Richter, Linda K. (1980a), "The Political Uses of Tourism: A Philippine Case Study," *Journal of Developing Areas*, 14 (January), 237–257.

Richter, Linda K. (1980b), "The Politics of Tourism: A Comparative Perspective," a paper presented at the Midwest Political Science Association Meeting, Chicago.

Richter, Linda K. (1981), "Tourism by Decree," *Southeast Asia Chronicle*, (78), 27–33.

Richter, Linda K. (1982), *Land Reform and Tourism Development: Policy-Making in the Philippines*, Cambridge: Schenkman.

Richter, Linda K. (1983a), "Tourism and Political Science: A Case of Not So Benign Neglect," *Annals of Tourism Research Special Issue on Political Science*, (October-December).

Richter, Linda K. (1983b), "The Political Implications of Chinese Tourism Policy," *Annals of Tourism Research*, (October–December).

Richter, Linda K. (1984a), "The Potential and Pitfalls of Tourism Planning in Third World Countries: The Case of Pakistan," *Tourism Recreation Research*, (March).

Richter, Linda K. (1984b), "The Politics of Tourism Development in the American States," a paper presented at the American Society of Public Administration meeting in Denver, Colorado, April 8–11, 1984.

Richter, Linda K. (1985a) with William L. Richter, "Policy Choices in South Asian Tourism Development," *Annals of Tourism Research*, Vol. 12, No. 2.

Richter, Linda K. (1985b), "Bureaucracy and the Political Process: Three Case Studies of Tourism Development in Asia," a paper presented at the International Political Science Association meeting, July 19, 1985, Paris, France.

Richter, Linda K. (1985c), "Tourism Development: Public Sector Careers for the 21st Century," a paper presented at the American Society for Public Administration meeting, Indianapolis, Indiana, March 25, 1985.

Richter, Linda K. (1985d), "Statement and Testimony before the Committee on Foreign Affairs, U.S. House of Representatives," March 6, 1985.

Richter, Linda K. (1985e), "State-Sponsored Tourism: A Growth Field for Public Administration," *Public Administration Review*, (November/December).

Rodenburg, Eric E. (1980), "The Effects of Scale in Economic Development: Tourism in Bali," *Annals of Tourism Research*, (November), 177–196.

Schuchat, Molly (1979), "State Tourism in China and the USA," *Annals of Tourism Research*, 6 (October/December), 425–434.

Stock, Robert (1977), "Political and Social Contributions of International Tourism to the Development of Israel," *Annals of Tourism Research*, (October/December).

Sturken, Barbara (1980), "The World Bank Well Runs Dry," *Travel Scene*, (November), 14–15.

Swain, Margaret Byrne (1978), "Cuna Women and Ethnic Tourism: A Way to Persist and an Avenue to Change," in *Hosts and Guests*, Valene L. Smith, Ed., Oxford, England: Basil Blackwell, pp. 71–82.

Turner, Louis (1976), "The International Division of Leisure: Tourism and the Third World," *World Development*, (March), 253–260.

Wilson, David (1979), "The Early Effects of Tourism in the Seychelles," in *Tourism: Passport to Development?*, Emanuel DeKadt, Ed., New York: Oxford University Press, pp. 205–236.

Wood, Robert E. (1984), "Ethnic Tourism, the State and Cultural Change in Southeast Asia," *Annals of Tourism Research*, 11(3), 353–374.

Young, George (1973), *Tourism: Blessing or Blight?* London: Pelican.

Young, Ruth (1977), "The Structural Context of the Caribbean Tourist Industry: A Comparative Study," *Economic Development and Cultural Change*, 25 (July), 657–672.

19

Environmental Design and Land Use

CLARE A. GUNN

Professor Emeritus
Recreation and Parks Department
Texas Agricultural Experiment Station
Texas A&M University
College Station, Texas 77843

As a very important aspect of the supply side of tourism, environmental development, including the landscape and built environment, is a comparatively new topic of research. In the past, designers and owners relied more on skill, tradition, and experience than upon research for land design and use decisions. Increased concern over the designed environment has come from more discriminating tourists, narrower margins of financial returns from tourism businesses, increased competition for land, and greater awareness of tourism's impact on the physical and esthetic environment. The future portends even greater emphasis on issues of better environmental design and land use for tourism.

A fundamental peculiar to tourism is that it is anchored to place. Therefore, how environments are used and how places are designed are critical tourism issues. Placeness is a tourism fact of life with many very important ramifications. No industry or social activity has as great a relationship to land—the givens of resources and the cultural modifications made by man. All other production industries distribute products to customers quite some distance from the origin. Most consumers have no notion whatsoever regarding the source location of the vegetables they eat or the clothing they wear. The reverse, the absolutism of the placeness of the tourism product, is extremely powerful—the very heart of tourism. The enticement of traveling to some place away from home and the satisfactions derived from being in that other place are basic to all tourism. Therefore, how places are identified, planned, and designed for tourism is vital to the best fit with resources and all other land uses, as well as to the success of tourism.

ENVIRONMENTAL PROBLEMS

Not long ago, the development of tourism was seen as a mounting resource use problem alongside industrialization and settlement. Mass travel expansion resulted in unprecedented growth in the development of land for tourism, especially in business. "However, a profit-maximizing orientation to tourism development can result in the deterioration of fragile ecosystems and attractive landscapes through overbuilding and excessive densities of visitors" (Dasman, Milton and Freeman 1973, p. 115). After many years of expounding the virtues of communicating with nature and enjoying the rewards of travel, the populace began to do so in such great numbers that environmentalists and governmental resource managers began to observe increased erosion of the resource base and conflict with other land uses. What was once seen as a positive social and economic movement became a negative environmental issue.

This conflict of tourist use of resource areas stimulated many expressions of opinion and some empirical studies of the consequences. Darling and Eichhorn (1969) outlined the impact on fragile sites by visitors destroying vegetation, collecting souvenir rock specimens, and causing trail erosion. Many research studies have shown negative environmental impacts to plants and animals by great numbers of visitors. Esthetic erosion of natural settings by poor building design, poor building siting, and even having visitor facilities within parks were criticized. Cursory review shows a combination of real and perceived problems of environmental deterioration, as illustrated in the documentation by Meyers (1976) of Hawaii's experience.

Much of the concern regarding tourism land use control in Hawaii stemmed from local, not visitor, worry over and observation of

> *the middle-class market Hawaii was attracting to their paradise... pollution, congestion, aesthetic blight, and what they saw as a declining quality of life.... Since the late 1960s, Waikiki has been undergoing a controversial wave of demolition to make way for new high-rise hotels. Vistas to both ocean and mountain, including the famed view of Diamond Head, are now blocked. Greenery and open space have been swallowed up by concrete, and Life of the Land did some unwelcome readings of pollution in the local water. Only two of the comfortable old hotels remain, so threatened by rising property taxes that special tax-exemption bills have been affectionately introduced in the state legislature to prevent their destruction. (Meyers 1976, pp. 88–89).*

When one adds to this the impacts tourism makes upon the cultural environment, the motivation for land use analysis and control becomes even clearer. Stated Baron Vaea, minister of tourism, Kingdom of Tonga:

> *When we examine other island tourist industries and the reappraisals which they are undergoing, we are inclined to hold back lest we are drawn into their trap of development for the benefit of developers whose sole purpose is the maximization of profits with only token regard for local participation and the social upheaval caused to the community by their development. (Ross and Farrell 1975, p. 153)*

Observations and readings suggest that similar concerns in other parts of the world have been strong motivating forces for exerting land use studies and controls for tourism. Obviously, these negative impacts, in the eyes of the motivators, demand regulation and control. Almost absent have been voices toward land use guidance that fosters rather than reduces tourism and yet protects basic environmental resources. Young (1973, p. 157) states, "These evil consequences are not *inherent* in the development of tourism; they just happen when tourism is developed in a thoughtless and casual way."

An example of these environmental issues was the impact of tourism development on the mangrove belt of the Florida coast. Studies by Odum (1971) and others showed that the food chain of valuable fish production is intimately linked with the decaying leaves of mangroves. When tourism development, especially for marinas and vacation homes in mangrove-lined coves, removes the mangroves, this valuable asset is destroyed. Robas (1970) showed that for every acre of estuary filled or dredged in Florida, two others are ruined for fish production (also important to tourism) by siltation, pollution, and other disruptions.

Of equal concern has been the cultural environment. Belisle and Hoy (1980, pp. 94–95) studied tourism impact upon the local population of Santa Marta, Colombia, and discovered that with positive economic and social impacts came inflated prices, increased robberies, drug traffic, smuggling, and prostitution. By means of controlled comparison (anthropological) research, Kemper (1979, p. 107) discovered that the impact of tourists upon Taos, New Mexico, was quite different from that upon Patzcuaro, Michoacan, Mexico, due primarily to the forms of governmental structure and tradition.

Descriptive and cause-and-effect research has proven that under certain conditions (most frequently poor planning and poor engineering) natural and cultural environments have been eroded or even severely damaged, not only by tourism but by many other land uses. While these studies were of value for better understanding and better planning for tourism, they were not sponsored by tourism interests. In fact, tourism leadership generally opposed such work on the grounds that it produced adverse publicity. Therefore, these groups were either negative or inactive on such issues. For example, the state tourism interests of Mississippi took no action and the local tourism businesses opposed the state health and pollution agencies' action to clean up polluted beaches (Cartee 1975).

Perhaps the most heavily criticized resource use has been that of coastal tourism. Waterfront resorting and recreation have historically dominated tourism destinations worldwide.

> *Hundreds of miles of coastline have been ruined irremediably by virtually uncontrolled building of hotels, restaurants, bars and houses. Beaches have been divided into unsightly allotments, and noise from jukeboxes, fumes from traffic and sheer human overpopulation pay witness to the chaos man has made of the organization of his leisure. (Young 1973, p. 157)*

Studies and conference deliberations (Ketchum 1972) of over 60 scientists culminated in coastal environmental issues and recommendations that formed the basis for the Coastal Zone Management Act of 1972. This act explicitly required the protection and planned development of tourism and recreational use of the coast.

POSITIVE DIRECTIONS

While most environmental tourism studies thus far have documented negative impacts on the environment, observations on the positive impacts have also been made. Perhaps the greatest impact has been an indirect one. Because millions of tourists have received personal benefits from their travels, they have been willing to provide political support for public park and recreation programs and direct contributions to nonprofit organizations important to tourism (Gunn 1973, p. 25).

For example, most states and provinces have improved their game and fish habitat, important to many tourists, through public support of natural resource agencies of governments. The array of historic buildings and sites is much greater today because of the efforts of cultural environmentalists in nonprofit organizations. Nelson (1974, pp. 235, 239), in his study of environmental changes in Banff National Park, Alberta, Canada, found that "the growth of recreation has helped foster protectionism. . . . The evolution of protectionism has largely depended upon the finances provided by recreation, the basic reason for creation of Banff and many other national parks."

Although resource protectionism was seen primarily as an obligation of the public sector, the private sector soon began making detailed studies and analyses before development. The development site of Walt Disney World, for example, underwent intensive environmental analysis before plans were developed. Sea Pines Plantation, a vacation home resort complex on Hilton Head Island, Georgia, also illustrates a high degree of sensitivity to the ecologically fragile sites by allowing building only on other areas.

A paradox of contemporary environmentalism has been historic and archeological investigation, protection, and restoration. This relatively recent surge of interest in our heritage is motivated not usually by a desire for more tourism but for cultural protection. Few research studies link the tourism implications— need for transportation, food, interpretation, and many ancillary tourist services—with the acts of historic and archeological development.

There is little doubt that environmental awareness of the last few decades has had much to do with tourism in both a negative and a positive way. As is true of all movements, there was more lay philosophizing, voicing of opinion, and legislative action than scientific research during this period. However, more serious systematic study of tourism and the environment, both cultural and natural, is now taking place and predictably will expand.

These introductory comments may serve to endorse the need for more and better environmental design practice and land use planning for tourism as well as research of this topic. Following this, two questions need to be asked. First, what are the main criteria for entering into more and better environmental guidance and who are the key decision-makers charged with the responsibility of creating improved environments? Second, what processes hold promise of accomplishing the desired goal, so important to the future of tourism? The remainder of this essay addresses these two questions.

ENVIRONMENTAL DESIGN CRITERIA

If environments of the supply side of tourism are to be designed to avoid the many problems and to meet the needs of tourism, certain criteria should be met. It is not enough to gather some financial resources, hire an architect, and let a contract for construction. These simple steps now need to be expanded into a range of several criteria that hold promise of better use of environmental assets and better provision for tourists.

Study of environmental design and land use planning for tourism suggests that at least the following seven criteria categories are important: functional design and planning, market acceptance, owner rewards, relevance to transportation, resource protection, local community goals, and environmental decision-makers.

FUNCTIONAL DESIGN AND PLANNING

Obviously, both managers and visitors prefer that all development functions properly. Nothing is more aggravating and costly to an operator than a facility that requires excessive maintenance and has too short a life. Equally aggravating to tourists are environments that do not work. Experience is showing that many functional problems (not all) can be anticipated and avoided best at the early design stages. But just telling a designer that you wish a functional design is not enough. Both owners and designers need to give consideration to at least three types of function.

All design must meet *structural* criteria. In an age of space shuttles and high technology, it seems redundant to stress the need for basic structural stability, and yet drives do erode, bridges do collapse, and sometimes hotel structural failures cause loss of life (Andersen 1981, p. 26). Although the incidence of these problems is very low, these examples do point up the need for concern over structural functionalism. Legislation may be less in need than greater precision, professionalism, and conscientious responsibility on the part of all involved in environmental design. By and large, research and testing as well as tightened regulation now offer little excuse for error in structural design. Buildings, drainage systems, drives, walks, and landscapes must be designed and maintained to withstand wear and tear as well as climatic conditions that would cause structural failure or shorten the life.

Another measure of design is that of *physical* function. By this is meant the capability of the designed environment, indoors and outdoors, to meet the physical needs of people, animals, automobiles, or any other units that will need to use the environment. For people-environments, designers need to be aware of the physical dimensions of the human body and how the various parts function (including the disabled and handicapped). In spite of the availability of design reference data books, generally derived from research, designers still give tourists noisy and uncomfortable heat and cooling, airline seats with unreachable controls, signs and directions on highways and in buildings that are illegible, and lockers that cannot be reached by some groups of travelers of short stature. In the landscape, the changing physical requirements of compact cars, recreation vehicles, tour buses, and large trucks must be considered in the site planning and overnight accommodations and food services for travelers. "In Monterey, California, as in many older towns, the primary tourist problems are parking and circulation coupled with a concentration of historic sites in a small area" (Edmunds 1980, p. 21). Owners and developers must continually insist upon efficient physical functional design for all their environments.

But environments can meet criteria of structural and physical needs and yet not fully satisfy the demands of tourism. How often one sees adjectives such as "comfortable," "pleasant," "beautiful," "luxurious," and "sparkling" in tourist promotional literature. These point up the need for a third category of criteria that all environments must meet—an *esthetic* or *cultural* function. Drab, institutional, plain, and unexciting landscapes and buildings are not acceptable even though sometimes more economical to build. For tourist appreciation, understanding, and enjoyment of natural settings, landscape architects must design walks, drives and overlooks with sensitivity to natural vistas and beauty. Sidestepping the engagement of creative and talented designers may appear to save money only to discover later that tourists patronize the better-designed competition. Some businesses, fearing decline in popularity of their design, regularly schedule remodeling of all exteriors and interiors.

Land use esthetics includes the appropriateness and beauty of areas surrounding major attractions—"the inviolate belt" (Gunn 1972b, pp. 40–41). An example of such intrusion is the controversial and "privately owned National Gettysburg Tower . . . and unless something is done in the near future, the Gettysburg area will lose its sense of place, and the things that make it very special will disappear—diminished, eroded, and erased by density, modernity, and sameness" (Gettysburg's Battle 1981, p. 20).

Managers and designers of tourist environments need to consider all three functions—structural, physical, esthetic—when developing new or remodeling older lands and buildings for tourists.

MARKET ACCEPTANCE

Environmental design and land use for tourism has a market side as well as a resource side. Land use is a social attribution as well as an activity based on physical assets. What visitors want to see and do—and they are not all alike in their tastes and interests—makes a difference. The sorting out of market diversity and translating it into appropriately created environments is no easy task. It is complicated by several factors.

First, there is a great difference in preference of destination activities between travelers. Studies variously classify travelers by whether they like active physical challenge or passive spectatorism, historic sites or natural resource areas, entertainment or solitude, and many other ways of sorting out the activity interests. This is further complicated by the difference in trip purpose and different interest by the tourist at different times.

Second, fad and fashion are powerful variables and can boom or break destinations. The capricious nature of some markets creates a volatile design and planning problem. Tourism activities grow out of culture's leisure patterns and therefore are extremely dynamic, not static. Early on, research of trends may be able to predict important "ins" or "outs" of travel trade.

Third, the vagaries of transportation technology and cost greatly influence the design and planning of destinations. Areas dependent upon automobile travel are subject to fluctuations of fuel cost, costs of vehicles, and changes of highways. They may also be affected by competitive fares of airlines, car rentals, and bus tours. Research of the comparative influence of transportation modes on travel can be valuable for all tourism destination management.

Fourth, some areas are blessed with natural resource assets in support of special activities much preferred by markets. No matter how much market analysis may suggest demand for winter sports, southern climes have difficulty in meeting this demand. Conversely, no matter how attractive some northern beaches may be, they cannot meet market demands for warm water, extended periods of sunshine, and high temperatures. Research of physical resource assets can assist managers in design and planning issues.

In addition to the above factors of market acceptance of designed tourism development, there is a temporal problem. Market research has resulted in a life-cycle theory for products (Buzzell 1966). For tourism, in which the product is fixed to place and has relatively high capital investment, this may mean a short life. Does the designer intentionally create flimsy environments that are to be flushed away after their usable life span? Can environments be designed with built-in flexibility that anticipates decline and therefore incorporates a chance for remodeling to meet new needs? Research has not yet provided adequate answers to these questions, but all managers must be aware of the anticipated life of built environments and have contingency plans available for meeting the new needs.

OWNER REWARDS

Both public and private owners expect certain rewards from their ownership and management and resist modifications for someone else's objectives. Those groups standing outside owners, such as advocates of greater environmental protection, must be able to translate their ideologies through the existing system of land ownership and development.

For the public sector in tourism, the greatest role as an owner-developer is that of holding and managing vast acreages of resource assets, functioning primarily as attractions. In the United States, federal agencies alone own and manage 85 percent of all outdoor recreation lands (Domestic Tourism 1973, p. 9), but considerable internal policy stress has developed because none of the agencies was originally given tourism as a significant function.

For the U.S. Forest Service, with over 188 million acres of land and some 234 million visitor-days a year (Van Doren 1982), forest production and watershed management were original mandates. However, this level of participation suggests a strong interest today in tourist use. Its policies of "multiple use" now include the building of tourist facilities as well as leasing lands to concessioners, such as for winter sports, resorts, and private organization camps. The fulfillment of its responsibility in providing for public recreation is its social reward for carrying out this land use policy.

The U.S. Army Corps of Engineers, not usually considered a member of tourism, owns over 10 million acres of land and controls over 28,000 miles of waterways. Policies on land use and development greatly influence tourism because these holdings include thousands of recreation sites, many boat launching areas, beaches, picnic areas, and concessions of camps, lodges, and other tourist services. The rewards to the agency are those of providing a social welfare service to the public.

The rewards to the National Park Service are twofold: providing visitor experiences for many millions of visitors each year and protecting outstanding natural resource assets for the national long-range welfare. Fulfilling these objectives influences greatly its policies on design and land use. Throughout its history, much controversy has centered on the extent of providing for visitors and at the same time protecting the resource. This has resulted in much vacillation in land use planning for the Service.

When one adds some 90 or more federal agencies to the hundreds of state, county, and city jurisdictions over lands used by tourists, the magnitude of governmental involvement in land development and use can be appreciated.

Rewards to the private nonprofit sector are prescribed by their individual organizational policies. For example, owners of the Alamo and Williamsburg seek to inspire in visitors a sense of national heritage understanding and pride as well as to restore and preserve important elements of national history. Much of the restoration of urban historic areas is motivated by altruistic rewards while greatly influencing the storehouse of development, land use, and profit to local tourism businesses.

Rewards to the free enterprise sector are commonly considered to be profitmaking, but those in business quickly point out that this is not an exclusive reward. Much social responsibility is felt and carried out, not merely for altruistic objectives but in order to function properly as a business. According to Drucker (1975):

There is no conflict between 'profit' and 'social responsibility'. To earn enough to cover the genuine costs which only the so-called 'profit' can cover, is economic and social responsibility—indeed it is the special social and economic responsibility of business. It is not the business that earns a profit adequate to its genuine costs of capital, to the risks of tomorrow and the needs of tomorrow's worker and pensioner that 'rips off' society. It is the business that fails to do so.

Profits cannot be an isolated goal, removed from service to tourists, protection of resources, or concern over social issues.

Regarding land use, all sectors are acting as brokers between visitors (with their preferences) and resources (with their intrinsic developable qualities). The more that research demonstrates the linkage between visitors and resources, the more that a closer balance between resource protection and use can be accomplished by all sectors. Their rewards are derived as much from visitor satisfactions as from other goals of the enterprise, public or private.

RELEVANCE TO TRANSPORTATION

An important criterion of environmental design for tourism—obvious but not well understood—is that of the relevance of transportation. This must be approached not only through the perception of the managers of the several modes (air, auto, rail, ship) but also through the perspective of the traveler. Research is demonstrating time and again that travelers do not stray very far from main thoroughfares. Even wilderness users have been found to congregate primarily at points of access penetration. Instead of citing this as a frailty of visitors, managers would do well to accept it as a principle and adapt destination design and planning thereto.

This does not mean that strip development is inevitable. It merely means that a transportation system that provides convenient, dependable, and affordable linkage between access and all points of interest to the tourist is important. Modern home-to-destination modes are dominantly automobile, tour bus, RV, and plane. (Cruise ships today are more destination resorts than modes of transportation.) At all exchange points (freeway exits, airports, bus depots), interconnecting modes—personal car, car rental, tour bus, tour ferry—become very important. At these points of intermodal connection, greater concern over integrated land use and information systems is needed. Research is showing that mastery of today's complicated regional airports is not for the infirm or faint-hearted.

The planning and development of future destinations should depend more heavily on studies of passenger transportation preferences and behavior than they have in the past.

RESOURCE PROTECTION

Polarized advocacy positions between resource protectionists—even "preservationists"—and developers has clouded the issue of environmental protection and tourism. Environmentalism, as a movement in the 1970s, has fostered greater awareness of the finite limits of natural resources. While abuse of resource assets by tourist developers can be cited, on balance much greater resource degradation has been caused by nontourism development, such as urban sewage disposal, industrial pollution, and mineral extraction. However, this does not in any way relieve the need to reduce resource abuse by tourism, especially in the realm of esthetics.

Poorly understood is the overwhelming dependence of tourism upon natural and cultural resource assets. Instead of opposing moves for resource protection, tourism managers could well lend their support not only for the long-range goals of society but also for their own self-interest. A good source of information on natural resource issues and concerns of value to tourism managers can be found in the work by ReVelle and ReVelle (1981).

Because *water* is so critical to so many tourist activities, its quality is of vital concern. Research is demonstrating the biological and physical needs for water waste treatment and ridding lakes and streams of many pollutants. Pollution from additives, such as her-

bicides, pesticides, and fertilizers used by farmers and lakeshore owners can be reduced. All body-contact water sports, such as swimming, diving, and water skiing, require water quality not injurious to health. Fish and other seafoods must not be contaminated by PCBs (polychlorinated biphenyls) or other elements injurious to man. Research is showing dramatic rehabilitation of waters, such as the Willamette River in Oregon and the Hudson River, following reduction of pollutants. All these water-protective moves are in the best self-interest of tourism.

Soils, usually thought of only in connection with agriculture, are equally important resources for tourism development. Massive vacation home plats, resorts, campgrounds, and marinas can destroy landscape beauty, pollute nearby waters, and threaten the stability of soils if improperly designed and built. Landscape architects and soils scientists have researched these issues and most of them have solutions. The problem is to stimulate owners and developers to heed their recommendations. Vacation home owners need not be threatened by landslides from heavy rainfall. Beaches need not be eroded due to thoughtless bulldozing of grass-covered foredunes. Resorts and campgrounds need not be void of ground covers and shade. Most of the soil compaction and erosion due to tourist use of land is due to poor design and maintenance of walks and drives used by high volumes of visitors. Managers must seek solutions to mass use of resource assets, especially soils.

Related to soil problems are those of *vegetative cover*. Tourism managers may believe they are far removed from issues of forest and game management but they are not. A significant number of tourists seek beautiful verdant landscapes, shaded campsites and parks, and even desert bloom. Less obvious are the valuable tourism functions of protected watersheds and wildlife habitat provided by vegetation. The term scenery appears at the top of most tourist preference lists but tourism managers are not always aware of practices and research that offer guidance on protecting and enhancing vegetative cover. For example, fall color tours are packaged by tourism wholesalers who do not always understand the land use policies of landowners that make such tours possible. Well aware of the responsibility in landscape esthetics as well as forest production is the U.S. Forest Service. Through its several experiment stations it has fostered the greatest amount of research today on outdoor recreation, especially as related to forests.

Far beyond the obvious importance of wild game for hunting is the entire resource of *wildlife*. Hunting of small and large game continues to be high on activity lists, especially in localized areas and at certain seasons. But, spurred by interest in amateur photography and nature appreciation, the esthetic aspect of wildlife is taking on even greater importance. Many land design issues are yet to be resolved through research and by the skill of the landscape architect to provide suitable interface between visitors and wildlife. Too heavy an intrusion upsets wildlife. Overmanagement of wildlife for tourists creates artificial settings, not unlike a zoo. Too severe restriction on visitor contact prevents personal enrichment and thrill from the experience. Continued research is needed to determine better interpretive mechanisms and perhaps the provision of vicarious experiences for the enjoyment of wildlife.

Emphasis must also be placed on *cultural* resources because of worldwide renewed interest in protection and restoration of past heritage. Tourism is regularly being expanded and enriched by forces outside its formal structure, such as from historians and archeologists. The renewal of cities, largely restoration of older plazas, parks, and historic structures, adds greatly to the store of tourism treasures. Throughout the United States and Canada, entire districts, once blighted and decaying, are being rejuvenated, restoring their attractiveness not only to local citizenry but to visitors as well. Baltimore, New Bedford, Charleston, Georgetown, and Savannah are some notable examples on the East Coast. These redevelopments are not only socially rewarding, but also provide the backdrop for many tourists who spend money. Redevelopment of Amish settlements in Pennsylvania has brought approximately 4 million visitors spending at least half a day in Lancaster County, thus making an impact of over $180 million (Buck and Alleman 1981, p. 44).

It behooves tourism management, then, to support research and management practices that protect and enhance the quality of natural and cultural resource assets.

COMMUNITY GOALS

Too often tourism is taken out of the context of basic community interest, activity, and goal-seeking. Since so much of tourism is directed to destination communities (even those resource assets in remote settings are served by local communities), it is necessary for tourism management to link all its efforts with the society, government, and traditions of cities. A polarized position such as that of Garland (1981, p. 19), "Tourism is a spinoff industry. . . . It should never be permitted to influence land use in any fundamental way," forecloses constructive environmental design and planning for the good of the community as well as for tourism.

Behind the obvious facade of tourism businesses—hotels, gas stations, airlines—lies the infrastructure of tourism. Because most development for tourism takes place at cities, research study of the economic input–output regarding infrastructure is needed. Expanded tourism brings in new revenues but it also requires more water, electricity, gas, waste disposal, streets, policing, fire protection, and even medical care. Com-

munities should have knowledge of added infrastructure costs as well as added returns before deciding on a positive or negative tourism development policy.

Because cities are where most people live, it is well for tourism management to be aware of what environmental development policies are important to local citizens. People value their cities, according to recent survey research (Kunde 1982, p. 10), because of their "economic opportunities and major enriching amenities." Cited among these amenities are cultural amenities (museums, symphonies, theaters), intellectual amenities (good schools, universities, institutes), economic amenities (diversified job opportunities, research facilities), and recreational amenities (parks, amusements, sports).

Coincidentally, most of these are the same elements that attract visitors and provide them with satisfactions. Therefore, essential is the careful design, planning, and management that reduces conflict between visitor and resident as each competes for the same amenities. Much of this may be resolved if the tourism interests (chambers of commerce, hoteliers, restaurateurs) communicate with city councils and citizen organizations when urban decisions are being made. A proactive stance by tourism has greater opportunities than the present reactive position in most communities. While environmental designers and planners extoll the virtue of diversity for all groups they also recognize the need for constant managerial interplay that maintains diversity with a minimum of conflict.

ENVIRONMENTAL DECISION-MAKERS

This discussion of environmental design and land use would not be complete without reference to the decision-makers. Popularly, professional designers are considered to have a major role. Perhaps they do in some instances, but research of this subject shows the important influence of several other segments. In fact, in today's complex environmental development process, it is not always easy to identify the true decision-makers—those who most directly influence how a specific piece of land is to be used and how final development is to appear. Therefore, it is equally difficult to identify present policy, to guide better future policy, and to guide future research.

Certainly, *owners* do have a major influence, whether they be hotel corporations, marina entrepreneurs, historical societies, national resource management agencies, or the individual with a cottage. For all land owners, public and private, certain owner objectives are very critical—speculation, specific business use, quasi-business use, tax reduction, social welfare, personal home. What actually is developed for tourists depends heavily upon the owner's intent, not only for the type of use but also the quality and quantity of use.

For government agencies, most are bound to their legal administrative mandates but exercise considerable freedom in their own land use policies within such mandates.

Today, *moneylenders* have a very strong influence on land use of tourism. Public and private financial sources have their own policies regarding land uses that they will and will not support. Moneylenders have great power and in many instances have stopped or changed drastically an owner's intended use of land. The influx of new coastal historical redevelopment in the United States is due largely to nonprofit and governmental funding for these uses but here also there are many constraints. Private finance is often very restrictive, especially for what is conceived as "high risk" development, such as for resorts and theme parks.

The *land development and construction industry* has a critical role in tourism land use. New methods and technology have reduced many limitations on environmental manipulation and building. But a most important control is the cost of construction. Many final decisions on uses of land and building design were dictated by how much the development would cost. Some land has never been developed for tourism because of this single factor. Especially in periods of inflation and recession, the availability and cost of labor and construction materials can dramatically influence decisions.

The *manager* of tourist lands frequently has an after-the-fact role in decision making on land use. Managers of parks, hotels, airports, campgrounds, and other tourist establishments have important design knowledge based upon experience. Frequently, however, they are brought into an active role only after most decisions on land use and design and even construction have been made by others. Hence, they face the dilemma of doing the best they can with the opportunities and constraints handed to them.

Perhaps the above review has shown that *designers and planners* do not have quite as much influence on decision making on land use as popularly believed. While it is true that professional designers and planners (architects, engineers, landscape architects, interior designers, urban planners) produce the sketch plans and working drawings and specifications for actual development of land, their freedom of choice is severely limited by other factors. Still, new environmental form and function, structure or landscape, is the realm of the creative designer.

One area of the designer–owner relationship needs to be emphasized. In most projects today there is often a gap between the owner's land and the designer's understanding of what is to be done with the land. The designer, whose last few projects likely were entirely different, expects information on *what* is to be done to come from the owner. On the other hand, the owner, believing that he is hiring the expert to design his land, relies on the designer. Neither one fully realizes the need for deeper research of the problem—a study of how many people, what level of market stratification, what seasons of intensity, tourism interests now and predicted, and many other program needs. The filling of this gap is becoming an important role of research by consulting firms.

Another important role of research, not being done very much today, is evaluation of design success after construction and use. Seldom are designers brought back in a research role to determine if the design really worked.

Finally, *publics* have entered into the process of land use decision making in several ways. Many agencies and private organizations, either because of legislation or voluntarily, use public involvement during the land use planning stage. Some publics have created specific organizations or worked through existing ones to lobby for legislation on land use. Many new rules and regulations on land use have been developed in recent years, from local to national levels, due to increased activity by private groups. An important public is the total of tourist users of developed land. Theirs is really the ultimate deciding factor regarding the success of design and land use.

This review of decision making and decision-makers in design and land use is intended merely to suggest the need for more and better research information on both improvement in the process and in the role of each sector.

PROCESSES

Throughout the discussion of environmental design and land use thus far, many solutions have been hinted at, even suggested. If better tourism environmental solutions are to be accomplished, what are some of the processes that can be employed? It is one thing to have noble goals, proper criteria, and decision-makers with the right policies for environmental design and land use; it is quite another to make them work. The complexity of tourism, as described above, suggests some of the problems of implementing desirable improvements in tourism development. But, progress is being made, both on the research side and the environmental design side. The following notes deal briefly with design and planning processes from several vantage points.

THE REGIONAL SCALE

Interest beyond-the-site has increased in recent years with greater recognition of the importance of large-scale factors that influence tourist business operators, the environment, and tourists themselves. This topic, involving planning principles as well as research techniques, paralleled the general interest in broad-scale planning, pioneered by works of Hills (1961), Lewis (1969), and McHarg (1969) (MacDougall and Brandes 1974, p. 14). McHarg's *Design with Nature* (1969) made the case for letting knowledge of the land resources strongly influence, or even dictate, the uses to which the land would be put.

In 1970, Steinitz compared 15 approaches to land analysis and came to the conclusion that they could be classified into the following:

Resource inventory.

Resource-centered analysis.

Analysis linked with demand studies.

Single-sector models which predict the effect of change.

Simulation models which can interact with other models in a general planning system.

But, he added, "one has the curious feeling that the several investigators are looking at the same objectively measurable data and idiosyncratically interpreting them . . . ." A valuable spinoff from these studies "is quite literally to frighten people into caring about environmental quality" (Steinitz 1970, pp. 103–105).

For tourism, a concept in 1965 (Gunn) suggested research of several physical characteristics of a region in order to identify potential destination zones, called "community-attractions complexes," illustrated by Fig. 1. A similar concept identifying "recreation centrics" (see Fig. 2) was used in the development of the Hawaii Comprehensive Outdoor Recreation Plan (Wolbrink 1970). In 1966, a team of economists and landscape architects used land research and analysis techniques to identify zones of greatest tourism development potential for Michigan's Upper Peninsula (Blank and Gunn 1965). Several countries of Europe developed regional analysis schemes to study tourism development potential. An example was that of Prikryl (1968), researching many resources and existing development for environmental planning of tourism in Czechoslovakia. No one purports these to be scientific ways of determining best tourism land use but these approaches are based upon research study of important factors rather than merely guessing at potential.

Forster (1973) identifies a "three-zone configuration" for environmental development of national parks and tourism. The core is the protected natural area with extremely limited or no access by tourists. Around this is a recreational zone where appropriate near-core activities are planned: camping, canoeing, interpretive tours, trails, and observation points. Outside this area is the perimeter zone where visitor services—accommodations, restaurants, shops—and intensive recreation are located. This approach is carried out in Canadian national parks, using the follow-

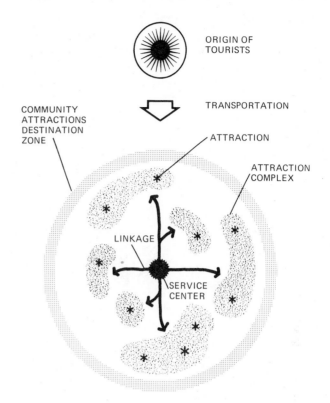

FIGURE 1 *Community–attractions complex.* A concept for a destination zone, encompassing attraction complexes, linkage, service center (city), and transportation. Source: Gunn 1972b, p. 47.

ing environmental design and land use policies (Forster 1973, pp. 61–62):

1 Outstanding natural features must be preserved for public benefit, education, and enjoyment.

2 Areas adjacent are to be protected.

3 Visitor facilities (for the main features) shall not intrude on features.

4 Tourist service centers (accommodations, restaurants, stores) shall be away from natural features or outside the park.

5 Staff residences shall be inconspicuous.

6 Maintenance facilities shall be concealed.

Environmental protection and tourism development are embodied in Scotland's assessment of resource potential (Travis 1974). Figure 3 shows a "twinning principle" that provides a commercial linkage between tourist demand and a protected natural resource area. By careful site design, services are concentrated in a supporting community and at the edge of the conserved attractions area.

Another illustration of a regional approach is that

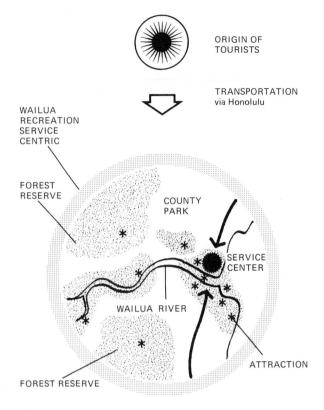

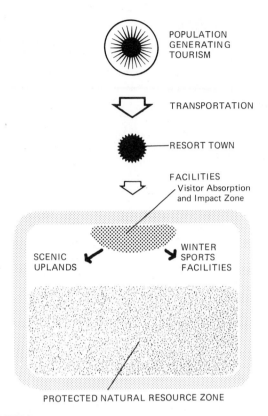

FIGURE 2 *Recreation centric.* A destination zone plan for Wailua, Kauai (Hawaii), including a service center, attractions, linkage (via river), and transportation. Source: Wolbrink 1970, p. 131.

FIGURE 3 *Twinning principle.* A destination zone concept with two main elements: a resort town as service center and a resource area with visitor attractions. Source: Travis 1974, p. 42.

of the environmental assessment of tourism potential for Ontario, Canada (Tourism Development 1977). Through a process that studied existing resources, 17 opportunity zones were identified. The criteria used were:

> Natural resource space.
> Population.
> Transportation.
> Attractions/events.
> Image/cohesiveness.
> Services/facilities.

One technique available to tourism regional planners utilizes a mix of research and planning principles, aided by computer mapping to identify zones of potential for tourism development (Gunn 1979a, b). The following five steps are involved:

1   Setting objectives.
2   Research of "physical" and "program" factors.

3   Synthesis and conclusions.
4   Concepts for development.
5   Recommendations and implementation (Gunn 1979b, p. 240).

Figures 4A and 4B show how destination zones are derived from computer mapping and summarizing of important physical factors. From this research information, investors and developers in the zones can then engage in more detailed feasibilities for individual enterprises—public parks, historic sites, recreation complexes, vacation home complexes, and their linkage with a service community. This approach does not deal with the site scale but identifies areas in which site developers should consider environmental assessment and design for their establishments. [More detailed explanation of the several research factors, their weighting and indexing, and the computer mapping process is offered in Gunn (1979b).]

Ferrario (1981) has developed an environmental and planning approach for tourism on a regional scale

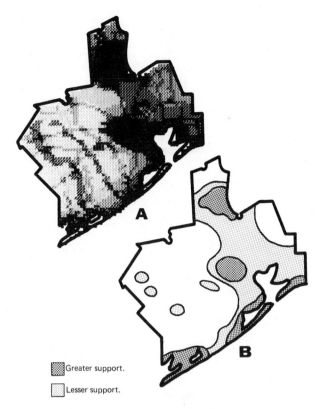

Greater support.

Lesser support.

FIGURE 4   *Potential destination zone.* (A) Aggregation of nine physical factors by computer. (B) Identification of priority development potential areas. An area surrounding Houston, Texas. Source: Gunn 1982, p. 26.

and recently applied it to KwaZulu and Natal in southern Africa. The following process was utilized:

1   Inventory of attractions.
2   Availability—seasonality, accessibility, admittance, fragility, popularity, local opinion.
3   Survey of tourist preferences—foreign, domestic.
4   Result analysis—indices and maps of potential.
5   Final considerations—development priorities.

Application of a pre-feasibility approach in Canada (Gunn 1982) led to emphasis on a process rather than a one-time reporting that annually updates guidance to all investors, developers, and tourism managers on environmental design and planning for tourism. It recommends that a national government is the logical sponsor for broad national research that annually produces popular information on this topic. Suggested are three publications, updated each year:

Annual Destination Report   Includes destination

zones based upon the several markets and resource assets.

Resource Foundations   Includes the research processes and results of necessary study of the resource foundations that led to the destination report.

Market–Economic Foundations   Annual update of economic and market conditions as a basis for destination report.

Regarding the regional scale of environmental design and land use, it would seem that tourism managers of all segments and sectors could gain by having a broad perspective of tourism in their region. No matter the technique used, investors and developers of projects need to know the overall environmental context of their projects. Individual businesses and the several kinds of park and recreation areas are never operating in isolation. Their success or failure is dependent upon many factors off the site. Studies that provide insight into these factors can assist greatly in individual decision making.

But such environmental research studies are costly, time-consuming, and require several highly specialized disciplinary inputs. Most of these are beyond the capacity of individual enterprise, especially small business, which is so very important to tourism. In some countries, this large-scale work is assumed by government. This seems to be a logical function for government provided that it maintains a positive and productive role for the good of tourism. It will not serve tourism well if it becomes entrenched in protecting its bureaucratic turf or loses contact with the several business and public elements so very important to the functioning of tourism. All regional environmental research and planning must foster individual project development and greater satisfaction to tourists at the same time that long-range protection to social, economic, and environmental values are maintained.

THE SITE SCALE

As important as a regional approach to tourism and environmental development is environmental design and planning at the site scale. Regional approaches can identify zones where development is logical and has potential, but studies at the site scale are necessary for individual projects.

Thus far in this chapter, volumes of tourists have been accepted as necessary to successful tourism—the more, the better. After all, businesses thrive on volume and need to be located (as well as managed) to favor volume patronage. The public sector, owner of extensive recreation and resource areas, gains better political support when more people can participate on their lands, and yet many studies by environmentalists (and resource managers) have shown deterioration of resource assets by masses of visitors. Increasingly, park managers are being pressured to curtail use. How can these seemingly conflicting positions be resolved? First, an examination of tourism clustering as a principle may be helpful.

CLUSTERING

A quick managerial response to increased wear-and-tear from too many visitors in one spot is dispersal. But now the problems of dispersal are beginning to show. Dispersal denies all the advantages of clustering, which is more functional from the standpoint of both visitors and services. As Balmer *et al.* (1977, p. 3) have described, clustering has merit from several perspectives:

From a development perspective The necessary infrastructure is much more efficient and certainly less costly in a developed area or where several developments are being planned. The viability of a new commercial tourism plant increases with the degree of travel and the size of the resident market. Experience has shown the marketing advantages of motels being located near other motels, food services near others, and other like groupings. Several developments from the same sector can create or ensure efficient use of necessary industry support services. For example, the California coastal plan "encourages the concentration of new development in those places that are already developed, so as to minimize resource damage, economize on public facilities and make nonautomobile transportation possible" (Healy 1976, p. 221).

From an economic perspective Longer stays in the area, generated by a variety of attractions, boost revenues in accommodation and food service sectors of the local economy. Diversity, both within the tourism industry and as tourism complements existing industry, increases the economic stability of the community. A large and mixed tourism industry will gradually create a skilled and reliable local labor pool. The more complete the local service (both to the tourist and to the industry) the smaller the possibility of "leakage." The benefits (direct and indirect through the multiplier effect) to the "primary impact area" increase with the size and diversity of the local tourism industry.

From a social perspective The opportunity for increased interaction between the resident and the tourist is enhanced by greater concentration. Traditional customs may be reinforced in an area. Many facilities, even though designed for the tourists, will be available to the resident population (specialty restaurants, convention centers, museums, theme parks).

From an environmental perspective Expansion of currently viable urban areas as tourism service centers is likely to alter rural and natural environments less than new development in those environments. Planners can become skilled in the direction of the tourism industry to ensure that unique and sensitive areas are protected, that adequate design standards are maintained, and that all necessary support services have been planned for and provided. Intensive site development and use is easier to control and manage with consequent protection and preservation of secondary impact areas. Clustering prevents sprawl and general visual pollution of key natural features (primary attractions in themselves).

From a promotional perspective The potential for "packaging" of diverse but complementary opportunities increases with the scale of local tourism investment. The possibilities of "themeing" to better convey the appeal of the area to the potential visitor are enhanced when a larger number of attractions and services exist. The synergistic effect of several attractions creates a natural ability to draw tourists over relatively large distances, thus increasing the market potential for each.

Clustering is an important principle for coastal tourism, very important in the United States and many other countries. The term "coast" implies a uniform linearity for great distances along the water's edge. Coastal tourism, however, functions primarily at nodes (see Lewis 1964 and Gunn 1972b). By designing for mass concentrations (meeting market needs for gregarious waterfront uses: beaches, festivals, marinas), better management, better control, and better guest satisfactions can be derived. Such concentration relieves the pressure on remote areas and provides greater solitude for the market segment desiring it.

PROBLEMS OF CAPACITY

Much writing in recent years has been directed to the other side of clustering and concentration—that of capacity. Even granting the environmental efficiencies and better visitor service through clustering, there have been many concerns expressed over exceeding maximum capacities of resources. A number of researchers have identified capacity problems: Stankey and Lime (1973), Edwards and Fowle (1955), Godschalk and Parker (1975), Wagar (1974), and Bouchard (1973). Stynes (1977, 1979) and others have grouped capacity problems into three categories.

Most commonly a source of concern among resource managers is the damage to a *natural resource* from volumes of visitors. Some plants cannot stand trampling and even forest trees have been damaged from excessive trail compacting of roots. Animal habitat is sometimes disturbed, reducing numbers or forcing migration. Therefore, planners are now realizing that they must consider resource carrying capacity when developing sites for tourism.

A second type of capacity is that related to the visitor's values, a *social* capacity. Some visitors thrive on crowds; others seek solitude. In the design of visitor environments, consideration must be given to the stratification of the market so that each site does not exceed its social carrying capacity.

Third, there are limits to the volume of visitors that *management* can handle. Both the private and the public sectors have constraints on budgets for capital improvements and operating staff. It is not always possible to cope with increased masses of visitors. With the great growth of recreation and tourism, this has probably been the greatest limitation.

While these environmental issues must be considered, much of the difficulty has been exaggerated, diverting attention toward curtailment of visits rather than toward design and management solutions. With creative design and better understanding of visitor interests and times of visits, solutions can be found to most of these problems. Rationing should be a last-resort solution, only after all other design and management solutions have been tried.

An example of how well site design and management can handle a capacity problem without curtailing visitors is the Wye Marsh Wildlife Refuge, located near Midland, Ontario. The visitor center and parking lot are located on a nonsensitive site within easy access of the highway. Thousands of visitors are able to gain an understanding of the marsh and its wildlife by studying the excellent exhibits, viewing an audiovisual presentation, or purchasing literature. Even without leaving the building, visitors gain a sense of place. For another market segment, very much smaller and willing to spend more time, self-guided or guided tours of the edges of the reserve can be taken. These offer a richer experience with opportunities of observing plant and animal life first-hand on trails, designed for heavy use, leading just a short distance from the visitor center. This leaves the bulk of the area, the ecologically sensitive portions, off-limits for nearly all visitors. Only biologists with scientific purposes are allowed into the heart of the reserve. This is a design—management solution to resource, social, and management carrying capacity without rationing visitor use.

LANDSCAPE RESEARCH-ANALYSIS

In the search for improved landscape planning, designers have increasingly sought new techniques. The state of the art is certainly in an experimental stage. The following discussions only touch upon some of the techniques that may have application to tourism. For individual site development problems, managers of tourism cannot view these as ready-made methods but rather as ways in which their designers may be thinking and approaching development.

In the United States, the Forest Service, U.S. Department of Agriculture, has been very active in the field of landscape research-and-analysis technology, especially for outdoor recreation. Certainly this has had an impact on many lands used as scenic and recreational attractions by tourists. Litton (1968) made a special study of the visual travel landscape and developed some classifications and techniques of inventory. Among the types, he identified the following: panoramic landscape, feature landscape, unclosed landscape, focal landscape, canopied landscape, detail landscape, and ephemeral landscape. Litton (1973) then made a refinement by developing a five-step procedure for analysis:

1 Establish landscape control points.
2 Plot visible landscapes.
3 Photograph panoramic view.
4 Prepare perspective.
5 Project impact of change.

This work utilizes a computer process, VIEWIT, developed by Elsner (1971), which produces an overlay of visible areas from a landscape control point.

A refined presentation of VIEWIT, suitable for direct application, was prepared by Travis *et al.* (1975) and describes the specific steps required to produce computerized visual images from landscape data. It provides basic landscape planning data for seen areas, slope, and aspect. Another computer design aid was developed by Myklestad and Wagar (1976) and allows visual presentation of proposed changes in the landscape. Even further refinement was developed by the Forest Service (Mosaic 1977) and is called "mosaic/photomontage."

But these techniques assume that data are available on viewer (tourist) preferences of landscape types. Experimentation in viewer perceptions of landscapes has been taking place and suggests the need for further research in market stratification. Studies of public response to landscape scenery have been performed by Carlson (1977) and Shafer *et al.* (1970, 1973).

Shafer and Brush (1977) developed a technique whereby photographs could be used in preference surveys. Each photograph was divided into three zones: immediate, intermediate, and distant. When results are obtained through statistical analysis, this model becomes a planning tool for making changes in the landscape.

Carls (1974), through sampling a population visiting outdoor recreation areas, found that there was a preference for a few people in the landscape rather than none but that great numbers reduced the preference. Water was consistently a landscape preference.

A guide to the use of environmental analysis approaches has been assembled by Marsh (1978). The importance of obtaining detailed information on slope, topography, soils, drainage, vegetation, floods, floodplains, and other land characteristics is described in this handbook for site designers.

A comprehensive view of the state of the art of analysis of the visual landscape is contained in the *Proceedings of Our National Landscape* conference (Elsner and Smardon 1979). Subjects covered are technology to solve landscape problems, computerized and quantitative problems, psychometric and social sciences approaches, and evaluation of visual assessment methods. Other subjects included application to special uses, such as for recreation and tourism. The techniques described have value but require implementation by specialists.

Review of the realm of landscape research-and-analysis shows that it is a combination of technique and art with some research processes applied to each landscape design and planning project. MacDougall and Brandes (1974) categorized the field in this way: natural sciences and planning, land resource inventory and analysis for planning, prototypical environmental planning studies, evaluation of scenic quality, and information systems. The effectiveness of the existing approaches depends greatly upon the collaboration between designers and decision-makers as well as upon the complexity of the development problem. The effectiveness of the several approaches by the many designers and planners is yet to be tested by research.

As was described at the outset of this chapter, increased public recognition of the limits of the physical environment is proving the need for controls. Increasingly, tourism is showing that "unique resources that are attractive for development are also highly perishable and vulnerable to irreparable damage" (Mertes and Skillern 1975, p. 59).

Recognizing that controls are necessary, opinions vary on the proper level for administering these controls. Concern over this was expressed succinctly by Ray (1973, p. 39), then governor of Iowa:

I believe the policy and the priorities related to land use should derive from the people in the most direct way possible .... I also believe that policy, implementation, and regulation should be based on the best facts possible.... As we begin the task of designing government to limit exploitation of nature, we must not accomplish our goal by means that will exploit our human resources.

Tourism and recreation may need a variety of land use controls in order to thrive. At the same time,

controls can have the effect of creating more problems. For example, Healy (1976, p. 183) states that "a virtually unrecognized area of potential intergroup conflict is the effect of land use controls on the distribution of recreation opportunities."

In the United States, both state and federal legislation on land use control, directly and indirectly, has become much more abundant in recent years.

STATE LEGISLATION

In spite of a free enterprise philosophy of land as a commodity, the United States has increasingly developed and implemented land use controls as necessary to the welfare of the nation. Tourism, as a major land developer, is affected by these controls. From the beginning, this was seen primarily as a city problem. With assistance from the federal government, most states enacted urban zoning enabling legislation in the 1940s and 1950s (Bosselman and Callies 1971). However, the states, because of different geographic characteristics and different felt needs, created different controls.

For example, Vermont enacted a comprehensive environmental control law in 1970 which has had an impact on recreational development of resources there (Bosselman and Callies 1971, p. 54). Through a permitting system, projects can be denied or accepted. It is based upon a land classification that identifies capability for agriculture, forestry, or mining, the existence of unique or fragile environmental conditions, and also places limits upon development.

In 1970, Maine passed a package of environmental legislation including a site location law requiring permits for certain land developments, such as housing subdivisions and many other uses. The prime objective is to protect fragile environments from development that could erode the quality of these resources.

Resort types of tourism have come under regulation in Wisconsin through the 1966 Water Resources Act, which required counties to enact controls. It authorizes the classification of lake shoreland into specific use zones.

Minnesota patterned its shoreland controls after Wisconsin. Land use management depends upon a classification by the Commissioner of Conservation: (1) "environment" lakes and streams, (2) "recreational development" lakes, (3) "general development" lakes and streams, and (4) "critical" lakes (Johnson and Fitzhugh 1976, p. 22).

Other states, such as Kansas, Michigan, Washington, and Montana, as well as special districts, such as Lake Tahoe and New York's Adirondack Park, have set up land use regulations for their waterfronts. These include guidelines and controls for tourist and resort development (Johnson and Fitzhugh 1976).

It is no coincidence that Hawaii, a major tourism

state, has the most stringent land use controls. Early, even before statehood, the citizenry of Hawaii realized the finite character of their land resources. Concern over esthetics came late but protection of agricultural land was of prime concern in 1961 when the land use law was enacted (Bosselman and Callies 1972, p. 7). This resulted in tight controls over forest and water reserve zones as well as agricultural, urban, and rural districts. Application of these land use controls has not been without conflict between the goals of preservation and development.

Two forces have had a major influence on tourism land use in Hawaii. The Oahu Development Conference, a private citizen planning organization for the island of Oahu, has had major input, mediating many conflicts between development and preservation. It was their recommendation that Waikiki Beach utilize a concept of "building envelopes" which would allow open spaces between highrise hotels for access and views toward the beach (Oahu Development Conference 1968–1969). While this has not been carried out literally, the Conference has had an impact upon land use decisions affecting tourism development. A second force is the Outdoor Circle, originally formed in 1913 as a conservation and natural beauty organization. It not only accomplished its goal in 1927 of ridding the islands of billboards (Campbell 1962) but has ever since kept a vigilant eye on all environmental land use legislation and implementation throughout Hawaii.

In Hawaii, this has resulted in a *State Tourism Plan* (1980), which includes not only land use but also related social and economic impacts. This enlightened approach is much broader than past zoning approaches to land use. The plan has three major goals:

1 A strong, viable economy, characterized by stability, diversity, and growth, that enables the fulfillment of the needs and expectations of Hawaii's present and future generations.
2 A desired physical environment, characterized by beauty, cleanliness, quiet, stable natural systems, and uniqueness, that enhances the physical and mental well-being of people.
3 Physical, social, and economic well-being for individuals and families in Hawaii that nourishes a sense of community responsibility, of caring, and of participation in community life (*State Tourism Plan* 1980, p. 2).

Among the land use issues addressed by this plan are concerns over improving the quality of existing destination areas, ensuring careful planning of development that is sensitive to local conditions, and better utilization of the state's physical resources. To avoid conflicts and redundancies, the several county plans and development plans are integrated into the overall state plan.

Meyers' (1976, pp. 104–105) assessment of the Hawaiian experience with land use controls includes several inferences for tourism. First, controls take time, time for development, testing and application. Second, legal forms of land use regulation have not necessarily produced the best decision making but have stimulated interest, discussion, and debate over the problems associated with land use. Third, "'Conservation' or 'preservation' cannot be a status-quo policy. Where such policies are appropriate, a management program must be developed." Finally, research is badly needed to provide sound information on the impact of development on resources and also on the effectiveness of controls.

It is important for all tourism developers and managers to be aware of how existing state controls may affect them as well as to be active in all control issues that may impinge upon tourism.

KEY NATIONAL LEGISLATION

Following is a brief discussion of federal legislation in the United States related to tourism land use. Certainly, managers should make much further investigation of these and other controls and also support research that proves or denies their effectiveness.

The National Environmental Policy Act (NEPA) of 1970 has many implications for tourism because it is a foundation declaration of national concern over how the resources of the country are to be used as well as protected. Basic provisions of the Act are

1 Fulfill the responsibilities of each generation as trustee of the environment for succeeding generations.
2 Assure for all Americans safe, healthful, productive, and esthetically and culturally pleasing surroundings.
3 Attain the widest range of beneficial uses of the environment without degradation, risk to health or safety, or other undesirable and unintended consequences.
4 Preserve important historic, cultural, and natural aspects of our national heritage, and maintain, wherever possible, an environment which supports diversity and variety of individual choice.
5 Achieve a balance between population and resource use which will permit high standards of living and a wide sharing of life's amenities.
6 Enhance the quality of renewable resources and approach the maximum attainable recycling of depletable resources (42 U.S.C.).

For assistance in policy formulation, the Council on Environmental Quality was formed. To assure that the objectives are carried out within all federal land use agencies, Environmental Impact Statements are required before any development takes place. Because tourism depends so heavily upon natural resource management, NEPA is having direct bearing on its development. Highways, stream channelization, waterfront development, parks, recreation areas, forest recreation, and many other tourism resource uses have felt the influence of NEPA (Moss 1977).

The Clean Air Act of 1970 requires the Administrator of the U.S. Environmental Protection Agency (EPA) to establish national ambient air quality standards. While its control of direct sources, such as manufacturing plants, is important to tourism, perhaps more significant is its control of indirect sources, such as from automobiles and airplanes. Much of this responsibility has been passed on to the states. The Clean Air Act has been a controversial issue because it tends to cut back on many activities that are important to commerce, including tourism. Part of the issue centers on preventing significant degradation of quality in areas where the quality is already very high.

The federal Water Pollution Control Act Amendments of 1972 created tighter controls on water pollution, no longer accepting lower levels of contamination because of the economic or social value of the activity causing the pollution. Several land use provisions, to be carried out by the states, are of significance to many tourism developments such as resort and vacation home complexes. Although difficulties have been encountered with administration, the impact upon all tourism water uses certainly should be beneficial. The Army Corps of Engineers was given the responsibility of issuing permits for filling and dredging, which is important to coastal waterfront development.

The Coastal Zone Management Act (CZMA) of 1972 is designed to stimulate and provide financial assistance to states for creation of plans for better management and control of coastal resources. In all, thirty states and four territories are eligible for grants under the Act. Included are the Great Lakes waters and states. The states are required to make provision for the preservation or restoration of specific areas for their conservation, recreational, ecological, or esthetic values. Of all the environmental acts in the United States in recent years, perhaps the CZMA is having the greatest impact upon tourism.

Another act that has implications for extensive types of tourism in the United States is the Wild and Scenic Rivers Act of 1968, which has since been amended to expand the program. This Act requires

that certain selected rivers of the Nation which, with their immediate environments, possess outstandingly remarkable scenic, recreational, geologic, fish and wildlife, historic, cultural, or other similar values shall be preserved in free-flowing condition, and that they and their immediate environments shall be protected for

the benefit and enjoyment of present and future generations (16 U.S.C. 1271).

This Act first included eight rivers and adjacent lands and was then in 1976 expanded to eight more. Proposals are being made for additions. Administration is being carried out by the Departments of Interior and Agriculture.

Other important federal pieces of legislation in recent years have been the national Flood Insurance Program, the Interstate Land Sales Full Disclosure Act, Endangered Species Act, Wildlife Coordination Act, and the Solid Waste Disposal Act.

Federal effects on land use have been classified by McDowell (1978, p. 28) into four broad categories:

1 The ownership and management of land by the federal government.
2 The location of federal employment and contractors.
3 The wide-ranging system of federal aid programs and their planning requirements.
4 Unplanned federal activities, including financial credit programs, taxes, and regulations.

Even this cursory analysis of land use legislation shows the need for research study in several areas relating to tourism: study of new legislative needs, research of existing overlap and conflict, and extent of excessive control of tourism development.

CONCLUSIONS

With greater taste discrimination of travelers and greater recognition of the role and limits of resources, environmental design and land use have increased greatly in managerial concern. What was viewed as a simple and private function of a market economy is now known to be much more complex. It involves characteristics of places, markets, transportation, owners, local citizens, and many other aspects of community and national life.

Research does not adequately prove what must be one of the most profound truths of tourism—placeness, and all the characteristics inherent in the location and development of tourism places. In many ways, tourism, the environment, and places are synonymous. All are important to tourists, to governments, to businesses, and to those concerned with perpetuating quality resource assets. The development and the promotion of the individuality of places may be tourism's greatest opportunity.

The creation of better environments has as one prime objective the protection of natural beauty and the assurance of more esthetically developed environments. While standards of beauty and taste are neither precise nor uniform, higher levels of tourism product development are possible through greater ordering by managers and better design by professionals.

The responsibility lies with all decision-makers, public and private. While legislation may be required for establishing a floor or performance, especially for health and safety, business and governmental developers can assume higher standards for their own self-interest. Resource assets are so intimately intertwined with tourism that anything erosive to them is detrimental to tourism. Conversely, support of environmental causes, by and large, is support of tourism.

Policies and practices for environmental design land use planning for tourism cannot be isolated from those for communities. Tourism is not a separate economy nor a separate part of society. Therefore, all that citizens aspire to for themselves—their quality of environment and quality of life—are the very foundations for a quality tourism.

Getting a better job done toward better environments has different processes at different scales, from broad to specific. At the regional level, research of basic tourism factors can reveal areas with greatest destination potential. Such areas then can be given more detailed examination at the site scale—to protect fragile resource assets as well as to develop greater volume and diversity of tourism. Better research and techniques are becoming more available for accomplishing these tasks. While most environmental protection and enhancement of beauty must come voluntarily from all decision-makers, not only for tourism but for all activity, broad-scale intervention has a role. Large-scale research, beyond the capability of the many fragmented elements of tourism, may have to be performed at the national level, either by government or by national tourism organizations.

But most control of environmental development at the site scale is best handled at the local level. It is becoming more and more evident that the creative, innovative, and entrepreneurial roles of business are best able to respond to the needs of tourists, but only within a framework of reasonable, long-range, and publicly accepted controls. This is in the best interest of tourists, of business, and of those controlling long-range environmental assets.

BIBLIOGRAPHY

Abrams, Charles, *et al.* (1953), *Urban Land Problems and Policies*, Housing and Town and Country Planning Bulletin 7, New York: United Nations.

Act 133, Relating to the Interim Tourism Policy Act (1976), Honolulu: Legislature of the State of Hawaii.

Andersen, K., *et al.* (1981), "Night the Sky Bridges Fell," *Time*, (118) July 27, pp. 26+.

Balmer, Crapo & Associates (1977), *A Review of Existing Tourism Zones and Suggested Primary Tourism Destination Zones*, Ottawa: Canadian Government Office of Tourism.

Belisle, Francois J., and Don R. Hoy (1980), "The Perceived Impact of Tourism by Residents," *Annals of Tourism Research*, 8 (1), p. 83.

Blank, Uel, and Clare A. Gunn (1965), *Guidelines for Tourism—Recreation in Michigan's Upper Peninsula*, Cooperative Extension Service, East Lansing, Michigan: Michigan State University.

Bosselman, Fred, and David Callies (1972), *The Quiet Revolution in Land Use Control*, prepared for the Council on Environmental Quality, Washington, D.C.: U.S. Government Printing Office.

Bouchard, Andre (1973), "Carrying Capacity as a Management Tool for National Parks," *Park News*, (9) 3, pp. 39–52.

Buck, Roy C., and Ted Alleman (1981), "Productive Coexistence," *Livability Digest*, (1) 1, pp. 44–45.

Buzzell, Robert D. (1966), *Competitive Behavior and Product Life Cycles*, Proceedings of the 1966 World Congress, Chicago: American Marketing Association.

Campbell, A.N. (1962), "How Hawaii Erased a Blot," from the archives of the Outdoor Circle, Honolulu: The Outdoor Circle.

Carls, E. Glenn (1974), "The Effects of People and Man-Induced Conditions on Preferences for Outdoor Landscapes," *Journal of Leisure Research*, 6 (Spring), pp. 113–124.

Carlson, A.A. (1977), "On the Possibility of Quantifying Scenic Beauty," *Landscape Planning*, 4, pp. 131–172.

Cartee, Charles P., *et al.* (1975), *A Case Study of Estuarine Pollution and Local Agency Interactions*, Water Resources Institute, Mississippi State University, Hattiesburg, Mississippi: University of Southern Mississippi.

Chapin, F. Stuart, Jr. (1976), *Urban Land Use Planning*, (2nd ed.), Urbana, Illinois: University of Illinois Press.

Clawson, Marion (1968), "The Development of Recreation in the United States and Canada and Its Implications in the National Parks," *The Canadian National Parks: Today and Tomorrow*, J.E. Nelson and R.C. Scace, Eds., Calgary, Alberta: The University of Calgary.

Darling, F. Fraser and Noel D. Eichhorn (1969), *Man and Nature in the National Parks* (2nd ed.), Washington, D.C.: The Conservation Foundation.

Dasman, Raymond F., John P. Milton, and Peter H. Freeman (1973), *Ecological Principles for Economic Development*, New York: John Wiley & Sons.

Ditton, Robert B., John L. Seymour, and Gerald C. Swanson (1977), *Coastal Resources Management*, Lexington, Massachusetts: D.C. Heath.

"Domestic Tourism: An Ambivalent Federal Policy" (1973), *Destination USA*, (4), pp. 7–18.

Driscoll, R.S., D.R. Betters, and H.O. Parker (1978), "Land Classification through Remote Sensing—Techniques and Tools," *Journal of Forestry*, 76 (October), p. 656.

Drucker, Peter F. (1975), "The Delusion of Profits," *Wall Street Journal*, February 5, p. 10, col. 4.

Edmunds, Francis (1980), "Controlling Tourism Impact," *Eleventh Annual Conference Proceedings*, Travel Research Association, Salt Lake City: University of Utah, p. 47.

Edwards, R.Y. and C. David Fowle (1955), "The Concept of Carrying Capacity," *Trans-North American Wildlife and Natural Resources Conference*, (20), pp. 589–598.

Elsner, Gary H. (1971), *Computing Visible Areas from Proposed Recreation Developments*, Note PSW-246, U.S. Department of Agriculture, Berkeley, California: Forest Service.

Elsner, Gary H., and Richard C. Smardon (coordinators) (1979), Proceedings, *Our National Landscape*, A Conference on Applied Techniques for Analysis and Management of the Visual Resource, Report PWS-35, U.S. Department of Agriculture, Berkeley, California: Forest Service.

Environmental Quality (1976), The Seventh Annual Report of the Council on Environmental Quality, Washington, D.C.: U.S. Government Printing Office.

Ferrario, Franco F. (1981), *An Evaluation of the Tourist Potential of KwaZulu and Natal*, Durban, Natal: KwaZulu Development Corporation.

Forster, Richard R. (1973), *Planning for Man and Nature in National Parks*, Morges, Switzerland: International Union for Conservation of Nature and Natural Resources.

Frayer, W.E., L.S. Davis, and Paul G. Risser (1978), "Uses of Land Classification," *Journal of Forestry*, 76 (October), p. 647.

Garland, Joseph E. (1981), "A New Englander Looks at Tourism," paper presented at "Tourism and New England Seaports," June 1980, *Livability Digest*, (1) 1 (Fall), pp. 18–19.

"Gettysburg's Battle for Dignity" (1981), Carole Rifkind, Ed., "Tourism and Communities: Process, Problems, and Solutions," *Livability Digest*, (1) 1 (Fall), p. 20.

Godschalk, David R., and Francis H. Parker (1975), "Carrying Capacity: A Key to Environmental Planning," *Journal of Soil and Water Conservation*, (30), pp. 160–175.

Gunn, Clare A. (1965), *A Concept for the Design of a Tourism–Recreation Region*, Mason, Michigan: B.J. Press.

Gunn, Clare A. (1972a), "Concentrated Dispersal and Dispersed Concentration—A Pattern for Saving Scarce Coastlines," *Landscape Architecture*, (62) 2, pp. 133–134.

Gunn, Clare A. (1972b), *Vacationscape: Designing Tourist Regions*, Bureau of Business Research, Austin, Texas: University of Texas.

Gunn, Clare A. (contributor) (1973), "Tourism and the Environment," 5, Special Studies, *Destination U.S.A.*, Report of the National Tourism Resources Review Commission, Washington, D.C.: U.S. Government Printing Office.

Gunn, Clare A. (1979a), *Tourism Development: Assessment of Potential in Texas*, Bulletin MP-1416, Texas Agricultural Experiment Station and Recreation and Parks Department, College Station, Texas: Texas A&M University.

Gunn, Clare A. (1979b), *Tourism Planning*, New York: Crane–Russak.

Gunn, Clare A. (1982), *Tourism Development Potential in Canada*, Ottawa: Canadian Government Office of Tourism.

Healy, Robert G. (1976), *Land Use and the States*, for Resources for the Future, Inc., Baltimore: Johns Hopkins University Press.

Hills, G.A. (1961), *The Ecological Basis for Land-Use Planning*, Research Report No. 46, Toronto: Ontario Department of Lands and Forests.

Hirsch, Allan, *et al.* (1978), "Land Classification—Where Do We Go from Here?" *Journal of Forestry*, 76 (October), p. 672.

Jensen, Clayne R., and Clark T. Thorstenson (1972), *Issues in Outdoor Recreation*, Minneapolis: Burgess Publishing.

Johnson, Corwin W., and Thomas C. Fitzhugh III (1976), *Legal Aspects of Land Use Regulation of Lake Shorelands by State and Local Governments for the Protection of Lakes*, Office of Water Research and Technology, U.S. Department of the Interior, Technical Report CRWR-142, Austin, Texas: College of Engineering, University of Texas.

Kemper, Robert V. (1979), "Tourism in Taos and Patzcuaro," *Annals of Tourism Research*, 6 (January/March), p. 91.

Ketchum, Bostwick H. (Ed.) (1972), *The Water's Edge*, Cambridge, Massachusetts: MIT Press.

Kunde, James E. (1982), "What the Polls Tell Us Citizens Want from Urban Policy: Livable Space" (reprinted), *Livability Digest*, (2) 1 (Spring), pp. 8–10.

Lewis, Philip (1964), "Quality Corridors for Wisconsin," *Landscape Architecture*, (54) 2, pp. 100–107.

Lewis, Philip H., Jr. (1969), "Ecology: The Inland Water Tree," *Journal of American Institute of Architects*, 51, pp. 59–63.

Litton, R. Burton, Jr. (1968), *Forest Landscape Description and Inventories—A Basis for Land Planning and Design*, Paper PSW-49, U.S. Department of Agriculture, Berkeley, California: Forest Service.

Litton, R. Burton, Jr. (1973), *Landscape Control Points: A Procedure for Predicting and Monitoring Visual Impacts*, Paper PSW-91, U.S. Department of Agriculture, Berkeley, California: Forest Service.

Lucate, D.S., and M.J. Romaine (1978), "Canada's Land Capability Inventory Program," *Journal of Forestry*, 76 (October), p. 669.

Lynch, Kevin (1960), *The Image of the City*, Cambridge, Massachusetts: Harvard University and Technology Presses.

MacDougall, E. Bruce, and Charles E. Brandes (1974), *A Selected Annotated Bibliography on Land Resource Inventory and Analysis for Planning*, Harrisburg, Pennsylvania: Department of Environmental Resources.

McDowell, Bruce D. (1978), "National Land Policies and Programs Affecting Transportation," *Proceedings, Transportation and Land Development* conference, Special Report 183, Washington, D.C.: National Academy of Sciences.

McHarg, Ian L. (1969), *Design with Nature*, Garden City, New York: Doubleday & Co.

Marsh, William M. (1978), *Environmental Analysis*, New York: McGraw—Hill.

Mertes, James D., and Frank F. Skillern (1975), "Planning and Legal Considerations Affecting Land Development," *Man, Leisure, and Wild Lands: A Complex Interaction*, Proceedings of First Eisenhower Consortium Research Symposium, Springfield, Virginia: National Technical Information Service.

Meyers, Phillis (1976), *Zoning Hawaii*, Washington, D.C.: The Conservation Foundation.

Mosaic: A System for Displaying a Proposed Modification before Its Impact on the Environment (1977), U.S. Department of Agriculture, Ogden, Utah: Forest Service.

Moss, Elaine (Ed.) (1977), *Land Use Controls in the United States*, New York: Dial Press, James Wade.

Myklestad, Erik, and J. Alan Wagar (1976), *Preview: Computer Assistance for Visual Management of Forested Landscapes*, Paper NE-355, U.S. Department of Agriculture, Upper Darby, Pennsylvania: Forest Service.

Nelson, J.G. (1974), "The Impact of Technology on Banff National Park," *Impact of Technology on Environment: Some Global Examples*, Studies in Land Use History and Landscape Change, No. 6, London, Ontario: University of Western Ontario, p. 201.

Oahu Development Conference: 1968—1969, Annual Report, Honolulu: The Conference.

Odum, William E. (1971), *Pathways of Energy Flow in a South Florida Estuary*, Sea Grant Technical Bulletin No. 7, Miami: University of Miami.

Outdoor Recreation for America (1962), A Report to the President and to the Congress by the Outdoor Recreation Resources Review Commission, Washington, D.C.: U.S. Government Printing Office.

Platt, John (1975), "The Future of Social Crisis," *The Futurist*, (October), p. 267.

Prikryl, Frantisek (1968), *Regions de Tourisme en Tchecoslovaquie*, Centre d'Etudes du Tourisme, Aix-en-Provence, France: Université d'Aix-Marseille.

Ray, Robert D. (1973), "On Personal Freedoms," *National Land Use Policy*, (proceedings of conference, November 27—29, 1972, Des Moines, Iowa), Ankeny, Iowa: Soil Conservation Society of America.

ReVelle, Penelope, and Charles ReVelle (1981), *The Environment: Issues and Choices for Society*, New York: D. Van Nostrand.

Robas, Ann K. (1970), *South Florida's Mangrove-Bordered Estuaries: Their Role in Sport and Commercial Fish Production*, Sea Grant Technical Bulletin No. 4, Miami: University of Miami.

Ross, Dianne Reid, and Bryan H. Farrell (Eds.) (1975), *Source Materials for Pacific Tourism*, Center for South Pacific Studies, Santa Cruz, California: University of California.

Shafer, Elwood L., Jr., and Robert D. Brush (1977), "How to Measure Preferences for Photographs of Natural Landscapes," *Landscape Planning*, 4, pp. 237—256.

Shafer, E.L., Jr., and J. Meitz (1970), *It Seems Possible to Quantify Scenic Beauty in Photographs*, Paper NE-162, U.S. Department of Agriculture, Upper Darby, Pennsylvania: Forest Service.

Shafer, E.L., Jr., and M. Tooby (1973), "Landscape Preferences: An International Replication," *Journal of Leisure Research*, 5 (3), pp. 60—65.

Standard Industrial Classification Manual (1957), Bureau of the Budget, Washington, D.C.: U.S. Government Printing Office.

Standard Land Use Coding Manual (1965), Urban Renewal Administration and Bureau of Public Roads, Washington, D.C.: U.S. Government Printing Office.

Stankey, George H., and David Lime (1973), *Recreational Carrying Capacity*, An Annotated Bibliography, General Technical Report INT-3, Ogden, Utah: USDA Forest Service.

State Tourism Plan (1980), Honolulu: Department of Planning and Economic Development.

Steinitz, Carl (1970), "What Goes Where? Landscape Resource Analysis," *Landscape Architecture*, (January), p. 101.

Stynes, Daniel J. (1977), "Recreational Carrying Capacity and the Management of Dynamic Systems," National Recreation and Parks Association Congress, Las Vegas.

Stynes, Daniel J. (1979), "A Simulation Approach to the Determination of Recreation Carrying Capacity," Proceedings, National Workshop on Computers in Recreation and Parks, National Recreation and Parks Association, St. Louis.

Tourism Development in Ontario: A Framework for Opportunity (1977), Balmer, Crapo & Associates, Inc., Toronto: Ministry of Industry and Tourism.

Travis, A.S. (1974), *A Strategic Appraisal of Scottish Tourism*, An Assessment of Resource Potential, Edinburgh: The Scottish Tourist Board.

Travis, Michael R., Gary H. Elsner, Wayne D. Iverson, and Christine G. Johnson (1975), *VIEWIT: Computation of Seen Areas, Slope and Aspect for Land-Use Planning*, Paper PSW-11, U.S. Department of Agriculture, Berkeley, California: Forest Service.

16 United States Code.

42 United States Code, Article 4331(b).

Van Doren, Carlton S. (1982), *Statistical Abstract on Outdoor Recreation*, Washington, D.C.: Forest Service.

Wagar, J. Alan (1974), "Recreational Carrying Capacity Reconsidered," *Journal of Forestry*, (72) 3, pp. 274—278.

Witmer, Richard E. (1978), "U.S. Geological Survey Land-Use and Land-Cover Classification System," *Journal of Forestry*, 76 (October), p. 661.

Wolbrink, Donald (1960), *Tourism Development Potential for Hawaii*, Honolulu: Department of Planning and Economic Development.

Wolbrink, Donald, and Arthur D. Little (1970), *Comprehensive Outdoor Recreation Plan*, State of Hawaii, Honolulu: Department of Planning and Economic Development.

Young, George (1973), *Tourism: Blessing or Blight?*, Middlesex, England: Penguin.

PART FIVE

AN INDUSTRY SECTOR PERSPECTIVE

The contents of Part Five of the Handbook are structured from a perspective with which the majority of tourism managers will be most familiar, namely, by industry sector. In contrast to Part Four, which reflects an academic orientation to the study of tourism, the chapters in the present section categorize research in a way that reflects the way in which the tourism industry is generally perceived by the bulk of the population. It also reflects the task-oriented concerns of individual managers who not infrequently view themselves as belonging to the hotel industry, the airline industry, the restaurant industry, and so on, rather than as part of the "tourism industry."

We have been particularly fortunate in this section to obtain the written views of several individuals who are actively involved in different sectors of the tourism business. As witness to this claim, Chapter 20 has been authored by David Wohlmuth, who has written and worked extensively in the field of travel retailing and wholesaling. Readers of this chapter, entitled "Research Needs of Travel Retailers and Wholesalers," very quickly become aware of both the author's knowledge of the field and his ability to present this knowledge in a stimulating manner. Mr. Wohlmuth begins his presentation by reminding us of the rapid changes that are occurring in all facets of our lives and particularly in areas related to travel. This opening set of comments leads into a discussion of the nature of research in the real world. Flowing out of this discussion is Mr. Wohlmuth's very broad definition of research as "any activity that provides useful information." Having taken this perspective, the author then provides a number of very insightful and practical guidelines for determining what kind of research is most appropriate in a given situation and for carrying out that type of research. This general discussion of practical research is then directly related to the information needs of the travel agent and tour operator. The manner in which this is done is both entertaining and informative.

Chapter 21 addresses the operation and research needs of the convention and meetings sector of the travel, tourism, and hospitality industry. As the title implies, this chapter, which is authored by James Abbey (University of Nevada—Las Vegas), describes the size and scope of the convention market and describes how it operates. Discussion in this area includes a review of the economic importance of conventions to a region and the manner in which associations and meeting planners choose the site for their activities. Subsequently, the author provides insight into the issues faced by suppliers of convention and meeting facilities. Following this description on the functioning of this sector, Dr. Abbey reviews the nature and extent of present research efforts in the convention industry including studies conducted by industry associations, those reported in trade publications, and those carried out in an academic setting. The chapter concludes with an overview of future trends and research needs in the convention and meetings sector.

Chapter 22 again presents the perspective of an experienced manager. Authored by Carolyn Carey (Knott's Berry Farm), this chapter reviews the research needs of operators in the events and attractions sector of the tourism industry. Ms. Carey's presentation makes several basic yet important distinctions. First, she distinguishes between the needs for ongoing research related to the monitoring of current performance of the event/attraction and the need for special research projects to deal with specific management concerns that may arise from time to time. The discussion also makes an important distinction between the manager's need to have information on present customers versus the need to acquire knowledge and understanding of individuals who currently do not patronize a particular event or attraction. Following this discussion at the microlevel of the individual operator, Ms. Carey then turns to a review of the research needs of the events and attractions sector taken as an industry. Here, after pointing out some of the difficulties involved in undertaking industry-wide research, the author reviews and categorizes the kinds of information that can be reasonably anticipated from a group of cooperating events and attractions. Ms. Carey draws upon her experience with the Southern California attractions committee to provide an example of how one region addressed its needs for research information in this important industry sector.

The research needs of the restaurant industry are addressed in Chapter 23. This chapter, authored by Robert Olson (University of Wisconsin—Stout) and Uel Blank (University of Minnesota) is again structured so as to provide guidelines for researching the operation of both the individual restaurant business and the restaurant industry taken collectively. Following an initial overview of the food service industry and its components, the authors identify the kinds of research which are appropriate to the individual restaurant operator. In doing so, the emphasis is upon information and analysis which provide the operator with measures of performance effectiveness or an indication of the profitability of a given market opportunity. As indicated above, the second part of this chapter provides a macro view of the overall research needs of the restaurant industry within a particular community, region, or country. The discussion here recognizes that different restaurant industry interests may vary widely and, therefore, the kind of information to be gathered can be extremely diverse. Having recognized this situation, the authors go on to provide guidelines concerning what information is appropriate to collect and how the required data can be gathered. Throughout, the emphasis is upon the assembling of information which is useful and which can be readily disseminated to interested restauranteurs. In this regard, a major ongoing consumer study sponsored by the National Restaurant Association is described.

The next two chapters in Part Five both deal with transportation-related research but from very different perspectives. Chapter 24, by Lawrence Cunningham (University of Colorado) and Lyonnel Barclay (American International University), discusses research related to personal transportation modes, while Stuart Robinson in Chapter 25 examines research needs in two important common carrier modes, namely, intercity bus and rail transportation. The personal transportation chapter by Professors Cunningham and Barclay first identifies priorities for research in the personal motor vehicle tourism area. It then discusses those major institutional issues which inhibit research in this area. The chapter then reviews statistics describing the personal motor vehicle tourist with a particular distinction being made between the tourist per se as compared with other travelers. This review is followed by a discussion of the various market segments which have been identified among personal motor vehicle tourists using a variety of segmentation criteria. Finally, the chapter examines a number of institutional issues which the authors believe have inhibited research related to personal transportation modes. In particular, the lack of overall research policies and direction at the international, federal, state, and local levels is cited as a major cause of present research inadequacy.

The Robinson chapter on research needs in the intercity bus and rail transportation industry takes a very different orientation from the previous chapter. It explains the responsibilities of selected managers within a corporation and specifies what information they need as well as how this information might be gathered. The chapter starts by reviewing regulatory policy in the intercity bus industry and its impact upon the functioning of that industry. Having clarified the rules of the game, Dr. Robinson identifies the responsibilities of marketing research in relation to the tasks facing senior management. As a means of presenting his case, Dr. Robinson describes how a market researcher can provide information which will help vice presidents in the areas of marketing, advertising, control, traffic operations, and passenger service.

The final chapter in this section is somewhat different from those previously discussed. Authored by Tyrrell Marris (English Tourist Board) and entitled "Research Needs of Small Tourism Enterprises," Chapter 26, does deal with "an industry sector" but one which cuts across the traditional functional definitions employed by the previous chapters. This chapter has been included because the small tourism enterprise represents an important component of the tourism industry and because it does have very specialized information needs, particularly in light of the resources available to assemble that information. The contents of the chapter start from the premise that owners of small enterprises often do not realize that they are part of a wider tourism industry. They are often also unaware of their need for information and for research. Accordingly, Mr. Marris attempts to identify the various types of rather straightforward information that the small enterprise should have available to it. Subsequently, he provides guidance on how the small tourism operator can get started doing research by identifying readily available internal and external sources of information. Throughout, the emphasis is on describing approaches that can be pursued personally by the owner of a small operation. This orientation has two main advantages. First, it limits the resources required to gather information, and perhaps more important, it ensures understanding and involvement on the part of the small tourism enterprise and its managers. The emphasis on simplicity and the provision of a typical questionnaire that might be used by a small enterprise make this chapter both unique and valuable.

20

Research Needs of Travel Retailers and Wholesalers

E.D. WOHLMUTH
Philadelphia, Pennsylvania

*T*he travel retailer and wholesaler have research needs that closely parallel the broader needs of all business entities, yet maintain unique characteristics unto themselves. The barrier to research implementation is not money or staff resources, but a complete understanding of what research is and how it can be applied in the real world of the travel distribution system. This chapter is recommended reading not only for travel agents and tour operators, but for anyone who would benefit from a practical knowledge of this phase of the industry.

As the travel distribution system enters the final third of the decade of the 1980s, the winds of change blow everywhere. The marketplace—and the technology available to serve it—are both being transformed by major forces.

To a degree unknown since World War II, political events have reshaped the list of potential destinations for both the business and vacation traveller. The Persian Gulf, Southeast Asia, and large chunks of the Middle East and Central America are now off-limits to all but the most necessary of itineraries; while China— the most forbidden of all destinations for over three decades—has now opened the doors of the world's most populous country to virtually all comers.

No less significant are the changes caused by economic forces. While the world's interlocked monetary system grows ever more complex, bringing with it the inevitable short-term changes in destination popularity caused by everchanging currency values, it is the long-term transitions that require the greatest study. A major realignment is taking place in the world economy. In America, we're rapidly moving from an industrial to a service-based economy—something that should be of as much concern to the Los Angeles travel agent as it is to the Pittsburgh steelworker.

Momentous as they are, however, these political and economic changes are only part of the total picture. A revolution in technology is also taking place. Just as the business world of the 1960s and 1970s was transformed by the arrival of the mainframe computer, the personal computer is drastically reshaping the marketplace of the 1980s. The technology now exists— and is being used—to transmit reservations data from suppliers directly to the desks of individual travel agents, and from travel agents directly to the desks of individual clients.

It is but one facet of a much larger, worldwide revolution: a revolution in communications. In America, the 800 toll-free phone line—the leading edge in telecommunications just a few short years ago—is rapidly becoming old hat. Today we have dedicated satellite channels, electronic bulletin boards, home-accessible data banks/bases, videotex, teletext, local networks, and self-dialing modems that permit even the smallest computers to talk to each other across continents—or oceans—without human intervention. Where it once took days, information is now being retrieved and exchanged in seconds. Where it once took weeks, transactions are now being initiated—and completed—in minutes.

What does all this mean for the travel agent and wholesaler? On the industry's side of the equation, it means the maximization of unit efficiency—and therefore profit—for anyone who understands and embraces the revolution. On the consumer's side of the equation, it may mean far different behavior and expectations. The lessons of automated teller machines and self-service gas pumps should not go unheeded: consumers do change behavior patterns with the arrival of new technology or the promise of monetary benefit.

When both items are present, as now is the case in the U.S. with discount brokerage houses operating on home computer networks, consumer behavior can change drastically, and overnight. The modern consumer is a very adaptable animal, shedding old buying habits and adopting new ones with great regularity. The travel product is no more immune to this phenomenon than anything else: a combination of the new communications technologies and discounted, no frills pricing could produce drastic changes in travel buying habits.

It would be a mistake, however, to assume that all patterns of travel purchase might change, or that all industry units would have to change with them. Travel is probably the most complex of all consumer items. It requires the expenditure of both money and time, and, in the case of vacation travel, an emotional investment as well. Face-to-face counseling will continue to be demanded by many clients and on many product lines. But which clients, and which product lines?

Some of the answers appear self-evident, but others are going to require insight into the relationship between the travel consumer and the travel product—and a high degree of advance planning by anyone wishing to remain viable in tomorrow's marketplace. It is the old marketing concept of "positioning," in this case to either attract more of the clients who will remain immune to the new technology or service the changing clients *with* the new technology. Either way, market research is the only sound basis on which such positioning and planning decisions can be made, just as it is the only sound basis in a stable marketplace.

It may be romantic and individualistic, but seat-of-the-pants decision making is as outmoded a vehicle in today's market as the horse-drawn milk wagon. Solid research is required. But what kind of research is either affordable or meaningful in the real world of the travel agency or tour operation? Perhaps it's time to rethink the entire research concept as it applies to the small business operator.

THE REAL WORLD OF RESEARCH

A few years back, first in a front page story in *The Wall Street Journal*, and later in the bestseller *Megatrends*[1] millions of readers learned of a unique service being offered to corporate America by researcher John Naisbitt and his colleagues. Using a World War II-developed technique called "content analysis," long-range trends in American life are identified via a method of deceptive simplicity: staffers search the pages of hundreds of local newspapers, measuring the amount of space editors devote to any particular topic. Trends are deduced when one topic starts inheriting space formerly devoted to another topic, with composite results being provided to subscribers on a regular basis.

The existence of this service tells us a number of important things, not least of which being what it says about the word "research." All too often, we tend to think of research in terms of fancy, statistical models—or extrapolations based on vast amounts of collected data—when the practical reality is frequently far different. A trend spotted in the back pages of local newspapers is no less important than a trend theorized through interpretation of thousands of special questionnaires. Research is any activity that provides useful information; from a series of short phone calls to thousands of hours poring over complex technical documents. It all depends on your needs, your resources, and how quickly the information must be obtained.

But, whatever it is, the research activity must be systematic. That's the second point raised by the content analysis method. Meaningful trends cannot be spotted by reading local newspapers just now and then. To be valid, the chosen activity must be regular and consistent. That may sound like a time-consuming proposition (especially in an industry where time is usually in short supply), but it really isn't. Regular activities lend themselves to great efficiency, just because they are regular. You simply learn to spot what's important, and eliminate anything that isn't.

Some people waste valuable time by reading every page of every industry trade journal. Not only is there the inevitable duplication of stories, but many items are of marginal or questionable value, and are soon forgotten, anyway. On the other hand, if you're clipping out those small but important articles—wherever they've been found—and passing them around to key staff members, you're performing a valuable research activity. As long as you do it consistently and not just now and then.

Point number three is that research does not require original material. We tend to think it does because projects based on original data (such as the Harris studies for *Travel Weekly*) are very highly publicized, and with good reason: they're expensive, and the sponsors want to get maximum mileage out of their investment. The projects you don't hear about are quietly conducted in-house by savvy agents and operators using data that already exist as a by-product of normal operations.

[1]*Megatrends: Ten New Directions Transforming Our Lives*, by John Naisbitt, Warner Books, 1982.

That's an important point: everything you need for a meaningful research program may be just a few feet away. The material may require some organizing, or collection in a slightly altered format, but it's there in your sales or accounting data. Are certain destinations waning in popularity? Are average vacation trips growing shorter? The keys to the future may lie hidden in your own sales figures, for the past two or three years, or the past two or three months.

Which brings us to point number four. The future almost always has its roots in what's happening now. Emerging trends are spotted by watching current— and sometimes quite ordinary—activity. That's what those research service staffers are looking for: the key to the future as reflected in the reporting of current events. The meaningful current events of the travel industry are *not* hotel openings and tour/cruise announcements. What *is* meaningful is what clients want at the inquiry stage, and how they react to what they get at the delivery stage, regardless of whether the trip is for business or pleasure. The information is yours for the asking, but you do have to ask.

Finally, and inescapably, productive research does not demand large expenditures of money. A simple methodology—clipping articles, or mailing postdeparture survey forms to clients—can be operated on a very modest budget and can produce results worth many thousands of times the investment. By the same token, meaningless or highly deceptive results can be obtained from expensive forms of data collection and interpretation. Success is not measured by the cost of the project but by the quality of the information obtained.

What would you like to know? What do you need to know? And if you can obtain the answers, how can they be adapted into practical, profitable actions?

WHAT THE TRAVEL AGENT NEEDS TO KNOW

An old axiom says that a mark of true intelligence is knowing what you don't know; in other words, being able to identify the areas where your knowledge is deficient. In the world of business, however, that's only a small portion of a larger truth: you must pinpoint the deficiency, know that you *need* the information, and be able to find a source to provide it.

The great majority of travel business failures can probably be traced to managers who didn't know what they needed to know. They were too overwhelmed by the routine, day-to-day details of the business: reservations that hadn't cleared, documents that hadn't arrived, personnel conflicts that hadn't been resolved, and so on. Add a constant barrage of cash-flow problems, visits from sales reps, and relatives demanding

Christmas reservations, and there wasn't room for anything else in the work week. In other words, the manager was indistinguishable from everyone else on the staff!

Staff members can afford to spend their time scurrying after hoary details, but the manager cannot. The future waits for no one, and it's the manager's responsibility to plan for it. But planning involves abstracts, and abstracts are difficult to grasp and veil the future in an impenetrable fog, while the small problems of the moment are highly visible, glowing with a seductive urgency.

To make the planning task just a bit less abstract, and demonstrate the importance of research to it, I've devised three small concepts. They're called "coming soon," "today only," and "starting tomorrow." Here they are:

COMING SOON

Coming soon is a very easy concept to grasp: your travel agency doesn't exist—yet. You've picked the location, signed the lease, and hired key personnel, but advertising, promotion, and operational details must still be decided. You have no clients. What do you need to know?

Before we get to the clients themselves, let's take a moment to consider what your agency will look like to outsiders. We live in a visually oriented society, where first—and frequently lasting—impressions are formed by our eyes. What type of image do you want to convey? Fun? Adventure? Professionalism? Consider the visual effect of every item you'll need in the office. What do you picture as your ideal "look?"

Now examine your agency as it actually exists. Does it bear any resemblance to what you'd put together at the coming soon stage of development? If not, you might want to make some alterations; perhaps in inexpensive areas such as window displays and general tidiness. At the other extreme, you might consider bringing in an interior designer (whose function is totally different from that of an interior decorator) to propose major changes. Either way, you've performed an important function of management by applying a simple planning concept.

Now, let's get to the guts of the matter—your clientele. Since your location is already fixed, you'll have to deal with the demographics that exist in and around that area. What are they? Who are the people who live nearby, and what levels of income and sophistication do they represent? Your entire advertising and promotion program may hinge on what you find. Or perhaps you'll discover that your location borders on several distinctly different neighborhoods, each suggesting a different marketing approach.

How about nearby businesses? What are they, and

what type of workers do they employ? There are opportunities here in both vacation and business travel, but you'll have to know the market to fully exploit either. A thorough survey may produce a surprise or two: office buildings can hide many different types of enterprise.

What about the traffic pattern that flows past your door? What is it, and where are people going? What are the transit routes? All of us fall into daily travel routines, and become so familiar (or bored) with them that we fail to see the changes taking place along the way. Many people who pass your door—on foot or in vehicles—may not know you're there; yet they represent solid potential.

Sound demographic research will answer these questions. Once you've developed the total picture of your area, compare it with what you thought all these years. What's the actual market potential, and how much of it still remains untapped? Your entire plan for the future might be shaped by the simple process of taking a good look around.

The beauty of coming soon is that it sweeps away all the natural prejudices and misconceptions we build through years of doing business in a certain way. The type of client you see most frequently may not be representative of the true demographics of your area, because your image or promotion is appealing to a narrow slice of the market. Perhaps you can build a solid new framework of clients, people who will come to you, and remain loyal no matter what the future holds. You won't know until you do your research.

TODAY ONLY

The world is coming to an end in exactly 24 hours! I'll leave this evening's activities to your imagination; meanwhile you have one complete business day to prove you're the world's greatest travel agency manager. What do you need to know?

There are two general measures of success in our society: profit and esteem. Since esteem is partly a function of financial success, we'll concentrate on profit, which, in turn, hinges on maximizing income and minimizing expense. Remember, you have just today. How can you maximize profit?

A quick walk through the office might reveal that your vacation counselors are working on sales of very limited potential, only because they're the next ones in order of departure date. Which would you prefer they handle, the quickie weekends coming up in a few days or the deluxe cruises due to depart next month? Either way, we'll credit you with earned commission as soon as the arrangements are complete (I know that's not the way it normally works, but when the world's coming to an end you're allowed these small deviations).

Did I hear you tell the staff to complete the cruise arrangements? If they move quickly, it might be possible to obtain the exact accommodations the clients want—rather than inferior offerings. Starting to get the idea behind today only? Good, let's move on.

The next stop is your business travel department and, as usual, the joint's jumping—every position busy with an incoming order. That's good; once again, we'll credit commission earnings as soon as each itinerary is completed. But what about that big pile of hotel vouchers waiting for commission collection follow-up? As you well know, some hotels won't pay a commission, but you won't know which ones until you try to collect. Worst of all, the staff members are using some of those very same hotels on today's bookings, and we'll have to deduct the deadbeats from the day's income. The answer, of course, is maintaining an up-to-date list of commission paying properties—as basic a research function as you'll ever encounter.

Finally, into the accounting department. Since every penny counts toward the day's profit, you're looking at the checking account for any excess balance that can be shifted to an interest-earning account, and you're also comparing present investments against possible higher returns in money-market funds, T-bills, or commercial paper.

As you can see, today only extends the familiar concept of the profit center by treating each day as if it were the last. By focusing on important planning considerations, rather than routine details, overall profit is maximized, and areas of deficient knowledge are quickly exposed.

STARTING TOMORROW

Years ago, a wise old real estate agent told me that the time to start looking for a new business location is the day after you sign your present lease. Starting tomorrow is an extension of that logic.

Let's suppose your landlord has just served notice that this is your last lease at this location (there's no stopping progress: they're tearing down your building to make way for a new porno movie house!). The big question is, do you want to remain in the general vicinity or move to a totally new location? Either way, you're forced to construct new quarters, so the expense will be about equal.

Our starting point is a big bonus provided by coming soon: you now know the complete demographics of your present location. You also know about an upcoming change: that new porno palace isn't going to do anything good for the neighborhood. Even allowing for that change, however, your immediate reaction is to concentrate on a nearby location, which will allow you to maintain your present clientele. On the other hand . . . .

A dynamite area, just begging for a new travel agency, may be just a few miles away. The commercial rental rates could be very reasonable, the demographics excellent, and the growth potential even better than your present location. Best of all, it could be close enough to be convenient for many of your present clients. But you're not sure; maybe you should stick to your original plan.

There are three problems at work here. First, there's a natural tendency for all of us to stay within familiar territory. Second, most of us have only surface impressions of nearby areas where we don't live or work. And finally, most retail enterprises have no idea whether customer loyalty and satisfaction are really sufficient to bring present clients to a less-convenient new address.

Starting tomorrow requires you to do your long-range homework; first by knowing everything there is to know about your entire community, and second by knowing all there is to know about your clientele. There's help in both areas (and others we've covered in these examples) coming up in a few seconds. Meanwhile, starting tomorrow offers substantial rewards as a planning concept: it prepares for the unknown, helps solidify relocation or branch-office expansion possibilities, and avoids the costly mistakes caused when sudden changes in the business climate yield inadequate planning time.

But enough of concepts, it's time to explore the research opportunities available in the real world of the travel agent.

PUTTING RESEARCH OPPORTUNITIES TO WORK

An incredible variety of research opportunities are available to the travel agency manager. They range from free, or low-cost, outside sources to in-house projects that can be devised and operated on modest budgets. The list presented here is by no means inclusive, but it does cover the major information areas explored earlier for agency planning needs.

Because no two agency operations are ever identical, some of these sources and projects may seem elementary to one manager and highly sophisticated to another. Whatever your initial reaction, I urge you to read this section in its entirety. Many of these items can be adapted to more- or less-sophisticated uses, depending on your actual needs.

CENSUS BUREAU

The U.S. Bureau of the Census is the single most overlooked source of free research information for the American small business operator. With branches in major urban centers throughout the country (see U.S. Government phone listing under Commerce Department), and extracts available at thousands of local libraries—and through data banks (explained later)

—the bureau can provide a wealth of vital information to the travel agent.

From statistics compiled in the standard population census taken every ten years, the bureau breaks down the demographics of the country by state, county, municipality, and even neighborhoods (called "census tracts"), providing personal income and lifestyle information on individual residents and family units. The information may appear to be complex, but a few minutes of instruction by bureau personnel, or a knowledgeable real estate broker, can provide important data for the travel agency manager.

The American population is changing, and it's important you know how, and how it's likely to affect future sales. For the first time in history, census bureau figures indicate that the number of senior citizens is larger than the number of teenagers and projections indicate that by 1990 the median age of all Americans will be 33 years old. Major merchandisers are paying close attention to these trends, and altering marketing plans—and products—accordingly. Just as the waist and seat measurements of Levi's jeans are becoming more generous to accommodate an aging customer base, so should your plans for the future be based on changes in client demographics. The bureau can help with these changes as they apply to your area.

In addition to population data, the bureau also collects business data in a less well known census of commercial enterprises conducted every five years (in years ending in 2 or 7). An examination of retail trade data for your community might indicate areas where other merchants are prospering, and where branch-office expansion should be considered—or, conversely, where others are beginning to experience downturns, and expansion into the market should be avoided.

The bureau can also provide the number of travel agency locations (Standard Industrial Classification code 4722) reported for any geographic area in the latest business census. From there, simple division into the population figure—which they'll also provide—gives the per capita coverage of average agencies in the vicinity (12,000 people per agency in my area at the moment). This is vital information that requires nothing more than a phone call and it's free.

Readers in other countries should investigate similar services (such as Statistics Canada) being conducted by governmental or private bureaus.

PRIVATE RESEARCH SERVICES

Private research companies, offering data collation and interpretation services, are located throughout the world. In addition to the long-term contracts generally favored by larger companies, many services also offer help on specific, one-time projects, and frequently at modest fees. Thus the agency manager who wants to consider all variables (including population data) before a branch-office commitment can usually contract with a local firm for such a service. In the U.S., see the business section of your classified phone directory under "market research" or consult the latest edition of *Bradford's Directory of Marketing Research Agencies* or *Consultants and Consulting Organizations* at your local business library.

LOCAL PLANNING AUTHORITIES

Every community has at least one public agency that acts as a repository for zoning variances, building permits, and the like. Yet, to hear realtors tell it, these agencies are the least likely candidates for prior research by small business operators who want to expand or relocate. The results are all too predictable: although it's on the public record—and available for anyone to see—the large chain's intention to open a new branch in the shopping center comes as a total shock to the small operator who's just opened across the street! It happens all the time, and to travel agents no less than anyone else in the business community. Do your research homework before signing that new lease: the minimal time involved is certainly worth it, in peace-of-mind if nothing else. Ask your real estate agent for the name of the proper authority in your area.

LOCAL BUSINESS AND LEGAL PUBLICATIONS

Every metropolitan area also has at least one source of public information on bankruptcies, new incorporations, real estate acquisitions, etc. Whether it's a legal newspaper, a local business publication, or a chamber of commerce monthly journal, it should be on your regular reading list. In particular, look for any trends that might affect your operation. Is your area losing business or industrial activity to another region? If so, why? Perhaps that all-important business client will be the next to go, and is already looking for a new site elsewhere. Forewarned is forearmed. On the other hand, you might spot a potentially lucrative new account (by keeping a sharp eye on real estate transactions) before they've even arrived on the scene! This is basic research for every agency handling commercial accounts.

THE WALL STREET JOURNAL

The Wall Street Journal is America's single most important source of business news (and, not incidently, superb writing). It should be required reading for every manager, or management-level employee, and at some companies it is. *Journal* articles profile industries and activities on the way up—as well as the way down—and give numerous insights into the way business conducts itself on all levels of operation. The coverage of consumer trends and fads is also unique, and extremely valuable to the travel agency manager.

The greatest value of daily reading, however, is that it's also where your business clients get their news—not only about their own industries, but about the travel business as well (the coverage of airfare changes is especially frequent). A year's subscription currently costs $114 for U.S. residents and is worth every penny.

DATA BASES

With its almost unlimited ability to store complex information, the mainframe computer can act as a vast, electronic encyclopedia, providing answers to millions of questions on demand. Using such technology, some 1,000 data bases (or data banks, as they're sometimes called), offering information on almost any conceivable subject, are available to American home computer and CRT users. The interconnection between home—or office—terminal and the master computer is made via the standard telephone network and a device called a "modem."

A degree of confusion exists about the two types of U.S. data base services. *The Information Bank* (New York Times Information Service) is a primary data base offering access to all *New York Times* articles— plus other data—through a single, mainframe computer. *The Source (Reader's Digest)* is a data base *network* service offering access to many different data bases (some 40 of them at the moment) depending on the particular type of information you need at the time. In either case, a flat, but variable, fee is charged for access, with most services offering reduced rates for off-hour use.

It doesn't take a crystal ball to see that the data base will be the public library of the future. Not only can reams of information be retrieved in a few seconds (all the flight schedules from North America to Europe, for example), but the technology already exists to transmit entire books from mainframe to home computer to home printer, also in a few seconds! (What that ultimately portends for the travel industry is anyone's guess; but it's good news for those of us who are authors. Tomorrow's "bookstore" will stock everything, no matter when it was originally published!)

For a complete rundown on who offers what in data base services, see the *Directory of Online Data Bases* at your public or business library.

PUBLIC LIBRARY INFORMATION SERVICES

Public libraries were among the first to recognize the potential of data base services and tap this vast resource through computer terminals of their own. Libraries throughout the U.S. now offer this computer-based service, with almost unlimited information on any subject available to all callers—first come, first served. The service is not only free, but it's usually very fast (once you get through the busy signal, that is). Library computer operators know not only the relative strengths and weaknesses of the many data bases at their command, but also how to access the best one for the task with maximum speed. If you need data, or have a question, but don't have access to a computer of your own, here's your answer. All it takes is a phone call.

SMALL BUSINESS ADMINISTRATION

The Small Business Administration wasn't chartered just to make loans (although many Americans think it was). It also assists small business operators with a wide variety of problems. In addition to the staffs on hand at local offices throughout the U.S., the S.B.A. also maintains an extensive library of publications, many of which are free for the asking. Subjects covered include everything from locating, or relocating, your office ("Using a Traffic Study to Select a Retail Site") to in-house research ("How to Analyze Your Own Business"). The agency's "small business bibliographies" are also of great value, pointing the way to dozens of other sources of information on many subjects, including market research.

For a list of free publications (SBA 115A), or for-sale booklets (SBA 115B), write: Small Business Administration, Washington, D.C. 20416, or visit your local office.

YOUR MAILING LIST

Whether it's computerized or on 3-by-5 cards, the agency mailing list is a valuable research tool. It can not only tell you who your clients are and where they live, but where they work and where they are moving.

One of the easiest ways to gain important information from your list is to sort it by home zip codes. You may see a definite pattern emerge, with two or three zones providing the bulk of your vacation customers and others providing just a smattering here and there. Targeted mass-mailings and door-to-door leaflet distribution are two natural uses of such information to add new clients.

A list that shows both home and work addresses can be even more meaningful, because it not only targets nearby work centers for additional promotion but also can be cross-sorted to show client transit patterns past your door. Armed with such information, you may decide on billboard or transit-route advertising to reach even more people who travel those same routes.

Other potential uses for mailing lists are for classifying family units by numbers and ages of children, identifying single clients of both sexes, and establishing special interests or vacation preferences for various types of targeted promotions.

NEWSLETTER FEEDBACK FORMS

Newsletters are an increasingly popular form of travel agency promotion that can yield even greater benefits when a customer "feedback" form is provided in each issue. Not only does this give clients a convenient method of asking for additional information on featured trips, but it can also provide a wealth of research information: articles found most appealing in the issue (don't be surprised if the gossip column about your staff is one of them), additional features they'd like to see included, when and where they'd like to vacation next, etc.

Experience has shown that the most efficient type of mail-back form is a lightweight postcard, with the return address and return postage indicia preprinted on one side and a grouping of numbers representing literature requests or question responses on the other (i.e.: "If you'd like more of this type of article, circle 99 on the reply card"). These cards are easy for clients to complete and mail, present a wealth of information in compact form, and avoid problems caused by poor or careless handwriting. Most users experience superior response rates when such forms are provided.

A word of caution, however: don't use such a form if you can't perform the necessary follow-up immediately. Clients consider themselves to be your top priority, and expect you to react likewise!

POSTDEPARTURE SURVEY FORMS

When it comes to obtaining information from actual travellers, the travel agent occupies the catbird seat among all industry units. No other segment of the industry has such complete access to the total travel picture: from airport limousine to flights, to hotel or cruise accommodations. Sadly, this incredible resource is wasted by the great majority of agents.

The few agencies using postdeparture survey forms usually report phenomenal results. Not only are response rates very high (in most cases better than 60%), but client loyalty and referrals almost always improve as a result. Everyone loves to be asked for his or her opinion, and the travel client more than most, for the agency conducting postdeparture surveying expresses an interest not only in the opinion but also in the welfare of the customer. The work involved is minimal: the form can be included with the document delivery, or mailed to the client's home a few days after departure. To ensure maximum response and client convenience, return postage is always provided, on either a preprinted envelope or a reply postcard.

In addition to the obvious benefit of spotting substandard services and accommodations very quickly, the postdeparture form allows the agency to nip complaints—sometimes serious ones—in the proverbial bud. Recent studies show that many people don't communicate their complaints to the source, preferring, instead, to remain silent— at least as far as the merchant is concerned. But these same people are anything but silent when it comes to friends and neighbors, telling them in detail how they were ripped off and by whom. The form puts an end to most of that. You may not be able to adjust the complaint to the client's complete satisfaction, but at least it's a positive start. After all, you took the trouble to ask how things went.

Once a complaint has been verified, the form can be used to back up a refund claim against a supplier or demonstrate to a carrier representative that there's good cause for the sales decline coming from your shop. On the other side of the coin, survey forms help isolate habitual complainers, particularly with respect to group arrangements (when you have their written comments it's much easier to prove that everyone did not think the food was rotten).

Finally, the forms can be used for market research, eliciting answers to questions such as "Where would you like to travel next?," "Do you prefer travelling with a group?," "Would you consider a trip with your children?," and other important data. As pointed out earlier, however, the information is of little value unless it's actually used in a coordinated plan of action: collation by destination or preference; or as review material for periodic staff meetings.

As with everything used for research, the postdeparture survey form is a tool, a good one, but still a tool. Obtaining the answer is only the first step along the road. You must know where you're going . . . and what you want to accomplish when you get there.

THE RESEARCH NEEDS OF TOUR OPERATORS

Among all the world's goods and services, the travel product stands alone with a unique characteristic: it is the only major consumer item that money, alone, will not buy. Time is also required. And, as every travel agent knows full well, many people have the money, but don't have the time. Nor is it meaningful to know, statistically, how many people do have the time—because of employer-assigned vacation dates. As with many things in life, it's the perception ("Can I afford to take the time off?") and not the reality that rules the game.

This unique money/time relationship makes the tour operator's task especially difficult, for it's not enough to know that people want to visit a specific destination. You must also know when they want to go there, how long they wish to stay (or, more accurately, be away from home), and how far in advance they'll make a commitment. Add to this the problems of obtaining sufficient, but not excessive, advance capacity, and maintaining prices at attractive levels, and the tour operator's task becomes rather formidable. But one must start somewhere and, obviously, it's with the destination.

TOURIST OFFICE AND PASSPORT STATISTICS

The tour operator in search of destination information can turn to two readily available sources, the U.S. State Department and individual regional or governmental tourist offices. In the first instance, statistics gathered by the State Department from passport applications can show broad trends in demand for those destinations requiring passports. There are three limitations, however: the information is voluntary, and not required for passport issuance; it only shows where people intend to go, and not actual travel behavior; and it only applies to the trip for which the passport is first issued, and not to future trips using the same document.

Tourist office information is usually based on actual arrivals, and therefore can be extremely helpful. In addition to highlighting lodging room/nights sold in various seasons (an indication of average length of tourist stay), the data can also show state or country of origin, method of arrival, size of family unit, and other pertinent data. Depending on specific needs, tour operators can develop sophisticated extrapolations from this raw information by applying cross-indexes of applicable lodging and/or transport costs, or economic indicators such as the consumer/price index.

Whether such information is totally valid as a forecaster of the future is another matter. Emerging or aging destinations present variables that can't always be predicted from current activity; and the everchanging political climate is always a factor.

POSTDEPARTURE SURVEYS

The use of a postdeparture survey form can be as valid for the wholesaler as it is for the travel agent. This is especially true for motorcoach tour brokers, where customer loyalty—and a high percentage of repeat business—can produce meaningful data on future destination choices. Escorted tours also lend themselves to this type of survey; but almost any operator can gain valuable information from enroute or just-returned clients.

In addition to seeking passenger comments on transport, accommodations, meals, and services, a number of firms seek demographic information on the tour participants themselves: average income, occupation, marital status, age, special interest data, and amount of annual vacation time. To assist in future advertising and promotion, some surveys also elicit information on magazines and newspapers read regularly, radio and TV habits, and the method by which the customer first heard of the tour company.

A clever p.r. step, but one that's never gained wide usage, is sharing individual client data with the travel agent who originated the booking. Not only does this make excellent promotional sense (as does any aftersale contact originated by the operator), but the retailer has the ability to follow up on any indication that the client might consider another of the operator's offerings, thus enhancing the possibility of additional revenue for both parties.

NEGATIVE FEEDBACK PROGRAM

Negative feedback programs are used to increase the conversion ratio of coupon-type advertising. At the end of each season, the tour operator's computer is asked to print out names and addresses of people who have requested literature but who haven't actually booked a tour. A reply form is then mailed to either everyone on the list or a representative sample.

The form begins by reminding the recipient that literature was requested and asking if it was received (a check not only on the efficiency of literature fulfillment but on the "memorability factor" of the literature as well). The respondent is then asked to check off any of a number of reasons why the tour wasn't purchased: "Too expensive," "Too many days," "Didn't cover the features I wanted" (followed by a request to specify which features), "Took another vacation" (again followed by a request to specify), etc.

One particularly important answer relates to the travel agent: "My agent recommended another trip (please specify)." A predominance of replies in this category might indicate all sorts of problems being experienced with the program by travel agents (some of which we'll cover in a few seconds) or, perhaps, a competitor offering substantial override commissions. Either way, the knowledge may be invaluable.

There are three keys to the success of a negative feedback program. First, the form must be perceived by the recipient as being both non-threatening and a genuine quest for information—and not just a sales ploy. This requires special attention to the design of the form and the wording of the introduction and questions. Second, the recipient must be convinced that cooperation will result in a better product not for the operator's benefit, but for the benefit of other travellers. Finally, the respondent must be encouraged to answer as honestly as possible (particularly with regard to tour cost), which is usually accomplished by an offer of anonymity, if desired.

Designed and used properly, the negative feedback program can be an important part of in-house research, improving not only the quality of tour literature and advertising, but also the selection of media for the ads themselves.

WHAT THE WHOLESALER NEEDS TO KNOW ABOUT THE AGENT

Show me a tour operator enjoying superior results at the retail point-of-sale and I'll show you a management

that has chosen to dig beneath surface impressions to learn about the real world of the travel agent.

It's a complex world where the next client will want who-knows-what, where the list of destinations and travel products stretches almost to infinity, and where the smallest supplier slipup can cause problems of traumatic proportions. It's a world where it's easy to become cynical about the true intentions of some principals to deliver a quality product, or—as with hotel or airline bumping—any product at all. Either way, it's the agent who will receive the ultimate blame, losing both hard-won clients and friends and relatives of clients as a result.

It's against this background that the situation of the wholesaler must be viewed. To be successful, the tour operator must penetrate the profusion of products, problems, and endless sales-pitches (not to mention airfare changes) to reach the people who will perform the actual selling. That it can and is being done by savvy operators is all the proof one needs that point-of-sale research pays handsome dividends. Here are the areas that beg for scrutiny:

THE TRAVEL AGENT'S MAILBAG

Agents receive a huge volume of mail, most of it unsolicited. A senior employee usually sorts the delivery each morning: client and commission checks, confirmations, debit memos, and documents into one pile; everything else into another. It's into this second pile that all tour operator promotional literature is placed, along with that received from everyone else. What happens to it from there? Many principals haven't the faintest idea, as is clearly demonstrated by the nature of the things they send.

Without question, the waste in printing, postage, and labor is in the millions of dollars annually.

The travel agent's mailbag is the point-of-entry into the retail marketplace. Successful principals know this, and view each prospective promotion not as artwork pasted to an ad agency's cardboard but one of many hundreds of promotional pieces which will arrive at the travel agency during a given period. Will it be read? Will the envelope even be opened? The only valid answers are those obtained through retail-level research. The principle involved is simple enough: you must know what works—and what doesn't.

What works for ad agencies and literature printers is anything the wholesaler will pay for; beyond that, it's his or her problem.

THE AGENT'S LITERATURE FILE

Given a choice between a trip to an ASTA convention or a tour of a typical agent's literature file, the travel principal should choose the latter. Agency file drawers are where the action is!

Bulk literature is the lifeblood of the travel agency business; without it, vacation sales just wouldn't take place. Yet most principals have only a vague notion of how much bulk literature to send—and how frequently to send it—and even less notion of how the stuff should be designed. The number of lost sales, for both retailer and wholesaler, is impossible to calculate.

Here's one of the best-kept secrets in the industry: in a well-designed tour brochure, the major features can be read upside-down! Why? Because when there's only one copy remaining in the office (as there frequently is), the brochure must be placed on the agent's desk *facing the client*. If you're a wholesaler, and didn't know that fact, you've just recovered your investment in this book, and then some.

But other bulk-literature design features are also important; and revolve around the way agents open, file, and retrieve current brochures—and the way they discard old ones (when they have time to do it, which isn't often, another well-kept, but important, secret). The well-designed brochure tells the agent everything he or she needs to know in a single glance: "Look at me, I'm new," "Throw me out, I'm old," "File me, I'm important." How do you express these thoughts as they relate to your new tour programs? You won't know until you do your point-of-sale research.

You also won't know how much to send, and when to send it, unless you do your homework. A few tour operators have developed sophisticated computer and research programs to provide these answers. The principle involved is easy enough to guess: when the prospect can't take the brochure home, you've sent too few; when the agent can't use what you've sent, you've sent too many.

THE RESEARCH OF DIALOGUE

Most retail sales personnel are creatures of habit, recommending the known, predictable products, and ignoring everything else. When tour operators build brand loyalty with travel agents, they're taking advantage of this potent selling force. Conversely, it's extremely difficult for a new operator to compete with an established, highly regarded wholesaler.

A great deal has been made of the use of override commissions to heighten travel agency awareness of various offerings, and it's true that such a program is better than simply mailing literature to everyone in sight. But in the contest between overrides and happy clients, the latter always win—hands down! Satisfied clients are the agent's stock-in-trade, providing not only the guaranteed profits of repeat business, but the valued prospects of referral business as well. In actuality, it's no contest at all; the agency that always opts for the override will not long remain a viable business entity.

Some nearsighted principals may think of travel agents as "order takers," but the truth is that the successful vacation agency faces the most difficult task in the entire industry: matching the client's expectations with the realities of the product. It is a business of constant compromise, and the task is made a hundredfold more difficult by the overblown prose that permeates much of travel advertising and literature. In this regard, the tour operator can be his own worst enemy.

These crucial sales factors—and many more—can be easily exposed by the tour operator who opens a meaningful dialogue with travel agents. The sales call, meeting, or junket that's specifically designed to create information flowing in both directions is as important a research activity as any on the face of the planet. "What do your clients want?" "Are we promising something we can't deliver?", "How can we create even happier clients for both of us?"

Basic questions. Find a way to ask them, frequently. And listen to the answers.

A PERSONAL AFTERWORD

Travel is a people business and, for that reason, our focus has been largely on people-oriented research. There's one built-in limitation to people-oriented research: the data become meaningless if you don't shed whatever prejudices you may have about those very same people.

My travel industry career included two decades of working with presentation audiences; and because my book on the subject[2] has received wide attention in the business press, I now spend much of my consulting time teaching the art of large-group presentations to a variety of business and professional clients. Many of them—from telecommunications giants to six-partner law firms—must be reminded that hunger is a basic human need. When it comes to demolishing an hors d'oeuvre table, a hungry group of diplomats can easily rival a hungry group of telephone retailers or law clients, or a hungry group of travel agents.

When some travel principals talk about the bad party manners of retailers, the carping is, by and large, ego-driven one-upmanship. It is by no means a unique phenomenon: you'll find similar prejudices in many industries and professions, wherever friction exists between the various levels of activity. And, lest I be accused of casting stones in one direction only, you'll hear carping from some travel agents about the bad party manners of their clients. Either way, allowing

---

[2]*The Overnight Guide to Public Speaking*, Running Press, 1983 (hardcover ed.).

ego to overrule common sense is a dangerous, frequently self-destructive, game. Blind prejudices do just that—they blind.

Bias, in any form, is the arch enemy of management. I hope you'll always be guided by that fact—and be reminded of it whenever you find yourself jousting with the crowd to get to the hors d'oeuvre table. And if, perchance, your progress toward the stuffed anchovies is impeded by a tall, bearded, consultant type, I hope you'll be patient as well. I get hungry too.

21

The Convention and Meetings Sector— Its Operation and Research Needs

JAMES R. ABBEY

College of Hotel
Administration
University of Nevada
Las Vegas, Nevada

The income potential available through the convention and meetings market can significantly affect the economics of virtually every city and resort setting. The monies generated from convention delegates benefit the entire community and for the most part represent revenues beyond the normal cash flow. This chapter introduces the reader to how the convention market operates, the present research efforts of the industry, and the future research needs of this sector.

HOW THE CONVENTION MARKET OPERATES: ITS SIZE AND SCOPE

Travel is stimulated by a number of motivators. One of the most significant and fastest growing is the need to attend meetings and conventions. Business and professional persons throughout the year travel from their home base to attend meetings. The economic impact of these travelers, the amount of money spent, and the needs and wants of these travelers are largely unexplored, despite their significance to the tourism industry.

The convention and meetings business is but one element of the tourism industry, but it is perhaps the healthiest and most growth oriented. Horwath and Horwath International, an accounting firm specializing in research of the lodging industry, lists the proportion of hotel guests who are conference participants worldwide to be 13.2 percent (1984). Pannell, Kerr, and Forster's "Market Trends" study reports that hotels with full-scale conference capabilities will reap substantial benefits from the growing convention market (1984).

Conference participants differ from the tour and travel segment. Unlike the tourist who seeks varied dining experiences and entertainment outside his lodging facility, at conferences the participants normally meet, sleep, and eat under the same roof. Another distinction is that growth in convention, business, and meeting travel frequently increases during times when the pleasure travel market is on the decline. The principal reason pleasure travel is outpaced during difficult economic times is because a poor economy actually stimulates nondiscretionary travel activity by creating the need for more direct contact among business associates.

One commonly held misconception of this market is that all conventions are large gatherings of thousands of people. There are more small meetings than large. Research conducted by the industry trade publications estimates that 75 percent of all corporate meetings have fewer than 100 in attendance. The fact that the majority of meetings never approach the thousand figure is significant because the convention and meetings sector represents a market potential for virtually every tourist center and city.

WHAT CONVENTIONS MEAN TO A TOURISM AREA

Hotels, restaurants, visitors and convention centers, retail stores, theatres, museums, airlines, and local governments all rely heavily on the revenues generated from convention/trade show sponsors and their delegates. Traditionally, the meetings market has been perceived as a major source of income for lodging establishments, but the delegates' expenditures are felt throughout the economy. The convention attendee not only spends dollars for lodging services but also contributes to local foodservice operations, cultural and sporting activities, sightseeing and tourism attractions, and local stores and gift shops, as well as benefiting local transportation firms. Furthermore, the benefits to the city or tourism area are twofold: not only are additional jobs created, but the tax revenues of the community are also increased by the influx of convention attendees.

The results of the International Association of Convention and Visitor Bureaus' Income Survey Update for 1983 reveal that the average delegate spends only 38.5 percent of his convention dollar on lodging. The balance of attendees' expenditures—food, entertainment, shopping, transportation—ripple through the entire local economy.

Additional advantages accrue to the tourist area through the meetings markets. Convention business can fill the gaps in slack months. Most tourism areas are faced with seasonal shoulder periods. Convention business can fill these soft periods. Second, group business is an excellent builder for repeat business. With conventions, a large number of potential repeat visitors become acquainted with a tourism area. If they are treated well and are pleased, they will not only advertise with word of mouth, but will also likely visit the area on other occasions.

CONVENTION PURCHASING— THE BUYER'S VIEWPOINT

In assessing the research needs of the convention sector it seems prudent to familiarize the reader with both the supply and demand side of the market, that is, from the buyer's and the seller's perspective.

WHO HOLDS MEETINGS

Several different buyer groups purchase convention services. Each group and each organization within these groups has needs that are not exactly identical. In fact, rarely does a single firm or organization have needs that are the same from one convention to the next.

In broad terms the meetings market can be separated into two categories: association-type meetings and corporate or company meetings. Within each group there are numerous further refinements.

The most visible convention organizers are the many associations throughout the country—indeed, throughout the world, because many of them are truly international. Associations vary in size and nature. They may be charitable, fraternal, educational, service, trade, union, or public organizations. Their scope ranges from small regional organizations through statewide associations to national and international ones. Trade associations are usually considered the most lucrative form of meeting business because their memberships are composed mostly of executives who have made it in business. It is a rare trade that doesn't have at least one association. The numerous associations in the professional and scientific fields also are inveterate meetings holders. Their subject range is far and wide, but they share a love for meetings and conferences.

Less visible, but of extreme importance, is the corporate meeting segment. Corporations have no need or desire to publicize their meetings, but meet they do. And often. They hold large meetings, small meetings, and middle-sized meetings. Insurance and appliance meeting planners frequently sponsor incentive trips for their top salespeople. Attending meetings is very definitely a part of business activity. Companies that stage meetings for dealers may deduct the cost of such events as business expenses. This has been a strong stimulant to meetings and conventions.

Figures 1 and 2 will help to put these two types of meeting segments in perspective. Figure 1 shows that in terms of number of meetings the corporate segment has an enormous 84% market share. Figure 2 reflects meeting expenditures by the two segments, showing that while association meetings are fewer in number, their size generates expenditures which outdistance the corporate market.

THE SELLER'S PERSPECTIVE

Many different names are given to properties that house conventions. Facilities chosen by meeting planners include: resort hotels, commercial hotels, suburban hotels, airport hotels, large motels and motor hotels, condominium resorts, cruise ships, universities, company meeting rooms, and specialized meeting centers.

The supply side of the convention industry is faced with two tasks in garnering the meeting and convention trade. The first and most obvious task is that of marketing and *selling* their community and facilities. The second is *servicing* the group by delivering what was promised. Securing a convention is only the beginning for the seller. Facilities should be much more concerned with how a convention goes out than with how it comes in.

NUMBER OF MEETINGS HELD ANNUALLY

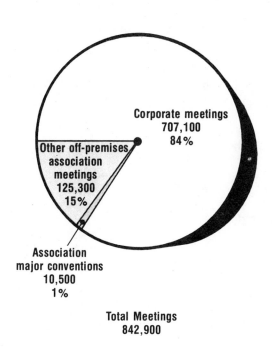

Total Meetings
842,900

FIGURE 1   Number of meetings held annually. Source: *Meetings & Conventions* 1981.

TOTAL ANNUAL MEETINGS EXPENDITURES

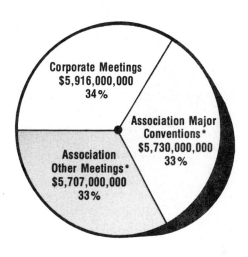

Total Expenditures: $17,353,000,000

FIGURE 2   Total annual meetings expenditures (asterisk denotes inclusion of delegate expenditures). Source: *Meetings & Conventions* 1981.

PRESENT RESEARCH EFFORTS IN THE CONVENTION INDUSTRY

To date, very little research has been conducted in the convention and meetings area. The limited research which has been undertaken has been done by three different groups: (1) by the industry itself through meeting associations, (2) by trade publications within the convention field, and (3) by universities.

STUDIES CONDUCTED BY INDUSTRY ASSOCIATIONS

The International Association of Convention and Visitor Bureaus periodically conducts what they term a Convention Income Survey. The IACVB serves as a clearinghouse for the exchange of industry data, ideas, and information. It represents the major convention cities throughout the world and has 228 member bureaus worldwide. The primary emphasis of its survey is to identify delegate expenditures. The first such sur-

vey took place in 1948 with subsequent research conducted in 1956, 1966, 1973, and 1978. Their next Income Survey is scheduled for publication in 1987.

The first four studies were concerned only with delegate expenditure information. The 1978-1979 survey, while collecting expenditure data, went beyond prior research efforts by collecting information on total travel party expenditures and the convention-related expenditures of exhibitors, associations, and exposition service contractors.

The United States Travel Data Center designed the survey methodology and analyzed the data for the 1978-1979 Convention Income Survey. The conventions sampled were chosen proportionately on the basis of four factors: (1) time of year, (2) scope (i.e., international, national, regional, or state), (3) whether exhibitors participated, and (4) attendance. The survey took place over the course of a year with fifty-five U.S. and two foreign cities participating.

Each bureau was instructed to survey 30 associations. A total of 1,402 conventions were sampled, including 666 national/international conventions and 736 state/regional groups. Each city was further instructed to survey 1,400 attendees and 300 exhibiting companies at the 30 conventions included in its sample. A systematic sampling procedure was used to produce random samples of attendees and exhibitors. Exhibitors and delegates were surveyed by mail questionnaire and completed questionnaires were returned directly to the U.S. Travel Data Center. Response rates for delegates and exhibitors were 38.3% and 32.3%, respectively.

In addition, the 1978–1979 Convention Income Survey collected expenditure data from two other sources: (1) associations sponsoring the convention and (2) the exposition service contractors which serviced the conventions. A total of 1,402 association and 441 exposition service contractors were contacted with response rates of 76.9% and 66.4%, respectively.

The results of the 1978–1979 IACVB survey are summarized in Tables 1 and 2. Convention attendees spent an average of $66.61 per day. Of this, 38.4% was spent for hotel rooms and incidentals; 26.5% for food, and 10.9% at retail stores. The results indicate the average length of stay per delegate to be 3.8 nights and the average party size to be 2.4 persons. Fifty-six percent used the airplane as the mode of transporta-

tion to the convention site while 39% arrived by private car, truck, or recreational vehicle.

The value of the Convention Income Survey is that it allows the industry to get a handle on its size and scope. It is designed to measure the monetary value of the convention business thus allowing a community or host city to get a picture of how much convention/trade show attendees are worth to an area. The results of the 1978–1979 Convention Income Survey provide a more comprehensive picture of the economic impact of conventions on city economics than ever before available, however, certain limitations need to be noted.

First, the geographical coverage of the survey is restricted principally to the continental United States and cities with IACVB members and does not extend to rural areas outside the influence of local convention bureaus. Second, the survey obtains data on conventions, trade shows, conferences, and meetings, but does not cover incentive trips, combination business/incentive trips, or the "nonoccupant" delegate (a delegate who stays for only one day and does not utilize lodging facilities). Moreover, only out-of-town delegates are represented. Further, only city conventions are covered, excluding resort settings which book considerable association convention business.

TABLE 1   Breakdown of Delegate Expenditures by Type of Expenditure

TYPE OF EXPENDITURE	ALL CONVENTIONS			NATIONAL AND INTERNATIONAL			STATE AND REGIONAL		
	% OF TOTAL	TOTAL EXPEND.	DAILY EXPEND.	% OF TOTAL	TOTAL EXPEND.	DAILY EXPEND.	% OF TOTAL	TOTAL EXPEND.	DAILY EXPEND.
Hotel rooms and incidentals	38.5%	$ 97.78	$25.64	39.0%	$107.04	$26.12	37.2%	$ 72.49	$24.28
Hotel restaurants	10.7	27.21	7.20	10.7	29.51	7.22	12.6	24.59	8.49
Other restaurants	15.8	40.24	10.61	16.0	43.97	10.85	13.5	26.25	8.53
Hospitality suites	4.5	11.54	3.26	4.5	12.37	3.44	2.6	4.99	1.75
Admission fees	1.2	3.06	0.78	1.3	3.49	0.83	1.2	2.35	0.76
Theatres/symphonies/movies	1.0	2.43	0.59	0.8	2.31	0.55	1.4	2.64	0.78
Recreational activities	0.4	1.05	0.26	0.4	1.11	0.25	0.5	0.88	0.26
Sightseeing	1.2	3.05	0.73	1.4	3.72	0.82	0.6	1.19	0.35
Nightclubs	3.7	9.36	2.48	3.7	9.98	2.49	3.6	6.93	2.38
Sports events	0.2	0.47	0.14	0.2	0.56	0.14	0.2	0.34	0.11
Retail stores	10.9	27.73	7.10	9.8	26.96	6.29	16.8	32.79	10.67
Local transportation	4.8	12.27	3.13	5.4	14.81	3.59	3.2	6.27	1.97
Gas/auto service	1.3	3.27	0.91	1.2	3.19	0.78	1.8	3.57	1.23
Other	5.7	14.50	3.78	5.7	15.62	3.88	4.9	9.64	3.16
TOTAL	100.0%	$253.96	$66.61	100.0%	$274.64	$67.25	100.0%	$194.92	$64.72

TABLE 2   Summary of Results—Delegate Survey

	ALL CONVENTIONS	NATIONAL AND INTERNATIONAL	STATE AND REGIONAL
Average total expenditure per delegate	$253.96	$274.64	$194.92
Average daily expenditure per delegate	$ 66.61	$ 67.25	$ 64.72
Average length of stay per delegate	3.8 nights	4.1 nights	3.0 nights
Average travel party size	2.4 people	2.3 people	2.4 people
Transportation usage (percentage of delegates)			
Airplane	56%	67%	32%
Train	1%	1%	2%
Bus	3%	3%	2%
Private car/truck/rv	39%	28%	63%
Other	1%	[a]	1%

[a]Less than 0.5 percent.

Third, because the 1978–1979 survey is more comprehensive than earlier studies, comparative analysis across the board cannot be made. However, by isolating delegate expenditure information, comparisons can be made with the 1973 study. For example, the 1978–1979 survey results reveal a 41.5% increase in total delegate expenditures over 1973 and the average stay per delegate increased from 3.59 days to 3.8 days.

A final question of concern with the IACVB's studies is whether they truly are income surveys. The IACVB derives its dollar data primarily from a survey of delegates' expenditures. Perhaps a truer measure of income would be derived from surveying the beneficiaries of convention business (i.e., hotels, restaurants, convention consultants, etc.).

The Hotel Sales and Marketing Association International in a joint effort with the American Society of Association Executives in 1983 conducted a study on association meeting trends. Three hundred ninety-six executives from professional and trade associations were questioned on various issues concerning the meetings market, such as the lead time for annual convention planning, the size and scope of educational seminars, and the use of teleconferencing. The survey is divided into six sections: (1) annual conventions, (2) expositions, (3) educational seminars, (4) board and committee meetings, (5) teleconferencing, and (6) general classification information, with each section giving statistical information related to its topic. The results

of the study are published in *Association Meeting Trends: A Perspective on the Future* (1983) and include over sixty tables of statistical data on the association meetings market.

TRADE PUBLICATION RESEARCH

Several of the trade journals in the meetings field conduct research on their subscribers. The leading publications and their research efforts are discussed below.

The most up-to-date information on the dimensions of the off-premises meetings market comes from a comprehensive, biennial survey of the corporate and association subscribers of *Meetings and Conventions* magazine. The major aspects that are explored in this study are the number and types of meetings held, the dollar expenditures, the number of attendees, the number of days duration of meetings, the lead time involved in planning meetings, the types of facilities used, the selection criteria used to choose destinations and facilities, the types of transportation used to and from and at the site of the meetings, and a profile of meeting planners' duties and responsibilities.

Because the sample is based on the magazine's circulation, the data contained in the report are not representative of the entire market. However, it is estimated by the research department of the publication that they reach virtually all of the associations which hold off-premises meetings and 70% of the corporations actively holding such meetings. The study includes trade shows.

Meetings and Conventions' 1983 survey of its subscribers projects the meetings and convention sector to be a $27.8 billion industry. In contrast to the survey conducted by the IACVB, *Meetings and Conventions* magazine explores the corporate market as well as associations. Of note in their 1981 *Meeting Market Study* is their finding that the corporate sector experienced a 50% expenditure increase between 1978/1979 and 1980/1981. Their 1983 study showed corporate recipients increased their spending by only 8% in the period 1981 to 1983.

According to the 1983 *Meetings and Convention* report, expenditures for corporate meetings were $6.4 billion. Of this, 50% was spent for hotels, food, and related items, 26% for air transportation, and 24% for miscellaneous expenses. The most frequently held type of corporate meeting was the training seminar, representing 24% of the total, followed by management meetings at 22%.

Two other publications which conduct similar research of their readers are *Successful Meetings* and *Meeting News. Successful Meetings* (1980) magazine segments the corporate and the association markets and presents data for both on type and number of meetings held, attendance, length of meetings, and site selection statistics. *Meeting News* (1980) has taken the lead in profiling the meeting planner. This publication has researched the demographic features of meeting planners including income, educational background, years of experience in meeting planning, and the like.

RESEARCH STUDIES BY UNIVERSITIES

A few researchers have attempted to determine the manner in which the association and corporate groups select sites at which to hold their conventions. One of the most definitive studies on the site selection process is the work done by Fortin and Ritchie titled *A Study of the Decision Process of North American Associations Concerning the Choice of a Convention Site* (1976). The study sampled all associations that were known to have held their convention in Canada over a five-year period as identified by *Successful Meeting's* Databank. The specific objectives of the research were

1 To obtain a descriptive understanding of the nature of the association convention site selection process (length, timing, etc.).
2 To measure the relative importance of a range of factors thought to influence the choice of a convention site.
3 To identify the different elements or subdecisions of the site selection decision process.
4 To measure the relative influence of different

groups involved in site selection within and across different stages of the decision process.
5 To identify major segments of the association convention market based on association characteristics, factors affecting site selection, and the structure of influence within the site selection decision process.

The findings of this research study are far too lengthy to discuss in this chapter but the authors' conclusions and implications section is particularly noteworthy and demands the attention of researchers in this meetings segment.

The directions for future research suggested by this study include

- A need to conduct a parallel study with the corporate meetings and the incentive travel markets.
- A need to measure the extent to which market segments are willing to trade off various combinations of site benefits.
- A need to more extensively study the roles, utilization, and impact of different types of information and information sources on the site selection process.
- A need to develop a methodology for assigning relative weights to the influence of site selection benefits in the decision process.

McCleary (1977) conducted similar, though not nearly as extensive, research of the corporate meetings market. The corporate meetings market is a potentially strong source of business for lodging facilities. Therefore, research to determine which facilities and services should be offered is extremely important to the tourism industry.

The corporate meeting market differs significantly from association meetings, having several unique characteristics which make it attractive.

- The majority of corporate meetings involve less than fifty persons. Thus smaller lodging operators can capture a portion of this market.
- Because corporate meetings are smaller, lodging facilities can take several groups simultaneously and may use small meetings to fill in around larger conventions.
- Corporate groups tend to meet more frequently, are not tied to a north−south−east−west geographic pattern as are many associations, and tend to spread their meetings throughout the year. This allows the lodging operator to use the corporate market to fill shoulder periods.
- Corporate meetings are generally better spenders, require fewer price concessions, and tend to utilize the other profit centers of the hotels, including the restaurants, lounges, and recreation areas.

McCleary's (1977) study was based on personal interviews with 15 corporate meeting planners and a like number of marketing persons from meeting facilities. The meeting planners were interviewed first, to establish their needs and compare them with the marketer's perception of these needs. The meeting planner was also asked to complete a questionnaire listing various attributes of meeting facilities. The final phase of the interview examined the decision process and criteria for site selection. Questions were structured to determine which factors affected satisfaction as well as the negative aspects of a meeting facility.

McCleary's findings indicated that the decision process for selecting corporate meeting sites is similar to the process for purchasing other industrial products. While multiple influences determine the corporate site decision, the major concerns for the planner were the meeting accommodations themselves, the supplier's staff, and location.

The Institute of Outdoor Recreation and Tourism at Utah State University conducted an image study of the Salt Lake Valley as a meeting site (Dalton 1978). The study was designed to gather information from national associations concerning their convention habits and needs and their perception of Salt Lake City as a potential convention site.

Based on interviews of over 140 associations, the Institute found that the hotel, the location of the host city, and the location of the convention facility were the three most pleasing qualities reported of the most recent convention site. The hotel was indicated by nearly one-quarter of the respondents. The climate, the hotel, and the convention facility itself were the three most reported least pleasing qualities of the most recent site. Meeting facilities were reported as the single most important item to be considered when selecting a convention site. The location of the site and sleeping facilities followed.

In an article on research in the meetings market, Margaret Shaw and Ellen Mazukina (1984) cite three independent research studies. In 1981, Heidi Bloom undertook a comparative study of hotel operators' current marketing programs and meeting planners' criteria for hotel selection; in 1983, Robert Lewis completed a study of the incentive travel market; and in 1984 Lisa Stavro and Thomas Beggs reported their findings of a study designed to identify the perceptions and motivations of meeting planners when booking meetings at hotels.

FUTURE TRENDS AND RESEARCH NEEDS

The convention and meetings market will continue to thrive as the need for communication within both associations and corporations increases in the years ahead.

Several industry trends and their need for research are identified and discussed in this section.

INTERNATIONAL MARKET

Very little research has been undertaken of the characteristics, trends, and implications of international congress-type meetings. Therefore, very little hard market planning data relevant to these visitors are available. The single exception is the work done by the Danish Institute for Transport, Tourism and Regional Science, which has done extensive research in the international convention field. The Institute under the direction of Ejler Alkjaer has conducted a number of studies on congress science including (a) feasibility studies and promotion plans for congress centers, (b) forecasts of the international congress business over 20-year periods, (c) global surveys of exhibitions and trade shows and their integration with congress activities, and (d) image research in congress tourism.

Researchers need to investigate the nature of this growing market and to segment out the convention traveler from the tour and travel international visitor. Possible areas to explore include; size of congress, visit duration, first time visitors, sources of planners' information, the strengths and weaknesses of the area as a meeting site, services and needs of international congress delegates, activities in the host area, and spending patterns, as well as demographic characteristics profiling the meeting group. The role the convention and meetings market might play in a developing country would certainly be well received research.

TELECONFERENCING

There is considerable evidence that communication facilities may soon be so advanced that there will no longer be a need for people to gather in one room or even in the same city for a meeting. A revolution in telecommunications is under way with four different types of communication services available to date.

1 Video teleconferencing via two-way voice and television communications.
2 Audiographics: two-way voice communications with the ability to exchange documents, drawings, etc., via facsimile or other graphic transmission devices. (In using this equipment the ability to exchange drawings, documents, etc., is an important user requirement.)
3 Computer conferencing: communicating through use of word processor computer terminals—a form of electronic mail.
4 Conference calls: telephone links among several people with no visual or graphic transmissions.

The *Meetings and Conventions* (1983) study, referred to earlier, questioned their sample of meeting planners on their use and intentions to use teleconferencing. While 8% of association planners and 8% of corporate planners have used telecommunications in the past, over 17% of both types of groups intend to make use of this technology in the "near future." When questioned as to their reason for employing the technique, planners cited the need to cut travel costs.

The impact of teleconferencing on future meetings raises a number of questions that need to be addressed by researchers. Is teleconferencing an adjunct, support system to existing methods of communicating or a substitute for the traditional methods? What is the attitude of convention delegates towards telecommunications as a substitute for attendance at meetings? What percentage of the business meetings can be conducted via telecommunications? What is the minimum number of participants to make teleconferencing cost-effective?

Extensive research identifying the pros and cons of substituting telecommunications for actual attendance at meetings needs to be undertaken. Words, body gestures, facial expressions, eye contact, and shared common space are all important ingredients in a successful meeting. Can teleconferencing overcome these benefits inherent in face to face communication? A reason frequently advanced for using teleconferencing is the rise in the cost of travel. Can telecommunications substitute for travel?

Lodging operators, as well as meeting planners, have many unanswered questions on the effect of this technology. What will be the impact of teleconferencing on sleeping room sales? Can hotels expect increases in banquet and beverage business, and use of ballrooms and other meeting rooms? What locations are best to install teleconferencing equipment? What are the costs/benefits of a system? How to market this new thing? What type of meetings will utilize teleconferencing? Can reservation information, telephone calls, entertainment, and staff training as well as teleconferencing be incorporated into a satellite system?

A third group concerned about teleconferencing is the airline industry. The Air Transportation Association commissioned a study on the potential impact of telecommunications technology on air travel. The key findings of this research include

- Telecommunications technology may begin to affect airline revenues by 1985, initially diverting away 1% of the travel market.

- Although saving in travel expense is often cited in studies of proposed new telecommunications systems, interviews indicate that savings in executive time is the real driving force.

- Even when teleconferences save money, unused travel funds are often diverted to other travel.

- The systems now being put into service will have little immediate effect on the rate of growth of air travel. Costs are still high, and the new telecommunications equipment and software cannot be delivered in quantity rapidly enough to make substantial immediate inroads.

- By 1985, business travel revenue will have grown to about $34 billion (up from $28 billion in 1980). As much as 5–10% of 1985 business travel in a few companies with telecommunications networks in place can be expected to be diverted. For the market as a whole, however, diversion of revenues to telecommunications will be much smaller.

NEGOTIATIONS AND CONTRACTS

Negotiations, including contracts, guarantees, and deposits, have become the most controversial subject of the meeting business today. There are no universally accepted industry standards governing the use of contracts and cancellations. What would be of tremendous value to the meetings industry is a state-of-the-art study identifying policies presently employed. Questions which might be addressed include: What is the liability of the lodging facility or convention center in the event of overbooking? What is the industry's policy on charging for function space? Is there a difference in the negotiating approach used by corporate meeting planners as contrasted to association planners? How does the state of the economy, energy, and labor costs affect negotiations?

In the past, the convention and meetings industry could run fairly effectively on gentlemen's agreement, but the handshake is rapidly giving way to the formal contract. The impact of the written agreement on the meetings industry has yet to be adequately researched. In fact, the entire area of negotiations and contracts cries for research.

IDENTIFICATION OF THE MEETING PLANNER

Future research efforts might be directed to the role and responsibilities of the meeting planner. *Meeting News*, a trade publication for the industry has undertaken such a study through polling its readership (1980). However, future research might track changes within this profession, suggest appropriate guidelines and channels for career planning, and identify academic programs and curriculums for developing the professional meetings manager.

Other areas for research might include profile studies of both corporate and association planners. Psychographics studies of meeting planners might be helpful in determining if there is a relationship between the decision-makers' lifestyle and the site selected. Comparative studies exploring how the wants, needs, and benefits sought by the association meetings market differ from those of the corporate market would be valuable.

SPOUSE ATTENDANCE AND ROLE IN DECISION TO ATTEND

Examination as to what part the spouse plays in convention attendance is an area of research which has not been touched. Most conventions make some effort to show the spouse a good time. The official feeling is that the conventioneer is there to work and the spouse is along for the ride. Is it possible that convention attendance can be increased by offering spouse programs consistent with the wants and needs of spouses? What role do spouses play in the convention decision process?

RESEARCH ON MEETING FACILITIES OF THE FUTURE

The design and layout of future conference facilities is an area in need of research. What will meeting rooms of the future look like? How will the new technology, including closed circuit, cable, and most recently satellite teleconferencing, affect state-of-the-art meeting facilities? Will future meeting facilities need to be reduced in size, yet with more sophistication and ingenuity required in their physical design?

How will changes in design alter management functions? It seems likely that the function rooms of the future will also necessitate more sophisticated conference service departments as meeting planners' needs become more complex. Research exploring the future might indicate that hotel facilities will need to include work areas for guests, copying centers, television studios, and photographic darkrooms.

Research into the most appropriate meeting environment has, to date, been sketchy. What of lighting, acoustics, sight lines, and air circulation?

THE SOURCES OF INFORMATION USED BY MEETING PLANNERS

Tourism destinations and individual lodging operators devote considerable expense to communicating benefits to meeting planners in an attempt to influence the planner's site selection. Very little is known about which sources of information meeting planners utilize in making their site decision. Fortin and Ritchie (1976) cite a need to more extensively study the impact of different types of information and information sources on the site selection process. Researchers might address the role of various information sources: information secured from other meeting planners, hotel convention collateral material, advertisements in trade publications, and direct mail pieces. Identification of those sources which most strongly influence the choice decision would offer the marketer opportunities to increase the probability of securing convention group business. A closely related research approach might be to identify the type of information sources used by particular types of meeting planners, i.e., corporate

versus association decision-makers. Also researchers might examine whether decision-makers in the area of meeting planning see impersonal or media sources of information as being more important than personal sources.

IMPACT OF CONFERENCE CENTERS

Conference centers—once viewed as dreary, dormitorylike facilities—have altered their product–service mix and become direct competitors of lodging properties. The conference center concept was created at Tarrytown House Conference Center in Tarrytown, New York, and has proliferated to locations throughout the country. Their reason for success is founded upon their creation of a self-contained environment for learning. The hotel meeting frequently involves a series of separate purchases. Lodging, meals, audiovisual, and support services are often arranged with different firms. In contrast to this piecemeal purchase of a meeting, conference centers provide lodging, food and beverage, meeting rooms, and most important auxiliary support services for a single package price.

While there is no clear-cut method of determining whether a property meets the requirements of a conference center, the International Association of Conference Centers, formed in 1981, has established certain guidelines. To call itself a conference center, a property must consider meetings their priority business—that is, they must do at least 60% of total volume in meetings. In addition, a conference center offers a total environment dedicated to meetings. The center's meeting rooms form the nucleus of the property. They are supported by lodging, food and beverage, and recreation. Often, but not always, the center is located in a quiet area—off the beaten path yet close to a major city or airport. Another distinguishing mark of conference centers is the number and quality of conference service professionals that are in their employ. Most conference centers fall into one of four basic categories as to type: Executive, Resort, Corporate, and College/University.

While little research has been undertaken on this active sector of the meetings market, Laventhol and Horwath has annually, since 1976, prepared a statistical and financial profile of the executive conference center. This study is designed to define the type of facilities, style of operation, source of customers, and financial profile of the typical conference center. Data are secured from clients of Laventhol and Horwath. The establishments which provide operating results are those that are specifically designed and operated as executive conference centers. A significant limitation of this work is its narrow sample. Further, since there are differences in the composition of the sample from year-to-year, comparisons of studies are not possible.

This rapidly growing sector is much in need of research. Research efforts identifying the wants and needs of the conference center customer would be beneficial in marketing these facilities as would attitude and awareness studies of the meeting planning industry. In the same vein, image and perception studies might be undertaken.

Research efforts should be directed to determine the size, composition, and pace of development of the executive conference center market. Site selection variables need to be explored and choice models developed. The levels of audiovisual and program support services required, as well as conference room design and flexibility, are areas that to date have not been researched.

CONCLUSION

The conventions and meetings segment of the travel industry is substantial and growing at an increasing rate. The International Association of Convention and Visitor Bureaus estimates that the association market segment generates an average of $140 per day to the host community (1984). In a more comprehensive study of both the association and corporate meetings industry, it was estimated that this market was approaching $28 billion (*Meetings and Conventions* 1983). The latter study further cites a threefold increase in the convention market between 1974 and 1983.

Not only is the market enormous and growing, it is also changing. New technology, the emerging importance of the professional meeting planner, the impact of teleconferencing, and the demand for more specialized meeting facilities are just some of the trends that promise to alter this segment of the tourism industry in the future.

Despite the importance of this market segment to both individual properties and host cities, relatively little research has been undertaken on its structure and workings. This lack of information is a severe handicap to operating managers and tourism officials responsible for marketing and promoting their product and services and also to the meeting and convention planners responsible for organizing and conducting effective meetings.

While this lack of research is, on the one hand, a hindrance to the convention and meetings industry, it presents a promising opportunity for researchers. Convention and meeting research is, for the most part, an untapped market for researchers. Considerable research is needed to increase our understanding of this important segment of the tourism industry.

REFERENCES

Alkjaer, Ejler (1976), "Images and Realities in Congress Tourism," *Journal of Travel Research*, 14 (Spring), 14–15.

Alkjaer, Ejler (1980), *The Congress Market of the 80's*, Institute for Transport, Tourism and Regional Science, Copenhagen.

Alkjaer, Ejler, and Jorn Eriksen (1967), *Location and Economic Consequences on International Congresses*, Institute for Transport, Tourism and Regional Science, Copenhagen.

American Society of Association Executives (1980), *Convention Liaison Manual*, Washington, D.C.

American Society of Association Executives and Hotel Sales Marketing Association (1983), *Association Meeting Trends*, Washington, D.C.

Astroff, Milton, and James Abbey (1978), *Convention Sales and Services*, Dubuque, Iowa: Wm. C. Brown Publishing.

Bloom, Heidi (1981), "Marketing to Meeting Planners: What Works?" *Cornell Hotel and Restaurant Administration Quarterly*, 22 (August), 45–50.

Dalton, Michael J. (1978), *The Image of the Salt Lake Valley Convention Analysis*, Institute of Outdoor Recreation and Tourism, Utah State University, Logan, Utah.

English Tourist Board (1974), *Report on a Survey of a Survey of Conference Venue Selection*, London.

Fortin, Paul A., and J.R. Brent Ritchie (1976), *A Study of the Decision Process of North American Associations Concerning the Choice of a Convention Site*, Quebec, Canada: Université Laval.

Horwath and Horwath International (1984), *Worldwide Lodging Industry*, New York.

International Association of Convention and Visitor Bureaus (1978) (1983, Update), *Convention Income Survey*, Champaign, Illinois.

Jones, James (1979), *Meeting Management: A Professional Approach*, Stanford, Connecticut: Bayard Publications.

Laventhol and Horwath (1982), *The Executive Conference Center: A Statistical and Financial Profile*, Philadelphia.

Lewis, Robert (1983), "The Incentive Travel Market: How to Reap Your Share," *Cornell Hotel and Restaurant Administration Quarterly*, 24 (May), 19–27.

McCleary, Ken W. (1977), "Factors Influencing the Marketing of Meeting Facilities: An Empirical Study of the Buying/Selling Relationship for Corporate Group Meetings," unpublished doctoral dissertation, Michigan State University, East Lansing, Michigan.

Meeting News (1980), *The Meeting Planner: An Emerging Specialist*, New York.

Meeting Planners International (1980), *Source Book for Meeting Planners: A Bibliography*, Middletown, Ohio.

Meetings and Conventions (1981, 1983), *Meetings Market Study*, New York: Ziff–Davis Publishing Company.

Pannell, Kerr, and Foster (1984), *Trends in the Hotel Industry*, Houston.

Shaw, Margaret, and Ellen Mazukina (1984), "The Meetings Market: Where the Research Is," *Hotel Sales Marketing Association Marketing Review*, (Fall), 27–30.

Stavro, Lisa, and Tom Beggs (1984), "Attributes of Significance a Priori and during the Meeting," published in the proceedings of the World Hospitality Congress II, March 25–28, Boston, Massachusetts.

Successful Meetings (1980), *Corporate and Association Meetings Market*, Philadelphia.

22

Research Needs for Developing Established Events and Attractions

CAROLYN CAREY

Manager, Market Research
and Promotion
Knott's Berry Farm
Buena Park, California

Events and attractions by their broadest definition could encompass anything that attracts an audience by appealing to specific tastes or desires. In the context of travel and tourism, this broad spectrum becomes limited to that segment of the industry which is unique to specific geographic locations. An event has a limited duration whereas an attraction is permanent.
This chapter covers the unique research needs for the marketing of established events and attractions. It covers analysis of customers and noncustomers and continuous and special basis research requirements. The types of research described satisfy needs for ongoing marketing activities as well as future planning at the individual and industrial level.

The research needs of events or attractions vary. This chapter will assume that the magnitude of the customer base can be estimated and the event or attraction is established. Three main areas of concern are ongoing marketing research, special research studies, and joint research compiled by the events and attractions industry. The objective of research is to maximize attendance and/or profitability through product improvement, marketing strategy, and long-range planning.

Key factors which make this research unique are: the joint and inseparable dependency on the resident and tourist population bases, the large array of competition for discretionary time and money, and the availability of a very large customer base at all times for research.

RESEARCH TECHNIQUES

Collection of historical data pertaining to existing customers is the first step in amassing information on events and attractions. Attendance and financial records provide valuable information about customer usage patterns. Correctly recorded data of this nature form a basis for future attendance projections and trending analysis relating to such factors as length of stay, per capita spending, "in facility" capabilities, ticketing structures, product improvement, and product component utilization. Along with appropriate additional secondary information, it also allows the multidimensional analysis of the effects of such external variables as weather, media exposure, economy, energy availability/cost, competitive activity, and airline deregulation.

Collection of secondary research data varies significantly with geographic location of the event and attraction and with government involvement. The geographic definition of the resident base for an event or attraction usually includes any household within an area which allows its members to visit the event or attraction and return home within one day. The nonresident or tourist base, therefore, includes anyone required to stay overnight in the area of the event or attraction in order to visit.

In most cases, the Census Bureau can provide all the secondary data required for the resident population, although as the time since the last census increases, the availability of updated data becomes fragmented and dependent on private sector updates. Data regarding the nonresident or tourist population are the major variable being entirely dependent on government involvement at a city, state, and national level. This involvement can range from extensive, as in the case of the State of Florida, to minimal, as in the case of the State of California. Where government involvement is extensive, the individual event or attraction can derive all the secondary data required for the quantitative demographic identification of the "noncustomer" within the nonresident or tourist base. Where government involvement is minimal, the individual event or attraction naturally has to identify an alternate source for their information. Their options are to subscribe to a national travel survey, or to initiate the collection of primary data either on an individual basis or in conjunction with other events or attractions. Neither of these options are totally adequate because of the primary nature of their data, their exclusion of the foreign tourist component for reasons of language, and their noncustomization to geographic designations.

Once all the existing secondary data are organized, the next step is to separate it by demographic component. The demographic components of greatest significance are geographic area of residence, age, race, sex, and customer party composition. In the case of larger events or attractions, primary or survey data must be collected. At this point, a decision has to be made regarding whether primary data should be collected by interviewing or by self-administered questionnaires. Many variables will affect this decision but where budgets permit the use of a personal interview is preferable to ensure valid and maximum responses, as well as facilitating quality control and the use of open-end questioning and screening techniques.

In determining the best method of personal interviews, the decision is based upon whether customers or noncustomers are being questioned. Whenever possible, the use of interviewers who are on the payroll of the event or attraction is considered preferable when interviewing customers. This ensures maximum cooperation and conduct compatible with the standards of the event or attraction as well as complete familiarity with the event or attraction. When noncustomers are being interviewed, it is recommended that an outside supplier be utilized to conduct the data collection by whatever means they advise as appropriate. Telephone surveys will usually be recommended for the resident "noncustomer" and their visiting nonresident friends or relatives, whereas in-person surveys at hotels or airports will usually be recommended for the nonresident or tourist. An outside supplier is better equipped to collect this type of data by virtue of their access to Watts lines, experience with telephone techniques, access to a larger and experienced interviewer base, and their ability to receive authorization for interviewing in public locations.

It is further recommended, in both situations, that the design and reporting of such a study should be handled by staff of the event or attraction for reasons of cost control, familiarity with the product, and feasibility of the recommendations.

ONGOING MARKETING RESEARCH

KNOWING YOUR CUSTOMER—QUANTITATIVE AND QUALITATIVE DATA REQUIRED

In conjunction with standard demographic data, other valuable customer-related data include: mode of transportation to the event or attraction, prior visiting patterns, reason for visit, awareness of the event or attraction geographic area, planning cycles, use of travel professionals or package tours, accommodation used, length of stay, and competitive visitations.

Qualitative information to be gathered from the customer about the visit to the event or attraction includes: overall satisfaction; satisfaction with components such as food, merchandising, employees, or rides; satisfaction with aspects such as landscaping, cleanliness, signage, layout, or public announcements; pricing; intent to return; and best and least liked features. If budget and time permit, psychographic characteristics of the customer should also be collected to ensure usable qualitative data.

These data form the basis of a quality control system where the strengths and weaknesses of the product relative to customer psychographics as well as demographics can be carefully monitored to ensure maximum product perception and, therefore, maximize word of mouth advertising and repeat visit factor. In collecting this data the guidelines in Table 1 should be kept in mind.

KNOWING YOUR NONCUSTOMER— QUANTITATIVE AND QUALITATIVE DATA NEEDED

The opinions and values of the noncustomers are required to identify their profiles. The basic reason for identifying the non-customers is to ascertain why they are not customers. These data are cross-referenced with demographic and geographic information. The data collection required to generate this type of information is fairly complex and costly and the benefits must be carefully assessed. The following represents the type of information which would be generated

TABLE 1   Guidelines for Reliable Demographic Data

- Minimum sample size, 2% of attendance during period of interest.
- Data collection schedule should coincide with every time frame part of the period of interest.
- Schedule should coincide with peak and nonpeak periods—two-hour periods are recommended.
- To maximize the random nature of response, projectionable demographic data should not be collected with other survey data.
- Interviewers should address the party unit rather than individuals to avoid the bias of the male adult responding on behalf of the other party members.
- Design questionnaires to allow cross-tabulation of demographics.
- Weigh the raw data in accordance to the actual attendance contributions during the day or day part it was collected.
- Customers are guests; sensitive demographics such as income or race should be avoided or collected by observation.

while identifying reasons for noncustomer status: perception of the event or attraction and its components; perceptions towards competitive events or attractions; effects of competitive activity; patronage of competitive events or attractions; and psychographics evaluation of the "noncustomer." Having compiled the reasons for the "noncustomer," status directions for product improvement or marketing strategy will become apparent and steps can be taken to broaden the customer base of the event or attraction.

QUANTITATIVE AND QUALITATIVE DATA NEEDED IN LONG-RANGE PLANNING

Long-range planning relies on historical and predictive demographic data. In most cases, resident population projections are available from Chambers of Commerce or private sector industries such as banking or housing. Data regarding the nonresident or tourist population projections are available through some state governments or industry trade groups.

Additional qualitative data needed on a continuous basis for predictive reasons relate to the ways in which the product can be adapted to maximize the penetration of the available population bases by the event or attraction in the future.

Product improvements are usually undertaken to maximize resident attendance. Data relating to the product should, therefore, be collected from the resident customer and "noncustomer" of the event or attraction, but for reasons of cost, it is recommended that as much preliminary data collection as possible be conducted at the event or attraction. Customer product improvements should be screened and rank-ordered by customers.

SPECIAL RESEARCH STUDIES

KNOWING YOUR CUSTOMER—QUANTITATIVE AND QUALITATIVE DATA NEEDED

Most events and attractions will have special periods where additional quantitative data become mandatory. Examples of such periods are periods of paid advertising on behalf of the event or attraction, periods where additional products are offered on a temporary basis, and periods of promotional activity.

Secondary data and secondary information variables such as paid media weights, admission discounts, attendance incentives, and media derived from publicity or tie-ins with noncompetitive ventures should be analyzed for the effect on the present event. The additional qualitative data required include satisfaction with the additional product offering, reactions to the various media campaigns, and reactions to the promotional activities. Such testing contributes in assessing the value of repeating the period of special activity and in maximizing attendance.

The next step is to relate this information to the demographic information collected during these special periods. Additional quantitative information required includes:

- The media through which the customer was informed about the event or attraction or its activities.
- The specific station or newspaper causing the awareness.
- The messages received through the media, generated on an open-end basis.

- The extent to which the media influenced the visit to the event or attraction.
- In the case of nonresidents or tourists, whether the media exposure occurred before or after leaving home.

Quantitative primary and secondary data of this type can serve to analyze: inter- and intramedia effectiveness as a ratio of cost and awareness; incremental business as a function of temporary product additions; and the extent to which customers would have attended the event or attraction despite the special activities.

KNOWING YOUR NONCUSTOMER— QUANTITATIVE AND QUALITATIVE DATA NEEDED

Identification of the "noncustomer" in relationship to special periods, unlike the identification of the "noncustomer" on a continuous basis, cannot rely on data for the population bases as a whole. Again the resident and nonresident or tourist bases must be addressed directly and the benefits to be derived from such a survey must be carefully considered relative to cost. Information generated from interviewing the "noncustomer" includes: media impact on the entire population; demographics of the "aware" population; and the extent of media impact on the nonresponding regular customer base.

The qualitative data can further serve to identify whether the product, the media, or some other factor contributed these strengths or weaknesses. Data of this type assist in determining the reasons for the response or nonresponse to a period of special activity, which, in the case of the quantitative data, essentially translates into what is commonly known in the consumer product industry as "Standard Advertising Testing."

QUANTITATIVE AND QUALITATIVE DATA NEEDED IN LONG-RANGE PLANNING

Additional data needed on a special basis for predictive reasons relate to the planning of media exposure and to the ways in which these periods of special activity can be adapted to maximize the penetration of the population bases by the event or attraction in the future. Special activities are usually undertaken by an event or attraction to maximize their resident attendance on the basis that the nonresident or tourist population would not be exposed to most of the periods of media or special activities. Although it relates only to the resident base, this research is further addressed for completeness.

Again, the needs from the resident and nonresident or tourist populations differ with quantitative data of this type only needed from the tourist population.

Data relative to quantitative media planning are required from the tourist population to determine the extent to which the individual event or attraction needs to rely on national or even international awareness to secure a place in the itinerary of a tourist entering the geographic area of that event or attraction. Data of this type can only be collected on a national or international level and are naturally also extremely costly. Studies of this type can be of value on an industry basis, and are discussed in the next section.

THE RESEARCH NEEDS OF THE EVENTS AND ATTRACTIONS INDUSTRY

The research needs of the events and attractions industry are equal to those required by individual events and attractions. However, unless the individual events and attractions are organized into a group, the amorphous nature of the industry precludes any research, needed or not. Under ideal conditions the events and attractions industry could provide much of the information already described for its individual members, eliminating the duplication of effort. However, under the extremely competitive conditions, there is considerable resistance to sharing of information. When the information affords the vehicle for enhancement of the customer base and the industry as a whole, at the expense of other leisure time industries, then there is a reason for cooperation. The following section describes the types of information that an organized industry could collect.

KNOWING YOUR INDUSTRIES' CUSTOMERS— QUANTITATIVE AND QUALITATIVE DATA REQUIREMENTS

The first step is to organize existing information about industry members. The organization does exist on a national level, but members are usually defined as those events and attractions within a geographic area. It is very significant to the industry to determine the strengths and weaknesses of their product as perceived by various market bases.

Availability of information depends upon the degree of cooperation and the publication of information for public relations or stockholder reports. Although it is doubtful that events and attractions will share all their individual data, they do have a mutual interest in determining how their products perform as an industry.

The nature of the data to be exchanged is usually limited to attendance rather than financial data. Any information of this type is extremely important in determining if attendance shifts are isolated or industry wide, market share, and external effects such as gasoline price, airline deregulation, or climatic changes. As an example of close cooperation, the Southern California Attractions Industry exchanges the following data: daily percentage shifts in total attendance with the seven largest attractions participating, monthly and yearly percentage shifts in total attendance of all major attractions, and monthly and yearly shifts in market share for all major attractions. To implement this exchange, one attraction takes responsibility for the collection and dissemination of data, in this case Universal Studio Tours (Steinberg 1971–1981).

On a national level, the United States Amusement Park Marketing Association's major attractions, with the exceptions of Disneyland and Disneyworld, exchange actual weekly attendance numbers. The Six Flags Corporation is responsible for this exchange (Delanoy 1972–1981).

The next step is to organize data by demographic components. This exchange will probably only occur very informally on a local level and is dependent on availability of data as well as cooperation. The Southern California Attractions Industry, having close cooperation and available data, has set up a relatively formal exchange at one of six yearly meetings. Also, the Southern California Attractions Industry has organized itself to conduct simultaneous surveys to collect identical data twice to three times a year with the objective of sharing the results. The data collected include: age of guest; geographic residence; party composition; media awareness; pattern of visits between member attractions; drive time to member attractions, arrival time, and length of stay; nonresidents' place of stay in Southern California; and questions relating to industry likes and dislikes.

This information is of significant value in planning the media message for joint media exposure. The data collection is controlled by Knott's Berry Farm, the data processing is undertaken by an outside supplier, and the report is issued on an individual and total basis to the participants (Carey 1972–1981). Although there are serious flaws with the collection techniques, these data become invaluable in determining strengths and weaknesses of individual attractions as well as the industry as a whole.

KNOWING YOUR INDUSTRIES' NONCUSTOMERS—QUANTITATIVE AND QUALITATIVE DATA REQUIREMENTS

Availability of quantitative data about nonresident or tourist populations is dependent upon government involvement. In situations of minimal government involvement, events and attractions are usually very willing to cooperate in generating this data as it benefits them all individually as well as the entire industry.

Southern California has minimal government involvement in collecting tourist demographics and, as well, there is no consensus as to the actual number of

tourists arriving in the area in any one year. Even the nationally available data as issued by the United States Travel Data Center (*Travel Printout*, *National Travel Survey*, and *Quarterly Travel Trends*) do not assist in that it is infrequently collected or reported too long after collection or addresses the entire state of California or addresses domestic arrivals only.

To overcome this problem, the Southern California Attractions Industry formed a committee in conjunction with the Greater Los Angeles Visitor and Conventions Bureau to initiate the collection of all available secondary data in an attempt to piece together a tourist count and profile (Baltin 1978–1981). The California State Office of Tourism later took over this project (Bousseloub 1980). The following information was amassed and indexed: airport arrivals; hotel occupancy rates; attraction attendance; highway travel; and fuel sales.

This index, however, did not give an accurate estimate of tourist numbers, particularly those originating in the United States. In addition, it certainly did not give any indication of tourist demographics or projections for the future. The committee, therefore, decided to initiate its own primary data collection. It was decided that a statistically representative mail panel was the most economical and practical method of data collection in assessing tourism originating in the United States. This is the first time in this chapter, therefore, that research outside the geographic area of the event or attraction has been required. In the case of Southern California, a quantitative assessment of tourism was considered impossible for anyone other than the State Office of Tourism, due mainly to the great number of access highways into the state, which account for a large portion of its tourist entries. The information collected from the mail panel, however, not only allowed quantification of domestic travel to Southern California, but also time of year visit occurred, composition of the tourist party, purpose of the visit, counties within Southern California visited, and future plans to visit Southern California (Haug 1978).

It was also decided by the committee that quantification of foreign tourism to Southern California would have to rely on airport arrival and Mexican border crossing information. This was acknowledged to be inaccurate in that it does not account for any foreign tourist passing through United States customs in any other state, nor does it account for non-Mexican foreign tourists arriving in Southern California by automobile, particularly Canadian nationals and those overseas residents arriving by air in another state. However, it was decided that in conjunction with statistics issued by the United States Department of Commerce (1971-1981), the above data were the only cost-effective way to quantify foreign tourism into Southern California.

These tourist assessments which were initiated in

1978 were repeated in a modified form in 1979 to determine the effects of the gasoline crisis on tourism in Southern California (Haug 1979). The study will be repeated in an expanded way in the future and should provide an invaluable base from which the individual event or attraction, as well as the industry, can determine their strengths and weaknesses relative to the available tourists.

Two pieces of information were still considered to be missing from this tourism assessment by some of the member events and attractions, so they independently sponsored additional primary studies. It was considered extremely important by the member attractions, in planning for industry as well as individual media exposure outside their geographic area, to assess the extent to which the nonresident or potential tourist markets needed to be educated as to the existence of that event, attraction, or industry. It was the feeling of these attractions that with the extremely high costs involved in national or even international media exposure, the media message must address the majority of the population bases.

A mail panel was selected to address awareness for participating attractions on a national level on the basis that domestic tourists already in Southern California would clearly exhibit a higher level of awareness. The information collected not only allowed for quantification of awareness levels, but also visiting history to the participating attractions, source of awareness, and future plans to visit the participating attractions (National Family Opinion, Inc. 1979).

This information became invaluable not only in the determination of media message but also in planning media placement, trade show participation, sales blitzes, publicity blitzes, and travel professional interaction. A second study was jointly sponsored to address the foreign or international tourist for similar reasons. However, the cost of such data collection outside the geographic area of the attraction is prohibitive. Interviewing was therefore conducted, with the acknowledged biases, at airport arrivals and departure terminals throughout California in the native language of the foreign tourist (Moore 1980).

The demographic and psychographic categories of the noncustomer are of interest in determining why these people do not become customers of the industry when they are in the "neighborhood." Although it is doubtful that events and attractions will in fact share such individual data, they do have a mutual interest in expanding their industry's overall attendance base. The Southern California Attractions Industry occasionally conducts spot surveys at area motels and hotels to address this problem among the available tourist base with the objective of sharing data. There is no need for data of this type from the Southern California resident population as it is widely known that almost its entire population base frequents at least one attraction in a year.

IMPLEMENTATION OF THE RESEARCH NEEDS FOR EVENTS AND ATTRACTIONS

Most of the research described in this chapter is conducted on a regular basis by Knott's Berry Farm. This amount of research is considered appropriate for an attraction such as Knott's Berry Farm, whose size, dependence on tourism, and location in a geographic area of minimal state involvement intensify these needs. To implement this amount of research, Knott's Berry Farm employs two research professionals, one clerical, and three interviewing personnel on a full-time basis. With this staff, Knott's Berry Farm's dependence on outside suppliers and nonlabor budgets is minimal despite it not being a member of a multipark corporation.

REFERENCES

Baltin, Bruce (1978–1981), *Southern California Tourism Index*, unpublished report, Pannell Kerr Forester, Los Angeles, California.

Bousseloub, Tiffany (1980), *California Travel Index*, unpublished report, California State Office of Tourism, Los Angeles, California.

Carey, Carolyn (1972–1981), *The Southern California Attractions Visitor Analysis*, unpublished report, Research Department, Knott's Berry Farm, Buena Park, California.

Delanoy, George (1972–1981), *The United States Attractions Marketing Association Attendance Exchange*, unpublished report, Marketing Division, Six Flags Corporation, Los Angeles, California.

Haug, Arne (1978), *Los Angeles/Southern California Vacationers Study*, unpublished report, Haug Associates, Inc., Los Angeles, California.

Haug, Arne (1979), *Southern California Travel Patterns: A Non-resident Visitor Survey*, unpublished report, Haug Associates, Inc., Los Angeles, California.

Moore, William (1980), *A Survey of International Vacationers in the State of California*, unpublished report, Tourmark, Ltd., Los Angeles, California.

National Family Opinion, Inc. (1979), *Awareness Analysis of Selected Southern California Attractions*, unpublished report, National Family Opinion, Inc., San Francisco, California.

Steinberg, Herbert (1971–1981), *The Southern California Attractions Leisure Time Index*, unpublished report, Marketing Division, Universal Studios Tour, Los Angeles, California.

United States Department of Commerce (1971–1981), *Profile Sheets in Major USTS Markets*, Washington, D.C.

United States Travel Data Center (1974–1981), *National Travel Survey*, Washington, D.C.

United States Travel Data Center (Monthly Newsletter), *Travel Printout*, Washington, D.C.

United States Travel Data Center (1980), *Quarterly Travel Trends*, Washington, D.C.

23

Research Needs of the Restaurant Industry

ROBERT P. OLSON

University of Wisconsin— Stout
Minomonic, Wisconsin

UEL BLANK

University of Minnesota
Minneapolis, Minnesota

*T*his chapter provides guidelines for researching the operation of an individual restaurant business or the restaurant industry of a community or region. Restaurants share much in common, hence maximum use should be made of existing industry data. But every individual operation and each community's restaurant industry is unique and must be separately researched. Many of the procedures treated by other chapters in this Handbook are applicable. This chapter brings them into workable focus upon restaurants.

THE ROLE OF RESTAURANTS AND THE FOOD SERVICE INDUSTRY

Food service away from home is essential to tourism. In the Minnesota setting, 30 percent of restaurant sales overall are estimated to be made to tourists. This leaves 70 percent of sales to residents of the local community (Blank and Olson 1982). The proportions will differ in each state, in each community, and for each restaurant.

In communities having a mixed economic base, a major part of the restaurant industry's output can be considered "industry support" (Blank 1982a). Most modern industry requires travel and work at a distance from home, thus restaurants play a required supporting role in providing food for these individuals. In the Minnesota setting, the industry support role is estimated to make up 50 percent of total sales, composed partly of sales to business tourists and partly to residents engaged in work patterns.

Restaurants provide a complex output in performing the above roles. In addition to food and beverage away from home, they provide convenience, communication settings, and a wide variety of outputs contributing to living quality. Among the latter are entertainment/diversion, the sweetening of social and business interactions, and ambiences contributing to variety in living experiences.

To produce its output, each restaurant purchases inputs. It is through these purchases, or "backward linkages" to the community, that the restaurant industry contributes to the local economy. A major type of input is labor, hence the restaurant industry is a major generator of jobs. The group of firms providing food and restaurant supplies has been found to be a substantial source of economic base in itself (Blank 1982c). Restaurants also support the community infrastructure through utility systems and local taxes.

Overall, the food service industry now provides about one-third of the meals eaten in the United States. In addition to its scale, it exhibits a pattern of dynamic growth not only in overall output but also in its employment pattern and in its service types. Table 1 shows a ten-year growth in dollar sales of all food of 165 percent; but "places of refreshment" increased sales by 472 percent. The latter corresponds roughly to short-order food operations. This growth indicates the need for those involved in the industry to remain abreast of current developments.

TABLE 1 Growth of U.S. Food Service 1967 to 1977

	1967	1977	PERCENT CHANGE
Sales			
Food ($ billion)	$23.8	$63.8	+165
All retail ($ billion)	310.2	723.1	+133
Employment			
Food (million)	2.4	4.1	+71
Employed U.S. (million)	74.4	90.5	+22
Places of Refreshment			
Sales ($ billion)	$3.4	$19.5	+472
Employment (thousands)	296.0	1157.0	+291

Source: U.S. Census of Business 1967, 1977.

DEFINITIONS: KNOW WHAT YOU ARE DEALING WITH!

Restaurants are part of an industry system, providing services to people away from home, that becomes progressively more general and broader as it moves from restaurants to food services to hospitality industry. Each of these is defined and discussed briefly below. A clear definition specifically applicable to each research situation should be devised by the research manager.

There can be and are many definitions for a *restaurant*. A place where food is served may be too broad. A place that serves food to the public is more restrictive and may be the appropriate one under some situations. If this is still too inclusive, how about a place of business serving food to customers with inside dining?

As we discuss travel/tourism-related research in this chapter, restaurants will be defined as enterprises having the following attributes.

- A commercial operation.
- Prepares and/or sells food (meals and snacks) to customers for consumption on premises (it may also provide take-out service).
- Open to the general public and/or restricted clientele, such as members. The element of choice on the part of the patron is a necessary but not sufficient consideration.
- Operates on a continuous basis (may close seasonally).

The term *food service* (or food and beverage service) is generally broader in scope than restaurant. It is often used to refer to all operations serving food (and/or beverages) to people away from home. As such, a food service not only includes restaurants as defined above but also hospitals and nursing homes, various kinds of noncommercial institutional food services, and sometimes occasional food services such as that provided by a church.

The *hospitality* industry is often defined as those businesses serving people away from home. The difference between hospitality and tourism is that in the case of the former, the operations are specialized to serve people away from home (department stores may be a part of tourism but not hospitality) and a hospitality service may occur in the home area or work area. A restaurant illustrates the distinction—it is always a part of the hospitality industry, but only that part of sales to people away from their usual residence or work area can be considered tourism. There is no universal framework recognized by governmental agencies, practitioners, or academicians that defines precisely hospitality industry components. Despite this, the classification as an industry generally holds. A common reference is to the hospitality service industries—the plural form denoting a collection including food services, lodging services, resorts, recreation centers, festivals, camps, attractions, and related operations.

The "service" aspect applied to restaurants, food services, and hospitality operations suggests a conscious level of appeal or dedication to those away from home. It also suggests the absence of a tangible product for ownership or consumption. The meal one purchases is a "product" accompanied by "services" that are necessary, rendered, and utilized for the execution of the complete transaction.

RESEARCHING THE INDIVIDUAL RESTAURANT OPERATION

WHO NEEDS INFORMATION ABOUT A RESTAURANT?

People requiring restaurant information will range from the owner or manager to its suppliers of goods and services, the financial sector, governmental and regulatory agencies, the business community, various associations, and the general public. Each of these will host different views of both the restaurant industry and individual restaurants, hence their research interests and needs will differ.

Managers, owners, and investors in a given restaurant need information to monitor ongoing operations and to guide potential improvements in markets and/or internal operations. Since each restaurant has a unique market and labor force, data from that individual operation or applying directly to it must be used in making decisions concerning marketing and operations.

MANAGER RESEARCH—MONITORING THE ONGOING OPERATION

Restaurant managers want to know how well the operation is doing in relation to

- Previous time periods
- Comparable units classed by size, type, geographic location, etc.
- Industry standards or averages
- What may be possible or desirable.

The comparisons could include such things as sales, market patterns, expenditures, productivity, energy usage, employee turnover, and many other enterprise-related questions.

A wealth of valuable data already exists in most, if not all, restaurants and it should not be overlooked. It would be prudent to review existing records to determine if they are current, complete, and accurate. In-house records should be organized to mesh with industry standards and norms so that meaningful comparisons can be made. Examples of restaurant records would be guest checks, sales records, banquet/group folios, accounting records and reports, production schedules, employee records, and purchase orders.

A number of questions need to be asked. Probably the most important is, who is going to use the information and for what purpose? Others are

- Are sales composed of food only, or is revenue from alcoholic beverages included?

- Are banquet and/or carry-away sales included, and should they be?
- Are guest checks used for all defined sales?
- Has the use of guest checks been consistently applied during the time period?
- Are there factors that inflate or deflate the average, such as lost or otherwise unaccounted for checks?
- Is a single guest check used for hundreds of people or dollars in group sales?
- Do units to which comparisons are to be made follow the same conventions?
- What is the accepted and preferred practice?

MANAGER RESEARCH—SALES AND SALES POTENTIAL

Another major concern of the manager is sales or the operation's sales potential, the latter term being the perceived share of the potential market. This potential market is defined as the total expected sales in a given geographic area for a measured period of time. A manager might want to increase sales. Reliable information concerning the market would be necessary to make a determination as to who the potential customers are, how many, and where they are located, along with their principal characteristics.

It may seem that everyone is a potential customer because everyone eats. This is not the case. It is important to be able to select out of the masses those with the inclination and resources to patronize a given restaurant. In planning sales and market research, the reader is referred to Part Two of the Handbook (especially Chapter 6), which deals with demand estimation, and Jane Fitzgibbon's chapter (Chapter 42) on market segmentation.

CONDUCTING A STUDY TO ESTIMATE MARKET POTENTIAL

One approach is to arrive at a description or profile of present satisfied patrons and use this to locate others that are similar in critical attributes. It is usually necessary to conduct a survey or study of present customers to determine their important characteristics. Principal ones are age, sex, education, occupation, income, marital status, and location of residence and/or workplace.

Surveys provide original data and may be conducted on site by personal contact, via a mail-out-return instrument, or by telephone. Other ways of gathering information may be the use of a guest register, prize drawings, or redemption of incentive coupons.

Data are usually gathered with the aid of a formal questionnaire (or instrument) in which information such as residence (state, city, zip code), menu preference, mode of travel to the restaurant, distance traveled, frequency of patronage, frequency of eating out, and much more may be requested. The hazard, of course, is that a questionnaire that is too long, complex, or personal may not be answered and, in fact, be a "turn-off." It is preferable to seek only the information that is necessary and immediately useful.

A survey is often a part of a larger research effort. Before undertaking a survey, all available information pertaining to the question should be gathered from secondary sources.

Since skills and finances are usually limited, it is important to employ all appropriate resources to accomplish the survey. These resources may be the manager and staff, specialized research firms, and individual consultants for part or all of the project.

It is desirable to seek counsel and assistance from a variety of sources, such as other owners or managers, trade associations, chambers of commerce, professional groups, governmental agencies, faculty of colleges and universities, and Service Core of Retired Executives (SCORE).

EXISTING DATA SOURCES

Before conducting a survey of a specific restaurant operation, there should be familiarity with existing sources of information. These are given in Table 2 of this chapter and in Chapter 15 by Charles Goeldner on data sources in tourism.

Data from existing sources can often be used as a preliminary or partial guide to operation of a given restaurant. Study of these data can also indicate what is considered relevant by management experts. In making comparisons of data from a specific restaurant with data from other existing sources, it is important that the same kinds of observations are being compared. Thus the implicit definitions contained in both sets of data must be well understood by the user.

PUTTING THE FINDINGS TO WORK

Data generated from research of a restaurant's operation do no good unless it is put to work. This is the

---

TABLE 2   Sources of Existing Restaurant Industry Information

A   United States Government Data and Research Methods

DEPARTMENT	BUREAU	PUBLICATION	TYPE OF DATA
Commerce	Census	Census of Population	Population, income, employment
		Current Population Reports	Population, income
		Population Estimates	Population
		Census of Business: Retail, Wholesale, Manufacturers, Selected Services	Employment, sales, number of businesses
		County Business Patterns	Employment
		Retail Trade Reports	Sales
		Wholesale Trade Reports	Sales
		Statistical Abstract	Varied
	Economic Analysis	Survey of Current Businesses	Income, sales, employment
Labor	Labor Statistics	Employment and Earnings	Employment, income
		Area Trends in Employment and Unemployment	Employment
Treasury	Internal Revenue Service	Statistics of Income: Individuals, businesses	Income, sales, taxes
Agriculture	Agricultural Research Service	Marketing Research Reports	Operating costs, labor requirement; food consumption, equipment; utilization and other selected topics.

TABLE 2 *(Continued)*

B *Canadian Government Data and Research Methods Sources*

DEPARTMENT	BUREAU	PUBLICATION	TYPE OF DATA
Industry, Trade, and Commerce	Office of Tourism: Marketing Research, Policy Planning, and Coordination Division	Special Reports Travel Trends Many others	Varied Food and beverage expenditures Trip purpose and travel modes Varied and comprehensive
	Statistics Canada: User Services	Restaurant, Caterer & Taverns Industry Survey	Food and beverage sales Numbers and kinds of restaurants and other food services
		Urban Family Food Expenditure Survey	Family restaurant expenditures
		Travel, Tourism, and Outdoor Recreation	Travel economics
		Canadian Travel Survey	Socioeconomic data on travel
Agriculture Canada	Food Markets Analysis Division	Food Market Commentary	Updates on expenditures for restaurant food

C *State and Provincial Data and Research Methods Sources*

TYPE OF DATA	POSSIBLE TITLES	POSSIBLE AGENCY NAMES
Population	Vital Statistics Population Reports Population Estimates	Health Department Department of Economic Development
Income	Economic Report Personal Income Per Capita Income	Department of Economics & Business Department of Administration Department of Revenue
Employment	Employment and Payroll Work Force Estimates Labor Market Statistics	Department of Employment Security Department of Human Resources Department of Manpower
Sales and Tax	Sales and Use Tax	Department of Revenue Department of Taxation Department of Treasury Department of Industry Department of Tourism Department of Travel

D *Government and Community Data and Research Methods Sources*

SOURCE	CONTACT	LOCATION
U.S. Department of Agriculture	Extension Service Statistical Reporting Service Agricultural Research Service	Washington, D.C.
Colleges and Universities	Cooperative Extension Service Faculty	Land grant universities
	Researchers in business	State universities and colleges
	Schools and Economics Departments	Community colleges
Libraries	Research librarian Electronic data librarian Professional journals Trade publications	Public and educational institution libraries

TABLE 2 *(Continued)*

E   Private Data and Research Methods Sources

ORGANIZATION TYPE	POSSIBLE TITLE	TYPE OF DATA
Accounting Firms	The Restaurant Industry (for city, region or county)	Numbers of operations, employees, total sales
	The International Restaurant	Trends in overall sales by type of operation
		Kinds of sales (food, beverages)
		Analysis of sales (per seat, per employee, etc.)
Publishing Firms	Magazine articles and reports of food services	Total sales, number of operations services
		Employment by firm categories or geographic regions
		Rankings by sales or number of operations
General Management and Restaurant Consultant Firms	Proprietary, may cover a wide range of topics, use only with permission.	May treat any type of restaurant industry and operating data
Professional and Trade Associations	Restaurant Association (national, state, local) Food Service Society Hospitality Association	May collect and disseminate membership and industry-wide data

payoff—what has been learned that can improve the restaurant's operation and marketing?

Use of the data depends, of course, upon the problem as originally defined. Problems could have been as widely different as efficiency of sales per employee, shrinkage of supplies, or employee turnover. Rather than treating all of the possible range, one example illustrating use of information from market research will be discussed.

Market research would deal with some of the following questions.

Who are the present customers?

Most restaurants, over time, have been able to appeal to and attract a relatively homogeneous clientele. This is an important ingredient to being successful. The purpose of conducting a survey is to develop a profile of present patronage.

Once a manager has a good understanding of who (by attributes) the customers are and that there will be no major change in the operation of the restaurant such as location, ambience, menu, services offered, etc., it is possible to locate and measure the potential market.

Who are the potential customers?

Potential customers can be defined as those persons in the population that are similar to present satisfied customers. This relationship underscores the importance of hav-

ing a well conducted survey based on a professionally designed survey instrument that accurately samples your present customers and their degree of satisfaction.

Fortunately, the important socioeconomic characteristics of the general population are readily available from a number of state and federal governmental sources which are listed in Table 2. These data sources make it possible to determine how many persons with selected characteristics are to be found in a given geographic area, such as state, province, county, or even census tract.

How can they be reached?

Knowing the size and location of the target group then begs the questions—How can I tell and sell them? There is no standard formula that can be applied to all situations to generate customers. Reaching potential customers with a marketing message will take a commitment of time, energy, and financial resources. The mix of these ingredients will vary depending upon, among other things, the marketing objectives, staff skills available, and funds to be dedicated.

Some of the ways to reach people are by radio, television, newspapers, other periodicals, speciality publications, direct mail, and handbills. Often, several approaches are necessary to realize expected results. It is wise to seek out professional assistance to design a marketing program.

Are there enough potential customers?   One may find out, after conducting a survey and analyzing the population data, that there are too few persons of the type that you are seeking. It may not be possible to satisfactorily increase customer count even if a disproportionately large share of those available were attracted.

Should this be the case, it would probably be advisable to carve out a different niche in the market and appeal to a different and larger or more responsive clientele.

RESEARCHING THE RESTAURANT INDUSTRY

In many situations, information is needed about not just one restaurant but about the restaurant industry of a community or region.

PLANNING FOR RESTAURANT INDUSTRY RESEARCH

Research of a community's restaurant industry must begin with a full understanding of the research purposes and the possible limitations to which it may be subject. It is suggested that three specific, interrelated questions be addressed as part of the planning process.

Who wants to know about the restaurant industry and what use do they plan for the information?   This question deals primarily with purpose—what questions are to be answered. The kinds of restaurant industry interests may vary widely and include such divergent groups as

- Restaurant industry leadership having interests in showing overall economic impact upon the community.
- Tourism development interests seeking information about tourism sales by the restaurants, or seeking means for better service to tourists.
- Potential investors investigating food service markets for the area and how well they are currently served.
- Restaurant users needing to know what types and qualities of eating experiences are available.
- Restaurant supply and service firms wanting to know the market for their services or products.
- Those having interests in employment opportunities, labor needs, manpower training, and teenage employment.
- Government agencies treating public health, etc.

All of the above and many others are possible research interests. No one study can supply information needs of all of these. To be certain that necessary questions

are treated, it is necessary to carefully define purposes at the outset, and then redefine them as progress into the research process dictates. (For example, it may be found that objectives must be scaled down to stay within cost limits.)

What is the applicable restaurant industry?   As purposes are defined, the industry to be studied will also be defined. One dimension is geographic: Is interest focused upon only a municipal neighborhood? A county? A Standard Metropolitan Statistical Area (SMSA)? An entire state or province? The way in which existing data are aggregated, such as by county, may influence this decision. Another question asks what components of the food service industry are to be included? If, for example, the purpose is to estimate supply needs, it may be desirable to include not only commercial operations but also in-plant feeders and not-for-profit institutional operations.

What data will be collected and how will this be done?   Having dealt with the "why" and "who" above, the "what" and "how" questions now involve the heart of the restaurant industry research process. The "what" and "how" require that one confront two issues: first, can "secondary data" (data collected and published by others) be used or must "primary data" (data which one collects) be gathered? The second issue asks if the actual research will be contracted or done by the person wanting the information. In considering these and related issues of "what" and "how" another set of interrelated questions must be dealt with. These must be considered by the person or organization making the basic decisions about the research and authorizing it, whether the actual work is contracted to another individual or firm or conducted in-house.

- What specific questions require answers? The precise information needs must be spelled out. These, in turn, determine what data are useful and dictate the nature of any new (primary) data gathered.
- How much time is available? If results are needed within one month, there is usually not time to gather new data and already existing information must be used.
- How much money is available? Available resources, together with time constraints, will often dictate how extensive the research can be and whether or not it must be done in-house using staff resources.
- How accurate must the findings be? A first response might be that any study should discover the truth! In fact, all data have limitations to their accuracy. If sales trends are to be charted, they will require reasonably accurate, consistent data. On

the other hand, estimates of demand for a new type of food offering may tolerate a modest margin of error.

- Does the information needed already exist? Needless time and effort can be spent gathering data or assembling it from partial sources when the job, or most of it, already has been done. In many studies, combinations of secondary and primary data are used.

EXISTING DATA SOURCES

The last question makes clear that any restaurant industry researcher must investigate fully the existing sources of information. Even in cases where primary data will be gathered, it is almost always necessary to use secondary data in the research design stages and to support and add further depth to primary research findings. Table 2 gives suggestions for sources of existing data that are specific to the restaurant industry. The reader should also consult Chapter 15 by Charles Goeldner in this Handbook.

Any data or conclusions about the restaurant industry from existing sources must be scrutinized for *relevance* and *accuracy* in deciding how to use them. Sometimes secondary restaurant industry data may be used as partial guides, even though they are not judged as fully relevant and/or accurate. *Relevance* as used here means "Are the definitions implied in the data compatible with your purposes and needs?" Every set of data has a built-in definition of industry, dependent upon how the information was collected. For example, (a) if a given state only licensed restaurants in communities of 2,500 or more, such a license list would contain few rural restaurants; (b) some restaurant lists include operations primarily serving alcoholic beverages, do these types fit your needs? and (c) many compilations may define a motel with a restaurant as either "lodging" or "food service" depending upon whichever sales figure is larger, thus all sales from both categories are attributed to the one business type. *Accuracy* can only be guaranteed by ensuring that proper statistical procedures were followed in compiling the data, and that the restaurant population of interest was sampled. In this step, the services of a statistician skilled in sampling and survey methods is a must. If a full picture of a city's restaurant industry is needed, it should be understood that this cannot be obtained simply from a few restaurants in the central business district or from the managers present at a local restaurant association meeting. Neither of these represent well the full range of the city's restaurant industry, and conclusions from such a survey could be misleading.

CONDUCTING YOUR OWN SURVEY

Despite the wealth of data that is available about the restaurant industry, a decision to gather primary data

might be made. There are a number of situations demanding this course.

- The restaurant industry of each community, state, or province is unique. A comprehensive description of your restaurant industry can only be obtained by gathering primary data.
- Specific qualitative data that are not available elsewhere might be needed. For example: The nature and composition of the restaurant work force. In studying the Minnesota food service industry, it was discovered that as many as one-fourth of the young people may have their first major employment experience in a restaurant.

Chapter 6 goes into extensive detail on how to set up research. This is very applicable to restaurant industry research.

MARKET AND EMPLOYEE STUDIES

As noted above, restaurant market and employee studies may be carried out through the restaurants. Often the firms already have a substantial amount of information about their markets and/or employees. In addition, a sampling may be made of customers while they are in the restaurant. Employees may be interviewed in person while in the restaurant or they may be interviewed at home, by mail, by telephone, or in person.

Market studies may also involve household surveys in the community, possibly combined with surveys of tourists (who, by definition, are not community residents).

Employee studies may also be conducted through household surveys. This is the origin of census of population employment data and of some labor/industry agency data.

PUTTING RESTAURANT INDUSTRY FINDINGS TO WORK

Time, effort, and money will have been invested in a study of a community's (city, county, state, or province) restaurant industry. What use will be made of it? Of what value to the industry will it be?

Part of the usefulness depends upon how well the purposes have been defined, how accurate and usable the data are, and how good an analysis has been made of the data. These original perceived needs for the research should direct use of the improved information that is now on hand. Important uses include:

- Highlighting the value of the restaurant industry, such as in terms of sales dollars, employment, and contribution to community living. Improved understanding can contribute to general public relations, restaurant association membership support, and appropriate restaurant industry legislation.
- Helping in managing the industry and directing its development

—regarding developing new markets among restaurants, local firms, and community tourists

—regarding promotion needs and practices

—regarding types of restaurant services needed

—regarding employment needs and employment legislation

—regarding supply systems, financing, and business management aids

—regarding the safeguarding of public health.

SPREAD THE WORD

Assuming that purposes have adequately been set up and research properly executed, there is much more to be done, that is, to get findings into the hands of those who can and will use them.

The first step toward getting the data into use started at the beginning—all of those who were expected to use the findings should have had a hand, or at least been represented, in setting up the purposes. They should have been updated regularly as progress was made and given opportunity to contribute to inputs of data. Finally, they should have been challenged to help interpret the data into usable terms. This requires major communications procedures, such as newsletters (perhaps an existing one can be used) or regular reports at association meetings.

A report of the findings should be published as early as possible. Consider a set of publications, each part covering a given special interest item, or each addressed to a specific audience. Use media to release some of the findings. Possibly a media event, such as a press conference, would be in order.

Perhaps the material can be used with managers and others in a workshop where it is combined with other inputs to help in management, legislative, and other decisions.

EXAMPLES OF FOOD SERVICE RESEARCH

CREST (Consumer Reports on Eating Share Trends) was initiated in 1974 by the National Restaurant Association (NRA) to learn about consumer attitude and behavior in the market place. These periodic studies gather data from national representative panels using mail surveys.

Some of the specific reports have dealt with topics such as:

- Consumer attitudes.
- Lifestyle and economic issues.
- Take-out purchases.
- Meal/snack purchases.
- Business travelers.
- Coffee shops.
- Fast food restaurants.

Restaurant Operation Report is published annually on a cooperative basis by the National Restaurant Association and Laventhal & Horwath, an international accounting firm.

Data presented are based on survey instruments sent to NRA members. Computation and analysis consider tenure of operation, type, location, sales, expenses, size, employment, and other characteristics.

The report is not intended to reflect standards but rather to present summaries that may be useful to managers as they consider their own enterprises.

Minnesota's Food Service Industry Study   This study was conducted by the hospitality group of the Agricultural Extension Service, University of Minnesota. It was designed to be a comprehensive study of all regularly operating food services in Minnesota, thus it covers not-for-profit as well as for-profit food operations. It was a mail survey to a sample of about one-third of all licensed establishments. About a 50 percent response rate was achieved. It gathered information about the types of operations, their age, size, employment, markets, advertising programs, and energy-conserving programs. Data are aggregated by types and by Minnesota development regions and tourism regions.

The Food Service Industry   This study of U.S. food service was conducted by the Marketing Economics Division, ERS, USDA. It was done by means of personal interviews with a national sample of 3,000 U.S. food service operations. It gathered overall data about sales by types. It especially concentrated upon kinds and quantities of food used by type and size of food service establishment.

Market Surveys of Individual Restaurants   As a service to local restaurants, the hospitality group at the University of Minnesota conducts a limited number of market studies for individual restaurants.

These are done by means of a one-page questionnaire which is completed by patrons while they are in the restaurant. A predetermined number of questionnaires are distributed on a random pattern throughout an entire week. These may be handled by the waitresses, by the cashier, or by university students.

Data are tabulated and results prepared by students and staff of the university. Reports are released to the management of participating restaurants on a confidential basis.

REFERENCES

Anon. (1974), *Youth and the Meaning of Work.* Manpower Research Monograph No. 32, U.S. Department of Labor, Manpower Administration.

Anon. (1976), *New Labor Force Projections to 1990.* Special

Labor Force Report 197, BLS, U.S. Department of Labor.

Anon. (1980), *Food Market Commentary*. Food Markets Analysis Division, Agriculture Canada. Vol. 2, No. 1, March 1980.

Anon. (1982a), *Minnesota Analysis and Planning Newsletter*. Vol. 14, No. 1, 1982. University of Minnesota.

Anon. (1982b), *Restaurants & Institutions Magazine*. Vol. 91, No. 1, July 1, 1982, p. 36.

Blank, Uel (1982a), *Life Style—Tourism Interrelationship of Minneapolis-St. Paul Residents*. Staff Paper 82. Department of Agriculture & Applied Economics, University of Minnesota, July 1982.

Blank, Uel (1982b). "Interrelationships of the Food Service Industry with the Community," *The Practice of Hospitality Management*. AVI Publishing Company, Westport, Connecticut.

Blank, Uel (1982c). *Minnesota's Food Service Industry Supply System*. Staff Paper P82-6, Department of Agriculture & Applied Economics, University of Minnesota.

Blank, Uel and Robert Olson (1982), *The Food Service Industry—A Major Minnesota Economic Sector*. Staff Paper P82, Department of Agriculture & Applied Economics, University of Minnesota.

Drake, Willis (1982), "Back-to-Basics Job Creation Lesson Needed," *St. Paul Pioneer Press*. July 18, 1982, p. 4G.

Fay, Clifford T., Jr., Richard C. Rhoads, and Robert L. Rosenblatt (1971), *Managerial Accounting for the Hospitality Service Industries*. Wm. C. Brown, Dubuque, Iowa.

Powers, Thomas F. (1979), *Introduction to Management in the Hospitality Industry*. John Wiley & Sons, New York.

Van Dress, Michael G. (1971), *The Food Service Industry: Type, Quantity & Value of Foods Used*. Statistical Bulletin No. 476, Marketing Economics Division, Economics Research Service, USDA.

24

Tourism Research Needs in the Personal Transportation Modes

LAWRENCE F. CUNNINGHAM

Associate Professor
Marketing and Transportation
University of Colorado
Denver, Colorado

LYONNEL J. BARCLAY

Research Associate
American International University
Glendale, Arizona

There are many research and institutional issues connected with the study of tourism using the personal transportation modes in general and the personal motor vehicle modes in particular. The research issues include determining the identity of the motor vehicle tourist, developing information and data bases about market segments of the personal motor vehicle tourist, exploring his/her planning and decision making, identifying the timing of personal motor vehicle tourist trips, uncovering data about trip habits, and investigating personal motor vehicle tourism research. There are also a number of institutional issues facing personal motor vehicle tourism researchers which inhibit their efforts. These issues include the role of the federal government in providing financial support for continued data collection by federal agencies. The consequences of this federal action are adversely affecting the quality of present research and will have a similar effect on future research as well. Another important issue is the lack of overall research policies and direction at the international, federal, state, and local levels. This chapter seeks to explore these issues and to propose insights and ways to deal with them.

INTRODUCTION

This chapter will seek to identify the major research issues and needs confronting researchers studying personal motor vehicle tourism. Personal forms of transportation appear most frequently in the highway mode, but also include certain forms of water and air transportation. Personal forms of highway transportation include the automobile, recreational vehicle, motorcycle, and even the bicycle. Personal water transportation forms include privately owned motorized boats and sailing vessels. Personal air transportation

modes consist of privately owned aircraft which are used for private enjoyment or personal business.

From an overall perspective, the privately owned auto and, to a more limited extent, recreational vehicles account for the majority of tourism expenditures by travelers using the personal transportation modes. For example, in 1982, all forms of automotive tourism generated total expenditures of $22 billion, surpassing the tourism-related expenditures of all other modes of transportation (Mina 1985).

In the context of this chapter, the term "personal motor vehicle" will encompass such personal highway

291

transportation modes as automobiles and recreational vehicles and will exclude other modes such as motorcycles, boats, and other segments having only minimal tourism-related impact.

CHAPTER SCOPE

The identification of future research needs in the area of personal motor vehicle tourism requires a careful examination of work conducted by international organizations as well as by governmental and private-sector organizations and agencies within the United States. At the international level, the chapter examines current research activities conducted by the United Nations, the Organization for Economic Cooperation and Development (OECD), and the countries of Canada and Mexico.

Domestically, the analysis examines research conducted by various agencies of the federal government, such as the U.S. Bureau of the Census and the U.S. Trade and Tourism Administration (formerly the U.S. Travel Service)—both branches of the U.S. Department of Commerce—as well as by the U.S. Department of Transportation. It also entails a careful examination of the research activities of such private and non-private organizations as the U.S. Travel Data Center, the Travel Industry Association of America (formerly the Discover America Travel Organization), and the American Automobile Association, among others.

In addition, the analysis includes a review of current research needs and future research directions of tourism offices and departments of transportation on the state level, as well as the research activities and requirements of private-sector firms, such as hotels and car rental companies, and such auxiliary services as magazines, advertising agencies, and consulting firms. The fundamental questions posed are the following.

1 What are the priorities for research in personal motor vehicle tourism?

2 What are the major institutional issues which inhibit addressing or attaining these research priorities?

PRIORITIES FOR RESEARCH ISSUES IN PERSONAL MOTOR VEHICLE TOURISM

WHO IS THE PERSONAL MOTOR VEHICLE TOURIST?

There is an extensive data base at the federal and national levels describing auto/truck and recreational vehicle trips and travelers in terms of demographics, as well as from the perspective of trip purpose.

Basically, the following trends emerge.

- Nearly 65% of auto travelers who undertook auto/truck trips had incomes less than $30,000 (U.S. Travel Data Center 1984).

- White travelers seemed to dominate auto/truck trips in proportions substantially in excess of normal population distributions (Bureau of the Census 1979).

- Trip-taking activity seemed to decline as individuals moved into older age categories. For example, 1983 study results indicate that individuals between 25 and 34 accounted for approximately 20% of all person-trips (a person-trip is one person taking one trip; a family of four traveling together would account for one trip and four person-trips), while individuals between 35 and 44 and 45 and 54 years of age accounted for 18% and 12% of all person-trips, respectively (U.S. Travel Data Center 1984).

- Auto trip-takers represented a lower proportion of noncollege graduates compared to trip-takers using other modes of transportation such as air, where college graduates were predominant. This seemed to be the case for both business and recreational travel (U.S. Travel Data Center 1984).

- From the perspective of family life cycle, nonmarried and married individuals without children were responsible for a large percentage of family travel in terms of miles. Families with children between 16 and 22 years of age were also responsible for a substantial percentage of trip-taking (Zimmerman 1981).

- Seventy-two percent of all travelers own their own homes (U.S. Travel Data Center 1984).

- The number of persons who typically undertook such trips alone constituted the largest percentage of trip-takers (U.S. Travel Data Center 1984). Seventy-three percent of all personal motor vehicle trips were taken by two persons or less. A small percentage (5%) of these auto/truck/RV trip-takers included five or more travel companions (U.S. Travel Data Center 1984).

- Travel parties in a majority (75%) of household trips involved no individuals under 18 years of age (U.S. Travel Data Center 1984).

- Personal motor vehicle occupancy was higher for recreational travel than for any other trip purpose, standing at 2.44 persons per vehicle versus 1.32 persons per vehicle for work-related travel and 1.95 persons per vehicle for educational and religious travel. As could be expected, the rate of vehicle occupancy increased as household income decreased and as size of the household expanded (Kuzmyak 1981b).

However, these data do not describe the personal mo-

tor vehicle tourist, but rather a sample of all travelers. Both federal agencies and national organizations have sought to maximize knowledge of the motor vehicle tourist by surveying travelers undertaking trips of 100 miles or more. Yet this research approach provides only limited understanding of who the motor vehicle tourist is.

The key challenge for researchers at the federal, state, and local political levels is to develop research approaches which focus on the personal motor vehicle *tourist*, as well as to develop a "richer" understanding of the individual(s). For example, market researchers recognized some years ago that it was impossible to predict potential purchasers based on demographic data. These researchers realized that greater predictability would likely ensue from a better understanding of the major facets of a purchaser's lifestyle or psychographics. Psychographics is a technique utilized by market researchers to measure lifestyle. It involves measuring the activities, interests, and opinions of subjects (A.I.O.).

Two basic types of A.I.O. questions or statements are used in psychographic research. One type, which is more common, employs general lifestyle items designed to ascertain the patterns or basic constructs that affect a person's activities and perceptual processes. These general statements provide market researchers with the opportunity to analyze an individual's overall perspective with regard to satisfaction with life, family orientation, price vs. quality trade-offs, levels of self-esteem, and attitude towards religion.

Psychographic or lifestyle research also includes questions or statements that seek to measure activities, interests, and opinions which are product-related. The specific approach may request information such as attitudes towards a product class, as well as frequency of use of a product or service, and media in which information is sought, etc.

While researchers can continue to work with existing demographic data bases until additional funds are available for the development of more specialized data bases, the current activity levels in the psychographic and attitudinal areas are minimal in the public, non-profit, and private sectors. Only one state (Massachusetts) has recently conducted psychographic research. At this time, attitudinal research regarding the motor vehicle tourist is conducted by only a limited number of states.

The best psychographic research that has been conducted is, to a large extent, either out of date or of a proprietary nature, rendering it unavailable for public consumption. One of the pioneering efforts in psychographics was a survey conducted by the 3M National Advertising Company, which combined demographics with limited psychographic evaluations of the auto traveler. The results were published only up to 1973. It is worth mentioning that no single private entity has duplicated 3M's past efforts in embracing a more effective micro and attitudinal approach intended to better understand auto travelers (1970a, 1972).

Some of the most pertinent and current psychographic research is being undertaken by Best Western International, a firm in the lodging industry. Their studies are designed to determine the relationship between psychographic properties of automobile travelers and the importance of roadside attractions along Interstate 80 between Chicago and San Francisco. While Best Western's activities appear to be the only current psychographic research in the area of motor vehicle tourism being conducted by either the public or private sectors, it is confidential and thus unavailable for public consumption (Wickliffe 1983).

In conclusion, a "richer" understanding of the motor vehicle tourist is likely to result only when federal and state data bases reflect a universe which more closely resembles the motor vehicle tourist and when researchers devote more attention to psychographic and attitudinal factors. In essence, psychographic and attitudinal analyses of more pertinent universes not only will tell us more about who the personal motor vehicle tourist is, but, more importantly, will also serve as prerequisites to the effective targeting of marketing resources.

WHAT ARE THE MAJOR MARKET SEGMENTS AMONG PERSONAL MOTOR VEHICLE TOURISTS?

Studies which have been conducted at the federal and national levels have provided an excellent working knowledge of personal motor vehicle travelers from an overall perspective. However, there is little knowledge regarding the various segments of motor vehicle tourists. Not only is demographic and psychographic information regarding these segments inadequate, but there is little information regarding the product attributes which are attractive to various segments.

It is reasonable to expect that certain market segments would find certain bundles of product attributes highly desirable. For example, recreational vehicle tourists might find different combinations of destinations, facilities, outdoor activities, and accessory services attractive, depending on their stage in life, marital status, number of children, hobbies, and ways in which they wish to spend their leisure time. Unfortunately, there is little empirical evidence beyond isolated studies to link these segments with product attributes.

The lack of market segment information cripples the research activities of members of both the academic and business communities. From the perspective of the academic researcher, there is a limited data base for use in developing hypotheses which describe the relationship between market segments and product attributes. Hence, valuable research resources are wasted on hypotheses which would be discarded in the presence of a better data base.

The lack of information is also a difficult problem for the business community. Market analysts who are assigned the task of determining the market segments which will buy particular tourism products will find the secondary data base highly limited. Besides limitations in the depth of secondary knowledge about market segments, there is also a certain awkwardness in the use of such information by business analysts. For example, in linking market segments to bundles of product attributes, the analyst would be forced to use a "top-down" and "bottom-up" approach. The analyst would descend through macrolevel data in an attempt to identify the specific gaps in the information base as they relate to the research objective. At the same time, the analyst would also have to piece together an information picture of a segment or segments from several isolated and unrelated studies of micro issues.

The limitation in the scope of the data and the awkward research approach suggest that the cost of such research at the segment level is highly inflated in comparison with the cost of identifying market segments in other consumer research involving nontourism topics. The limitation also suggests that research in personal motor vehicle tourism requires significant marketing research skills because of these problems.

While the Reagan administration would suggest that academic and business researchers are able to justify the additional cost of acquiring information because of sponsor need or the chance for profit, the limitations in available data impose additional costs on many governmental users as well. It is probably even possible to stretch the cost-shifting argument to suggest that state government and, hence, the people of a state should pay the cost of attracting tourists. Unfortunately, the cost-shifting argument completely ignores the fact that tourism from the state perspective is often interstate commerce. As such, federal involvement is at least justified and perhaps warranted. It is also interesting to note that tourism is a mechanism which generates employment in states and which often lowers the need for federal assistance in such areas as employment training for the unskilled. However, the most important argument against cost-shifting is that private sector, university, and state researchers may have neither the capability nor the statutory authority to undertake either the data collection or the analysis.

PLANNING AND DECISION MAKING

The first two potential research areas which have been discussed have basically entailed an extension of existing research activities. A third area for future research involves planning and decision making on the part of the personal motor vehicle tourist. The existing data

and body of knowledge about this subject, at least in terms of publicly available studies, are extremely limited. What knowledge there is has been dependent upon specific tourism studies and general principles based on consumer behavior models developed by marketing theorists. Unfortunately, such studies have been extremely limited, and the general principles of consumer behavior are too broad to be of much value. In short, very little is known about how individuals go about planning their trips.

This lack of information is at least partially the result of the minor role played by intermediaries in the planning and decision-making process of motor vehicle travelers. While tourists using other modes of transport often consult with a transport company representative or with a travel agent at some stage of the decision-making process, the motor vehicle tourist usually plans his or her trip in private, with little assistance from intermediaries. This is unfortunate from the standpoint of researchers, as intermediaries often serve as a fertile ground for the collection of primary data at reasonable costs.

Intermediaries sometimes used or contacted by personal motor vehicle tourists, which might be tapped by researchers, include state tourism offices, the American Automobile Association, and those conducting roadside surveys. However, such data should be treated with some suspicion, since those patronizing or responding to such intermediaries may prove to be members of self-selecting samples.

An alternative method for gathering planning and decision-making data about the personal motor vehicle tourist would involve sampling the general public. Essentially, this is the technique used by the Census Bureau and the Federal Highway Administration to gather data. However, such a technique is expensive.

One area of study that researchers might focus upon is that of family influence. Family influence constitutes an important element of planning and decision making in modern American society. While the airline industry has made a major effort to understand family interaction and its influence on decisions related to airline trips, there is scant information available about the roles played by different family members in the decision-making process related to personal motor vehicle tourism.

TIMING OF TRIPS

Our knowledge regarding the timing of trips is rather basic in nature and has evolved from federal and selected state data bases. The federal data which concentrate on trips of 100 miles or more suggest that 49% of all auto/truck trips of such distance occurred on weekends, while the remainder occurred during the work week. Vacation trips accounted for approximately 50% of all trips (U.S. Travel Data Center 1984).

An examination of federal data bases for auto/truck

trips suggests that the bulk of personal motor vehicle tourism, especially auto trips, occurred during the summer months. The study indicated that more vehicle miles were driven during the summer than during any other season. However, more auto trips were taken during the spring. As could be expected, automobile travel was at its lowest point during the winter, in terms of both numbers and distances of trips (Strate 1972c).

The major difficulty in assessing the data base for the timing of trips is the lack of demographic and psychographic information regarding the market segments. While it is known that the bulk of personal motor vehicle tourism occurs during the summer months, one has little ability to predict empirically why certain segments or groups of individuals will vacation during this period.

The key issue is to determine which segments prefer to vacation during seasons of the year other than summer. In many cases, the seasonality of personal motor vehicle tourism is dictated by inflexible job and school vacations. However, there are a tremendous number of market segments which have job vacation flexibility and are not encumbered with the problem of school vacations. In essence, there is little knowledge about the primary factors which motivate these segments to take their vacations during seasons other than the traditional summer vacation time.

Another problem for researchers in the area of trip timing is the limited understanding of weekend trips. While much information exists about the purposes of weekend trips, it is difficult to define precise market segments by trip purpose for many activities. For example, market segments associated with sightseeing and visiting friends and relatives may prove virtually impossible to identify. On the other hand, it is usually possible to identify the market segments which patronize ski resorts on weekend trips.

Another research issue is the overall relationship between frequency and timing of trips. Several studies have investigated trip frequency, while other studies have considered trip timing, however, few studies have sought to link the two variables in a comprehensive fashion. As a consequence, there is limited understanding of ways to exploit the trip timing of the frequent personal motor vehicle tourist, who represents the most lucrative market in automobile tourism.

TRIP HABITS

Traditionally, the urban transportation planner has checked travel habits through such mechanisms as travel diaries. These mechanisms, combined with origin–destination surveys, have enabled urban planners to assess the nature and intent of trip-taking activities within urban areas.

Researchers in the tourism field have used similar types of techniques to monitor travel habits of motor vehicle tourists. However, the task in this research area is more difficult because it is important to know the travel habits of the many diverse segments among the personal motor vehicle tourists.

From the perspective of expenditures, it is possible to identify how the motor vehicle traveler "votes" with his pocketbook in terms of food and lodging. This technique, however, often fails to address several key issues. For example, such studies, while they often include demographic profiles, frequently fail to develop a psychographic profile. As a consequence, there is often an ill-defined linkage between trip habits and market segments.

Another fundamental research deficiency is that while there is a good understanding of how the personal motor vehicle tourist spends his funds, there is little information regarding why he decides to patronize particular types of food and lodging establishments. This issue is largely unaddressed in publicly available studies.

While at first glance this research issue may seem to be private sector in orientation, it also seems to have implications for the public sector. For example, it would seem to be of importance to federal planners who are charged with the responsibility of assessing the magnitude and types of facility needs on public lands. It is also of considerable importance to state officials seeking to create incentives for constructing tourist superstructures, i.e., hotels and restaurants. When there is a proper allocation of capital, such investments will maximize spending from tourists in the state and, hence, tax revenues from tourism.

THE INTERNATIONAL ARENA

The interrelationship between personal transportation modes and tourism is receiving varying degrees of attention from various countries around the world. While most nations recognize the potential of tourism to generate export income, they are aware that, in the vast majority of cases, personal motor vehicle tourism contributes a relatively small proportion of tourism exports. When viewed from the perspective of an individual nation, a country's stage of industrial, economic, and road infrastructure development and population density determine, to a large extent, the contribution to the nation's GNP made by tourism from the personal transportation modes. Needless to say, only nations with a substantial tourism contribution from the personal transportation modes may justify the undertaking of such research.

It is also interesting to note that the importance of tourism generated by the personal transportation modes is also determined by qualitative factors. For example, worldwide traveling habits differ significantly from those found in the United States. In no other country but the United States has the personal automobile achieved such a paramount societal, economic, and even cultural role. In addition, other nations with different population densities possess adequate transportation alternatives for tourism which may affect the appeal of personal transportation modes for purposes of tourism. In France, for example, most employers and the government substantially subsidize vacation travel costs, provided the elected transportation mode is the nationalized railroad.

These criteria limit the importance of the personal motor vehicle tourism issue to a small number of advanced industrialized countries, such as Canada and certain Western European nations, to countries bordering such nations (e.g., Mexico), and to such international organizations as the OECD and the United Nations.

CANADA AND MEXICO

Canadian research in personal motor vehicle tourism offers some interesting similarities and contrasts with the experience of U.S. researchers.

The most important Canadian effort at the federal level is by *Statistics Canada*, which provides, on a quarterly basis, statistics on personal motor vehicle tourism, as well as on various economic activities, including the number of U.S. visitors. Many of these statistics resemble measures already collected by the U.S. Census of Transportation and closely parallel U.S. Federal Highway Administration efforts in both scope and content.

At the provincial level, Canadian research activities are varied and seem more numerous than those at the U.S. state level. All provinces seem to undertake some form of personal transportation research. This research includes

1 Origin–destination studies.
2 Studies regarding levels and types of tourist spending within each province.
3 Inventories of tourism resources.
4 Evaluation of the psychographic profile of the automobile traveler in some limited cases.

A major orientation of this research at both the federal and provincial level is analyzing U.S. traffic into Canada, because these tourist flows represent a sizable amount of export income. These flows are highly influenced by exchange rates, as was demonstrated during the summer of 1983 when it was estimated that U.S. tourist flows into Canada set new records (Reeves 1983).

From the perspective of Mexico, the emphasis on U.S. traffic flows is accentuated. This is due primarily to the fact that the impact of domestic personal transportation mode tourism is economically negligible and that export income (especially in U.S. dollars) has become a principal concern.

There is basically no personal transportation tourism research tradition in Mexico. Indeed the only figures available constitute what can be described as usually inaccurate raw data.

From a true international perspective, several organizations are involved in research in the personal transportation modes in general and in personal motor vehicle tourism in particular. Although the OECD does not undertake any tourism research, it does publish economic reports which include specific attention to specific tourism statistics. In addition, results of extraordinary research or experts' opinions regarding tourism are frequently published.

The OECD does publish tourism studies such as the *Tourism Policy and International Tourism in OECD Member Countries* (1981). This study assesses tourism policies and discusses tourism flows between member countries. Unfortunately, it does not disaggregate the statistics by transport mode.

The OECD has published a study entitled *The Future of the Use of the Car* (1982). While this publication included forecasts for ownership and use of automobiles, the average cost of using an automobile, and the interrelationship between car usage and space/time patterns, it did not address the tourism issue.

While the United Nations and the World Bank have pursued some research in tourism-related areas, the bulk of this activity has little to do with personal motor vehicle tourism.

Certain key conclusions and, hence, issues arise from this rather cursory analysis of the international arena. It is obvious that the research issues surrounding motor vehicle tourism primarily apply to a small handful of countries in North America and Europe.

Unfortunately, the magnitude of the tourism generated by the personal motor vehicle modes seems to be much larger in North America than in European countries. This is probably true because the former has a limited alternative transportation infrastructure, e.g., a well developed train system. From the perspective of Mexico and Canada, their primary concern is with the impact of traffic flows across borders with the United States, since such interborder flows produce the bulk of tourism expenditures. As a consequence, the major issues facing both Canada and Mexico are to determine the precise impacts of domestic versus international motor vehicle tourism from the United States and to develop mechanisms to use to attract more tourists from the United States.

In essence, the key international issue—*attraction* of more motor vehicle tourists—is not unlike the issue faced by various states, municipalities, and attractions within the United States itself.

INSTITUTIONAL ISSUES

FUNDING ISSUES

The majority of data collection and research activities in the area of personal motor vehicle tourism in the United States are undertaken by the Bureau of the Census, the Federal Highway Administration, the United States Travel and Tourism Administration, and the U.S. Travel Data Center.

The Bureau of the Census probably makes the most significant contribution to the data-gathering activities of the Federal Government. In particular, the *National Travel Survey* of the Census of Transportation provides information on the volume and characteristics of nonlocal auto/truck travel by the civilian population. Although the *National Travel Survey* can be considered to be relevant only as a source of macro-secondary data, it is, nonetheless, essential in that it provides comprehensive and timely data regarding the interrelationship between personal motor vehicle tourism and levels of economic activity.

The United States Travel and Tourism Administration (formerly the U.S. Travel Service) was a joint sponsor of the 1977 *National Travel Survey*. The U.S. Travel Service provided each state with NTS highlights for their areas of jurisdiction, but this consisted only of a retabulation of existing data (U.S. Travel Service 1979).

The Federal Highway Administration's *Nationwide Personal Transportation Study* consisted of a series of reports covering questions administered by the Bureau of the Census as part of the National Travel Program.

The U.S. Travel Data Center is one of the most important nonprofit organizations at the national level which conducts tourism research in a wide variety of areas, including motor vehicle tourism. The organization publishes a number of research studies which are particularly relevant to personal motor vehicle tourism, including the *Annual National Travel Survey* and the *Proceedings of the Travel Outlook Forum*, as well as other reports specified in Appendix 1.

The *Annual National Travel Survey*, published as full-year and quarterly reports, provides substantial information and comparisons with data from preceding years and describes such aspects of travel activity as modal splits, destinations, trip purposes, distances and durations of trips, and demographic characteristics of travelers. *The Travel Outlook Forum* is a gathering of industry personnel, academics, and consultants who try to predict the course of the travel industry over the next 12 months. These sessions often contain the results of research activities in particular areas, including personal motor vehicle tourism. For example, the results of an empirically based study of historical and future automobile traveler patterns was presented at the *1982 Travel Outlook Forum*.

The U.S. Travel Data Center also performs customized research services for members, as well as for nonmembers, for a fee. These services can range from a travel economic impact model for local or state entities to access to the U.S. Travel Data Bank, which can provide a sound source of secondary data.

Unfortunately, the Reagan administration has radically changed the role of the actors in this overall equation. The objective of the budget-cutting activities at the Bureau of the Census was to shift the cost and burden of data collection to the private sector and data users themselves. Specifically, these cutbacks have led to the cancellation or postponement of critical data-gathering activities, including the *National Travel Survey* conducted by the Bureau of the Census and the *Nationwide Personal Transportation Study*.

The U.S. Travel Data Center has willingly tried to breach this research gap by compiling quarterly and annual national travel surveys, however, it is obvious that statistical quality will suffer as a result of more limited resources, and not as a result of any lack of expertise or dedication. The research directions suggested in this document are, in most cases, predicated upon the existence of basic data bases. The failure to have these basic data bases as departure points for further research in public or quasi-public form in the coming years will leave federal, state, and private researchers in the "dark ages" regarding knowledge of personal motor vehicle tourism.

LACK OF OVERALL RESEARCH POLICIES AND DIRECTION AT THE INTERNATIONAL, FEDERAL, STATE, AND LOCAL LEVELS

The lack of overall research policies and direction at the international, federal, state, and local levels can be attributed to the unique nature of personal transport. Personal transport modes are usually operated on publicly financed and publicly provided rights-of-way (e.g., interstate highways in the United States) in privately owned vehicles. The actual routing of these vehicles is a function of individual decision.

The nature of the individual decision-making process has precluded research funding by private-sector firms involved in carrier transportation, although firms engaged in activities that benefit from personal transportation, such as hotels, have made some efforts to estimate the interrelationship between their businesses and tourism generated by motor vehicles. The majority of research funding for such activities, however, has been provided by public-sector entities.

Public-sector agencies need to understand the effects of motor vehicle tourism expenditures to ascertain the economic contribution of this form of tourism.

However, the wide geographic scope of motor vehicle tourism has prompted research activities by a multitude of nonprofit and public-sector agencies operating at various levels of jurisdiction, i.e., federal, state, and local.

Simply stated, the involvement of these nonprofit and public-sector organizations has created a fundamental research problem in analyzing the current knowledge and future direction for tourism research within the scope of personal motor vehicle tourism: a lack of coordination among research agencies. There is simply no master plan for research in the field, nor is there a central coordination agency or organization.

Research activities by federal agencies and national organizations have suffered from several policy and directional weaknesses. For example, federal agencies, such as the Bureau of the Census and the Federal Highway Administration, have primarily sought to develop data bases, some of which describe different characteristics of motor vehicle travelers and the utilization of their vehicles. However, there has been no consistent or comprehensive effort to analyze the implications of the data. In addition, federal agencies have failed to initiate research programs designed to expand knowledge of the interrelationships between personal motor vehicles and tourism.

According to the *Survey of State Travel Offices*, published by the U.S. Travel Data Center (1981b), most states are involved in monitoring traffic flows to and through their states. A significant number of states use traffic counts to determine attendance at public and private facilities. Many states also monitor such factors as length of stay in the state, travel industry sales and receipts, levels of tourism expenditures, hotel occupancy, and travel-generated tax revenues and employment.

Within the scope of state surveys, the parameters most often established are of a demographic nature, paralleling federal agency statistics in orientation. Nonetheless, these data, as they are published, form only a rudimentary basis for states to use as a tourism/travel marketing tool.

The gap in federal information pertaining to micro-origin—destination studies is partially filled by state research efforts. These market research studies are most often broken down by mode of transportation and, within the area of motor vehicle tourism, compile information such as trip and traveler characteristics, length of stay, and hotel facilities used. The research entities most often used by states for such studies are the U.S. Travel Data Center and universities.

One criticism of most federal and state research is that it generally overlooks the local level. This could prove to be a serious flaw for local entities in ascertaining the true nature of the personal motor vehicle tourist. California has established a decentralized tourism promotion/research system whereby some of the limitations of a macro-statewide approach are reduced. This is accomplished by providing local political entities with study models to use when conducting their own research (Wassenaar 1981). This alternative not only addresses the need for a micro-approach but also reduces dependence on state budgets. However, the problem then becomes a lack of state macro-data regarding origin—destination trip characteristics and traveler demographics for statewide tourists.

This brief description of the research activities at the federal, national, state, and local levels serves to highlight the nature of the organizational problems which affect relationships between such entities. For example, there is no overall policy direction or guidance mechanism to provide a target for entities at these various levels to aim at. This is true whether one considers major activity areas, such as economic research, and/or psychographics, or demographic data base development. Hence, it is fair to say that there is little rhyme or reason to personal motor vehicle tourism research by either the public or private sector in the United States today.

To a large extent, the federal government must bear the burden of blame for this problem. Government at this level has the capability to initiate policies which guide research activities by both the public and private sectors. Perhaps more importantly, it has the resources at its disposal to create incentives for state and local governments and the private sector to pursue meaningful research topics. These incentives can, of course, take the form of matching grants for meritorious data collection efforts or for specific research studies.

While an argument can be made that the federal government has little capability to generate these incentives without congressional action, this argument offers little explanation for the lack of a coherent overall policy. Furthermore, it also constitutes a poor excuse for the constant infighting and working at cross purposes which characterizes the relationships between many federal agencies engaged in direct or peripheral research in personal motor vehicle tourism.

These organizational problems also plague the relationship between the public and private sectors in the area of personal motor vehicle tourism research. The position of the private-sector regarding such research issues has traditionally been to consider the material proprietary in nature. As a consequence, the company is the prime beneficiary of both the findings and conclusions of the research and the methodological developments of the study. Government has offered little incentive or assistance to ensure that research which is nonproprietary or of a marginally proprietary nature is circulated to researchers in the academic, state government, or business communities. For example, with encouragement and reimbursement, private industry might be willing to release parts of internal research documents to such researchers. Without such moral support and financial incentive, such sharing of information is highly unlikely.

Of course, there are other ways in which the organizational problems between the public and private sectors can be solved. For example, government is often aware of business entity studies of specific personal motor vehicle tourism research areas. These areas, in many cases, also happen to hold high priority for state and federal researchers. Instead of bemoaning the fact that the private sector will not share the results with the public sector, it would probably make more sense to have more cost-sharing arrangements between the government agencies and the private sector entity in order to facilitate the release and dissemination of selected research results. Hence, both parties would share in the research results and enjoy lower costs.

CONCLUSION

There are a variety of research and institutional problems connected with tourism-related research in the personal transportation modes in general and personal motor vehicle tourism in particular.

One of the key research questions is "Who is the motor vehicle tourist?" While we do have some rudimentary knowledge about the automobile traveler, we have only limited knowledge about the motor vehicle tourist. The identification of the latter is likely to occur only when federal and state research efforts are expanded beyond their traditional emphasis on data collection to include the development of psychographic profiles for various market segments.

Another issue is the need to develop information and data bases regarding market segments of the personal motor vehicle tourist. The current lack of information increases the cost of tourism research in this area for both the academic and research communities.

The Reagan administration has instituted cost-cutting measures reducing the amount of research available to these two groups. In theory, these measures are designed to ensure that research sponsors and businesses pay the full cost of acquiring data. In reality, it also imposes hardships upon state governments as they seek to understand and promote a form of interstate commerce.

The research areas of planning and decision making constitute an extremely difficult topic because we know so little about them. In the area of planning motor vehicle tourism, the general lack of information is at least partially the result of the limited role intermediaries play in assisting the personal motor vehicle tourist in planning his trip.

In addition, there is little knowledge about how the principles of consumer behavior apply to personal motor vehicle tourism. While there are fairly sophisti-

cated models, they have not been empirically tested in areas related to planning and decision making.

The timing of personal motor vehicle tourist trips is an important issue because the tourist superstructure has to supply adequate capacity at the times tourists demand service. Federal data bases suggest that a great number of trips occur on weekends and during the summer months. However, the key research issue in this area involves determining why individuals who can exercise great discretion in the timing of tourist trips choose off-peak times.

While there is at least some knowledge of when and how the personal motor vehicle tourist spends his or her money when traveling, there is little information in publicly available research regarding why he decides to patronize particular types of food and lodging establishments. This issue seems to have importance for both private- and public-sector entities in their planning of facility needs.

There is a limited interest in personal motor vehicle tourism from an international perspective. Such research is primarily limited to a handful of countries, such as the United States, Canada, Mexico, and several of the more advanced industrialized countries of Europe. In reality, the United States and Canada seem to have fairly well developed programs, although the U.S. program seems to suffer from lack of policy and direction, while the Canadian program devotes substantial attention to border flows.

There are a number of institutional issues which seem to affect the ability of researchers to adequately address the research issues which have been identified. One institutional issue is the question regarding the withdrawal of federal funding for the Bureau of the Census. This funding reduction has led to a reduction in federal data collection efforts related to personal motor vehicle tourism. The U.S. Travel Data Center has sought to bridge some of the gap, but its coverage is less comprehensive and involves more costs for users.

The research effort in the United States also suffers from a lack of overall policy and direction. Federal efforts have traditionally involved data collection rather than analysis. State efforts have suffered from a limited identification of national priorities and from parochial interests.

APPENDIX   List of Other U.S. Travel Data Center Reports Relevant to the Topic of Personal Motor Vehicle Tourism: 1983 Program

1   The monthly *Travel Printout* newsletter presents research findings of the Data Center and other national organizations. It attempts to uncover trends in the industry and regularly features travel indicators, levels of attendance at national parks, and the travel price index that reflects future predictions of price changes for categories of travel costs, including gasoline, transportation, food and lodging (1983a).

2 The monthly *Travel Price Index* forecasts the costs of travel as presented above (1983b).

3 *The Economic Review of Travel in America* (1982–1983), published in the summer of 1983, presented and projected travel expenditures and traffic information. It also emphasized tourism's economic impact in terms of travel-generated employment, tax revenues, and other related parameters (1983c).

The following is a series of publications with material pertinent to personal transportation modes which the U.S. Travel Data Center deleted from its program for 1983.

1 *1979–80 Quarterly Travel Trends* contained data pertaining to travel in general and contained information on the domestic supplies of petroleum, and attendance figures at U.S. parks and attractions were presented (1980a).

2 *The 1980 and 1981–82 Economic Reports on Travel in America* emphasized the economic role of tourism in the U.S. and provided gasoline consumption figures relevant to the automobile (1980b, 1982b).

3 *The 1977 and 1979 National Travel Expenditure Studies* summarized U.S. traveler spending figures for trip and traveler characteristics similar to those presented in the annual *National Travel Survey* (1978b, 1980c).

4 *The 1979 National Travel Barometer* contained quarterly data regarding attendance at national and state parks, as well as at private attractions at over 1,000 facilities. While short term in nature, this report seemed to offer substantial information for researchers in the personalized transportation modes (1980d).

5 *The 1979 Gasoline Shortage Impact* was a study of the impact of gasoline shortages (1980e).

REFERENCES

Asim, Ruth H. (1974), *Purpose of Automobile Trips and Travel*, 1969–70 Nationwide Personal Transportation Study Report No. 10, U.S. Department of Transportation, Washington, D.C.: U.S. Government Printing Office.

Asim, Ruth H. (1982), *Rural vs. Urban Travel*, 1977 Nationwide Personal Transportation Study Report No. 8, U.S. Department of Transportation, Washington, D.C.: U.S. Government Printing Office.

Asim, Ruth H. and Paul V. Sverci (1974), *Automobile Ownership*, 1969–70 Nationwide Personal Transportation Study Report No. 11, U.S. Department of Transportation, Washington, D.C.: U.S. Government Printing Office.

Belden Associates (1978), *Identifying Traveler Markets, Research Methodologies*, Washington, D.C.: U.S. Government Printing Office.

Better Homes and Gardens (1976), *Pleasure/Vacation Travel*, New York: Meredith Corporation Publishing Group.

Better Homes and Gardens (1979), *The Highlights: Comparison of Consumers Opinion on Gas, June 1979 vs. September 1979*, New York: Meredith Corporation Publishing Group.

Bousseloub, Tiffany (1983), Travel Research Director California, Telephone Interview 3/2/83.

Bryan, William R. (1981), "Improved Mileage, Discretionary Income and Travel for Pleasure," *Journal of Travel Research*, 20 (Summer), 28–29.

Bureau of the Census, U.S. (1979), *1977 Census of Transportation, National Travel Survey, Travel During 1977*, Washington, D.C.: U.S. Government Printing Office.

Bureau of Outdoor Recreation, U.S. (1973), *Outdoor Recreation—A Legacy for America*, U.S. Department of the Interior, Washington, D.C.: U.S. Government Printing Office.

Cadez, Gary, and John D. Hund (1978), *A Comparison between Port of Entry Visitor Center Users and Nonusers*, Logan, Utah: Institute for Outdoor Recreation and Tourism, Utah State University.

Corsi, Thomas M., and Milton E. Harvey (1979), "Changes in Vacation Travel in Response to Motor Fuel Shortages and Higher Prices," *Journal of Travel Research*, 17 (Spring), 7–11.

Curtin, Richard T. (1980), *The RV Consumer*, Chantilly, Virginia: Recreation Vehicle Industry Association, University of Michigan Survey Research Center.

De la Pena, Jerry (1983), Mexican Tourist Office official, Phoenix, Arizona, Telephone Interview 8/26/83.

Dopkowski, Ronald (1983), Demographic Survey Division Director, U.S. Department of Highways, Telephone Interview 3/30/83.

Duricka, Laura A. (1983), VP PR DATO Telephone Interview 3/22/83. Energy Research and Development Administration (1977), *Transportation Energy Data Book*, Washington, D.C.: U.S. Government Printing Office.

EC Info (February 1981), *European Documentation*, Brussels, Belgium: European Communities Information Commission.

EC Info (November 1982), *European File*, Brussels, Belgium: European Communities Information Commission.

Garpo, Bill (1983), VP PR RV Industry Association Telephone Interview 3/23/83.

Goeldner, C.R., and Karen Dicke (1980), *Bibliography of Tourism and Travel Research Studies Reports and Articles*, Boulder, Colorado: University of Colorado and the Travel Research Association.

Goley, Beatrice T., Geraldine Brown, and Elizabeth Samson (1972), *Study of Household Travel Patterns in the U.S.*, 1969–70 Nationwide Personal Transportation Study Report No. 7, U.S. Department of Transportation, Washington, D.C.: U.S. Government Printing Office.

Hall, Dave (1983), Ford Motor Company, Marketing Projects Department, Telephone Interview 3/4/83.

Hartung, Melita (1983), Research Staff AAA, Telephone Interview 3/2/83.

Krerr, Earl (1983), Motor Vehicle Manufacturers Association Research Staff, Telephone Interview 3/2/83.

Kuzmyak, Richard J. (1980a), *Characteristics of Licensed Drivers and Their Travel*, 1977 Nationwide Personal Transportation Study Report No. 1, U.S. Department of Transportation, Washington, D.C.: U.S. Government Printing Office.

Kuzmyak, Richard J. (1980b), *Purposes of Vehicle Trips and Travel*, 1977 Nationwide Personal Transportation Study Report No. 2, U.S. Department of Transportation, Washington, D.C.: U.S. Government Printing Office.

Kuzmyak, Richard J. (1981a), *Household Vehicle Utilization*, 1969-70 Nationwide Personal Transportation Study Report No. 5, U.S. Department of Transportation, Washington, D.C.: U.S. Government Printing Office.

Kuzmyak, Richard J. (1981b), *Vehicle Occupancy*, 1977 Nationwide Personal Transportation Study Report No. 6, U.S. Department of Transportation, Washington, D.C.: U.S. Government Printing Office.

Mandlestein (1983), Marketing Research Staff, Avis Rent-A-Car, Telephone Interview 3/22/83.

Mina, Nancy (1985), U.S. Travel Data Center, Telephone Interview 4/29/85.

OECD (1981), *Tourism Policy and International Tourism in OECD Member Countries*, Paris, France: OCDE/OECD.

OECD (June 1982), *The Future of the Use of the Car*, ECMT Roundtable 55, 56, 57, Paris, France: OCDE/OECD.

Randill, Alice, Helen Greenhalgh and Elizabeth Samson (1973), *Modes of Transportation and Personal Characteristics of Tripmakers*, 1969–70 Nationwide Personal Transportation Study Report No. 9, U.S. Department of Transportation, Washington, D.C.: U.S. Government Printing Office.

Reeves, J. (1983), Department of Transport Canada, Ottawa, Ontario, Telephone Interview 8/25/83.

Roskin, Mark E. (1980), *Purposes of Vehicle Trips and Travel*, 1977 Nationwide Personal Transportation Study Report No. 3, U.S. Department of Transportation, Washington, D.C.: U.S. Government Printing Office.

Strate, Harry E. (1972a), *Automobile Occupancy*, 1969–70 Nationwide Personal Transportation Study Report No. 1, U.S. Department of Transportation, Washington, D.C.: U.S. Government Printing Office.

Strate, Harry E. (1972b), *Annual Miles of Auto Trips and Travel*, 1969–70 Nationwide Personal Transportation Study Report No. 2, U.S. Department of Transportation, Washington, D.C.: U.S. Government Printing Office.

Strate, Harry E. (1972c), *Seasonal Variations of Automobile Trips and Travel*, 1969–70 Nationwide Personal Transportation Study Report No. 3, U.S. Department of Transportation, Washington, D.C.: U.S. Government Printing Office.

Sweenee, Mary (1983), PR American Car Rental Association, Telephone Interview 3/21/83.

Travel Data Center, U.S. (1977), *1977 Travel Outlook Forum Proceedings*, Address by James J. Gibson, Marketing Director, 3M National Advertising Company, Washington, D.C.: U.S. Travel Data Center, pp. 86–90.

Travel Data Center, U.S. (1978a), *Travel Data Locator Index, Second Edition*, Washington, D.C.: U.S. Travel Data Center.

Travel Data Center, U.S. (1978b), *1977 National Travel Expenditure Study*, Washington, D.C.: U.S. Travel Data Center.

Travel Data Center, U.S. (1978c), *1978 Travel Outlook Forum Proceedings*, Address by James A. Imwold, Marketing Operations Manager, 3M National Advertising Company, Washington, D.C.: U.S. Travel Data Center, pp. 93–102.

Travel Data Center, U.S. (1979), *1979 Travel Outlook Forum Proceedings*, Address by Robert C. Olney, Vice President and General Manager, 3M National Advertising Company, Washington, D.C.: U.S. Travel Data Center, pp. 93–101.

Travel Data Center, U.S. (1980a), *1979–80 Quarterly Travel Trends*, Washington, D.C.: U.S. Travel Data Center.

Travel Data Center, U.S. (1980b), *1980 Economic Report on Travel in America*, Washington, D.C.: U.S. Travel Data Center.

Travel Data Center, U.S. (1980c), *1979 National Travel Expenditure Study*, Washington, D.C.: U.S. Travel Data Center.

Travel Data Center, U.S. (1980d), *1979 National Travel Barometer Quarterly*, Washington, D.C.: U.S. Travel Data Center.

Travel Data Center, U.S. (1980e), *The 1979 Gasoline Shortage: Lessons for the Travel Industry*, Washington, D.C.: U.S. Travel Data Center.

Travel Data Center, U.S. (1980f), *1980 Travel Outlook Forum Proceedings*, Address by Gregg P. Ganschaw, National Manager of Publications, Marketing & Travel Market Research, 3M National Advertising Company, Washington, D.C.: U.S. Travel Data Center, pp. 83–91.

Travel Data Center, U.S. (1981a), *1980 National Travel Survey: Full Year Report*, Washington, D.C.: U.S. Travel Data Center.

Travel Data Center, U.S. (1981b), *1981–82 Survey of State Travel Offices*, Washington, D.C.: U.S. Travel Data Center.

Travel Data Center, U.S. (1981c), *1981 Travel Outlook Forum Proceedings*, Address by Gregg Ganschaw, Director of Marketing, Color Arts, Inc., Washington, D.C.: U.S. Travel Data Center, pp. 95–105.

Travel Data Center, U.S. (1982a), *1982 Outlook for Travel and Tourism*, Address by Gregg Ganschaw, Vice President of Marketing, Color Arts, Inc., Washington, D.C.: U.S. Travel Data Center, pp. 97–105.

Travel Data Center, U.S. (1982b), *1981–82 Economic Report on Travel in America*, Washington, D.C.: U.S. Travel Data Center.

Travel Data Center, U.S. (1982c), *1982 Travel Outlook for Travel and Tourism*, Address by Barbara Wickliffe, Director, Best Western International Advertising Division, Washington, D.C.: U.S. Travel Data Center.

Travel Data Center, U.S. (1983a), Monthly *Travel Printout*, Washington, D.C.: U.S. Travel Data Center.

Travel Data Center, U.S. (1983b), Monthly *Travel Price Index*, Washington, D.C.: U.S. Travel Data Center.

Travel Data Center, U.S. (1983c), *The Economic Review of Travel in America*, Washington, D.C.: U.S. Travel Data Center.

Travel Data Center, U.S. (1984), *1983 Full Year Report: National Travel Survey*, Washington, D.C.: U.S. Travel Data Center.

Travel Service, U.S. (1977), *Analysis of Travel Definitions, Terminology and Research Needs among States and Cities*, Washington, D.C.: U.S. Travel Service.

Travel Service, U.S. (1979), *1977 National Travel Survey Highlights for Each State*, Washington, D.C.: U.S. Travel Service.

Wassenaar, Dirk J. (1981), *California Visitor Impact Model*, Sacramento, California: California Office of Tourism, Department of Economics and Business Development, San Jose State University.

Wickliffe, Barbara (1983), Director Market & Research Advertising Division, Best Western International Hotels, Telephone Interview 3/1/83.

Worby, Tim (1983), VP Market Research, Hertz Rent-A-Car, Telephone Interview, 3/22/83.

World Bank (annual), *Urban Transport*, Sector Policy Paper, Washington, D.C.: World Bank Publications.

Zimmerman, Carol (1981), *A Life Cycle of Travel by the American Family*, 1969–70 Nationwide Personal Transportation Study Report No. 7, U.S. Department of Transportation, Washington, D.C.: U.S. Government Printing Office.

3M National Advertising Company (1970a), *Greater Nags Head Chamber of Commerce Visitors Study*, Argo, Illinois: 3M National Advertising Company.

3M National Advertising Company (1970b), *Impulse Travel: Changing Trends in Auto Vacation Travel*, Argo, Illinois: 3M National Advertising Company.

3M National Advertising Company (1972), *Psychographics of the Auto Traveler*, Argo, Illinois: 3M National Advertising Company.

25

Research Needs in the Intercity Bus and Rail Transportation Industry

STUART N. ROBINSON

Stuart N. Robinson and Associates, Inc.
Richmond, Virginia

*T*his chapter describes the travel information needs of managers in rail and bus companies. It explains the responsibilities for selected managers within the corporation and it specifies what information they need. The needs of five managers are discussed. The Vice-President of Passenger Marketing needs information that will help price tickets and travel services, develop and evaluate marketing promotions, and forecast passenger miles, passenger revenues, and profits. The Vice-President of Advertising needs research support for testing advertising copy, developing media plans, and tracking advertising. The Marketing Controller needs help in evaluating the costs and benefits of marketing programs. The information requirements of the Vice-President of Passenger Service focus on receiving ratings of passenger service on a timely basis and the Vice-President of Traffic and Operations needs to be kept apprised of changes in preferred origins and destinations.*

This chapter describes the research needs in the intercity bus and rail transportation industry and defines the functions of the market research staff in a transportation company. It predominately addresses the intercity bus industry since this market is more competitive than intercity rail. Most everything described about the bus market, however, is relevant, if not directly parallel, to the rail market except when noted otherwise.

MARKET RESEARCH RESPONSIBILITIES

The dynamic nature of the intercity bus market requires all companies to develop marketing plans in an atmosphere of considerable uncertainty and these plans must be flexible enough to adapt quickly to a constantly changing market. The major responsibility

[1]The author would like to acknowledge the efforts of Mr. Tom Robinson and Miss Karyn Heemann in the preparation of this manuscript, which could not have been completed without their help.

of the corporate market research department, therefore, is to help senior managers develop strategies that can be changed and modified at a moment's notice.

Most of the time, senior managers do not realize they lack the information they need to make a management decision until it's time to make the decision. The market analyst who has a complete understanding of the functions and responsibilities of the senior managers he supports eventually learns to anticipate their needs for information quickly and to satisfy their requests completely. This approach is very different from the classical problem solving mode of providing market information after someone in the company asks a question. To be efficient and cost-effective, the market research department must act, not just react, and plan, not just respond.

The following examples will demonstrate this need. Each example will show a senior manager, inside or outside of the marketing department, who needs information and is looking to the market research department to supply it. After briefly describing his function and the stresses to which he is subjected, the section describes how a market researcher can provide information which will help him complete his tasks.

VICE-PRESIDENT OF MARKETING

One of the major responsibilities of the Vice-President of marketing is to develop a pricing strategy. He usually asks the market research staff to develop a price–volume curve. The curve will usually look something like the one shown in Fig. 1, which shows travel volume decreasing as fares increase. This curve, however, is limited because it predicts tendency to purchase under the most simplistic and static conditions. It does not consider competitive pricing, it does not consider changes in the economy, and it does not consider changes in consumer motivation that are not related to price. Worse yet, however, is that no one seems to care. Most senior managers have learned to accept these deficiencies especially when they need the information right away. This complacency is also the result of market researchers, who find these curves easier to present to naive managers than something more complicated and harder to explain or sell.

The demands of planning in a changing market require a price–volume curve which incorporates market dynamics like the graph in Fig. 2. It not only shows how volume varies with price, but also predicts how this price–volume relationship is affected by competitive pricing. It describes the relationship between fares for air, bus, and train between two cities. The air fare stays constant at $100 and the train fare stays constant at $70, but the bus fare is allowed to vary

from $50 to $90. The graph shows that at $50 the bus can capture 65% of the market, but at $90 loses substantial market share to airlines and at $80 loses market share to trains. Other price–volume relationships can be estimated considering the effects of various external influences like the price of gasoline or the rate of inflation.

The methodology to generate these types of price–volume curves most often incorporates conjoint measurement or trade-off analysis procedures which are described elsewhere in this book. The research project needed to develop these curves requires more time and funds than most. It can easily cost $50,000 per project and require a minimum of three months to complete. The pricing information they generate, however, can be retabulated every time the competitive environment changes.

VICE-PRESIDENT OF ADVERTISING

Most ad directors come up with a new ad campaign at the mere suggestion of a new fare or a change in route structure. They need guidance that will direct and focus their apparent unlimited creativity. They do not need ideas and ad copy, and will not cooperate or support market research analysts who forget their role as researchers and try to develop ad campaigns.

Ad tracking studies monitor the effects of advertising on a number of measures. They relay the consumer feedback that provides the guidance an advertising manager needs to continually fine-tune his advertising.

Most often ad tracking data are collected via telephone interviews and the results are reported in percentage of total people interviewed. The percentage of people who are aware of the advertising without being prompted is called unaided ad awareness; the percentage who were aware of the advertising after being prompted is called aided awareness. The assumption is that increases in ad awareness reflect increases in advertising effectiveness or the successful communication of advertising messages.

Figure 3 shows how ad awareness of one bus company increased as a result of its advertising campaign. It shows that most increases followed campaigns which were aired on both national and local (spot) television as opposed to either national or local television. It does not indicate the effects of changing the messages of the advertising or the effects of the competitive advertising. Both are important factors which must also be monitored.

Finally, advertising effectiveness can be evaluated using a number of performance measures. Ad campaigns will often show positive performance on one measure and negative on another. Research managers should report performance on a number of measures and recommend corrective actions on each.

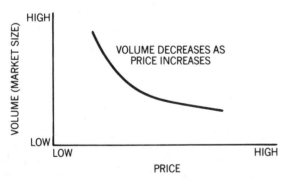

Weaknesses	Does Not Consider
Simplistic	Competitive Pricing
	Complexities of Buying Decision
Static	Shifts in Economy
	Changes in Consumer Motivation

FIGURE 1   V.P. Marketing price/volume curve. Source: Stuart N. Robinson and Associates, Inc., 1980.

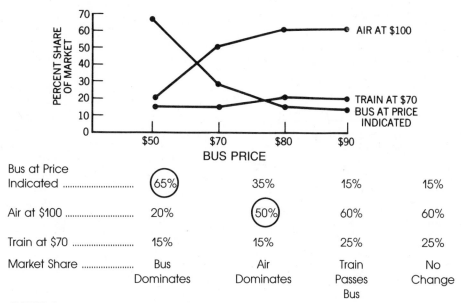

Bus at Price Indicated	(65%)	35%	15%	15%
Air at $100	20%	(50%)	60%	60%
Train at $70	15%	15%	25%	25%
Market Share	Bus Dominates	Air Dominates	Train Passes Bus	No Change

FIGURE 2   Dynamic price/volume curve. Source: Stuart N. Robinson and Associates, Inc., 1980.

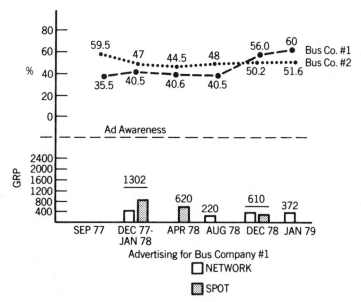

FIGURE 3   Ad awareness total sample. Source: Stuart N. Robinson and Associates, Inc., 1980.

To expect advertising to increase sales *directly* is asking quite a lot. Some people will not see the ads and some will see one or two exposures but no more. More will not pay attention, even though they see the ad, and even more will not remember what they were.

Still more people will not "learn" the message well enough to recall at a later point in time and fewer will be prompted to change their minds about service. Finally, even fewer will actually modify their habits and thereby increase sales. A complete performance evaluation should track all these measures. Only when each effect is measured over time will you know what modifications increase sales as well as promote attention or communicate information.

MARKETING CONTROLLER

The Marketing Controller must develop long-range travel forecasts, detailed financial analyses of a competitor's financial status, and regional market analyses to help determine priorities with regard to market expansion. By far the most critical information that a researcher can provide a Marketing Controller is that which will help him perform a costs–benefits analysis of marketing promotions. The main difficulty in performing a costs–benefits analysis is that, in most instances, the benefits cannot be clearly identified. Market research must operationally define and measure the individual items identified under the "benefits" column so the market controller can assign a cost to each.

Costs–benefits analyses also require teamwork. Here management techniques which promote cooperation and cooperative task orientation are very useful. Many of these can be found in management texts (Drucker 1974) as well as in various industrial psychology and social-organizational psychology textbooks (Siegel 1969, Whyte 1969).

VICE-PRESIDENT OF TRAFFIC OPERATIONS

Traffic managers make sure that the buses are where the people are, when they are needed. Without expertise there would be utter chaos. The major difficulty in determining the demand profitability of different routes arises from the complex nature of a transportation system where profit on one route is dependent on volume from another. This means that routes must be considered as a network, not just as independent

routes linked together. Figure 4 provides an example of a transportation network analysis. It shows a hypothetical bus line from the small community of Elkin, Maryland, to Wilmington, Delaware, continuing on to Philadelphia, Pennsylvania. On a typical bus run, 10 people ride the full route from Elkin to Philadelphia, 2 ride only the Elkin–Wilmington segment, and 20 ride the Wilmington–Philadelphia segment. If the route segments are viewed separately, the Elkin–Wilmington segment with just 12 passengers looks unprofitable, while the Wilmington–Philadelphia segment with 30 passengers seems considerably more lucrative. Yet, if the bus company were to drop its Elkin–Wilmington service, it would risk losing the 10 passengers on the Wilmington–Philadelphia run who embarked in Elkin. Because they would have to find alternative service from Elkin to Wilmington to catch the bus there, these passengers would be inclined to switch modes for the entire trip. The Wilmington–Philadelphia segment would be left with only 20 passengers which at best would be only marginally profitable.

VICE-PRESIDENT OF PASSENGER SERVICE

The Vice-President of Passenger Service must establish which customer services are most important. He has to satisfy everyone and needs guidance as to who needs what, when, and how. He has a variety of service options readily available, but without priorities he can rarely use this potential. When inadequately supported by the market research department, he knows too little, too late and never has enough people to sell tickets when demand increases.

He is often faced with questions such as: "Should this schedule leave five minutes early to attract 12 more passengers from our competitor's terminal across the street, or should it be held up twelve minutes for thorough cleaning?" "Should we dump the johns at 3:00 in the morning at Bugtussle, Iowa, or schedule a

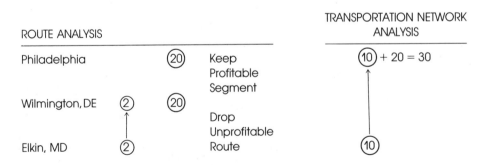

- Network Approach Will Guarantee Maximum Profitability
- Very Few Communities Will Lose Service. Many More Will Gain Service.
- Rural Traffic Subsidizes Major Routes.

FIGURE 4   Transportation network analysis. Source: Stuart N. Robinson and Associates, Inc., 1980.

late and long dinner stop the night before?" Such priorities can only be made with the benefit of passenger preference data. But the data alone are not enough. As with the price—volume curves discussed earlier, this preference information must be collected and analyzed in such a way that it remains a source of information that will be as good tomorrow as it is today. This information should suggest a set of recommendations based on current passenger preferences. However, when the market expands or new fares are introduced, the same passenger responses need to be retabulated in light of the new priorities which address the new marketing environment. Keep in mind that the market changes too often to implement new research projects, even if the research funds were available, which they are not.

This situation calls for another trade-off analysis which shows how much one service is specifically desired relative to a set of other services. Each preference is given a specific value and since these scores are developed on a linear scale, they may be added, combined, or subtracted from each other at will.

Figure 5 shows what services can be compromised with the least effect on passenger satisfaction. It indicates that a manager can make arrivals less convenient if he keeps his buses clean and departures convenient. If this is not possible, then his next best option is to keep his buses clean, arrival times convenient, and make his departures less convenient.

MARKET RESEARCH MANAGEMENT

In each case described above, the solutions presented were always flexible and adaptable to change. Price—volume curves considered changing competitive prices; ad tracking guided and helped course correct advertising; route analyses considered transportation systems as networks; and service strategies considered changing preferences.

Flexibility is easiest to maintain if a systems approach is used which establishes ongoing, continuous data collection systems which allow periodic market analysis. More importantly, such systems allow a periodic analysis and can update the information anytime the market dynamics require. Once established, these systems prove to be more cost-effective than research on an as-needed basis.

Table 1 gives some examples of these transportation systems. It indicates that on-board passenger surveys, advertising evaluations, origin—destination studies (ticket studies), and secondary source literature reviews are the four primary market information systems.

THE FUTURE

Deregulation of the intercity bus industry has meant the removal of most route and price regulation by the Interstate Commerce Commission and by state regula-

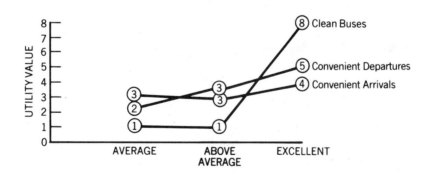

Optimum Service	Clean Buses	Convenient Departures	Convenient Arrivals	
1st Trade-off	Excellent	Excellent	Excellent	
	8 +	5 +	4	= 17
2nd Trade-off	Excellent	Excellent	Above Average	
	8 +	5 +	3	= 16
3rd Trade-off	Excellent	Above Average	Excellent	
	8 +	3 +	4	= 15

FIGURE 5   Service trade-offs. Source: Stuart N. Robinson and Associates, Inc., 1980.

TABLE 1 Projects for Transportation Companies and Travel Organizations

1. *On-Board Passenger Surveys*

   Objective—Measure passenger preferences, attitudes, characteristics, and travel habits.

   Purpose—Develop and track national marketing, advertising, and media plans on a yearly basis.

   Procedure—One to three administrations per year.

2. *Ad Tracking Studies*

   Objective—Monitor consumer awareness of T.V. advertising and of corporate image.

   Purpose—Evaluate effectiveness of advertising and advertising agency performance and modify when appropriate.

   Procedure—One to five telephone polls a year.

3. *Ad Pretesting*

   Objective—Pretest rough copy of newsprint magazine, radio, and T.V. ads.

   Purpose—Modify early versions to maximize communication effectiveness.

   Procedure—Administered on an as-needed basis.

4. *Sales Analysis and Forecasts*

   Objective—Track and analyze sales on a monthly basis, make yearly sales forecasts, and modify monthly.

   Purpose—Identify or predict weak sales areas or seasons and recommend marketing strategies to counter them.

   Procedure—One to four times a year.

5. *Schedule Analysis*

   Objective—Track and analyze passenger volume on all schedules between all origins and destinations in the system.

   Purpose—Weed out small revenue producers and provide more transportation to big revenue producers.

   Procedure—Same as with sales analysis.

6. *Advertising Analysis*

   Objective—Evaluate the effects of advertising on sales.

   Purpose—Evaluate and judge the performance of the advertising agency.

   Procedure—Costs−benefits analysis weighing ad costs versus sales generated.

7. *Energy Reports*

   Objective—Monitor extent and effects of gasoline shortages or gluts.

   Purpose—Modify operations accordingly.

   Procedure—Monthly reports

8. *Competitive Reports*

   Objective—Monitor activities, marketing, financial condition, and advertising of all major competitors.

   Purpose—Alter marketing and promotions to match or better competition.

   Procedure—Monthly report.

9. *Market Intelligence Reports*

   Same as above but for market/industry information.

TABLE 1   *(Continued)*

10. *Site Analysis*

Objective—Evaluate pros and cons of alternative sites for new terminals relative to their potential.

Purpose—Help select sites for new terminals.

Procedure—Administered as needed.

11. *Special Travel Studies*

Objective—Measure changes in travel habits as a result of gasoline shortages, competitive discounts, economy, etc.

Purpose—Predict extent of sales increases due to gasoline shortages and recommend modifications to market and advertising plans.

Procedure—Monthly reports.

12. *Seasonality*

Objective—Determine when sales go up consistently and when they go down consistently each year.

Purpose—Identify trends in sales so that media plans can support both low and high sales periods accordingly.

Procedure—Monthly reports.

13. *Market Segmentation Study*

Objective—Identify major target market segments.

Purpose—Develop target marketing plans.

Procedure—Factor analysis, perceptual mapping, and multidimensional scaling of psychographic, behavioral, and attitudinal data. Quarterly reports.

14. *Promotion Evaluations*

Objective—Evaluate effectiveness of promotions to increase sales.

Purpose—Modify or cancel current marketing promotions.

Procedure—Administered as needed.

15. *Secondary Source Reports*

Objective—Compile, evaluate, and report on all available current secondary source information of the travel or transportation industry.

Purpose—Continuous market information data base.

Procedure—Monthly.

16. *Media Planning*

Objective—Identify who (passenger characteristics) reads, listens to, or watches which newspapers, magazines, radio stations, or T.V. shows.

Purpose—Develop media plan.

Procedure—Administered on a quarterly basis.

17. *Origin–Destination Reports*

Objective—Determine who goes where, when, etc.

Purpose—Modify old routes and establish new routes.

Procedure—Administered on a monthly basis.

18. *New Service Concept Evaluations*

Objective—Develop new services to customers.

Purpose—Identify needs of passengers not being adequately satisfied and develop services which provide better satisfaction.

Procedure—Administered on an as-needed basis.

Source: Stuart N. Robinson and Associates, Inc., (1980).

tory agencies. This has marked the beginning of a whole new "ball game." Now companies can introduce new fares and establish new routes almost whenever and wherever they want. The market research department that is most flexible under a deregulated market will provide the best support to its company.

REFERENCES

American Bus Association (1978), *America's Number One Passenger Transportation Service*, Washington, D.C.

Drucker, Peter F. (1974), *Management: Tasks, Responsibilities, Practices*, New York: Harper & Row Publishers Inc.

Stuart N. Robinson and Associates, Inc. (1980), *Marketing Research Study*, unpublished in-house report, Dallas, Texas.

Siegel, Laurence (1969), *Industrial Psychology*, Georgetown, Ontario: Irwin-Dorsey Limited.

Whyte, William Goote (1969), *Organizational Behavior—Theory and Applications*, Georgetown, Ontario: Irwin-Dorsey Limited.

26

Research Needs of Small Tourism Enterprises

TYRRELL MARRIS[1]

English Tourist Board
London, Great Britain

*T*his chapter concentrates on market research for the small enterprise working in tourism. Market research attempts to discover more about the enterprise's customers: who they are, what they want from the enterprise, and whether what they bought seemed a fair value for the money. A small enterprise is directly in touch with its customers, and therefore market research should be practicable and—unless he be a genius—should help to turn the owner's hunches or "guestimates" into valid insights or sound estimates. The aim of this chapter is to condense just enough ideas, knowledge, and simplified techniques both to interest the reader and yet require few resources to turn the information to practical use.

Small enterprises need market research information similar to large ones: there is much they can do to help themselves. The published sources of tourism statistics provide a context for the small enterprise's own comparable researches. Because small enterprises are in close touch with their customers, there are realistic ways to achieve their own surveys, which are described herein. They can proceed step by step, learning from the most useful results of previous research.

For simplicity, this chapter will refer to the "enterprise" as the best single name to describe a business, or company, or whatever. The "owner" will describe the main decision taker, who might in fact be a manager or partner. Also, the "owner" of the "enterprise" will be nominated a "he": in many small enterprises the owner might equally be a she or that sometimes most successful combination of wife and husband.

[1]The author thanks the English Tourist Board, of which he is an Assistant Director, for permission to write this chapter and for use of the Board's many published sources. Nevertheless, the opinions and advice given here are the author's own, without implied or expressed agreement by the Board.

There is no easy definition of "small." It really means, in this context, an enterprise that has not the resources to have its own research department, nor the finance to buy much custom-designed research from outside agencies. So, are such enterprises helpless when they need research? This chapter aims to show that—on the contrary—there is much research that the owner can have to help him.

WHO IS IN TOURISM

An enterprise that is small in size can still think big. The owner, who will usually be the manager too, can very well think of the wider opportunities in the industry of which his own enterprise is a small part.

Owners of small enterprises might not realize that they are part of this wider tourism industry. Hoteliers or campsite operators probably do realize this because they sell lodgings for the night; but they need also to realize that most tourists want something to do during the day. Vice versa, owners of other enterprises are often more deeply in the tourism industry than they realize; for instance, archeological sites, boats for hire, boutiques, cafes, discos, exhibitions, fishing lakes, golf courses, hairdressers, information centres, and many more, right through the alphabet to yacht marinas and zoos.

Because the tourist wants a great variety of things to do and see, owners of all those enterprises are directly contributing to the customer's satisfaction. The customer does not see the enterprises as competing, to him they are largely complementary. That even applies to very similar enterprises: an area of the town where most of the restaurants are to be found is often a much greater attraction to having a meal out than any individual place would be on its own. The sense of excitement and entertainment in such an area can add to everybody's enjoyment and hence to increased sales.

Anyone planning to start a new enterprise can easily research his best location by going to see where existing tourist attractions are. Location is known to be crucial, and that will be reflected in site values. Simple observation of where tourists stay, eat, have their fun, or conduct their business and how they travel can help the new owner choose the best site he can afford. A good way for an owner to observe is to be a tourist himself, in and around the area he has in mind, imagining where other tourists would want to find the service he plans to offer.

WHO NEEDS RESEARCH

Wherever an enterprise's sales depend on the general market of consumers, it needs market research to aid its other skills and energies. Many vast business enterprises choose to spend enormously on market research because they cannot be directly in touch with their millions of customers by any other means. But in tourism, many sales are made directly to the customer. That is especially true of small tourism enterprises. Also, what a small enterprise sells is not like an extensively advertised branded item. Small tourist enterprises sell something uniquely their own: their motel at this particular site, their composition of fish menus, their pony treks on these ranges, this style of hand-thrown pottery, and so on.

Because these tourist attractions or facilities or services are so unique, it is wise to research what the "market" wants so as to understand their customers' special needs. It is dangerous to rely on guesswork or tradition. This chapter on market research means to interest, in particular, those who provide accommodation or food or special goods or entertainment or stimulus or relaxation to the tourist—and who would like to do it better.

Small enterprises need similar information about their customers as big ones. A small enterprise has the advantage of much closer contact between the owner

and his customers than the big businesses. But small or big the aim is the same: to discover what makes a happy customer likely to come back for more. It is necessary to identify customers in a systematic way. A good way is for the owner to write what he already knows about present customers under headings relevant to the enterprise, for instance:

- What they do at or buy from the enterprise
- The proportion on vacation, on business, on social trips
- Their sex, age, party size, and if children included
- Spending pattern and income
- Duration of stay
- Frequency of visit
- Mode of travel
- Where they come from
- How they found out about the enterprise
- What attracts them to the enterprise, to the locality.

Having done that, the owner should ask himself: "Do I really know or am I guessing?" His research is just starting.

STARTING TO RESEARCH: INTERNAL SOURCES

Some of those headings will be more important to his type of business than others. If the owner detects an information gap that is obviously important to him and his customers, then it should be filled if possible. Widespread, thorough, custom-designed surveys cannot be afforded by small enterprises but previously published market surveys can be useful for filling gaps. They need not be expensive to buy or borrow. An example of relevance to vacation farms, typical small tourist enterprises, is the research of Pizam and Pokela (1980). Researches of that sort might be located through local reference libraries. More likely, the owner will need to consider other sources. His own financial records will be a good starting point. Charles Goeldner in Chapter 15, Travel and Tourism Information Sources, discusses secondary sources extensively.

Using his financial records, the owner can make simple calculations such as spending per customer or spending per day. Seasonal variations or weekend versus weekday comparisons can be revealing. Some calculations might seem promising but impossible to do because the records are not kept in suitable form. A way to improve the usefulness of financial records is to contrive simple coding of the paper or ink color used on payment slips. Thus, different types of customer, or times of day, or categories of sales can be picked out for special analysis. All this will help to identify the largest revenue-earning aspects of the enterprise.

Where customers came from and how they knew about the enterprise are other questions needing other sorts of research. A hotel, for instance, has the opportunity to modify slightly its advertising in each medium used so as to identify the sources of its visitors. Potential tourists can be invited to write for the hotel brochure using differently coded coupons in each advertisement to identify different media. It is simple to see, from the codes of coupons returned, whether local or national newspapers are attracting more potential customers. In the same way, alternative layout or wording of advertisements can be tested for pulling power. Chapter 41, by Ilkka Ronkainen and Arch Woodside, covers conversion studies more extensively.

An occasional refinement of those methods is to make the same tests but based on actual sales attributable to the advertisement rather than on returned coupons which are only potential sales. It might be helpful to concentrate on those coupons which do convert into immediate sales if the hotel is advertising a short period offer—for instance, a Spring price reduction. But generally, advertising has a longer-term aim, not just to create a sale here and now, so the simple return of a coupon with its consequent opportunity to mail a brochure or other follow-up literature to the potential customer may usually be taken as a valid test.

Calculations of the interval between when advertisements are published and when and how many replies are received will help to appraise how best to time promotional activity. The location of replies will help pinpoint how far afield to go. The style of the media generating replies to advertisements also tells something of the style and tastes of customers. All those items of information can be had from the enterprise's internal sources, if advertisements are coded.

STARTING TO RESEARCH: EXTERNAL SOURCES

None of the research methods described so far will have done much to answer questions about why the customers chose the particular enterprise, or the general locality, or why they chose to come away from their hearth, home, and television set to spend their time and money as tourists. Well-informed opinions of the owner can be a good starting point for finding answers, but opinions need to be tested. Preconceived ideas can mislead or overlook new opportunities.

A good test is, first, to use the observation method. Looking at and listening to the enterprise's customers is informative. Doing the same in competitive and complementary enterprises adds a new dimension to that information. The time and location of other enter-

prises' advertising, opening and closing times, and peak and off-peak pricing are all revealing to the owner of a small enterprise. A question for the owner to consider is whether to do the same as others or whether deliberately to choose a different policy for his enterprise.

The importance of recognizing the complementary nature of tourism enterprises was stressed above. That has a relevance to probing the "why" questions about customers' tastes and choices. Owners of the local restaurant, general store, and camping site will find they have many customers in common. By exchanging ideas and opinions and concrete statistical facts about their enterprises, each owner can gain entirely new insights of why tourists come in the first place and what makes them happy to stay and what might bring them back.

The second readily available source of external research is published statistical information. Local tourism statistics are published by various town, state, provincial, or regional bodies, or their national and regional tourist offices. Local tourism information often comes from national surveys whose results have been broken down to provide statistics for smaller parts of the country. There are many such surveys in tourist destinations with highly developed economies and established research agencies. Examples are:

- The National Travel Survey (U.S. Travel Data Center, 1980), which has been made monthly since 1979 and which covers trips of 100 miles or more (one way).
- The Canadian Travel Survey (Canadian Government Office of Tourism, 1981), which has been made quarterly since 1978 and which covers trips of 50 miles or more.
- The British Tourism Survey (English Tourist Board and British Tourist Authority, 1985), which has been made monthly since 1972 and which covers trips of any distance of 24 hours duration or more.
- The statistical publications of many other government bodies or statistical services such as those of Statistics Canada and the United States Travel Service (see list of references).
- Hotel occupancy surveys (see below).

A selection of tourism surveys is given in the references for further reading at the end of the chapter. A feature of many such surveys, which makes them appealing to small tourism enterprises, is that the results are inexpensive or freely published. Usually they are frequent enough for the owner to compare his business trends with national and local trends.

More rarely, collections of many tourism statistics from several sources are available for particular areas.

An example is the Tourism Regional Fact Sheets (English Tourist Board), which are usually published yearly. They are digests of regional information on the volume and value of tourism, its origin and season, the demographic characteristics of tourists, the main tourist destinations, the use of accommodation, the occupancy of hotels, and visitors to particular attractions. A reading list is included, so that the owner of any enterprise can see where to look for more detailed facts and figures. The British Tourist Authority publishes a digest of tourism statistics for the whole of Britain.

A very comprehensive source of tourism statistics for the North American market is the updated edition of *Travel Trends* in the United States and Canada (Goeldner and Dicke, 1984). It is a compendium, rather than a digest, of a great range of statistical sources, and likewise includes a listing of where and from whom to find more detailed facts. Local libraries might have or get it for reference.

The major tourist bodies often publish books or booklets to advise small enterprises. They can give the owner ideas for research and practical information that save having to do so much of his own research. It might not always be obvious which bodies to go to for information. Seeking such bodies and investing in stamps or telephone calls to find what they have to help the small tourism enterprise is part of the research process.

DOING YOUR OWN RESEARCH

When the owner has seen what can be gotten from analysis of his own internal records, and carefully examined competitive or complementary enterprises, and sought out what can be gotten from other local sources and from bodies promoting tourism, there will be a pile of research facts to consider. The character and seasonality and so forth of the enterprise's customers can be compared with past and recent trends for similar localities or types of tourist. But such comparisons are difficult if there are still large gaps in knowledge about the enterprise's own customers.

The owner may now use simple surveys to fill the gaps. The way to do that with the full rigor of a professional market research survey is explained in countless books, however, they will presumably take more time to read and resources to apply than the small enterprise can afford. There are three other possible methods described below. The first two are really simplified versions of the full survey; they can never be as good as the real thing. But on the principle that half a loaf is better than no bread at all, they do offer a realistic solution to the owner's need for better knowledge. Other sections of this book go into more detail on how to develop and administer survey methods.

FIRST: DO-IT-YOURSELF QUESTIONS

When there are just a few bits of marketing information needed, it can be simple and reliable to ask brief questions of only a hundred or so customers. The method requires talking to those particular customers in a more deliberate and controlled way than usual. The owner and other staff must all do this in the same way, noting customers' answers in a form that is easy to add up. Also, there has to be an impartial way of selecting customers to void the risk of not getting a fair answer because only the more approachable ones have been questioned.

For example, an owner might need to know more about repeat customers. So for one week, at the start of each month, the person served nearest to the hour is asked: "Is this the first time we have served you here or have you come before?" If "before": "How often?" Immediately afterwards the answer is noted down. Naturally those questions will be preceded and followed by the normal courtesies of conversation (but avoiding opening remarks that could influence the answer). Such a survey is not designed to give precise information. It need continue only long enough to show a roughly steady proportion of repeat/first-time customers—or any other topic chosen for survey.

SECOND: DO-IT-YOURSELF MINISURVEY

When an enterprise needs a range of market information, the owner will need to use a more formal way to get it. Seldom will he or his staff have the time to ask customers all the necessary questions, and it is unlikely that he will have the skill to conduct formal interviews: that calls for a personality and training not normally found amongst owners. The way to get the information will be by means of a questionnaire filled in by the customers themselves. Postal return of questionnaire is both inefficient and subject to unknown bias, response rates below 50% being likely. So it is best personally to ask the selected customers to complete and return the forms near the end of their stay, but before they are in such a hurry to leave that they will not answer all the questions before they do leave. Where the customer spends only a short time at the enterprise, for instance at a restaurant, the questionnaire has to be correspondingly shorter and therefore quicker to complete.

People approached the right way at the right time can feel that it is a compliment to be asked their opinions. It matters that the questionnaire is given to selected customers personally, by the owner or responsible staff, making clear that there is a special need for that customer's response: "I/the manager would really value *your* response, madam." And that is indeed true because, when a carefully written questionnaire is necessary, it becomes very important that customers are selected properly. With a steady flow of guests throughout the week, questionnaires might be given to one member of all parties leaving on a Monday in one week, on a Tuesday the next week, and so on. Any practicable method of selecting customers, that is impartial, is valid.

Ideally, one particular member of a party of customers should be selected to fill in the questionnaire, but without experienced interviewers that is unrealistic for a small enterprise. Anyway, in such circumstances, a good questionnaire can be so interesting that many members of the party will want to help complete it—even if dad or the boss or the person paying the bill has the final say.

An example of a questionnaire including a range of questions suitable for a small hotel is shown in Appendix 1. The owner must take care to ask just those questions from which the information is needed and to cut out everything unnecessary to him or perhaps annoying to his customers.

The limit on the number of questionnaires issued is most likely to be set by the ability of the owner to add up and analyse all the answers returned. Although the process is straightforward, it is bound to be time-consuming. As a rule of thumb, experience shows that more than a hundred completed questionnaires are necessary to establish roughly valid answers but more than three hundred are unnecessary for a first mini-survey. It is always possible to make repeat surveys to examine, say, other topics or other seasons of the year.

Assuming that there are between one and two hundred questionnaires to tabulate, results are obtained by adding up the number of ticks in the answer "boxes" and simply expressing the number as a percentage of all responses. Where the questionnaire asks for written answers, it is surprisingly easy to thumb through them to get a first impression of frequent types of written reply. You then list typical replies and allocate the actual written answers accordingly, always being conscientious about extending the list rather than forcing a particular reply where it does not really fit.

The adding up and percentaging is aided by a simple electronic calculator. Everyone will find their own best method: it needs a clear day, a clear head, and plenty of paper and pencils. As an alternative to his own or his staff's efforts, the owner might find a local high school willing to help with tabulating answers (but not with interviewing or similar jobs—student labor needs too much supervision).

When the main findings have emerged, it might be worth breaking down some answers for different types of customers such as vacation/business, repeat/first-time, origin, etc. Without a programmed computer, it is a laborious process, so only a few breakdowns should be attempted at any time. The simplest method is to deal the questionnaire forms into piles, for instance, adults on their own/adults plus child/adults only, and then retabulate.

THIRD: OCCUPANCY SURVEY

The third possible method of research that is easily applied to a small enterprise is the occupancy survey. The merits of this are three:

- Information is gotten that has obvious practical value for the day-to-day management of the enterprise.

- Partly because of the first, existing methods of record-keeping will probably need little modification to make the survey possible.

- There are occupancy survey results published freely, or at small cost for many countries which make useful comparisons.

The essence of the occupancy survey is that it gives an accurate record of how fully the enterprise's accommodation is used. Daily, weekly, or monthly figures can be calculated of which the last is the most frequently published. The ability to compare the enterprise's own monthly performance with the average for similar enterprises in the same locality, or of the same type, is invaluable. Some of the many published sources are given as references at the end of the chapter. If there is no readily available published source for a locality, but there is a strong desire amongst the industry for information, then a local association of owners can organize its own survey. To ensure proper confidentiality of individual figures, the occupancy returns necessary for the survey should be sent to some reliable third party such as a firm of accountants for monthly addition and issue.

The form on which occupancy should be recorded for a small hotel is shown in Appendix 2, together with an example of the arithmetic needed to calculate average room occupancy, average bed occupancy, and duration of stay. All three pieces of information can be revealing: for instance, if occupancy of beds is below average, the cause might be that guests are staying a shorter than average duration at the hotel, rather than that there are fewer than average arrivals. If stays are short, perhaps there is too little to keep the guests amused in or near the hotel. Alternatively, if arrivals are below average, there might be too little to attract guests in the first place. The full diagnosis of what the trouble is and therefore what should be done will depend on a variety of factors. Undoubtedly, having sound information on which to base the diagnosis is a vital starting point for marketing action.

CONCLUSION

The information needs of a small enterprise are very like those of a large one. The disadvantage is that a small enterprise lacks the resources of time and money to buy its own custom-made research services. The advantage is that the owner and his family or staff are so much closer to their customers that do-it-yourself research is a real possibility for the small enterprise. It needs market research to keep in touch with its customers' needs.

Starting to research requires that the owner recognizes the sort of industry in which he works. Many other small enterprises must be regarded as complementary to the total experience a tourist is buying. Observing the enterprises of other owners and exchanging information with them about customers is the start of research. An oversensitivity to competition is a mental barrier to be discarded: much mutual benefit can be had from cooperation.

There are various simple calculations possible, using the enterprise's own financial records, which can pinpoint the greater or lesser revenue-earning aspects of the business. Slight changes in methods of record-keeping can make the financial records more adaptable to such calculations.

Before embarking on more elaborate methods of do-it-yourself research, the owner should see what is published about tourism in his locality or for his type of enterprise. Specialist libraries, tourist bodies, and other professionals might be available to help that search. In some areas there might be a danger of being swamped by all that is available, and in others there might be almost nothing useful. Some attempt needs to be made to look for and use what information is already available.

The small enterprise can do its own research both to fill gaps of knowledge and to get information comparable to what is published. It is quite practical for the owner to question his customers in an effective, structured way so as to improve his knowledge. The resulting market survey, for such it is, can range from one or two questions asked informally of fifty customers to a dozen questions on a printed questionnaire asked of two hundred or so. A step-by-step approach is wisest, so that more elaborate methods are not tried until the simpler ones have been achieved. Amongst the simplest, and most useful for enterprises offering accommodation, are occupancy surveys.

Market research for small tourism enterprises aims to help them, like larger tourism enterprises, to provide customers with satisfaction. When outlining research ways and means it is possible to mention only a few of the results that might come out of research, and how those results are applicable to meeting customers' needs. Many owners of small enterprises, until they have experience of research, will have little preconceived idea of how much they could be helped by surveys. They will be well advised to enter into research gradually, always assessing which previous results have been valuable to them before getting any more. Equally, they are well advised not to reject

research as a complicated irrelevance, but to welcome it as a greatly useful possibility.

REFERENCES

Some sources of national tourism surveys which include useful breakdown of the statistics are:

Australian Government Tourist Bureau (Canberra City, Australia) for results of their *Domestic Tourism Monitor*, etc.

Bahamas Ministry of Tourism (Nassau, Bahamas) for their annual report.

Belgium: Westvlaams Ekonomisch Studiebureau (Brugge, Belgium) for their annual survey of Belgian holiday taking.

Bermuda Department of Tourism (Hamilton, Bermuda) for their tourism statistics.

Canadian Government Office of Tourism or Statistics Canada (Ottawa, Canada) for their many publications.

Denmark Statistics (Copenhagen, Denmark) for their *Statistical News*, etc.

English Tourist Board (Hammersmith, London, England) for the *British Tourism Survey* and *Regional Fact Sheets*, etc.

Finnish Tourist Board (Helsinki, Finland) for their twice yearly statistical publications.

France: Institut National de la Statistique et des Etudes Economiques (Paris, France) for their annual survey of French holiday taking.

Germany: Studienkreis fur Tourismus (Starnberg, Germany) for their annual *Deutsche Reiseanalyse*.

Hawaii Visitors Bureau (Honolulu, Hawaii) for their annual research report.

Japan National Tourist Organization (Tokyo, Japan) for their annual statistical analyses.

Kenya Ministry of Finance and Economic Planning (Nairobi, Kenya) for their *Statistical Digest*.

Netherlands Central Bureau of Statistics (Voorburg, Holland) for their annual survey of Dutch holiday taking.

Pacific Area Travel Association (San Francisco, California, U.S.A.) for their annual reports.

Spanish Ministry of Tourism Information (Madrid, Spain) for their annual statistics.

Switzerland: Institute for Tourism and Transport (St. Gallen, Switzerland) for travel market surveys.

United States Travel Data Center (Washington, D.C., U.S.A.) for the *National Travel Survey*.

United States Travel Service (Washington, D.C., U.S.A.) for their many publications.

Some sources of occupancy surveys of tourist accommodation, particularly hotels, are given below. Many national sources are listed and a selection of local ones to show the range of information available.

Denmark Statistics (Copenhagen, Denmark).
English Tourist Board (London, England).

Harris/Pannell Kerr Forster & Company (New York, New York, U.S.A. and elsewhere).

Hong Kong Tourist Association (Hong Kong).

Horwath & Horwath International (New York, New York, U.S.A and elsewhere).

Las Vegas Convention/Visitors Authority (Las Vegas, Nevada, U.S.A.).

Mexican National Tourist Council (Washington, D.C., U.S.A.).

Newfoundland Department of Tourism (St. John's, Newfoundland).

New Zealand Tourist Department (Wellington, New Zealand).

Northern Ireland Tourist Board (Belfast, Ulster).

Nova Scotia Department of Tourism (Halifax, Nova Scotia).

Tourism Development Company of Puerto Rico (San Juan, Puerto Rico).

Scottish Tourist Board (Edinburgh, Scotland).

Wales Tourist Board (Cardiff, Wales).

There are many researches about particular types of enterprise in particular areas. They can be found in bibliographies of tourism research such as those published by:

Business Research Division, University of Colorado (Boulder, Colorado, U.S.A.).

Centre des Hautes Etudes Touristiques (Aix-en-Provence, France): searches and lists are available from a computer-based index.

Commonwealth Agricultural Bureaux (Oxford, England): Leisure Recreation and Tourism Abstracts; searches and lists are available from a computer-based index.

Particular sources named in the text are:

Goeldner, Charles R., and Karen Dicke (1984), *Travel Trends in the United States and Canada*, Boulder, Colorado: University of Colorado.

Pizam, A., and J. Pokela (1980), *The Benefits of Farm Tourism to Rural Communities: The Massachusetts Case*, Massachusetts Agricultural Experiment Station.

APPENDIX 1   The Minisurvey

Example of a self-completion questionnaire, handed personally to one guest in each tourist party, for return anonymously in a sealed envelope before departure. The questions are designed for an enterprise providing overnight accommodation and meals. They could easily be adapted to other needs.

All unnecessary questions should be deleted: the shorter a questionnaire the better. It is vital to try out an experimental version on a dozen or so guests to see if any aspects need improvement, such as the wording or layout or the way it is issued to or collected from customers.

The "Lake" Hotel Customer Quiz

PLEASE ANSWER BY TICKING THE BOX OR WRITING IN THE SPACE

Q.   For what reason are you staying here?
   on business ☐
   on holiday/vacation ☐
   visiting friends or relatives ☐
   a mixture, or other, please say _____
Q.   About how frequently do you stay here?
   three or more times a year ☐
   twice a year ☐
   once a year ☐
   most years ☐
   less often ☐
   first stay ☐
Q.   What was the main method of transport you used to get here?
   Auto ☐   Train ☐   Plane ☐   Coach ☐   Other ☐
Q.   Did you set out meaning to come here? ☐

or decide during the journey?   ☐
or just stopped when you saw us?   ☐

Q. Can you remember how you first got to know about us?
saw your advertisement   ☐   if so please say where _____
just chanced to stop   ☐
mentioned by friends or relatives   ☐
mentioned by business colleagues   ☐
other, please say _____

Q. Did you have any difficulties on the journey? for instance
heavy traffic on the way   yes   ☐   no   ☐
finding us was   difficult ☐   easy   ☐
somewhere to park   difficult ☐   easy   ☐
public transport or taxi   scarce   ☐   plenty   ☐

Q. How big is the party staying here together with you?
just me ☐   two ☐   three ☐   four ☐   five or more ☐
they are   all adults ☐   adults and children ☐

Q. Have you found things to do and see during your stay?
plenty, some left for next time   ☐
enough for a good holiday/vacation   ☐
sometimes short of things in bad weather   ☐
sometimes short of things in the evening   ☐
not really enough   ☐

Q. Could you list the three highlights of your stay?
1. _____
2. _____
3. _____

Q. Have you found enough choices in our menu?*
great variety, things left to try next time   ☐
enough for a good meal   ☐
rather restricted starting courses   ☐
rather restricted main courses   ☐
rather restricted final courses   ☐
not really enough variety   ☐

Q. Could you list your three favorite things about eating here?
1. _____
2. _____
3. _____

*Other wording could be used for wine lists, displays, entertainments, sports facilities, or other features of competitive importance.

Q. Please write down the price on your bill _____ which covered this number of people ____ . Are there any other things or services which you think should be provided? If so, do please describe and say how much extra, if any, you would be willing to pay for them. _____
_____

Q. Please describe anything at all we ought to have done better to improve your stay. _____
_____

Q. Have you read our brochure?
No, didn't know there was one   ☐
No, not truly interested in brochures   ☐
Yes, but I don't remember much about it   ☐
EITHER
Yes, I liked these features _____
_____

OR Yes, and I would have liked
written description   more ☐   less ☐   OK ☐

pictures	more ☐	less ☐	OK ☐
maps	more ☐	less ☐	OK ☐
about the surroundings	more ☐	less ☐	OK ☐
about the place itself	more ☐	less ☐	OK ☐

Any other comments on the brochure? _____

_____

Q.   Please would you record some personal details?

age under 16 ☐	female ☐
16 to 24 ☐	male ☐
25 to 34 ☐	
35 to 44 ☐	paid employment ☐
45 to 54 ☐	homemaker or ☐
55 to 64	unpaid work only ☐
65 or over ☐	retired ☐
☐	student or other ☐

Q.   If you have paid work, what is your job? _____

_____

Q.   Where do you live?   Country _____

Province/County/State _____

Town _____

Date of Departure _____

THANK YOU FOR YOUR HELP, PLEASE COME AGAIN. THERE IS NO NEED TO WRITE YOUR NAME ON THIS FORM. PLEASE SEAL IT IN THE ENVELOPE AND RETURN TO THE RECEPTION DESK.

APPENDIX 2   The Occupancy Survey

An enterprise offering tourist accommodation can carry out its own occupancy survey in a way comparable with most published occupancy results. Actual occupancy of the enterprise is recorded on the form shown on the next page, which is completed daily. In a small hotel the items recorded are:

- The number of new arrivals that day
- The number of rooms let that night
- The number of beds let that night.

At the end of the month, those items are added to give *total arrivals*, *total rooms let*, and *total beds let*.

The month's Room Occupancy percent is calculated as:

$$\frac{\text{total rooms let} \quad \times \quad 100}{\text{rooms in the hotel} \times \text{nights in the month}}$$

Taking the example given on the next page the calculation is:

$$\text{Room Occupancy} = \frac{634 \times 100}{28 \times 30} = 75.48\%$$

A similar calculation is made for bed occupancy, which will nearly always be lower than room occupancy because double or family rooms are sometimes filled with fewer people than the beds could accommodate.

The month's Bed Occupancy percent is calculated as:

$$\frac{\text{total beds let} \quad \times \quad 100}{\text{bed-spaces in the hotel} \times \text{nights in the month}}$$

Taking the example given on the next page the calculation is:

$$\text{Bed Occupancy} = \frac{1024 \times 100}{52 \times 30} = 65.64\%$$

The month's Average Duration of Stay is calculated as:

$$\frac{\text{total beds let}}{\text{total arrivals}}$$

Taking the example given on the next page the calculation is:

$$\text{Duration of Stay} = \frac{1024}{125} = 8.19 \text{ nights}$$

The occupancy of camp sites or chalets may be simply calculated each week as: the total number of pitches/units let that week divided by the total capacity of the site and multiplied by 100 to give the percent.

RECORD FORM FOR MONTHLY OCCUPANCIES AND ARRIVALS

This hotel, for example, has 10 single rooms (10 bed-spaces) plus 15 double or twin-bed rooms (30 bed-spaces) plus 3 family rooms (12-bed spaces). Total capacity is therefore 28 rooms (10 + 15 + 3) with 52 bed-spaces (10 + 30 + 12). You can see the hotel has a weekly cycle of customers.

Hotel Capacity   *28* rooms   *52* bed-spaces

June date	daily ARRIVALS	ROOMS filled	BEDS filled
1	0	9	12
2	4	10	16
3	4	11	16
4	0	11	16
5	0	10	14
6	16	15	24
7	3	18	27
8	0	18	27
9	0	18	27
10	6	24	33
11	0	24	33
12	0	24	33
13	15	18	31
14	5	23	36
15	0	23	36
16	0	23	36
17	3	26	39
18	0	26	39
19	0	23	36
20	31	22	41
21	6	25	47
22	0	25	47
23	3	28	50
24	0	28	50
25	0	28	50
26	0	25	44
27	24	23	40
28	0	22	38
29	5	27	43
30	0	27	43
31	not applicable	not applicable	not applicable
TOTAL	125	634	1024

PART SIX

ASSESSING THE IMPACTS OF TOURISM

Part Six of the Handbook focuses on a number of different research approaches having one common underlying theme, namely, the measurement of tourism impacts. Those impacts included are economic, employment, social, and environmental impacts. In total, six chapters are involved.

Of the six chapters, three are devoted to the assessment of economic impacts. The importance accorded to this area is related both to the traditional importance of economic impacts to tourism planners and to the willingness of one of the industry's leading experts in this area to contribute extensively to the Handbook. The first of the three chapters authored by Douglas Frechtling (U.S. Travel Data Center) provides readers with an introduction to travel impact estimation. In this introduction, Dr. Frechtling examines the nature of direct and indirect economic repercussions related to travel expenditures. In doing so, he stresses the need for definitional clarity. The chapter subsequently discusses the two main approaches used for estimating economic impacts, namely, direct observation and simulation. It then provides some guidelines concerning the criteria to be used for judging the utility of these alternative approaches. The chapter concludes by providing an overview of the nature of the economic benefits and costs associated with travel, tourism, and hospitality as well as the uses to which economic impact studies can be put.

Chapter 28, "Measuring Economic Benefits," provides the reader with a much more in-depth review of the various approaches to measuring economic benefits and the difficulties encountered in doing so. This discussion will be particularly valuable to managers and researchers who have an active interest in the estimation of economic impacts of travel, tourism, and hospitality. Dr. Frechtling, in presenting his material, provides a very thorough discussion of a large integrated model (the Travel Economic Impact Model) developed by the U.S. Travel Data Center to produce detailed estimates of the economic benefits of travel on the U.S. economy as well as state and local areas.

The final of the three chapters authored by Dr. Frechtling addresses the issue of economic costs associated with tourism and the means of measuring these costs. After pointing out the need to measure such economic costs, the author provides an in-depth discussion of both the fiscal and quality of life costs that may be incurred as a result of tourism development. Again, the distinction is made between direct and indirect impacts. While some readers may find certain parts of the discussion (notably that related to the social rates of discount) somewhat technical, we believe that it is an important contribution to increasing the rigor of tourism research and tourism management. It is our belief that, taken together, these first three chapters of Part Six will become a benchmark and a constant source of reference for tourism planners and researchers.

Next to the measurement of expenditures on tourism, it is the study of the employment impacts of tourism which has traditionally attracted the greatest degree of interest on the part of researchers and particularly on the part of policymakers and politicians. In Chapter 30, Randyl Elkin (West Virginia University) and Randall Roberts (Louie Glass Company) examine this important area and the nature of research which is required. This research falls into two major categories, human resource requirements and employment impact studies. Accordingly, the first part of the chapter reviews human resource requirements research which in turn includes two main categories of enquiry. These are "methods of job analysis," which involves the collection and analysis of data about jobs within a tourism organization with a view to job restructuring, training program development, standards development, performance evaluation, employee counselling, and salary administration, among others, and the second category is that of "projecting and forecasting labor demand and labor supply." The purpose here is to provide some understanding of the kinds of programs that will be needed to meet the employment requirements of the tourism industry of the future. In the latter part of the chapter, the authors discuss research designed to estimate the employment impacts of travel expenditures. In this case, the authors refer back directly to the Travel Economic Impact Model developed by the U.S. Travel Data Center and its ability to predict employment impacts as part of its overall estimation procedures.

A related and yet distinctively different examination of the social impacts of tourism, particularly as they relate to developing rather than developed regions, is presented in Chapter 31 by Louise Crandall (National Capital Commission, Ottawa, Canada). In the first part of her chapter, Ms. Crandall provides a comprehensive overview of the social impacts which can potentially affect developing nations. For purposes of discussion, these impacts are reviewed under the rubric of socioeconomic impacts and sociocultural impacts. In the second part of her paper, the author turns to an examination of the methodologies appropriate to social impact assessment. While a number of the techniques discussed are familiar (such as surveys and Delphi studies), others are not traditionally included in the tourism research repertoire. Such approaches as the use of key informants/community leaders and the participant observation approach, while well known in the field of sociology, have not received widespread attention in tourism. It is anticipated that Ms. Crandall's explanation of the use of these techniques will encourage their further application in tourism. This may also be true to a lesser degree of the use of secondary sources for estimating social impacts which may result from the examples provided by Ms. Crandall. The approaches discussed are the content analysis of newspapers and the analysis of government records and other public documents. In brief, Ms. Crandall provides the reader with another perspective on the measurement of social impacts which, because it has been conceived in relation to developing countries, is substantially different from that outlined by Dr. Frechtling.

The final chapter in Part Six is concerned with the evaluation of environmental impacts of tourism, particularly as these pertain to the physical carrying capacity of a region. Chapter 32, which has been authored by Peter Williams (Ryerson Polytechnical Institute), provides a framework for conducting research and for assessing and managing the environmental impacts of tourism. As the author indicates, his focus is specifically upon the impacts of tourism on the physical environment in general and ecological impacts in particular. The chapter starts with a discussion of the nature of environmental impacts and how they may be classified and defined to permit meaningful research to be undertaken. An important follow-up to this initial discussion is a review of the various methodological constraints which must be faced by researchers who wish to systematically explore or measure the extent of environmental impacts. Having identified these constraints, Dr. Williams proceeds to outline a functional classification of environmental assessment approaches, how they may be used in different settings, and how the data resulting from them can or should be analyzed. For readers who are interested, a detailed example of the environmental impact of one type of tourism example is provided. The chapter concludes with an in-depth discussion of the concept of carrying capacity, a key but controversial concept associated with the physical planning of tourism areas.

27

Assessing the Impacts of Travel and Tourism—Introduction to Travel Impact Estimation

DOUGLAS C. FRECHTLING
Director, U.S. Travel Data Center
Washington, D.C.

*E*conomic impact, the direct and secondary costs and benefits of travel, and the travel industry are defined. Two general methods of approaching travel and tourism impact estimation are presented, along with detailed criteria for judging alternative approaches. Uses of economic impact studies in travel are also discussed.

Economic impact studies in travel and tourism are undertaken to determine the effect of specific activities in a given geographic area on the income, wealth, and employment of that area's residents. They are conducted for cities, counties, towns, states, provinces, and nations, and usually relate to an annual period, although seasonal and event impact studies are not unknown. The results indicate the contribution or cost of tourism activity to the economic well-being of residents, usually in monetary terms.

In the broadest sense, economic impact studies can indicate the gross increase in resident wealth resulting from the activity, the reduction in wealth resulting as well, and the net of the two influences. The wealth effects are traced through household or personal activity, such as employment and income, and through the business and government sectors serving the area.

While implicit in economic impact studies, explicit consideration of the wealth effects of tourism is seldom found. Rather, measurement is limited to the impact on income. Since wealth is created primarily through income, it is clear that concentrating on the latter is consistent with the objectives of economic science.

As discussed here, economic impact studies are understood to include objective analyses of travel ac-

tivity's impact on resident wealth or income in a defined area. On the benefit side, this normally means the study provides estimates of travel spending and the impact of this spending on employment and income. On the cost side, this means estimating the costs, sometimes nonmonetary, to government and residents of travel activity in the area.

A great number of studies have been limited to estimating travel spending in an area, often through direct surveys of travelers or households. No attempt is made in these studies to trace the effects of this spending on area employment, income, or other economic variables.

Such travel expenditure studies are specifically excluded from this discussion. However, the broader impact studies which are considered here include the essential elements of the limited expenditure studies, so the reader will gain an understanding of them in what follows in this and the following two chapters.

The reason for this exclusion is that travel expenditures tend to obscure the impact on resident wealth and income. Although such expenditures may be substantial in an area, they often have little to do with resident earnings and employment. The extreme case is represented by a hotel in an underdeveloped economy, owned by nonresidents, staffed with nonresident employees who send their earnings home, and serviced by imported goods and services. Travelers may spend millions of dollars in the hotel each year, but the contribution to the wealth or income of the residents is virtually nonexistent.

A similar case can be found in the developed economy. Consider a popular self-service gasoline service station in a resort area. Visitors purchase gasoline and oil provided by nonresident suppliers. The station itself is owned by an oil company headquartered elsewhere. The employees may be residents, but it takes only one to oversee the sale of several hundred thousand dollars of petroleum products a year. The dollars spent are a poor guide to the impact on resident wealth or income.

The point is that travel expenditures can be quite misleading in evaluating the economic benefits or the economic costs of travel and tourism in an area. They are best viewed as merely the initial monetary activity that begins the production and measurement of true economic impact on the economy.

DIRECT AND OTHER IMPACTS

Economic impact should be understood to include both direct or primary costs and benefits and secondary costs and benefits. The former occur as a *direct* consequence of travel activity in the area. Travel expenditures become business receipts which in turn are used to pay wages and salaries and taxes. Visitor use of recreation areas requires expenditures on services for the visitors as well as on redressing any environmental damage: these are direct costs. These benefits and costs are directly related to the travel activity.

In addition, there are secondary effects of travel activity. On the benefit side, entrepreneurs spend part of their receipts on goods and services they require to serve customers, including investment in new equipment and structures. In turn, their suppliers must purchase certain items from others. As this chain continues in an area, income and employment are produced *indirectly*.

The other type of secondary benefit is *induced*. Here we track the consumption spending of the wage and salary income directly generated by the travel expenditures on goods and services produced in the area. The induced effects can also include government expenditures in the area induced by the tax revenue generated by travel spending.

We can also speak of secondary costs of travel. These are related to the public goods and services required to serve those businesses and employees that are impacted at the secondary level. Very little work has been done in this area due to its complex and often obscure nature.

DEFINITIONS AND DATA

At first glance, travel economic impact estimation appears quite complex and arcane. This is due to the heterogeneous nature of what we call travel demand and the travel industry. The "travel industry" cannot be defined the way industries normally are. Industries are generally understood as collections of business firms or establishments with the same "primary activity, which is determined by its principal product or group of products produced or distributed, or services rendered" (Office of Management and Budget 1972, p. 12).

This "type of product" classification system is not consistent with the definition of travel and tourism as "end-use" activities, that is, defined by the purpose of the personal or business purchase. We view travel expenditures as those made by people traveling away from home. They cut across many type-of-product industries, and only occasionally account for the bulk of such an industry's output. More often, travelers purchase a minority portion of a product-type industry's output.

It is difficult to square the end-use definition of travel with the type-of-product statistics available from government. Government data indicate total restaurant sales, for example, but not those attributable to travelers. Consequently, travel economic impact studies are confronted by an unusual challenge at the outset: to determine the impact of an end-use activity in a world of product-type data. That this is not easy is readily indicated by the number and complexity of approaches to measuring the economic impact of travel.

This and the two succeeding chapters are designed to cover all aspects of travel's economic impact, including measures of both costs and benefits. The discussion reflects a broad range of studies and other literature on the economic impact of travel, including the U.S. Travel Data Center's contributions. The following pages discuss the major approaches to economic impact measurement, criteria for judging them, appropriate impact measures, estimation methods, and secondary measures of travel's impact.

As the discussion notes, there is a great deal more basic and applied research required in travel economic impact estimation to resolve significant issues in data collection estimation design. It is hoped that these chapters will provide both a guide to what we have learned and a stimulus to others to teach us more.

TRAVELERS AND VISITORS

It is important to clarify whether the study objective is to measure the economic impact of travelers or of visitors. At the national level, we are generally interested in travelers, that is, all people traveling away from home and the industry that serves them. Occasionally, a study will concentrate on visitors to a country from other countries. More often, we are concerned with the business receipts, employment, income, and tax revenue generated by all people traveling away from home.

Studies conducted for smaller geographic areas often concentrate solely on visitors: that is, nonresidents entering the area on a trip away from home. Because the researchers are interested solely in the economic contribution of outsiders to the community, they are not concerned with travel expenditures by residents, such as purchase of common carrier tickets and other items preparatory to taking a trip.

The distinction is vital because it determines the expenditure categories and travel industry components to be included. If we are concerned with the impact of visitors to an area, we should exclude air tickets purchased by that area's residents traveling to outside destinations. The employment and payroll of travel agencies in the area are generally not included in a *visitor* impact study, since they primarily service *resident* consumers and businesses.

In developing an economic impact model or reviewing someone else's it is important to keep this distinction in mind.

DIRECT OBSERVATION AS AN ESTIMATION METHOD

There are two primary ways of producing estimates of travel's economic impact. The more self-evident is *direct observation*. By this approach, we observe the behavior of travelers and determine the effects on the area economy, both positive (income, employment, and tax revenue) and negative (costs to government and individuals).

Observation of benefits could involve analyzing existing secondary data on travel expenditures and the response of business and government to this spending. Such data do not generally exist in a form useful for determining travel's economic impact. Government data available on personal consumption activity, for example, do not distinguish between the type of product purchased and the end-use of that product. We know the U.S. government estimates consumers spent more than $90 billion on gasoline and oil in 1983, but we cannot separate spending on local auto transportation from that on auto travel away from home. Similarly, we cannot segregate travel use in government data on food purchases, amusement and recreation, incidental purchases, and auto rentals.

Even if we could determine travel expenditures from analysis of secondary data, the information necessary to determine the impact of this spending on income, employment, and tax revenue does not exist, nor are data generally collected on the cost effects of travel in the normal course of economic statistics-gathering.

The other method of direct observation is through sample surveys. Travelers can be interviewed concerning their expenditures on trips away from home, and the sample data projected to provide population estimates. While this is frequently done, the results are often poor. Moreover, the approach falls far short when surveys are extended to business owners and operators and government officials to try to determine the effect of travel on income, employment, tax revenue, and costs. The businesses and agencies involved cannot distinguish between activity attributable to travelers and that produced by local residents.

Direct observation approaches are apt to be segmentary, that is, they virtually always focus on one measure, often travel expenditures, rather than following the impact of this activity on income and employment down through the primary and secondary links in the chain.

It is conceivable that someone could observe employees in travel-related establishments, account for how much time on the job they spend serving travelers, and then apportion their compensation accordingly. It is also possible to observe how much of retail sales taxes collected are generated by travelers for an indicator of total retail sales tax revenue attributable to this activity.

However, it is obvious that this is a cumbersome and costly approach. Moreover, it tends to break down in estimating secondary impact on suppliers and the effects of travel-related employees spending their income in the area under study.

Attempts have been made to survey business operators to obtain their estimates of travel-generated receipts as a proportion of total receipts (West Virginia University 1981; Division of Tourism 1974). However, this has not proved a viable method in examples available to date.

ESTIMATION BY SIMULATION

The second major way of producing economic impact estimates is through *simulation*. In simulation, a model is built to represent the major relationships operating in the world. The model is necessarily a simplification embodying only the most important relationships. What is deemed most important varies among those building the models, depending upon their perceptions of the world and their analyses of existing data available to them describing travel activity and impact.

Models vary between being simple and complex and explicit and implicit. Explicit models are composed of clearly stated relationships, usually in the form of equations. Implicit models lack comprehensive statements of relationships and are often judgmental, that is, reflect the views and experiences of the estimator regarding travel magnitudes rather than mathematical relationships among objective variables.

Methods of estimating travel's economic impact are numerous and vary widely in their approaches and output. It is important to judge the approaches by some formal criteria, as discussed in the following section.

CRITERIA FOR JUDGING ECONOMIC IMPACT METHODS

It is vital to judge an approach used for travel economic impact estimates as objectively as possible. We should be especially interested in the relevance, coverage, efficiency, accuracy, and applicability of the approach suggested for use.

RELEVANCE

The approach should measure travel's economic impact and not that of some other activity. For example, a study of the economic effects of restaurants in a community would not represent travel's impact because most of the business could be derived from local residents. Or an approach that uses data on recreation activity as input would include purely local-origin effects as well as those of travelers.

Specific attention should be directed to ensuring that an impact estimation method and the data used in it represent the community, city, state, region, or other area under study. Estimated economic benefits should truly accrue to the residents of the area, and these residents should truly bear any costs estimated from travel. We should be particularly interested in three aspects of the approach in terms of relevancy: Does it relate to travel alone? Does it represent the area under study? Does it cover the time period under study?

COVERAGE

The approach should also cover all of the travel away from home and related activities. On the economic benefit side, the impact of purchases in anticipation of a trip as well as those during the trip should be included in a travel impact study. Anticipatory purchases include major consumer durables such as recreational vehicles and vacation homes and minor items such as tennis rackets and camping equipment. Expenditures during the trip should cover all types of transportation, accommodation, food consumption, entertainment and recreation, and incidental purchases such as souvenirs. But again, the distinction

between visitors and travelers should be observed and the expenditures should truly occur in the area under study.

EFFICIENCY

Since funds available for economic impact estimation are generally limited, the approach should make maximum use of existing data commensurate with satisfying the other criteria. Primary data collection is costly and difficult to do well. It should be avoided wherever possible in favor of relevant, comprehensive, and accurate secondary data.

ACCURACY

We should also judge the approach on the basis of its accuracy. Are the input or survey data accurate measures of travel activity? Does the approach accurately reflect real relationships? Are the results reasonable? This involves investigating the techniques used to generate primary or secondary data. It also includes comparing the results with other, independent measures of travel impact wherever possible. Since these other measures generally do not pass these five evaluation criteria themselves, a good deal of judgment is often required to assess the accuracy of an approach and its output.

APPLICABILITY

The approach should be applicable over different geographic areas and different time periods rather than requiring data unique to one particular case. It should also be sensitive to differences in travel patterns, industry structure, and prices in different places and times. The main objective here is an approach that is feasible in different areas for different time periods and produces consistent results in varying contexts.

These five criteria should be applied to the structure of the estimation procedure, the input data, and the results. They should also be applied to sample design, questionnaires, interview models, expansion factors, and weighting in surveys. The user can weight the criteria based on his own requirements regarding relative importance.

ECONOMIC BENEFITS OF TRAVEL AND TOURISM

An "economic benefit" is best understood as a gross increase in the wealth or income, measured in monetary terms, of people located in an area over and above the levels that would prevail in the absence of the activity under study, *ceteris paribus*.

We are interested in "gross" increases because we will estimate the costs of the activity separately. Subtracting the gross costs from the gross benefits produces a measure of net economic benefit, either positive or negative.

We concentrate on the economic benefits (or costs) for the sake of convenience only, not because other, nonmonetary benefits are insignificant. Economic benefits are measured in terms of money and are amply documented in available data. It is far more difficult to measure the psychic benefits of travel, such as a relaxed feeling, lower blood pressure, or enjoyment of beautiful surroundings. Techniques to measure these nonmonetary benefits are beyond the scope of these chapters. Indeed, little work has been done in this area. This does not mean these nonmonetary benefits are insignificant, only that we have few objective means of measuring them at the current time.

It is important to understand that economic benefits should actually accrue to the people located in the area under study. If we want to estimate the economic benefits of travel to the people who live or work in Missouri, we should be sure the economic benefits actually redound to these people.

Our analysis assumes the absence of these benefits if travel did not occur in the area, *ceteris paribus*. One could argue that with the cessation of tourism in an area, other industries would spring up to provide the same amounts of employment and income. However, this is by no means assured. Employees and proprietors skilled in tourism service could not necessarily find immediate employment in a manufacturing plant. We want to know what travel is contributing to the economy of an area under certain conditions. Analysis of alternative industries that could replace tourism should tourism disappear is beyond the scope of the study of travel's economic benefits.

Finally, a word about terms used to represent economic benefits. The one most often found in economic discussions of travel is "travel expenditures." However, a little thought reveals that expenditures mean little in themselves to the income and wealth of a community.

If travelers purchase all their goods and services from residents who employ labor and supplies originating solely in the area, then travel expenditures represent income to the community. However, it is far more common for travel-related businesses to purchase most of the supplies they need, and often labor as well, from sources outside the community. The gasoline station operator must buy gasoline from a supplier usually refining oil many miles away. Expenditures on an airline ticket do not remain in the community for long, but rather are remitted to some central office to pay for salaries, depreciation, fuel, and other items not found in the community where the ticket was bought.

Many of the goods purchased by travelers are likely to have high import content, that is, consist primarily of intermediate goods produced outside the community. Even services, especially common carrier transportation, may have few linkages with the local economy. Consequently, to focus on travel expenditures as the measure of economic benefits to an area's residents is to grossly misstate the actual benefits generated in the area in many cases.

For a more accurate view, we must calculate the personal income and corporate profits generated by travel spending. We can also look at employment as an important economic policy objective. Government revenue generated by travel expenditures is a valuable measure as well, for it helps convince governments to include tourism in public economic development strategies and to treat tourism fairly in energy, regulatory, and other public policies.

Travel expenditures are an initial cause of economic benefits, but should not be confused with these effects. Table 1 provides a comprehensive outline of the major types of economic benefits derived from travel and tourism.

ECONOMIC COSTS OF TRAVEL AND TOURISM

We normally think of the "costs of travel" as the explicit prices the traveler pays for his trip, his "private costs." He purchases transportation, lodging, food, entertainment, and numerous other goods and services, all at explicit prices in the marketplace.

However, it is important to recognize that all of the costs associated with a trip are not paid explicitly by the traveler. Some are paid explicitly and implicitly by others. These costs borne by others but related to the traveler's activities fall into the general class economists call "spillover effects" or "externalities." The distinction is between the "private costs" of the trip, those paid explicitly by the traveler for goods and services in the marketplace, and "social costs," which represent all other values that must be sacrificed, all the disutility generated by the production process that is not recompensed by traveler purchases (Heilbroner and Thurow 1978, pp. 229–235).

To the extent that we can make all spillover costs explicit and include them in the costs the traveler pays, we will maximize welfare. The traveler then faces higher costs which reflect all of the costs of his trip, and on this basis chooses whether to purchase travel or not. The higher costs are also a signal to industry that competitive advantage can be gained by producing at lower than the prevailing costs, through greater efficiency either in directly serving the traveler or mitigating the externalities generated by the traveler. However, in practice, there will always be uncompensated externalities to deal with.

As Table 2 indicates, we can make a useful distinction between the "private costs" of visiting a commu-

TABLE 1   Economic Benefits of Travel and Tourism

A.   Primary or Direct Benefits
    1.   Business Receipts
    2.   Income
       a.   Labor and proprietor's income
       b.   Corporate profits, dividends, interest, and rent
    3.   Employment
       a.   Private employment
       b.   Public employment
    4.   Government Receipts
       a.   Federal
       b.   State
       c.   Local

B.   Secondary Benefits
    1.   Indirect Benefits generated by primary business outlays, including investment
       a.   Business receipts
       b.   Income
       c.   Employment
       d.   Government receipts
    2.   Induced Benefits generated by spending of primary income
       a.   Business receipts
       b.   Income
       c.   Employment
       d.   Government receipts

TABLE 2   Outline of the Costs of Travel and Tourism

I.   Private Costs
II.   Social Costs
    A.   Direct social costs
       1.   Life quality costs
          a.   Congestion
          b.   Pollution
          c.   Danger to life, health, and property
       2.   Fiscal costs
          a.   Public services
          b.   Public investment
    B.   Indirect social costs
       1.   Life quality costs
       2.   Fiscal costs

nity and the "social costs" depending upon whether the visitor explicitly pays the market prices for travel goods and service or the costs are borne by the residents of the community as a result of the visit.

Frequently, other distinctions are made in discussing the overall costs of tourism: economic costs, social costs, environmental costs, fiscal costs, and life quality costs. These distinctions are valid if we are interested in who initially bears the burden, or what is initially sacrificed. They are also useful for actually measuring the costs associated with tourism. However, it should

be recognized that these distinctions are not very useful for determining who *finally* bears the burden of visitation to a community. Instead, they reflect how a given community has decided to allocate the social costs of visitors at a given point in time.

The term "economic costs" covers all costs, both private and social, explicit and implicit, and refers to the value of what must be sacrificed (called the "opportunity cost" by economists) to provide the visitor experience. It is important to remember that we are interested in the sacrifice of *scarce* goods and services to provide the experience. The fact that a visitor breathes air or absorbs the sun is not a cost to the community, because the residents are not giving up anything scarce that they own and value.

The term "social costs" is used to cover all of the implicit externalities of the visitor experience, as noted above. "Environmental costs" are reductions in the quality of air, water, land, flora, and fauna in our area. These are initially imposed upon those who "consume" them, either directly (e.g., breathing air) or in recreation and enjoyment. "Fiscal costs" are those imposed by government on residents or visitors through taxes, user fees, license fees, fines, and admission charges. "Life quality costs" are those that reduce our standard of living in some nonmonetary way. For example, highway congestion increases the time I must spend commuting to and from work. Since I do not enjoy time spent commuting, this is a reduction in the quality of my life. Virtually all environmental costs are life quality costs, but not all life quality costs are environmental costs.

Environmental costs, fiscal costs, and reduction in resident standards of living or quality of life are all social costs, and denote which group or entity is initially bearing the cost at the current time. They do not designate who finally sacrifices value.

An example will make this clear. Tourists crowd a park that I enjoy visiting in my town. If nothing is done, then I bear the burden as a reduction in the quality of my life. I do not enjoy visiting the park as much as I would in the absence of the visitors. The visitors may also pollute the stream running through the park, again reducing the quality of life for us residents. If nothing is done about this, we residents directly bear these costs and the visitors do not.

However, as residents we have several options. For one, we can persuade the government to impose admission fees for the park. This will not only limit visitor demand somewhat and reduce crowding, but also provide funds for cleaning up the stream and hiring park attendants to prevent pollution. If the admission fees now reduce crowding to its previsitor level and provide funds for returning the environment to its previsitor state, then the environmental life quality costs have become private costs and have been shifted to the visitors and residents who use the park. (In actual practice, it is unlikely that admission fees will both reduce visitor demand significantly and provide enough funds for cleaning up the park, since these are conflicting objectives: we achieve fewer visitors at the expense of revenue.)

There is another option. The residents can vote to spend public funds on enlarging the park and fencing in the stream. If successful in returning the park to its previsitor level of congestion and environmental quality, this tactic has turned one type of social cost (life quality) into another (fiscal). However, in the absence of higher admission fees, the citizens run the danger of attracting even more visitors than before, and there is no guarantee that the taxes required to pay for the park enlargement will be generated by the visitors or local users. The fact that the costs are now fiscal instead of life quality does not tell us who finally pays them. It could be that the residents have just transformed the costs but still must bear them on behalf of the visitors.

Residents can also attempt to reduce congestion and other ill effects of tourism by treating visitors in a repellent manner. In this way, travelers may be dissuaded from returning. It is not clear that negative resident attitudes are effective in reducing visitation, but the resident may not approach this issue in a rational manner (Pizam and Acquaro 1977, pp. 7–11).

Measuring the economic costs of tourism and comparing them to the economic benefits are discussed in a following chapter.

USES OF ECONOMIC IMPACT STUDIES

Measurement of the economic benefits and costs of travel and tourism can help meet a variety of objectives for both marketers and planners.

These studies can inform public officials and business managers of the net benefits of investing in travel promotion or tourism and recreation facilities. The studies can also show how the costs and benefits are distributed geographically and among residents.

Economic impact studies can help tourism marketers evaluate the effectiveness of marketing efforts and the effects of additional facilities on demand for current ones.

Estimates of tourism's economic impact can educate travel-related employees about their role in economic and business development and how their services contribute to the economic health of their communities.

By displaying the net returns to promotional and facility investment, these studies can encourage both business and government to seek out cooperative ventures with other organizations for mutual benefit.

By demonstrating the effects of travel development to the general public, economic impact studies can help citizens rationally choose whether to encourage or resist additional tourism marketing or development efforts.

Economic impact studies also aid public officials in developing laws and policies that best promote the economic, social, and cultural health of their citizens and in avoiding decisions that would threaten this health.

In short, the estimation of the economic benefits and costs of travel and tourism activities permit consumers, business, and government to make efficient and effective marketing and development decisions.

BIBLIOGRAPHY

Division of Tourism, California (1974), *Tourism Employment Study*, Sacramento: State of California Department of Commerce, 76 pp.

Heilbroner, Robert L., and Lester C. Thurow (1978), *The Economic Problem*, fifth edition, Englewood Cliffs, N.J.: Prentice–Hall, 710 pp.

Office of Management and Budget, U.S. (1972), *Standard Industrial Classification Manual*, Washington, D.C.: U.S. Government Printing Office, 649 pp.

Pizam, Abraham, and Ernest J. Acquaro (1977), *Some Social Costs and Benefits of Tourism to Rural Communities, The Cape Cod Case*, Amherst, Mass.: Massachusetts Agricultural Experiment Station, 84 pp.

West Virginia University (1981), *Creating Economic Growth and Jobs through Travel and Tourism*, Washington, D.C.: Government Printing Office, 315 pp.

28

Assessing the Impacts of Travel and Tourism—Measuring Economic Benefits

DOUGLAS C. FRECHTLING

Director, U.S. Travel Data Center
Washington, D.C.

*D*irect observation as a travel impact estimation method is discussed, including the disadvantages of surveys for estimating travel spending and other impact measures. Simulation models are presented and the Travel Economic Impact Model is evaluated in detail. Measuring secondary benefits is also discussed, including alternative techniques for estimating multipliers.

The economic benefits of travel and tourism in an area are the gross contributions to resident income and wealth resulting from the presence of travelers. Normally, this income will result from traveler expenditures in the area. One could conceive of increased resident wealth in the absence of any visitors, say through construction of a tourist facility in anticipation of visitors who never arrive, but this is an unlikely exception that tests the rule.

Resident wealth may be augmented through labor earnings, rising real property values, or returns on capital invested in tourist facilities. As a practical matter, economic benefit studies focus on labor income and generally ignore the other two. This is primarily due to the difficulty of estimating increases in property values from tourists (indeed, values sometimes *decline* with rising visitor volume) and returns on tourism capital. Moreover, these wealth increases often accrue to nonresidents of the area as absentee owners.

There is an implicit consensus in economic benefit studies that we wish to determine the benefits accruing to residents. These are the people needing employment if tourism is viewed as an economic stimulant, and these are the people who choose the area's political leaders and representatives. While tourism development projects sometimes end up benefiting absentee owners more than residents, it is unlikely the

residents and local government had this objective in mind.

The following pages discuss methods of estimating the direct economic benefits of tourism in an area, with a brief explanation of one approach and its evaluation by the criteria established in Chapter 27. Methods of quantifying secondary benefits are introduced and evaluated as well.

No single chapter can exhaustively discuss measuring the economic benefits of travel and tourism. It is hoped that the reader will explore the individual references listed at the end of this chapter for further treatment of individual issues.

DIRECT OBSERVATION OF TRAVEL EXPENDITURES AND BUSINESS RECEIPTS

There appear to be two ways to apply the direct observation approach to estimating travel expenditures, which become business receipts from travelers. One is to actually observe the traveler purchasing food, gasoline, lodging, and other items, either by following him around or by asking the seller to keep records. It would, of course, be quite expensive to follow the traveler even if he would allow this. Moreover, this method could distort travel spending patterns that would occur in the absence of the observer, as the traveler reacts to the observer.

The sellers of air, bus, rail, and cruise transportation can estimate sales to travelers with a high degree of reliability due to the nature of their business. It is unlikely that restaurateurs, gas station operators, or entertainment and recreation facility managers can do so, however. Even hotel and motel operators do not have an easy time making such estimates. In a study conducted by the State of California in the San Diego area, hotel/motel operators were asked to estimate the percentage of their business arising from tourism. The responses ranged from 40 percent to 100 percent (Division of Tourism 1974, p. 21). It seems fair to conclude that following the traveler is not feasible, and business operators do not know distribution of their receipts between visitors and local residents (West Virginia University 1981, p. 52).

The second and most popular direct observation method is to survey travelers either while traveling or in their homes. The results from questions on expenditures can then be projected to produce estimates of business receipts in various types of businesses. Surveys of travelers can be conducted as they enter an area (entry surveys), as they leave the area (exit surveys), or while in the area under study (visitor surveys). In addition, *enroute* surveys can be conducted by common carriers while passengers are traveling on an airplane, train, bus, or ship.

Among these, entry surveys are the least satisfactory, because they cannot obtain information on actual expenditures in the area, only amounts intended.

RECALL BIAS

Exit surveys are superior to visitor surveys if one assumes no decline in respondent recall as the time elapsed between expenditure and interview increases. The recall issue is the most crucial in travel-generated business receipt estimation and has received increasing research attention. If one believes there is little or no loss of recall as a function of the time lapse between purchase and interview, then it makes little difference when the interview is conducted. Travel expenditure estimates derived from household surveys conducted months after the trip are just as accurate as those done in transit.

However, if one believes recall declines precipitously as the duration between purchase and interview increases, then the most accurate direct observation results are obtained only through interviewing travelers while traveling.

A number of researchers argue that because of the great number of travel purchases made in the course of a trip, respondents cannot recall expenditures accu-

rately after the fact.[1] Moreover, currency may not change hands when the purchase is made. Travelers may pay with personal checks, traveler's checks, vouchers, credit cards, or direct billing to home or office. It is difficult to believe the traveler can remember each of the cash or noncash purchases he makes, and the amount as well.

In addition to problems with the human memory, the traveler may never know what some of his expenses were. Many expenses of business travel, convention trips, and incentive travel are paid directly by an employee's firm. Apparently, this type of travel spending produced the lowest response rates among the expenditure questions in the U.S. Census Bureau's 1977 National Travel Survey (Bureau of the Census 1979c).

There is one last difficulty in obtaining reliable expenditure information from travelers. Package tours provide transportation, accommodations, meals, entertainment, or any combination of these for a single price. The traveler cannot usually tell how much of the tour price is attributable to items provided in a given locale. Consequently, he cannot give the interviewer reliable information on his expenditures in the area under study.

Objective evidence on the scope of the recall problem in travel spending is available. In the 1977 National Travel Survey, respondents who took trips involving public transportation, commercial accommodations, or a package tour were asked to report their expenditures for each of the categories. The elapsed time between the trip and the interview was as long as three months. Among those who took package tours, the tabulated data suggest only 70 percent could respond with any cost estimate at all. For public transportation and lodging, the response rates were higher: 85 percent and 92 percent, respectively. These rates only indicate the proportion of those with eligible trips who reported some expenditures. They do not suggest the degree of underreporting of expenditures that may have taken place (Bureau of the Census 1979c, pp. 54, 59).

A comparison of visitor expenditure estimates in Hawaii derived from diaries kept by visitors and from questionnaires sent to former visitors one month after they returned home found that "relative to the diary method, visitors who recall their vacation spending some time after returning home generally underestimate their expenditures" (Mak, Moncur, and Yonamine 1977). While the diary method may have been biased, it intuitively appears to have the better chance

---

[1]See the following for discussions of this recall bias: Haynes (1975), Steel (1981), Bureau of Management Consulting (1975a, p. 41), Church (1969), Lansing and Morgan (1971, pp. 123–126), Mak, Moncur, and Yonamine (1977), Ritchie (1975, pp. 3, 5), and Meyburg and Brog (1981, p. 47).

of capturing visitor expenditures due to the shorter recall period.

In a study of the impact of the amount of elapsed time between an intercity trip and the report of the trip on reported trip volume, Meyburg and Brog found that the longer the elapsed time, the smaller the proportion of actual trips reported. For example, more than 4 percent of actual intercity trips were unreported six to nine months later, and 13 percent were unreported nine to twelve months after they occurred (Meyburg and Brog 1981, p. 48). We may fairly conclude that if there is underreporting of trips, there must be underreporting of expenditures while traveling away from home six months or so earlier.

One other source of direct comparison between short and long recall period surveys is the U.S. Travel Data Center Study of the 1973–1974 Consumer Expenditure Survey (CES), conducted by the U.S. Bureau of the Census (Travel Data Center 1978, pp. 162–164). The CES obtained expenditure information on travel purchases by personal interview once every three months over a two-year period. It was estimated that U.S. residents spent an average of $2.7 billion on foreign travel per year during the survey period.

The U.S. Department of Commerce Bureau of Economic Analysis (BEA), which is responsible for deriving estimates of U.S. travel spending in foreign countries for balance of payments purposes, annually uses self-administered questionnaires distributed to returning residents, keeping the elapsed time between expenditure and report to a minimum. Through this technique, BEA estimated an annual average of $7.2 billion in consumer expenditures for foreign travel for 1972–1973. U.S. consumer spending on foreign travel, then, may have been underestimated by more than 60 percent through the CES because of recall bias associated with the long elapsed time between expenditures and interview.

More objective evidence is needed before handing down a final verdict on this important issue. However, the evidence that is available, along with intuition, suggest estimates of travel expenditures suffer as the elapsed time between purchase and interview increases. Moreover, for some types of travel, such as business or package tours, the respondent may never have knowledge of his actual travel expenses in an area.

This author believes poor recall substantially biases travel expenditure estimates derived from interviews more than a day or two after the purchase. Consequently, exit, visitor, or enroute surveys where the expenditure recall period is limited to the previous 24 hours appear to be better choices than entry surveys. The Florida Division of Tourism has conducted such surveys since 1974 with apparent satisfaction with the results (Haynes 1975; Schultz and Stronge 1980a).

Visitor surveys can suffer from "length-of-stay" bias. If visitors are interviewed while they are in an area rather than when they enter or leave, the probability of being selected increases with the length of stay. A visitor staying ten days in Washington, D.C., has ten times the probability of being interviewed as a visitor staying one day, *ceteris paribus*. This should be adjusted for in enroute surveys, or multiplying length of stay by daily travel expenditures is likely to produce estimates significantly biased upward (Archer and Shea 1975).

One other problem may frequently be encountered in traveler surveys. Sometimes the estimates are distorted by a few travelers who make unusually large purchases while in the area and bias the results of a small sample survey substantially upward. The motorist forced to buy a new set of tires while at his destination is one such case. A traveler who requires hospital care for an unexpected illness is another. This can be accounted for by asking both actual expenses during the previous 24-hour period and which of these were atypical. However, it would be unfair to remove completely the atypical expenditures because they do indeed constitute travel spending. Rather, samples over time can yield the correct probability of encountering these, and this is used to adjust the survey results for these expenses (Haynes 1975).

HOUSEHOLD SURVEYS

The conduct of surveys in the household have been discussed at length elsewhere.[2] The recall problem regarding travel expenditures as discussed earlier is a prime weakness of this approach. A strength is that sampling frames for household surveys are readily available, and it is a simple matter to project sample results to the total population for absolute estimates, something traveler surveys do not readily permit.

There is an analogue to the length of stay bias in household surveys. Those people who travel the most are by definition least likely to be home to be interviewed. Repeated call-backs and adjusting for probability of being at home can be used to reduce this potential source of bias.

Another drawback of the household survey is that it misses travelers in an area who do not belong to the population being sampled. For example, a survey using a probability sample of the U.S. population cannot provide information on foreign visitors in a locality. This requires either surveys among foreign resident populations or a traveler survey.

There are three basic modes of household surveys: mail contact, personal interview, and telephone interview.

[2]For example, see Lansing and Morgan (1971), Babbie (1973), Ferber (1978), and Bureau of the Budget (1969).

Mail surveys are the least expensive, allow the largest sample size within a given budget, avoid not-at-home bias, and allow respondents to consider their answers carefully, perhaps checking with other household members to ensure accurate information. On the other hand, mail surveys are the slowest of the three modes, often adding four weeks or more to the survey process. Moreover, they permit the least control over question completion, are subject to loss in the postal system, do not permit interviewer probing for detailed recall, and produce the lowest response rates. The last caused the U.S. Census Bureau to switch from mail to personal interview in its 1977 National Travel Survey (Bureau of the Census 1979c, p. xxi).

The low response rate in mail surveys produces trip volume bias. There is evidence that nonrespondents to mail surveys tend to be less mobile in terms of trip frequency than respondents (Hunt and Dalton 1983; Woodside and Ronkainen 1984). However, this bias cannot be easily removed by adjusting sociodemographic weighting procedures (Brog and Meyburg 1980). The Data Center noted similar evidence in mail surveys conducted from 1974 through 1976 (Travel Data Center 1975, 1976, 1977).

Personal interviews have the virtues of shorter elapsed time between interview and processing relative to mail, more uniformity in question interpretation if interviewers are properly trained, and high response rates either through repeated call-backs or by substituting similar households. The drawbacks of this mode are the high cost of interviewing, the difficulty of obtaining interviews in some areas due to crime or exclusivity, and poor interviewer supervision. In some cases, interviewers have been known to falsify interview records to achieve interview quotas (Ferber 1978, p. 426).

Compared to personal interviews, telephone surveys are considerably less costly, produce results more quickly, and provide direct supervision of interviewers. Response rates are similar and can be higher through increased ease and lower cost of repeated call-backs.

Telephone surveys cannot be easily or accurately conducted among populations relatively inaccessible to the instrument. In the U.S., it is estimated that 97 percent of U.S. households have telephone service, making this an effective interview mode (Bureau of the Census 1981, p. 585). Another drawback is that telephone surveys do not permit lengthy interviews or questions with many choices or with exhibits.

Compared to mail surveys, telephone interviews are more costly. However, they are superior in minimizing lag between interview and processing, maximizing response rates, and providing control over the interview.

When considering an interview mode, it is important to determine whether the interviews will be conducted among a probability sample of the population or among a preselected panel of potential respondents. Panel surveys are frequently found in the mail mode because they produce high response rates.

These panels are large files of households that have agreed to be included in consumer surveys conducted by research firms. When a survey is to be conducted, a sample of necessary size is drawn to reflect the characteristics, usually demographic, of the population as a whole. This approach generally produces significantly higher response rates than a "cold" probability sample.

The failure of this approach is due to the basically upscale nature of the preselected panel. People interested in participating in surveys are apt to be more active in many aspects of life than those who do not, regardless of income or level of education (Lansing and Morgan 1971, pp. 59–62). The U.S. Travel Data Center's 1974 and 1975 National Travel Surveys were conducted among mail panels and found a considerably higher incidence of travel among nearly all groups than the Census Bureau's probability sample (Travel Data Center 1975, 1976).

Moreover, since all households in the population do not have a known chance of participating in the panel, techniques for estimating sampling variability cannot be applied. Confidence intervals at different numbers of standard deviations from the mean cannot be computed, so this guide to the reliability of the survey in reflecting actual population behavior is not available (Dommermuth 1975, p. 19; Cochran 1977, p. 135).

In summary, among the direct observation methods of estimating travel expenditures, exit surveys are the best at limiting recall bias. However, the difficulty in projecting sample results to the total population is not resolved in any of the three kinds of traveler surveys.

Household surveys solve the projection problem, but fall short on the recall bias issue. If a household survey is the chosen direct observation method, telephone surveys with minimum recall periods (one month at most) among national probability samples are the preferred mode.

This author believes none of the interview methods discussed above can provide reasonably accurate travel expenditure information, with the possible exception of the exit survey limited to 24-hour recall. It is argued in ensuing sections that simulation produces better results in estimating expenditures on trips and their impact.

DIRECT OBSERVATION OF OTHER BENEFIT MEASURES

Travel and tourism produce a demand for a variety of different goods and services. In a travel impact study, we are interested in the end use of these items rather than the type of product produced. For example, we should examine data on gasoline purchased for travel away from home, not all gasoline sales; or meals purchased by visitors, not all meals sold.

The *end-use* focus of travel impact studies prohibits employment of the direct observation approach for measures other than travel expenditures and business receipts. It has been documented, if we did not intuitively know, that we cannot expect employers or employees to accurately estimate how many of their jobs are attributable to tourism. Similarly, there is not direct way to determine travel-generated profits, tax revenue, or income, except in cases of industry segments or individual business establishments where it can be documented that virtually all receipts are attributable to travelers or visitors.

This group is small relative to the universe of businesses and items affected by travel and tourism. It includes Amtrak (although some studies suggest a substantial proportion of receipts are derived from daily commuters), air passenger service (when it can be separated from cargo and other nonpassenger airline activities), commercial lodging guestroom rentals, intercity bus service (if passenger revenue can be separated from that of other services), cruise lines, and arrangers of passenger transportation (travel agents, tour operators, etc.). For these travel industry segments, some information can be derived on travel's economic contributions from tax, business, and employment data through the application of direct observation.

However, we should not focus on a segment just because it is easy to measure. A far more comprehensive and accurate picture of travel's economic benefits must come from examination of all business types, goods, and services affected by travel demand.

SIMULATION MODELS OF TRAVEL'S ECONOMIC BENEFITS

The essence of building a simulation model for estimating the economic benefits of travel and tourism in an area is the embodiment of the major relationships among travel activity, expenditures, employment, earnings, profits, and tax revenue. Most of these relationships are straightforward, and vary only by the quality of the input data. For example, a given amount of travel-generated employment in a business in an area will produce a certain amount of wage and salary income. The objective is to obtain the best data quantifying the relationship.

Some relationships, however, might be termed "provisional" or even "speculative." These are primarily found when trying to estimate the relationship between the act of taking a trip and the expenditures related to it. The problem here is to quantify the linkage between trip-taking activity and travel expenditures.

There are, again, two major approaches. One is direct observation, through surveys of travelers either enroute or at home. In a number of cases, direct observation is used to estimate travel spending, and then relationships to measures of economic benefit are simulated in a model. The drawbacks of this approach have been discussed earlier in this chapter.

The other method is simulation of travel spending. Sample survey interviewing is conducted to obtain certain measures of travel activity on the theory that respondents can more accurately recall many nonmonetary characteristics of their trip, such as destination, length of stay, mode of transport, and season of the year, than they can the money spent.

Simulation models vary in the degree that they rely upon survey results to produce the estimates of economic benefit. At one end of the scale is true direct observation, where the expenditure estimates are derived solely from the survey. At the other end is true simulation, where no survey data are used at all. In the opinion of this author, the better models fall near, but not at, the simulation end of this spectrum.

The other common characteristic of simulation models is the degree to which they rely upon information on the purchase and use of commercial lodging facilities: hotels, motor hotels, motels, and tourist courts. Practically all guestroom rentals in these establishments are attributable to travelers (some small percentage may be due to local residents needing rooms for receptions, dinners, or other sorts of local entertainment). Consequently, data on guestroom rentals are virtually all travel-related and are often relatively easy to obtain through tax and business records.

Simulation models often link information on lodging receipts or guestroom rentals to other travel activity and expenditures. A relatively common technique is to use a travel expenditures survey to estimate the ratio of commercial lodging purchased to total travel expenditures including lodging. By multiplying this ratio by lodging industry guestroom receipts from tax or business records, an estimate of total travel expenditures is derived (West Virginia University 1981).

This procedure can provide very misleading estimates if:

1 The survey sample is not large enough to produce relatively accurate estimates of the lodging-to-total-expenditure ratio.

2 Recall bias distorts this ratio.

3 Surveys are conducted only at long intervals on the assumption that the ratio remains stable over time.

4 The tax data on guestroom rental receipts for a particular year are distorted by payment of past taxes and penalties for previous periods, or underreporting.

5 Respondents report all travel expenditures on the trip rather than only those in the area under study.

Consequently, it is important to examine how heavily the expenditure estimates from a given model depend upon guestroom rental data, an issue under the accuracy criterion of the evaluation procedures detailed above. Users should be leery of models that are based primarily on this single input. Travel activity and the economic benefits derived from it are too complex to be estimated from a single datum.

INTEGRATED VERSUS SEGMENTARY MODELS

We can develop methods to estimate one aspect of economic impact, such as travel expenditures or travel-generated employment. These may be called *segmentary* models. Alternatively, we can develop an *integrated* model that simulates the linkages among travel spending and a number of its economic effects, including employment, income, and tax revenue.

The segmentary model has the advantage of being simple and inexpensive compared to the integrated model. Fewer input data are required, less behavior and fewer interrelationships among variables need to be simulated, and a fixed amount of time and money can produce higher-quality estimates.

The major disadvantage, and it is a large one, is that the one economic magnitude estimated is emphasized at the expense of other aspects of impact. Segmentary models are most frequently built to estimate travel spending, and less frequently travel-generated employment. Travel expenditures tell us very little about the economic contribution travel makes to an area. In the extreme case, such as small island economies which import nearly all productive goods, services, and capital, travel expenditures produce little or no economic benefit for the residents.

Travel-generated employment is a useful measure of economic contributions of travel to a community. There is an explicit commitment at all levels of government to fostering employment opportunities for residents. This commitment has spawned several segmentary models aimed at estimating only the employment attributable to travel and tourism (Kahn 1975; Mueller 1977; Ellerbrock and Hite 1980).

It is a mistake to raise this measure above others characterizing travel's economic benefits. In the final analysis, we are not interested in the jobs generated for their own sake but for the earnings these jobs provide. Community leaders should prefer one thousand travel-generated jobs paying $10,000 each to two thousand jobs paying $4,000 each.

Jobs generated by travel and tourism run the gamut from the lowest hourly wages (eating and drinking places in the U.S.) to the highest (air transportation). Knowing how many jobs are attributable to tourism may well be a highly misleading indicator of the actual income earned by those holding them, and it is income that is the more revealing measure of travel's contribution to economic well-being, although not sufficient in itself.

Integrated models, admittedly more difficult to construct and more expensive to operate, have the advantage of simulating a number of relationships in the economic world. Relationships among the important economic measures of travel's contributions—business receipts, employment, earnings, profits, tax revenue—are specified. We then have a number of measures of travel's economic benefits to work with in evaluating the importance of this activity to the residents of an area, with all measures consistent with one another. Moreover, all of the relationships in the model can be examined for validity.

The segmentary mode is attractive in its simplicity, but misleading in emphasizing one measure of economic benefit at the expense of others.

TRAVEL ECONOMIC IMPACT MODEL

The Travel Economic Impact Model (TEIM) is a large, integrated model developed by the U.S. Travel Data Center to produce detailed estimates of the economic benefits of travel away from home by U.S. residents on the U.S. economy, as well as on state and local areas. It is an attempt to satisfy the five evaluation criteria discussed in the previous chapter.

Development of the TEIM began in 1972, when the Data Center assembled a team of researchers to design the National Travel Expenditure Model. This model, later renamed the National Travel Expenditure Component (NTEC) of the TEIM, aimed to provide annual estimates of U.S. domestic traveler spending on a consistent basis for each state and the nation.

In 1975, the Data Center added the Economic Impact Component and the Fiscal Impact Component to the TEIM and extended it to produce estimates for counties and cities. This work was initially done under a contract with the Bureau of Land Management, U.S. Department of the Interior (Frechtling *et al.* 1975a,b). In subsequent years, the Data Center has revised the model to incorporate additional information on U.S. travel spending and its economic contributions.

TEIM estimation starts with travel expenditures in the benchmark year through the National Travel Expenditure Component. In 1977, and every fifth year thereafter, the U.S. Bureau of the Census conducts a National Travel Survey and Censuses of Service Industries and Retail Trade (Bureau of the Census 1979a,b,c). These provide data down to the state and local level on travel activity and the structure of the travel industry.

Travelers can travel by air, bus, rail, ship, personal motor vehicle, or some combination of these. They can spend the night in the homes of friends or relatives, hotels/motels, campgrounds, own second or vacation homes, or enroute. They can take taxicabs, rent cars, purchase meals, consume entertainment or recreation, and buy gifts and other incidentals. All of these activities give rise to travel expenditures, and are included in the TEIM.

Table 1 lists the travel expenditure categories and the activities used to represent them derived from the National Travel Survey. The U.S. Standard Industrial Classification codes, designed to classify establishments by the type of activity in which they are engaged, are shown in parentheses.

The activity level for each expenditure category is derived for each state form the National Travel Survey.

The cost per unit of activity is derived for each category in each state from industry sources, U.S. Travel Data Center surveys, government data, and other reliable sources. These per-unit cost factors, adjusted for certain variables expected to influence each factor, are multiplied by the activity levels to produce the expenditures in each category in each state.

An example may make this clear. The 1977 National Travel Survey indicates the number of hotel/motel and other commercial lodging room-nights purchased by travelers with selected characteristics in each state. The number of room-nights for each travel type in a state is multiplied by the cost per room-night for that traveler in the state, and summed for all hotel/motel lodging in the state.

The equation is

$$NHLS_s = \sum_p \sum_h HLN_{s,p,h} \cdot HLC_{s,p,h} \qquad (1)$$

TABLE 1 Expenditure Categories and Related Industry Categories in the Travel Economic Impact Model

ACTIVITY OF EXPENDITURE	TYPE OF BUSINESS (SIC CODE)
Transportation	
Air	Air transportation (45)
Taxicabs/limousines	Taxicab companies (413)
Automotive operation	Gasoline service stations (554)
Camper/trailer operation	” ” ”
Automobile ownership	Automotive dealers (55 except 554)
Camper/trailer ownership	” ”
Auto rental	Passenger car rental and leasing without drivers (7512)
Boat/ship	Water transportation (44)
Bus/motorcoach	Intercity highway passenger transportation (412)
Train	Amtrak (National Railroad Passenger Corporation)
Other	Average for transportation businesses
Lodging	
Hotels/motels	Hotels, motels and motor hotels (701)
Camping	Camps and trailering parks (703)
Own second or vacation home	General contractors and builders (152)
Other	
Entertainment/recreation	Amusement and recreation services, including motion picture theatres (783, 79)
Incidental purchases	General merchandise and miscellaneous retail stores (53, 59)
Gifts	” ” ”
Meals	Eating and drinking places (58)
Travel agent bookings	Arrangement of passenger transportation (4722)

where

s = one of the 50 states or the District of Columbia

p = travel party size

h = high or low season for rates

$NHLS$ = traveler spending on lodging in a hotel, motel, or other rental accommodation, NTS basis

HLN = travel party nights spent in the above types of lodging

HLC = cost per room-night.

Other expenditure categories are similarly treated, using the appropriate measures of activity and cost factors.

The expenditure data resulting from the National Travel Expenditure Component cover only those trips to places 100 miles or more away from home, the basic trip definition used in the 1977 National Travel Survey (NTS). Consequently, these results understate U.S. travel expenditures on all overnight trips and day trips of 100 miles for two reasons. First, only 100-mile trips are included in the 1977 NTS and the expenditures estimates based upon it. Second, the 1977 NTS may have underestimated travel activity, with resulting expenditure estimates based upon it underestimated as well for a state.

To correct for these potential sources of underestimation, the results of the NTEC for each state are calibrated using estimates provided by the U.S. Census Bureau's 1977 Census of Service Industries (CSI). The NTEC estimates of traveler spending for commercial accommodations are compared to the CSI estimates of hotel/motel receipts from room rentals, and the state travel expenditure estimates for each category are adjusted by the ratio of the CSI estimates of hotel/motel room rental receipts in a state to the NTEC estimates of travel spending on commercial accommodations in the state. The results are adjusted travel expenditures in each of the 18 categories for each state, which represent expenditures on overnight trips away from home and day trips to places 100 miles or more away from home.

The TEIM then sums across all adjusted expenditure categories to produce a total estimate of travel spending by U.S. residents in the state, and sums across states to obtain the national total.

The next component of the TEIM begins by estimating the payroll earnings attributable to travel spending in each category in each state. Data from the Censuses of Service Industries and Retail Trade indicate the ratio of payroll to business receipts for most relevant industry categories in each state during the benchmark year. The necessary common carrier data

are not available from this source but are estimated from other data.

The relevant equation for hotel/motel lodging is

$$THLP_s = THLR_s \cdot (HLP_s / HLR_s) \qquad (2)$$

where

s = one of the fifty states or the District of Columbia

$THLP$ = hotel/motel payroll attributable to traveler spending on lodging

$THLR$ = hotel/motel business receipts attributable to traveler spending on lodging

HLP = total payroll of hotels/motels

HLR = total business receipts of hotels/motels.

It should be noted that business receipts are defined to exclude sales taxes, use taxes and gross receipts taxes that are included in travel expenditures. The removal of these from travel expenditures to produce travel-generated business receipts will be discussed later.

Next, employment generated by travel spending is estimated by relating jobs to payroll. In effect, the proportion of a job supported by a dollar of payroll is estimated for each industry in a state, and multiplied by the travel-generated payroll estimated in the previous component.

The relevant equation for the lodging section is

$$THLE_s = THLP_s \cdot (HLE_s / HLP_s) \qquad (3)$$

where

s = one of the fifty states or the District of Columbia

$THLE$ = hotel/motel employment attributable to traveler spending on lodging

$THLP$ = hotel/motel payroll attributable to traveler spending on lodging

HLE = total payroll employment for the hotel/motel sector

HLP = total payroll for the hotel/motel sector.

Detailed employment and payroll data by industry segment are available from the U.S. Bureau of Labor Statistics each year. The employment estimates are of jobs in the industry, including both full and part time jobs.

Travel-generated employment for other sectors of the travel industry are similarly estimated. Employment is then summed across sectors to obtain the total for the state, and summed across states for the national total.

The Fiscal Impact Component of the TEIM develops estimates of the following types of taxes at the federal, state, and local levels:

Excise taxes.
Sales, use, and gross receipts taxes.
Individual income taxes.
Employment taxes.
Corporate income taxes.
Property taxes.

The rates prevailing for these taxes in each state and the industry segments to which they apply are determined and entered into the Component. The following details the general approach for the above types of taxes.

For excise, sales, use, and gross receipts taxes, the general equation for the hotel/motel sector is

$$THST_{s,g} = THLS_s \cdot [t_{s,g} / (1 + \sum_g t_{s,g})] \quad (4)$$

where

s = one of the fifty states or the District of Columbia

g = federal, state, or local government

THST = excise, sales, use, or gross receipts tax revenue attributable to traveler spending on hotel/motel lodging

THLS = traveler spending on hotel/motel lodging

t = tax rate on guestroom rentals.

The final term in equation (4), $(1 + \sum_g t_{s,g})$, removes tax payments included in the travel expenditure so the rate is applied to the purchase price not to the price plus the sales tax.

At this point, business receipts attributable to travel spending can be computed. Business receipts are defined to be net of sales, use, or gross receipts taxes to be consistent with the benchmark Bureau of the Census data. The TEIM computes travel-generated business receipts for an industry in a state by subtracting sales, use, and gross receipts taxes from travel expenditures, as indicated in equation (5):

$$THLR_s = THLS_s - \sum_g THST_{s,g} \quad (5)$$

where

s = one of the fifty states or the District of Columbia

g = federal, state, or local government

THLR = hotel/motel business receipts attributable to traveler spending on lodging

THLS = traveler spending on hotel/motel lodging

THST = sales, use, or gross receipts tax revenue attributable to travel spending.

Travel-generated individual income and employment tax revenue is estimated by developing the average rate of these taxes as a percentage of personal income in the state and applying this to travel-generated payroll. The equation for the hotel/motel sector is

$$TIIHT_{s,g} = THLP_s \cdot (IIT_{s,g} / PY_s) \quad (6)$$

where

s = one of the fifty states or the District of Columbia

g = federal, state, or local government

TIIHT = individual income tax and employment tax revenue generated by hotel/motel payroll attributable to traveler spending on lodging

THLP = hotel/motel payroll attributable to traveler spending on lodging

IIT = total individual income tax and employment tax collections

PY = personal income.

To estimate corporate income tax revenue attributable to travel spending, data are collected from the U.S. Internal Revenue Service and the states on the relationship of corporate income tax payments to business receipts, by industry segment. Equation (7) presents the method used for the hotel/motel sector:

$$TCIHT_{s,g} = THLR_s \cdot (HCIT_{s,g} / HBR_s) \quad (7)$$

where

s = one of the fifty states or the District of Columbia

g = federal, state, or local government

TCIHT = corporate income tax revenue attributable to traveler spending on hotel/motel lodging

THLR = hotel/motel business receipts attributable to traveler spending on lodging

HCIT = corporate income tax collections from hotels/motels

HBR = total business receipts of hotels/motels.

Local governments generally rely most heavily on

property taxes for revenue. Property taxes are normally paid by residents out of personal income. The income earned by residents in a location enables them to pay their annual property taxes. It is assumed that the amount of property tax a resident pays is proportionate to his income, including that earned in a job attributable to travel spending.[3]

Equation (8) details the estimation technique for employees of the hotel/motel sector:

$$TPHT_{s,g} = THLP_s \cdot (PT_{s,g} / PY_s) \qquad (8)$$

where

s = one of the fifty states or the District of Columbia

g = state or local government

$TPHT$ = property tax revenue attributable to traveler spending on hotel/motel lodging

$THLP$ = hotel/motel payroll attributable to traveler spending on lodging

PT = property tax revenue

PY = personal income.

This completes the TEIM estimates of travel's economic contributions at the state and national level. To produce county or city estimates of travel impact, the state totals in each impact category are distributed to a particular locality based upon available measures of business activity in the area. For travel expenditures on hotel/motel lodging, the relevant expenditure equation is

$$THLS_1 = THLS_s \cdot (HLR1 / HLR_s) \qquad (9)$$

where

1 = any locality in state "s"

s = one of the fifty states or the District of Columbia

$THLS$ = traveler spending on hotel/motel lodging

HLR = total hotel/motel receipts.

Data are not generally available on the relationships among business receipts, payroll, and employment by industry at the local level. Consequently, the state-wide relationships are assumed to hold, and equations

---

[3]The same approach to estimating local property tax revenue attributable to the presence of a specific economic activity in an area was used in the economic impact model developed by the Commission on the Review of the Federal Impact Aid Program, *A Report on the Administration and Operation of Title I of Public Law 874, Eighty-first Congress*, Washington, D.C., 1981, 153 pp., H-6.

similar to equation (9) are used to distribute travel-generated payroll and employment by industry among the localities.

Federal and state tax revenue attributable to travel are similarly distributed among the localities. However, local sales, excise, gross receipts, individual and corporate income, and property tax rates are entered for each locality and estimated directly.

Care is taken to specify whether the local estimates are of traveler impact or of visitor impact. If the latter, state-level travel expenditures for each industry sector are adjusted to represent the amount attributable to nonresidents entering a locality. This is particularly important for common carrier expenses, auto ownership costs, and travel agency services.

UPDATING THE BENCHMARK ESTIMATES

Once the benchmark estimates of travel's economic benefits are complete for every state, they are updated each successive year. The update procedure involves applying growth factors to expenditures and their relationships to payroll, employment, and taxes, by state and by industry segment. At the county and city level, distribution matrices specific to the year are entered to reflect changes in the patterns of travel's impact within the state.

The update factor for a category of travel spending in a state is based upon available measures of change in the activity over the previous year. For example, spending on commercial lodging in the benchmark year is updated each year by the percentage increase in a state's lodging tax revenue over the previous year, adjusted for tax rate changes. If a state cannot break out lodging taxes on guestroom rentals, then total sales tax revenue data for the lodging industry are used. In the few states where these are not available, regional data from the U.S. Travel Data Center's National Travel Surveys are used along with measures of change from similar states to develop the estimate of percent increase.

Travel-generated payroll is updated by adjusting the ratio of payroll to business receipts for each industry in each state, and multiplying this by expenditures. As a practical matter, there are annual data on business receipts by industry available from only a few states. More often, changes in the national or regional ratios are used.

Travel-generated employment is similarly estimated for a post-benchmark year by adjusting the previous year's ratio of employment to payroll, and multiplying by current year's travel-generated payroll. Here, data are available for each industry in each state on an annual basis in the U.S.

Travel-generated tax revenue is estimated by introducing appropriate tax rates, both explicit and implicit, for the year under study.

EVALUATION OF THE TEIM

The evaluation criteria developed in the previous chapter can be applied to assess the quality of the Travel Economic Impact Model.

RELEVANCE

The TEIM was developed to provide estimates of travel or visitor impact alone. It is based upon surveys of travel activity, rather than receipts of travel-related businesses. A number of studies begin with explicit estimates of the proportions of hotel/motel, restaurant, entertainment services, and other business receipts attributable to travelers. These proportions are generally subjective, and often approach pure conjecture. In the TEIM, such proportions can be implicitly derived from the output but are not input assumptions in the model.

Ensuring that the economic impact estimates actually relate to the geographic area under study is difficult in travel research. Some travel expenditures are made at home in anticipation of the trip, some are made enroute, and some may even occur after the trip (e.g., developing photographs of the trip). Moreover, travelers may pay for their trip at home or enroute by currency, check, or credit card. Determining where travel expenditures should be allocated requires special research effort.

The primary rule or convention for travel spending in the TEIM is that the expenditure takes place where the goods or services are actually consumed. If this rule cannot be applied, then the expenditure is assumed to take place where the service is purchased.

The primary rule works well for all items except common carrier transportation. Hotel expenditures are assumed to take place where the traveler spends the night. Gasoline purchases are made where traveler visits by car, truck, or recreational vehicle. Meals, amusement and recreation, and incidentals are similarly handled.

In common carrier transportation, the service is consumed across as many geographic boundaries as the traveler passes. It is not feasible to allocate this spending over all such areas. Instead, the travel expenditure is assumed to take place where the ticket is purchased in the TEIM. Since most common carrier tickets are for round-trip travel, most of this spending occurs at the traveler's origin, and only a minority is allocated to the destination.

While this particular convention works reasonably well for expenditures, its applicability to the other measures of impact is not so clear. While I may purchase a round-trip ticket in Washington, D.C., for a trip on United Airlines to San Francisco, this gives rise to employment and income in Washington, San Francisco, Chicago (where United's headquarters are), and other cities housing maintenance facilities, flight personnel, training centers, and regional offices. Research has not been done that traces the overall geographic impact of airline ticket purchases. Even if it were, it would be difficult and costly to truly allocate this spending across all geographic areas affected.

In the TEIM, the employment, payroll, and tax impacts of common carrier transport purchases are allocated to the origin and destination areas based upon the allocation of expenditures. This may overstate the actual employment associated with my trip in Washington and San Francisco and understate it in Chicago, but there seems no preferable alternative at the current time.

By carefully choosing the input data, the TEIM can closely approximate actual travel benefits, and only travel benefits, in a given area for a given time.

COVERAGE

This criterion is applied to determine how comprehensive a model is in providing estimates of all economic impacts of travel. A segmentary model will necessarily provide incomplete coverage of benefits. An integrated model may fail to treat certain classes of impact, and this can be due to either lack of necessary input data or deficiencies in the model's structure.

Two important classes of travel-related expenses are not estimated in the TEIM due to lack of sufficient data. Consumers purchase certain goods and services in anticipation of a trip away from home. These include sports equipment (tennis racquets, skis, scuba gear, etc.), clothing (tennis clothes, ski togs, bathing wear, etc.), travel books and guides, and services such as language lessons and lessons for participatory sports (tennis, skiing, underwater diving, etc.). Although the magnitude of these purchases in preparation for a trip cannot be quantified, it is probably significant relative to overall travel expenditures.

The second type of spending not covered due to lack of sound, relevant data is the purchase of major consumer durables generally related to outdoor recreation on trips. While recreational vehicles (campers, motor homes, trailers, and mobile homes) are covered, spending for boats and boating supplies and off-road recreational vehicles such as trail bikes, dune buggies, and snowmobiles are not. Further research is required in this area to estimate the average spending on items such as these by travelers.

The TEIM records travel expenditures only for those states where travelers spent the night, originated, or were destined. Due to the nature of the Census Bureau's 1977 National Travel Survey, expenditures could not be allocated to states passed through in a single day. It is believed these expenditures may be quite significant to certain "bridge" states between major population concentrations and major destinations.

Among the benefit measures, the TEIM does not provide estimates of travel-generated profits, dividends, or interest payments in an area. Rent, the other component of personal income, is partially covered. The rent paid by travelers to owners of second homes, vacation condominiums, and like properties is included. However, the rent paid by a travel-related business to the owner of the structure housing it is not. Again, lack of data is the problem.

The smaller the area under study, the less of a problem exclusion of dividend, interest, and rent payments attributable to travel may be. Travel may generate this income, but it is unlikely to accrue to residents of a small area. A hotel operator may borrow money from a bank in another city, and pay interest income that does not accrue to any resident of his area. Vacation home owners are virtually all nonresidents of the area where the home is located, and their rental income should not show up in the area being studied.

Until 1984, little was known about the types and geographic distribution of foreign visitor expenditures in the U.S. However, the U.S. Travel and Tourism Administration's (USTTA) survey of international air travelers, begun in late 1982, provides a sound basis for estimating these expenditures by state and expenditure category (U.S. Travel and Tourism Administration 1984).

Utilizing this data base and similar data on Canadian visitors from Statistics Canada and the TEIM, the U.S. Travel Data Center prepared estimates for USTTA of the economic impact of foreign visitors on each of the fifty states and the District of Columbia for 1984 (U.S. Travel Data Center 1985). Future editions of these estimates are anticipated, subject to funding.

The TEIM does not include a module for estimating public or government employment attributable to travel and tourism. This is because the relationship between travel activity and government employment is not clear.

Perhaps similar relationships could be established between travel activity and employment in regulatory agencies and in government programs for constructing and maintaining travel-related facilities and rights of way. It is more difficult to speculate on the links between tourism promotion agency employment and travel activity, however.

It may be that firm relationships cannot be established at all. Governments frequently cut back on employment in travel-related agencies for budget considerations even while travel is rising. In any event, the appropriate research on the link between travel and government employment has not been conducted.

Until it is, this sector will not be included in travel economic impact models.

The TEIM measures tax revenue generated by travel for federal, state and local governments. It does not similarly measure travel's contribution to other government revenues. These include user fees, license fees, and fines.

Travelers pay park entrance fees, purchase hunting and fishing licenses, and pay traffic and other fines. These are all government revenues attributable to travel. However, accounting for these in a national model is a difficult task. It requires examination of detailed revenue data for each level of government to determine the appropriate relationships. The U.S. Travel Data Center conducted such a study for the State of Delaware, but the cost makes it prohibitive for comprehensive application across all states (Travel Data Center and Fothergill/Beekhuis 1979, pp. 69–104).

The TEIM as currently configured does not include components for measuring the secondary benefits of travel expenditures in an area. While the appropriate structure could be added, the difficulties of finding relevant and accurate interindustry data to develop the necessary input relationships would continue to be an obstacle. The regional input–output modeling system developed by the U.S. Bureau of Economic Analysis provides total requirements output and earnings multipliers for multicounty regions and may prove to be a good basis for estimating tourism multipliers (U.S. Bureau of Economic Analysis 1984).

The TEIM covers all U.S. travel away from home overnight and day trips to places 100 miles or more away. It does not measure the impact of travel to destinations less than 100 miles from the traveler's home with a return within the same day. While there may be a great number of trips of this type that may be of interest to the travel industry and others, the average expenditure per traveler is quite low, since no overnight lodging is purchased, little common carrier transportation is consumed, and other expenditures are likely to be small, being confined in a period less than one day. It is likely, therefore, that for most areas, excluding day trips of less than 100 miles will bias the economic impact estimates little, if at all (West Virginia University 1981, p. 54).

In summary the TEIM fails to cover certain direct impact due to lack of the necessary input data. Secondary benefits will soon be covered if the relevant input data prove satisfactory. However, the TEIM does provide estimates of travel-generated labor income, employment, and tax revenue for all types of businesses serving the traveler while away from home.

APPLICABILITY

The TEIM was designed to provide estimates of travel's economic impact for any state, country, or major city in the U.S. for 1977 and subsequent years. The same approach has been adapted for use in Canada by federal and provincial governments, and in New Orleans (Bureau of Management Consulting 1975a,b; Crawford and Nebel 1977). This suggests that the model can be applied in different geographic areas.

As it is quite complex, adapting the model to a certain country or other area is a difficult task. Moreover, it requires a good deal of input data which may not be readily available, particularly in lesser-developed countries.

In short, the TEIM can be used throughout the United States, through either the U.S. Travel Data Center or an adaptation of the original model. Applicability in other countries, particularly lesser-developed ones, is questionable.

EFFICIENCY

The TEIM was designed to be efficient. It does not require extensive primary data collection, but rather uses information available from existing government and industry data-gathering projects. It is flexible in accepting alternative sources of input data when necessary.

It has been the Data Center's experience that the Travel Economic Impact Model can provide economic benefit estimates for states, cities, and counties at costs considerably lower than other simulation or direct observation approaches.

ACCURACY

We can judge the accuracy of an approach's estimates by examining the structure and input data of the approach. We also judge its accuracy by comparing the estimates produced with independent estimates.

The TEIM structure is consistent and logical. The input data include survey results that are subject to sampling and nonsampling errors. However, survey-based data constitute a part of the input, not the whole. Other input data are derived from administrative records and complete censuses.

There are few independent estimates of travel impact we can refer to in judging the validity of the output. The TEIM was developed precisely because travel economic impact data did not exist. In the few cases where valid comparisons can be made, the TEIM appears to be somewhat conservative in its estimates, reflecting its basic assumptions.

SECONDARY ECONOMIC BENEFITS

When the traveler purchases goods and services, he produces the direct economic benefits detailed above. These direct or primary effects produce secondary economic effects as well that add to the community's economic well-being.

The secondary economic benefits of travel activity include *indirect* benefits and *induced* benefits. The indirect benefits occur as the travel-related business operator, say a restaurateur, purchases goods, such as food and drink, and services, such as electricity and building maintenance. These purchases generate output. Moreover, those supplying the restaurateur must, in turn, purchase goods and services from their suppliers. This chain of buying and selling continues in an area until the initial purchase leaks out of the area, through taxes, purchases from suppliers outside the area (imports), business savings, and payments to employees. The greater the proportion of spending that leaks from the community's spending process, the smaller will be the secondary impact.

The measures of indirect impact of travel activity in an area are the output or transactions, income, employment, and tax revenue generated as businesses purchase from suppliers in order to sell to the traveler.

The other type of secondary impact is the *induced* economic effect of the travel activity. This results as the employees in the travel-related businesses, and those of suppliers along the chain of indirect impact, spend a part of their earnings in the area under study. This spending itself generates output and additional induced impact throughout the area.

The sum of indirect and induced effects constitutes total secondary impact of travel activity.

IMPACT MULTIPLIERS

We can develop the concept of the *multiplier* from the understanding of the nature of secondary impact. The multiplier is simply the ratio of the sum of primary and secondary impact to primary impact alone. It is important to understand that a multiplier can be static or dynamic, relate to any of the measures of economic benefits discussed above, and vary according to the measure of primary impact used as the divisor in the ratio (or the multiplicand to which the multiplier can be properly applied). Confusion over these different multipliers has limited the usefulness of a number of secondary impact studies (Archer 1982).

We can compute transactions or output multipliers, which relate the total sales in an area resulting from the initial travel purchase, to the travel purchase itself. We can also compute employment, payroll or earnings, profits, and even tax multipliers. The distinguishing feature is the measure of benefit we obtain by applying the multiplier to our measure of initial impact.

Very often, travel impact studies including estimation of a secondary multiplier are vague regarding the measure of initial impact used in the divisor, that is, the variable the multiplier is applied to. On the one hand, we could calculate what have been termed *ratio* multipliers, representing the ratio of a primary plus secondary measure of impact, to the primary measure of that same impact. For example, a ratio employment multiplier would equal all employment in an area, both primary and secondary, generated by travel spending divided by employment generated directly. If the resulting multiplier were 2.0, we could say that for every job directly attributable to travel spending, another job is generated by the secondary effects, for a total of two jobs.

On the other hand, a *normal* or *Keynesian* multiplier relates the total measure of impact, such as earnings, to a different measure of initial impact, often travel expenditures. In a study of foreign visitor impact in the U.S., the U.S. Travel Data Center found that the ratio of earnings generated by foreign visitors to foreign visitor spending in the U.S. was 0.779: for every dollar the visitor spends, 77.9 cents in wage and salary income is generated from direct, indirect, and induced effects (Travel Data Center 1980).

Normal multipliers are quite useful to those developing travel and tourism to improve area economies. By focusing on the relationship of travel expenditures to employment, earnings, taxes, and profits, the analyst can directly estimate the total economic benefits of attracting an additional one thousand dollars in traveler spending.

Care must be exercised in using ratio multipliers. They do not indicate the total impact from traveler spending in an area, but only the ratio of total impact to direct impact. In some cases, this ratio can be less than unity or even negative in extreme cases. Indeed, one authority flatly states that by themselves "'ratio' income multipliers have little or no practical value" (Archer 1977b, p. 10).

Multipliers are usually *static* as estimated in travel impact studies, that is, they include only the impact resulting from the current productive facilities, without any provision for expansion or improvement of those facilities through investment. The *dynamic* multiplier includes investment expenditures generated by travel sales, as the restaurateur enlarges his dining rooms to accommodate business from growing travel demand.

Dynamic multipliers are more elegant than static ones, but are quite different to measure given the data usually available on an area. Since researchers are generally interested in the overall multiplier impact rather than the effects at a given point in time, and since the stimulus of travel expenditures in a local area generally exhausts itself in four or five rounds because of heavy leakages, we do not lose much by focusing on static multipliers to the exclusion of dynamic ones (Archer 1977b, p. 42).

Great care must be exercised in applying a multiplier developed for one area to another, because multipliers can vary considerably (Archer 1977b, pp. 58–61; Archer 1982). The broader the interindustry linkages in an area, that is, the lower the proportion of spending leaked at each round, the higher will be the multiplier. This is because more of the dollar stays in the area after each round to provide stimulus for another round of spending.

The size of the multiplier also depends on the configuration of the travel bill of goods. The multiplier will be higher where a greater proportion of the spending is in sectors with strong linkages to other area industries and will be smaller where more is spent in weak-link or high import-content sectors.

Generalizations can be misleading. However, the larger and more economically self-sufficient an area is, the higher will be the multiplier. This indicates that multipliers estimated for a country will always be larger than those estimated for one region of that country. And the more travelers spend on goods and services with high labor content, the higher the multiplier for a given area will be (Archer 1982).

TURNOVER VERSUS THE MULTIPLIER

In speaking of transactions or output multipliers, it is common to discuss the "turnover" of the travel dollar. This term refers to the process where the dollar spent by the traveler becomes a receipt to a business and a portion of it is, in turn, respent for goods and services. The suppliers of these goods and services also respend part of the receipts they receive, and this continues until leakages reduce the original dollar to near zero.

There is a definite relationship between the transactions multiplier and the number of times the original dollar spent turns over before disappearing from the area. An example can make this clear. If 50 percent of the dollar disappears in leakages each time it is respent, then the initial dollar expenditure would produce one dollar in transactions or output directly, 50 cents in the first round of the indirect impact, 25 cents in the second round, 12.5 cents in the third round, and continue in this manner until it disappears. The equation for the total impact transactions multiplier is

$$TM = 1 + \sum_t (1 - L)^t \qquad (10)$$

which is equivalent to

$$TM = 1 / (1 - L)^t \qquad (11)$$

where

TM = transactions multiplier
L = average leakage per round of spending as a percentage of spending
t = number of the round.

Applying equation (10) to our 50 percent leakage example and working it out for each round, we find that the amount of the dollar left to be respent drops below one-half of one cent after the eighth round, that is, it effectively disappears.

Consequently, a multiplier of 2.0 is equivalent to eight rounds of dollar turnover. Unfortunately, the terms are sometimes confused, and we find someone stating that for every dollar spent by tourists eight additional dollars are generated by turnover in the area, when the correct estimate is two dollars.

ESTIMATION METHODS

There are three basic techniques available for estimating the secondary and total impact of travel spending. These are the input—output model, the economic base model, and what Archer calls the "ad hoc" model (Archer 1973, p. 44).

INPUT—OUTPUT

Input—output is a means of analyzing the interindustry relationships in the production process in an economy. It displays the flow of goods and services from one producer to another and from the final producer to the final buyer. It covers all production, both final and intermediate, and provides a detailed understanding of the linkages among industries that we cannot obtain from analysis of the value of final production sold to the final buyers alone (Ritz 1979).

Input—output analysis starts with the development of a *direct use table*. The use table shows the sales in dollars of the total output of an industry to all other industries in the economy. By convention, the rows of the table show the sales of the industry listed at the left to every other industry listed at the top of the columns. By reading down the column, we can see how much input every industry requires from every other industry.

From the use table, we develop the *direct requirements table*. Each column in the direct requirements table shows the inputs required by the industry listed at the head from the industries listed at the beginning of each row to produce one dollar of the column-industry's output. Reading down the 1972 U.S. input—output direct requirements table for eating and drinking places, we see that for every dollar of output, these establishments buy 32 cents worth of food and kindred products, 6 cents of trade services, 4 cents of real estate and rental services, and about 2 cents of electric, gas, water, and sanitary services. Eating and drinking places buy less than 2 cents worth per dollar of their own output from each of 32 other industries. They pay 32 cents to their employees, and nearly 7 cents in indirect business taxes. Each of these values is an *input coefficient* for the eating and drinking place industry.

By manipulating the direct requirements table through matrix algebra, we obtain the *total requirements table*, which can be used to obtain indirect transactions multipliers and ultimately to estimate total secondary impact. (Archer 1977a).

The total requirements table shows the output required, both directly and indirectly, from each industry listed in the rows by the industry at the head of the column to deliver a dollar of output to final demand. It summarizes all of the intermediate transactions required for an industry to produce for retail. Consequently, by summing the coefficients in the columns, we obtain an indirect transactions multiplier that can be applied to industry sales at producers' prices to obtain the total output required.

The total requirements table also shows the amount of employee compensation per dollar of final demand. Summing the total employee earnings generated by travel spending and its indirect effects, and apportioning this among personal consumption expenditure categories, savings, and taxes, we can introduce the induced impact. The personal consumption expenditures by category are treated as final demand for analogous industries and run through the total requirements table to obtain additional estimates of indirect output and earnings. This is reiterated until the travel-generated earnings leak out of the system completely in the form of savings, taxes, and imports.

In input—output structures treating the household as a processing sector similar to business, the indirect and induced impact would be generated by one iteration of the process, rather than the repeated iterations necessary for the U.S. tables.

As indicated, total primary and secondary output and payroll generated by travel spending is produced through the input—output process. Employment can be added by developing ratios of employment to earnings, as in the Travel Economic Impact Model, for all of the industries with substantial impact. The TEIM approach to estimating direct travel-generated profits and tax revenue can be similarly applied to the total output and payroll estimates to obtain the appropriate multipliers.

Input—output analysis is the most powerful tool for estimating secondary impact, and the appropriate tables are generally available at the national and often the regional level on a periodic basis (U.S. Bureau of Economic Analysis 1984). Its limitations include assumption of fixed input coefficients when these may actually vary depending upon the size of the travel expenditure injected in the system, lack of detailed industry disaggregations to accommodate the sectors of the travel industry, and the fact that input—output tables are available only after substantial lags, often four to five years. These limitations will be discussed more fully in the section below evaluating the three secondary impact estimation techniques.

ECONOMIC BASE MODELS

Commonly used to estimate multipliers, the economic base approach divides the local economy into two segments: (1) firms serving markets outside the region and (2) firms serving markets within the region (Archer 1977b, pp. 14–16; Tiebout 1962).

The goods and services firms are selling outside area boundaries are considered exports and are assumed to be the prime mover of the local economy. If sales and employment serving this export market rise, sales and employment serving the regional market are presumed to move in the same direction. For example, the more a restaurant can sell to nonresident visitors, the greater the employment of residents and the more money will be spent by these employees and the restaurant operator in the local economy for goods and services.

This approach recognizes that industries and firms within industries may sell their products in both regional and extraregional (export) markets. For each industry in the area, employment is divided between basic (export) and nonbasic (local) markets. Ratios are then developed of total employment or earnings in a region to basic employment or earnings to estimate the multiplier.

To develop these multipliers, data from sources such as the U.S. Census Bureau's censuses of retail trade and service industries are used to divide sales, employment, and payroll between basic and nonbasic markets by industry sector in an area. The amounts allocated to basic markets are summed and used as the denominator, with the total for the magnitude (output, employment, or earnings) in the area as the numerator. The resulting multiplier is then applied to the direct travel-generated measure of economic impact.

The advantage of this approach is that it is simple and straightforward, employing data generally available even for small areas such as counties. Its disadvantages include the often subjective nature of allocating industry activity between basic and nonbasic markets, the assumption that all types of export sales to basic markets have the same multiplier effect regardless of their type of industry source, and the assumption that the growth in an area economy is attributable primarily or totally to export sales.

THE AD HOC MODEL

Adaptation of the Keynesian income multiplier to estimating the income multiplier for travel expenditures has been termed the *ad hoc model* by Archer.

The ad hoc model concentrates on the income generated in an area by the initial travel expenditure in the area through the consumption expenditure patterns of its residents. Archer presents the following equation as the most useful form of the ad hoc model (Archer 1977b, p. 22):

$$\sum_j \sum_i Q_j \cdot K_{j,i} \cdot Y_i \cdot 1 / (1 - c \sum_i X_i \cdot Z_i \cdot Y_i) \tag{12}$$

where

j = types of travelers

i = type of traveler outlet or business directly serving travelers

Q = proportion of total each type of traveler spends

K = proportion travelers spend in each type of traveler outlet

Y = direct and indirect income generated per dollar by each type of traveler outlet

c = propensity to consume of residents

X = distribution of resident consumer spending among different types of consumer outlets

Z = proportion of income spent within the area by residents.

The ad hoc model requires a substantial amount of data to be collected through surveys. For example, in addition to estimates of income generated per dollar of travel expenditure for each type of travel-related business (Y), the distribution of resident consumer spending (X) must be developed, as well as proportion of income spent in the area by residents (Z).

Moreover, additional structures need to be specified to develop the other types of multipliers, such as employment and transactions multipliers.

EVALUATION OF SECONDARY IMPACT ESTIMATION METHODS

We can apply our criteria for evaluating economic impact techniques to the three approaches to measuring secondary and total impact.

RELEVANCE

The ad hoc model is the only one of the three developed specifically for travel impact. However, by carefully estimating the traveler's "bill of goods," or the items the traveler buys, the input–output approach can be used as well. In both cases, multipliers can be developed for each type of traveler or type of accommodation to compare secondary and total impact of various traveler types.

The economic base model treats all sources of export purchases as having the same impact and does not distinguish the singular effects the travel bill of goods will have on the area economy. This makes it inferior to the other two approaches.

COVERAGE

The coverage is as good as the initial travel bill of goods and the structure of the secondary multiplier model. All three approaches include travel-related businesses, but the economic base approach is the least likely to include the industry detail found in the other two.

In terms of the ability to provide both ratio and normal multipliers for output, employment, earnings and other income, and taxes, the input–output approach is the best. It allows for explicit development of secondary impact estimates consistent with the primary impact estimates. The economic base model can produce consistent estimates if the output, employment, and earnings data are consistent with one another. If, as is usually the case, the data are developed from different sources with different industry classifications, the multipliers will not be mutually consistent.

The ad hoc approach is specifically designed to estimate income multipliers for areas. Presumably, output and employment could be appended, but this would require additional conceptual design work.

APPLICABILITY

The economic base model is the easiest to apply across varied areas. The input data needed are generally available on a timely basis. The ad hoc model requires surveys to be conducted among travelers, residents, and businesses and will produce consistent results across different areas if the surveys are conducted uniformly. However, given the budget constraint, it is likely that the relationships developed for one place and time will often be applied to others where they are not valid.

National input–output tables are not applicable to local or regional areas. However, the U.S. Bureau of Economic Analysis can now provide input–output tables for multicounty or city areas (U.S. Bureau of Economic Analysis 1984). These are based upon the quinquennial updating of the national tables, and consequently may be five years or so behind. However, given evidence that the production coefficients do not change substantially over time, this may not be a problem here (Ritz 1979, p. 37).

EFFICIENCY

The economic base model is most efficient in using readily available data. Where input–output models have been constructed or adapted for use in local areas this approach is efficient.

The ad hoc model, however, requires substantial amounts of data to be developed through surveys. Travelers must be surveyed to determine their type of accommodation and their expenditure patterns among types of businesses, and whether purchases were made inside the area or outside. Business operators must be surveyed regarding their receipts, payroll, and purchases from other businesses within the area. This is expensive and difficult to accomplish satisfactorily, particularly in an urban area.

ACCURACY

The economic base model does not appear to be a reasonable reflection of area economic structure. It assumes that all economic growth in an area results from export sales. Since economic growth is possible from internal sources as well, such as through greater demand for local products from tax reductions for residents or through changes in consumption patterns, this approach tends to overestimate the impact of export sales, such as visitor purchases.

Moreover, this approach assumes all injections of demand from outside the area have the same impact, regardless of the bill of goods. But it is clear that a visitor dollar spent on gasoline in an area will produce less secondary impact than a visitor dollar spent on a restaurant meal, since the latter has far higher labor and other local-origin content.

The ad hoc model comprises a reasonable structure. However, it requires a great deal of input data developed through surveys of consumers and business operators. The structure may be accurate, but the input data may not, producing misleading results. It should be clear that the ad hoc model must be constructed from the ground up for each area studied, and should be done by researchers well-versed in economic theory and economic survey sampling.

Archer has discussed the following limitations of input-output multiplier analysis (Archer 1977a):

1 Input–output assumes linear production functions, that is, any additional final demand will be met by an industry through purchasing inputs in the same proportion from the same suppliers: this may particularly be a problem where the supply of a certain input is limited;

2 All additional income resulting from additions to final demand will be spent in the same proportions on the same consumption items, with the same split between intraregional purchases and imports: this is analogous to the assumption of a linear production function in (1); while this can be overcome by disaggregating resident purchases in an area, this is quite expensive;

3 Interindustry relationships change considerably

over a period of perhaps five years, yet most input—output data are older than this;

4 Travel spending items may not be consistent with the industry or   commodity groups in the input—output tables.

All four of these are serious considerations in applying the input—output model to estimating the total impact of travel expenditures in an area. However, it should be noted that the first two limit the usefulness of the ad hoc and economic base models as well.

The question of aged data (limitation 3) has not been resolved, although at least one study has found that input—output coefficients change little over time. However, it seems clear that the ad hoc model is superior to the input—output approach limitations 3 and 4. The data needed to develop the ad hoc multipliers can be timely and gathered to fit travel spending patterns and area industry structures.

In sum, if an input—output model exists for the area under study, it should be used. If no such model exists, the ad hoc model will provide reasonable accuracy for less cost than constructing an input—output model from scratch. The economic base model, while cheap, provides estimates worth less than the cost of deriving them.

REFERENCES

Archer, Brian (1973), *The Impact of Domestic Tourism*, Bangor, Wales: University of Wales Press, 128 pp.

Archer, Brian (1977a), "Input—Output Analysis: Its Strengths, Limitations and Weaknesses", *Eighth Annual Conference Proceedings*, Salt Lake City: The Travel Research Association, pp. 89—101.

Archer, Brian (1977b), *Tourism Multipliers: The State of the Art*, Bangor, Wales: University of Wales Press, 85 pp.

Archer, Brian (1982), "Value of Multipliers and Their Policy Implications," paper delivered to the Surrey International Conference on Trends in Tourism Planning and Development, University of Surrey, Guildford, Great Britain, September 1—3, 1982, 19 pp.

Archer, Brian, and Christine B. Owen (1972), "Towards a Tourist Regional Multiplier," *Journal of Travel Research*, 11 (Fall), pp. 9—13.

Archer, Brian, and Sheila Shea (1975), "Length of Stay Problems in Tourism Research," *Journal of Travel Research*, 12 (Winter), pp. 8—10.

Babbie, Earl R. (1973), *Survey Research Methods*, Belmont, California: Wadsworth Publishing Company, 384 pp.

Brog, Werner, and Arnim H. Meyburg (1980), "Nonresponse Problems in Travel Surveys: An Empirical Investigation," *Transportation Research Record 775: Travel Demands Models: Application, Limitations and Quantitative Methods*, pp. 34—38, Washington, D.C.: Transportation Research Board, National Academy of Sciences.

Bureau of Economic Analysis (1977), *Industry Specific Gross Output Multipliers for BEA Economic Areas*, Washington, D.C.: U.S. Government Printing Office, 135 pp.

Bureau of Economic Analysis (1984), U.S. Department of Commerce, "RIMS II, Regional Input—Output Modeling System, A Brief Description," May 1984, 7 pp.

Bureau of Management Consulting, Canadian (1975a), *Tourism Expenditures Model, A Functional Planning and Policy Making Tool*, Ottawa: Department of Supply and Services, 111 pp.

Bureau of Management Consulting, Canadian (1975b), *Tourism Impact Model*, Ottawa: Department of Supply and Services, 94 pp.

Bureau of the Budget, U.S. (1969), *Household Survey Manual*, Washington, D.C.: U.S. Government Printing Office, 237 pp.

Bureau of the Census, U.S. (1979a), *1977 Census of Retail Trade, Geographic Area Series*, Washington, D.C.: U.S. Government Printing Office.

Bureau of the Census, U.S. (1979b), *1977 Census of Service Industries, Geographic Area Series*, Washington, D.C.: U.S. Government Printing Office.

Bureau of the Census, U.S. (1979c), 1977 *Census of Transportation, National Travel Survey, Travel During 1977*, Washington, D.C.: U.S. Government Printing Office, 406 pp.

Bureau of the Census, U.S. (1981), *Statistical Abstract of the United States 1980*, Washington, D.C.: U.S. Government Printing Office, 1060 pp.

Church, Donald E. (1969), "A Proposed Model for Estimating and Analyzing Travel Expenditures," *Western Council for Travel Research Bulletin*, 8 (Summer), pp. 1—6.

Cochran, William G. (1977), *Sampling Techniques*, 3rd edition, New York: John Wiley & Sons, 428 pp.

Cournoyer, Norman G., *et al.* (1976), *Travel and Tourism in Massachusetts, 1975*, Amherst, Massachusetts: University of Massachusetts, 250 pp.

Crawford, William D., and E.C. Nebel III (1977), "The Importance of Travel Activity to the New Orleans Economy," *Louisiana Business Survey*, (July), pp. 1—5.

Division of Tourism, California (1974), *Tourism Employment Study*, Sacramento: State of California Department of Commerce, 76 pp.

Dommermuth, William P. (1975), *The Use of Sampling in Marketing Research*, Chicago: American Marketing Association, 37 pp.

Ellerbrock, Michael J., and James C. Hite (1980), "Factors Affecting Regional Employment in Tourism in the United States," *Journal of Travel Research*, 18 (Winter), pp. 26—32.

Ferber, Robert (Ed.) (1978), *Readings in Survey Research*, Chicago: American Marketing Association, 604 pp.

Frechtling, Douglas C. (1978), "A Brief Treatise on Days and Nights," *Journal of Travel Research*, 18 (Fall), pp. 18—19.

Frechtling, Douglas C., *et al.* (1975a), *Travel Economic Impact Model, Volume I, Final Economic Analysis*

Methodology, Washington, D.C.: U.S. Travel Data Center, 108 pp.

Frechtling, Douglas C., *et al.* (1975b), *Travel Economic Impact Model, Volume II, Final Demonstration Report*, Washington, D.C.: U.S. Travel Data Center, 119 pp.

Haynes, Landon G. (1975), "A Known and Equal Chance," *Sixth Annual Conference Proceedings*, Salt Lake City: The Travel Research Association, pp. 95–97.

Hunt, John D., and Michael J. Dalton (1983), "Comparing Mail and Telephone for Conducting Coupon Conversion Studies," *Journal of Travel Research*, 21 (Winter, pp. 16–18.

Kahn, Terry D. (1975), "Employment in the Texas Tourist Industry," *Western Economic Association Annual Conference*, June 25, 1975.

Lansing, John B., and James N. Morgan (1971), *Economic Survey Methods*, Ann Arbor, Michigan: Institute for Social Research, 430 pp.

Mak, James, James Moncur, and David Yonamine (1977), "How or How Not to Measure Visitor Expenditure," *Journal of Travel Research*, 16 (Summer), pp. 1–4.

Meyburg, Arnim H., and Werner Brog (1981), "Validity Problems in Empirical Analyses of Non-Home-Activity Patterns," *Transportation Research Record 807: Travel Demand Forecasting and Data Considerations*, pp. 46–50, Washington, D.C.: Transportation Research Board, National Academy of Sciences.

Mueller, Raymond W. (1977), "When is a Job a Job?" *Journal of Travel Research*, 16 (11), pp. 1–5.

Office of Business and Economic Development, District of Columbia Government (1981), *District of Columbia Tourism Development Policy Study Report*, Washington, D.C., 114 pp.

Ritchie, J.R. Brent (1975), "Some Critical Aspects of Measurement Theory and Practice in Travel Research," *Journal of Travel Research*, 14 (Summer), pp. 1–10.

Ritz, Philip M. (1979), "The Input–Output Structure of the U.S. Economy," *Survey of Current Business*, (February), pp. 34–72.

Schultz, Ronald R., and William B. Stronge (1980a), "Social and Economic Effects of Tourism in Florida," *Business & Economic Dimensions*, (2), pp. 5–13.

Schultz, Ronald R. (1980b), "Tourism's Impact Is Not All Positive," *Business & Economic Dimensions*, (2), pp. 14–21.

Steel, Brian F. (1981), "Measuring Tourist Expenditures—A Discussion Paper," unpublished manuscript, New Zealand Tourist and Public Department, 11 pp.

Tiebout, Charles M. (1962), *The Community Economic Base Study*, Washington, D.C.: Committee for Economic Development, 84 pp.

Travel and Tourism Administration, U.S. (1984), *Survey of International Air Travelers, Overseas and Mexican Visitors to the United States, Survey Period: October–December, 1983*, Washington, D.C.: U.S. Government Printing Office, unpaginated.

Travel Data Center, U.S. (1975), *1974 National Travel Survey Full Year Report*, Washington, D.C.: U.S. Travel Data Center, 130 pp.

Travel Data Center, U.S. (1976), *1975 National Travel Survey Full year Report*, Washington, D.C.: U.S. Travel Data Center, 130 pp.

Travel Data Center, U.S. (1978), "An Analysis of Data on Travel Expenditures," unpublished manuscript submitted to the U.S. Travel Service, U.S. Department of Commerce, April 4, 194 pp.

Travel Data Center, U.S. (1980), *The Economic Impact of Foreign Visitor Spending in the United States*, Washington, D.C.: U.S. Travel Service, 33 pp.

Travel Data Center, U.S. (1985), *Impact of Foreign Visitors on State Economies, 1983*, Washington, D.C.: U.S. Travel Data Center, 65 pp.

Travel Data Center, U.S., and Fothergill/Beekhuis Associates (1979), *Delaware Tourism Policy Study*, Dover, Delaware: Delaware State Travel Service, 252 pp.

West Virginia University (1981), *Creating Economic Growth and Jobs through Travel and Tourism*, Washington, D.C.: U.S. Government Printing Office, 315 pp.

Woodside, Arch G., and Ilkka A. Ronkainen (1984), "How Serious Is Nonresponse Bias in Advertising Conversion Research?" *Journal of Travel Research*, 22 (Spring), pp. 34–37.

29

Assessing the Impacts of Travel and Tourism—Measuring Economic Costs

DOUGLAS C. FRECHTLING

Director, U.S. Travel Data Center
Washington, D.C.

*T*he relationship of two kinds of social costs of tourism, fiscal costs and life quality costs to a community, is discussed. A method of estimating the direct and secondary fiscal costs is presented, as well as comparing these costs to benefits. The correct approach to discounting future costs and benefits is also detailed.

In a world of scarce resources, measuring the economic benefits of tourism in an area without measuring the costs risks serious misappropriation of limited public funds. The danger goes beyond the mere wasting of money that might have been more productively spent elsewhere. Concentrating on the benefits of a project and ignoring the costs can produce serious damage to the environment, rapidly escalating costs of public services needed to support visitors, and dramatic declines in the quality of life of residents.

Public officials cannot survive many projects that cost their constituents far more than they return. Nor can the tourism industry maintain its credibility after selling such projects to residents and their officials. Beyond the increased efficiency in using scarce resources, it is a wise policy for public officials and the tourism industry to properly estimate the economic costs as well as the benefits of tourism projects.

There appear to be two main cases where we should apply cost analysis to travel and tourism. One is to examine the current situation to determine how much additional cost visitors are imposing on the community relative to conditions without visitors. The other is to estimate the additional costs imposed by more visitors to a community, either from natural growth or produced by a prospective development, such as a new park, additional transportation capacity, or new marketing programs. It is the second case that has received

the most attention, especially in public water resource development projects, where the costs and benefits of a proposed project are estimated as part of the determination whether to proceed with the project or not.

If we are interested in the reduction of life quality, including deterioration of the environment and increases in government expenditures resulting from visitors, we must be careful to analyze the additional costs imposed by visitors over conditions without visitors. Alternatively, we may be interested in the marginal costs of serving additional visitors over the number we are currently serving. This "before and after" method of analysis is helpful in evaluating the impact of prospective tourism development projects.

There is a trade-off relationship between the two major types of social costs: fiscal and life quality costs. The community can reduce its life quality costs associated with visitors by increasing its fiscal costs through financing higher public expenditures, or it can refuse to raise fiscal costs and accept the burden of a lower quality of life.

Table 1 lists a number of categories used in studies to distinguish different social costs of tourism. The table makes clear that any type of cost can initially fall on the government (fiscal costs) or the residents (life quality costs), including reductions in the quality of their environment. If tourists visit my town and dirty its streams, pollute its air, raise its noise level, and

TABLE 1 Alternative Direct Fiscal and Quality of Life Costs Associated with Visitors

FISCAL COSTS	QUALITY OF LIFE COSTS
Highway construction and maintenance	Traffic congestion
Fish and game regulation	Destruction of wildlife, human life, and property
Construction, operation, and maintenance of park and recreation facilities	Destruction of flora, fauna, and natural and scenic beauty; congestion
Police services	Traffic congestion and destruction of life and property
Construction, operation, and maintenance of museums and historical sites	Destruction of historical and cultural heritage
Construction, operation, and maintenance of port and terminal facilities	Traffic congestion
Regulation of environmental impact	Destruction of flora, fauna, and natural and scenic resources; noise pollution
Forestry maintenance	Destruction of flora, fauna, and natural and scenic resources
Watercraft regulation	Destruction of life and property
Planning and zoning	Destruction of natural and scenic resources and historical and cultural heritage; noise pollution; resident income decline
Water supply and sewage treatment	Destruction of water resources and limits on water usage
Fire protection	Destruction of life and property
Trash and litter disposal	Destruction of health and natural and scenic resources
Health and sanitation	Destruction of health and life
Public transportation (local)	Traffic congestion and air pollution

litter its streets, these directly reduce the quality of my life, unless government redresses them through regulation, taxation, direct expenditures, or any combination.

SCOPE OF COST STUDIES

Study of the costs of travel and tourism should consider all of the direct social costs indicated in Table 1. It may well be that the nature and volume of the visitors will not produce any costs in several of the categories listed. For example, visitors to New York City will not impose costs on residents related to regulation of hunting and fishing or forestry management, and if an area is developing a facility or service that would attract few additional visitors, then the contribution to social costs in many of the categories may be negligible. However, the point is that the potential cost of visitors in each category should be explicitly examined if a study of the social costs of tourism is to be comprehensive.

So far, the costs of visitors have been described only at the primary level, that is, those costs directly attrib-

utable to visitors. However, there are also indirect or secondary cost effects that can operate, as indicated in Table 2.

If the development of a new tourism facility attracts enough additional visitors, there may be an increase in the number and size of business establishments in the community, requiring an increase in the labor force and thus the resident population. As resident population increases, this imposes additional fiscal and life quality costs on the community. Some of the costs of additional residents will be similar to those imposed by additional visitors, and can be categorized as in Table 1. We can then use the same measurement techniques for assessing their impact.

Often, some of the costs imposed by additional residents to serve a larger visitor volume may not appear to residents to be travel-related. For example, the children of the additional residents will require an increase in educational expenses in the community. They may also require additional hospital facilities as well (Baumol *et al*. 1970, pp. 161–177).

One of the most troublesome areas of indirect costs is in welfare or income maintenance programs. For

TABLE 2 Alternative Indirect Fiscal and Quality of Life Costs Associated with Visitors

FISCAL COSTS	LIFE QUALITY COSTS
Education	Uninformed electorate; danger to life and property
Hospital construction, operation, and maintenance	Danger to life and health
Housing and urban renewal	Danger to life and health; decline in property and scenic resources; congestion
Public welfare	Danger to life, health, and property
Economic development	Longer job search or unemployment; reduced income growth

example, it has been alleged that tourism in certain regions provides highly seasonal job opportunities, attracting a work force that settles in and requires unemployment compensation and other income transfer programs during off-peak seasons (Cournoyer 1975, pp. 205–227).

Table 2 shows the indirect fiscal and life quality costs that might be imposed on a community by an increase in the work force to serve an increase in visitor volume. They differ from those costs identified in Table 1 in that they are not generated directly by visitors, only indirectly. The two tables are intended to be exhaustive, but additional costs may be identified by others.

The larger resident population will impose an increased burden on education and hospital facilities. If these are not expanded, the community as a whole deteriorates somewhat as the ignorant and sick threaten to increase in number. The additional population may put increased pressure on already declining neighborhoods and require more urban renewal to prevent an increase in crime and street congestion, with concomitant declines in property values and the visual aesthetics of the community.

If the work force expands to take on additional, highly seasonal jobs, welfare payments and counseling costs may increase; otherwise, crime and disease may well grow. Finally, the population increase may expand the work force considerably more than the additional jobs produced by visitors, as the spouses and children of the travel-related employees look for work. In the absence of economic development programs, long-term residents may experience declines in opportunities for employment and income growth available to them.

The presence of visitors gives rise to indirect social costs as the business and labor population expands to meet increased demand. These indirect costs may be fiscal or life quality, depending on how the residents decide to handle them. There is an additional set of public expenditure programs, however, that do not have direct counterparts on the life quality side. These

might be termed "fiscal overhead expenditures" and relate to the operation and management of government. They include financial administration, general control, and interest on the general debt.

It is not immediately evident whether these government expenditures should be included among travel-generated fiscal costs. On the one hand, we could argue that fiscal overhead costs are sensitive to the size of government, and that part of government is attributable to servicing travel and tourism activity. On the other hand, we could argue that government primarily exists to serve its citizens, and that these overhead costs should not be allocated to nonresident visitors: they would continue unabated in the absence of visitors. Moreover, public officials are occasionally able to cut back on these overhead expenses while the costs of servicing visitors is rising.

If we decide to include fiscal overhead costs in our accounting of travel-generated fiscal costs, we could allocate them by the proportions that travel-related and non-travel-related fiscal costs bear to the sum of these two items. For example, if an exhaustive study of fiscal costs attributable to visitors indicates that one-third of the government's expenditures relate to their presence, then one-third of the fiscal overhead costs could be attributed to visitors as well.

There is another area where it is unclear whether additional social costs for the community as a whole are involved. This includes the redistribution effects of tourism projects. A new highway or transportation terminal located far from the old one may well cause a decline in the receipts of those businesses established near the obsolete facilities. However, businesses near the new road or terminal will thrive.

As another example, the hotels located in a community may be enjoying very high occupancy rates. Then a government program (low-interest loans, loan guarantees, special infrastructure) stimulates additional hotel construction. After the new property opens, the original hotels suffer declines in occupancy and in return on investment.

As one other, the additional visitors generated by a

new public visitor-related facility may push up wage rates and property values in the community. Now employers must pay their workers more, and those wishing to buy property must pay more to those who already own it.

These are distributional aspects of increased visitor demand. Income or wealth is transferred from one group in the community to another. Since we have no objective way of determining whether the community is better or worse off as a result of this transfer, and no additional output has been produced by the transfer, it is recommended that this be excluded from cost analysis (Prest and Turvey 1967, p. 160).

We can make one judgement here, however. If it can be shown that a new project primarily benefits nonresidents at the expense of residents through shifting benefits to the former away from the latter, then the project is clearly costly from the residents' point of view. This can happen, for example, if locally owned and staffed hotels lose business to properties owned by absentee owners, staffed by imported labor and operated with imported goods and services. It is clear here that the gross economic benefits of the project are not benefits to the residents, and some are actually costs in terms of lost jobs and income.

It is important that the range of costs of tourism that is examined is consistent with the spectrum of benefits. It is not correct to calculate the indirect costs of additional visitors without recognizing the indirect benefits in terms of additional income and tax revenues in the community. It may be that the study of the costs and benefits of a given tourism project must be limited by available funds to the direct implications to the community. In such a case, the researchers must make sure that the cost and benefit implications are consistent, and that the scope of one side is not expanded beyond the scope of the other.

It should be clear that the optimum scope of cost analysis of tourism-related projects can be summarized as broad, deep, and long: broad in covering all social costs in the community; deep in including the indirect costs from population increases for an expanded work force to meet enlarged visitor demand; and long in including the distant as well as the near future. This last aspect will be covered more fully in a succeeding section on the appropriate social rate of discount.

MEASUREMENT

The first issue in actually estimating the cost of visitors relates to direct versus indirect costs. It is difficult to measure the direct costs of travel and tourism. Many simplifying and sometimes subjective assumptions must be made to arrive at final figures. As the state of the art progresses, the subjective content can be reduced to produce the reliable objective estimates that are most useful.

Measuring the indirect costs is even more difficult, requiring an additional analytical step. First, assumptions must be made about the link between visitor demand and the resident businesses and individuals who service this demand. Once this is established, we must then determine the relationship between those servicing visitors and the social costs of their activities. This two-step process may increase the subjective content of the estimates and reduce their accuracy.

It is quite important to be consistent in the scope of both the cost and benefit analyses we apply. If we are measuring the secondary benefits of travel and tourism and we wish to determine whether this activity provides net benefits to the area or community, we should measure the indirect costs as well. To only measure the secondary benefits and not the secondary costs is to bias the results of a cost–benefit analysis.

Little work appears to have been done in measuring the indirect costs of travel and tourism. This subject needs more serious attention before it can be considered as accurate as measurement of secondary benefits.

FISCAL COSTS

Measurement of the costs of visitors to the community involves apportioning some of the fiscal costs in each category listed in Table 1 to visitors and imputing life quality costs imposed on the residents by the visitors. The final estimates of visitor-related social costs will be quite sensitive to the measurement method employed, so special care should be taken to develop objective and accurate techniques.

Looking at the direct fiscal costs of visitors, there are two basic issues. One is how to measure the *net* fiscal costs of visitors. Many of the program costs listed in Table 1 are at least partially offset by user charges in the community. Street and highway construction and maintenance programs are funded by motor gasoline taxes. The costs of developing and operating museums, historic sites, parks, and recreation areas may be offset by admission or user fees. The cost of fish and game regulation may be financed entirely by license fees. The question is, should we subtract the revenue from user charges and deal only with the net costs of each program, or address user charges paid by visitors on the benefit side and deal with the *gross* costs of each program attributable to visitors on the cost side?

If we are only interested in the cost side, the former approach might be preferable. This gives us the net costs of visitors which must be picked up by the residents. However, we do run the risk of neglecting to include travel-generated fiscal revenue not directly attributable to specific programs, such as sales and gross receipts taxes. Since these taxes are usually not earmarked for offsetting specific costs (i.e., are a general benefit), they are apt to be excluded in calculating the net costs of each visitor-related public service.

It seems far more advisable to maintain a strict distinction between costs and benefits. All of the fiscal costs generated by visitors should be totaled on one side, and all of the fiscal revenue derived from visitors should be summed on the other, and then comparisons made. This has the advantage of including all revenue items, whether related to a specific service or not, on the benefit side with other benefits. Similarly, we can compare gross fiscal costs with other social costs. All is laid out explicitly, with no "off balance-sheet accounting" to worry about.

Table 3 presents the units of measurement suggested for apportioning public service costs between visitors and residents. In each case, we need to estimate both total use and visitor use. We then distribute the total program costs in each category to visitors according to the proportion of use generated by visitors.

It should be understood that in many cases the measurement units suggested are imperfect indicators of actual visitor consumption of public services. However, they have the virtue of being readily available from visitor surveys and resident population data. Further research is required on better indicators of visitor use of public services.

The fiscal cost categories are drawn from Table 1. Alternative units of measurement are sometimes given, in estimated descending order of accuracy.

While most of the units of measurement are self-explanatory, a few words about the "daily census" measure are required. The "daily census" is the average number of people present in the area under study for some period, usually a year. If the area studied is a local community, commuters from outside the community boundaries should be included along with residents and visitors. If the area is a state, it is unlikely that commutation will add much relative to the total of residents and visitors.

The daily census measure is the sum of the number of visitor-days spent in the area plus the product of resident population and 365 days in the year, plus a measure of commuter-days. This latter might be represented by the number of daily commuters multiplied by one-third of a day, the product multiplied by 236 days as an average work year, recognizing weekends, holidays, and vacations as nonwork days without commuting.

The daily census approach assumes that the cost of a given public service is a function of the number of people present in the area daily. The costs of the service can then be apportioned between visitors and others in the same way that the daily census is composed (Baumol *et al.* 1970, pp. 149–160).

It is attractive to the researcher to apply the daily census approach to estimating all or nearly all public program costs (Office of Business and Economic Development 1981). However, this tendency should be

---

TABLE 3   Suggested Units of Measurement for Direct Fiscal Costs of Visitors

FISCAL COST CATEGORY	UNIT OF MEASUREMENT
Highway construction and maintenance	Vehicle-miles Vehicle-days Daily census
Fish and game regulation	Licenses sold
Park and recreation facilities	Site visitor-days Site visits (admissions)
Police services	Daily census
Museums and historic sites	Site visits (admissions)
Port and terminal facilities	Arrivals
Environmental regulation	Daily census
Forestry maintenance	Site visitor-days Site visits
Watercraft regulation	Watercraft registrations Dock and mooring fees
Planning and zoning	Pro-rata share of fiscal costs
Water supply and sewage treatment	Daily census
Fire protection	Daily census
Trash and litter disposal	Daily census
Health and sanitation	Daily census
Public transportation	Passengers Daily census

resisted in favor of measures that more accurately represent actual visitor usage of the program or facility. This allows for valid estimation of public costs related to visitors even if visitor activity patterns change but visitor volume does not.

While it is a very simple concept, the daily census approach appears to be a pretty good one for a number of public services. For example, it is difficult to conceive of a better way to apportion costs of police protection or sewage treatment between visitors and others in the community.

The overhead costs of administration, financial control, debt service, and other programs that support the public services listed above can be prorated between the visitor and resident fiscal costs as discussed above.

LIFE QUALITY COSTS

Putting actual dollar values on the life quality costs is quite difficult. One conceptual approach is to estimate what residents would be willing to pay to return to their previsitor level of risk of destruction of flora, fauna, human life and health, natural and scenic beauty, historical and cultural heritages, and amount of crowding and congestion. However, we cannot actually ask the residents hypothetical questions because what they respond they would pay and what they would actually pay for reducing each visitor-related life quality cost are likely to be quite different.

Moreover, the cost categories require trade-offs since the resident has a fixed budget and visitor-related costs would have to be accommodated within it, along with maintenance, nurture, recreation, and other expenses. Finally, the resident has an incentive to understate the amount he would be willing to pay for collective goods, such as police protection and pollution control. Since the amount of these services each consumes is equal and unrelated to the cost each would pay, each resident would hope to get someone else to pay more than he does by understating the value he puts on it (Prest and Turvey 1967, pp. 167–168).

The measurement of life quality costs associated with travel and tourism in a community has not been adequately addressed in past research. Some investigators have tried to estimate relative life quality costs of alternative activities. These have generally been limited to environmental consequences of visitation and suggest that certain classes of visitors pursuing certain activities have lower benefit–cost ratios than others (Tatzin 1978; Northeast Markets *et al.* 1974, pp. 155–174). However, these studies incorporate large subjective components in the estimation methods.

It could be argued that the residents have the ability to redress life quality costs of visitors by transferring them as fiscal costs through taxes and fees on the visitors. If they do not choose to do so, this reasoning goes, then the life quality costs cannot be significant to the residents. Therefore, the calculation of fiscal costs is sufficient to cover social costs.

A counterargument to this one is that residents do the benefit–cost calculus on their own and a majority decide that the life quality reduction suffered is more than offset by personal economic benefits attributable to visitors. But this does not resolve the issue of whether the community is collectively better off with additional visitors or without them. It may be that the majority of voters feel they are better off, but that the minority, which may well bear most of the cost burden or value the quality of their environment most highly, bear net costs large enough to offset the majority's net benefits.

Further study of such reasoning and its implications, and methods of quantifying life quality costs of tourism, is required before this issue can be settled.

OTHER ISSUES

There are additional issues in analyzing the costs of travel and tourism that deserve study. However, so little attention has been given them so far that it is difficult to suggest even conceptual solutions at this time.

It was mentioned earlier that the redistributional aspects of a development project in a community can be ignored since income and wealth would be transferred among community members. However, if it could be shown, for example, that the construction of a new terminal would benefit absentee property owners while demolition of the old terminal would hurt resident owners, then the community would experience a net cost from this aspect of the project.

Moreover, in some communities there may be a broad consensus that all public projects should help the poor rather than the rich. In such a community, if a project reduced the business and employment opportunities of the poor, say around an old terminal, and increased those of the more advantaged around the proposed site for new construction, then it would have redistributional costs from the community's standpoint.

As another issue, we have assumed that the fiscal costs of redressing certain effects of visitation do not exceed the life quality costs the resident would endure in the absence of these fiscal costs. The amount a community is willing to tax itself or its visitors to limit congestion or protect the environment is assumed to be fairly representative of the life quality cost that would be imposed on the residents. However, this may not always be true. Inefficient public programs could cost the community or its visitors far more than they return in redressing life quality costs.

We have not addressed the point that certain kinds

of visitors are more costly to service than others. For example, one study has found that convention visitors to a city produced some of the highest costs (Tatzin 1978). Such information would be useful if a community were deciding whether to attempt to change the mix of visitors to reduce costs and increase benefits. However, in estimating the current benefit and cost relationships actually obtained in an area, this information is not important.

In this chapter, we have sometimes talked in terms of the additional costs of attracting additional visitors. Optimally, this should be in terms of the *marginal* costs of these visitors, that is, how much additional social cost would be imposed by one thousand more visitors. Usually this question is answered by assuming the *marginal* cost of serving one thousand more visitors would be the same as the *average* cost of serving one thousand current ones. This may not be true. If visitors, such as convention delegates, are served by a project with a large fixed cost such as a convention center, then the marginal cost of servicing an extra thousand could actually be less than the average cost. In other cases, the marginal cost could exceed the average cost because a facility has reached its service capacity. Far more study is required before we can be completely comfortable with our projections of the cost implications of additional visitors.

Finally, further research is required on measurement of the social costs of travel. Much is conjectural at this point. Better measurement techniques will help ensure better decisions.

COMPARING BENEFITS AND COSTS

Once the economic benefits and the economic costs of travel have been computed on a sound and consistent basis, then we are in a position to determine whether tourism is good for an area in economic terms or whether it costs residents more than they gain. Similarly, we can analyze whether additional visitor promotion provides net benefits, and what direction this promotion should take (Travel Data Center and Fothergill/Beekhuis 1979).

Estimation of the ratio of benefits to costs is straightforward once these two magnitudes have been measured. However, there is one additional issue that relates to the timing of costs and returns from public investment projects designed to serve travelers, such as highways, lodges, and recreation areas.

THE SOCIAL RATE OF DISCOUNT

When residents through their government contemplate investing public funds in a travel-related development project, such as a park or recreation area,

highway, or visitor information facility, they should examine the total construction, operation, and maintenance costs of the project. These costs, as well as benefits from the project, stretch out into the future as far as the useful life of the facility.

They should seek a measure of the total costs of the project. However, we cannot simply sum over the time stream of costs because a dollar's worth of cost five years from now is not worth the same as a dollar's worth of cost today. We need a factor that will put all costs, no matter what year they occur, in terms of a consistent "present value." Benefits should be similarly treated.

A great deal has been written on devising a "discount rate" for valuing the streams of benefits and costs of a public investment project (Mikesell 1977). The debate has been quite technical and is not settled to the satisfaction of all. However, there is a strong case to be made for adopting a single approach for determining the "social rate of discount," the interest rate for collapsing all of the costs and benefits of a project over time into a consistent current value.

Government should be interested in maximizing efficiency in the use of the area's total economic resources. Specifically, this means that a dollar's worth of resources withdrawn from the private sector for public investment should earn the same rate of return as it would in the private sector. If the dollar earns less in the public project, then society is worse off after the public investment than before because a less productive alternative has been implemented.

Consequently, in evaluating the cost stream, government should determine the "opportunity cost of capital" in the private sector, that is, what the investment funds required for the public project would have earned if left in the private sector. This interest rate is then used to discount future benefits and to compound present and future costs.

On the benefit side, a dollar's worth of some benefit, say income, in the future is worth less than a dollar received today (Heilbroner and Thurow 1978, pp. 434–437). There are several ways of justifying this position, but one of the most lucid is to consider that a dollar received today can be invested in the private sector and earn a return, such as interest or dividends. So we say that a dollar received today is worth five percent more than a dollar received one year from now because we can invest today's dollar and earn five percent in a year. The other side of the coin is that the dollar received one year from now is worth five percent less than the dollar received today.

In the general case, if the interest rate or rate of return is r, and the number of years we are awaiting to receive the dollar's worth of income is n, then a dollar's worth of benefit received today is worth $\$(1+r)^n$ at the end of n years. This is also a measure of the return foregone by waiting to year n to receive our dollar's worth of benefit, that is, a dollar's worth of benefit in year n is worth $\$1/(1+r)^n$ today.

Of course, once the benefit is received, it can earn a return from investment just as a dollar received today. If a project has a useful life of 50 years, and we consider the worth of a dollar's benefit in the tenth year, this dollar can earn the return over the last 40 years. So the sooner a dollar's worth of benefits is received, the less income foregone to wait for it, and the more income earned from its investment. On the other hand, the later a dollar's benefit is received, the lower its present value.

The resulting general equation for computing the present value of future benefits is

$$PVB = B_0 + B_1/(1+r) + B_2/(1+r)^2 + \cdots + B_n/(1+r)^n + S/(1+r)^n \quad (1)$$

where

PVB = present value of benefits

$\quad B_t$ = dollar value of benefits in time period t

$\quad r$ = opportunity cost of capital or some other social discount rate

$\quad n$ = life of the project in years

$\quad S$ = salvage value at end of project life.

While there is little disagreement over the proper way to discount benefits into the present, measurement on the cost side does not enjoy such unanimity. The popular approach is to discount the current and future costs of a project in the same manner that benefits are discounted. However, the opportunity cost of capital approach does not allow this reasoning to be applied on the cost side. Whereas future benefits can be invested once they are received and all that is lost is the return foregone waiting for them to arrive, on the cost side there is no return to be gained by investment of future amounts. All such income is foregone beginning the year in which the cost is incurred. If we had invested the money represented by the cost in the first year the project is begun, over the life of the project it could have earned a compounded amount at the given interest rate. All of this income is foregone when the money is invested instead in the public project.

The correct method of computing the present value of costs over the life of a public investment project, recognizing the opportunity cost of capital, is (Mikesell 1977, p. 53)

$$PVC = C_1(1+r)^n + C_2(1+r)^{n-1} + \cdots + C_n \quad (2)$$

where

PVC = present value of costs

$\quad C_t$ = dollar value of costs in time period t

$\quad r$ = opportunity cost of capital

$\quad n$ = life of project in years.

The comparison of the costs and benefits of a public investment project is very sensitive to the discount rate employed. Most of the costs are incurred early in the project's life, so the present value of the costs increases directly with the discount rate employed. On the other hand, the benefits flow over the life of the project rather than at the front end, many accruing far into the future. Thus the present value of benefits *declines* rapidly as the discount rate increases.

It has been a common practice in some public investment areas to keep the discount rate low to maximize the ratio of benefits to costs and ensure project acceptance (Mikesell 1977, pp. 3-6). All that this ensures is that investment resources are wasted as they are taken from their higher return use in the private sector to be used in lower return projects by the government.

To determine the opportunity cost of capital in the private sector relevant to a given project, we first determine whether the project has private sector counterparts. Campgrounds, resorts, transportation terminals, and several other types of public investment projects are often financed by the private sector. In this case, the appropriate social rate of discount is the comparable real before-tax rate of return for the same project in a similar risk class.

If there is no private sector counterpart to the project being studied, then it is suggested that the average real rate on long-term U.S. government bonds be used, with additional premiums to account for the risk of the investment and the average corporate tax rate on total returns to private capital investment.

This approach will help ensure that the social rate of discount is not set too low, thus distorting the flow of investment funds in the private sector and reducing economic welfare in general.

When all is said and done, benefit–cost analysis is just one fairly blunt tool in the decision-makers kit. In wielding this tool, it would be well to note the following perspective:

Cost–benefit analyses can seldom provide complete answers. They are intended primarily to provide more information to decision-makers concerning the major trade offs and implications existing among the alternatives considered. This information would then be available for use by decision-makers, along with any other information available—e.g. that pertaining to political, psychological, and other factors which may not have been included in the cost–benefit study. (Senate Committee on Government Operations 1967, p. 4)

CONCLUSIONS

The preceding three chapters have attempted to address the nature, classification, and measurement of the economic benefits and costs of travel in a comprehensive manner. This broad coverage of issues and alternatives necessarily prohibits detailed examination of any one topic. However, the sources used are amply documented for those who wish to learn more about a single subject.

More attention has been devoted to the benefit side of tourism than the cost side. This is not because determining benefits is more important than understanding costs, but rather reflects the research resources that have gone into the two areas. Future efforts are best directed at developing better techniques to measure costs in an objective manner for it is here our knowledge is weakest. This ignorance gives rise to radical attacks on tourism as an activity and an industry from time to time, attacks that are ill-founded but capture the public's attention. We would all be better served by objective cost measurement rather than the speculation that has characterized many cost discussions so far.

One theme that runs through these chapters is that surveys of travelers should be used only sparingly to develop economic impact information because they are quite expensive, are difficult to conduct well, and may well produce biased results even under the best conditions. It is this author's view that exhaustive examination of data available from government surveys, administrative records, and industry compilations are better sources of necessary information. Moreover, the limited resources available for economic impact estimation are more efficiently devoted to making better use of existing wheels rather than to inventing new ones.

BIBLIOGRAPHY

Baumol, William J., et al. (1970), *The Visitor Industry and Hawaii's Economy: A Cost–Benefit Analysis*, Princeton, N.J.: Mathematica, 30 pp.

Cournoyer, Norman G., et al. (1976), *Travel and Tourism in Massachusetts*, Amherst, Mass.: University at Massachusetts, 250 pp.

Heilbroner, Robert L., and Lester C. Thurow (1978), *The Economic Problem*, fifth edition, Englewood Cliffs, N.J.: Prentice–Hall, 710 pp.

Mikesell, Raymond F. (1977), *The Rate of Discount for Evaluating Public Projects*, Washington, D.C.: American Enterprise Institute, 64 pp.

Northeast Markets, Arthur D. Little, and William Fothergill (1974), *Tourism in Maine: Analysis and Recommendations*, Yarmouth, Maine: Northeast Markets, Inc., 250 pp.

Office of Business and Economic Development, District of Columbia Government (1981), *District of Columbia Tourism Development Policy Study Report*, Washington, D.C.: D.C. Government, 114 pp.

Prest, A.R., and R. Turvey (1967), "Cost–Benefit Analysis: A Survey," *Surveys of Economy Theory, Volume III, Resource Allocation*, New York: St. Martin's Press, pp. 155–207.

Senate Committee on Government Operations, U.S. (1967), *Criteria for Evaluation in Planning State and Local Programs*, Washington, D.C.: U.S. Government Printing Office, 42 pp.

Tatzin, Donald L. (1978), "A Methodological Approach to Estimating the Value of Public Services Consumed by Tourists," *Ninth Annual Conference Proceedings*, Salt Lake City: The Travel Research Association, pp. 53–60.

Travel Data Center, U.S., and Fothergill/Beekhuis Associates (1979), *Delaware Tourism Policy Study*, Dover, Del.: Delaware State Travel Service, 252 pp.

30

Evaluating the Human Resource (Employment) Requirements and Impacts of Tourism Developments

RANDYL D. ELKIN[1]
West Virginia University
Morgantown, West Virginia

RANDALL S. ROBERTS
Louie Glass Company, Inc.
Weston, West Virginia

Human resources research in travel and tourism falls broadly into two categories: human resource requirements and employment impact studies. Human resources requirements research done internal to the firm often deals with problem and planning areas. This in-house research includes job restructuring to eliminate dead-end jobs and redundant tasks; turnover analysis to reduce recruiting, screening, and training costs; and training development programs to reduce turnover and to meet future human resource needs. Research done external to the travel firm is generally done for planning purposes. Industry trade associations, government agencies, and in particular those private and public units charged with providing training and education services plan classes and programs according to industry needs. They project or forecast the number and skills of employees both needed and available for future industry growth. Projected skills shortages are moderated through education and training programs.

Employment impact studies are used to determine past, current, and possible future effects of travel and tourism on employment and earnings. They are usually done by trade associations, universities, and government agencies and are often too complex and costly for an individual firm to undertake. Uses include planning for industry expansion (e.g., identifying viable markets with a readily available labor supply), substantiating applications for loans and government grants, and most commonly for travel promotion and public relations. The results can generate funding from government agencies (to provide training programs or development money), elicit community and resident support, and attract new businesses to the travel industry.

INTRODUCTION

THE NATURE OF THE LABOR MARKET

Economists view the labor market as the arena of interaction between demand and supply. The supply of labor side of the market consists of people. Conceptually, it is the quantity of work hours individuals are willing to work at specific wage rates. For travel research purposes studies usually seek to determine the number of people available to work who have the skills demanded by the travel industry. The quantity dimension of labor supply is number of people and the wage they will work for. The quality component relates to their skills and abilities.

[1]The authors wish to thank Dr. Paul Baktari for his technical assistance in the preparation of this manuscript.

363

On the demand side of the labor market are the firms which employ or wish to hire labor. The demand for labor is a derived demand, that is, firms hire labor because there is a demand for the firms' products. The demand for labor then is a reflection of the demand by the public for travel goods and services. The quantity dimension of labor demand is the number of workers employers are willing to employ at the various wage rates they are willing to pay. The quality dimension relates to the skills and abilities required to do the job. Demand and supply interact to produce employment. Labor cost to the firm is income to its employees.

When examining labor at the firm level, the idea of the internal labor market (ILM) will prove useful. Jobs internal to the firm are relatively isolated from the external (outside) labor market. According to the theory, jobs are often related to one another as a progression of skills requirements. Employers employ new hires only for selected entry-level jobs. Vacancies in positions other than entry level are filled internally by promoting and transferring employees already on the payroll. In a unionized setting these movements are often controlled by a posting and bidding contract clause whereby the positions are filled by current employees on the basis of seniority and ability. The employee assuming the open position is already partially trained for the job via on-the-job training (OJT).

The firm then is pictured as mobility clusters of jobs linked together by technology and custom. An employee starts at the entry-level job and progresses through OJT to better jobs (higher pay, more security) in the cluster. The internal labor market exists more or less in almost all firms. It is a matter of degree. Businesses characterized by many entry-level jobs and short promotion ladders have a stronger external and less internal market orientation. Enterprises which have few entry-level jobs and which have lengthy promotion ladders filled from within are more nearly internal labor markets.

CHOOSING THE RIGHT METHOD

The choice of the appropriate research method depends upon the goal of the research, the amount of money available to finance it, the time allotted to do the study, the expertise available to design, conduct, and analyze it, and the will of the buyer of the results to do something with them.

The primary problem faced by those who conduct human resource research is lack of a well defined goal. All too often consultants are hired by managers who have only hazily defined goals for research. The managers know they have a problem or an interest but cannot set concrete goals for research. The first step is to define the problem at hand. For example: "Our problem is excessive turnover. Our costs of turnover are too high. What can we do to decrease the costs of turnover?" The more specific the statement, the better. Such general statements as "Our labor costs are excessive" aren't very helpful to the person assigned the research. "We're faced with a cutback in government support for travel bureaus. We need to determine what impact travel has on community wages and employment. We need credible research to have clout politically." This is a succinct goal statement for impact research.

The more general statement can be honed to specific research goals after examining the other parameters of the decision such as available money and methods. For example, after a review of finances and research resources, a trade association might conclude, "We want a range of projected demand for chefs under varying industry growth assumptions for each year over the next decade. We have $10,000 to put into the study and will have to contract with a consultant who has computer services available." Further discussion with the researcher can delineate the specifics of estimation.

The ends must be defined with an eye toward the means to achieve them. Research has a cost associated with it and the decision to do or not to do research is no different from any other business decision. The key consideration is still the bottom line. Do the benefits of the proposed analysis outweigh the costs? Most travel businesses do not have the resources for pure research—knowledge for knowledge sake. Thus the more specific the goals and means can be determined the greater is the likelihood that the research will pay off.

Research takes money, but it also has a time cost. A schedule for conducting the study and receiving the results should be included in the proposal. Information after a budgeting or other decision-making date is like old news. If the study is to be done in-house, the time of the person doing the research must be considered as should the time required of management and the employees who may be the targets of the effort. Whether the study can be done in-house will also depend upon resident expertise. Most small businesses and agencies simply do not have employees skilled in research methods or the sophisticated computer hardware needed to do extensive research projects.

Here are three rules of thumb on costs of research. First, there is a trade-off between accuracy and cost. General estimates are less costly than very close estimates. For public relations purposes, it may be sufficient to know the provincial or state employment impact within the nearest 1000. Knowing to the nearest 10 is a waste of resources.

Secondary sources of information are much less costly than primary sources. Don't reinvent the wheel. The information needed may already be available at little or no cost. Impact and human resources requirements studies are done constantly by government agencies, universities, trade associations, banks, and large businesses. The problem with secondary information is that it may be too general to be of much value. In that case, gathering primary data may be necessary. Very often research internal to the firm requires primary data collection and analysis. Turnover analysis at firm A and at firm B will very likely use the same method, but the data and analysis will be unique to the firm. Primary research is much more costly when measured in time and money.

Finally, without the managerial will to use the research results, research is a waste of money. Knowledge isn't a panacea in and of itself. It is only a tool. A turnover analysis forced by higher management on lower levels will neither be successfully conducted nor the results implemented.

HUMAN RESOURCE REQUIREMENTS RESEARCH

Human resource requirements research falls broadly into two categories: (1) methods of job analysis and (2) projections and forecasts.

JOB ANALYSIS

Job analysis is merely the collection and analysis of data about jobs within the firm. Its applications include job restructuring, training program development, qualifications standards development, test development, performance evaluation, employee counseling, safety and hazards identification, and wage and salary administration, among others. The focus here is on job content and worker skills uses.

There are numerous systems of job analysis (Rohmert and Landau 1983). Consultants, often managers or industrial engineers, sell systems of job analysis. One method suitable for small businesses is readily available (U.S. Department of Labor 1972b). Other methods use similar techniques.

Jobs are viewed as a hierarchical collection of positions, tasks, and elements. The basic building block is the element or smallest step work can be divided into. Tasks are combinations of elements which are steps in performing work. A position is the total of tasks which constitute a work assignment. A job is composed of positions that are identical in most tasks.

Jobs are analyzed according to five categories of information: (1) worker functions, (2) work fields, (3) machines, tools, equipment, and work order, (4) materials, products, subject matter, and service, and (5) worker traits. Worker functions are used to identify the complexity of jobs on the belief that all jobs involve some level of relationship to "data," "people," and "things." Worker functions in the data area include such items as synthesizing and compiling. People relationships include negotiating, supervising, and serving, for example. The things functions vary from handling to setting up.

Work fields are methods of production that have either a technological basis (e.g., characteristic of machines) or a socioeconomic one (e.g., providing a service). Materials, products, subject matter, and services refer to the raw materials, final goods, types of specialized knowledge (e.g., math), and services associated with the job. Machines, tools, equipment, and work aids are self-explanatory.

One of the most useful categories is worker traits. These are requirements the job demands of the employee. They include training time, aptitudes, temperaments, interests, and physical demands. Training time has a "General Education Development" (GED) component which refers to an employee's learned ability to reason, follow directions, and knowledge of such tools as language and mathematical skills. The "Specific Vocational Preparation" (SVP) component specifies the amount of vocational learning time required to do the job. Aptitudes are composed of such individual capacities as verbal, spatial, numerical, manual dexterity, and others.

Job restructuring, education and training analyses, and turnover studies illustrate several uses of job analysis.

JOB RESTRUCTURING

By using job analysis, comprehensive job descriptions can be produced and logical job interrelationships identified. This has the virtue of regularizing pay and progression schedules, relates to employment and affirmative action in that hiring standards can be directly related to occupational requirements, and provides a basis for human resources planning (e.g., training and recruitment).

The U.S. Department of Labor method for job restructuring consists of four steps (1972b). The system makes extensive use of both the worker functions (data, people, and things) and the worker traits (GED, SVP, and aptitudes) to rate job complexity and to identify occupational patterns. First the occupations are examined for their task composition and are rated on the appropriate worker function scales. There usually tends to be a layering of occupations by complexity scores. Then the patterns that evolve are modified to take into account work flow, plant layout, plant technology, and other considerations relating to the firm's production process and organizational goals. Finally, the system is revisited to establish an internal mobility structure that will facilitate training on the job. What emerges is a system of effective job descriptions ordered in a logical fashion.

EDUCATION AND TRAINING ANALYSES

Associated with each job structure is a training and education structure. Using the GED, SVP and aptitudes information on each occupation, it is possible to develop a human resource program. Career ladders emerge as a set of related jobs at progressively higher levels in the same occupational category. Dead-end jobs can be identified and logical transfers from one mobility cluster to another can be seen. It should become apparent that recruiting, screening, and training costs can be decreased by relying on OJT to prepare employees for movement internal to the firm. Knowledge of the productivity and track record of the individuals already employed cuts down the expense and uncertainty of recruiting new hires from the outside for positions which can better be filled internally. Entry-level jobs can be identified and training programs can be devised for use on a regular basis for new hires.

A survey of job analysis techniques and applications identified common problems with job analysis (Wilson 1974). Both the conduct and implementation of job analysis are hampered if the goals of the analysis are not well defined. Where the goal is lower turnover and absenteeism or increased mobility, it should be made as specific as possible from the start and modified if necessary as the study is conducted. The study and its implementation must have the support of management, employees, and, in a union setting, the labor organization. Where management itself is not of one mind as to the utility of the research, it is doomed to failure. Some managers may resent job analysis for reasons of indifference (it's a gimmick), insecurity (endangers their job), or prestige (dilutes authority). Some management attitudes are incompatible with job analysis. Managers may believe in use of the stick, not the carrot, to improve productivity. Others may fear loss of quality employees to better jobs and empire builders see mobility as a threat. Finally, lack of managerial support is likely to result in insufficient funding, time, and expertise to do the job right.

TURNOVER ANALYSES

High absenteeism and turnover are both costly and disruptive. Professors Cawsey and Wedley in a study of Canadian manufacturing firms estimated partial turnover costs from $400 to $3,732 (1979). The average for production workers was in excess of $1,000 per turnover. As a proportion of the total wage bill, turnover cost varied from 3.3% for low turnover firms to 31.4% for high turnover firms. Turnover costs for professional employees may be in the five and six figure range.

Cawsey and Wedley suggest a method for turnover analysis. The five steps include: (1) define turnover, (2) identify the relevant cost components, (3) determine measurable and unmeasurable costs, (4) determine controllable and uncontrollable turnover, and (5) calculate total turnover cost.

The definition of turnover should take into consideration the expansion or contraction of the firm, student employees, and part-time employees. The cost components include the cost of exit (severance pay), recruiting and screening, orientation and training, equipment underutilization, and lost production and lost productivity due to training (managerial and trainee). Lost production and productivity are the most difficult to estimate because they are an opportunity cost. Dollar estimates for the first categories are usually visible, measurable, direct costs retrievable from business records. Controllable turnover includes separation for another job, to return to school, or due to the nature of the work, working conditions, and wages. Uncontrollable turnover may be due to retirement or for health, death, or family reasons. Discharge, personal reasons, and turnover for other reasons might be classified in either category depending upon the situation. Calculation of the total cost of turnover is confined to summing up the costs of avoidable turnover.

Armed with the knowledge of turnover cost and the reasons for controllable turnover (Thompson and Terpeniay 1983), management can devise a policy or continue to research a method (job restructuring) for cost reduction. Cawsey and Wedley suggest an accounting budgeting system which makes first line supervisors responsible for a turnover budget.

PROJECTIONS AND FORECASTS

Projections and forecasts of labor demand, supply, and employment are done by a variety of public and private entities. The primary use of these is for planning purposes. The Canadian and American governments pump millions of dollars into education, training, and other human resource programs each year. Private businesses and trade associations do so as well. The nature of most education and training is such that the education itself as well as the payoff are long term. Efficient use of resources mandates projections of the demand for and supply of trained and educated people in the future.

Before considering the common techniques, a distinction is appropriate. From data, projections and forecasts are made. Data may include historical employment by occupation, number in the labor force, business receipts, etc. Projections are an "if. . . , then . . ." statement. The "if" part states the assumptions that have to be made to do the projection (e.g., "If we assume that there will be an occupancy rate of 80% capacity, . . ."). The "then" part is the projection (". . . hotel and motel restaurants will hire 200 short-order cooks.") Forecasts, in contrast to projections, state that the estimates will actually occur. For example, "Business conditions will be such that over the next four years grocery stores will hire 150 check-out trainees."

SURVEYS

Surveys are a commonly used method for gathering primary data. They are usually expensive. Methodologically, a survey requires a goal statement, selection of the target population, choice of a sample or census of the population, derivation of a questionnaire, administration of the questionnaire, and analysis of it.

The problems and pitfalls of obtaining useful survey data are many. They usually require the services of an expert. To do a survey of employment in the travel industry, one would first have to identify travel employers. The industry cuts across many types of employers who attribute varying proportions of their sales revenues to travel. Added to that problem is the fact that most travel businesses are small businesses. A sample of businesses is usually required. If a reasonably complete list of travel and tourism businesses can be had, it then becomes necessary to sample to save on cost. The scientific selection of the sample calls for the skills of a statistician to ensure that the data obtained are accurate. Questionnaire length, exact wording of the questions, and the layout to facilitate computer coding are matters best handled by experts. The same must be said for questionnaire administration. Often a pilot or minisurvey is used to get the bugs out of the questionnaire and the technique. Questionnaires may be by mail, telephone, or personal interview. Questionnaire analysis usually requires statistical methods and the use of a computer.

If possible, survey data should be obtained from secondary sources skilled in all aspects of survey methodology. Area skills surveys are generally available from national, provincial, and state government agencies. In the U.S., the Occupational Employment Statistics (OES) program provides useful survey data. Systematic surveys of nonfarm establishments collect wage and salary information by occupation. The system surveys 20% of the universe of establishments on a three-year cycle. From the surveys come total employment estimates by occupation and industry for state and substate area for over 2000 occupations. These are available in the OES *Occupational Staffing Patterns* and *Occupational Employment Statistics* publications.

The authors did a survey and analysis which illustrate one application of the methodology. This was part of a larger study to assess the potential held by development of the travel industry for employing the hardcore unemployed (Elkin and Roberts 1981). The goal of the survey was to provide data on the internal mobility clusters in travel and tourism businesses. The

target population was all travel-related employers in a specific labor market area in West Virginia. A sample was drawn by industry classification and by size of employer. The population from which the sample was drawn was garnered from local travel association records, the telephone yellow pages, and trade listings. Because the person to be interviewed was a busy personnel manager or person in charge of employment, the questionnaire had to be short. All the information that could be gathered from secondary sources (especially the OES *Staffing Patterns*) was done before the interview. The interview was used to close information gaps. Trial interviews were conducted. A letter from the area Chamber of Commerce and travel association preceded a telephone call to schedule the on-site interview. The interviews were completed in an orderly and timely fashion.

Table 1 is a typical research summary generated by the survey. The design complements the purpose of the interview—to generate data on mobility clusters and associated entry-level occupations and their training requirements.

ORGANIZING THE BASIC DATA

The hotel/motel and other lodging industry is very closely tied to the travel industry. It also characterizes much of the nature of employment in travel. The first column lists the major occupations. The next column indicates the percentage of total industry employment in that occupation. For example, 20% of the people employed in the hotel/motel industry are maids. The numbers in the next column show how many persons are predicted to be in each occupation: total industry employment multiplied by the percentage figure in the preceding column. For maids, $48 = 243 \times 0.20$. The Wages column has two figures. The first is starting pay ($2.65 for maids) and the second is pay after being on the job one year ($3.00 for maids). Seasonality or employment is indicated next. Maid employment is seasonal. The recruitment column shows maids to be recruited externally (from the Job Service, walk-ins, want-ads) and by promotion from within (from what job isn't known) so the entry reads "both." An entry-level "yes" indicates a potential entry-level job and a "no" means the job is only filled internally by promotion. The growth column shows actual employment change from one year ago and for maids was "stable" (no appreciable change over the year).

Promotion affords an application of the internal labor market concept. As noted earlier, a firm characterized by an internal labor market has mobility clusters or job ladders of promotability connected by on-the-job training. These clusters are insulated from outside (external) labor market pressures. Jobs beyond the entry level within a cluster are filled by promotion from within. Pay, skills, and responsibility increase

TABLE 1 Survey Results

INDUSTRY OCCUPATION SIC 70 HOTEL/MOTEL	EMPLOYMENT (INDUSTRY) (243) %	#	WAGES START	AFTER 1 YR	SEASONALITY	RECRUITMENT AND SOURCES	GROWTH OCCUPATION	PROMOTION	EMPLOYER'S PERCEPTION OF AVAIL. JOBS	ENTRY REQUIREMENTS REQUIREMENTS EDUC.	EXPER.	EMP. TRAINING TIME	PROGRAMS OJT	CT
Manager	2.8	7	Salary	Salary	None	External	Stable	Regional Director	Adequate	12–16	6 mos.	8 wks		
Accountant/Auditor	2.8	7	3.50	9.00	None	Both	Stable	Asst. Mgr.	Adequate	12–14	1 yr.	3 wks–1 yr.		
Housekeeper	2	5	4.50	7.00	None	Internal	Stable	None	Adequate	12	6 mos.	3 wks. –6 mos.		
Maid	20	48	2.65	3.00	Yes	Both	Stable	Housekeeper	Adequate	0–12	0	3 days–4 wks.		
Janitor	6.2	15	3.00	NA	None	Both	Stable	Maintenance	Adequate	0	0	3 days–4 wks.		
Bartender	6.2	15	3.00	NA	None	Internal	Stable	None	Adequate	12	0	10 days		
Busboy	2.8	17	2.65	NA	None	External	Stable	Waiter/Front Desk	Adequate	0	0	2 days		
Kitchen Helper	6.2	15	2.65	3.00	Yes	External	Stable	Cook	Adequate	0–12	3 mos.	2 days–2 mos.		
Waiter/Waitress	27.6	67	1.50	1.75	Yes	Both	Stable	Hostess	Adequate	0–12	0	10 days–2 wks.		
Cook, S.O.	4.8	12	3.00	NA	None	Internal	Stable	None	Adequate	0	3 mos.	3 wks.		
Cook, Rest.	4.1	10	3.00	7.50	None	Both	Stable	Supervisor	Adequate	0	3 mos.	3 wks–1 yr.		
Maintenance Person	2.1	5	4.00	4.50	None	Both	Stable	Regional Maintenance	Adequate	0	5 yrs.	5 days–1 yr.		
Cashier	2.1	5	3.00	NA	None	Internal	Stable	Front Desk	Adequate	12	0	4 days		
Bookkeeper	1.3	3	4.50	5.00	None	Both	Stable	Operational	Adequate	12	0	6 wks.–3 mos.		
Hostess	1.3	3	3.50	NA	None	Internal	Stable	Front Desk	Adequate	NA	NA	2 wks.		
Chef	0.7	2	Salary	Salary	None	External	Stable	None	Adequate	16	0	4 yrs		

with progression up the job ladders. Maids are promotable to housekeepers. The Employer's Perception of Available Jobs column is a measure of the employer's perception of the ease with which vacancies can be filled in the current labor market. The market supply of maids is "adequate."

Entry Requirements has three columns. The first is what the employer requires by way of education for an employee taking the job whether recruited externally or promoted from within. Employers require a high school education or less for maids. The next column shows prior experience an entrant must possess. Becoming a maid requires none (0). The last column is an indication of typical, average on-the-job training put into those people becoming maids. The last two columns are blank but could be filled in by users of the matrix. The entry would indicate the type of training program recommended, if any, and training time.

The individual subindustry occupational matrices provide thumbnail sketches per industry, but are also the fundamental building blocks for more extensive analysis useful for both job development and human resource planning activities. Table 2 shows the mobility clusters derived from Table 1 for the hotel/motel industry.

Entry-level positions are numerous, tend to be near the minimum wage for unskilled and semiskilled jobs, and for these workers require 12 years of education or less and little or no experience. Employer training time is short—a few weeks. The more skilled workers, such as chef, have much longer training times, are salaried, and require a higher educational attainment.

Few are hired. Look further at the mobility cluster. Except for the busboy/busgirl cluster with five occupations, the rest are short. The numbers in parentheses indicate the relatively low probability of promotion and upward mobility. Pay starts near the minimum wage and for unskilled and semiskilled jobs progresses somewhere but remains relatively low. The survey results suggest to employers that job restructuring and turnover analysis might decrease employment costs. To training and education planners it suggests occupations for potential training classes and others to which training moneys should not be allocated (Connor and Pelletier 1981).

PROJECTIONS AND FORECASTS

Most of the analyses of elements of future labor demand and supply are projections, not forecasts. Forecasts contain a judgment factor as to what actually will happen in the future. Rather than commit to a specific forecast, most analysts use an "if-then" format and leave it to the user to select the most likely "if." Problems for users of projections arise when either the analyst does not clearly specify the assumptions made (the if) to get the projection or when the user treats the projection as a forecast.

Projections and forecasts are made up mechanically of a data base and a method for extrapolating that base into a future time period. So it is true that a projection is only as good as its data and all projection methods must rely on the stability of some relationship between the phenomenon to be projected and the data used as a predictor.

TABLE 2   Mobility Clusters in the Hotel/Motel Industry

CLUSTER	ENTRY LEVEL	PROMOTION TO	PROMOTION TO
One	Maid (20%/$2.65)[1]	Housekeeper (3%/$4.50)	
Two	Janitor (6.2%/$3.00)	Maintenance Person (2%/$4.00)	Regional Maintenance NA
Three	Busboy/Busgirl (2.8%/$2.65)	Waiter/Waitress (2.8%/$1.50) Desk Clerk (6%/$3.25)	Host/Hostess (1.3%/$3.50) Desk Superintendent NA
Four	Kitchen Helper (6.2%/$2.65)	Cook (4%/$3.00)	Supervisor NA
Five	Chef (1%/Salary)		
Six	Accountant/ Auditor (2.8%/$3.50)	Assistant manager	
Seven	Manager (2.8%/Salary)	Regional Director	

[1]Percentage of employees in the occupation, starting pay.

Projections are either direct or derived. Direct projections include surveys and curve fitting techniques. There are no intermediate variables between the base data and the projected results. For example, past employment is used to project future employment. Derived projections include an intermediate variable. For example, output would first be projected and then future employment would be derived from the output estimate. Derived projection methods include the use of econometric models, input—output models, and industry—occupation models.

SURVEYS AND CURVE FITTING

As mentioned earlier, surveys are really data collection devices. They become projections by asking respondents what they believe the future holds for the phenomenon in question. This type of analysis is subject to the greatest error because few employers plan far ahead when it comes to employment and because their expectations are overly pessimistic or optimistic depending upon the current business situation.

Curve fitting techniques take historical data and literally fit a curve to the data and extend that curve out into a future time period. There are several methods for fitting the curve to the data (Morton 1968). Two methods are eyeballing a straight line between data points and regression models which minimize the square of the distance between the fit curve and the data points.

The hidden assumption which underlies this type of projection is one of historical constancy. As the OPEC experience has shown, this may not be an adequate long-term assumption. Projections of this sort are most useful for short-run decision making. Longer-term planning requires a more sophisticated methodology.

ECONOMETRIC MODELS

Econometric models use either a single-equation or multiequation format. The equation postulates a stable relationship between what is to be projected and some intermediary economic variables. For example, long-term labor supply projections often assume some type of stable relationship between the labor force and population. Long-run demand projections postulate a relationship between output and employment.

A common single-equation model uses a production function. The production function has many possible forms but in each case makes the production of final goods and service (output) a function of resource inputs such as labor and capital. By making assumptions about the likely future levels of production and assuming the relationship estimated from historical data holds into the future (the if), then future levels of labor required to produce the output can be projected (the then).

Multiequation models build systems of equations which are supposed to represent the workings of the economy. They may consist of a few equations or hundreds of them as does the Brookings econometric model of the U.S. economy. Whether they are single-equation or multiequation models, most econometric projections require the use of a computer and knowledge of economics and regression analysis. The travel employer would do well to obtain these projections as secondary information and be very careful to understand the assumptions upon which the projections are made.

INPUT—OUTPUT MODEL

The advantage of input—output models is that they provide both direct and indirect estimates of human resource requirements, that is, they allow for interindustry economic actions and reactions, and they can be used to disaggregate employment into occupation changes and requirements. On the other hand, this type of model assumes a static economic structure. It assumes that there is one production method in each industry, that there is no change in the prices of resources one relative to another, that each industry produces only one output, and that the method of production does not change.

Input—output analysis subdivides the economy into industries. Each industry uses resources (inputs) to produce a single industry output. What emerges is a table with industries (outputs) across the top and inputs along the side. The cells of this "transaction" matrix show what dollar amount of the total revenue generated by an industry is spent on each input. This transaction matrix is then divided out by the total revenue figure to yield a "coefficient" matrix that shows the percentage of a dollar of output which can be attributed to an input. The coefficient matrix is then manipulated to obtain its "inverse." The inverse shows the direct and indirect requirements placed on all inputs to produce and support a final demand of one unit of output from each industry. The matrix indicates the direct input needs from its own industry and the indirect needs from other industries. These needs can then be transformed into a human resources needs matrix given knowledge of the occupational composition of the industries in the table.

Input—output models present a more realistic view of the interrelatedness of the sectors in the economy. It can provide direct and indirect estimates of total human resource requirements by occupation by industry. It assumes, however, that the input—output coefficients in the table will not change, i.e., that the economy is in a steady state. Changes in productivity, production methods, and hours of work which violate those assumptions can make the coefficients and the derived estimates in need of revision. Travel employers should obviously treat input—output estimates as a secondary information source.

INDUSTRY—OCCUPATION ANALYSES

Industry—occupation matrices are used widely by themselves or as a step in other models (e.g., the input—output approach just discussed). Each industry is decomposed into its occupational structure. The first column of Table 1 was a type of industry—occupation matrix. Industries run across the top of the table to head up columns of occupations which run down the side of the table. Coefficients show either the number or percentage composition of employees in a particular occupation in a particular industry.

Publications such as *Tomorrow's Manpower Needs* (U.S. Department of Labor 1972c) use a national industry—occupation matrix. They first estimate national output for the future. Then the total GNP is disaggregated into expenditures by type of demand and from there in a process similar to input—output analysis into future national occupational requirements.

These national figures are frequently used to make state and local estimates. A local area base period industry—occupation matrix is developed. The change factors from the national matrix are applied to the local matrix out to some future period. The matrix is then multiplied by base period employment figures by occupation to get estimates of future local employment by industry and occupation. The greatest leap of faith required by this method is that the assumption made to get the national estimates will be valid in the subnational area.

TRAVEL EMPLOYMENT IMPACT MODELS

Travel has an impact on business receipts as travelers and tourists buy final goods and services. Travel also has an impact on the employment and wages of those who work in travel and travel-related industry as a result of the labor demand generated by travel demand. The focus of this section is on the estimation of the impact travel has on wages and employment.

The results of such studies are used for planning for the effects of travel on human resources when the industry contracts or expands. They are the meat of public relations and promotion campaigns. Requests for loans and government support are supported by a credible impact study.

The methods for assessing the employment impact of travel are the same methods used to determine the human resources requirements. The difference is one of outlook. The human resource requirements perspective is on what quantity and quality of labor travel

businesses need *to produce*. The employment impact model sees the same set of figures as employment *produced by* the travel industry.

Travel impact models generally have a scope of inquiry beyond employment. Other sections of this research volume address the more general types of studies (see Chapter 27). A Department of Commerce manual, *Creating Economic Growth and Jobs through Travel and Tourism* (1981), assesses the research methods for determining impact. It also critiques the various methods and details methods for household, traveler, and travel business surveys.

The same input—output models which generate requirements information also provide impact estimates. Once again, the advantage of input—output models is their ability to use the economic interrelationships to generate direct and indirect travel effects. These indirect effects can be substantial. In the absence of a method of estimating these, travel impacts on employment can be severely understated. For example, a West Virginia study cited in the manual mentioned earlier found the direct economic impact of travel to be $579,119,000. The indirect figure was $197,651,000. The total impact would have been understated by 25% without a measure of indirect effects.

THE TRAVEL ECONOMIC IMPACT MODEL

The travel economic impact model (TEIM) was developed by the U.S. Travel Data Center (1974) to estimate the impact travel has on the national, state and local economies in the U.S. It is a basic econometric model with input—output features that allow estimates of the impact of travel on business receipts, taxes of all kinds, employment, personal consumption, and personal income. It generates both primary and secondary effects.

The estimation process takes several steps. First, survey data on the number and types of travel trips are combined with average cost data to yield a national travel expenditure model. The results include expenditures on 15 categories by state. These figures are then augmented with short trip data to correspond with a more generally accepted definition of travel than was used by the initial survey. The result is a data set of total travel spending by state (or county) which is then categorized to become business receipts for 13 travel industries.

By using coefficients which show the number of jobs generated in each industry per dollar of business receipts, the business receipts figures can be multiplied to obtain the primary (direct) effect on employment. Knowing the blue collar, white collar, and service occupation distribution of each industry, the employment estimates yield direct occupational employment figures.

The secondary (indirect) effects of travel on employment are found by using a secondary economic impact component. This is done by separating earnings and employment into categories: basic and nonbasic. Basic employment is that which services entirely local consumption. Nonbasic employment generates goods and services which are exported out of the local economy. Employment multipliers are calculated which relate employment to travel earnings. The multipliers are used to generate the secondary employment impacts.

Obviously such involved calculations of travel employment impacts are beyond the resource availability of most travel entrepreneurs. The results of impact studies such as the TEIM model are best treated as secondary information. They can be purchased or are otherwise available from the researchers.

The impact models are mirror images of the human resource requirement models. Therefore, all of the caveats about the human resource requirements methodologies apply to the same types of impact research models. The admonitions regarding the costs and uses of research apply equally to both human resources requirements and uses of research.

REFERENCES

Cawsey, Thomas F., and William Wedley (1979), "Labor Turnover Costs: Measurement and Control," *Personnel Journal*, February, 90-95.

Connor, Samuel R., and May Beth Pelletier (1981), *The Handbook for Effective Job Development: Placing the Hard-to-Employ in the Private Sector*, Work in America Institute, Scarsdale, New York.

Elkin, Randyl D., and Randall S. Roberts (1981), "A Study of the Potential for Economic Development in the Travel and Tourism Industry to Provide New Employment Opportunities for the Chronically Unemployed," Economic Development Administration, U.S. Department of Commerce, Employment and Training Administration, U.S. Department of Labor, Washington, D.C.

Morton, J.E. (1968), *On Manpower Forecasting*, The W.E. Upjohn Institute for Employment Research, 300 South Westnedge Avenue, Kalamazoo, Michigan 49007.

Rohmert, Walter, and Kurt Landau (1983), *A New Technique for Job Analysis*, International Publications Service, New York.

Thompson, Kenneth R., and Willbunn D. Terpeniay (1983), "Job-Type Variations and Antecedents to Intention to Leave: A Content Approach to Turnover," *Human Relations*, July, 655−681.

United States Department of Commerce, Economic Development Administration (1981), *Creating Economic Growth and Jobs Through Travel and Tourism: A Handbook for Community and Business Developers*, Washington, D.C.

United States Department of Labor, Bureau of Labor Statistics (1972a), *A Handbook for Analyzing Jobs*, Washington, D.C.

United States Department of Labor, Bureau of Labor Statistics (1972b), *A Handbook for Job Restructuring*, Washington, D.C.

United States Department of Labor, Bureau of Labor Statistics (1972c), *Tomorrow's Manpower Needs*, Washington, D.C.

United States Department of Labor, Bureau of Labor Statistics (Yearly), *Occupational Outlook Handbook*, Washington, D.C.

United States Department of Labor, Bureau of Labor Statistics (1980), *Methodology for Projection of Industry Employment to 1990*, Washington, D.C.

United States Department of Labor, Employment and Training Administration, Bureau of Labor Statistics, Research and Statistics Section (Yearly), *Occupational Employment Statistics*, Washington, D.C.

U.S. Travel Data Center (1974), *Travel Economic Impact Model*, Vol. 1, *Final Economic Analysis Methodology*, Washington, D.C.

Wilson, Michael (1974), *Job Analysis for Human Resource Management: A Review of Selected Research and Development*, National Technical Information Service, Springfield, Virginia 22151.

31

The Social Impact of Tourism on Developing Regions and Its Measurement

LOUISE CRANDALL

National Capital Commission
Ottawa, Ontario, Canada

*T*ourism affects the society and culture of a receiving country as well as its economy and environment. This is especially true of developing countries that are reliant on the tourism industry as a mainstay of their economies. This chapter presents an overview of the various types of social impacts that could be found in a tourism destination area and describes a number of methodologies that can be used to examine them.

As a tourism industry develops and grows it usually has an impact on a number of sectors of society. A tourism industry or, on a smaller scale, tourism attractions such as beach resorts and theme parks are often developed with two main thoughts in mind—to attract as many tourists as possible and to maximize revenues. This is sometimes especially true of developing countries with few resources that are seeking to diversify their economies. These countries are generally islands or are small in size and rely on the export of one or two primary products for foreign exchange earnings. They often have little to sell except these products and their sun and sand. In many instances governments, having heard about the potential economic returns from tourism, jump into tourism development wholeheartedly with little analysis of potential impacts on their economies, on their environment, or on their people. Tourism can, however, be a major agent for change in the social, political, and cultural system of a destination area as well as in the economy and environment.

For years tourism was accepted as a boon to local economies, and there was little realization on the part of government and residents that it leads to social change and, sometimes, to social problems. This social change can be gradual, or rapid and large scale. Some governments are now starting to realize that the welfare of the public should be considered along with the needs of tourists and investors. In the sixties and seventies, riots and civil disturbances erupted in formerly peaceful countries. In many of these countries, such as St. Croix, Trinidad, Bermuda, and Jamaica, in the West Indies, the tourism industry acted as a catalyst in the disturbances (Turner and Ash 1975). Tourism is generally developed to meet one or more of the objectives of society, usually economic growth. When, after a number of years of disruption in their way of life, residents see few improvements except that a small minority has grown richer, questioning and frustration can erupt. Social stress and disorganization could already have developed through changes in the structure of local society. This is especially prevalent in traditional societies which have been forced to adapt rapidly to modern ideas, values and technologies.

Rarely is an effort made to determine social as well as economic costs and benefits when the performance of tourism is being evaluated or when new developments are planned. The assessment of social impacts is very complex because one cannot quantify social impacts, subtract costs from benefits, and arrive at a conclusion, as in an economic cost/benefit analysis. It is also sometimes difficult to differentiate between social and economic costs and benefits, since they are so intertwined. Furthermore, the tourism industry will not have the same impacts on the economy and society of any two countries, no matter how similar they might appear. The potential impacts of the tourism industry depend on a large number of criteria; not only on the numbers of tourists, but on the historical, social, cultural, economic, and political background of the host country.

The first part of this paper presents a broad overview of the various negative and positive social impacts one could potentially find in a country with a developed tourism industry. They are divided into socioeconomic and sociocultural. The main focus is on small, developing countries where, for many reasons, negative impacts are more prevalent than in large developed regions with a mature and stable economy. The second part of the paper presents a discussion of some of the various methodologies that can be used to assess the social impact of tourism on a receiving area.

THE POTENTIAL SOCIAL IMPACTS OF TOURISM ON DEVELOPING NATIONS
SOCIO-ECONOMIC IMPACTS

While the tourism industry has definite effects on the economy of a country in terms of job creation, increased foreign exchange earnings, or a growth in the import bill, there are also indirect socioeconomic impacts, many that have both positive and negative aspects to them (as set out in Exhibit A).

Economic Independence

In most tourism areas the majority of jobs, particularly the unskilled ones, will be filled by women and young people, many of whom are earning money for the first time. This can cause conflict in traditional societies where parents and/or husbands have always held more power or status. They sometimes find it hard to accept the fact that family members have both economic independence and exposure to new and threatening ideas. Studies have shown this to be the case in areas like Malta, Cyprus, and the Seychelles (de Kadt 1979a; Boissevain 1977; Cleverdon 1979).

Labour Force Displacement

In many countries, especially those limited in size, local populations have been displaced by tourism developments that are often built in the more scenic areas (i.e., a type of competition for resources). Migration could occur because of the razing of a squatter townsite to build a resort, or the flooding by tourists of a beach formerly used by fishermen, and as a result family and economic patterns can be broken. Examples of this occurred in western Mexico when resorts such as Ixtapa and Zihuatanejo were developed in the seventies on the sites of small undeveloped villages (de Kadt 1979a). The opposite phenomenon can also occur. In Cancun, in the Yucatan, the pattern of migration was towards the development rather than away, and many of the people working in the hotels are probably earning their first salaries. Labour force migration can therefore have both positive and negative effects. In undeveloped regions it can mean paid employment; in urban areas, such as Acapulco, it can lead to further crowding, higher rates of unemployment, and the growth of slums.

Changes in Forms of Employment

A frequent impact in areas with growing tourism developments is that local residents will leave traditional forms of employment, such as agriculture and fishing, to work in the hotels or restaurants. While they might become wage earners for the first time, the primary sector of the economy may be adversely affected by a loss of labour. In the Seychelles a shift from jobs in the agriculture sector to those in the tourism and construction industries eventually resulted in higher food prices (de Kadt 1979a). Second, many jobs in the tourism industry are seasonal, so that the worker must either remain unemployed throughout a number of months of the year or find supplementary work, which is often hard to do. These same people can also find themselves permanently unemployed if demand for their destination area shifts, a frequent occurrence in tourism.

Changes in Land Values and Ownership

A common occurrence in areas beginning to develop a tourism industry is the skyrocketing of land values, which can cause conflict over land use and displacement of local residents from land that often goes into the hands of a group of powerful nationals or foreigners (Perez 1974; Cleverdon 1979). This is especially true where a tourism development is planned in a formerly untouched area. In parts of Barbados the price of land rose almost 50 percent annually in the early seventies (Crandall 1976).

Improved Standard of Living

A major beneficial impact of tourism is that local residents can take advantage of improvements made in health services, airports, water and sewage systems, and recreational facilities that might have been built primarily with the tourist in mind, or that are paid for by local governments with the surplus from tourism revenues. Another example is the new roads that can facilitate access to markets for local farmers. A frequent cost of tourism growth, however, is that prices are often driven up as a result of tourists who are willing to pay more for many items. While a "two price system" may be in effect, more often prices remain at the higher tourist level. This inflation can sometimes negate the positive impact of flows of tourism revenue into a region.

EXHIBIT A   Potential Social Impacts of Tourism

IMPACT	POSITIVE ASPECTS	NEGATIVE ASPECTS
Socioeconomic		
Individual economic independence	Wages	Conflict in traditional societies
Labour force displacement	Migration to tourism region for employment	Forced migration of residents from region
Changes in employment	Employment in tourism sector	Seasonal unemployment; abandonment of traditional forms of employment
Changes in land value	Increased value of land	Higher land prices; conflict over land use changes in ownership
Improved living standards	Improved services, facilities, infrastructure	Inflation generated by tourism
Changes in political–economic system	Growth of new elite; growth of depressed regions	Splits in national unity
Sociocultural		
Growth in undesirable activities	—	Growth in crime and prostitution
Social dualism	Cross-cultural exchange; widened dimensions	Conflicts in values
Demonstration effect	Stimulation to improve living standards	Frustration; increased spending; growth in import bill
Culture as a commercial commodity	Preservation of cultural heritage; growth of pride	Culture loses meaning as it is commercialized for tourists
Growth of heritage	—	Growth of resentment and hostility; servile attitude growth on the part of residents

Changes in the Political–Economic System

The development of tourism on a large scale can sometimes help to shift political and economic power from traditional groups to a new elite of businessmen who own the resources needed by the industry. Tourism growth can also lead to development of previously economically depressed regions, such as Mexico's Yucatan and certain Caribbean islands. This can have beneficial economic and social impacts, or can lead to splits in national unity as one region gets precedence over another in terms of resource allocation (de Kadt 1979b; Cleverdon 1979; Butler 1975).

SOCIO-CULTURAL IMPACTS

Growth of Undesirable Activities

Many people in tourism destination areas believe that tourism will bring in or help facilitate undesirable activities, such as gambling, drug trafficking, and prostitution, which will result in changes in the local system of sexual values (Young 1973). One phenomenon

that the industry has brought to many countries is growth in the number of "beachboys," young men who do not look for jobs because they know that they can be supported by the female visitors in the area (Turner and Ash 1975). The church and many local residents in developing countries are especially bothered by this and place much of the blame on the tourists. Local residents are also often offended at the brief attire of tourists, women wearing shorts into town or bathing suits in the street. (However, this varies region by region and even city by city.) Another fear is that crime will increase as the tourism industry grows and affluent tourists are envied by poor residents. Studies carried out in Mexico and Hawaii have shown this to be the case (Jud 1975; Fujii, Mak, and Nishimura 1978).

Social Dualism

Another social cost of tourism is what has been called the "premature departure to modernization" (Jafari 1973). Foreign values and ideologies come to be accepted by and influence the lives and behaviour of local residents. Some may copy tourist behaviour and attitudes and ignore cultural and religious traditions. There may be abrupt and disruptive changes in social customs and patterns, for example, women leaving their homes for the first time to work in the hotels as maids or cooks. Studies in Hawaii have linked this occurrence to a sharp increase in the rate of divorce (Lundberg 1974). This can interrupt the slow, normal, and unique process of development, and it is claimed that social dualism can result in a person who is partly westernized and partly holding onto traditional values. Disruptions in societies and split families can often occur as a result (Cowan 1977).

On the positive side, tourism is credited with beneficial cross-cultural exchanges that can result in international understanding and widened dimensions on the part of both local residents and tourists to whom new ideas have been transmitted.

Demonstration Effect

The demonstration effect is basically the adoption by local residents, especially the young, of tourist behaviour and attitudes and consumption patterns. It can be beneficial when locals might see what else is available in the world and be stimulated to work harder and get a better education in order to improve their living standards. However, this is only a social benefit when the opportunities for upward mobility are there to be exploited, such as the existence of jobs and schools. Otherwise, the result will be increased frustration as young people go to school or move to the city in the expectation of a better life but find a lack of employment opportunities. The demonstration effect can also lead to spending on diverse items, such as blue jeans, records, fast food items and sunglasses, even though the means to do so are not there. Some locals adopt the marks of affluence, wear foreign fashions, eat imported food and drink imported liquor. Not only do they live beyond their means, but the consumption of imported goods is further increased (Turner and Ash 1975; de Kadt 1979b; Cleverdon 1979).

Culture as a Commercial Commodity

Another potential impact of tourism is that art, ceremonies and rituals, music, and traditions can become marketable commodities and lose relevance to the local people. (Examples are Haitian Voodoo ceremonies, Balinese religious ceremonies, Hawaiian fire dances, and Canadian Indian rain dances put on mainly for the benefit of visitors.) Moreover, remnants of the colonial past, such as forts and plantations, become tourism attractions. As well as lowering the dignity of the people and their culture, a deterioration of the standard of local arts and crafts and a "watering down" of local music, crafts, and ceremonies for mass tourist con-

sumption can result. Ceremonies and rituals, which once had great importance for a native people, now become meaningless and are used primarily to attract tourists who feel no respect for the local beliefs or traditions (de Kadt 1979a; Perez 1975; Cleverdon 1979).

On the more positive side, however, the tourist industry is also credited with helping to revive or preserve the cultural heritage of a destination area—monuments, ceremonies, arts and crafts, and traditions which otherwise might have been forgotten or died out. A sense of inferiority can be alleviated and a sense of pride in one's country promoted as tourists seek things not found elsewhere (Cowan 1977).

Growth of Hostility to Tourists

A major phenomenon seen in many tourist destination areas, but especially in the developing regions, is growth of resentment and hostility towards the tourist on the part of the local resident. One author wrote "the poorer the host country, the greater irritants (such as arrogant displays of wealth and disregard of the host's values and sensitivities) are likely to be" (Gray 1970). Two other factors influence relationships between the people of developing countries and the tourist: the fact that the former are often ex-colonies of the tourist-generating countries and, second, that the people are of different racial backgrounds (Turner and Ash 1975; Perez 1975). Fears have been expressed by West Indian writers that a form of neocolonialism is developing as former "slaves" serve former "white masters" and that a servile attitude or negative self-image could grow on the part of a black, newly independent population (Theuns 1973). For example, one author stated: "We find in the Caribbean predominantly coloured people recently emerged from a colonial status, seeking an identity free from the legacy of slavery, colonial dependency, and the plantation economy, who are suddenly thrust into having to serve rich, white tourists who either intentionally or unintentionally begin to dictate the shape of the environment to meet their leisure needs" (Doxey 1973).

Resentment and hostility to tourists can also grow as hordes of people descend on regions with limited space, leading to strains on infrastructure such as roads and water and sewage systems. Services such as health clinics and police can be overtaxed; beaches become crowded and polluted; traffic jams become common, as do long lines in stores. These phenomena are especially prevalent in areas which are tourism "ghettos" (i.e., where tourism is the major activity) or those with a short tourism season (Theuns 1973).

Irritation at these occurrences is a major sign that the saturation point of a destination area has been reached. The saturation point in most host countries is a vague undetermined point of diminishing returns at which the benefits from tourism start to be outweighed by the socioeconomic costs. The saturation point is extremely hard to measure and depends on many variables, of which volume of tourists is just one. The following factors were identified by Butler (1975) as the major ones which influence the tourism saturation point of a country.

VISITOR CHARACTERISTICS

1 Volume: A major factor is volume of tourists. A small number of visitors to a country with a large population will have little effect, while a large number of tourists visiting a small island or resort town, especially over a short season, will have a major impact.

2 Length of stay: The longer the visitors stay, the greater will be their contact with the host population and their socioeconomic penetration.

3 Racial characteristics: The greater the differences between the tourists and locals in terms of colour, language, and culture, the greater will be their impact.

4 Economic characteristics: The greater the difference in levels of affluence, the stronger will be the resentment and desire for equality on the part of local residents.

5 Activities of tourists: Their activities determine the amount of contact, i.e., visiting local hangouts versus spending a week on the beach and in "tourist only" bars. The type of tourist is also a factor: the institutionalized mass tourist who seeks familiarity and does not stray from what has been called his "environmental bubble" to mix with locals versus the "explorer" or "drifter" (according to Cohen's typology (1972) who wishes to experience other cultures fully.

CHARACTERISTICS OF A DESTINATION AREA

1 Economic development: A general rule is that the more developed the local economy, the less the dependence on the tourism industry and the less its impact.

2 Spatial characteristics: This includes size of the destination area, size of population, location of resorts (i.e., close to or distant from local settlements), capacity of facilities, number of hotels, area of beach, miles of roads, and other physical variables. Ratios are then calculated between arrivals and the population and land area (including total and peak arrivals), and between tourist nights to land areas, beach areas, road mileage, and restaurant capacity. Obviously, the higher the ratios, the more likely it is that friction will occur. (The concept involved here is the absorptive capacity of the host country.)

3 Degree of local involvement: The amount of contact is also a function of whether tourist enterprises are run and owned by local or foreign companies. (The former situation is better for the economy, of course.)

4 Strength of local culture: The stronger the local culture (i.e. unique, clear traits) and language, the better the ability to withstand the impact of a foreign culture.

5 Other: This can include the political attitudes and degree of nationalism in the host country, as well as its historical background (i.e., a long, stable history versus recent independence and a market of former "colonizers").

All these factors affect the penetration and pressure on the daily life of the local inhabitants of a resort area and the demand tourism has on their habitat. The physical saturation point, whether it be a tourist/resident ratio of 1:1 or 10:1, is different in every destination area because of the variables involved. It is, however, virtually impossible to arrive at a total saturation point because psychological attitudes are difficult to quantify. The point of physical saturation can perhaps be determined, but equally important, social attitudes must also be taken into account, since what one person finds irritating often does not bother someone else.

METHODOLOGIES OF SOCIAL IMPACT ASSESSMENT

The preceding pages presented an overview of the various types of social impacts and unwanted consequences one could find in a country that has a fairly advanced tourism industry, especially a country that is undergoing the process of development. These impacts can be examined or assessed in many ways, and a brief description of a number of nonstatistical methodologies follows. Most are derived from social science, and, more specifically, from social impact assessment methodology. The bulk of social impact assessments, however, deal with natural resource developments and are carried out before the fact, with the aim of forecasting potential impacts and recommending mitigative measures. Although many of the initial processes in a social impact assessment are relevant to a study of the tourism industry, the latter is usually done after the fact, that is, when tourism has been in place a number of years and negative impacts are starting to be evident. Ideally a government would carry out a Social Impact Assessment (S.I.A.) when the industry, or a particular development, was in the planning stages.

A social impact assessment has been defined as: Any study which attempts to determine the impacts of a particular physical development on the day-to-day quality of life of persons whose environment is affected by the development, other than those whom the development is expressly designed to serve; such a study may be prospective or retrospective (Boothroyd 1975).

There are many approaches that can be used to examine social impacts; no one way is best. To carry out a proper study two points are important: the research should be carried out within the sociocultural context of the impacted group, and more than one methodology should be used. Exhibit B indicates some of the primary methodologies which can be used to collect data on each of the social impacts discussed in previously. Since social impact assessment is an area in which much of the data available is qualitative, it is important to develop multiple lines of evidence with which to examine each potential impact. The researcher will undoubtedly face a number of problems, among them: (1) the difficulty in defining or quantifying the subject matter, (2) the wide variety of methodologies available, (3) the question of validity of qualitative data, (4) the lack of complete, adequate data, and (5) the problems posed by potentially conflicting interests, values, and perceptions of the impacted population, the government, and those in the industry.

Two major ways in which social science research is carried out are through (1) interviews/surveys and (2) analysis of secondary sources including written documentation and statistics.

SURVEYS/INTERVIEWS

Surveys and interviews are key methods for collecting information about a community. Specific techniques that can be useful in assessing the social impact of tourism include attitude surveys, use of key informants, use of the Delphi technique, and, while not technically a survey, participant observation.

Design of Surveys of the Public

Since many potential impacts of tourism are only negative if so perceived by the local residents, it is important to discover his or her attitudes and perceptions towards tourism. Depending on the stage at which it is carried out, a survey can either serve as a "benchmark" for a later assessment of change or as a measure of current perceptions. The survey should test the researcher's theories on what impacts tourism may have had, but it is also important that it be designed with the

EXHIBIT B Primary Data Collection Methods for Potential Impacts

| IMPACT | SURVEYS/INTERVIEWS | | | | SECONDARY SOURCES | |
	SURVEYS	KEY INFORMANTS	DELPHI	PART. OBS.	DATA ANALYSIS	CONTENT ANALYSIS
Socioeconomic						
Economic independence	X	X			X	
Labour force displ.		X			X	
Employ. changes	X	X	X		X	
Change in land values		X	X		X	
Improved living standards	X	X			X	
Changes in pol. – econ. system		X	X		X	
Sociocultural						
Undesirable activities	X	X		X	X	X
Social dualism	X	X	X	X		X
Demonstration effect	X	X		X		
Commercialism of culture	X	X	X	X		
Hostility	X	X	X	X		X

values of the impacted area in mind, i.e., what is important to the community.

Surveys are especially relevant for studying all the sociocultural impacts, as well as economic independence, changes in employment, and improvements in living standards. They can be carried out by telephone, mail, or in-person. Local residents to be surveyed can be chosen randomly to be representative of the population or in a purposefully biased way if only a participant group is to be surveyed. Different questionnaires can be administered to local residents and to employees in the tourism industry, since their involvement and perceptions will vary. (It is believed that attitudes to tourism may vary with dependency on the industry and there is evidence to suggest that those who work in tourism or benefit from it will likely identify more positive than negative impacts (Brougham and Butler 1981; Pizam 1978; Rothman 1978).) It is also important to note that surveys measure perceived impacts, which can be different from actual impacts (Pizam 1978; Belisle and Hoy 1980).

A number of researchers have carried out surveys of attitudes of local residents to assess tourism impacts (Pizam 1978; Murphy 1981; Thomason, Crompton, and Kamp 1979). A minority of these attitude surveys have been carried out in developing countries—Sethna in the Caribbean (1977), Doxey in Barbados (1972), and Belisle and Hoy in Colombia (1980). The survey methodology is quite similar in all of the studies. The first step is usually to devise a questionnaire based on the hypotheses to be tested. Hypotheses should be based on the types of social impacts which may be present in the host country. Data with which to examine the relationship between social impacts and various socioeconomic and demographic variables of residents (income, age, sex, language, education, etc.) can also be built into the survey. For example, the Belisle and Hoy study (1980) hypothesized that perceptions of tourism impacts vary with the distance from the tourist zone and with socioeconomic status. (The first hypothesis was judged to be proven while the second was not.) Hypotheses from which questions can be formed may also be derived from unstructured, open-ended interviews with residents that can provide a range of attitudinal concepts, perhaps in the form of frequently repeated phrases (Knox 1978; Thomason, Crompton, and Kamp 1979).

The actual questionnaire may have a number of sections. The first section can contain socioeconomic and demographic data on the respondents and should identify his/her contact with tourists. This data is useful for categorizing residents and later correlating perceived impacts with different variables.

If desired, a second section of the questionnaire can elicit opinions on such things as perceived benefits or disadvantages of tourism with open-ended questions. In this way, factors which might have been overlooked

in the survey design will be picked up. A survey carried out by the English Tourist Board (*Report* 1978) contained a number of probes such as "What in your opinion are the most important benefits/disadvantages to London/yourself from tourism?" and "Precisely what problems do you suffer from tourists in London?" Open-ended questions though may not elicit negative, complete, and/or relevant comments and responses, and also are difficult to quantify.

A third section of the questionnaire can contain a survey of attitudes. This entails close-ended questions to be answered on a scale. (Bipolar scales, using adjective pairs with opposite meanings, are called semantic differentials and are a common method of measuring perceptions.) Attitude surveys can be used alone, but are especially useful in getting indirectly at information which could be asked directly in a probe of opinions. One common technique is to set out statements which are to be rated on a scale somewhere between strong agreement to strong disagreement. (For a list of 100 attitudinal questions which can serve as a starting point in an attitude survey, see Knox (1978).) The attitudinal statements can be grouped into a number of areas. An attitude survey carried out on seven Caribbean islands (Sethna 1980) contained 56 attitudinal statements grouped into seven areas: financial, moral, religious, social, physical, human, and cultural. Respondents were asked to rate a typical attitudinal statement on a five-point scale; for example, "Local people working in the luxury hotels or big shops do not treat the local people as nicely as they do tourists."

A second method which can also be used is to set out a list of potential developments such as "an increase in the cost of seafood" (Belisle and Hoy 1980) or "occurrence of prostitution" (Pizam 1978). The responses to this type of statement can be rated on an eleven-point scale ranging from -5 to +5, with zero equating to no impact from tourism on the item. A third method is to use a semantic differential scale but vary the possible responses according to the item; for example, "winter visitors are beneficial−harmful," and "their presence results in crowded−uncrowded hotels/beaches/restaurants" (Thomason, Crompton, and Kamp 1979).

The next step in the survey is to pretest the questionnaire for reliability and validity and modify questions, if necessary, to make them more relevant. The questionnaire is then administered to the sample of respondents selected. The data collected can be analyzed very simply using means, medians, or percentages, for example, or with any one of various statistical data analysis techniques such as multiple regression (Pizam 1978), discriminant analysis (Murphy 1981), Thaid technique (Brougham and Butler 1981), analysis of variance (Thomason, Crompton, and Kamp 1979), common factor analysis, stepwise regression, or chi-square analysis (Belisle and Hoy 1980).

Use of Key Informants/Community Leaders

Interviews of key informants/community leaders can be used to elicit factual data as well as opinions and attitudes towards tourism. The same questionnaire as used for the survey of the public can be administered, although a slightly more focused questionnaire would probably prove to be of more use. Key informants are defined as people who work in the tourism industry, in the government, or in key jobs in the area (e.g., the police, the mayor, local businessmen, etc.). Key informants can also be used to identify those people they think represent the community. (Each person is asked to identify community leaders, and those people who are mentioned a number of times are chosen to be interviewed.) While the responses are likely to be similar to those interviewed in the public survey, they will likely be more informed. Key informants can probably provide relevant information on all the potential impacts caused by the growth of tourism in their region.

Delphi Study

A Delphi study is another way in which information can be gathered that is factual and/or attitudinal. It is a method of polling experts in order to arrive at a consensus of informed opinion on current or, more usually, future occurrences. In a Delphi study, a panel of experts is assembled who can be community leaders, tourism industry employees, government employees, or academics. They are often first given background information on possible tourism impacts and statistics on the tourism industry in the area. The panel members are then sent a questionnaire in which the various hypotheses to be tested are formed into questions, e.g., "Has hostility to tourists increased in the past two years with the recent growth in tourism?" The Delphi technique would probably provide the most relevant information on changes in land values, employment and the political−economic system, social dualism, commercialization of culture, and hostility to tourists. Unstructured opinions and factual data can also be elicited. Responses are analyzed and synthesized and then sent back to respondents, who are given a chance to reconsider and change their answers if desired on the basis of this feedback. Answers are once again analyzed and a third round of mailouts is sometimes carried out before the final analysis. (For an example of a Delphi study related to tourism, although not to tourism impacts, see *Tourism in Canada—1986* carried out by L.J. D'Amore and Associates (1977).)

Participant Observation

Participant observation is a useful technique when carrying out a case study, especially when it is utilized along with surveys and data analysis. It can provide first-hand data on various ideas or theories the researcher wishes to study (especially sociocultural impacts of tourism) while allowing access to "informants" who might not be represented in a survey (often anonymously in a casual, social situation). Participant observation uses an intuitive approach. The researcher, either overtly or covertly, observes a social system in order to (1) explore the society looking for possible predetermined social impacts, (2) develop new ideas and hypotheses, and (3) look for new data to test them. It is especially useful if the researcher has detailed knowledge of an area before tourism developed, either through a baseline study or preferably through first-hand experience. In this way a type of longitudinal (i.e., before and after) study can be carried out and the intensity and impacts of change can be examined.

The data collected are usually somewhat subjective, however, which is why other techniques that provide more objective information should also be used. The problems with participant observation are that there are no checks on possible bias or distortion on the part of the researcher, there is no sampling design, and the introduction of an observer can, in itself, affect what is being studied (the control effect, see Riley (1963).)

ANALYSIS OF SECONDARY SOURCES

Two of the ways in which analysis of secondary sources can be carried out are (1) content analysis of newspapers and (2) analysis of quantifiable data found in government records and other public documents.

Content Analysis

Content analysis of newspaper articles, news items, advertisements, photos, and letters to the editor can provide a very good picture of developments in an area over time. It is possible to compare information over a period of years or decades; in other words, to "reconstruct" a community or region, identify changes over time, and determine their content. Content analysis can also serve to check the validity of other types of data, especially information related to social attitudes and behaviour patterns (for example, social dualism, hostility, and the growth of undesirable activities).

Information collected by content analysis can be analyzed descriptively (i.e, thematic analysis) or quantitatively, using frequency counts of symbols or items. The main problem is that data can be biased, fragmented, and incomplete.

The first step is to identify questions to be answered and types of information sought. Categories must be devised to record the information for later analysis. The second step is to determine the best newspaper(s), the time period to be covered, and the number of issues to be reviewed. The newspapers are then examined for references to tourism and especially to its social impacts. It might be necessary to classify certain items as having equivalent meaning in order to fit them into the predetermined categories. All mentions to social impacts are then recorded as a frequency count (i.e., as a check in the appropriate category box) or as a quote for later thematic analysis. If certain potential social impacts are referred to a number of times, it is often possible to draw inferences as to when and why they developed and compare them to quantitative data such as annual tourist arrivals.

Data Analysis

Analysis of various types of statistics usually collected by governments can provide excellent information on past trends. A review of these often provides useful insights on the impacts of a growth in tourism, assuming the statistics are available at the level of the region studied. Results from analysis of statistics can quantitatively reinforce results of qualitative research methodologies, such as participant observation. It is especially relevant for looking at the socioeconomic impacts of tourism discussed previously although somewhat less so for examining most of the sociocultural impacts.

The first step in statistical analysis should be to analyze tourism arrivals (including cruise ship arrivals if relevant) by year and month to chart their growth. These figures can be compared with population and land area (including roads, beaches, number of facilities, water supply, etc.) to determine the tourism density by month, and thereby the pressure on both local people and infrastructure. The average length of stay and daily expenditure of tourists should also be calculated. (These are some of the factors which help determine the saturation point of tourism.) Other factors, such as racial characteristics, activities of tourists and strength of local culture, can usually be determined through participant observation and surveys. In this way a number of quantitative and qualitative lines of evidence can be utilized to estimate the saturation point of tourism. As already stated, however, it is a rather indefinite concept and cannot be pinpointed exactly.

Once arrival trends have been established, they should be compared with a number of other types of statistics in order to draw inferences and perhaps conclusions about the impact of tourism on the society and economy of the destination area. For example, the growth of undesirable activities can be analyzed statistically through crime figures usually available in local police headquarters. They should be examined to see if crime has increased in certain categories which can involve tourists, such as indecent assault, prostitution, break-ins, drug use, theft, rape, and robbery. Although figures do not differentiate between crimes against tourists and those against locals, it would be surprising if the majority of break-ins in some regions,

for example, did not involve tourist hotels and apartments since they are often accessible and apt to contain valuables. As an example, in Barbados break-ins increased 1,381 percent between 1971 and 1974, while indecent assaults increased 225 percent. In the same time period tourist arrivals, including cruise visitors, increased 30 percent (Crandall 1976). If a number of observations are available, statistical analysis (regression analysis, etc.) can be used to determine the relationship between crime and tourism growth rates.

It is similarly possible to examine socioeconomic impacts through the analysis of directly relevant statistics or, if necessary, proxies. Changes in land values as a result of tourism developments may be estimated by analyzing the amount of development or redevelopment and land sale figures. These are usually available in local planning and tax assessment offices. Such statistics may also indicate whether migration into or out of an area has taken place.

Government labour force distribution statistics by sector can indicate growth of employment in the tourism sector, and if it is the only industry in the area, these may be used as a proxy to ascertain economic independence for youth and women and overall improvements in standards of living. These figures can also indicate if other forms of employment have been abandoned (e.g., agriculture or fishing) or if workers have jobs only a few months a year. They can also show the growth of a newly wealthy elite or a middle class which formerly did not exist.

The retail price index is a good indication of how tourism growth might have affected the cost of living in a destination area, after inflation has been taken into account. For example, the retail price index in Barbados rose from 100 in 1965 (the base year) to 279.6 in 1974. Although these statistics do not take into account inflation, it would be surprising if tourism (which rose 250 percent in the same period) did not play an important role. On the more positive side, statistics on government spending for social services, such as health and education, should also be analyzed. Revenues from the growth in tourism can enable the government to accelerate spending on social services which improve the standard of living of local residents. In this case, it would be useful to compare changes in expenditure levels for all categories to determine the government's priorities and areas of greatest impact.

Through analysis of statistical data, over half of the social impacts discussed previously can be examined and in some cases conclusions may be drawn. Where evidence is less conclusive or where it is not possible to extract factors unrelated to tourism which also influence these indices, inferences can often be made. These, however, should be tested against other sources of data to derive a better estimate of their validity.

SUMMARY AND CONCLUSION

The first section of this paper described briefly many of the potential social impacts that tourism can have on the society of a destination area, particularly one that is a developing country. These can be socioeconomic: economic independence, labour force displacement, changes in employment, changes in land values, improvement in living standards, and changes in the political–economic system; or sociocultural: growth in undesirable activities, social dualism, demonstration effect, commercialization of culture, and growth of hostility. Most of the social impacts contain both negative and positive aspects, which might or might not balance the other.

The second part of the paper examined various social science methodologies which can be used to look at the impacts of tourism. They are divided into surveys: attitude surveys, public surveys, key informants, Delphi studies, and participant observation; and analysis of secondary sources: content analysis and statistical analysis. Since the concept of social impact is still fairly subjective and nebulous it is difficult to arrive at concrete conclusions. Therefore, a combination of a number of methodologies (or all of them if feasible) should be used to assess social impacts. Most of the methodologies provide somewhat qualitative information (even the results of surveys and content analysis contain fairly subjective data), therefore, they can best be used as aids in attempts to define and understand the social impacts of tourism.

BIBLIOGRAPHY

Belisle, F., and D. Hoy (1980), "The Perceived Impacts of Tourism by Residents, A Case Study of Santa Marta, Colombia," *Annals of Tourism Research*, 7 (1), 84–100.

Boissevain, J. (1977), "Tourism and Development in Malta," *Development and Change*, 39.

Boothroyd, P. (1975), *Review of the State of the Art of Social Impact Research in Canada*, Ottawa, Ontario: Ministry of State for Urban Affairs.

Brougham, J.E. and R.W. Butler (1981), "A Segmentation Analysis of Residents' Attitudes to the Social Impact of Tourism," *Annals of Tourism Research*, 8 (4), 568–587.

Bryden, J. (1973), *Tourism and Development: A Case Study of the Caribbean*, Cambridge, U.K.: Cambridge University Press.

Butler, R. (1975), *Tourism as an Agent of Social Change*, Occasional Paper No. 4, Peterborough, Ontario: Department of Geography, Trent University.

Cleverdon, R. (1979), *The Economic and Social Impact of International Tourism on Developing Countries*, E.I.U. Special Report No. 60. London: Economist Intelligence Unit Ltd.

Cohen, E. (1972), "Toward a Sociology of International Tourism," *Social Research*, 39.

Collins, C. (1979), "Site and Situation Strategy in Tourism Planning," *Annals of Tourism Research*, 6 (July/Sept.), 351–366.

Cowan, G. (1977), "Cultural Impact of Tourism with Particular Reference to the Cook Islands," in *A New Kind of Sugar*, B. Finney and K. Watson, Eds., Honolulu: East–West Center.

Crandall, A.L. (1976), "The Impact of Tourism on Developing Countries—A Case Study of Barbados," unpublished M.A. thesis, Ottawa, Ontario: Faculty of International Affairs, Carleton University.

D'Amore, L.J., and Associates (1977), *Tourism in Canada—1986*, Montreal: for the Canadian Government Office of Tourism.

Doxey, G. (1972), *The Tourist Industry in Barbados*, Kitchener, Ontario: Dusco Graphics.

Doxey, G. (1973), *Ensuring a Lasting Tourist Industry*, Fiji: PATA Research Seminar.

Doxey, G. (1975), *The Impact of Tourism*, Sixth Annual Travel Tourism Research Association Conference.

Farrell, B., Ed. (1977), *The Social and Economic Impact of Tourism on Pacific Communities*, Santa Cruz, California: Center for South Pacific Studies.

Finney, B., and K. Watson, Eds. (1977), *A New Kind of Sugar*, Honolulu: East–West Center.

Finsterbusch, K., and C. Wolf, Eds. (1977), *Methodology of Social Impact Assessment*, Philadelphia: Dowden, Hutchinson and Ross Inc.

Fujii, E., J. Mak, and E. Nishimura (1978), *Tourism and Crime*, Tourism Research Project, Occasional Paper No. 2, Honolulu: University of Hawaii.

Goode, W., and P. Hatt (1952), *Methods of Social Research*, New York: McGraw–Hill Book Co.

Goodrich, J. (1977), "Differences in Perceived Similarity of Tourism Regions: A Spatial Analysis," *Journal of Travel Research*, 16 (Summer), 10–13.

Gray, H. (1970), *International Travel—International Trade*, Boston: Heath Lexington Books.

Haywood, K. (1975), *Criteria for Evaluating the Social Performance of Tourism Development Projects*, Guelph, Ontario: Department of Geography, University of Guelph.

Hiller, H. (1976), *Some Basic Thoughts about the Effects on Tourism of Changing Values in Receiving Societies*, Seventh Annual Travel Tourism Research Association Conference.

Hills, T., and J. Lundgren (1977), *The Impacts of Tourism in the Caribbean*, Working Paper, Montreal: McGill University.

Hudman, L. (1980), "Proposed System Analysis Model for Assessing the Potential Impact of Tourism," *Tourism Marketing and Management Issues*, Washington, D.C.: George Washington University.

Jafari, J. (1973), "Role of Tourism in the Socio-Economic Transformation of Developing Countries," published M.A. thesis, Ithaca, New York: Cornell University.

Jud, G. (1975), "Tourism and Crime in Mexico," *Social Science Quarterly*, 56.

Jud, G., and W. Krause (1976), "Evaluating Tourism in Developing Areas," *Journal of Travel Research*, 15 (Fall), 1–9.

de Kadt, E. (1979a), *Tourism, Passport to Development*, Washington, D.C.: Oxford University Press.

de Kadt, E. (1979b), "Social Planning for Tourism in the Developing Countries," *Annals of Tourism Research*, 6 (Jan/March), 36–48.

Kaplan, A. (1964), *The Conduct of Inquiry*, Philadelphia: Chandler Publishing Company.

Knox, J. (1978), *Classification of Hawaii Residents' Attitudes towards Tourists and Tourism*, Honolulu: University of Hawaii.

Laflamme, A. (1979), "The Impact of Tourism, A Case Study from the Bahamas," *Annals of Tourism Research*, 6 (April/June), 137–147.

Linton, N. (1972), *Proceedings, Caribbean Travel Association Seminar*, San Juan, Puerto Rico.

Lundberg, D. (1974), "Caribbean Tourism," *Cornell H.R.A. Quarterly*, (February/May), 30–45, 82–86.

MacCannell, D. (1973), *The Tourist*, New York: Schocken Books.

Murphy, P. (1981), "Community Attitudes to Tourism," *International Journal of Tourism Management*, (September), 189–195.

Nettleford, R. (1975), "Regional Seminar on Tourism and Its Effects; Cultural Impact," *The Cultural and Environmental Impact of Tourism with Reference to the Caribbean*, Barbados, W.I.: Caribbean Tourism Research Centre.

Perez, L. (1973/1974), "Aspects of Underdevelopment: Tourism in the West Indies," *Science and Society*, 37 (4), 473–480.

Perez, L. (1975), "Tourism in the West Indies," *Journal of Communication*, 25 (2), 136–143.

Pizam, A. (1978), "Tourism's Impacts: The Social Costs to the Destination Community as Perceived by Its Residents," *Journal of Travel Research*, 16 (Spring), 8–12.

Report on Survey of London Residents' Opinions on Tourism, (1978), London: English Tourist Board Market Research Department and N.O.P. Market Research Ltd.

Riley, M. (1963), *Sociological Research, A Case Approach*, New York: Harcourt, Brace and World Inc.

Robinson, H. (1976), *A Geography of Tourism*, London: MacDonald and Evans Ltd.

Rothman, R. (1978), "Residents and Transients: Community Reaction to Seasonal Visitors," *Journal of Travel Research*, 16 (Winter), 8–13.

Sethna, R. (1977), "The Caribbean Tourism Product—An Appraisal," *Inside Barbados*, (October).

Sethna, R. (1980), "Social Impact of Tourism in Selected Caribbean Countries," *Tourism Planning and Development Issues*, Washington, D.C.: George Washington University.

Smith, V. (1977), *Hosts and Guests, An Anthropology of Tourism*, Philadelphia: University of Pennsylvania Press.

Theuns, H. (1973), "Conditions and Effects of International Tourism," *Tourist Review*, No. 3.

Thomason, P., J. Crompton, and D. Kamp (1979), "A Study of the Attitudes of Impacted Groups within a Host Community Toward Prolonged Stay Tourist Visitors," *Journal of Travel Research*, 17 (Winter), 2–6.

Turner, L., and J. Ash (1975), *The Golden Hordes*, London: Constable.

Waiten, C. (1981), *A Guide to Social Impact Assessment*, Ottawa, Ontario: Department of Indian and Northern Affairs, Canada.

Wu, C. (1982), "Issues of Tourism and Socioeconomic Development," *Annals of Tourism Research*, 9 (3), 317–329.

Young, G. (1973), *Tourism, Blessing or Blight*, Middlesex, U.K.: Pelican.

Zehnder, L. (1978), *Tourism and Social Problems*, Ninth Annual Travel Tourism Research Association Conference.

32

Evaluating Environmental Impact and Physical Carrying Capacity in Tourism

PETER W. WILLIAMS

Ryerson Polytechnical Institute
Toronto, Ontario, Canada

*T*his chapter provides a framework for conducting research with respect to assessing and managing the environmental impact of tourism. Rather than addressing assessment techniques associated with all spheres of environmental impact (e.g., economic, social, cultural, political, etc.), the focus is specifically upon the impacts of tourism on the physical environment in general and the ecological impacts in particular. Part one briefly describes the nature of tourism's impact on the physical environment. The second segment suggests the methodological problems inherent in most physically based impact assessment research. Part three describes alternative research assessment frameworks suited to studying the physical impact of tourism. The fourth segment discusses the concept of carrying capacity and the inherent research requirements associated with it in a physical impact context. The final section provides an example of how carrying capacity methodologies can be applied in a lake environment setting.

Tourism development has experienced tremendous expansion in the past two decades. It now touches most parts of the world and its spatial penetration continues to intensify. The growth of tourism development has brought with it a wide variety of impacts ranging from those which are economic and/or sociocultural in character to those which are ecological in nature. While the overall environmental impact of tourism is probably less than that of most other industries developed on a similar scale, the significance of its impact lies in the fact that it frequently impinges upon the most fragile, sensitive, and/or interesting segments of an area's landscape. What in absolute terms would normally represent a minor environmental disturbance could be of considerable significance because of where it occurs. With more recent trends toward the development of massive and intensive year-round tourism developments, it is conceivable that the environmental consequences of some tourism projects could rival those of other industries.

Particularly as the scale of tourism development increases, an appreciation of its potential environ-mental impact becomes a necessity to planning and management. As this need for an understanding of tourism's environmental impact becomes increasingly recognized, and in some instances legally required, so the need for information on the environmental effects of tourism and frameworks for conducting research with respect to these impacts will become more pressing. Without such frameworks, decision making with respect to tourism development planning will lack in both its content and process.

TOURISM AND ENVIRONMENTAL IMPACT

Because tourism is such a highly differentiated phenomenon that occurs in a wide variety of environments, it is dangerous to refer to the physical effects of tourism in general terms. It is more appropriate to isolate those factors peculiar to the tourism situation and then evaluate the impact of each. Considerable research related to the physical impact of tourism exists. With the notable exception of work by Cohen (1978) few attempts have been made to integrate the findings. In most situations, the environmental impact of tourism can be related to such factors as the intensity of site development and use, the resiliency of the ecosystem, the time perspective of the developer, and the transformational character of tourist development.

ECOSYSTEM RESILIENCY

Not all physical environments can equally withstand tourism influxes. Urban centers are normally more resilient than are seminatural or natural settings. The worst environmental effects of tourism typically occur in the least resilient ecosystems. The most sensitive ecosystems tend to be associated with:

A   Coastal systems such as sand dunes and salt marshes, which represent early and very vulnerable ecosystem successional stages with unstable substrata.

B   Montane habitats where growth and self-recovery capability is reduced by climatic influences.

C   Landscapes with shallow (e.g., chalk grasslands), nutrient-deficient (e.g., lowlands), and/or excessively wet soils (Goldsmith and Munton, 1974).

Such locations are often intensively developed for tourism because of their innate attractiveness for tourists as well as their limited capability for other forms of economic development.

SITE-USE INTENSITY

Tourist flow levels (Bateille, 1968), length of stay (Cohen, 1978), activity patterns (Wall and Wright, 1977), and degree of facility development (Barbaza, 1970) all represent intensity factors which correlate positively with negative environmental impact in tourist areas. Generally, the need for tourism infrastructure grows with increases in the volume of tourism traffic and the intensity of site use (Cohen, 1978). As time passes, the central areas of these intensively developed tourist centers become dramatically transformed, and peripheral staging areas accommodating those persons visiting the core of development are also changed (Christaller, 1964).

Typically a pattern of ribbonlike tourist development emerges which becomes particularly difficult to control. It frequently infringes upon less resilient seminatural and natural areas. (Barbaza, 1970).

DEVELOPMENT MOTIVATION

Much of the rationale for tourism development is based upon the economic exploitation of natural and heritage-associated resources. These resources represent the "draw" for tourism enterprises and it is reasonable to assume that developers should be con-

cerned with the protection of these environments. However, tourism entrepreneurs frequently possess only a limited view of the total situation and are unable to grasp the implications of their activity on the overall environment. Competition for the most attractive sites frequently forces them into locational choices which in the long run are detrimental not only to the environment but also to their own interests. Developers with a commitment to the long-run viability of a business are more apt to show a greater sensitivity to environmental concerns than will those with short-run profits in mind (Cohen, 1978). Areas where speculative tourism booms have occurred reveal considerable disdain for environmental concerns (Williams, 1978).

SITE TRANSFORMATION

It is doubtful that a natural environment can be completely preserved without any transformation and still be intensively used for tourism. Some transformation of the environment takes place even when care is taken to minimize the negative environmental impacts of tourism development (Goudie, 1981). Whether associated with the planning and design phase (e.g., the impact of uncertainty and speculation associated with theme park development upon surrounding land-use practices (Cameron and Bordessa, 1981)), the construction phase (e.g., the destruction of and/or damage to aquatic habitat associated with coral reefs and marina development (Speight, 1973)), direct operation of the facility (e.g., the trampling of soft volcanic stone in tourist activity areas (Cohen, 1978)), or indirect impacts associated with the operation of a facility (e.g., air pollution in ski area developments (Jerome, 1977)), an element of transformation of the environment is found in most tourism developments serving mass tourism.

METHODOLOGICAL CONSTRAINTS

While the broad types and rates of environmental change caused by tourism can be related to certain recognized influences, specific impacts associated with any kind of environmental assessment are difficult to clearly specify. This situation is attributable to methodological problems associated with the determination of base points for comparative change analysis, man-environment entanglements, spatial and temporal discontinuities, and environmental interaction complexities.

BASE LEVEL DETERMINATION

To assess environmental impact it is important to compare what the effects of tourism are or will be against some base level or previous stable situation. In most areas other land uses have existed well before the introduction of tourism development. This makes the determination of tourism-induced environmental impacts particularly difficult to disentangle from other influencing factors (Goudie, 1981). For example, increased nutrient buildup in a lake environment may be due to tourist resort development or other land uses such as agriculture, fishing, or a combination of all of these (Lund, 1972). Tourism's contribution to lake eutrophication in such an instance can only be hypothesized.

MAN–NATURE ENTANGLEMENTS

Natural environments are in perpetually changing states (Goldsmith and Munton, 1974). Determination of a base assessment level is at best hazardous under these conditions. From an environmental impact perspective, this problem is compounded because tourism impacts frequently correspond with the flow of normal environmental processes. Tourism development might only hasten what was bound to occur naturally. Wave erosion is a natural process in lake environments but it can be accentuated by the presence of tourism-related motor boat operations (Hails, 1977). The processes may remain the same, but the rate at which they occur may be altered radically.

SPATIAL AND TEMPORAL DISCONTINUITIES

Environmental impact associated with tourism projects is hampered by spatial and temporal discontinuities between "cause and effect" (Wall and Wright, 1977). For instance, seemingly harmless meltwater runoff associated with artificial snowmaking practices in large ski area developments may result in the destruction of key elements of aquatic life habitat several miles downstream from the resort site (Jerome, 1977). From a temporal viewpoint, considerable time may pass before the full impact of an activity is apparent. The impact of tourism on a coral reef's organism diversity may take years to appear (Clare, 1971).

ENVIRONMENTAL COMPLEXITY

The complexity of interactions between different components of the environment make tourism's actual environmental impact almost impossible to measure. Changes in water quality due in part to boating activity associated with a resort development may lead to adjustments in aquatic vegetation, which in turn may generate changes in fish habitat, causing adjustments to sport fisheries capability (Hansmann *et al.*, 1974). Thus primary impacts sometimes generate secondary and tertiary impacts which may cause several successive repercussions throughout the ecosystem. Such complexities in ecosystem interaction make the assessment of cause and effect relationships associated with tourism development particularly nebulous (Wall and Wright, 1977).

METHODOLOGICAL APPROACHES

Despite the difficulties associated with assessing the environmental impacts of tourism, a variety of applicable analytical methodologies are available. The approaches can be categorized according to either their analytical function (Dickert, 1974) or the techniques of analysis that they employ (Warner and Bromley, 1974).

ANALYTICAL FUNCTIONS

Analytical functions associated with environmental assessment can be separated into three categories. They are identification, prediction, and evaluation. Each function has its own methodological thrust and suitabilities in impact assessment. They are described in Table 1.

Identification functions are designed to assist in specifying the range of impacts that might occur, in-

TABLE 1 Functional Classification of Environmental Assessment Approaches

FUNCTION	METHODOLOGICAL THRUST
Identification	Description of the existing environmental system
	Determination of the components of the project
	Definition of the environment modified by the project (including all components of the project)
Prediction	Identification of environmental modifications that may be significant
	Forecasting of the quantity and/or spatial dimensions of change in environment identified
	Estimation of the probability that the impact (environmental change) will occur (time period)
Evaluation	Determination of the incidence of costs and benefits to user groups and populations affected by the project
	Specification and comparison of the trade-offs (costs or effects being balanced) between various alternatives

Source: Cantor (1977).

cluding their spatial distribution and duration. They seek to clarify the components of a tourism project as well as what environmental elements may be affected by these project components. Tourism projects have three broad components (planning and design, construction, and operation) which create direct and indirect environmental impacts. The elements of the natural environment which can be influenced include the physical and chemical characteristics of the land (Liddle, 1975), air (Jerome, 1977), and water (Barton, 1969), the biologic condition of the flora (LaPage, 1962) and fauna (Dorrance et al., 1975), the condition of surrounding land use (Cameron and Bordessa, 1981), and more complex ecological relationships.

There are essentially two types of identification methods. They are checklists and matrices/networks (Dickert, 1974). Checklists contain environmental factors which should be considered with respect to the impact of tourism development. From a master list of environmental factors associated with tourism projects, researchers select and evaluate those impacts expected from a particular type of development under study.

Matrices are two-dimensional checklists which identify normal project component actions and their potential impacts on environmental elements. They might identify the indirect influence of a ski area resort operation upon air quality (Jerome, 1977). Networks assist in recognizing interrelationships between affected environmental elements. They might flag interrelations between tourism-related vegetation trampling in national parks or a reduction of wildlife numbers and species (Myers, 1972).

Predictive methodologies are designed to forecast the quantity and/or spatial dimensions of environmental impact, as well as the probability of impact occurrence. They involve the greatest application of technology. Using "controlled" environments for testing purposes and technological aids (e.g., artificial tramplers, stream tables, wind current tunnels, computerized models, etc.), they attempt to simulate the influence of visitor traffic and facility development upon a proposed development area (Wagar, 1961). Their application in assessing the influence of physical development upon air, water, and noise quality is well documented. From a tourism perspective, their application in marina development (Isard, 1972), ski area design (Bugel and Tybutski, 1979), and trail system planning (Lime and Stankey, 1972) is well recognized.

Evaluative methodologies seek to determine the costs and benefits of proposed developments upon affected environments. They attempt to specify and compare the trade-offs between various forms of development. Evaluative techniques might be applied to tourism situations in which competing development strategies associated with the development of hotels and tourist facilities in a fragile environment such as Bali (Hanna, 1972; Kwee, 1972) might be assessed on a common basis. Two particularly promising and well documented approaches to this type of assessment are the Battelle environmental evaluation system (Dee, 1972) and the Georgia optimum pathway matrix (Odum, 1971). Using systematic analytical procedures, they both provide aggregate indices of environmental impact for each alternative under investigation.

TECHNIQUES OF ANALYSIS

Five main techniques of environmental impact analysis are identifiable for tourism-related studies. They are ad hoc procedures, overlay techniques, checklists, matrices, and networks. Information collected by all five techniques is valuable in signalling the magnitude and importance of tourism's environmental impact as well as potential areas of future research.

AD HOC

Ad hoc procedures involve assembling a team of "specialists" to identify impacts in their areas of expertise. Normally such teams are given minimal guidance beyond the parameters as established by related environmental planning authorities. Typically such an approach is evident in those regions possessing neither the incentive nor the human and economic resources to undertake extensive investigations.

OVERLAY

Overlay approaches involve the use of well established techniques frequently employed in land use planning and landscape architecture. They use a series of overlay maps to depict environmental elements or other land resource factors which may be sensitive to development schemes. The overlay process provides a visual means of filtering through the natural environment of an area in order to separate environmentally durable from ecologically sensitive areas. In a tourism context, overlay techniques involving both manual environmental mapping procedures (Laventhol and Horwath, 1982) as well as computerized graphic techniques (Gunn, 1979) have been successfully employed to identify key tourism development areas in strategic planning exercises.

CHECKLISTS

Checklist approaches involve the use of master lists of different types of impacts typically associated with different kinds of physical developments. Each type of physical development should have its own particular master checklist which provides the main factors to assess in the impact investigation. An example of an environmental impact checklist for a tourism project involving the creation of an artificial lake could include but need not be limited to the factors listed in Table 2.

TABLE 2   Potential Tourism-Related Environmental Impact Elements Associated with Water Impoundments

    I.   Direct loss of land and/or productivity
          A.   Specified land uses
               1.   Agricultural or grazing land
               2.   Forests or timberland
               3.   Wetlands or marshes
          B.   Commercial productivity
               1.   Mineral resources (gravel, limestone, oil, gas, etc.)
               2.   Commercial fisheries
   II.   Loss or relocation of built structures and other archeological or historical sites
          A.   Archeological or historical sites
          B.   Homes or villages
          C.   Highways, railroads, and other transportation facilities
          D.   Cemeteries
          E.   Recreation facilities
  III.   Loss of wildlife habitat
          A.   Specification of habitat type
          B.   Change in hunting opportunities
  IV.   Aesthetic impacts
          A.   Decreased aesthetics
          B.   Increased aesthetics
   V.   Loss or inundation of the natural stream
          A.   Loss of the stream fishery
          B.   Loss of recreation and tourism potential
  VI.   Lake-related environmental impacts
          A.   Substitution of a lake environment for a stream environment
          B.   Creation of a warm-water fishery
          C.   Change of wildlife habitat
 VII.   Water quality impacts
          A.   Thermal stratification
          B.   Growth of algae
          C.   Impoundment of nutrients and wastes
               1.   Decrease in water quality
               2.   Increase in rate of eutrophication
VIII.   Dam-related impacts
          A.   Increased sediment deposition
          B.   Loss of anadromous fish runs
  IX.   Impacts due to spillways
   X.   Downstream effects
          A.   Decreased silt or sediment in downstream channel
               1.   Increased erosion downstream
               2.   Increased water quality downstream
          B.   Improvement or enhancement of downstream fishery
          C.   Flow regulation
               1.   Improvement of water quality downstream
               2.   Improvement of downstream aesthetics
               3.   Improvement of recreation and tourism downstream
               4.   Reduction of mosquito problems downstream
  XI.   Effects on groundwater recharge
 XII.   Effects of fluctuating shorelines
          A.   Adverse effects on wildlife
          B.   Adverse effects on vegetation
          C.   Decreased aesthetics at low lake stages

The master list for a ski area development would probably be quite different. However, comprehensive lists of 50 to 100 different environmental factors that are generally considered when conducting an impact assessment are available from those government agencies dealing with environmental matters (Warner and Preston, 1973). From such lists a master checklist suited to a particular form of tourism development can be established.

These checklists can be structured in a variety of ways. Essentially they are simple, descriptive, scaling or scaling-weighting in character.

Simple checklists (Table 2) provide a basic list of assessment parameters. They do not provide guidelines concerning how the impact of each development action is to be measured and interpreted with respect to each environmental element being assessed. They can be organized by category of impact, temporal phase, spatial boundaries, or a combination of any or all of these. For instance, the structure of Table 2 focuses solely upon categories of impact. On the other hand, Table 3 provides a simple checklist organized not only by category of impact but also temporally as to the phase of the project's development. The project checklist could be associated with the assessment of the impact of a proposed shoreline-oriented marina/resort complex.

Descriptive checklists include both an identification of environmental elements and guidelines concerning how each type of environmental impact is to be assessed. Using Section V.B of Table 3 as an example, a descriptive checklist might require the researcher to assess the impact of the marina/resort development impact upon fauna by identifying important wildlife species in and immediately adjacent to the site; indicating their habitat distribution and relationship to other species; noting rare or endangered species which exist in or near the site; discussing the current degree of ecological succession in terms of its impact upon current and future wildlife production; and defining any other preexisting environmental stresses (e.g., surrounding land uses) which might influence the future fauna characteristics of the area.

Scaling checklists are similar to descriptive lists except for the addition of a subjective scaling of environmental impact values. A scaling approach used in the comparative analysis of alternative transportation projects (Adkins and Burke, 1974) provides a prototype for the analysis of alternative tourism development strategies. It involves scaling the impact of alternative tourism development actions such as those described in Table 3. Scaling is conducted on a relative basis on a scale ranging from minus five to plus five. The summary of the overall evaluation is based on the number of plus and minus ratings, as well as their algebraic average rating.

Scaling-weighting checklists are similar to scaling

checklists except that they provide researchers with information concerning how to subjectively evaluate each potential environmental impact parameter with respect to every other factor. They also suggest how to express these weighted factors in equivalent units for comparative purposes (Dee, 1972). For example, in Table 3, a scaling-weighting checklist would subjectively indicate that the weighting of this form of tourism development impact upon III.A (i.e., groundwater elements) should be considered to be three times as significant as its influence upon III.B (i.e., surface water elements). The application of this methodology is well documented (Dee, 1972) and appears to be very applicable in a tourism context.

MATRICES

Matrix approaches to environmental impact assessment incorporate both a list of project activities and a checklist of potentially impacted environmental elements (Leopold, 1971). The matrix is usually composed of project actions along one axis, and environmental elements along the other axis (Fig. 1). Where an impact upon an environmental element (e.g., alteration of drainage on a ski hill slope) is anticipated because of a project action (e.g., construction of ski area cables and lifts), the matrix is normally marked with a diagonal line in the interacting matrix cell (Fig. 1).

The interaction between actions and the environment in terms of their magnitude and importance (Fig. 1) are assessed. The magnitude of an interaction refers to its extensiveness or scale. It is described by the assignment of a numerical value ranging from one to ten, with ten representing the largest impact in terms of scale and one being the least extensive. The development of Florida's Disneyworld would receive a high score in terms of its scale or extensiveness, while many of the resort developments within Canada's National Parks would receive lesser magnitude scores because of their smaller areal extent.

The importance of an interaction is related to the significance of the consequent relationship. Importance ratings also range from a high of ten to a low of one. The extreme transformation of physical environments by tourism development in Waikiki (Kent, 1971) might receive a high importance rating, while tourism's impact upon old British spa resort communities (Patmore, 1968) would be significantly less important. The numerical value is normally based upon subjective judgment.

Summation of the values assigned to those interacting cells within rows and columns of the matrix can offer insights into tourism's impact and the interpretation of that impact from a development perspective. Matrix procedures can be structured like simple checklists designed to identify impacts both tempo-

TABLE 3   Environment Checklist for Potential Environmental Impact of a Proposed Marina/Resort Complex

CATEGORY OF IMPACT	PLANNING AND DESIGN	PROJECT PHASE	
		CONSTRUCTION	OPERATION
I. Noise impacts			
A. Public health			
B. Land use			
II. Air quality impacts			
A. Public health			
B. Land use			
III. Water quality impacts			
A. Groundwater			
1. Flow and water table alteration			
2. Interaction with surface drainage			
B. Surface water			
1. Shoreline and bottom alteration			
2. Effects of filling and dredging			
3. Drainage and flood characteristics			
C. Water quality aspects			
1. Effect of effluent loadings			
2. Implication of other actions such as			
a. Disturbance of benthic layers			
b. Alteration of currents			
c. Changes in flow regime			
d. Saline intrusion in groundwater			
3. Land use			
4. Public health			
IV. Soil erosion impacts			
A. Economic and land use			
B. Pollution and siltation			
V. Ecological impacts			
A. Flora			
B. Fauna (other than humans)			
VI. Aesthetic and visual impacts			
A. Scenic resources			
B. Urban design			
C. Noise			
D. Air quality			
E. Water quality			

rally and spatially. They can also be organized like scaling checklists to note detrimental impacts. This involves the use of positive and negative symbols or verbal notations (e.g., high, medium, and low significance) rather than ratio designations.

NETWORKS

Unlike their purely matrix approach counterparts, network approaches to environmental assessment examine the secondary and tertiary effects associated with project actions. A stepped process in which primary

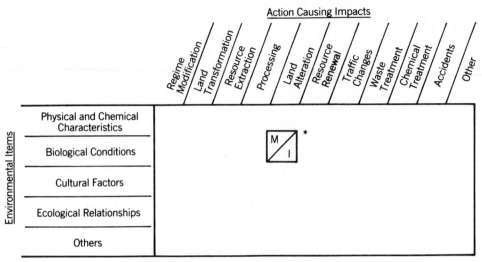

FIGURE 1 Environmental assessment matrix format. Source: Leopold, 1971.

and direct impacts are depicted as leading to other secondary and tertiary indirect impacts is a particularly popular form of network analysis (Sorenson, 1971). The direct action of dredging a coastal submerged shoreline for the development of a marina/resort complex harbour facility can be assessed from an impact perspective using this technique. The dredging operation may lead to the primary impact of increasing water depth. This in turn may lead to the secondary impact of inhibiting normal aquatic vegetation growth. This action could create such tertiary impacts as the destruction of fish habitat and the loss of a significant commercial sport fishery crucial to the long-run viability of the proposed marina/resort complex (Sorenson, 1971). An example of a network analysis framework for dredging projects which might be related to tourism projects along coastal shorelines is described in Fig. 2.

SUMMARY

The preceding discussion has described the primary methods and research starting points for assessing the environmental impact of tourism projects. Given the typical kinds of methodological constraints associated with such research, each technique must be used with care. Sound professional judgment must guide both their application to particular situations and the interpretation of the information that they generate. This professional judgment is frequently subjective in nature. Assessments often boil down to a matter of degree rather than a single correct or wrong decision.

CARRYING CAPACITY

While changes in the environment due to tourism development are inevitable and environmental impact

research can provide an appreciation of these consequences, the determination of a carrying capacity for a development area can help to plan the degree and direction of environmental change. Once a carrying capacity for an area has been established, controls (Wolbrink and Associates, 1973) and management policies (Ehrlich and Vaccaro, 1972) can be enacted to put restrictions on unhampered growth. The concept of carrying capacity and its determination in a tourism-related lake planning context will be discussed in the following paragraphs.

Carrying capacity is a key but controversial concept associated with the physical planning of tourism areas (Myers, 1972). The controversy focuses on the value judgments and the subjective decisions which characterize it (Schreyer, 1976). Carrying capacity calculations for a site involve determining a continuum of use intensities that may be suited to that environment. The polarities of the continuum range from no direct tourism use, as illustrated in tourism strategies for the Caribou lands of northern Yukon (Wolman and Associates, 1978), to unlimited and environmentally destructive tourism use, as exemplified by the exploitation of Majorcan olive trees for tourism souvenir product production (Graves, 1965).

Carrying capacity statements have both prescriptive and descriptive characteristics. In a prescriptive context, they can be used to assign to a tourism site a preferred type and amount of use. For instance, they can be used to indicate the type of ski market appropriate for a landscape and the number of skier days suited to that environment given the capability and preferences of the skiers (Farwell, 1974). From a descriptive perspective, carrying capacity can describe the relationships between the quantity (e.g., number of novice skiers) and the quality (e.g., length of ski lift line

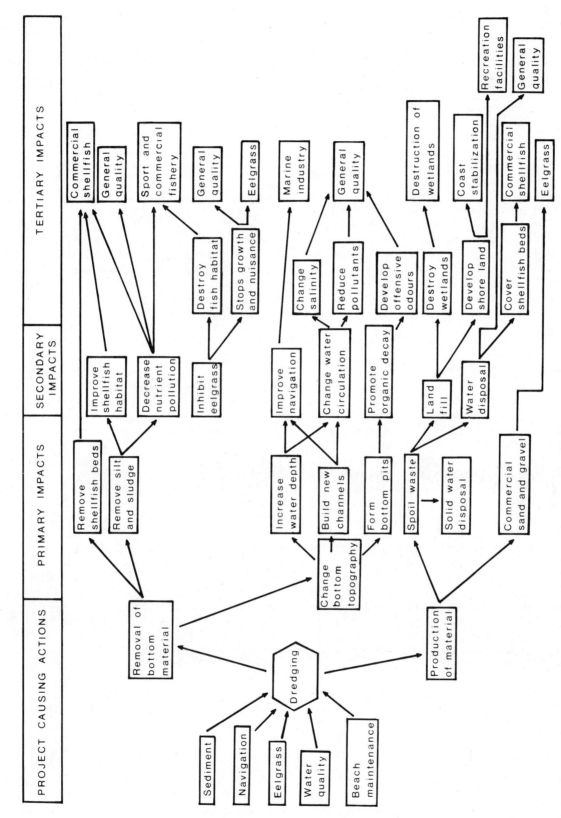

FIGURE 2 A network analysis framework for coastal dredging projects. Source: Sorensen, 1971.

waiting time) of use in an area.

The common theme associated with most carrying capacity statements concerns their role in establishing the level of use possible within a given environment without unacceptable environmental deterioration and use quality losses. A corollary to that theme is that carrying capacity statements reflect decisions concerning the environmental degradation and use quality diminishment seemingly acceptable as the cost for the use of a site. In any tourism development project, there is no single carrying capacity figure, but rather a range of use intensities and use-type management alternatives, each with its own consequences on the environment and the tourist. As well, for each alternate mix of uses, separate carrying capacity continuums apply. To complicate matters further, the dynamics of constantly changing environmental conditions as well as user experience preferences dictate the need for periodic reviews of previously established use intensity levels.

Carrying capacity statements seek to establish acceptable use intensities from a variety of different perspectives. Physical/ biological carrying capacity methodologies attempt to determine the attributes of a physical environment and the amount of use it can withstand without severe degradation (Frissel and Duncan, 1965). They have been used to examine water quality changes that occur with changing intensities of cottage development in lake environments (Michalski and Conroy, 1972). Management-based carrying capacity statements seek to determine a level of tourist activity for a site that is efficient and safe for users given the human and fiscal resources available to the managing agency (Schreyer, 1976). Psychological carrying capacity estimates try to determine the most acceptable and pleasurable density of site usage as perceived by the users. Sociopsychological carrying capacity studies have been conducted to establish optimum use levels for whitewater float-trippers in the Western United States (Schreyer and Nielson, 1978). All of these approaches to establishing the appropriate site-use intensity for a tourist site have merit in a management context. Any defensible policy decision prescribing a certain carrying capacity of use types and intensities should consider all three approaches. Unfortunately, the sophistication of carrying capacity as a management tool is still crude in a tourism planning context. Indeed, carrying capacity determinations tend to be based upon the use of a single approach rather than an integrative strategy (Jaakson, 1979). It should be noted that the integrative approach is not always the most appropriate methodology. In special situations, it may be more suitable to use an exclusionary carrying capacity strategy. Instead of a management decision being based on the integration of a number of capacity considerations, a single capacity constraint may overrule all the others. This single constraint excludes the others from further consideration. For instance, a biologically based exclusionary carrying capacity would be one in which a fragile lake ecosystem might have a particularly low ability to accommodate the higher use intensities established by management and psychologically based methodologies without suffering irreversible deterioration. In such a case, the biological sensitivity of that environment would mean the exclusion of the other carrying capacity estimates.

LAKE CARRYING CAPACITY APPROACHES

Because so much of tourism development is associated with the use of water resources as well as locations situated adjacent to water bodies, considerable research has focused upon creating methodologies suitable for establishing lake carrying capacity. Much of the early research in lake planning and use intensity determination attempted to define lake carrying capacity in terms of an acceptable density of human activity or development. One set of studies centered upon attempting to develop minimum water surface space standards for a variety of water-oriented activities. Using observations of boating density as well as interviews with boaters concerning acceptable crowding levels, the approach which is commonly referred to as the boat-limit technique has been used extensively (Threinin, 1961; Jaakson, 1968). Essentially it involves employing boat-limit water surface space standards to establish a maximum amount of associated land-use development (e.g., cottaging). A second early research thrust involved the Lake Alert method (Ontario Ministry of Natural Resources, 1970). In this approach, six water quality parameters (e.g., algae cover) along with six other constraining factors (e.g., shoreline swimming zones) are combined by using a subjectively determined weighting factor to establish the development limitations for lake environments.

Other lake carrying capacity research has aimed at identifying physical environment capacity determinants. Water quality-based carrying capacity estimates are usually measured by a series of indicators which allow the quality of a lake environment to be measured on a composite scale. Carrying capacity methodologies have been established based upon the combined influence of proposed development intensities, aesthetics, and the biological capacity of the lake to absorb wastes (Seppanen, 1974). Another system employs several different water quality-based parameters to calculate the phosphorous concentration of a lake, which is in turn used to establish the summer chlorophyll a concentration. This index is then compared with the maximum permissible chlorophyll a for the lake being considered for development (Dillon, 1974). The result of the method is an index of the allowable number of cottages on a lake.

Other methodologies are also available for such investigations. For instance, the "shoreline capacity" approach bases capacity on the development potential of the lakeshore as recorded in land inventory surveys (Ontario Ministry of Natural Resources, 1968). Another technique, the "water quality index" system, defines lake carrying capacity in terms of its trophic status and in relation to an aggregate index of six parameters. However, a weakness common to all of the previously described research methods is that management decisions regarding carrying capacity are based upon single indices, when in fact most capacity decisions are multifaceted in nature.

Probably the most integrative technique for establishing use intensity estimates is the spectrum approach (Jaakson 1979). The spectrum model uses four capacity estimation equations, combines this information and then expresses the results as a spectrum of planning alternatives. The alternatives are based upon estimates derived from shoreline reserve, shoreline capability, theoretical boat density, and observed boat density methodologies. The suitability of each carrying capacity methodology varies with the water body under investigation. For instance, normally as the water surface of a lake diminishes, the importance of boat-limit calculations relative to shoreline methods increases (Jaakson, 1979). Consequently, the relative significance of the various carrying capacity measures employed should be weighted according to the lake environment with which they are being associated. If the water body under study was relatively large, the ratio weighting of the two boat-limit calculations to the two shoreline related approaches might be subjectively set at 1:4. In the hypothetical example illustrated in Table 4, the weighted mean carrying capacity so calculated would be 960 boats or 397 cottages. Consequently, instead of using a single estimate as the basis for lake planning, a range of capacity estimates are provided. This procedure makes it possible to consider a series of development alternatives.

SUMMARY

The results generated by this approach must be used with caution. The estimates provided show merely a range of carrying capacity alternatives based upon factors not incorporating key water quality or psychological considerations. Its main focus is on boating density and shoreline capability for physical development. However, the spectrum approach could be extended quite easily to integrate these other concerns. In all cases, the results only represent broad guidelines for managerial decisions regarding man's impact upon the physical environment.

TABLE 4 Summary of Spectrum Carrying Capacity Methodology

APPROACH	CARRYING CAPACITY ESTIMATES	
	BOAT	COTTAGE
Shoreline reserve	1,100	440
Shoreline capability	750	300
Theoretical boat density	1,380	552
Observed boat density	817	453
Unweighted mean	1,012	436
Shoreline weighted mean	960	397

CONCLUSION

The preceding discussion has focused upon research methods for assessing and assisting in the management of tourism's impact upon the natural environment. The impact methodologies presented provide a means of systematically filtering through the complex interactions which typify tourism−environment relationships. They describe tourism−environment relationships in relative and frequently subjective terms. As such they require experienced professional judgment in both their application and interpretation. Knowledge of tourism's physical impacts is limited despite the numerous research studies on the subject. Tourism research dealing with environmental impact as discussed here requires the involvement of many disciplines so that a better appreciation of its penetration into the environment can be understood.

Carrying capacity research approaches are equally as subjective in character. It is highly unlikely that precise numerical carrying capacity indices can be calculated which meet the needs of all groups associated with tourism development. Perhaps it is more practical and meaningful to direct research toward the establishment of tourism development thresholds beyond which significant environmental changes occur. Certainly the need for better approaches will intensify as tourism expands.

REFERENCES

Adkins, W.G., and D. Burke, Jr. (1974). "Social, Economic and Environmental Factors in Highway Decision Making." Research report 148-4. College Station: Texas Transportation Institute, Texas A & M University.

Barbaza, V. (1970). "Trois types d'intervention du tourisme dans l'organization de l'espace littoral," *Annales de Geographic*, pp. 446−468.

Barton, M.A. (1969). "Water pollution in remote recreational areas," *Journal of Soil and Water Conservation*, 24:132–134.

Bateille, R. (1968). "Tourisme et milieu rural montagnard: l'example de Pitztal (Tirol autrichien)," *Revue de Geographic Alpine*, 56: 367–376.

Bugel, L., and D. Tybutski (1979). "Making a mountain out of a computer," *Ski Area Management*, 18:46–47.

Cameron, J.M., and R. Bordessa (1981). *Wonderland through the Looking Glass*. Maple, Ontario: Belstein Publishing.

Canter, L. (1977). *Environmental Impact Assessment*. New York: McGraw–Hill.

Christaller, W. (1964). "Some considerations of tourism in Europe: The peripheral regions—Underdeveloped countries—Recreation areas," *Papers of the Regional Science Association*, 12:95–105.

Clare, P. (1971). *The Struggle for the Great Reef Barrier*. London: Collins.

Cohen, E. (1978). "The impact of tourism on the physical environment," *Annals of Tourism Research*, 5 (2):215–237.

Dee, N. (1972). "Environmental Evaluation System for Water Resource Planning." Report prepared by Battelle-Columbus for Bureau of Reclamation, U.S. Government.

Dickert, T.G. (1974). "Methods for environmental impact assessment: A comparison," in Thomas G. Dickert and Katherine R. Domeny (Eds.), *Environmental Impact Assessment: Guidelines and Commentary*. Berkeley: University of California, pp. 127–143.

Dillon, P.J. (1974). *A Manual for Calculating the Capacity of a Lake for Development*. Toronto: Ontario Ministry of the Environment.

Dorrance, M.J., P.J. Savage, and D.E. Hulf (1975). "Effects of snowmobiles on white-tailed deer," *Journal of Wildlife Management*, 9:563–569.

Ehrlich, H., and M.A. Vaccaro (1972). "Disney's new world," *The Asia Magazine*, 24:3–12.

Farwell, T. (1974). "Ski area capacity: The critical design parameter," *Ski Area Management*, 13:40, 41, 56.

Frissel, S.S., and D.P. Duncan (1965). "Composite preference and deterioration in the Quetico–Superior canoe country," *Journal of Forestry*, 65:256–260.

Goldsmith, F.B., and R.J.C. Munton (1974). "The ecological effects of recreation," in P. Lavery (Ed.), *Recreational Geography*. New York: John Wiley, pp. 259-269.

Goudie, A. (1981). *The Human Impact: Man's Role in Environmental Change*. Oxford: Basil Blackwell, pp. 187–238.

Graves, R. (1965). "Why I live in Majorca, 1952," in R. Graves and P. Hogarth (Eds.), *Majorca Observed*. London: Cassell.

Gunn, C.A. (1979). "Assessing community potential: Land analysis for tourism planning," in *A Decade of Achievement—Tenth Annual Conference Proceedings, Travel Research Association*, pp. 179–183.

Hails, J.R. (1977). *Applied Geomorphology*. Amsterdam: Elsevier.

Hanna, W.A. (1972). "Bali in the seventies. Part 1. Cultural tourism," *American Fieldstaff Reports, Southeast Asia Series*, 20(2).

Hansmann, E.W., D.E. Kidd, and E. Gilbert (1974). "Man's impact on a newly formed reservoir," *Hydrobiologia*, 45:185–197.

Isard, W. (1972). *Ecologic–Economic Analysis for Regional Development: Some Initial Explorations with Particular Reference to Recreational Resource Use and Environmental Planning*. New York: Free Press.

Jaakson, R. (1968). "Lakeshore Recreation Planning for Cottage Development." Unpublished M.Sc. Thesis, Toronto: Department of Urban and Regional Planning, University of Toronto.

Jaakson, R. (1979). "A spectrum model of lake recreation carrying capacity estimation," in J. Marsh (Ed.), *Water-Based Recreation Problems and Progress*. Occasional Paper 8. Peterborough, Ontario: Department of Geography, Trent University, pp. 63–83.

Jerome, J. (1977). "Skiing and the environment," *EPA Journal*, 3:11–14.

Kent, N. (1971). "Escape mecca of the world," *Hawaii Pono Journal*, October: 32-35.

Kwee, M. (1972). "Indonesia ready to start $80 million Bali tourism project," *Straits Times*, 6.2.

LaPage, W.F. (1962). "Recreation and the forest site," *Journal of Forestry*, 60:319–321.

Laventhol and Horwath (1982). "Tourism Development Strategy for the Peterborough–Haliburton Tourism Zone. Report prepared for the Ontario Ministry of Industry and Tourism.

Leopold, L.B. (1971). "A procedure for evaluating environmental impact," *Geological Survey Circular*, 645.

Liddle, M.J. (1975). "A selective review of the ecological effects of human trampling on natural ecosystems," *Biological Conservation*, 7:17–34.

Lime, D., and G.H. Stanley (1972). "Carrying capacity: Maintaining outdoor recreation quality," in *Northeastern Forest Experiment Station Recreation Symposium Proceedings*. Upper Darby, Pennsylvania: Northeastern Forest Experiment Station, pp. 174–183.

Lund, J.W.C. (1972). "Eutrophication," *Proceedings of the Royal Society of London*, 180B:371–382.

Michalski, M.F.P., and N. Conroy (1972). *Water Quality Evaluation, Lake Alert Study*. Toronto: Ontario Ministry of the Environment.

Myers, N. (1972). "National Parks in Savannah Africa," *Science*, 178: 1255–1263.

Odum, E.P. (1971). *Optimum Pathway Matrix Analysis Approach to the Environmental Decision-Making Process*. Athens, Georgia: Institute of Ecology, University of Georgia.

Ontario Ministry of Natural Resources (1968). *Methodology for Ontario Recreation Land Inventory*. Toronto: Queen's Park.

Ontario Ministry of Natural Resources (1970). *LAKE ALERT, Phase 2, Methodology*. Toronto: Queen's Park.

Patmore, J.A. (1968). "The spa towns of Britain," in R.P.

Beckinsole, and J.M. Houston (Eds.), *Urbanization and Its Problems*. London: Blackwell, Oxford, pp. 47–69.

Schreyer, R. (1976). "Sociological and Political Factors in Carrying Capacity Decision-Making." Paper presented at Visitor Capacity Conference, National Park Service, Ft. Worth, Texas.

Schreyer, R., and M. Nielson (1978). *Desolation/Westwater Whitewater River Recreation Study*. Logan, Utah: Institute for the Study of Outdoor Recreation and Tourism.

Seppanen, P. (1974). *Determination of Summer Cottaging Capacity of Lakes*, Eripaninos Aqua Fennica.

Sorenson, J.C. (1971). *A Framework for Identification and Control of Resource Degradation and Conflict in the Multiple Use of The Coastal Zone*. Berkeley: University of California.

Speight, M.C.D. (1973). "Outdoor Recreation and Its Ecological Effects: A Bibliography and Review." Discussion Papers in Conservation No. 4. London: University College, p. 18.

Threinin, C.W. (1961). *Some Spatial Aspects of Aquatic Recreation*. Madison: Wisconsin Conservation Department.

Wagar, J.A. (1961). "How to predict which vegetated areas will stand up best under active recreation," *Recreation*, 1.

Wall, G., and C. Wright (1977). "The Environmental Impact of Outdoor Recreation." Publication Series No. 11. Waterloo, Ontario: Department of Geography, University of Waterloo, pp. 1–3.

Warner, M.L., and D.W. Bromley (1974). "Environmental Impact Analysis: A Review of Three Methodologies," Technical Report, Wisconsin Water Resources Center, University of Wisconsin, Madison.

Warner, M.L., and E.H. Preston (1973). "A Review of Environmental Impact Assessment Methodologies." Report prepared by Batelle-Columbus for the U.S. Environmental Protection Agency, Washington, D.C.

Williams, P.W. (1978). "Retirement community impacts," *Utah Tourism and Recreation Review*, 7(3):1–4.

Wolbrink, D., and Associates (1973). *Physical Standards for Tourism Development*. Honolulu: Pacific Islands Development Commission.

Wolman, F., and Associates (1978). *Tourism Industry Development Strategy*, Whitehorse, Yukon: Yukon Territory Government.

PART SEVEN

DATA COLLECTION METHODS OF PARTICULAR RELEVANCE

Part Seven of the Handbook contains seven chapters dealing with data collection methods which have achieved a particular prominence or are considered especially useful in the field of travel, tourism, and hospitality. The first of these, enroute surveys, which is described in Chapter 33, is discussed by Fred Hurst (Port Authority of New York and New Jersey). As those in the travel industry are aware, the enroute survey provides a data collection context which is unique. Starting from this perspective, Mr. Hurst first examines the characteristics of enroute surveys as compared with other data collection approaches. He subsequently provides an overview of the methodology underlying the enroute survey and the characteristics of their common users. Recognizing that there is a bewildering array of possible enroute survey methods, Mr. Hurst then examines some of the methodological difficulties likely to be encountered in executing enroute surveys and provides guidelines for dealing with these difficulties. The chapter concludes with a very detailed example of an application of the enroute survey method. Individuals who are interested in developing their own enroute surveys will find the details provided by Mr. Hurst in this example to be extremely useful.

Chapter 34 deals with a methodology which, while not developed for or unique to tourism, has proven to be particularly relevant to the field. As a result, it has received fairly widespread application and is likely to continue to be a basic methodological approach for tourism planners. The methodology in question is the Delphi technique, an approach which attempts to provide planners with forecasts of probable states of the future. The chapter describing the Delphi technique has been authored by George Moeller (USDA Forest Service) and Elwood Shafer (The Pennsylvania State University). The chapter first reviews the value of attempting to forecast the future and identifies some of the difficulties associated with attempting to do so. Following these introductory remarks, the authors review other forecasting techniques which have been used to predict the future prior to their discussion of the Delphi technique itself. In this discussion, the authors provide a description of the Delphi technique as well as a critical review of its strengths and weaknesses. The latter part of the chapter provides a specific example of an application of Delphi in the area of recreation planning. Again, it is expected that readers will find this example extremely helpful should they actually be required to undertake a Delphi study.

In Chapter 35, Wilbur LaPage (New Hampshire Parks and Recreation) examines another research methodology which has been developed outside the field of tourism but which has been found to be particularly relevant for the collection of certain kinds of data. In this case, we are referring to the use of panels for travel, tourism, and hospitality research and their particular value for trend monitoring, test marketing, impact assessment, and future assessment. The author then discusses the relative advantages and disadvantages of this approach as compared with other methods that might be employed. The chapter concludes by providing guidelines for prospective panel developers concerning the factors that need to be considered in the design and maintenance of such a panel.

The fourth chapter in this section of the Handbook continues with the theme of adapting general research approaches to travel, tourism, and hospitality. In this chapter, Karen Peterson (Davidson-Peterson Associates) reviews the use of qualitative research methods as an aid to understanding consumer behavior in the field. Ms. Peterson first examines the general characteristics of qualitative research and the particular research situations for which it is best suited. In doing so, she takes care to provide readers with an understanding of the limitations of the method. The remainder of the chapter provides a brief overview of the variations which exist in qualitative research methods and then discusses in some depth the steps that researchers can take to enhance the quality of this kind of research.

Chapter 37 introduces readers to a research technique which has been widely utilized in the fields of planning and consumer behavior but which has received relatively little attention in tourism until recently. Authored by Brent Ritchie, this chapter describes the nominal group technique (NGT) with an emphasis upon its role as a tool for assisting in policy formulation. The chapter first describes NGT as it is normally employed. This general discussion is followed by an example describing the manner in which the method was applied in one case of consensus planning. This example includes an examination of some of the data analysis issues which are peculiar to this type of research. Subsequently, a discussion is presented concerning the potential applications of NGT in other areas of tourism and research planning. The chapter concludes with an assessment of the relative strengths and weaknesses of NGT compared to other commonly used planning/research approaches.

Chapter 38 continues the transition from qualitative to quantitative research techniques which started in the previous chapter on NGT. In this chapter, James Rovelstad (University of Wisconsin– Parkside) examines the use of model building and simulation as research tools for assisting managers and government officials in analyzing and understanding their markets, the travel consumer, and the facilities and resources for which they are responsible. As Dr. Rovelstad points out, both qualitative and quantitative models are available to assist such individuals. It is from this perspective that the author reviews the scope, nature, and range of uses of models in the field of tourism. The chapter starts out by examining the nature of modelling itself and discussing the different types of models that can be employed. These include physical and economic impact models, input–output models, and behavioral models. The chapter next provides two examples designed to provide a more substantive understanding of the applications and benefits related to modelling in tourism. The chapter concludes with a brief discussion of the relationship between models and the process of management.

The final chapter in Part Seven again describes how a general research technique developed in other fields has been adapted to tourism. In this case, however, the technique described, namely, conjoint measurement, is more quantitative in nature. This chapter, which has been authored by John Claxton (University of British Columbia), presents conjoint measurement as a technique for assessing the trade-offs which travellers make when choosing among alternative destinations, travel modes, accommodation, and so on. After positioning conjoint measurement as a tool which can help us understand consumer trade-offs, Dr. Claxton describes in some detail the specific nature of conjoint measurement by use of an example drawn from the field of transportation. He also summarizes a number of other examples where conjoint measurement has been applied to enhance understanding of travel-related behavior. The chapter concludes by providing managers with a general appreciation of the major issues involved in the use of conjoint measurement as a research approach as well as an understanding of the manager's role when employing the technique.

33

Enroute Surveys

FRED HURST

Port Authority of
New York & New Jersey
New York, New York

*T*his chapter reviews the growing use of enroute survey methods, who uses them and why. Key factors to consider in the design and implementation of enroute surveys are described. The significance of control over the sample selection procedures is described insofar as it relates to the quality of the survey product. Additionally, some guidance is offered in assessing the value of enroute survey research to the travel manager, particularly with regard to the three most important parameters of any survey plan: cost per interview, sampling error, and control. The interrelationships among these values reveal that low cost per interview does not necessarily represent the best value to a travel manager, on the contrary, it is sometimes a symptom of poor quality.

Travel industry managers need timely information about the travel market to optimize their continuing performance in a changing world. Some of this information is gotten from:

1 *Financial reports* of airline and other carrier revenues, hotel/motel revenues, tax reports, etc.
2 *Traffic statistics* of passengers using planes, buses, ships, hotels/motels, national parks, and other attractions, etc.
3 *Household surveys*, where a selection of people are interviewed either personally or by telephone at home or asked to complete a questionnaire and then mail it back.
4 *Surveys of people while they are away from home*, where a selection of travelers is made while they are enroute in planes, buses, trains, or ships, visiting attractions or stopping over at hotels/motels, and interviewed or asked to do a self-completion questionnaire either to be mailed back or collected on site.

Financial and traffic statistics are widely available and provide a vast resource of basic information useful to travel managers often at little or no cost. Customized surveys are never available without cost. Investments in surveys, however, are part of many sound management programs because they yield valuable information that cannot be obtained from any other source: information about the travelers—their residence, income, family status, and other demographics; and information about their trip characteristics—nights away, travel group composition, travel itinerary, modes used, and attitudes about facilities; knowledge that successful travel managers recognize as providing the vital edge for achieving outstanding results. This chapter will review the conditions that can lead to a decision to sponsor a survey, particularly an enroute survey.

SURVEY COSTS

Unlike financial or traffic statistics, surveys do not require that observations be made on every element of the "population." Surveys are designed to provide estimates of population characteristics based on a relatively small selection of carefully chosen population elements. These estimates can be brought as close to the population values as desired by suitable design of the selection procedures. More importantly perhaps, the survey can be designed to yield only as much accuracy as the user needs and, therefore, the costs can be controlled.

Surveys are usually undertaken to provide hard facts in lieu of judgments. Investments in surveys are first made when it begins to appear to a manager that the cost of a survey might be less than the value of the information derived, particularly when it is considerably less. There frequently is synonymous evidence that judgments are inadequate, e.g., "trial and error" is becoming a noncompetitive strategy.

HOUSEHOLD SURVEYS VERSUS ENROUTE SURVEYS

Household surveys are probably most well known. The selection of people for inclusion in a household survey proceeds through various stages of sampling: a selection of geographic areas to represent the total area of the United States, for example, within selected areas a selection of households, and finally a selection of people within selected households. Highly sophisticated control of selection procedures throughout these stages of selection can assure quality results at minimum but still very high costs. If instead of sending an interviewer to each selected household a self-completion questionnaire is sent, costs can be still further reduced. Telephoning a selection of households has still further cost advantages. These cost-induced alternatives generally entail quality trade-offs that must be given careful consideration before opting for one or another.

Household surveys provide valuable perspectives on the incidence of travel and can identify useful relationships between travel and various other factors such as income, occupation, education, composition of the household, etc. When they are repeated from time to time, they can reveal switches in mode, e.g., from car to air, or indicate switches in vacation destinations, e.g., from Europe to the Caribbean for U.S. residents, as well as many other significant shifts in the market place.

One of the problems with surveys of people at home insofar as the interests of travel industry management are concerned is that frequent travelers are frequently not at home. Another problem is recall. Details about the respondent's last trip are sometimes forgotten, particularly as the interval between the trip and the survey interview increases. This problem, of course, assumes even greater significance for trips before the "last" trip. When the lasting impressions are the only ones of importance this is not a serious problem, but sometimes the casual encounter of a bad experience during a travel episode is not remembered, only the quality is recalled and this information may be considerably less useful to travel industry management than specific problem area definition. Although methods have been devised to cope with these problems, enroute surveys are uniquely free of these "not at home" and "recall" factors. Also enroute methods are more effective than household surveys in locating specific markets. For example, United States residents visiting Europe (or vice versa) are easier to find on transatlantic flights than they are by looking into a random selection of households.

ENROUTE METHODOLOGY

Enroute survey methods are designed to select travelers on the move, while they are making their trips. The quality of the response, however, depends very importantly on soliciting responses at the right time in their travel. One "right time" to approach a traveler, for example, has been found to be when he is enjoying the comfort and security of his accommodation, not while he is waiting impatiently on check-in lines or during the harried rush to claim errant baggage. The point at which a traveler is selected for inclusion in an enroute self-completion or interview survey is a vitally important consideration in the design of the sampling methodology. When the selected traveler is asked to mail back his or her self-completion questionnaire, this consideration may not be quite as important. Hopefully the traveler will pick a convenient time to complete the questionnaire and mail it back. With mail-back surveys, however, it has been found that many travelers forget to complete and/or mail back the questionnaire either because they have gone on to other facets of their trip that obscure their interest in the surveyed factor or they wait until their return home where routine responsibilities sweep the trip factors from their minds. High nonresponse rates indicate a significant probability that the people who respond are different from those who do not in ways that are important to an evaluation of the survey results. Again methods have been devised to cope with high nonresponse to mail-back surveys but self-completion questionnaires with on-site collection or interview surveys are not as liable to this hazard. Enroute survey response rates are optimized by choosing the traveler at a propitious point in his/her trip and collecting the information *in situ*. Response rates of over 90% are quite possible when due attention is given to these factors.

USERS OF ENROUTE SURVEYS

Enroute surveys have been used with increasing success for more than thirty years. Airlines such as Eastern and Pan Am were among the early pioneers of this method, using it to evaluate in-flight services and profile their air passenger markets. The Port Authority of New York & New Jersey used enroute surveys as long ago as 1948 to help assess facility needs at Newark International, La Guardia, and John F. Kennedy International Airports and to provide a demographic base for a forecast of air passenger traffic, as well as for determining the characteristics of bridge and tunnel users as far back as the early sixties. A little later it started using enroute surveys for identifying the passenger market using the midtown Manhattan bus terminal and, also in the sixties, the Port Authority in cooperation with the New York Central Railroad used in-train (enroute) surveys to identify a sector of the rail passenger market. The Port Authority during the full year of 1973 also used a variant of the enroute survey principles to find the origin, destination, and commodity type for air cargo that flowed through its airports by abstracting key information from a sample of waybills.

The airlines have continued to be the most notable users of enroute survey methodology. Some have used regular ongoing programs, yielding results on a periodic basis, e.g., quarterly. The key to the success of their surveys has been the in-flight completion of questionnaires by the passengers, a most propitious environment for soliciting passengers' responses to travel questions. The flight crews distributed the questionnaires, solicited response on the cabin public address systems, and collected the completed questionnaires. In more recent years, however, with the increasing size of aircraft, and the proliferation of in-flight surveys, the administrative problems became formidable and response rates plummeted. To address this problem one airline introduced in-flight survey administration as part of their new crew training program and thereby assured that one person on each selected flight (a crew trainee) would have sole responsibility for the survey. British Airways used a seat sampling plan administered by the in-flight service manager. Some nonairline users of the in-flight environs have bypassed busy flight crews altogether by distributing questionnaires to all boarding passengers and collecting the completed results from deplaning passengers at their next destination. The unique advantages of in-flight surveys continue to be exploited with innovative modifications to overcome new problems.

Enroute survey techniques have been applied in a wide variety of circumstances to measure characteristics of the automobile passenger travel market: by highway administrations to identify the origin and destination of traffic flows, by state and city tourist commissions to measure these tourist markets, and visitor surveys at national parks and attractions. In some rigorous cases, a sample of cars was selected and stopped (occasionally by police car pursuit) for a few brief questions. In others, mail-back questionnaires are distributed at key points.

Some difficult investment decisions for travel management are in the realm of what to do next season, next year, or a few years down the road. Increasing numbers of travel managers are finding that enroute surveys provide them with a better understanding of their market today so that they can plan effectively for tomorrow, particularly because enroute surveys are an efficient way to target their own segment of this dynamic market.

CONSIDERING A "FIRST" SURVEY

Faced with the bewildering array of possible enroute survey methods, how does the travel manager who has no previous experience with survey techniques approach the question of whether he can profit from them? First the manager has to bring into focus the characteristics of his/her market that are or might be important to his/her developmental efforts. This usually results in a sharper definition of "population" as well. Together these two factors, a set of measurement objectives and a "survey population," are the cornerstones of a survey proposal. These factors will probably undergo some modifications and certainly clearer specificity as the consideration of a survey enters the active stage of a proposal.

Some travel managements have the personnel resources to develop their own sampling plans and perform the analysis. Many do not. Many go to consultants and professionals with demonstrated expertise in market studies. Sometimes travel managers solicit a few survey proposals from different consultants in order to select a proposal representing the best value.

Judging the value of an enroute survey proposal is based on cost as well as on the prospects that a proferred plan will satisfactorily answer the need. These are not easy judgments to make. Some unfamiliar language will undoubtedly come up, terms such as "sampling error" and occasionally "bias."

SAMPLING ERROR

Whether a sampling plan will meet the needs of the user can be partially expressed in terms of sampling error. How close the survey estimates can be expected to come to the values that would be obtained if "everyone" instead of just a relatively few were queried is possible for a professional to estimate with a good degree of confidence once the sampling plan has been carefully designed. More specifically the professional can give a range of values for an estimate within which the results from, say, 95% of the repeated application of the same design will fall, if the design is implemented exactly as prescribed. Sometimes a few field tests are needed to estimate the sampling error from a particular survey plan. Better value is obtained by the user when he/she isn't asked to pay for more sampling error than he/she requires.

CONTROL: BIAS/NONRESPONSE

In addition to sampling error, almost all sampling plans are liable to other problems encountered in executing the design. Most enroute sampling designs, like household surveys, define a procedure for selecting people through stages of sampling; e.g., for an in-flight survey: a sample of work shifts for the survey representatives, then a sample of flights scheduled to depart during a selected shift, then a sample of passengers enplaned on the selected flights. Failures can be encountered at any stage: e.g., a field survey representative gets sick and doesn't make his work shift, an interviewer fails to find a selected flight, or a selected passenger fails to respond to a questionnaire.

Failures at any stage of the sampling design when duly recorded and summarized are measures of how well the sample design is implemented. If the sampling at one or more of the stages of selection in the design goes out of control, the quality of the ultimate estimates is jeopardized. Estimates of sampling error are not always adequate to signal such an event. The postsurvey estimates of sampling error are made on the basis of observations actually included in the sample. The fact that all women might have been left out, for example, would not enter into sampling error estimates.

The measure most often used for control problems is nonresponse rates or its counterpart, response or return rates. Most commonly these nonresponse rates are used only in the final stage of sampling—nonresponse among people selected for inclusion in the sample. Nevertheless, in auditing the performance of any survey the user should review the control performance measure at all stages of the selection procedure. Good designs incorporate stages of selection which have been chosen because the professional expects to have good control problems at these stages. Additionally, a good design will prescribe in advance alternate procedures to use when failures are encountered, procedures intended to minimize the chance that the quality of the ultimate estimates will be weakened.

A nonresponse rate of 50% means that only half of the intended population actually got into the sample. It can result in "biased" estimates. For example, if all women are inadvertently excluded, the estimates are biased to males. Since little or nothing is usually known about nonrespondents except their share of the intended population, the best protection against bias is to keep nonresponse as low as possible. Failing in that endeavor, many survey designs provide methods for trying to get information about nonrespondents. Subsampling mail-back failures with telephone follow-ups

where possible is one way. There are many other ways used by creative professionals.

QUESTIONNAIRE

Another area where bias may be encountered is in the most vital survey instrument—the questionnaire—particularly in self-completion types. The phrasing of a multiple choice question for occupation, for example, has been found to be biased towards "executive" if that term is included among the multiple choices. Whether or not it should be included depends on how the results are to be applied. Questions must be carefully phrased so as to preserve the intent of the survey. A recall bias can be encountered when asking for "frequency of travel over the past year." In questionnaire design, many problems can be avoided if the inclusion of questions is stringently disciplined to provide only the information most pertinent to the survey objectives. Some respondents find that qualitative judgments require a substantial amount of effort and they selectively avoid these questions. Selective avoidance of specific questions within a questionnaire can assume significant proportions. In the end, a questionnaire developed under strong discipline, carefully worded, and tested will be shorter and probably elicit a higher response rate than long questionnaires loaded with redundancy and asking for marginally useful judgments on an extensive scale. Careful structuring of the question sequence so as to ease the response is also important to reducing the incidence of wrong answers and increasing response rates. Short, businesslike questionnaires that are easy to follow and understand are important in any survey, but particularly so in enroute surveys where response time may be limited.

RANDOMNESS

When the elements drawn at each stage of the survey design are selected with known probabilities, the result is a random sample. There are many methods for drawing probability samples, all characterized by objective selection procedures at each stage. The population elements are identified with a random number series in such a way as to assure that the probability for each element's inclusion is known. Sample estimates then are simply derived by "weighting" the elements included in the sample by the reciprocal of their probability of inclusion in the sample.

When observations on some selected sample elements are not completed, nonresponse is encountered. If nonresponse is "small," a judicious adjustment of the weightings is often introduced so that the survey estimates apply to the originally intended population, rather than the "slightly" reduced one actually included in the sample.

A random procedure is characterized by an objective selection method: every nth passenger with a random first selection. More completed questionnaires per interviewer hour are obtained in some methods by assuming that a surveyor's uncontrolled selections are random—with an increased risk of bias.

Random selection control procedures are developed for one purpose, to assure that the sample represents the intended population and thus the consequent survey estimates will apply to the whole market as originally intended. Sampling error estimates in such a case have real meaning in describing the quality of the survey estimates. When selection procedures are not under control, the sampling error estimates apply to an unknown part of the intended population and the results may be misleading with only the nonresponse rate to indicate the existence of this hazard.

SUMMARY

A travel manager who is considering the use of enroute surveys wants estimates of market characteristics in which he can have more confidence than the traditional use of his/her own judgment and appreciates the value of such information. A survey sampling plan and its analysis provide the basis for estimating the cost of this information. The quality of the product is specified by an expected level of sampling error together with the expected ultimate sample size and, very importantly, how the sample was selected. One of the most common mistakes in survey design is probably the assumption that quality of the estimates and sample size go hand in hand. This emphasis neglects the critical function of design: How were the observations obtained? How were the people selected? Large sample sizes cannot correct for a bad design, one that is not in control at every stage of selection. Before accepting the survey results, the survey user must be assured that the original specifications for sampling error and control at all the stages of sampling have been reasonably met. The quality of a sampling design can have a strong professional and theoretical basis but it is up to the user to be assured at final report time that control had been maintained as stipulated at the time of the agreement.

Thus the cost of the information developed by enroute surveys is an integral function of the demonstrated quality of the result. If the travel manager chooses not to use an enroute survey, it is probably because he values his/her own judgment higher than the cost of the survey (see Fig. 1).

Figure 1 may help to make visible the quality of the relationship between sample size and sampling error (standard deviation). It depicts the standard deviation for an estimate of a proportion from samples of size 20 or so to 10,000 where the observations are selected by simple random sampling (e.g., from an urn). The standard deviation is greatest for estimates in the neighborhood of 50% and least for those around 10% or so. The error in "high estimates" like 90% are described by their complement, 10%; or to put it another way, 75% has the same standard deviation as 25%, etc. Thus these two lines describe practically the full range of errors that might be expected in sampling for proportions. The chart reveals that sampling error falls off rapidly for sample sizes of up to 800 or so—and beyond 2,000 there is hardly any reduction in error left to achieve by increased sample size. A logarithmic scale for sample size is used to emphasize this quality.

Most surveys are based on multistage sampling designs which are less efficient in this error sense but nevertheless less costly. Sample sizes in most surveys are given in terms of the ultimate sampling unit, a questionnaire or an interview. The sampling error relationship in these cases often requires two, three, and even four times as many observations to yield the same standard deviations as depicted in Fig. 1. for simple

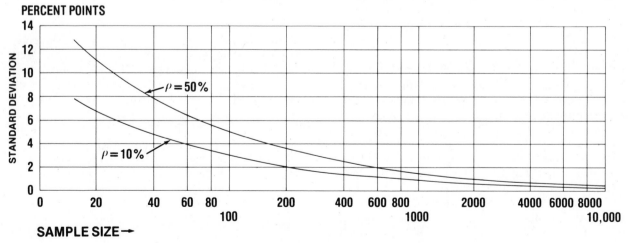

PERCENT POINTS

FIGURE 1 Standard deviation as function of sample size (SRS for proportions $\sigma = \sqrt{pq/n}$).

random sampling. Nevertheless, even at four times as many observations sample sizes in excess of, say, 8,000 ($4 \times 2,000$) don't do much to improve the quality of the estimates.

Perhaps the main point to be derived from this cursory review of sample size is that large sample sizes can be hazardous; they increase the processing costs and might divert attention and resources from two of the most important factors of survey work, control of the sampling procedures and editing of the questionnaires. Careful editing of responses is a time-consuming but vital part of the survey process.

AN EXAMPLE OF THE ENROUTE SURVEY METHOD

This section describes how an enroute survey is conducted. It does this by example. A model is developed from applications in the airline industry. The airline model is chosen because in-flight surveys provide the richest background for gaining a broad perspective on the methodology that can be useful for interpreting the results from completed enroute surveys, or considering the feasibility of further applications. An in-flight survey for an airport is used.

THE MODEL—AIRPORT X

Airport X has reached a stage of growth where the need is recognized for a more intense understanding of the passenger traffic flows to enhance the ability of management to plan and coordinate the development of their facilities more effectively. About a million passengers are enplaned on about 10,000 scheduled flight departures per year. The airport is served by five or six scheduled airlines. The use of an in-flight survey is being considered. The following is a detailed development of a practical proposal for an in-flight survey which provides the necessary flexibility for negotiating its implementation under highly variable conditions.

IN-FLIGHT SURVEYS: A SCALAR MODEL

Airport operating and planning problems generally have two significant facets: physical and economic. Physical problems generally emphasize "peak hour" flows while economic problems depend on round-the-clock traffic activity and revenue generation. An in-flight survey will give results in both these areas by providing a model of the total operations with a scalar factor about equal to the sampling rate. Peak hours will come into the model with the same significance they have in the population and peak period measurements will derive their strength from repeated observations over the time span of the survey.

AIRLINE COOPERATION

A successful in-flight survey program requires the cooperation of virtually every airline serving Airport X. Accordingly, the proposal must be prepared so as to minimize the impact on any airline's ongoing operations and yet be specific enough to clearly describe the extent of their involvement under the simplest conditions. At the same time, the proposal must be flexible enough to adapt to variable procedures insofar as they are unique to each airline. Some airlines have their own in-flight survey programs. Some are conducted periodically and systemwide, others on an ad hoc basis. Some airlines do not do in-flight surveys.

For those airlines who do not conduct in-flight surveys, the services of a survey representative to meet the flight crew of selected flights and supply them with questionnaire "kits" including addressed pouches for returning completed questionnaires to the originating airport via airline company mail services are almost a necessity. Some airlines could not participate unless this service was provided. The survey field representative is also needed to instruct the chief cabin crew member on the method—most simply, to distribute a questionnaire to everyone aboard the plane as it leaves Airport X, ask for cooperation on the PA system, and be responsive to questions about the survey.

The representative then collects the load statistics for the flight: the number of throughs and enplaned revenue and nonrevenue passengers for response rate analysis and weighting completed questionnaires. The representative also picks up kits from the airline ticket counter that have been returned from earlier flight selections. Flight crew cooperation is improved if their airline management provides advance notice that their flight has been included in the sample selection for Airport X's in-flight survey. For this reason, the airline must receive notice of the flight selections as much in advance of the contact date as possible; by the middle of the month preceding a month's selections is a practical schedule for flight sample selections and clearing with the airlines.

Airlines with in-flight survey programs of their own may participate in Airport X's in-flight program with the proviso that their own in-flight selections have precedence. They may still, however, welcome the services of a field representative to reduce the extent of their participation in Airport X's survey. Others among them may prefer to board Airport X's survey kits themselves without the intervention of a field representative. Still others may have their own in-flight passenger sampling schemes that they are willing to extend for Airport X's program, again without the intervention of a field representative.

Airline cooperation, then, may take various forms. One way to approach the problems this might create is to prepare a proposal consistent with the lowest common denominator before soliciting airline cooperation. A basic proposal would include the services of a field representative, a completely designed questionnaire, and a specific plan for selecting flights for inclusion in the sample with the time span and total flight sample size clearly specified together with an estimate of the number of flights needed from each airline. Then when it comes to soliciting each airline's cooperation, the basic proposal can be modified to accommodate individual airline requirements. The following is a development of such a basic proposal for an airport with a million passenger enplanements per year on 10,000 scheduled flight departures operated by six airlines.

OUTBOUND FLIGHTS ONLY

Providing a field man as an integral part of a basic in-flight design limits the feasibility of survey coverage to flights outbound from Airport X only. Otherwise delivering survey kits to all upline airports for inbound flights involves additional costs that are not usually commensurate with the value of the information added, since virtually all passengers found at Airport X use it at least twice on each trip—once in and once out. Therefore, the amount of unique information provided by inbound passengers may be only hour of arrival and expected mode of egress.

TIME FRAME

An in-flight survey program can be thought of as a "model" of Airport X's passenger market that can be used for both short- and long-term analysis. Its utility is enhanced if the sample covers all seasons, days of week, and hours of day so as to minimize the amount of projection and extrapolation that will be necessary in applying the results to real problems. The simplest survey design assumption is that the survey shall span a full year. This provides results that are reasonably free from otherwise unknown seasonality. It also allows the necessary amount of sampling to be done at the lowest level of ongoing activity, thus minimizing the interruption of normal operations and maximizing control over the field work. It also reduces the number of different people who must be trained to work on the survey while providing optimum conditions for ongoing feedback in a wide range of survey operating characteristics, e.g., flight crew cooperation, in-flight response rates, and questionnaire design, as well as yielding interim results on a timely basis. The design can be made in building blocks of time that can be assimilated for full year coverage—or truncated at a half, third, or even quarter year without inordinately jeopardizing the quality of the results. The damage done to the estimates by not finishing a full year can be limited to little more than that which arises from incomplete control over seasonality.

QUESTIONNAIRE DESIGN

The model questionnaire given on the following pages illustrates some of the problems encountered with self-completion in-flight surveys. It is structured on the assumption that it will be given to all passengers aboard a selected flight after it leaves Airport X, but it is not limited to that condition.

The easiest questions are put first to encourage response. "Where did you board this flight?" seems obvious, but some flights contain "through" passengers who stayed aboard the aircraft while it stopped at Airport X to enplane passengers. This question provides the information necessary to segregate them from analyses of Airport X enplanements. It is also protection against distributions that occur after the flight has made another stop and new enplanees erroneously receive questionnaires.

Question #3 "Where will you leave this plane?" is almost as simple. Some transfer passengers will give their ultimate destination and forget about a change of planes enroute. For some purposes this ultimate destination today is more important. It depends, for example, on whether the adequacy of through service is being evaluated. Question #4 elicits this information.

Together, Questions #2 and #3 provide the basic means for identifying the population being studied.

Question #5 "Where do you live?" is vital to a meaningful analysis of airport access modes. Generally the passenger has a car available for the trip to the airport nearest his home and more often public modes at the other end of his trip. The clarification addenda are not necessary for most of the passengers. Question #6, residence ZIP code, gives adequate geography in easy to code numerics that are known by virtually all passengers who live in the U.S.A.

Question #7 is a simple purpose question liable to some ambiguity, but used in conjunction with Question #8 "Nights Away" provides a qualitative basis for market analysis. Other types of survey research may require more detail in this question.

Question #9, travel group composition, is liable to more response error than the foregoing questions because of the many possibilities for travel group arrangements and because it is not altogether unreasonable to suppose that each passenger is "traveling with" everyone else on the flight. It is also somewhat ambiguous: Some people travel "alone" in a group tour and some travel with their spouses in a group tour. It is structured to provide a basis for qualitative classification.

Question #10, mode of airport access and local origin, is also a difficult concept to communicate in a self-completion questionnaire, e.g., business visitors with a number of stops don't know where to say their trip to the airport "originated" and some visitors on personal trips don't know the ZIP Code of the home they visited and are reluctant to give a street address. Part C is useful for converting passengers into the number of different people using Airport X.

Questions #11, #12, and #13 are common ingredients of almost all population surveys. When age is open-ended instead of multiple choice (as herein presented), it encounters a little more nonresponse but provides a more definitive distribution. The incremental nonresponse has not been found to be localized in any particular age brackets.

Question #14, occupation, is structured to identify nonrevenue passengers and to classify passengers on broad occupation bases of particular significance in travel studies.

Question #15, household income, generally has the most nonresponse, about 15 percent, but it is usually localized among females and students, while the response from male business travelers is high. Open-ended income questions increase the nonresponse to 20 percent or 25 percent but expedite the handling of comparisons with other distributions. Again, the incremental nonresponse has not been found to be localized in any particular categories.

In any effort to shorten the model questionnaire, there are some obvious candidates for omission because they are not of interest to the majority of passengers. The appended remarks to Question #5 (residence) are directed towards passengers who are moving or going to or from school. The last box for Question #8 (nights away) is only for people who are changing residence. Questions #9A and #9B are primarily directed towards passengers traveling in groups, while about half the travelers are generally found to be traveling alone. If these questions are dropped, the people who need them may be annoyed by this apparent ambiguity. As a result they may not complete the questionnaire. On the other hand, those who don't need these questions may fail to respond because of the clutter introduced by having the questions included.

Dilemmas of the above sort are common in the design of self-completion questionnaires. Explanations, clarifying remarks, and other extraneous notations on self-completion questionnaires add to the complexity of the instrument and consequently increase nonresponse, perhaps significantly.

Sometimes pretesting the questionnaire provides enough reliable information to permit rational decisions in these problem areas. Often, however, the pretest is not sensitive enough; the sample size is inadequate and/or the selection of pretest "groups" misses some important components of the population or includes too many of another group.

Another way to handle problems of this sort is to use more than one questionnaire type. Half the questionnaires can be produced in ultimate simplicity—the other half could be produced with technical precision. The two questionnaires can then be collated on an every other one basis so that half the respondents get one questionnaire and the other half get the other. Since reliability of the sample estimates is about as good from half the respondents as it is from the two combined, one questionnaire result can be used for very sensitive corrections to the other and best estimates can be obtained from their interaction if significant defects in population coverage are discovered. A technique like this, together with careful attention to original questionnaire design and survey goals, can sometimes yield detailed results while still protecting the ultimate estimates from significant response bias. For example, an open-ended income question can be run with a multiple choice income question. The multiple choice questionnaires would maximize response while the open-ended questionnaires would provide fine detail for alternative income groupings. The former provides protection against response bias while the latter provides details for better comparisons of the results with other information sources. Open-ended age against multiple choice is another example for applying this technique.

AIRPORT INFLIGHT SURVEY—SELF-COMPLETION (OUTBOUND FLIGHTS ONLY)

1. WHERE DID YOU BOARD THIS AIRPLANE? _____ _____ _____
                                                      Airport/City   State/Prov.   Country

2. Airport/city above is ☐ Where you live—or the nearest suitable airport
                               ☐ Where you visited—or the nearest suitable airport
                               ☐ An airport that you used only to change from a plane boarded in another city; which city?
                   _____ _____ _____
                     City   State/Prov.   Country

3. WHERE WILL YOU LEAVE THIS AIRPLANE? _____ _____ _____
                                            Airport/City   State/Prov.   Country

4. Airport/city above is ☐ Where you live—or the nearest suitable airport
                               ☐ Where you will visit—or the nearest suitable airport
                               ☐ An airport that you will use only to change to another plane going to another city; which city?

          _____   _____   _____
             City   State/Prov.   Country

5. WHERE DO YOU LIVE? _____ _____ _____
                              City   State/Prov.   Country
        Note: If you are changing residence, check here ☐ and give last address above.

                 If you are making a temporary change of residence (school or extended work assignment), check here ☐ and give permanent address above.

6. If you live in USA—give ZIP Code. ☐☐☐☐☐

7. IS THIS A BUSINESS TRIP?   Yes ☐   No ☐

8. HOW MANY NIGHTS WILL YOU HAVE BEEN AWAY by the time this trip is completed?
                   ☐ No nights—a one-day trip
   Number of nights: _____
             or ☐ A one-way trip; a permanent change of residence, moving.

9. A. Are you traveling in a charter or tour group today?   Yes ☐   No ☐
      If yes: About how many in the group? 20 or less ☐   21 or more ☐
   B. Your PERSONAL travel party—Are you making this trip:
      ☐ With your spouse   ☐ With friends or business associates
      ☐ With other relatives   ☐ Alone
   C. If you are *not* making this trip alone—How many others are in your PERSONAL travel party?

         _____ _____ _____ _____
         (adults) (teenagers) (children) (infants)

10. If you boarded this flight at Airport X, answer A, B, and C below; if you didn't, check here ☐ and go on to Question #11.
   A. IN WHAT KIND OF TRANSPORTATION DID YOU ARRIVE AT THE AIRPORT TODAY?
      ☐ Private CAR   ☐ Taxi
      ☐ Company CAR   ☐ Bus
      ☐ Rent-a-CAR   ☐ Limousine
           Other, please specify: _____
   B. Where did you board the above transportation—or, if you used more than one mode, WHERE DID YOU START YOUR TRIP TO AIRPORT X TODAY?
      ☐ Your home   ☐ An office
      ☐ Another private house ☐ A hotel/motel
           Other, please specify: _____

    LOCATED AT: ☐☐☐☐☐ ZIP code; or if you don't know ZIP
    Street Address: _____
               (or name of hotel, nearest street intersection, etc.)

    City/Town: _____

C. How many times did you *board* a flight at Airport X during the past 12 months?

☐ Once, just this flight or   ☐☐☐   Number of other flights boarded at Airport X.

11. AGE: ☐ 12–21   ☐ 22–39   ☐ 40–64   ☐ 65+

12. SEX: ☐ Male   ☐ Female

13. MARRIED: ☐ Yes   ☐ No

14. WHAT IS YOUR MAIN OCCUPATION?
☐ Student
☐ Military
☐ Homemaker
☐ Retired
☐ Airline employee or
   family thereof

☐ Travel agent
☐ Self-employed
☐ Employed by government
☐ Employed by industry
☐ Employed by nonprofit
   organization

15. What is your approximate HOUSEHOLD INCOME?
Yours plus that of your spouse, parents, etc., in U.S. dollars:
☐ to $5,000   ☐ to $25,000
☐ to $10,000   ☐ to $50,000
☐ to $15,000   ☐ to $75,000
☐ to $20,000   ☐ $75,000 plus   ☐ Don't Know

THANK YOU!

SAMPLING PLAN

One of the basic sampling elements in a manned in-flight survey is a field representative's working shift. During a selected work shift, the field survey representative would be expected to contact the flight crews from a selection of six or so flights. Any day's outbound schedules at Airport X, for example, will probably all fall easily within two eight hour shifts: 6 A.M. to 2 P.M., and 2 P.M. to 10 P.M. The definition of the two shifts hinges on the choice of afternoon hours—2 P.M. or 3 P.M., whichever divides the schedules into most nearly equal parts. The other end of the shifts is determined by the fact that activity between 10 P.M. and 6 A.M. is usually nil. For any shift then all scheduled flight departures will be listed in chronological order and a random start systematic selection of six flights for inclusion in the sample will be made.

If flight schedules are fairly evenly distributed over the shift period from 6 A.M. to 2 P.M. then the interval between sampled flights will be about an hour or so. If they are not, listing them in chronological order before making the sample selection assures maximum intervals between flight selections. If the schedules are highly clustered, it may be necessary to reduce the flight sample size in the shifts or use a more complicated sampling scheme.

Thus two shifts cover a day's flights at Airport X; fourteen shifts cover seven days' flights in any given week. Since Saturday and Sunday activity before 2 P.M. or 3 P.M. is usually weakest, these shifts might be pooled and covered by one field work shift scheduled on either Saturday or Sunday—alternately as the sampling plan is replicated. This is one way to draw a sample of shifts—stratify first by day types. Schematically the resultant thirteen day types can be depicted as follows:

	MON.	TUES.	WED.	THURS.	FRI.	SAT.	SUN.
Day (to 2 P.M.)	1	3	5	7	9	–11–	
Night (from 2 P.M.)	2	4	6	8	10	12	13

Since there are 13 weeks in a quarter year, a reasonable shift sampling scheme would be to schedule a different day-type shift each week thus covering all day types in a quarter. If they were scheduled in the order numbered above, e.g., day type #1 (Monday day shift) in week #1, day type #2 (Monday night shift) in week #2, etc., weekends would not be covered until the last month of the quarter year. One way to reduce risks inherent in selecting a shift sample this way is to introduce an element of random sampling for the quarter by using a permutation of the numbers 1 through 13.

WORKING SHIFT SAMPLE

A shift schedule for one full year based on one such random permutation is given below. It selects one shift per week.

FLIGHT SAMPLE

Each flight scheduled to depart during a shift selected for inclusion in the shift sample is listed in chronological order of departure time. Each month's schedules are usually listed in the month prior to contact so that problems with schedule changes are kept to a minimum. A random start systematic selection of six flights is made from these flights. For example, if there are 12

Full Year's Shift Schedule
(Q1 = First Quarter, Q2 = Second Quarter, etc.)

WEEK	MON. D	MON. N	TUES. D	TUES. N	WED. D	WED. N	THURS. D	THURS. N	FRI. D	FRI. N	SAT./SUN. D	SAT. N	SUN. N
1			Q4				Q1		Q2				Q3
2	Q4			Q1			Q2				Q3		
3	Q3			Q4			Q1				Q2[a]		
4		Q3			Q4				Q1			Q2	
5	Q1			Q2			Q3			Q4			
6		Q2			Q3			Q4				Q1	
7			Q1			Q2			Q3			Q4	
8	Q2			Q3			Q4				Q1		
9			Q1			Q2			Q3				Q4
10			Q3			Q4			Q1				Q2
11		Q1			Q2			Q3			Q4[a]		
12		Q4				Q1			Q2			Q3	
13			Q2			Q3			Q4				Q1

[a] = Scheduled on Sunday; other two on Saturday.

If it was necessary to reduce the span of the survey to a half year, the same array could be adapted in the following way: For two shifts per week (a one-half year survey) quarters #1 and #2 could be collapsed to read as quarter #1 and quarters #3 and #4 could be collapsed to read as quarter #2. It also follows that to reduce the survey to only a 13-week period (one quarter) the four shifts for each week could all be done in one calendar week. For practical purposes, it is usually appropriate to change holiday shifts to the same day type in an adjoining week so that holidays are not covered in the sample. This is usually a tolerable omission because holidays are relatively few and are especially light air travel days. If this option is chosen for a Monday holiday for example, there would be only 12 Mondays in that quarter instead of 13.

The fact that Saturday and Sunday day types are pooled into one day type implies that results from these shifts are doubled at some point during the ultimate weighting procedures. Otherwise each shift result is multiplied by 13, simply because there is one shift selected of each day type in each 13-week period (assuming the survey extends for the full year). The Sat./Sun. day type then is multiplied by 26.

flights scheduled, divide by six and find that every second flight will be selected for inclusion in the flight sample. To select the first one, a random source for selecting the first or second flight is used. The results obtained from the six flights are multiplied by two (or whatever the sampling fraction was in each shift) in the ultimate weighting procedures to bring the statistics up to full shift level. Because the flight sample is selected from schedules, cancellations are not failures. The basic survey design is intended to describe what happens to flight schedules and cancellations are a real consequence of some schedules. Replacing them would bias the results. In an analogous sense extra sections to a flight schedule should also be covered as well as the original flight section.

PASSENGER SAMPLE

Although it is assumed that each passenger receives a questionnaire, completed questionnaires are not received from each passenger on a flight. Some passengers never receive a questionnaire from the flight crew; some don't fill them out when they get them and some completed questionnaires are not returned. The ratio of the number of completed questionnaires received to the number of passengers on the flight can be called the "response rate" but it includes coverage as well as "response" gaps. The reciprocal of this ratio yields a "weight" that can be given to each questionnaire to bring it up to the full flight load.

In the above sense, it may be said that there is sampling within flights. The term "sampling" is, in theory however, associated with an objective process of selection that is made under controlled conditions. A controlled random sample can rarely be generated without the interjection of a random numbers generator (book or computer) at one point or another in the design. The sampling within flights as herein described is not under control and therefore its objectivity is not assured. Initially, however, it might be assumed that the results produced are not significantly different from a random sample. Subsequent audits of field procedures can be used thereafter to identify departures from this assumption and corrections introduced.

The risk that biased selection of respondents within a flight will have a significant effect on estimates is a function of response rates; higher nonresponse rates give rise to greater risk of significant bias. A lower limit for "acceptable" flights can be implemented to protect resulting estimates from damage introduced by extremely bad flights. If that standard is set at a minimum of 20% response, experience indicates that about two-thirds of the flights selected will meet the standard: more if they are domestic flights, less if international; more if short haul, less if long haul; and more on small aircraft, less on large aircraft.

WEIGHTING

Each questionnaire processed is assigned a weight that is calculated as the product of sampling at three stages: shifts, flights, and passengers within flights. For example, each of the questionnaires completed by 50 passengers on a flight of 100 passengers selected from a weekday day shift of 12 scheduled departures where four out of six selected flights met the 20% response standard would be given a weight of 78, that is, the product of the shift weight 13 times the flight weight 3 (12 schedules divided by 4 "successful" flights) times 2, the ratio of completed questionnaires to passengers on the flight. A similar questionnaire obtained from a flight sampled during a Saturday/Sunday shift would be weighted with twice that value, e.g., 156. The sum of the weights on all the questionnaires will provide an estimate of the number of passengers enplaned at Airport X during the time spanned by the survey. The number of passengers enplaned at Airport X is generally known from traffic statistics. The first meaningful statistic then is the enplaned passenger total. If it compares reasonably well with the traffic statistics the

two sources are compatible; if not, one or the other is measuring different things and a problem of reconciling the estimates is created.

SAMPLE SIZE

The foregoing design yields a sample of one shift per week, 52 for a year. Each shift yields a selection of 6 schedules or 312 departure schedules for the year. With a minimum standard of 20% response within flights, this might result in about 200 successful flights yielding an average of about 50% response. With an average plan load of 100 passengers enplaned at Airport X the total number of completed questionnaires could be expected to reach about 10,000. Of course, the same sample size results would also hold if the schedules were condensed to just one quarter.

If only every other questionnaire was processed and the weights doubled, most estimates could be expected to remain virtually unchanged from the estimates obtained with the full processing of 10,000 questionnaires (see Fig. 1) but processing costs might be halved. Even if the full processing option is chosen, it might be instructive to reproduce the report based on using only every other record. Based on the result of a half sample report, a judgement could be made about the value of full versus half sample processing.

Adequacy of the sample size is normally evaluated on the basis of sampling theory formulae. Most are based on the assumption that the sample is randomly generated. The validity of this assumption depends on the adequacy of control over field work.

Since the sample design is implemented in three stages—shifts, flights, and passengers—the error in the estimates has components attributable to time, flight schedules, and people. The quality of an estimate of the proportion of Airport X's passengers destined for City Y is largely determined by the flight sample size assuming almost all the passengers on a given flight depart at a given city. In the extreme case, the sample need include only one passenger from each flight going to City Y, together with the flight load, to estimate route volume. Local access mode, however, can depend on whether the passenger lives around Airport X or is visiting the area, not so much on the destination. In this sense, the number of respondents within each flight is important and the hour of departure is significant; residents tend to enplane in the morning, visitors in the evening. It is apparent, then, that the quality of destination estimates depends on flight sample size while the quality of local access mode estimates might depend more on sample size within flights.

Simple random sampling is more efficient for many classes of estimates than the sampling design put forth here for Airport X. The Airport X in-flight design contains cluster effects that can result in errors two and three times as big as those graphed in Fig. 1. The importance of the figure, however, is in depicting the extent to which large sample sizes are not productive in reducing error, particularly when field control problems probably increase nonlinearly with very large sample sizes. The figure may be interpreted then as evidence that effort spent in editing the questionnaires and in the field control of in-flight surveys as herein depicted is likely to be more cost-effective than expenditures to increase the sample size.

NON-RESPONSE PROBLEMS

A random sample is drawn with known, not necessarily equal, probabilities. This implies strict controls so that at each stage of the selection process—shifts, flights, and passengers—elements are drawn into the sample by a rigorous probabilistic procedure. Invariably a random number source is required at each stage except where entire clusters are assimilated, e.g., a full flight load of passengers. Random numbers are available in a number of different books, by computer program, various algorithms, or from analogue processes like flipping a coin. The choice among sources is not so important as the fact that one is necessary to the generation of a random sample. When control is weak, the resulting sample may be assumed to be random, but this assumption is not a substitute for the assurance that it is derived from appropriate attention to control in drawing the sample. Confidence limits for error in the estimates derived from sampling theory formulae depend on the validity of the assumption. Rigorous control of the field work provides assurance that such confidence limits are valid.

In the foregoing model development, simple random processes for selecting shift and flight samples are used. Many more sophisticated variations could be used to generate more efficient sampling at these two stages of selection. Such efficiency gains, however, are relatively small compared to the hazards encountered at the third stage—passengers on a flight.

Nonresponse as used in the preceding development encompasses all of the departures from random sampling encountered in implementing the design. There are many. The quality of a sample is determined by the extent to which these departures are minimized. Sample size in practice is a relatively small consideration in generating estimates that can be used with confidence. Large sample sizes cannot correct the damage that can be done when control of the field work is weak or ineffective.

Failures to maintain the integrity of a random sample can result in bias, or wrong estimates. At the first stage of selection, for example, the field representative might fail to cover some shifts. If there are "many"

such failures, they might tend to be weekend shifts—or rainy days. One might try to correct this by rescheduling for the same type of shift lost in another week, but the replacement schedule will be different, *and* hopefully not significantly.

At the second stage of selection—flights within shifts—there can be errors in the source flight listing, or in the record of flights selected. If the schedule is not found when the field representative looks for the flight, a departure from random sampling is encountered. Intensive control over the flight selection procedure is necessary to minimize this problem.

In practice, the third stage of selection—passengers—is where control is the weakest. The successful return of a completed questionnaire depends on a chain of events fraught with frail links, any one of which can result in the failure to complete an observation on a randomly selected element. Thus the sample that results—the final collection of completed questionnaires—becomes the result of a "selection" process that has many nonrandom elements. This is where the most important sources of possible bias can be encountered, where wrong estimates are born.

The field rep meets the chief cabin attendant before flight departure time to deliver enough questionnaires for each seat on the flight (to assure that there are enough for all enplaned passengers) in a return addressed envelope or pouch designed to survive the return trip to Airport X and remain there until the rep retrieves the kit at a later date. The chief cabin attendant must be contacted because there can be thirteen or more cabin attendants involved and good supervision of the in-flight phase is critical to proper coverage. Although the contact is brief, it is obviously important that the communication be effective. It is most effective if the time and place of meeting are carefully coordinated with airline procedures. Nevertheless, some flight crews will refuse to accept the survey kit and a contribution to nonresponse is encountered. While rescheduling the same flight a week or so later is clearly desirable, it may not be practical.

Even after accepting the survey, the flight crew may not choose to implement the in-flight phase—because of bad weather, a full flight, or other reasons—and more nonresponse is encountered. Again rescheduling might be desirable, but at best it would be delayed a few weeks until the absence of the returned flight kit gave evidence of the failure to perform the in-flight phase. It might still not be practical to reschedule.

In-flight distributions may fall short, far short, of the intended 100% for a variety of reasons that are rarely documented. The only evidence available is the number of completed questionnaires finally received versus the load statistics. The questionnaires may have been given only to passengers in aisle seats, who might tend to be experienced business travelers, or they might have been given only to passengers in window seats, who might tend to be new travelers on vacation. These are just two of the obviously many possibilities for bias in an undisciplined selection of passengers on the flight. Similarly there may be gaps in the collection of completed questionnaires, adding further to the nonresponse problems. Numbering the questionnaires provides information for evaluating problems of these kinds.

The last level at which nonresponse is encountered is from the passenger. This too can be strongly influenced by the flight crew—by whether response is solicited on the PA system and, if an announcement is made, the quality of the appeal. Again, numbering the questionnaires provides information that can be used to identify the contributions to nonresponse from passengers themselves.

SOME PERSPECTIVES ON RESPONSE RATES

Some qualitative inferences about the relative significance of these various components of nonresponse accumulated over years of in-flight surveys may be useful to someone contemplating an in-flight survey (or using results from one). Domestic in-flight surveys during the late 1950s produced a 96% success rate on flight contacts; 96% of the flights selected for inclusion in the sample came back with a 50% or better response rate from within the flight. The response rate within successful flights was 92%. Overseas (transatlantic and western hemisphere) in-flight surveys were weaker: 78% of the flight contacts came back with a 50% response rate or better and the response rate from within successful flights averaged 80% (with multilingual questionnaires).

Ten years later, in the late sixties, domestic in-flight success rates were down to 80% of the flights coming back with 50% or better response, and response within successful flights (having 50% or better) was 80%. Among transatlantic flights, the success rate went down to 68% of the sampled flights coming back with 50% or better response and down to 63% response within successful flights.

Another ten years later, in the late seventies, performance criteria had been further eroded. The standard for an acceptable flight had to be lowered from 50% to 20% and rescheduling of flight failures completely abandoned. Only 40% of domestic flight contacts were "successful" under the old standard of yielding a 50% or better within flight response while only about 20% of the overseas flight selections met the same standard. By reducing the standard to 20% for within flight response, the successful flights became 67% in domestic and 55% in overseas.

In summary, the increasing problem with in-flight survey response can be described by the following table describing the share of all flights drawn into the sample yielding a 50% or greater response rate from passengers within the flight:

Proportion of Flight Contacted
Yielding 50% or Better Response

	DOMESTIC	OVERSEAS
1958	96%	78%
1968	80%	68%
1978	40%	20%

It has been shown that the nonresponse problem is a function of the increasing size of aircraft. The administrative problems of distributing and collecting questionnaires on jumbo aircraft are formidable. Airlines are coping with this problem in a variety of ways. One approach taken is to designate a specific cabin crew member to deliver questionnaires to an occupant of a preselected random sample of 8–10 seats instead of attempting 100% coverage. Another approach is to interject flight survey assignments in the curriculae of stewardess training programs so that all passengers are covered on a small selection of flights by one cabin attendant trainee whose prime function is to conduct the in-flight phase of the survey.

Other methods of improving control of the in-flight phase of these surveys will no doubt appear as problems with the old methods are further amplified. The most likely improvements will probably hinge on the fact that quality is more effective than quantity, that more effort put towards the selection and inclusion of a few carefully chosen passengers or flights will lead to estimates commanding more confidence than dissipating effort in the accumulation of large samples of doubtful origin. In any case, it is rather clear that a designated survey representative is necessary in each selected flight.

There has not yet occurred a clear case of conflict with the assumption that current in-flight surveys are random samples. Of course, the opportunities for such evidence are rare. A demonstration requires that the survey estimates can be compared with independent sources of information that are known to be correct. The surveys, however, are undertaken to obtain information available from no other source but occasionally an overlap with other sources occurs.

The Port Authority of New York and New Jersey made one such comparison with in-flight survey results from a year-long study in 1978 and it confirmed the validity of the assumption that the sample was free of bias in one area. The comparison was made with parking lot statistics from the airport. A similar comparison with INS statistics on Aliens vs. Citizens was attempted but yielded ambiguous results because both sources had inherent weaknesses. Nevertheless, it is clearly in the best interests of travel researchers to maintain as much fidelity with the theory of random sampling as practical so that the wealth of theoretical implications can be brought to bear on the analysis of results and the survey results can stand on their own feet.

SAMPLING ERROR

Among the theoretical implications of a well founded random sample is the ability to describe confidence intervals around the estimates. A wide variety of estimating functions for error due to sampling are available. The simplest are the replicated sample types that are best accommodated in the early stages of sample design. The plan described herein can be adapted to these formulae with relatively modest constraints, but added complication, nonetheless. It is beyond the scope of this elemental exposition to give adequate attention to sampling error or attendant considerations for efficiency. It may suffice to state that the design as herein proposed could yield estimates within a few percentage points of true values for the sample universe.

EXTENSIONS

The model in-flight survey proposal developed in the foregoing can be easily extended to encompass another airport, say, Airport Y, if there is sufficient community of interest to support a cooperative in-flight survey program for two airports—or three or four airports. Cooperative programs among airports can produce efficiencies which will lead to lower unit costs and enhance the value of the information derived.

REFERENCES

Kish, Leslie (1965), *Survey Sampling*, New York: John Wiley and Sons.

Kish, Leslie, and Martin R. Frankel (1970), "Balanced Repeated Replication for Standard Errors," *Journal of the American Statistical Association*, 65, 1071–1094.

Kish, Leslie, and Martin R. Frankel (1974), "Inference from Complex Samples," *Journal of the Royal Statistical Society*, B36, 1–37.

The Port Authority of New York/New Jersey (1965), *New York's Domestic Air Passenger Market*. A report of a one-year survey conducted April 1963 through March 1964.

The Port Authority of New York/New Jersey (1970), *New York's Domestic Air Passenger Market*. A report of a one-year survey conducted June 1967 through May 1968.

The Port Authority of New York/New Jersey (1980), *Airport Access Survey*. A report of a one-year survey conducted among all scheduled airline passengers at La Guardia, J.F. Kennedy, and Newark Airports during the calendar year 1978 in collaboration with the F.A.A.

34

The Delphi Technique: A Tool for Long-Range Tourism and Travel Planning

GEORGE H. MOELLER

Assistant to the Deputy Chief
for Research
USDA Forest Service
Washington, D.C.

ELWOOD L. SHAFER

Chairman, Recreation and Parks
The Pennsylvania State University
University Park, Pennsylvania

*T*ourism and travel planning and management requires that we look to the future for events that are likely to influence current decisions. The rapid change that underlies future tourism and related travel activities is frequently attributed to advancing technology. This paper examines the state-of-the-art methodologies to forecast future tourism and travel activities as they may be affected by developing technology and discusses the results of a study that uses some of these methodologies. Future events in this study are separated into five categories: natural resource management, wildland recreation management, environmental controls, population–work force–leisure, and urban environments.

WHY STUDY THE FUTURE?

The future was once a kind of never-never land that had nothing to do with practical matters like earning a living, making a success of one's life, or managing an organization. But today events are occurring rapidly and the future has become part of the present! If measured by the time between events, time is actually speeding up. To cope with this accelerated rate of time, we need to plan to meet anticipated change. Tourism planning and management requires that we look to the future for events that are likely to influence current decisions, as well as to evaluate future impacts of our current decisions. To cope, we must focus our attention on the future, not on the present or the past, because these are beyond our power to change. Never in history have human beings been subjected to so

many changes in so short a time. Few agree on where all this change is leading or what its ultimate result may be. But it is clear that a hurricane of change is sweeping through all human institutions—particularly in the fields of recreation and tourism. If planners and managers are to cope, they must focus on the future and plan to meet it through today's program decisions.

The rapid change that underlies future states of tourism and travel is frequently attributed to advancing technology. People often think of technology as consisting of such things as machinery and chemicals. But, in a broader sense, it includes practical knowledge as well as the social and political arrangements found effective to implement developing technology.

Advancing technology has greatly intensified an ancient problem: the unintended consequences of any action or plan. Every action radiates forward in time and outward in space, eventually affecting almost everything else. Recent technology influencing tourism and travel has convincingly demonstrated that the consequences of a new technology are often far different and far greater than the users of that technology may have first dreamed. The automobile, for example, did much more than just provide people with a way to travel rapidly, easily, and inexpensively from their homes to their places of business. The social and economic changes brought about by the automobile form a long list—effects on the family, on jobs, on entertainment, on the landscape, and, obviously, on tourism and travel. What are the implications of other emerging changes on the future of tourism and travel? Is there anything we can do about this—and, what approaches can be taken to assessing future change and its impact on travel and tourism?

It is not possible for anyone to come up with a neat, effective master plan for the future of tourism; and if anyone tried, it would be either farcical or dangerous. Changes in tourism systems take place on so vast a scale they cannot be easily controlled by a handful of experts or politicians. The process of change occurs at a million points at once—in transportation systems, in businesses, and in communities, as well as in government, and it involves millions of ordinary people, as well as specialized or elite groups. Nevertheless, futurism can make a significant contribution to solving tourism planning and management challenges in the next decade and beyond.

THE UNCERTAINTY BARRIER

There is a period of time, perhaps three years, beyond which our ability to understand and suggest future events becomes extremely hazy and uncertain. How uncertain? More uncertain than we care to admit! More uncertain than we can afford to be in making some of the decisions we must make! We are faced, for instance, with committing to energy conservation (10- to 20-year commitments) while lacking the ability to foresee the effects of related government policy (or lack of it) on tourism activities even two years ahead.

Future studies give some comfort, but not much. Experience suggests that such studies substantially understate future uncertainties. For one thing, there are few "experts" to call on in gauging future political compromises or in assessing public sentiment, which is whipsawed so erratically, sometimes by modern media. Additionally, growing world interdependence and intercommunication have grossly complicated the "models" and the number of parameters involved in the study of future tourism environments. This complexity alone presents a barrier to how far our insight can reach into the future.

Admittedly, we face limits imposed by a type of "uncertainty principle" applied to planning for the future of tourism. This might be stated as a trade-off between time and detail. In other words, the further ahead we try to look, the less discrimination there is in our understanding. Is this a hopeless situation? No. But it is a very tough one—one that should compel us to rethink our tourism planning methods and objectives.

FUTURES METHODOLOGIES

The time-honored way to deal with change has been to take it as it comes and then adjust to its impact. But, under today's conditions of rapid change, the time available for such evaluation and adjustment has decreased. Fortunately, scientists have started to develop methods for investigating the future that do not require the future to merge with the present before action programs can be developed.

TREND EXTRAPOLATION

The most common way to make projections is to extrapolate historical experience or past trends. Such projections are based on the assumption that the future will be a logical extension of the past. The approach has severe limitations (Rescher 1967). The effects of technological innovation and predictable future political–social events cannot be incorporated into extrapolations. Extrapolation techniques are based on the restrictive assumption that causal relationships that have produced past trends will continue to operate in the future. Yet, we can be reasonably certain that the future will be nothing like the past. This method of forecasting is used not only by people in their everyday lives but also by city planners, economists, demographers, and other specialists who first identify a trend and then make a projection suggesting where that trend will lead.

SCENARIOS

A scenario is simply a series of events intertwined to form a concept of the future. Our everyday thinking continuously takes ventures into the mysterious world of next week's or even next year's scenario. We may begin a scenario by asking, "What would happen if we went to the theatre on Saturday night?" With the question posed, we can begin to imagine the various consequences of the action. First, it would require certain preparations: for example, transportation to the theatre would be needed. Then, if the event does occur, further consequences might arise, such as missing a relative who may drop in unexpectedly for a visit.

A scenario awakens us to potential problems that might accompany a proposed action. It helps us to decide whether we want to do something and how to do it. Many policy analysts working for various governments now use scenarios to explore alternative policies that their governments might pursue. In effect, a scenario provides us with a way to shape our futures more intelligently.

ANALYTICAL MODELS

A host of analytical approaches to projections of the future have developed with the advent of rapid data-processing and associated improvements in mathematical and systems-modeling techniques. Analytical models are based on mathematical relationships between relevant elements that are thought to produce or influence the outcome of the process of interest. Although based largely on past relationships, analytical models are flexible so that relationships between modeled elements and the absolute levels of elements themselves can be changed for estimating the effect on the performance of a system. Such analytical models provide a powerful tool for investigating the future and evaluating outcomes of alternative courses of action.

EXPERT OPINION

When we consider taking an important course of action, we usually solicit the advice of other people—often people who have some special knowledge of our proposed venture. These people will give us their judgments of what will likely happen in response to our actions. In effect, these "consultants" make forecasts for us based on their own special insights and knowledge. Their counsel helps us to understand what we may encounter in the future and how we can deal with it. Top leaders in business and government use this forecasting technique. For example, the President of the United States may describe a number of alternative courses of action to his cabinet and get their views on the consequences of each.

Scholars in research institutes ("think tanks") use the above methods, plus others, to explore the future. In recent years, they have made many improvements in the naive methods of forecasting that most of us use. Yet the basic principles remain the same.

THE DELPHI TECHNIQUE

Any or all of the above-mentioned techniques can be used to predict the future of tourism and travel. But whatever the method used, judgment is required, even in sophisticated analytical models where expert opinion is needed to specify future levels of the model components. Judgment must be based on knowledge, opinion, or speculation. Knowledge, of course, provides information on which to make a firm judgment. Opinion is informed judgment based on limited evidence or a thought process that can be opened to discussion. Thus, opinion can be altered as new evidence becomes available. Speculation does not provide a valid basis for judgment, because it is not based

on knowledge or other tangible evidence (Dalkey 1968b). Thus, without knowledge, opinion is the next best insight on which to base futures evaluations.

DESCRIPTION

The Delphi technique is a method used to systematically combine expert knowledge and opinion to arrive at an informed group consensus about the likely occurrence of future events. The technique derives its importance from the realization that projections of future events, on which decisions must often be based, are formed largely through the insight of informed individuals rather than through predictions derived from well-established theory (Helmer and Rescher 1960).

The Delphi technique is based on the assumption that although the future is uncertain, its probabilities can be approximated by individuals who are able to make informed judgments about future contingencies. It is intended to provide a general perspective on the future rather than a sharp picture.

Instead of the traditional approach to achieve consensus of opinion through face-to-face discussion, the Delphi technique "eliminates committee activity altogether, thus . . . reducing the influence of certain psychological factors, such as specious persuasion, unwillingness to abandon publicly expressed opinions, and the bandwagon effect of majority opinion" (Helmer and Rescher 1960).

The Delphi technique encourages individual input by maintaining anonymity among those who take part in the process. Information relevant to the development of consensus is systematically fed back to participants by the Delphi study director. Several rounds of rethinking the problem, with information feedback provided after each round, usually results in a convergence of a group opinion (Dalkey 1968a).

The Delphi technique replaces direct open debate with a series of questionnaires sent to a selected panel of experts. The general procedures used to conduct a Delphi investigation are outlined in Table 1. Successive questionnaires contain opinion feedback summaries from previous panel responses (Weaver 1969). Feedback information includes summaries of reasons given by individuals for their responses about the probability, desirability, interaction, or impact of future events. This information serves to stimulate further thought about points that other panel members may have overlooked and allows them the opportunity to reconsider arguments they may have at first thought to be unimportant.

Delphi study results are summarized graphically to show the interquartile range of predictions (Fig. 1). The median is most often used as the most probable year of occurrence because half the predictions fall above and half below that point. Independent events are then often woven together to form an abstract concept of the future or to develop scenarios.

TABLE 1   Steps in Conducting a Delphi Study

STEP	PROCEDURE	
Identify relevant events	Determine events from theoretical models, futures scenarios, or literature. Panel members may also suggest events.	
Prepare event statements	Statements must be clear and precise.	
Select and establish panel of experts	Select panelists from area of expertise suggested by the problem. Expertise based on contributions to the literature and peer recognition.	
Mail Delphi questionnaires	Questions asked of panel members	Summary information sent to panel members
Round 1 questionnaire	Assign probabilities and dates to events. Add events to list. Solicit information on ambiguous statements.	Edit event statements. Prepare response summary distributions showing individual responses.
Round 2 questionnaire	Ask individuals to reevaluate their round-1 responses based on summary distributions. Ask panelists to provide reasons for changing or not changing their responses if they remain outside interquartile range.	Prepare interquartile response summaries for round-2 questionnaire. Edit reasons given by those outside interquartile range.
Round 3 questionnaire	Ask individuals to evaluate their round-2 responses based on summary information. Ask panelists to provide reasons for changing or not changing their responses if they remain outside interquartile range.	Prepare summaries of interquartile distribution of round-3 questionnaire responses. Edit reasons given by those outside interquartile range.
Round 4 questionnaire	Give individuals final chance to reevaluate their round-3 responses based on summary information. Ask panelists to rate their expertise, evaluate desirability of each event, evaluate interactions between events, and evaluate social impact of each event.	
Other rounds	Questionnaires should continue until a consensus prediction begins to emerge.	
Data analysis	Prepare event summaries showing event distributions, probabilities, impacts, desirabilities, and interactions. Use median prediction as most probable year of event occurrence. Prepare summaries of interquartile distributions. Prepare futures scenarios.	

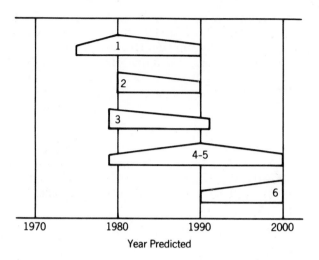

Year Predicted

Key to Events:

1. Different recreation activities allocated specific time periods for the same recreation management area.

2. Computers used to advise recreationists where to go for recreation.

3. Tax credits to industries that practice pollution control.

4. Consumers accept major cost of pollution control.

5. Most homes have videotape systems.

6. Five hundred miles is a reasonable one-way distance to travel for a weekend.

FIGURE 1 Example, graphic summary of Delphi results: medians and interquartile ranges of panel predictions.

CRITIQUE

The Delphi technique has been subjected to much criticism (Weaver 1972). Identification of panel experts and evaluation of their expertise present problems. Experts are usually busy people, and it is difficult to get them to serve on a Delphi panel for an extended period of time. Panel attrition can be severe. The effect of dropout has not been adequately evaluated.

The Delphi study director can have a strong effect on study results. The events he chooses to include in the study and the way in which he phrases event statements can easily lead to misinterpretation (Salanick *et al.* 1971). The study director can also influence results by editing panel response—feedback information.

The Delphi technique has been criticized because it usually treats events as independent of one another (Dalkey 1968a). It does not provide a way to evaluate the interaction between events. An event's probability of occurrence depends largely on the general perspective assumed by panel members when they make their evaluations. If panel members do not share common perspectives, resulting predictions of events will be based on different criteria.

The Delphi technique has not been extensively tested in predicting events other than those directly related to technology. It has been shown to be most accurate in predicting technological events related to space and medical developments and in forecasting political alliances. The technique has had limited application for predicting events that involve human interaction.

Although based on many restrictive assumptions, the Delphi technique is useful where decisions have to be made quickly with limited knowledge. Indeed, in such situations, there may be no alternative. The need to make decisions today to meet tomorrow's leisure needs provides an example. As professionals in recreation, for us it is easy to get tied up with our everyday problems. Seldom can we see beyond our next year's operating budget. But, if changing leisure needs are to be met, we must take a longer look into the future. The Delphi technique can help focus our thinking.

AN EXAMPLE—APPLICATION OF DELPHI TO RECREATION EVALUATION

Following is an example of how the Delphi technique was used in a study to probe for social, managerial, and technological events that are likely to shape the future of park and recreation management to the year 2000. Although study results are somewhat dated, they have strong implications for future tourism and travel planning and management.

In 1974, we asked 900 experts in the biological sciences, ecology, conservation, and fields related to population dynamics, recreation resource management, and environmental technology to take part in the study. Selection of panel members was based on their contributions to the current literature on environment and technology.

The panel of experts was asked to list events that they felt had a 50–50 chance of occurring by the year 2000. They were instructed to consider only those events that related to their own areas of expertise. Responses were summarized and resubmitted to the panel through four rounds of questionnaires (Table 1). Each time, panel members were given the opportunity to reevaluate their previous predictions in light of these summaries.

Results were summarized by grouping events by the median year of prediction—the year falling at the midpoint of the distribution of panel predictions. Fifty percent of the experts felt that the event would occur on or before the median year, and 50 percent felt it would occur on or after the median year or never occur. Descriptive information returned to panel members in each round included the median and interquartile distribution of panel responses for each event.

Events fell into five categories: Natural Resource Management, Wildland Recreation Management, Environmental Controls, Population—Work Force—Leisure, and Urban Environments. More detailed results of this study have been reported elsewhere (Shafer and Moeller 1974).

NATURAL RESOURCE MANAGEMENT

The panel predicted an expanding role of government in directing natural resource management. It forecast that by 1980 economic incentives would be offered to private landowners who manage for fish and wildlife. Although not precise, it appears that this panel prediction was reasonably accurate. Several states have enacted laws that allow tax revenues to be diverted directly toward fish and game management activities. Federal cost-sharing has also been made available to support fish and wildlife habitat improvement projects. The panel further predicted that these programs would broaden by 1985 to include tax incentives for providing scenic amenities.

The panel anticipates that the federal role in coordinating natural resource planning will expand from establishing the first land, water, and air use plan in 1990 to a comprehensive national land use zoning plan in 2000. By 2000, environmental planning will be effectively coordinated among all levels of government and private interests. Also by 2000, land use patterns will stabilize and land preempted for one use will be replaced with comparable land. All land resources, including marine and estuarine areas, will be under intensive management.

WILDLAND RECREATION MANAGEMENT

In this area it was forecast that by 1980 restrictions would be placed on recreational use of wildland areas. Again, this prediction was relatively accurate. Permits are now required for use of many remote recreation areas. It is also a common wildland recreation management practice to restrict and allocate particular kinds of recreation use to specific areas and times, and to allow use of only certain kinds of recreation equipment. The panel also predicted that by 1980 computers would be used to advise people on where to go for resource-based outdoor recreation. Such computerized information systems are now commonly available.

By 1985, it was predicted that limits would be placed on the number of people allowed to use all wilderness and remote recreation areas and that maximum noise levels would be established for recreation vehicles. It was further forecast that the outdoor recreation experience would change: that facilities such as cable TV hookups would be available at most camp-

grounds. Also by 1985, it was expected that economic incentives would be offered to private landowners who open their land for public recreation.

Growing demand will require further restrictions on recreation use by 1990. Restrictive management techniques will be employed to reinforce heavily used recreation sites and to direct use patterns. Public recreation areas will be assigned maximum carrying capacities and use will be kept at or below these levels. Reservations will be required for use of developed public recreation facilities. Maximum sizes will be established for boat motors used on public water bodies. Licenses will be required for all types of saltwater fishing.

By 2000, wilderness management policy will change to allow for more intensive recreational development. Permits, used to control all forms of wildland recreation, will also require certification for certain user groups. The wildland recreation area of 2000 will be vastly different from that of today. Only transportation systems that have a minimum physical and visual impact on the natural environment will be allowed and only recreation vehicles that employ nonpolluting propulsion systems will be permitted in wildland recreation areas. Heavily used areas will be serviced by air, and parks will be aesthetically improved by underground placement of utility lines.

Technology will aid the park manager of 2000. For example, artificial lighting will extend use of recreation facilities and remote-sensing devices will be used to monitor park use. Waste-disposing bacteria will be incorporated into recreation area equipment to reduce sanitary disposal problems. Extensive irrigation of arid regions will broaden and enhance recreational opportunities.

Technology will also create challenging management problems. For example, the experts felt that by 2000, small private recreational submarines, hovercraft, jet-powered backpacks, and one-man helicopters will be in common use.

The wildlife manager will utilize captive rearing to raise endangered species for release. He will monitor wildlife migrations by satellite. Controls will be placed on hunting, and motorized vehicles will be excluded from all public hunting areas during hunting seasons. But, by 2000, wildlife resources will be used primarily for nonconsumptive purposes such as photography.

ENVIRONMENTAL CONTROLS

Most experts felt that by 1980, tax credits would be available to industries that meet pollution control standards. Indeed, many kinds of tax credits have become available to industries to retrofit plant and equipment for pollution abatement. But by 1990, the panel felt that standards will be strongly enforced and companies that do not comply will be closed.

It was expected that concern for landscape aesthetics would lead to half the states passing legislation to control outdoor advertising by 1985. Also by that year, experts foresaw that effective controls would be placed on auto and airplane exhaust emissions, and that all consumer products judged to have adverse impacts on the environment would be banned from production.

By 1990, data collected through a nationwide monitoring system will be incorporated into models that accurately simulate the environmental effects of pollutants. Consumers will accept the major costs of effective pollution controls. By 1995, all consumer products will be packaged in biodegradable containers.

By 2000, strict international pollution-control standards will be established and an international environmental monitoring agency will be organized. Although predictions varied considerably among panel members, other events predicted for the turn of the century include: setting exact human tolerance limits for various pollutants; allowing only biodegradable chemicals to be discharged directly into the environment; and restricting federal reserve chartered banks from financing companies that are known polluters.

POPULATION—WORK FORCE—LEISURE

A growing population with changing attitudes toward leisure will have a major impact on recreation programs. By 1985, experts predicted we would have an average 4-day, 34-hour work week and that most employers would provide leisure counseling services. By 1990, data on leisure activities and interests will be a regular part of the U.S. decennial population census. In response to changing leisure patterns, public schools will operate year-round, with staggered vacation periods. Most homes will be equipped with videotape systems for entertainment and education.

By 2000, panel members felt that 500 miles would be a reasonable one-way distance to travel on weekend recreation trips. Tax incentives will be available to employers who include recreation facilities in the design and construction of new plants.

By 2000, "weekends" will be distributed throughout the week. With an average retirement age of 50 years, more total leisure time will be available during retirement. In response to this abundant leisure, the role of public schools will expand further to serve the recreation needs of the entire community. Middle-income families will vacation as commonly on other continents as they now vacation in the United States. Panel members also felt that by 2000, the work ethic would have assumed a lesser role in society and leisure would become an acceptable lifestyle. An attempt will be made to control population growth through tax incentives, but panel members felt that a mandatory population control program would eventually be established.

URBAN ENVIRONMENT

Improved planning and technology will combine to make future urban environments much more enjoyable than they are today. It was predicted that by 1985 more emphasis would be placed on providing recreation services for specific urban population groups. For example, experts predicted that most urban areas will have special fishing areas for the handicapped, elderly, and children.

By 1990, private aircraft will be excluded from all metropolitan airports. Ten years later, only non-air-polluting vehicles will be allowed in downtown urban areas. Computers will be used to control the movement of individual vehicles. More urban land will be provided for leisure enjoyment; cemeteries, water reservoirs, and planned open space will be available for recreation. Facilities, like city parks and play fields, will be covered with artificial turf to sustain heavy recreation pressure, and some will be covered with transparent domes to allow year-round use. Natural environments will be simulated inside man-made structures to provide urban residents with recreation opportunities now available only in the outdoors.

SUMMARY OF STUDY RESULTS

Results of the example Delphi study should not be taken as indisputable fact. Individual items may be grossly inaccurate. But taken as a whole, the predictions represent a future perspective, with clearly identified underlying trends. This future perspective and the trends on which it is based is perhaps the most valuable product of a Delphi.

What are the trends in these Delphi predictions? Action will be taken at all levels of government to face environmental pressures brought about by increasing demands of a growing population with more time and money. Rational resource planning will be coupled with rigid, enforced controls. How much controls will affect individual freedom cannot easily be determined.

Taken as a whole, our panel of experts predicted an optimistic future. The events are certainly possible and even probable; some have already occurred. But whether or not they occur will depend on the route we select along the road to the future. Man cannot suddenly be expected to become more rational than he has been in the past. But, through better understanding, he can become more aware of the consequences of his decisions and can choose his own future.

IMPLICATIONS OF FUTURES PERSPECTIVES

All of us working in the rapidly changing field of tourism and travel face hundreds of problems, each demanding from us more than we can possibly give.

Pressed by the urgent tasks of the moment, we often feel a little impatient with anyone who suggests that we should think about the future. A natural reply is, "How can you ask us to think about the future when we're trying to deal with a crisis right now?"

Yet, the fact that we are experiencing a crisis today offers one of the best reasons for thinking about the future. Almost always, the crisis has resulted from a failure to deal with a problem before it became a crisis. In retrospect, it is generally easy to see how a modest amount of thought and effort—if invested earlier— could have forestalled a crisis and saved the subsequent money and grief.

Identifying the potential crises of the future in order to avert them is one important function of the study of the future. In effect, the systematic exploration of future possibilities serves as an early warning system, permitting us to deal with problems before they become disasters.

A study of the future of tourism and travel can help provide us with reasonable assumptions about what the future may hold. At the same time, it can help us identify future dangers and opportunities, giving planners and managers a set of perspectives with which they can respond to a rapidly changing world. The futures perspective should be reinforced through an understanding that:

1 The future is not fixed but consists of a variety of alternatives from among which we choose to meet our goals.

2 Choice is unavoidable; refusing to choose is itself a choice.

3 Small changes today can become major changes through time.

4 The future world of tourism and travel will be drastically different from the present one.

5 Planners and managers in tourism and travel are largely responsible for the tourism and travel of the future; that future will not just happen to them, they will create it!

6 Methods successful in the past probably will not work in the future.

In an era when momentous long-term decisions about man and his environment must be made, similar attention should be given to the underlying prediction process upon which all tourism planning must be based.

For example, the United States Government staked $20 billion on inventing a future that included placing a man on the moon by 1970. Similarly, many other potential futures are open to man.

Short-term (2- to 5-year) analysis—upon which many of today's tourism management decisions are based—has the advantage of being able to extrapolate from existing trends. But in many tourism systems, long-range analyses are needed that consider future breakthroughs in technology that may appear and interact before a specific future event occurs. Thus, the variables and contingencies of most futures beyond 5 years from now can only be assessed intuitively. The use of intuitive "forecasting" as a basis for long-range tourism planning is unavoidable.

The Delphi technique, along with the other futures forecasting methods reviewed here, provides a useful tool with which to probe the future so that individuals, organizations, and public agencies concerned with tourism and travel can work together in a framework of cooperation and desired progress.

REFERENCES

Dalkey, Norman C. (1968a), "Experiments in Group Prediction," Paper P-3820, Santa Monica, California: Rand Corp., 40 pp.

Dalkey, Norman C. (1968b), "Predicting the Future," Paper P-3948, Santa Monica, California: Rand Corp., 20 pp.

Helmer, Olaf, and Nicholas Rescher (1960), "On the Epistemology of the Exact Sciences," Paper R-353, Santa Monica, California: Rand Corp., 40 pp.

Rescher, Nicholas (1967), "The Future as an Object of Research," Paper P-3593, Santa Monica, California: Rand Corp., 35 pp.

Salanick, J.R., William Wenger, and Ellen Helfer (1971), "The Construction of Delphi Event Statements," *Technology Forecasting and Social Change*, 3:65–73.

Shafer, Elwood L., Jr., and George H. Moeller (1974), "Through the Looking Glass in Environmental Management," *Parks and Recreation*, 9(2):20–23, 48, 49.

Toffler, Alvin (1971), *Future Shock*, New York: Bantam Books, Inc.

Weaver, Timothy W. (1969), "Delphi as a Method for Studying the Future: Testing Some Underlying Assumptions," Syracuse University, Sch. Educ. Policy Res. Cent., 22 pp.

Weaver, Timothy W. (1972), "Delphi: A Critical Review," Syracuse University, Sch. Educ. Policy Res. Cent., Res. Rep. 7, 63 pp.

35

Using Panels for Tourism and Travel Research

WILBUR F. LaPAGE

Director
Division of Parks and Recreation
State of New Hampshire
Concord, New Hampshire

While relatively little use has been made of panels for travel and tourism research, this method offers enormous potential for improved understanding of travel market trends and tourism promotion analysis. Panels of consumers and of producers of travel experiences are discussed from four specific research objectives: trend monitoring, test marketing, impact assessment, and future assessment. The advantages and disadvantages of panels are discussed and several examples are cited. Considerations for the design and maintenance of panels are presented and references included for a variety of panel studies and analysis techniques.

Consumer panels have played an important role in studies of consumer purchasing patterns, including such leisure interest trends as television viewing and dining out. Less well known are the numerous industry panels of dealers, agents, retailers, and various professionals that also are valuable sources of market trend insight.

Although panels are usually viewed as a longitudinal survey technique, they do have important uses other than trend monitoring. For example, many new products arriving on the market have received extensive testing by panels. Because of their "standby" capability, panels also are valuable for assessing the social impacts of unforeseen events, and voter panels as well as panels of specialists have been used effectively for short-term predictions. Each of these uses has potential applications for travel and tourism research.

PANELS FOR TREND MONITORING

Reliable facts and figures on trends in tourism are surprisingly scarce in light of the high values placed on

such data by planners and investors. While available indicators such as park visits, passports issued, commercial lodging, vacation trips, airline travel, and gasoline consumption provide gross estimates of tourism trends, their value for planning purposes is limited. Questions of travel market shifts, interactivity substitutions, changing travel interests and frequencies, planned equipment purchases, and travel intentions reflect a more ideal level of detail for corporate planning. This kind of data, along with documented trends in tourism developments and profitability, could spell the difference between sound and superficial planning. Such trend data can best be generated by longitudinal studies of specific populations.

Longitudinal studies of tourists can be classified broadly as (1) independent samples (resurveys) of a given population at two or more points in time or (2) repeated measurements of the same sample (panels) over time. Both approaches have distinct applications for the study of travel and tourism depending on the specific research objectives. In general, resurveys are best for monitoring gross changes in large populations over extended time intervals; panels tend to be more commonly used for sensitive monitoring and in-depth studies of the factors (attitudes, interests, etc.) that may have contributed to those changes.

Most commonly, longitudinal studies take the form of periodic resurveys in which a new sample of the population is drawn for each survey. The National Boating Surveys (U.S. Coast Guard), the National Hunting and Fishing Surveys (U.S. Fish and Wildlife Service), the National Camping Market Surveys (USDA Forest Service), and the National Outdoor Recreation Participation Surveys (U.S. Department of the Interior) are federally sponsored resurveys conducted at approximately 5-year intervals. A number of states, industries, and nonprofit research centers also conduct periodic travel and tourism surveys. For example, the U.S. Travel Data Center conducts a telephone survey of 1,000 adults each month to gather information on travel behavior. The Commerce Department's periodic Surveys of National Travel, Retail Trade, Purchase of Durables, and Consumer Expenditures all provide opportunities for analysis of tourism-related trends. While obviously better than the available indicators, population resurveys are still basically descriptive and have a limited capability for explaining trends and shifts in leisure-related travel.

For longitudinal studies with greater explanatory capability it is sometimes desirable to periodically recontact the same sample of respondents. Panels are superior for providing in-depth answers to questions of why market shifts and trends are taking place. An 8-year-long travel-oriented panel study conducted by the USDA Forest Service (LaPage and Ragain 1979) to document trends in camping participation showed clear relationships between family life cycle stages and styles of camping participation. The study also documented the impacts of crowding on camping frequencies and destinations.

Panels of tourist businesses are more common than panels of tourists and have provided useful indexes of changes in business volume and profitability. One of the longest such series (13 years) is the Economic Analysis of North American Ski Areas conducted by the University of Colorado's Graduate School of Business Administration. This survey uses essentially the same sample of respondents each year (Goeldner and Farwell 1980). A similar survey of the commercial campground industry that has been in operation since 1979 provides a biweekly occupancy index (National Campground Owners' Association 1981).

A number of long-term market research panels are in use by industries, university research groups, and government agencies. The Census Bureau's Consumer Buying Expectation Survey, the University of Michigan Index of Consumer Sentiment, and the Chicago Tribune Panel are well known and proven tools for monitoring changes in consumer behavior and attitudes. Several large companies such as General Electric (Carman 1974) maintain their own national panels to monitor such items of consumer behavior as brand loyalty, which can influence their market share. A number of independent research organizations (e.g., Market Facts, Inc., Market Research Corp. of America, J. Walter Thompson, and National Family Opinion) maintain large consumer panels to provide their clients with up-to-date information about consumer purchases, purchase intentions, product recognition, and the likely acceptance of new products, services, packaging, and delivery modes. The 10,000-member CREST (Chain Restaurant Eating-Out Share Trend) panel, using diaries, has monitored market shares and regional and seasonal purchasing changes among patrons of the nation's chain restaurants since 1975.

PANELS FOR TEST MARKETING

The availability of existing consumer panels, whose primary purpose is to track changes in purchasing patterns or in television viewing, provides an ideal opportunity for the test marketing of new products. "Pilot" television shows are evaluated in just this way to determine their potential for development into a continuing series. Comparisons of competing household products are frequently made by panels of homeowners who receive unidentified product samples for "blind" testing. Such panels can require intensive researcher−client interaction, including lengthy interviews, diary records of expenditures and use of time, and even the installation of recording instrumentation in the home, such as television audiometers.

While most panels exist with the full knowledge of the panel members, it is also possible, in fact highly likely, that most of us have served on informal test marketing panels without knowing it. Mailing lists of credit card holders, or college alumni, may be sent brochures offering "discount" rates for vacation tours. The response rates are analyzed and, if favorable, the list becomes targeted for additional promotions—a de facto "panel" whose responses are purchases instead of opinions! In a similar fashion, buyers of chainsaws, garden tractors, television sets, guns, campers, and snowmobiles are often provided with a warranty containing a brief questionnaire which must be returned to the manufacturer for validation. The buyer gets his warranty and the sales department gets a mailing list, a purchaser profile, and a test marketing panel.

The possibilities for establishing both formal and informal panels of travelers and tourists are clearly unlimited—every reservation, registration, and most equipment purchases and travel tickets can contribute to a potential master list for sampling and promotional targeting. The advantages of these informal panels are that they are already "in the market" and are inexpensive to establish. The disadvantage is that they can tell the researcher little about the market's potential size and distribution—critical facts for large-scale test marketing.

While the emphasis on panel research has been in the realm of long-term trend monitoring, the value of panels for short-term studies and experimental uses should not be overlooked. For example, entry and exit surveys at recreation areas or on cruise ships constitute a form of short-term panel ideally suited to matching visitor expectations and satisfactions. Short-term panels, using diaries, have been effective in studying seasonal changes in leisure behavior (Moeller 1975). Club memberships, subscription lists, and visitor registration afford outstanding opportunities for experimental panels to test the effectiveness of different promotional strategies. In terms of available sampling frames, the opportunities for using short-term panels to assess consumer acceptance of new travel products and tour promotion packages have too often gone unrecognized.

Panels are ideally suited for a true before—after experimental design and, therefore, are capable of generating some of the strongest cause—effect data available to the social scientist. Once a panel's levels of travel expenditures, travel behavior, and travel attitudes have been determined, the panel can be subjected to stimuli in the form of promotional materials, price incentives, or new information, and then the panel's response can be determined. Sophisticated, split-sample designs can introduce the elements of control and of multivariate analysis. In this way, the images of various tourist destinations and travel modes can be determined and the effectiveness of a variety of measures to enhance those images can be assessed. Or the effectiveness of different tourism promotions might be assessed by first determining a base level of interest among the panel, distributing different brochures in a randomized block design, and subsequently recontacting the panel to determine new interest levels, trip plans, or actual trips taken. Obviously, subjecting a panel to this type of experimental use may compromise the future use of that same panel for trend monitoring purposes, or even for further experiments.

The "standby" capability of a panel to assess the impact of unforeseen events is often a case of "planned serendipity"! Voter panels established for the sole purpose of charting changing voter sentiment during an election campaign are frequently used to provide instant impact assessment of potentially significant turning points in the campaign. Since every campaign has its share of blunders, good and poor speeches, perceived ethnic slurs, and surprising revelations, today's astute political analyst will have a panel poised and ready for rapid feedback. Travel and tourism panels could provide the same type of impact analysis for such unforeseen (but highly probable) events as a series of

airplane crashes, labor disputes at tourist attractions, hotel fires, bear attacks in national parks, or volcano eruptions!

In addition to assessing the impacts of real events, research on the effect of assumed or imagined events could prove useful in demonstrating the real costs to a tourist economy of erroneous news reporting or faulty weather forecasting. Again, the panel with its known behavior patterns provides a superior analytic model to the "what if" approach of an ad hoc survey.

Using panels for impact assessment is clearly a variation of the experimental design in which the intervening stimulus in the before—after sequence is not induced by the experimenter. This means that inferences from the data may be questionable. Specifically, all of the panel members are unlikely to have had equal exposure to the stimulus. Some may have been totally unaware of it and others may have received biased second- and third-hand accounts of it. The imaginative researcher may, however, be able to partially account for some of these sources of variation by careful questioning of the panel.

PANELS FOR FUTURE ASSESSMENT

Although the use of expert panels to provide a window on the future is discussed elsewhere in this Handbook, it is important to recognize that formal Delphi techniques are but one panel approach to developing probable future scenarios. An excellent model study of future leisure environments that uses the Delphi method has important implications for travel and tourism planners (Shafer et al. 1974).

At least two major national surveys have used panels to estimate future consumer impacts on the economy: the Consumer Buying Expectations Survey (Census Bureau) and the Index of Consumer Sentiment (University of Michigan). Both surveys include two to four panel contacts per year for assessing expectations of major consumer purchases and consumer confidence in the economy. Planned purchases of cars, campers, and boats, along with probability estimates for taking vacation trips, are important indicators for the tourism and travel industries. To the extent that these expectations can be correlated with actual past consumer behavior (via a trend-monitoring panel), their utility and reliability can be greatly extended.

In addition to panels of experts and panels of consumers, important future insights can be generated through the imaginative use of producer panels. Panels composed of equipment dealers, travel agents, park managers, airline stewardesses, and almost any group having constant contact with the traveling public are potential sources of information about tourists' unmet needs and dissatisfactions. It is safe to assume that there is a direct link between unmet needs and future market declines or shifts in market shares. The "front line" is an information source that is so obvious that it is all too often ignored by many market researchers and most managers!

ADVANTAGES AND DISADVANTAGES OF PANELS

The decision of whether to use a panel for tourism and travel research is a complex one. The panel approach must be appropriate to the objectives of the research and be viewed in terms of organizational commitment. For trend-monitoring purposes, a simple listing of panel advantages and disadvantages is not very helpful to the researcher who must choose between a panel and periodic resurveys. The kind of detail desired in trend monitoring is far more important to the decision than the possibility that a panel, once established, might be useful for test marketing or for its standby potential.

Panels are often credited with being more economical than resurveys because sampling is only done once, and secondary contacts are often by mail. In fact, to be representative, the panel's composition must be constantly monitored and procedures must be established for introducing replacements to the panel. Even if the follow-up contacts are by mail, the costs of panel maintenance may well offset that economic advantage. It is increasingly common for panel members to be paid for their services. Because of their continuing relationship, panel members often request follow-up information from the researcher. Unless one responds promptly to these requests, the panelists may lose interest and drop out.

Panels do provide a distinct advantage over other types of surveys in that they can tell the researcher a great deal about the nonrespondent. As members drop out of the panel over time they leave behind a useful file of their characteristics and predropout purchasing/participation patterns. And if budget restrictions require a mail survey rather than personal interviews, panels do tend to produce very high rates of mail response. In the Forest Service camper panel study, 65 percent of the initial panel members continued to respond to the annual survey after five years. After eight years (and a three-year lapse between contacts), 53 percent of the panelists responded.

Panels are, of course, ideally suited to minimizing the error in social surveys that result from faulty memory recall. And where the study objectives require detailed responses about quantities purchased, prices paid, dates, brands, expectations, and satisfactions, carefully designed panel procedures can serve to shorten the gap between the event and its reporting. For example, waves of questionnaires can be timed to follow seasonal fluctuations in travel, rather than using one survey to cover a full year. Frequent participants, such as a panel of skiers, may be asked to record their activities in a specially prepared diary format. The simple fact of being a panel member can make the subjects more alert to remembering the kinds of travel facts being asked of the panel.

Because panels are expected to provide detailed data, there is a concern that the panel may lose its representivity as it becomes sensitized to the objectives of the survey. Panelists may assume that their price reactions might help to lower prices. They may "fine-tune" their comparisons, becoming far more discriminating than normal, as their awareness and analytic abilities are tested. Panels of hotel owners may overreport their occupancy and panels of restaurants may overreport meals served if they assume that the data might be interpreted as a gain in their market share. In fact, underreporting, by consumer panels at least, is more of a problem than overreporting. No matter how carefully the researcher designs his study, humans forget. In general, the bias from underreporting due to forgetfulness is a constant and will have little impact on trend findings. It does, however, become important in the case of test marketing and procedures are available for estimating its impact (Hyett and McKenzie 1976).

Because panels are considered sensitive social measurement instruments, undetected errors can have serious consequences. So it is essential to undertake panel research only with a strong organizational commitment to the method to ensure awareness of the many potential error sources. By understanding the potential problems of panels, the researcher may be able to compensate for them, rather than discard the method. For example, concern relative to sensitization of the subjects can be countered by a panel design which includes "controls" of different question wording and small sample validity checks. Any survey contact produces a degree of sensitization to the study objectives and may generate bias due to the respondent trying to please the researcher. As a suspected limitation of panels, sensitization to the study objectives is probably exaggerated. In the case of the Forest Service camper panel, increasingly large numbers of campers were reporting that they were dissatisfied with conditions and planned to drop out of the market. Sensitization was suspected; however, in comparing panel responses with those of a national market survey conducted during the eighth year of the panel's existence, there were no significant differences in camper attitudes or participation patterns between panel members and nonmembers.

If sensitization is the most overrated source of bias in panel studies, selective dropout is probably the most underrated. Panel mortality is often related to the factors under study. Camper panel members would sometimes report that they had lost interest in camping and would no longer be responding. In assuming that their contribution to the panel was now unimportant, they seriously compromised the panel's potentially most significant findings regarding the nature and duration of market dropout. Similarly, those panelists who are most interested and involved are also more likely to be panel losses simply because they may be too busy to participate. In a panel of travelers, these may be the most important and most difficult panel members to retain.

While incentives and compensation may help to avoid potential panel losses, they are likely to do so not because of value received but because that value convinces them that their contribution is important. Stressing that importance, for example, with telephone follow-ups to nonrespondents, is probably the single most important guideline for panel maintenance.

Panels are clearly useful devices for travel and tourism research, both for long-term trend monitoring and short-term experimental testing. Long-term panels require considerable maintenance effort on the part of the researcher and are subject to a variety of sources of error from selective mortality, nonresponse, panel conditioning, initial selection bias, and underreporting. The potential effects of these errors on the survey results must be carefully considered in deciding whether to use panels or population resurveys. Despite the problems associated with them, panels are an effective and efficient way of developing indicators of change. There are many instances where consistency of bias is a reasonable trade-off for representivity, particularly when complete sampling frames are nonexistent, making representivity an impossible objective.

DESIGN AND MAINTENANCE OF PANELS

Panels are a powerful technique for understanding the process of social change and should be designed to take maximum advantage of that power. If only the volume of change and its mathematical time-series description are obtained, the panel approach would be underutilized and probably inappropriate. In designing panel studies it is essential to consider (1) the kinds of changes that may be taking place, (2) the measurement units of change that are appropriate to describe that change, (3) the period of time that is realistic to expect the change to occur, and (4) the natural variation that exists within the population. For example, a panel designed to monitor changing leisure travel patterns must consider, at a minimum:

1 Kinds of Changes
   a. Increasing, decreasing, or constant travel levels.
   b. Longer or shorter trips.
   c. Shifting modes of travel.
   d. Expanding or shrinking range of destinations.
   e. More business and vacation combinations.
   f. Greater use of travel agents and information services.

2 Measurement Units
   a. Trips, days in travel, dollars spent, and number of destinations.
   b. Total miles traveled, average miles per trip, and states or countries visited.
   c. Incidence and frequency of travel by auto (owned or rented), plane, ship, train, or bus, organized tours, and types of accommodations.
   d. Number, types, and distances of destinations considered/visited per time unit.
   e. Frequency of personal/household trips per time unit. Conventions/convention centers visited. Use of time while away from home.
   f. Incidence, frequency, and nature of contacts with travel bureaus, tourism promotional offices, etc. Travel mailings (information units) received/requested.

3 Change Factors
   a. Personal influences such as financial, family, occupational, and residential limitations.
   b. Opportunity influences, such as improved residential location, availability of business trips, and personal invitations to visit or use another's facilities.
   c. Social influences, such as the travel experiences of friends and relatives.
   d. Informational/incentive influences, such as specialized media exposure and the availability of free or low-cost travel and/or accommodations.

4 Time Periods
   a. Are there normal cycles involved in personal travel, such as a major trip in alternate years?
   b. To what extent do annual business cycles (conventions, etc.) affect personal travel patterns?
   c. Are there seasonal cycles at work: spring fishing, summer camping, fall hunting, winter skiing?
   d. What is a realistic recall period for the type of data being collected: daily exposure to promotional materials; weekly participation in recreation travel; monthly purchases of travel magazines and travel-related clothing/equipment; annual vacations; biennial foreign travel?

5 Normal Variation
   a. How much variation around a long-term trend line is normal? How many units of difference produce a significant increase or decrease?
   b. How many consecutive time periods of declin-

ing travel are necessary to conclude that a real decline exists?

c. What shifts, alterations, and substitutions occur that may tend to obscure or exaggerate a real trend?

Obviously, not all of the above questions can be answered in advance; if they could, research might be unnecessary. To the extent that the researcher designs his panel procedures around such questions, his analysis will be easier and his conclusions more defensible. Suggestions for the analysis of panel data are provided in a number of references cited at the end of this chapter (Ahl 1970; Carman 1974; Hyett and McKenzie 1976; Parfitt and Collins 1968).

Ignoring any one of the four "M's" of panel design—methods, measures, meaning, and maintenance (La-Page 1979) will clearly compromise the panel's utility. Problems of panel maintenance are most likely to be overlooked. Panels are somewhat more difficult to establish than normal population surveys. Special populations lists, e.g., travelers, may not exist, and will have to be developed through a screening phase of a general population survey. The recurring nature of the panel needs to be carefully explained to prospective panelists—and even then many will agree to cooperate without realizing what is involved, or will agree with little or no commitment to actually cooperate. Incentives to encourage cooperation commonly used include commemorative stamps, coins, raffles, samples, discounts, free information, and monetary compensation.

Since much is usually known about panel members' backgrounds, it is often possible to develop a sense of panel cohesiveness and loyalty by the use of occasional newsletters, birthday cards, "anniversary" specials, and other discount offers. If the panel is supplying information that is potentially critical to the success of corporate decisions, a commitment to invest in that panel is appropriate.

SUMMARY AND CONCLUSION

Panels are neither inexpensive nor an alternative way of engaging in longitudinal research on changing behavior patterns of large populations. They are an extremely potent means for understanding social change, for test marketing new services and products, for assessing the impact of unforeseen events, and for short-term forecasting. However, these are their uses, not their "advantages," and no one panel could logically be used to monitor naturally occurring changes, to react to experimentally induced changes, or to provide in-depth understanding of the factors producing changes.

Initiation of panel research requires a substantial commitment on the part of the researcher. Maintenance of a panel's representivity and response rates requires careful planning and often a substantial investment in time and incentives. Analysis of panel data requires an exceptional degree of advance planning and study design—particularly if the panel is to be used for explanatory or experimental purposes.

Despite the costs, complexity, and commitment associated with panels, they are distinctly appropriate to the problems of travel, tourism, and leisure research. The magnitude of change in people's leisure behavior patterns, and their receptivity to new leisure opportunities, appears to be far greater than would be true for household purchases—a field where panel research has been most conspicuous.

Panels of repeat visitors to popular tourist attractions could provide a sensitive measure of trends in the quality of service and its impacts on visit length and repeat visitation. Panels of purchasers of expensive hunting and fishing equipment could be used for test marketing of remote sporting lodges. Panels of motor home buyers could provide a sensitive monitor of new features that prospective buyers are looking for. A panel of former visitors to Spirit Lake Lodge at Mt. Saint Helens could have provided unique information on the dispersal of clientele when their favorite vacation spot is no longer available. And panels of campground owners could provide immediate feedback on the impacts of gasoline shortages and price increases. The monitoring, standby, marketing, and forecasting opportunities for travel and tourism research are limitless, and because of the relatively large changes that are possible in discretionary leisure spending, there is a distinct opportunity for travel and tourism panels to make a major contribution to our understanding of the processes of social change.

REFERENCES

Ahl, D.H. (1970), "New Product Forecasting Using Consumer Panels," *Journal of Marketing Research*, 12 (May), 160–167.

Carman, J.M. (1974), "Consumer Panels," in *Handbook of Marketing Research*, Robert Ferber, Ed., New York: McGraw–Hill.

Hyett, G.P., and J.R. McKenzie (1976), "Effect of Underreporting by Consumer Panels on Level of Trial and Repeat Purchasing of New Products," *Journal of Marketing Research*, 13, 80–86.

Goeldner, C.R., and Ted Farwell (1980), *Economic Analysis of North American Ski Areas 1979–80 Season*, Boulder, Colorado: University of Colorado, Graduate School of Business Administration.

LaPage, W.F., and D.P. Ragain (1974), "Family Camping Trends—An Eight Year Panel Study," *Journal of Lei-*

sure Research, 6 (Spring), 101–112.

LaPage, W.F. (1979), "Research Problems in Monitoring Recreation Trends," in *Dispersed Recreation and Natural Resource Management Symposium Proceedings*, Joan Shaw, Ed., Logan, Utah: Utah State University, College of Natural Resources.

Moeller, G.H. (1975), "Identifying Leisure Behavior Patterns of Onondaga County Adult Residents," Ph.D. Thesis, Syracuse, State University of New York.

National Campground Owner's Association (1981), *American Campground Industry 1979 Economic Analysis and 1980 Occupancy Data*, Washington, D.C.: NCOA.

Parfitt, J.H., and B.J.K. Collins (1968), "Use of Consumer Panels for Brand Share Prediction," *Journal of Marketing Research*, May, 131–145.

Shafer, E.L., G.H. Moeller, and R.E. Getty (1974), *Future Leisure Environments*, Broomall, Pennsylvania: USDA Forest Service.

36

Qualitative Research Methods for the Travel and Tourism Industry

KAREN IDA PETERSON

Davidson-Peterson Associates Inc.
New York, New York

*T*he methods of qualitative, exploratory, and developmental research widely used in the general marketing world are today underutilized in travel and tourism marketing research. There are steps in the marketing research process for travel and tourism for which qualitative research methods are uniquely suited. The purpose of this chapter is to review five basic questions: What is qualitative research? What purposes does it serve? What are its limitations? What are the techniques of qualitative research? What is good qualitative research?

WHAT IS QUALITATIVE RESEARCH?

Qualitative research is the foundation on which strong, reliable research programs are based. It is most often the first step in a research program—the step designed to uncover motivations, reasons, impressions, perceptions, and ideas which relevant individuals have about a subject of interest. Unlike more quantitative methods of research, qualitative research involves talking in depth and detail with a few individuals. The goal is to develop extensive information from a few people.

With the quantitative types of research, the goal is to develop important—but limited—information from each individual and to talk with a sizable number of individuals in order to draw inferences about the population at large. The characteristics of qualitative research on the other hand include small samples, extensive information from each respondent, and a search for meaning, ideas, and relevant issues to quantify in later steps of the research program.

WHAT PURPOSES DOES QUALITATIVE RESEARCH SERVE?

Qualitative research is used to address a number of different types of objectives in the research process.

Some are purposes related to using qualitative research as the first step in a research program.

TO DEVELOP HYPOTHESES CONCERNING RELEVANT BEHAVIOR OR ATTITUDES

Qualitative research is used very often to generate hypotheses to suggest solutions to marketing problems when a travel researcher is faced with a marketing problem such as: Why are my rooms not full? Why has occupancy in this resort been declining over the past two years? What are the primary reasons for visiting my destination area? These questions may trigger the decision to do a research project. The travel marketer may well have some hypotheses, some possible answers. However, before proceeding to do major quantitative work to address those hypotheses, the researcher may suggest doing some qualitative work to search for additional hypotheses and new consumer-based ideas as to why the change has occurred.

TO IDENTIFY THE FULL RANGE OF ISSUES, VIEWS, AND ATTITUDES WHICH SHOULD BE PURSUED

Qualitative research serves often to broaden the researcher's views and to uncover issues and topics which should be considered in quantitative evaluations. Since the small samples used in qualitative research are in no way projectable to the population at large, an idea expressed by one individual may be critically important to the success of the final study. Thus, the purpose of the qualitative work is to explore the full range of views, developing the range of issues which need to be addressed in the final study.

TO SUGGEST METHODS FOR QUANTITATIVE INQUIRY

Qualitative research can also direct the methodological decisions which will be made for quantitative studies. For example, if in-depth conversations with travelers suggest the importance of the role of the travel agent in a particular decision, the research design might be adjusted to include a sample of travel agents where none had been planned. Or in-depth discussions may indicate that a new product is so difficult to understand that the study to project market size cannot be done on the telephone but rather must use a personal interview. Or if in individual discussions those who have taken a particular vacation trip find it extremely difficult to reconstruct the decision process they went through prior to taking that particular trip, it may be necessary to interview decision-makers for the confirmatory study during the time period after the decision is made but before the trip has been taken. All such inputs from qualitative research guide the selection of specific quantitative methods.

TO IDENTIFY LANGUAGE USED TO ADDRESS RELEVANT ISSUES

In the travel industry, the specific language used by operators, travel agents, and travelers to describe the same phenomenon is quite different. One cannot talk with a travel agent using the traveler's language and vice versa. Thus, qualitative research is an important way of learning just how the relevant groups talk about the issues, what language they use to describe their understanding of the topics.

TO UNDERSTAND HOW A BUYING DECISION IS MADE

In any marketing task, one of the key issues is how to influence a competitive buying decision. Unless the marketer understands how the buyer makes the decision, he is unlikely to be able to influence that decision. Thus, qualitative research contributes through understanding in depth and detail what steps are undertaken, allowing the marketer to quantify that process and direct his strategies toward influencing a particular segment of the market.

To this point we have seen the purposes of qualitative work as a first step in the research process. In those situations the qualitative work is generating issues, attitudes, language, and hypotheses for later confirmation, rejection, or use in quantitative survey methods.

In addition, however, qualitative research methods may be used to guide the marketing efforts for a company or destination in the travel industry. The purposes which qualitative research can fill in this area include:

TO DEVELOP NEW PRODUCT, SERVICE, OR MARKETING STRATEGY IDEAS

For a travel-related company anxious to broaden its market share or enter new fields, qualitative research can contribute importantly to developing new products or services which the company might consider. Even in qualitative research, however, no consumer or travel trade professional can create the new product alone. What needs to be done is to explore in-depth problems, dissatisfactions, dreams, wishes, concerns, etc. Then, the analyst can create new product/service opportunities based on expressed consumer needs.

TO PROVIDE AN INITIAL SCREENING OF NEW PRODUCT, SERVICE, OR STRATEGY IDEAS

Once new product/service ideas are developed, qualitative research is often used to explore the strengths and weaknesses of alternate ideas, to cull out those which offer the least opportunity, and to suggest which ought to be developed further or pursued in further quantitative assessments. Qualitative research should NOT be used to select the single alternate which will be marketed, but rather to eliminate the least interesting and suggest a group of ideas or concepts which should be subjected to further modification and evaluation.

TO LEARN HOW COMMUNICATIONS ARE RECEIVED—WHAT IS UNDERSTOOD AND HOW

Qualitative research is used extensively in the development of advertising strategies and approaches in learning what messages intended recipients take from proposed advertising in order to suggest how wordings and approaches might be improved. Again, however, qualitative research should NOT be used to judge which of several alternatives is best, but rather to explore what each communicates. In addition, qualitative research can shed no light on the intrusiveness of advertising, its attention-getting values, etc. Qualitative research makes its contribution in what the advertising or promotional material communicates, not in whether it will gain attention from the intended audience.

Clearly, then, there are a number of specific purposes which may be addressed by qualitative research in the travel and tourism market.

WHAT ARE THE LIMITATIONS OF QUALITATIVE RESEARCH?

The findings from a qualitative research effort must usually be regarded as informed hypotheses, not as proven facts. The samples which are used are quite small, and usually selected in a purposive rather than a probability sampling procedure. Thus, the inferences which are made based on qualitative research are normally subjected to evaluation using quantitative procedures. Hypotheses, issues, ideas for new product/ services, or communications strategies need to be confirmed on more reliable samples before major decisions are made on the basis of qualitative research.

In addition, qualitative findings may be limited by the skill, experience, and understanding of the individual gathering the information. Thus, the skill of a group session moderator to draw out all participants, to reduce domination by some members of the group, and to develop sufficient rapport to gain truthful information from participants must be assessed in judging the value of a group session study. Additionally, when individual interviews are used in a qualitative research effort, the interviewers asking the questions and probing responses may also influence responses and perhaps bias the results. A number of interviewers each doing a small number of interviews helps to control for this potential bias.

WHAT ARE THE TECHNIQUES OF QUALITATIVE RESEARCH?

Two basic methods of data collection are used in qualitative research: the individual interview and the focused group discussion. Let's look at the advantages and limitations of each.

FOCUSED GROUP DISCUSSIONS

In a focused group discussion, eight to ten relevant individuals are gathered together to discuss a topic under the leadership of a trained moderator. One key benefit of this approach is the interaction among respondents. Each individual is free to argue, disagree, question, and discuss the issues with others in the room. Thus, the group session becomes most useful when exploring a broad range of attitudes and views, when searching for a variety of responses, and when interaction is a plus for the study.

Additionally, group sessions in most locations can be done in professional facilities with one-way mirrors and sound systems so that the discussion can be observed by others. So, if observation by one or more members of the management or research team is desirable, focused groups discussions would be suggested. Care must be taken, however, to ensure that hearing a few customers discuss a topic does not lead management to make premature decisions on the subject.

On the liability side, the major drawback to using groups in the qualitative research process is that despite the efforts of a trained moderator, some individuals may dominate the discussion, leaving open to question whether the views obtained are biased or prejudiced in any way because of the group dynamics or the group "leader." Concern with biasing of this type is most important in studies designed to screen out products/services which offer limited opportunities for development. In cases where the goal is to develop a range of views or attitudes, the problem is not so serious, though it may mean that one or more groups have been less productive than would have been hoped.

INDIVIDUAL INTERVIEWS

Individual interviews are used most often in qualitative research when the interaction of a group is not desirable, when the goal of the research effort is to understand a process or an event in which each individual must talk at length about how he or she went about doing something. For example, individual interviews are particularly useful in travel research when the goal is to understand how travelers go about making a decision to take one vacation trip versus another. To gather that information, it is necessary to delve into each person's decision process at length—to learn where the idea originated, what information was gathered, who was consulted, whose views were sought out, and, finally, what led the individual to make a choice for one opportunity and to reject the others.

Where this type of information is sought from each individual, the group process breaks down. It is reasonably boring and uninteresting for each participant in a group session to sit and listen to the process another went through. Interaction is of little importance in these types of studies and therefore groups are replaced with a series of individual interviews.

On the limitation side, individual interviews require that a reasonably careful topic guide be written prior to the start of the interviewing. Since a number of interviewers will conduct the interviews, the process has to be reasonably well defined prior to the start of interviewing.

Each interviewer uses the general questions posed and probes with his or her own additional questions to gather more meaning. Thus, with a number of interviewers, the probing questions may differ, and each may get slightly different information. In a qualitative study, such variations are often beneficial since they bring to light a broad range of views and insights.

In comparison with groups, it is much more difficult for interested marketers and researchers to observe such individual interviews, and these interviews can frequently be quite costly. Interviewers must be specifically trained to conduct these types of interviews and that training cannot be amortized over too many interviews since each interviewer does only a small number.

WHAT MAKES GOOD QUALITATIVE RESEARCH STUDIES?

The criteria for successful qualitative research differs somewhat for focused group discussions and for individual interviews. Let's look at some of the key elements in the assessment of each type of qualitative research.

FOCUSED GROUP DISCUSSIONS

Several steps are key to having a successful focused group discussion:

First, all respondents must be relevant to the topic under discussion. It is critical that prospective participants be selected using a screening questionnaire which establishes their relevance to the topic. For example, should the study be designed to understand the full range of attitudes toward and impressions of a destination area, it is likely that all participants should have visited that area in the recent past.

To the extent possible, the screening questionnaire should be "blind"—that is, the respondent should not be able to detect just exactly who is sponsoring the study, what behavior is being explored, and what attitudes will be sought. Naturally, it will be clear to respondents that the concern is with travel, but the specific destination or property should not be easily identifiable by the respondent during the screening process.

Additionally, anyone with special knowledge of or interest in the topic or the technique should be excluded. Those involved in advertising, market research, or any aspect of travel should not qualify as participants in a traveler group. Similarly, those who have participated in a group session or been interviewed individually in the past six months should be eliminated.

Second, to permit good information exchanges, good interaction and a lively discussion, all participants must feel comfortable presenting their views during the discussion. People are simply more comfortable discussing topics with "their own kind." Thus, one goal should be to do separate groups in most cases, with younger and older people, with white collar and blue collar families, with experienced international travelers and inexperienced ones, etc. Such homogeneity is important in establishing psychological comfort for the respondents. This psychological comfort can be achieved with people of different demographic backgrounds if they have shared similar experiences recently which are relevant to the subject of interest to the researcher.

In designing a focused group discussion study, one group session with any population subgroup is seldom, if ever, sufficient. While a second session with the same subgroup may not be identical in content, if there are signs of consistency and commonality, we can confirm that neither is truly aberrant or deviant and thus be comfortable with inferences from the groups. In addition, should there be a need to conduct more than eight or ten groups (four or five different population groups) then it would appear that another, perhaps more quantitative research approach should be used. Upon completion of a group discussion study, the researcher still has only informed hypotheses, judgments, and ideas—not confirmed facts. Thus, spending time and dollars to conduct more than eight or ten focused groups and still not having facts on which to base a marketing decision is usually wasteful.

Third, the role of the moderator is critical in producing a good focused group discussion. The moderator is a director, but also a facilitator. He or she must develop rapport with the group participants, help them to relax and speak freely with each other, draw out the reluctant contributors, and keep natural leaders from dominating the conversation. The moderator's job is also to guide the discussion so that all important topics are covered, and to probe and question (usually in a nonthreatening manner) to elicit the broadest range of information and views.

The moderator's topic guide should be thoroughly and completely worked out prior to the beginning of the session. The outline of questions should include the researcher's best thinking on the topics which must be addressed and the likely order in which they will emerge during the discussion.

The moderator, however, must be fully cognizant of the goals and objectives of the research, knowing which topic areas are most critical to cover in-depth and which could be treated more lightly. In addition, the moderator must be sensitive to the emergence of unexpected information, ideas not anticipated at all by the research team, and decide if and how to pursue those issues. One of the benefits of focused group research is that the moderator is free to gather new ideas, pursue new directions, and achieve new insights during the course of the session itself.

Fourth, the physical comfort of respondents in the group discussion period should be of primary concern. Comfortable chairs and a well-ventilated room at the appropriate temperature are often as important in setting the tone of the session as are proper recruiting procedures and a good moderator. When appropriate, serving light refreshments also contributes to the development of the relaxed and informal atmosphere which is essential. Since most group discussions will last from an hour and a half to just over two hours, respondents need to be comfortable physically as well as psychologically.

Finally, the analysis and interpretation of the focused group sessions contribute importantly to the assessment of a successful study. The way in which the findings are approached and interpreted depends, of course, on the purpose for which the study was designed. Thus, it is not possible to suggest rules of interpretation which would apply to all analyses.

In reviewing the report on a focused group session study, however, the researcher/marketer should probably note whether the objectives have been addressed, whether the analysis covers the broad range of issues and ideas which emerged in the discussions, whether generalizations and conclusions are based soundly on the session input, etc. The key assessment criteria should probably be: How useful are the results? How well do they guide and inform further steps in the research and development process?

INDIVIDUAL INTERVIEWS

In designing a qualitative study which includes individual interviews, several steps are important to a successful study.

First, as with groups, the participants need to be carefully selected so as to be relevant to the problem under study. For example, should the issue be learning about the vacation decision process, then all participants should have taken the appropriate vacation, been involved in the decision process, and should have done so recently enough to remember the steps they went through.

The screening questionnaire designed to identify these individuals should be carefully constructed to find only appropriate individuals and to eliminate those who could contribute only marginally to the study objectives. When only a few interviews will be conducted (15 to 30 is often an appropriate sample size), it is clearly critically important that each one contribute to the overall study goal.

Additionally, since studies in which qualitative research is accomplished through individual interviews usually seek to gain an understanding of behavior or decision making from a variety of points of view, it is often important to include individuals with a variety of demographic characteristics to ensure that all population subgroups of importance are included in the qualitative research.

Second, the development of the interview guide is critically important. The careful assessment of all issues likely to arise in the conversation, ordering of topics into a likely sequence, and listing of possible probe questions are critical to the success of an individual interview qualitative project.

Third, the selection and thorough training of the interviewers who will conduct the interviews form a crucial step in the individual interview study. It is likely that the professional researcher who will ultimately analyze the responses to these interviews should conduct at least some of the interviews.

Interviewers being trained to conduct the interviews should observe the initial interview by professional researchers and be further trained in the goals and objectives of the project. They will need to ask additional questions and probes as they proceed through the interview as ideas emerge and are discussed.

Finally, interpreting the results of individual interviews is likely to be as varied as the purposes for which they were conducted. If the goal is to understand a decision process, then the results should include the variety of typologies which seem to occur in the process. If it is to understand motivations and reasons for particular behaviors, again the interpretation should include the array of ideas gathered from the individuals who are included in the study.

Again, however, the interpretation and analysis are best judged on the basis of how useful the findings and recommendations are to the study as it progresses.

The following series of questions may be used by a travel researcher/marketer in assessing the quality and effectiveness of qualitative research conducted. For the most part, the questions can be used for studies employing either focused group sessions or individual interviews.

- Are the objectives for the qualitative research clearly stated, appropriate for the techniques used, and targeted toward the marketing/research needs of the study?
- Is the number of groups and/or interviews appropriate for the problem? Are the population segments under study carefully delineated?
- Is the screening questionnaire tightly designed to eliminate all who will not be relevant to the project and all who might create bias?
- Does the moderator's guide/interview guide show clear and careful thinking about the issues to be explored and the logical flow of questioning?
- Is each group session conducted in facilities and with accoutrements which will generate both physical and psychological comfort for the respondents?
- Is the moderator/interviewer well versed in the goals and objectives of the study? Is he/she well trained and experienced in the professional skills required?
- Are the respondents comfortable, able to talk with each other, and the moderator without pretense?
- Are the topics of interest covered in sufficient depth and detail in each session/interview?
- Do the analysis and report reflect the full range of views expressed and generalize to the level of meaningful conclusions for further steps in the

research effort or the marketing strategy development?

- Are all elements of the qualitative research effort handled in a professional manner?

If a travel researcher/marketer can answer these questions in the affirmative, the qualitative research study should have contributed importantly to the solution of research and marketing problems.

BIBLIOGRAPHY

Axelrod, Myril D., "Marketers Get an Eyeful When Focus Groups Expose Products, Ideas, Images, Ad Copy, etc., to Consumers," *Marketing News*, (February 28, 1975), 6–7.

Axelrod, Myril D., "10 Essentials for Good Qualitative Research," *Marketing News*, (March 14, 1975), 10–11.

Bellenger, Danny N., Bernhardt, Kenneth L., and Goldstucker, Jac L., "Qualitative Research Techniques: Focus Group Interviews," (Chicago, Illinois: American Marketing Association, (1976), pp. 7–18.

Calder, Bobby J., "Focus Groups and the Nature of Qualitative Marketing Research," *Journal of Marketing Research*, Vol. 14, No. 3 (August 1977), 353–364.

Caruso, Thomas E., "Moderators Focus on Groups: Session Yields 7 Hypotheses Covering Technology Trend, Professionalism, Training, Techniques, Reports, etc.,"
Marketing News, (September 10, 1976), 12–18.

Dichter, Ernest, "Depth Interviewing," in *Handbook of Consumer Motivations* (New York: McGraw–Hill Book Co., 1964), pp. 413–417.

Goldman, Alfred E., "The Group Depth Interview," *Journal of Marketing*, Vol. 26, No. 3 (July 1962), 61–68.

Hess, John M., "Group Interviewing," in Robert L. King (Ed.), *1968 ACR Fall Conference Proceedings* (Chicago, Illinois: American Marketing Association, 1968), pp. 193–196.

Merton, Robert K., Fiske, Marjorie, and Kendall, Patricia, "The Group Interview," in *The Focused Interview* (Glencoe, Illinois: The Free Press, 1956).

Payne, Melanie S., "Preparing for Group Interview," in Beverlee Anderson (Ed.), *Advances in Consumer Research* (Ann Arbor, Michigan: University of Michigan, 1976), pp. 434–436.

Sampson, Peter, "Qualitative Research and Motivation Research," in Robert M. Worchester (Ed.), *Consumer Market Research Handbook* (Maidenhead, England: McGraw–Hill Book Co. (U.K.), Ltd., 1972), pp. 7–27.

Smith, Joan Macfarlane, "Group Discussions," in *Interviewing in Market and Social Research* (London and Boston: Routledge and Kegan Paul, 1972).

Walters, J. Hart, "Structured or Unstructured Techniques?," *Journal of Marketing*, (April 1961), 58–62.

Wells, William D., "Group Interviewing," in Robert Ferber (Ed.), *Handbook of Marketing Research* (New York: McGraw–Hill Book Co., 1974), pp. 133–146.

37

The Nominal Group Technique— Applications in Tourism Research[1]

J.R. BRENT RITCHIE
The University of Calgary
Calgary, Alberta, Canada

*T*his chapter introduces tourism researchers and policymakers to a group planning and research process which has achieved considerable recognition in other fields while being largely ignored in tourism. This procedure, termed the Nominal Group Technique (NGT), was originally developed by Delbecq, Van de Ven, and Gustafson (1975) as an organizational planning technique. Although the developers indicated that NGT may be useful in a wide variety of planning tasks, no applications were found in relation to tourism. Accordingly, this chapter describes the use of NGT as a tool for consensus planning at the regional level with a view to demonstrating its strengths as a research procedure within this and other areas of tourism.

The discussion that follows is divided into five major sections. The first section describes the nominal group technique (NGT) as it is normally employed. This general discussion is followed by a description of the manner in which the method was applied in the case of consensus planning by the Tourism Industry Association of Alberta (TIAALTA). The third section focuses on issues of data analysis peculiar to this type of research. Subsequently, a discussion is presented concerning the potential applications of NGT in other areas of tourism research and planning. The final section provides an assessment of the relative strengths and weaknesses of NGT compared to other commonly used planning/research approaches.

NOMINAL GROUP TECHNIQUE

The NGT procedure, as used for program planning, is normally implemented in six stages. Participants are first presented by the session moderator with an initial statement of the topic area to be discussed. For example, top management of a corporation might be asked to indicate what directions future diversification would take. Once it is clear that participants understand the issue, further discussion is halted.

Participants are then directed to reflect individually on the topic and to record their personal responses on a worksheet containing a written statement of the issue being addressed. This period of individual reflection and recording of responses usually lasts from 5 to 20 minutes, depending on the complexity of the topic under discussion.

The group moderator subsequently asks a participant, chosen at random, to state one of the responses he or she has arrived at individually. This response is written in a concise yet complete manner on a large flipchart. At this point, the participant is allowed to explain his/her response briefly, so that its meaning is clear to other participants. This process is repeated in round-robin fashion until all participants have had a chance to express a response. Second and third rounds may follow, depending on the number of ideas identified by members. Participants are allowed, and even encouraged, to express additional ideas that have been stimulated by the remarks of others.

[1]Material in this chapter was originally published in *Tourism Management*, Vol. 6, No. 2, 1985. Permission to reprint is gratefully acknowledged.

439

The next stage involves consolidation and review of the complete set of ideas. At this point all flipchart sheets are posted so that all responses are visible. The moderator reviews the responses recorded on the flipcharts to eliminate duplications and to ensure that all responses are clearly understood by participants. Each response is then assigned an identifier code, such as a letter of the alphabet.

Participants are subsequently requested to establish the relative importance that should be accorded to each of the response ideas. This importance may reflect, for example, the desirability of a given idea for corporate diversification. Although various approaches may be employed to establish the importance of each response (Delbecq *et al*., 1975), a commonly used method is to instruct each individual to first select a certain number of responses (e.g., eight)[2] that he considers to be most important. The participant then writes each of these responses on a 3-×-5 card along with the alphabetic identifier, and is asked to rank the eight responses in terms of their relative order of importance.

The final stage is compilation of the results. In this stage, the rankings accorded to the various ideas by each participant are aggregated to provide a measure of overall importance. As per the Delphi technique (Linstone and Turoff, 1975), these results may be presented to participants and a second round of ranking undertaken to permit individuals to adjust their judgments in the light of the earlier evaluations. However, this round is not essential unless the initial judgments were highly variable or the purpose is to achieve a reasonable level of group consensus.

To summarize, the NGT process is a systematic approach designed to provide two specific types of output. First, it provides a list of ideas relevant to the topic in question. Second, the technique provides quantified individual and aggregate measures of the relative desirability of the ideas raised in the session.

AN APPLICATION OF NGT TO TOURISM RESEARCH AND PLANNING

THE RESEARCH/PLANNING CONTEXT

The private sector of the tourism industry in the province of Alberta, Canada, is composed of a broad range of firms and organizations dispersed geographically throughout the region. While each of these firms and organizations has its own goals, they all share in and benefit from one common objective—the growth and development of tourism to and within Alberta.

For the growth and development of tourism in the province to be successful, it is essential that the efforts

of the private sector be complemented by the activities of government. Indeed, the partnership which exists between the public and private sectors is an important characteristic of tourism in Alberta and in Canada as a whole. As in any such relation, it is important that each partner fulfills its role effectively and contributes equitably to the partnership.

From an operational standpoint, the public/private sector partnership roles in tourism at the provincial level in Alberta are formally carried out respectively by Travel Alberta and the Tourism Industry Association of Alberta (TIAALTA). In the past, this partnership has functioned reasonably well. However, several trends have indicated that significant modifications to the management of provincial tourism may be required to meet the challenges of the future. These trends include:

- A stabilization, and even a decline in tourism to Canada and to Alberta. Among the reasons for this situation is a dramatic increase in competition from other international destinations.

- A movement towards increased privatization of numerous functions previously carried out by governments in response to growing pressures on public expenditures.

- A recognition of the need to develop and expand the tourism industry in the province as part of an overall industrial strategy aimed at providing a broader range of employment opportunities for Albertans (Government of Alberta, 1984).

As a result of these trends and other factors, TIAALTA concluded in 1983 that the private sector in Alberta must accept a greater role in developing and managing tourism in the province. To do this, however, it was essential that the Association formulate a coherent statement of its views concerning the directions which tourism development in the province should take. While it was recognized that the size and diversity of the private sector would never permit the preparation of the type of unanimous report that is possible from a government agency, TIAALTA saw the need to develop a consensus of its members' views which would serve to focus Association efforts and to prioritize its actions. It was with this need in mind that TIAALTA undertook a three-phase program designed to set out the views of the private sector concerning provincial tourism development and promotion. The contents of each phase were defined as follows:

- Phase I: Definition of priority issues and problems facing tourism in the province.

- Phase II: Identification of initiatives, actions, and programs to deal with the priority issues and problems facing Alberta tourism.

---

[2]Delbecq *et al*. (1975) suggest having respondents select and rate 7 ± 2 preferred ideas.

- Phase III: Monitoring of recommendations concerning initiatives, actions, and programs for tourism development to ensure timely and effective implementation.

This chapter describes Phase I of the program, which undertook to identify those issues and problems that private operators view as most seriously affecting the future development of tourism in the province (TIAALTA, 1984). The process involved, which is discussed below, was one in which an overall consensus was derived from inputs obtained from the many tourism regions (zones) and industry sector associations which constitute TIAALTA.

In Phase II of the program, TIAALTA is undertaking to identify solutions to the most serious issues facing the industry, to determine how those solutions can be most effectively implemented, and to define what individual group or organization should assume responsibility for solution implementation.

Finally, in Phase III of the program, TIAALTA seeks to establish a process to assist in monitoring the degree of progress and the level of success in relation to its recommendations for actions and programs to further develop tourism in Alberta. The intent here is to actively work with government to ensure timely and effective implementation of those initiatives judged most critical to the success of tourism in the province.

SPECIFIC OBJECTIVES OF PHASE I

While the objectives of Phase I of the study are implied in the foregoing discussion, they may be explicitly stated as follows:

1 To identify the most significant issues, problems, and concerns currently facing the development of Alberta tourism
   (a) at the provincial level
   (b) within the various zones
   (c) within various industry sectors.
2 To establish the relative priority which members of TIAALTA attach to the seriousness of the issues, problems, and concerns identified above.

STUDY PARTICIPANTS

Participants in the study were drawn from among members of the Boards of Directors of the Zone and Industry Sector associations which make up TIAALTA. A total of 16 sessions were conducted during the period June 1983 to June 1984. Of this total, 11 sessions involved zone organizations and 5 sessions obtained inputs from industry sector associations. The size of the groups ranged from a minimum of 6 to a maximum of 19 with the average number of participants per session being between 9 and 10. As such,

data for the study were obtained from a total of 153 active leaders from the private sector of tourism in Alberta.

DATA BASE

The raw data obtained from each NGT session were of three types:

- A list of problems, concerns, and issues facing Alberta tourism as identified by session participants.
- A list of the problems, concerns, and issues facing tourism within the zone or industry sector as identified by session participants.
- A selection and ranking by each participant of the ten problems/issues/concerns that he/she judged to be most significant at both the provincial and zone/industry sector level.

As might be anticipated, the number, the nature, and the wording of the concerns emanating from each of the 16 sessions varied across the different NGT groups. The number of provincial issues identified per session ranged from a minimum of 12 to a maximum of 29, with the average being 18 (for a total of 288 issues). An example of actual problem statements resulting from an individual session are given in Table 1. For present purposes, the detailed analysis reported below focuses only on data related to the 288 provincial tourism issues.

ANALYSIS OF NGT DATA

Analysis of data obtained from the NGT process involves a combination of qualitative and quantitative procedures requiring four basic steps:

- Categorization of initial problem statements into problem themes.
- Regrouping of problem themes within a conceptual model to form major problem dimensions.
- Calculation of a score or index reflecting the importance of each problem theme.
- Ranking of problem themes according to their importance index.

IDENTIFICATION AND CLASSIFICATION OF PROBLEM THEMES

The purpose of the first step was to identify ideas or themes that were common across the statements obtained from each of the group sessions. These themes were subsequently regrouped according to a framework describing major managerial functions in tourism. The framework employed in this case corresponded to the various areas of functional responsibility within TIAALTA.

TABLE 1   Example of Provincial Problems/Issues Resulting from a Zone Session

---

A   Provincial campsites are too small and overcrowded.

B   Government regulations, e.g., Sunday liquor laws.

C   Government red tape discourages development.

D   Less than desirable quality of hospitality by front line staff.

E   Need for higher wages/more qualified people for interpretive staff in provincial parks.

F   Need for business in general to understand the importance of the tourism industry.

G   Difficulties in identifying the most important market targets.

H   Lack of liaison and continuity among zones—need for more exchange of information.

I   Shortage of professionally trained people in the tourism industry—need for additional educational programs and greater industry input to programs.

J   Better signage on highways for facilities and attractions.

K   Need for more rest stops.

L   Need by public in general to understand financial impact of tourism on their communities.

M   Lack of key destination areas in the province—too much reliance on Banff. Need for "nonmajor" destination areas.

N   Too much competition between government and the private sector (e.g., golf courses, standards for campsites).

O   High level of taxation has made Alberta/Canada non-competitive with the United States.

It is useful at this point to note the difference between identifying problem themes and the subsequent classification of these themes according to the TIAALTA managerial framework of Fig. 1. The purpose in identifying themes is to aggregate across group sessions statements that express essentially the same idea, a process conceptually similar to content analysis (Holsti, 1969; Kassarjian, 1977). On the other hand, the classification according to the dimensions of the managerial framework is done with a view to provide a structure relating the themes, a process similar to taxonomic analysis (Green and Wind, 1973).

The foregoing analysis resulted in the identification of 35 problem themes which were subsequently classified within the four major components of the TIAALTA management model. Of this total, the majority of the themes identified from the problem statements of the private sector participants (13 of 35) were found to be related to tourism development issues. Nine themes concerned difficulties involving overall policy issues, while eight themes pertained to perceived shortcomings in the area of marketing and promotion. Finally, six themes addressing concerns in the area of human resource development were identified. The original report (TIAALTA, 1984) contains a detailed listing by management function of each of the 35 themes as well as the individual problem statements

falling under each of the themes. Table 2 provides a selected example of one problem theme and associated problem statements.

INDEX OF THEME IMPORTANCE

The index of theme importance which was developed was designed to reflect two different measures of importance, namely, the *frequency* with which a prob-

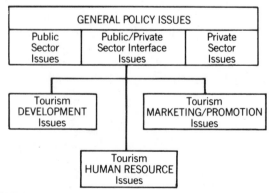

FIGURE 1   Structure of the managerial areas of responsibility within TIAALTA used as classification framework for problem themes.

TABLE 2   Human Resources

THEME: LACK OF EDUCATION AND TRAINING PROGRAMS NECESSARY TO IMPROVE PROFESSIONALISM
AND EFFECTIVENESS OF THE TOURISM INDUSTRY

11 mentions
$$3 \times 5 = 15$$
$$2 \times 3 = 6$$
$$2 \times 2 = 4$$
$$4 \times 1 = \underline{4}$$
Index of Theme Importance = 29

SESSION RANK	SESSION SCORE/ AVERAGE	PROBLEM/ISSUE	ZONE/ ASSOCIATION
3	51/9 = 5.7	Service industry staff not properly trained to handle public—need more educational programs.	Z7
3	49/10 = 4.9	Need for provincial subsidies to educational system to train people in hospitality industries (need to return some of the revenues).	AR/E
4	54/11 = 4.9	Shortage of professionally trained people in the tourism industry—need for additional educational programs and greater industry input to programs.	Z4
5	53/16 = 3.3	Lack of qualified private sector manpower to develop and sell tourism.	Z5
7	20/8 = 2.5	Lack of training/tourism studies program for province. No return business because of poor attitudes and service.	AHA
9	24/7 = 3.4	Need for improved training and educational facilities for industry at provincial level.	AR/C
11	30/13 = 2.3	Lack of education/training programs to raise quality of staff and service in industry.	Z9
12	25/11 = 2.3	Need for higher wages/more qualified people for interpretive staff in provincial parks.	Z4
13	19/10 = 1.9	Need for industry training programs for staff and management.	H
15	27/13 = 2.1	Tourism operators/businesses not sufficiently educated on how to deal with wholesalers.	Z9

EXHIBIT 1   Procedure for Developing Index of Theme Importance

Step 1: Session Score

Calculation of average importance ranking of each statement within total set of statements from a single session.

Step 2: Session Rank

Ranking of each statement within a session from most to least important as determined by session score.

Step 3: Statement Index Score

Assignment of points to the relevant theme in which a statement was classified according to the following scale:

Session Rank of 1– 4 . . . . . 5 points
5– 7 . . . . . 3 points
8–10 . . . . . 2 points
11 or more . . . . . 1 point

Step 4: Theme Index Score

Calculation of total points assigned to all problem statements with a given theme.

lem had been mentioned across the 16 sessions and the *priority* accorded to it when it was mentioned in a session. Thus, a theme which had been identified in most sessions and which had been ranked highly by most participants would receive a high index score; one mentioned frequently but considered less important, or mentioned less frequently but judged important by certain participants, would receive an intermediate index score; and, finally, a theme mentioned infrequently and accorded little importance would receive a low index score. In the present study, the Index of Importance for each theme was developed according to the procedure described in Exhibit 1 on the previous page.

RANKING AND PRIORITIZING OF THEME IMPORTANCE

Based on the Index of Theme Importance, it was possible to rank the 35 themes in order of perceived priority as rated by the entire sample. Because this overall ranking was somewhat too detailed for managerial purposes, the themes were further classified into two levels of priority. The classification was made after examining both the distribution of the Indices of Importance for all 35 themes and the characteristics of the themes judged most significant. This classification, which is partially summarized in Table 3, was carried out according to the following criteria:

- Priority 1: Includes 15 themes which identify the most serious problems currently facing tourism in Alberta. As seen from Table 3, each of these themes tended to address fundamental issues affecting virtually all aspects of provincial tourism. As such, it is these concerns which are the object of further in-depth review and study within Phase II and whose resolution provides the focus for TIAALTA's ongoing efforts.

- Priority 2: Involves the remaining 22 themes. These themes were identified as important but not as critical as those categorized as Priority 1. In general, these themes tended to involve more specific issues. Problems related to these themes will receive attention by TIAALTA to the extent that time and resources permit. In particular, an effort will be made to resolve a given problem in cases where an opportunity for substantial progress within a reasonable time frame appears possible.

OTHER APPLICATIONS OF NGT

The foregoing discussion has provided one detailed example of how NGT can be used as a consensus formulation tool at the initial or problem definition stage of the planning process. The potential tourism applications of NGT, however, go far beyond the single example described in this paper. These applications may be categorized as other planning situations and more general research uses.

OTHER PLANNING SITUATIONS

At least two other planning tasks lend themselves to the application of the nominal group technique. The first of these relates to *organizational goal setting*. In this context, the process serves first as a means of eliciting a set of statements defining the mission and the objectives of the organization. In the case of a private sector tourism operator, these goals would normally relate to the overall direction of the firm and the specific achievements it hopes to realize within a specific time frame. For a public sector organization, the process would normally involve attempting to specify the economic and social contributions it is hoped to achieve through tourism development. In both cases, once the organizational goals have been defined, the NGT process provides a mechanism for determining the relative priority which top management wishes to accord to the various goal statements which have been proposed.

A further area of application relates to the *identification and evaluation of alternative courses of action* for resolving a management issue. In this situation, NGT can first be used to generate a range of possible solutions to the problem or opportunity facing a management team, and then subsequently employed to rate the perceived effectiveness or desirability of the options generated. It is this approach which is relevant to Phase II of the present planning process. In this context, special task forces have been formed to identify initiatives, actions, and programs which might contribute to the resolution of the priority problems or issues which were defined in Phase I. The judgments of task force members concerning the desirability and feasibility of the ideas proposed will serve to determine which initiatives, actions, and programs will be endorsed by TIAALTA for implementation.

RESEARCH APPLICATIONS OF NGT

In addition to being employed as an internal tool for organizational planning, NGT can be very effectively employed in *consumer research* as an alternative means of data collection. In this regard, NGT provides a methodology which falls between unstructured focus group techniques and structured survey methods. Ex-

TABLE 3   Prioritization of Tourism Problem Themes—Priority 1

INDEX OF THEME IMPORTANCE	OVERALL RANKING	THEME DESCRIPTION	TIAALTA AREA OF RESPONSIBILITY
50	1	The high cost of travel in Alberta/Canada has crippled our ability to compete in tourism markets.	Development
46	2	The present structure for managing Alberta's tourism system does not involve the private sector adequately or early enough in the planning process. The result is a perceived lack of cooperation, coordination, and effectiveness.	Policy —Public/Private Interface
44	3	Despite some recent progress, governments are still perceived as failing to acknowledge the current or the potential importance of the tourism industry to the well-being of the province.	Policy—Public
42	4	Lack of appreciation on the part of supervisors and front line staff of the critical role that positive attitudes, hospitality, and quality service play in the success of the tourism industry—and a pressing need to rectify the situation.	Human Resources
37	5	Lack of adequate funding for the promotion of Alberta as a tourism destination.	Marketing/ Promotion
36	6	Government legislation, regulation, and bureaucracy are perceived as major deterrents to the successful development and functioning of the tourism industry in Alberta.	Policy—Public
32	7	Lack of adequate funding and funding mechanisms for tourism development.	Development
31	8	Need to substantially improve the level of cooperation, liaison, and communication among all tourism zones and industry sector associations.	Policy—Private
29	9	Lack of education and training programs necessary to improve the professionalism and effectiveness of the tourism industry.	Human Resources
29	9	Lack of public awareness of the importance and significance of tourism to the socioeconomic well-being of Alberta.	Human Resources
27	11	Ineffective and inappropriate expenditure of those funds which are available for the promotion of tourism to Alberta.	Marketing/ Promotion
27	11	Need to upgrade the quality of information, particularly road signage, available to visitors to Alberta.	Marketing/ Promotion
24	13	Need to develop additional facilities, attractions, events, and activities in the province so as to make Alberta a more viable and competitive tourism destination.	Development
24	13	Need for a greater degree of creativity and innovation in marketing and promotional efforts which will result in a well focused, recognized image/theme for Alberta as a tourism destination.	Marketing/ Promotion
20	15	Government is perceived as having access to a disproportionate share of tourism planning and development resources, thus placing the private sector in a disadvantaged position.	Policy —Public/Private Interface

amples of the kinds of consumer research that might be addressed by NGT would include:

- Studies to identify and establish the relative importance of factors which consumers view as critical in determining the quality of service in a hotel, a ski resort, or other tourism facility;
- Studies to identify and establish the relative importance of information sources used by consu-

mers when choosing among alternative types of tour packages;

- Studies to identify the dimensions which are important in defining the images of different countries as travel destinations.

By extension, it is seen that NGT can be adapted for use in the study of most research questions in which individuals are required to generate ideas and subsequently provide some rating of their relative desirability.

A second research application of NGT is an alternative to the Delphi technique (Linstone and Turoff, 1975) when attempting to obtain *expert consensus* on a given research topic. While the Delphi method is effective when respondents are geographically dispersed, it is somewhat cumbersome and time-consuming unless it can be conducted in an electronic format. In contrast, in situations where experts can be physically brought together, NGT provides a very effective data collection approach. Examples of potential applications in this area include:

- research to identify and determine the relative importance of factors influencing the choice of meeting and convention sites;
- research to examine how wholesalers assess the attractiveness of proposals submitted by different travel destinations and suppliers when assembling their tour packages;
- research to identify those regulations and laws which are most severely impacting on the success of private tourism operators.

Again, as in the case of consumer research, NGT is appropriate in situations where it is required to gather and structure information from a defined group of respondents who can be brought together for a limited period of time.

STRENGTHS AND WEAKNESSES OF NGT AS A PLANNING AND RESEARCH METHODOLOGY

To this point the discussion has described the nature of NGT and provided a number of examples of its use or potential uses. As for any methodology, however, NGT has its limitations. The remainder of this chapter will assess the relative strengths and weaknesses of NGT as a tool for tourism planning and research and will attempt to show where NGT fits relative to other data collection procedures.

Several strengths can be identified. First, although a group method, NGT provides structured output that can be analyzed at an individual level. The term nominal group technique is intended to suggest that the method is nominally viewed as group based, though for the most part the activities and output focus on individual efforts. The early stages of the process provide respondents with the opportunity to hear the views of others as they are thinking through the topic under discussion—similar to other group methods. On the other hand, the final stages require respondents to sort and rank the items generated in earlier stages.

Thus, the data output is more structured than is usual with group methods.

Second, the NGT process results in high respondent involvement and commitment. This commitment develops as respondents express their views to others in the group and realize that they are sharing in the identification of items to be evaluated. This advantage can be particularly useful when participants need time to think through their responses. This is not to imply that they are thinking up new ideas in a creative sense. Rather, when asked to recall behavioral experience, it is probable that respondents have had little experience identifying the various steps that were involved in the behavior. In other words, although the behavior of interest may be current or even habitual, the process of articulation requires time and commitment to recall the various components.

Third, the process of identifying and scoring problem themes, as developed in this application, makes it possible to study both intra- and intergroup differences.

The major disadvantage of NGT relates to sampling. Because participants have to agree to come to a central meeting location, attempts at probability sampling are met by a serious level of non-response, as discussed further in the following sections.

COMPARISON WITH FOCUS GROUP INTERVIEWS

A number of authors provide reviews of qualitative research methods (Bellenger, Bernhardt, and Goldstucker, 1976; Bogdan and Taylor, 1975; Higginbotham and Cox, 1979). One of the most insightful of these reviews has been presented by Calder (1977) in which he distinguishes among the exploratory, clinical, and phenomenological dimensions of qualitative research. Although NGT possesses some characteristics of each of these dimensions, it is perhaps closest to what Calder defines as exploratory research. As he points out, a major strength of exploratory methods is the ability to identify major issues or attributes associated with a particular research problem. However, there are several characteristics of standard focus groups that restrict this method to exploratory applications. First, the output of the session is relatively unstructured. Although the session can provide an extensive list of attributes, the process does not facilitate establishing attribute priorities. Second, a small subset of the participants may be outspoken and dominate or intimidate the rest of the group. Third, to minimize this potential domination and to ensure the desired depth of coverage, a highly trained session leader is required. Finally, the necessity to bring participants to a meeting room virtually precludes the use of probability sampling procedures. However, the quota sampling methods usually adopted are entirely consistent with the exploratory nature of the focus group process.

Nominal group technique shares with exploratory focus groups the facility for identifying issues relevant to target consumers, and also adds a number of other very useful features. First, in addition to providing an extensive listing of issues or attributes, NGT enables the researcher to identify priorities for each individual session participant. Second, an advantage of NGT is that the structuring and establishing of priorities makes it possible to analyze similarities and differences across multiple NGT sessions. Third, because of the procedural rules established at the outset of the session, the NGT session leader is able to ensure that all participants have an equal voice in the session. Fourth, the author's experience indicates that the added structure of NGT sessions simplifies the process of training session leaders. In other words, session leadership is somewhat less of an art than appears to be the case with focus group sessions. Despite these advantages, it must be remembered that NGT shares with focus groups the need to assemble participants in the meeting room, and hence the necessity to adopt quota sampling procedures.

COMPARISON WITH STRUCTURED SURVEY METHODS

Although NGT is not seen as a substitute for structured survey methods, it is useful to draw several contrasts. A summary of the major strengths of structured research methods would be: (1) ability to cover a large number and range of items, (2) use of probability sampling, and (3) structured output that facilitates analysis. The difficulties associated with these methods include problems inherent in establishing questions or items that are relevant to intended respondents and maintaining control of the interview setting. The former problem is handled by careful exploratory research and pretesting. However, despite methodical preliminary efforts, most researchers have experienced studies in which some aspect of the research problem has been undermeasured. The second problem mentioned, controlling the interview setting, is related to the use of a large number of interviewers. In a field situation, interviewers often feel a pressure to hurry the interview and, as a result, respondents are not encouraged to think out their answers. Further, as the questionnaire length increases, the interviewer has increasing difficulty maintaining respondent interest and commitment.

The strengths and weaknesses of NGT methods are almost the mirror image of those associated with survey methods. The advantage of probability sampling is not available with NGT. Although both methods provide structured output, the range of topics that can be covered is reduced with NGT. On the other hand,

the problem of establishing items that are relevant to the intended respondents is enhanced. Furthermore, the control of the interview setting is simplified by the highly structured NGT process. This latter point can be emphasized by noting that in the application discussed earlier, each session lasted a total of three hours. At the end of the sessions, respondents continued to express a keen interest in the research, and felt a strong sense of achievement for their efforts.

To restate an earlier comment, the intention is not to suggest NGT methods as a substitute for structured surveys. However, the added structure of NGT, not normally available in group methods, together with the judicious use of multiple quota based groups, may provide an opportunity to go considerably beyond the usual exploratory research.

COMPARISON WITH THE DELPHI METHOD

As indicated earlier, NGT and the Delphi method may be viewed as alternatives when it is required to gather information from industry experts. While both approaches are often referred to as "consensus planning" techniques, the nature of the process associated with each provides different benefits and limitations.

The most obvious difference pertains to the need to physically assemble NGT participants. In contrast, the Delphi method usually assumes that experts are geographically dispersed. Since such dispersion is not unusual when dealing with a select group of experts, the Delphi method may be the only option available. Increasingly, however, professional groups are finding that it is very effective to schedule what are effectively different types of research sessions as part of national or international conferences which by their nature attract experts in sharply defined fields. One example is a recent focus group sponsored by the Marketing Science Institute which attempted to identify the key success factors for organizations involved in the marketing of services (Schmalensee *et al.*, 1983). In this type of context, NGT might prove to be a useful alternative to either focus groups or the Delphi method for reasons outlined above.

Another advantage of the Delphi method is that by its nature it allows for more information to be provided to respondents and for more time to consider and reflect upon that information prior to making judgments. Conversely, there is no control over respondents and thus no guarantee that judgments across respondents will be made with the same degree of care. In this regard, NGT data are gathered under more controlled conditions with the opportunity for discussion and direct explanations. As such, a reasonable argument can be made that the judgments underlying NGT data are at least as considered and reliable as those available from the Delphi approach.

Another advantage of both NGT and Delphi is that

they lend themselves to phased research and planning programs in which data are gathered sequentially. This approach enables planners/researchers to benefit from respondent learning and to develop a cumulative knowledge base on which to formulate policy and make decisions. While this benefit is theoretically available from focus groups and structured surveys, the reality appears to be that respondent commitment is more difficult to obtain using these approaches.

CONCLUDING REMARKS

The quality of research and planning activities is no better than the quality of information on which these activities are based. In turn, the quality of this information depends upon the use of methods of data collection which provide appropriate, reliable inputs which can be analyzed and interpreted to provide meaningful insights and conclusions. This paper has attempted to familiarize readers with one technique which the author has found to be extremely useful and which it is believed deserves wider recognition and use by those involved in tourism research, tourism planning, and tourism management. In addition, it is hoped that the contents of this article will stimulate greater levels of interest and debate concerning the relative merits of different planning and research techniques as tools for improving management effectiveness in tourism.

REFERENCES

Bellenger, Danny N., Kenneth L. Bernhardt, and Jac L. Goldstucker (1976), *Qualitative Research in Marketing*, Chicago: American Marketing Association.

Bogdan, R., and S.J. Taylor (1975), *Introduction to Qualitative Research Methods*, New York: John Wiley & Sons, Inc.

Calder, Bobby J. (1977), "Focus Groups and the Nature of Qualitative Marketing Research," *Journal of Marketing Research*, 14, 353–364.

Delbecq, Andre L., and Andrew H. Van de Ven (1971), "A Group Process Model for Problem Identification and Program Planning," *Journal of Applied Behavioral Science*, 7, 4.

Delbecq, Andre L., Andrew H. Van de Ven, and David H. Gustafson (1975), *Group Techniques for Program Planning*, Glenview, Illinois: Scott, Foresman and Co.

Government of Alberta (1984), *Proposals for an Industrial Strategy for Albertans, 1985 to 1990*, Edmonton, Alberta, Canada.

Green, Paul E., and Yoram Wind (1973), *Multiattribute Decisions in Marketing*, Hinsdale, Illinois: The Dryden Press.

Higginbotham, James B., and Keith K. Cox (1979), *Focus Group Interviews: A Reader*, Chicago: American Marketing Association.

Holsti, Ole R. (1969), *Content Analysis for the Social Sciences and Humanities*, Reading, Massachusetts: Addison–Wesley Publishing Co.

Kassarjian, Harold H. (1977), "Content Analysis in Consumer Research," *Journal of Consumer Research* 4, 8–18.

Linstone, Harold A., and Murray Turoff (Eds.) (1975), *The Delphi Method*, Reading, Massachusetts: Addison–Wesley Publishing Co.

Schmalensee, Diane H., Kenneth Bernhardt, and Nancy Gust (1983), "Focus Group Examines Keys to Services Success," Marketing Science Institute, Cambridge, Massachusetts.

Tourism Industry Association of Alberta (1984), *A Program for Furthering Tourism Development in Alberta—Phase 1*, Calgary, Alberta, Canada.

38

Model Building and Simulation

JAMES M. ROVELSTAD

Director
Center for Survey & Marketing Research
University of Wisconsin—Parkside
Kenosha, Wisconsin

The use of models and simulation has grown rapidly. Both qualitative and quantitative models are available to assist managers and government officials in analyzing and understanding their markets, the travel consumer, and the facilities and resources for which they are responsible. This chapter provides an overview of the scope, nature, and range of uses of models in tourism. Several examples are provided to suggest the diversity and value of models available. However, their ultimate value to the individual firm or agency depends on management's interest, understanding, and acceptance.

Many of the chapters in other sections and most in this section directly or implicitly incorporate models in some form or another. This chapter describes some of the concepts employed in model building, and a rationale for their development and use. It is not the purpose here to provide a comprehensive and definitive guide for the design of models or their use, but it is hoped that this discussion will provide the reader with an understanding of what models are, ways that they can be used in general—by tourism-related organizations in particular—and their roles and relationships vis-à-vis management.

SCOPE AND LIMITATIONS

The following sections provide an overview of the major types of models being used in the travel industry and in other related fields, and describe some of the uses of models in the travel and tourism field. The role of models in the management process is defined, with special attention on the interface and balance between theory and quantitative analysis on the one hand and managerial judgement on the other. Finally, two models developed by the author are described in some detail, including both the methods employed in their construction and their uses.

As noted earlier, this chapter is dedicated to the user, or potential user, of models—not to the model builder. Its purpose is to encourage an awareness and interest among those who may have had little exposure and/or are skeptical, or even cynical, about the value of investing time and resources in what appear to them to be theoretical exercises.

Only a few of the relevant examples of the models from travel and its component functional fields such as economics, marketing, finance, and the other management sciences can be included here. However, the interested reader will find some useful references for further study at the end of the chapter. Some of the examples described come from industries not specifically confined to travel, but these models have significant application potential for travel-related organizations.

The final caveat is that (through a heroic effort in restraint and self-control on the part of the author) no attempt is made to offer value judgements as to which of similar modeling concepts is better. This is really dependent on many external factors including but not limited to the availability of resources, time pressure, and the level of expertise to which the organization has access.

WHAT IS MODELING?

DEFINITION OF A MODEL

The term "model" as used here is defined as a simplified representation of a more complex process or condition (Markin 1974, pp. 78, 79). It may be quantitative or qualitative, normative or descriptive, and many range from simple to very complex.

Moreover, a model may be static and serve primarily to aid the understanding of the user; it may be dynamic and interactive, permitting manipulation of its components to test alternative actions or predict future conditions; or it may synthesize a whole from an incomplete set of component parts as is the case in one of the examples in the latter part of this chapter.

Although the design and use of models is a science that has a long history, especially at the theoretical level and in the physical sciences, it is of much more recent vintage in its broad use for practical business applications. The latter is a phenomenon that corresponds roughly with the growth in the population of professionally trained managers and the increased availability of electronic data processing—a development mainly of the 1960s and 1970s. This explosion of knowledge and capability also produced a gap between many of the younger managers and the decision-makers in higher management.

GENERAL TYPES OF MODELS

While all models do not fit neatly into one category or incorporate cleanly defined attributes, it is helpful to know what some of the possible dimensions might be. Perhaps the broadest division can be made between the quantitative and the qualitative.

Qualitative

Qualitative models commonly are employed in the analysis and prediction of consumer behavior. These might, for example, describe the ways that individual personality characteristics relate to purchase behavior. One notable research study disclosed that in sales situations the level of a person's self-confidence is inversely related to his or her persuasibility, i.e., the degree to which the sales person will be able to influence a change in choice of competitive product purchased (Cox and Bauer 1971).

Personality along with other variables has been combined to form complex models of purchase behavior to provide a conceptual basis for understanding the process and variables involved for a consumer in making the ultimate decision to, say, take a trip, to where, by what means, and including which components. With nearly all of these models the user of the model is aided in design of marketing strategy, but not "delivered" a set of quantitative criteria—how much to spend on advertising, price, the resulting sales volume. One of the more comprehensive and well developed of these is the Howard–Sheth model of consumer behavior (Howard and Sheth 1969). Table 1 illustrates the nature and scope of variables incorporated in this model.

Quantitative

Quantitative models have the capability of providing the user with numerical outputs. These might be measurements of traveler flows and expenditures, forecasts of return on investment, estimates of changes in market share, and the like.

Quantitative models generally are more limited in

TABLE 1   Variables Involved in Consumer Purchase Decision

MARKET INPUTS	ENVIRONMENTAL	CONSUMPTION
Variety of brands available	Importance of purchase	Information search
Quality		
Price	Personality	Sensitivity to information
Distinctiveness		
Availability	Social class	
Service		Perceptual bias
Warranties	Culture	
		Evoked set
Commercial information	Organization	
Advertising		Predisposition
Personal sales	Time pressure	
Publicity		Prior satisfaction and experience
	Financial status	

Source: Adapted from Howard and Sheth (1969).

the range of situations in tourism for which they can be constructed than the behavioral or qualitative models. This is due to the difficulty in quantifying many of the variables relating to human behavior and to the fact that statistical data for the travel and tourism industry have not been thoroughly and systematically collected and maintained, and these historical data often form the basis for designing and/or evaluating a model.

These models often are designed around or with general statistical or mathematical models such as linear programming, probability theory, regression, Markov chains, Bayesian theory, factor analysis, and many others. The use of these theories and tools at the model design stage does require persons with relatively high levels of technical training and experience, and for many potential users of models presents a barrier. But with the wide availability of computer services and specialized consultants this should not be a significant deterrent.

Other model attributes may be described under one or more of the following dichotomies (Markin 1974, p. 85).

- Partial/comprehensive: Represents only a part of the situation, say, the role of personality; or focuses on the complete process.
- Normative/descriptive: Provides a prescriptive guide to optimal action; or a picture or measurement.
- Macro/micro: Describes a group; or an individual situation.
- Static/dynamic: Provides a "snapshot" at one point in time; or indicates interactive relations or flows over time.
- Hypothetical/concrete: Based on theoretical vs. empirical evidence or data.

Simulation is a special type of quantitative modeling that may incorporate several of the types of modeling concepts discussed above. However, it includes the additional feature that a number of variables can be examined under differing dynamic conditions over simulated periods of time, with the outcome, say, profits, determined through the process rather than providing a single solution.

> *Simulation seeks to develop a realistic model of a real world system or process rather than just a problem solving procedure. Simulation models differ from mathematical models in that simulation abandons the requirement that an (unique) analytical solution for the mathematical structure must exist. (Day and Parsons 1971, p. 635)*

It is a reasonable generalization to state that nearly all simulation models are computer-dependent tools. This is due to the volume of numerical computation that typically is required. They also require a high level of technical sophistication in their initial construction.

However, once developed and programmed for the computer, simulation models often can be used readily by those having little technical background. Some of the types of simulation models useful in tourism include:

Economic systems.

Intraorganizational, communication, decision making.

Competitive markets.

Group dynamics.

Distribution/location strategy.

USES OF MODELS IN TRAVEL

The potential applications of models in travel are infinite in variety and in type of user. Probably the heaviest users are government agencies and the larger private corporations. This no doubt is due more to the availability of persons in the organizations with training and familiarity with models and their value than it is to size or scale as a precondition for utility. Internal access to a computer is another enabling—*but not prerequisite*—factor.

It is true that the design and implementation of some of the more complex specialized quantitative models require the commitment of substantial time and resources. But much of the work in model building that has been published, say, in the marketing field, can be of great value to even the smaller entrepreneur with limited or no further investment in original research or data collection. This is particularly true in the use of models as a basis for designing and implementing consumer-oriented marketing strategies.

Some of the more common areas of application include market measurement and analysis, process or project monitoring and control, communications, consumer behavior analysis and prediction, management decision analysis, and training of personnel. The following examples are only suggestive of the range of possibilities.

Physical and economic impact models of tourism flows provide estimates of the size and composition of tourism activity within, and to and from, their jurisdictions. They may also measure changes in size, traveler origin destination, and the like in order to evaluate promotional efforts and/or assess changes in the demand in different markets.

The U.S. Government (Bureau of Economic Analysis) has used a model based on a sample drawn from international visitors to estimate the total and net impact of such travel on the U.S. balance of payments (Wynegar 1980). The quinquennial U.S. *National Travel Survey*, discontinued in 1982, used a statistical model of the U.S. population to translate a sample survey of households into a measure of the size, nature, and distribution of domestic travel in the U.S. Similar information is developed in the intervening years by a statistical model using a different statistical approach designed and implemented by the U.S. Travel Data Center (U.S. Travel Data Center *National Travel Survey*).

State governments also make use of the outputs from these models. In addition, the federal government, and many states, has need for models to estimate the economic impact of tourism. Several different models, generally based on one or more types of survey research, have been developed (Rovelstad 1974; U.S. Travel Data Center 1975). Each has some limitations in comprehensiveness or accuracy, but provides data that are of great value in assessing the role of tourism in the economy, justifying support for tourism developmental appropriations in legislative bodies, and providing essential basic market data for potential private sector developers. Such information also has great importance in generating the support of the residents of host communities.

Input/output models of an economy also are used by government agencies to estimate the impacts of tourist expenditures on various sectors of an economy. It is possible, for example, to show how a dollar spent in a hotel is respent in wages, with supplier firms such as food suppliers, and to estimate the multiplier effect. Such models may be developed as general models of all economic activity for a country, state, or region (Seastrand 1963) or for tourism specifically (Archer 1977).

Generally, input/output (I/O) models have been developed by government agencies for purposes of economic planning and development. The level of detail in breaking down individual component sectors—hotels and motels, automobile services, eating and drinking places, etc.—varies from state to state in the U.S. Also these models need to be updated from time to time as the relative mix of businesses sector productivity and other factors change. However, the use of I/O tables is relatively simple, and permits tracing of, say, one dollar of tourist expenditure through the various types of businesses affected, state and local taxes created, wages paid, labor hours required, and payments (leakages) to out-of-region recipients.

Behavioral models developed specifically for tourism, or derived from other consumer research, provide important insights for the design of marketing strategies for all sectors of the travel industry. These may be very general or highly specific as to application.

One general model of long standing is the motivational model specified by A.H. Maslow. He postulated that behavior is the result of five basic needs. In order of decreasing importance they are physiological, safety, love, esteem, and self-actualization. But once the more basic needs (physiological and safety) have been *adequately* satisfied they cease to be impor-

tant motivators, and the "higher" needs predominate (Maslow 1954).

Maslow's model does not help to produce numbers—estimates of profits, market share, etc. It does provide important insight as to what factors to look for in marketing a discretionary product such as pleasure travel to an affluent population. Of course it also shows why an unusual situation such as political unrest and violence in a destination area creates such intractable short-run market problems.

A Transactional Analysis model has been proposed to explain the underlying reason why people decide to travel and the process which promotional efforts must undertake in order to motivate a decision to take a pleasure trip. This starts, it suggests, by "hooking" the "I want" child ego state (Kennedy 1977). This model does not conflict with Maslow's but provides further insight as to how the higher-level needs can be aroused.

The Howard–Sheth model mentioned earlier has been applied as a basis for determining how travelers choose among alternative, competitive destinations, once they have decided to travel. This model helps those with the responsibility to promote a destination to understand the differing promotion needs as a function of traveler awareness level vis-à-vis the destination. It suggests levels of "evoked sets" of consumer awareness which a travel destination must pass through in order to achieve market success, and the most feasible targets for each stage (Woodside and Ronkainen 1980).

A further aspect of the Howard–Sheth model is the grouping of purchasing behavior into three patterns: *Extensive Problem Solving (EPS)*—the buyer seeks a great deal of information as in the case of a product where the buyer has little or no prior similar experience; *Limited Problem Solving (LPS)*—the buyer is considering a new product which is comparable to previous experience and the buyer therefore knows the information and criteria for decision making; and *Routinized Response Behavior (RRB)*—the buyer repeats previous product choice(s), selecting the same product or one of a small group of products based on price availability or even whim. Two points are salient. A person/household in RRB with respect to a particular product, say, vacation destination choice, will require a very strong cue from the market, a new destination, to revert to LPS or EPS, and the extent and persuasibility of the information will have to be high. It has been shown that while there always is a potential for a change, the tendency for most people is to go to and stay in the behavioral pattern that involves the least effort and perceived risk, i.e., RRB (Lehman, Moore, and Elrod 1982).

The idea of evoked set might be the basis of specific individual studies by destinations, hotel chains, airlines, etc., to measure the level of specific consumer/

awareness and determine appropriate market segmentation strategies. As an example, a state may learn that in many parts of the nation it has no significant image or awareness. In general no reasonable level of general mass media promotion will be effective, however, tightly targeted efforts on small segments could be.

International tourism is increasingly viewed as a vital element in a country's trade account. A family of mathematical models for foreign travel expenditures in the U.S. was derived which shows the relative importance of such factors as price levels, per capita incomes, exchange rate, and unique special events (e.g., Olympic Games). The models also show how these factors' influence varies for different countries of origin (Loeb 1982). Models such as these not only aid governments in policy and economic areas, but also provide guidance to private businesses as to where they may expect their marketing efforts to be most effective at any given time, and which factors will have the greatest promotional impact.

Some models have been designed for highly specific uses, for example, casino gaming. Planning, equipping, and staffing a casino, especially deciding which games and how many positions of each, are critical to the business' success. Dandurand (1982) has suggested a modeling approach that could be useful in projecting the demand for each.

A general group of models described collectively as Multidimensional Scaling and Conjoint Measurement is among the newer tools in marketing, and has been used for tourism applications. In brief, these methods provide a means of product positioning vis-à-vis specific markets and market segments. They also can be used to predict which combination of product attributes is most likely to be preferred by various segments. Bjorklund and King designed a model for determination of the best mix of hotel facilities for a new resort area (1982).

A conjoint model has even been applied to evaluation of restaurant menus. This model included such variables as menu mix—appetizers, entrees, and desserts—and prices, in the context of consumer background variables—place of residence, demographics, general food preferences, frequency of eating out, and even whether on a weight-reducing program or not (Green and Wind 1973).

Most of the preceding discussion of uses for models has centered on marketing. Other travel-related applications include recreational land management/development optimization (Gundermann 1980), determining trends in demand for different types of recreational activity (O'Leary and Dottavio 1980), and demand forecasting for international tourism (Edgell and Seely 1980). The list is much longer, and covers nearly every facet of tourism activity.

Simulation models designed specifically for tourism applications are not yet numerous. Of course many of the general business and economic simulation models are directly applicable to travel industry needs. A few of the existing travel-specific simulators are described here.

Before doing so, it may be useful to note the most important value of simulation models, that is, that they allow the user to conduct a "laboratory experiment" with differing mixes and types of decisions and actions under varying environmental conditions (e.g., consumer, competition, economic conditions, etc.) to learn probable business outcomes. This can be done without the market cost or risk required by a real market test, with no time cost, and without exposing future strategies to competitors.

One of the most difficult problems for major portions of the travel industry has been and continues to be designing strategies to deal with deregulation in the U.S. transportation industry. A simulation model has been developed that permits airline management to evaluate alternative actions with regard to fleet composition and route and schedule changes, and also provides a tool for executive training. This model, called CASS (Competitive Airline Strategy Simulation), also has been used by the FAA to study slot allocation problems for capacity-limited airports (Archer 1980).

Simulation also is used by recreation and park system planners to evaluate prospective development and resource management strategies. In this application changes in such factors as visitor density can be "tested" without substantial cost or exposing the natural resources involved to perhaps irreversible environmental damage (Shecter and Lucas 1980).

EXAMPLES OF MODELING APPLICATIONS

The preceding review of some of the models in or related to the travel industry provides a sense of the range of types and uses of models in the travel and tourism industry. Following are two examples, both developed by the author, which are presented to provide a more substantive understanding of the applications and benefits in modeling.

VACATION DESTINATION CHOICE—A QUALITATIVE EXAMPLE

The most important factors in marketing discretionary or vacation travel are those which affect the choice of a place to go. From these are derived the development of destination facilities, transportation systems and routes, and the marketing efforts and support of the trade channels—wholesalers and retailers.

One of a continuing series of research studies conducted for the state of West Virginia yielded useful insights as to why vacationers choose a particular destination, and led to a conceptual model of this process. This model was derived by grouping survey respondents' answers to the open-ended question, "What three factors do you consider most important in choosing a vacation spot?" The factors fell into four groups, which were identified as "Facilities," "Aesthetics," "Time/Cost," and "Quality of Life" (Rovelstad 1975).

While this is a qualitative rather than quantitative model, it can be expressed in mathematical form as

$$V = f\ (F,A,C,Q)$$

where

V = number of vacation or pleasure travelers to a destination

f = a function of

F = quality and quantity of facilities (lodgings, attractions/activities, outdoor facilities, roads, etc.)

A = perceived aesthetic qualities, perhaps also including those encountered en route (scenery, historical sites, weather, atmosphere of isolation, relaxation)

C = travel time and costs to reach and stay at destination

Q = perceived quality of life at the destination (people/residents, lack of pollution).

Moreover, in terms of the relative importance of these factors, it was found that

$$F > A > C > Q$$

For each person or household there would be some maximum or minimum threshold for each of the factors, which if exceeded (or unmet) would make that factor an absolute barrier, regardless of its relative importance when within the range of acceptability. Thus, for a person with only two weeks for vacation, a trip/destination requiring more than this is eliminated no matter how well it rates in the other three areas. This model also will explain why attractions with a strong facilities image may bring visitors in spite of high costs, relatively poor aesthetic qualities, and quality of life factors that are perceived to be poor.

The model provides substantial insight for tourism planners and marketers, even though it does not yield precise numerical answers. For example, when applied to West Virginia in conjunction with a field survey of travelers, the strengths and deficiencies of the state become apparent. Figure 1 shows these results which led to reorientation of the state travel development agency's marketing plan. The importance of improved facilities spurred new development, and market targets were geographically revised.

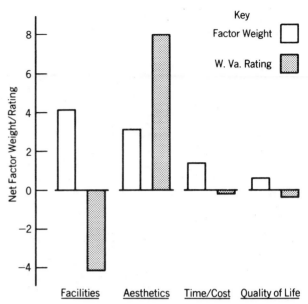

FIGURE 1 Evaluation of West Virginia on vacation choice factors. (Source: Adapted from James M. Rovelstad *Behavior Based Marketing Strategies for Travel and Tourism.* (Morgantown: Bureau of Business Research, West Virginia University 1975).

ECONOMIC IMPACT MEASUREMENT— A QUANTITATIVE EXAMPLE

Accurate measures of the economic impacts of visitors to an area are important for planning, evaluation of strategy, gaining government support, and many other reasons. The direct impacts include the jobs and wages created for community residents, the profits received by local businesses from sales to travelers, the direct net revenues received by local, state, or federally owned facilities such as state parks or beaches, and the taxes paid to local, state, and federal governments from wages and sales created by travelers' purchases.

The direct impacts (sales, profits, jobs, and taxes) also create indirect impacts, which themselves can be very significant. For example, a hotel employee uses the after-tax wages earned to purchase goods and services from businesses, government agencies, and other organizations, as does the business owner with his or her profits. Also, the hotel purchases goods and services to support its sales to travelers. The size of these indirect effects varies from community to community, depending on the local availability of merchants and suppliers. They can total several times the size of the original tourism sale, especially if the effects of the repeated recycling of the travel sales dollar are considered; for example, the purchases made by the sales clerk whose wages come from the store that sold products to the hotel employee.

The model described here was designed originally for the state of West Virginia to obtain measures of the size and dynamics of its travel and tourism industry.

The principal goal was a model to be used on a state-wide basis, but the outputs provide useful information down to the county level. This approach has been in use in West Virginia since 1972 and has been one of the principal planning and evaluation criteria used by that state's travel industry (Rovelstad 1974). An improved version of the model is now being used in New York and Wisconsin.

Obtaining data to measure either potential or actual travel market performance is especially difficult because of the fragmented nature of the industry and a variety of definitional problems. Indeed, the industry is a collage of various size firms from many industries. The types of businesses involved include hotels, motels, tourist courts, and campgrounds, which receive nearly all of their revenues from travel and tourism, and gasoline stations, movie theaters, and liquor stores, which receive only part of their income from travel and tourism.

Three criteria were central factors in development of the model:

1 *Reliability and continuity*—The measurement should be made in a way that can be repeated in successive periods and reliably show the changes that have occurred in the amount and type of travel in the area.

2 *Comprehensiveness*—Measurements should cover all relevant and significant kinds of travel activity.

3 *Community/area sensitivity*—Since the interests of the planners are assumed to be in a relatively small geographic area, the method employed should make disaggregation to this level possible.

The West Virginia model incorporates:

1 A model of traveler expenditures as a function of lodgings choice and a model of lodging choice as a function of trip purpose, both developed primarily by means of traveler surveys.

2 A lodging model based on an annual survey of private and publicly operated lodging places and campgrounds.

3 A distributive model derived from secondary sources that provides an estimate of the impact of day trips, visits with friends and relatives, and trips using other types of lodgings (sleeping in car, owned or rented vacation home) as a percentage of commercial lodging sales.

These serve as inputs to determine total travel industry sales revenues, and from these are projected indirect impacts, employment and tax receipts using an input/output model, plus actual tax rates.

The model is used to project responses from an annual survey of lodging facilities (hotels, motels, resorts, and state park cabins and lodges) and camp-grounds (privately and publicly owned) into a measure of total overnight space sales revenues by class of lodging. It also serves as an input to the TRavel Industry Analysis and InformaTion System (TRAITS).

There are two versions of the lodging model: one for campgrounds and one for hotels, motels, and state-owned accommodations. They are very much alike, and input variables for the hotel/motel sector are:

Number of units (rooms, cabins, etc.).

Average single rental rate ($).

Average double rental rate ($).

Charge per additional person above two ($).

Average occupancy rate (%).

Average party size, or number of guests per unit per night when a unit is occupied (person-nights/unit-nights).

Number of nights open for business per year.

Percentage of out-of-state guests (%).

A special computer program, TRAITS, was designed for this application. It was possible to incorporate the SPSS software package for some of the tabular reporting program. Thus, TRAITS is in fact a hybrid, consisting in large part of specialized routines for state travel data analysis and in part of the standard routines from SPSS.

Table 2 is a sample of one of the types of tabularized reports produced by the TRAITS program. A table is provided for each type of establishment (hotel, camp, park) for each county, travel region, and the entire state.

Some of the general uses of this impact information include the following:

Planning and implementation
   —identification of markets and potential markets
   —benefit/cost and business forecasts
   —assessing results of development process
   —early identification of changes in traveler behavior
Promotion and public relations
   —gaining attention and support from government agencies and elected officials
   —gaining community business and resident support
   —attracting potential new travel industry entrepreneurs and investors
Basis for credibility
   —obtaining debt capital from lending institutions
   —obtaining grants from regional, state, and federal agencies
   —gaining support for improvement/development of public infrastructure
   —influencing legislation favorable to travel industry operations

TABLE 2   Sample TRAITS Report

West Virginia Travel Industry Quarterly Regional Summary
Lodging
Entire State
Second Quarter, 19XX

	THIS PERIOD	LAST PERIOD	1 YEAR AGO	CUMULATIVE AVERAGE[1]
Occupancy rate	73%	77%	76%	66%
Average guest per unit	1.55	1.23	1.43	1.01
Revenue (thousands)	$98,765	$87,654	$76,543	$65,432
Out of state	98%	97%	96%	95%
Average room rate	$55.00	$54.00	$53.00	$52.00
Person-nights	98,765	87,654	76,543	65,432

Source: Rovelstad (1975).
[1]Calcualted for 27 samples.

Information is organized and presented in different forms and levels of detail for each of these uses. Table 3 is an example of a presentation included in an eight-page color brochure summarizing the annual measurement in West Virginia and designed primarily to serve the third category—especially with the state legislators.

The brochure also serves secondarily as a promotion and public relations piece. But more impact is gained by selecting specific figures such as total sales, employment, or taxes collected and using these in press releases or documented interviews. It is important in communicating the desired message that the major points don't become lost among too many less directly meaningful bits of information.

MODELS AND MANAGEMENT

The growth in variety and quality of business/management models over the past two decades has been great, but this has not been accompanied by proportionate growth in their acceptance and use. Some of the reasons for this include the normal lags between theory and practical application, inadequate communications to potential users, and lack in some organizations of personnel trained to use these techniques. Time may ultimately narrow these gaps to some extent.

But the relatively limited use appears to have additional causes that might be remedied more quickly. Among these is the reluctance of many in senior management to accept these ideas because they don't understand them—and may even view them as a threat. This probably is more true for the smaller business and those having less intrinsic involvement with advanced technology of other kinds. Frequently these managers have little or no advanced formal education themselves.

A related factor is reluctance to invest time and resources in "soft" projects (or personnel) which in themselves do not produce a profit. It may appear more attractive to devote whatever resources are available to activities which, however risky, *can* produce a direct return.

While there are many other potential reasons for management reluctance to make use of appropriate modeling and simulation techniques, perhaps one of the more significant is that the wide availability of low-cost data processing is not fully comprehended. This probably is simply because of the rapid growth in supply and substantial decline in costs for service and equipment over a very short time. This has made it possible for even the small business to own its own computer for not much more than the cost of an electric typewriter.

Barriers such as these will best be resolved by understanding what modeling techniques can do, and where their limits are. Perhaps the most important point to note is that models do not make management decisions, they only help to organize the available knowledge and information and therefore to permit better focus on those facets of problem solving and decision making where judgment and experience are most needed.

This chapter started with a definition of models, noting that they are simplifications of reality. Given this, no model can fully incorporate all of the variables and dynamics of the real world. What they can do is help management to understand and deal with complex situations more effectively and thoroughly. It is just as vital, in fact, that management not be lulled into overreliance on cranking out numbers and accepting them on blind faith.

Benefits from the use of models in the planning, monitoring, and evaluation process include the following:

TABLE 3   Travel Council Area Sales, Employment, and Wages and Salaries

TRAVEL COUNCIL	TOTAL SALES (MILLION $)	EMPLOYMENT	WAGES AND SALARIES (MILLION $)
Country Roads	42.3	2,247	11.5
Eastern Gateway	52.1	2,772	11.5
Moutainaire	192.8	10,251	52.6
Mountaineer Country	90.2	4,798	24.6
Nine Valley	209.7	11,153	57.2
Potomac Highland	77.9	4,144	21.3
Upper Ohio	49.8	2,649	13.6
State Total*	715.0	38,017	195.0

Travel Sales by County

COUNTY	SALES (MILLION $)	COUNTY	SALES	COUNTY	SALES
Barbour	3.2	Jackson and Roane	6.7	Pleasants	1.1
Berkeley	30.1	Jefferson	15.1	Pocahontas	9.8
Boone	1.4			Preston	3.6
Braxton	6.3	Kanawha and Clay	127.0	Putnam	4.3
Brooke	5.1	Lewis	2.3	Raleigh	32.9
Cabell	51.2	Lincoln	.1	Randolph	25.0
Calhoun	.8	Logan	8.8	Ritchie	2.9
Clay— see Kanawha		McDowell	4.1	Roane— see Jackson	
Doddridge— see Harrison		Marion	12.5	Summers	13.3
		Marshall	4.3	Taylor	4.9
Fayette	8.1	Mason	6.2	Tucker	17.2
Gilmer	.8	Mercer	41.1	Tyler	1.5
Grant	4.6	Mineral	3.3	Upshur	10.6
Greenbrier	84.0	Mingo	7.5	Wayne	3.2
Hampshire	9.7	Monogalia	32.3	Webster	2.0
Hancock	7.5	Monroe	.3	Wetzel	4.3
Hardy	1.4	Morgan	6.9	Wirt and Wood	22.0
Harrison and Doddridge	20.8	Nicholas	5.1		

*Totals may not add due to rounding.

—Forces early organization of information, identification of potential problems, and location of information gaps and needs.

—Enables management to reduce the number of factors of uncertainty on which subjective judgment must be used.

—Increases understanding of the operational environment(s).

—Reduces risk and probability of wrong decision.

Caveats to the use of modeling and simulation methods have been identified in this and earlier sections, and with some additions include the following:

—Management acceptance is imperative.

—Limitations of the models must be identified and understood in interpretation of results.

—Models, especially quantitative, are derived from empirical information, and therefore have to be updated and revalidated as environments change.

—Limitations in data, especially in the travel industry, may be difficult to overcome.

—The simplest *useful* model probably is best—level of complexity should increase as problem is more fully defined.

SUMMARY

This chapter has provided an overview of the nature, uses, and concepts of models used for the travel and tourism industry. Simulation is a special type of modeling concept and was described as a valuable tool for planning, evaluation, and training.

While *modeling* may require persons with special and highly technical skills, the *use* of models does not. In some applications access to computers is needed, but this should not be considered a barrier with the wide availability and low cost of using such services today.

One of the biggest barriers is likely to be gaining the interest and acceptance of management. The rapid growth of modeling knowledge and technology appears to have opened a gap that serves to inhibit the use of these tools. It is therefore important for senior management to become aware of and receptive to the potential that modeling and simulation offers for increased tourism revenues and profits.

REFERENCES

Archer, Brian (1977), "Input—Output Analysis: Its Strengths, Limitations and Weaknesses," *The 80's Its Impact on Travel and Tourism Marketing*, Proceedings of the Eighth Annual Conference, Salt Lake City, Utah: The Travel Research Association, pp. 89—108.

Archer, Brian (1980), "CASS, Competitive Airline Strategy Simulation," an unpublished descriptive summary by Flight Transportation Associates Inc., Cambridge, Massachusetts.

Bjorklund, Richard A., and Barry King (1982), "A Consumer-Based Approach to Assist in the Design of Hotels," *Journal of Travel Research*, Vol. 20, 4 (Spring), pp. 45—52.

Cox, Donald F., and Raymond A. Bauer (1971), "Self Confidence and Persuasability in Women," *Marketing Models: Behavioral Science Applications*, Ralph L. Day and Thomas E. Ness, Eds. Scranton, Pennsylvania: Intext Educational Publishers, pp. 62—76.

Dandurand, Lawrence (1982), "Incorporating Casino Game Preference Market Segmentation Data into Marketing Plans," *Journal of Travel Research*, Vol. 20, 4 (Spring), pp. 15—19.

Day, Ralph L., and Leonard J. Parsons, Eds. (1971), *Marketing Models: Quantitative Applications*. Scranton, Pennsylvania: Intext Educational Publishers.

Edgell, David, and Richard Seely (1980), "A Multi-Stage Model for the Development of International Tourism Forecasts for States and Regions," *Tourism Planning and Development Issues*, Donald E. Hawkins, Elwood L. Shafer, and James M. Rovelstad, Eds., Washington, D.C.: George Washington University, pp. 407—410.

Green, Paul E., and Yoram Wind (1973), *Multiattribute Decision Making in Marketing: A Measurement Approach*, Hinsdale, Illinois: The Dryden Press.

Gundermann, Egon (1980), "The Question of Optimal Densities of Forest Land in the Tourist Regions of Central Europe," *Tourism Planning and Development Issues*, Donald E. Hawkins, Elwood L. Shafer, and James M. Rovelstad, Eds., Washington, D.C.: George Washington University, pp. 149—159.

Howard, John A., and Jagdish N. Sheth (1969), *The Theory of Buyer Behavior*, New York: John Wiley & Sons, Inc.

Kennedy, John L. (1977), "A Transactional Analysis Model for Understanding Travel Decisions," *The 80's Its Impact on Travel and Tourism Marketing*, Proceedings of the Eighth Annual Conference, Salt Lake City, Utah: The Travel Research Association.

Lehman, Donald R., William L. Moore, and Terry Elrod (1982), "The Development of Distinct Choice Process-Segments Over Time: A Stochastic Modeling Approach," *Journal of Marketing*, Vol. 46, 2 (Spring), pp. 48—59.

Loeb, Peter D. (1982), "International Travel to the United States: An Econometric Evaluation," *Annals of Tourism Research*, Vol. 9, 1, pp. 7—20.

Markin, Ron J., Jr. (1974), *Consumer Behavior: A Cognitive Orientation*, New York: Macmillan Publishing Co. Inc.

Maslow, Abraham H. (1954), *Motivation and Personality*, New York: Harper & Row.

O'Leary, Joseph L., and F. Dominic Dottavio (1980), "Recreation Activity Clusters in Resource Settings: A First Approximation," *Tourism Planning and Development Issues*, Donald E. Hawkins, Elwood L. Shafer, and James M. Rovelstad, Eds., Washington, D.C.: George Washington University, pp. 161—178.

Rovelstad, James M. (1974), *Analytical Measures of Travel and Tourism: The West Virginia Model*, Morgantown, West Virginia: Bureau of Business Research, West Virginia University.

Rovelstad, James M. (1975), *Behavior Based Marketing Strategies for Travel and Tourism: The West Virginia Model*, Morgantown, West Virginia: Bureau of Business Research, West Virginia University.

Schecter, Mordechai, and Robert Lucas (1980), "A Park Visitor Travel Simulation Model as a Management Tool," *Tourism Marketing and Management Issues*, Donald E. Hawkins, Elwood L. Shafer, and James M. Rovelstad, Eds. Washington, D.C.: George Washington University, pp. 379—390.

Seastrand, Frans (1963), "New York State Economic System: The Interindustry Structure of the New York State Economy," Data and Systems Bureau, Office of Planning Services, Albany, New York.

U.S. Department of Commerce, U.S. Travel (periodically), "Summary and Analysis of International Travel to the U.S.," Washington, D.C.: U.S. Travel Service.

U.S. Travel Data Center (1975), "Travel Expenditure Impact Model," Washington, D.C.: U.S. Travel Data Center.

U.S. Travel Data Center (annual), *National Travel Survey*, Washington, D.C.: U.S. Travel Data Center.

Woodside, Arch G., and Ilkka A. Ronkainen (1980), "Tourism Management Strategies for Competitive Vacation Destinations," *Tourism Marketing and Management Issues*, Donald E. Hawkins, Elwood L. Shafer, and James M. Rovelstad, Eds., Washington, D.C.: George Washington University, pp. 3—22.

Wynegar, Don (1980, 1981), "International Outlook," *Proceedings: 1981 Travel Outlook Forum*, Washington D.C.: U.S. Travel Data Center. pp. 157—174.

39

Conjoint Analysis in Travel Research: A Manager's Guide

JOHN D. CLAXTON

Faculty of Commerce
University of British Columbia
Vancouver, British Columbia,
Canada

*C*onjoint analysis has been put forward as a procedure for evaluating the relative importance that buyers place on the various components of a product or service. This chapter discusses the advantages and pitfalls associated with the application of these procedures and highlights manager versus researcher roles in this type of study.

A traveller wanting to go from the airport to downtown may be faced with a number of public transport options: a local bus that costs $2.00, makes many stops and takes 60 minutes; an express bus that costs $5.00, is nonstop, and takes 45 minutes; or a helicopter service that costs $25.00 and takes 10 minutes. The trip characteristics that might be considered by travellers choosing one of these options include waiting time until next service, travel time, comfort enroute, cost, baggage handling, sights enroute, and possibly many others. Each traveller weighs the pros and cons and makes a choice. Since all three services attract customers the implication is that all travellers do not make the same trade-offs. In other words, each traveller makes *trade-offs* that suit individual values and preferences.

In 1973 a research paper titled "Forecasting Traffic on STOL" introduced conjoint analysis as a method of evaluating transportation user trade-offs (Davidson, 1973). Since then conjoint analysis has become widely used with numerous applications in the travel and transportation field. The purpose of this chapter is to describe some of these applications with a view to helping research users assess the merits of this research approach. In other words, this chapter is not written for researchers, but rather for managers who

use research to guide decisions and are interested in understanding the potential strengths and pitfalls of conjoint analysis.

The discussion is presented in the following sequence. First, there is a discussion of the range of travel-related situations where user trade-offs are of interest. Second, a conceptual description of conjoint analysis is presented. Third, a number of travel-related applications of conjoint analysis are reviewed. The final section presents a number of suggestions for managers when working with research specialists on the design and evaluation of user trade-off studies.

USER TRADE-OFFS

THE TRADE-OFF VIEW OF USER CHOICES

The purpose of this section is (1) to provide a conceptual description of user choice as a trade-off process and (2) to suggest examples of travel situations where user trade-offs are of concern. First, to introduce the idea of trade-offs consider the following examples:

- Why do some people drive their car to work, even though parking is expensive and a bus stops a block from their home?

- Why do some people make their own travel arrangements, while their neighbors use a travel agent?

- Why do travellers have individual preferences for one airline over another?

- Why does one municipal government decide on a bus system and another opt for rail rapid transit?

- How do travellers decide on one hotel over another?

- Why does one tour operator decide on a fleet of GM vehicles rather than Ford?

- How does a department of tourism decide whether to emphasize low-cost camping holidays or luxury resort vacations?

At the root of each of these decisions is the issue of attribute trade-offs. In some sense the decision-maker must give up one attribute (or characteristic) to gain another—give up low price to gain flexibility, give up convenience to gain satisfaction, give up frequent departure times to gain better meals, give up shorter travel times to gain low capital costs, give up convenient location to gain quieter surroundings, give up fuel economy to gain better dealer service, give up attracting tourists to cities to gain tourists in rural regions. Although each of these is hypothetical, jointly they indicate that attribute trade-offs are of concern in a broad range of travel-related situations.

The second point to be made is that trade-off decisions can usefully be viewed as a process where *a decision-maker implicitly sums up the value (or utility) of various "parts" of each alternative, and then selects the alternative with the "greatest net utility"*. Returning to the situation of the traveller wishing to travel from the airport to downtown, it is clear that some travellers place a very high utility on speed of service. These travellers are willing to spend five times the price to shorten the trip from 45 to 10 minutes. At the other extreme some travellers consider it extremely important to minimize their travel costs. Between these extremes there are those who are willing to pay an extra $3.00 to reduce the trip time from 65 to 45 minutes, but are not willing to pay an increment of $20.00 to shorten the trip an additional 35 minutes.

The implication of this example is that users can be viewed as having certain values or utilities for various levels of each attribute, and that for each alternative the utilities of the parts (the "part worths") are in some manner combined. The alternative chosen will be the one with the highest net utility. Table 1 provides a simple numerical illustration of part worths and net utilities. This example does not imply that users explicitly keep scorecards on each alternative being considered, rather this summing up of pros and cons is done in a very implicit fashion. Further, this summing up is equivalent to making a series of trade-offs, giving up less import aspects to gain more important ones.

The third point to be made regarding user trade-offs is to reinforce the view that faced with one particular set of alternatives *different users have different utility profiles and thus make different decisions*. As was pointed out with the airport to downtown example, the value placed on the various attributes differs from one traveller to another. As a result the net utility for the alternatives will differ and, therefore, so will the alternatives selected. The implication of this for trade-off research is the importance of identifying user segments with various attribute preferences, that is, various utility profiles. In the airport to downtown example the size of the segment that has very high utility for short travel time will determine the feasibility of a helicopter service.

In summary, user trade-offs are of concern in a broad range of travel-related situations. User trade-off can be viewed as a process whereby users consider the value of the various parts of each alternative, in some manner combine these "part worths," and select the alternative with the greatest net value (utility). Finally, because users differ in terms of the trade-offs they would prefer to make, segmentation on this basis can be used to assess the viability of specific travel services.

USER TRADE-OFF SITUATIONS

Before leaving the discussion of user trade-offs it is important to emphasize the range of travel- and leisure-related situations where this type of information can be of importance to management decisions. As outlined in Table 2, both private and public sector managers might be faced with situations where user trade-offs are of concern. Further, the focus could be either trying to increase market share within a particular mode or trying to shift travellers from one mode to another. An intramode (market share) example would be a hotel manager considering whether a discount price, a room—meals—entertainment package, or some other alternative would be the most effective way to improve his share of the weekend guest market. An intermode (market growth) example would be a government program to switch commuters from private autos to public transit. In both of these examples a clear understanding of user trade-offs with respect to various mode characteristics is of critical importance to the mode manager. As noted in Table 2, *mode* is used in this discussion to refer to any particular travel product or service.

CONJOINT ANALYSIS

The discussion of this point has not considered how to obtain information on user trade-offs but rather has

TABLE 1 The Concept of Part and Net Utilities: Airport to Downtown Example[a]

PART WORTH UTILITIES

	ATTRIBUTE 1: TRIP TIME			ATTRIBUTE 2: COST		
	SLOW (60 MIN.)	MODERATE (45 MIN.)	FAST (10 MIN.)	LOW ($2.00)	MODERATE ($5.00)	HIGH ($25.00)
Traveller A (placing high value on speed)	2[b]	3	10	6	5	4
Traveller B (placing high value on low cost)	4	5	6	9	6	0
Traveller C (placing value on both)	2	6	7	8	5	2

NET UTILITIES

	LOCAL BUS (SLOW−LOW)	EXPRESS BUS (MODERATE−MODERATE)	HELICOPTER (FAST−HIGH)
Traveller A (will go by helicopter)	8[c]	8	14
Traveller B (will go by local bus)	13	11	6
Traveller C (will go by express bus)	10	11	9

[a]In this example it is assumed that only two attributes, travel time and cost, influence user choice.

[b]Entries indicate the value between 0 (low value) and 10 (high value) that Traveller A places on each possible attribute level.

[c]It is assumed that part worths are simply added to obtain net utilities. Other combinational approaches such as multiplication could have been assumed.

TABLE 2 Examples of Travel and Leisure Situations Where Information about User Trade-Offs Can Have Impact on Management Decisions

	INTRAMODE[a]	INTERMODE
Private Sector	• an airline trying to improve its service relative to other airlines • a bus manufacturer trying to interest a city in its model of buses • a hotel attempting to increase its share of the weekend market	• a train system attempting to attract auto travellers • a boat manufacturer association trying to increase the number of families that buy boats • a symphony company attempting to attract a broader cross section of attendees
Public Sector	• a municipal bus company trying to decide on the price of an express bus service • a "miles per gallon" campaign attempting to shift car owners to energy-efficient vehicles	• a subsidy program to facilitate the introduction of a rapid transit system • grants to enable the operation of a cultural organization

[a]*Mode* is used in a general sense to refer to any particular travel product or service.

only argued that this type of information can be useful. This section discusses the use of conjoint analysis for the evaluation of user trade-offs.

Conjoint analysis was first developed in the field of mathematical psychology (Luce and Tukey, 1964). It was introduced to consumer research a decade ago (Green and Rao, 1971) with the first transportation-related study being reported by Davidson in 1973. An example is used here to explain the nature of conjoint analysis. The example was selected because it dealt with a transportation issue, the purchase of an electric vehicle, and because the conjoint analysis utilized two different data collection procedures.

ATTRIBUTE TRADE-OFFS BETWEEN ELECTRIC AND CONVENTIONAL VEHICLES

It is clear that even when an electric vehicle could meet usage requirements, a consumer may not switch from a conventional vehicle. Several additional attributes come into consideration. Electric vehicles represent a new propulsion system. Consumers who enjoy innovation may consider this desirable, but consumers who prefer to stay with the tried and true may be deterred. Electric vehicles, at least initially, will be priced at premium. On the other hand, electrics will have lower operating costs and will offer very low levels of air and noise pollution, both desirable attributes. The study of interest here (Hargreaves, Claxton, and Siller, 1976) used conjoint measurement to assess the relative importance of these attributes.

Table 3 describes both a conventional and an electric vehicle in terms of five major attributes. The research issue is to assess the relative importance of these five attributes on consumers' vehicle preferences. Unfortunately simply asking consumers to choose between a conventional versus an electric would not indicate which attribute(s) influenced preference most. However, if hypothetical vehicles were specified with various combinations of the five attributes, consumer preferences for these hypothetical vehicles would reveal attribute importance.

In the electric vehicle study each of the five *attributes* was specified by two levels. All combinations would result in $2 \times 2 \times 2 \times 2 \times 2 = 32$ hypothetical vehicles. Since conjoint analysis requires only rank preference data, consumers would be asked to rank 32 vehicles if all alternatives were included. Clearly, as the number of attributes and number of levels increase the ranking of all alternatives becomes onerous. However, the use of a balanced subset reduces the respondent task and still allows evaluation of attribute importance (Green, 1974). As indicated in Table 3, the electric vehicle study had consumers rank a subset of 16 hypothetical vehicles. The selection of the 16 was based on an experimental design referred to as an orthogonal array.

The method employed to obtain consumers' preferences was to prepare sets of 16 cards, each card containing one of the attribute-level combinations. Consumers were asked to sort the set from most to least preferred.

TABLE 3   Attribute-Level Specification: Electric Vehicle Study

ATTRIBUTE	LEVEL A	LEVEL B	CONVENTIONAL VEHICLE	ELECTRIC VEHICLE
Speed and range	40 miles and 40 mph	Unlimited	[B][a]	[A]
Operating costs	10 cents/mile	5 cents/mile	[A]	[B]
Initial price	$8,000	$5,000	[B]	[A]
Air and noise pollution	"normal"	"zero"	[A]	[B]
Propulsion system	"gas engine"	"new system"	[A]	[B]

ATTRIBUTE-LEVEL COMBINATIONS USE IN ELECTRIC VEHICLE STUDY[b]

	1	2	3	4	5	6	7	8	9	10	11	12	13	14	15	16
Speed and range	B	B	B	B	A	B	B	B	B	A	A	A	A	A	A	A
Operating costs	B	B	B	A	B	B	A	A	A	B	B	B	A	A	A	A
Initial price	B	B	A	B	B	A	B	A	A	B	A	A	B	B	A	A
Pollution	B	A	B	B	B	A	A	B	A	A	B	A	B	A	B	A
Propulsion	A	B	B	B	B	A	A	A	B	A	A	B	A	B	B	A

[a]The attribute-level combination for a conventional vehicle is: level B on speed and range, level A on operating costs, level B on initial price, level A on pollution, and level A on propulsion.

[b]For example, "Card 1" was specified as: Unlimited speed and range, 5 cents/mile, $5,000, zero air and noise pollution, and a gasoline engine.

Analysis of the rank preference data was done using MONANOVA (Kruskal, 1965). This computer program searches for values (utilities) for each of the 10 attribute-levels such that when the utilities are added together, the net utilities for each of the 16 combinations will correspond to the original preference rankings. This analysis can be based on either the rankings of individual consumers or the composite ranking of a group of respondents.

For the electric vehicle study analysis of the composite rankings of all respondents produced the "part worth" utilities of the 10 attribute-levels indicated in Table 4. Also indicated are the net utilities resulting when the part worth utilities are combined for conventional and electric vehicles.

The net utilities indicate that electric vehicles capable of only 40 miles and 40 miles per hour, and priced at $3,000 premium, will be seen as inferior to conventional vehicles even when operating costs are reduced by 50 percent and pollution eliminated. However, the part worth utilities also indicate that only one of the electric vehicles' impediments need to be eliminated for consumer preferences to be reversed.

AN ALTERNATIVE DATA COLLECTION APPROACH

The foregoing study indicates a data collection approach referred to as *full profile* or *concept evaluation*, that is, the respondent compares alternatives specified in terms of all of the attributes of interest. A second conjoint measurement approach involves evaluating two attributes at a time and is referred to as a *trade-off matrix* approach. An example of this is also provided by electric vehicle study.

When the importance of operating capacity became apparent, further attention was directed to this characteristic. Electric propulsion technology limited operating capacity in terms of speed, range, and number of stop−start cycles. However, technology did make possible various combinations of these three characteristics. Thus, it was important to assess consumers preferences in this regard.

Figure 1 indicates the trade-off matrices used to evaluate the three capacity attributes. With this approach consumers were asked to rank the nine cells each of the 3x3 matrices from one (most preferred) to nine (least preferred). Analysis similar to the earlier example was then used to assess the part worth utilities for the three levels of each of the three attributes.

CONJOINT ANALYSIS SUMMARY

The assessment of consumer trade-offs via conjoint analysis can be divided into five steps. The first, and most critical, is the careful identification of the attributes that are important to consumers. For example, assessment of consumers' trade-offs when selecting a resort hotel will only be valid if the measurement process asks about attributes of concern in the actual choice situation.

The second step is to specify the levels to be evaluated for each attribute. Again the criterion should be specification that is consistent with the actual choice situation. For example, if air travel choices were being evaluated and an attribute of concern was price, the price levels used for trade-off assessment should be consistent with feasible price levels on the route of interest.

The third step is the design of a data collection approach. As indicated earlier the research can be based on full profile or trade-off matrices. The trade-offs can be presented in a verbal or pictoral format. Consumers can be asked to respond using a paper and pencil approach or by means of an interactive computer display. These and other design issues are discussed further in a later section of the paper.

The fourth step is the data collection process. It is clear that this process is influenced by the choice of trade-off measurement procedures. Sorting of full profiles from most to least preferred places two constraints on the data collection process. Use of full profiles

TABLE 4   "Part Worth" Utilities of Attribute-Levels

ATTRIBUTE	LEVEL A	LEVEL B	CONVENTIONAL VEHICLE	ELECTRIC VEHICLE
Speed and range	−1.43	+1.43	+1.43	−1.43
Operating costs	−0.93	+0.93	−0.93	+0.93
Initial price	−0.90	+0.90	+0.90	−0.90
Air & noise pollution	−0.54	+0.54	−0.54	+0.54
Propulsion system	−0.02	+0.02	−0.02	+0.02
		Net[a]	+0.84	−0.84

[a]Comparison of conventional and electric vehicles indicates that the attribute-levels of conventional have a high net utility.

SPEED

		25 m.p.h.	40 m.p.h.	55 m.p.h.
	20 miles			
RANGE	40 miles			
	60 miles			

SPEED

		25 m.p.h.	40 m.p.h.	55 m.p.h.
	10			
STOP—STARTS	40			
	70			

RANGE

		20 miles	40 miles	60 miles
	10			
STOP—STARTS	40			
	70			

FIGURE 1 Trade-off matrix approach. Consumers respond by ranking the 9 cells from 1 (most preferred) to 9 (least preferred).

requires careful explanation by the interviewer, and a flat surface to spread out the concept cards. Similarly, use of computer display places a restriction on interview location.

The final step in conjoint analysis applications is parameter estimation. In the electric vehicle study attribute-level utilities were estimated using monatonic analysis of variance. As discussed later, other procedures, including regression analysis, can also be applied.

TRAVEL-RELATED APPLICATIONS

A study sponsored by the Research Branch of the Canadian Transport Commission provided several examples of the application of conjoint analysis in travel-

related applications (Strachan, 1978). The purpose of the study was to interview managers who had used conjoint analysis. The applications reviewed included four studies of air traveller trade-offs and three studies of rail traveller trade-offs. These are summarized here to indicate the approaches utilized and some of the problems encountered.

The Appendix indicates for each of the seven studies the study objectives, the method of attribute specification, the sampling method, the measurement approach, and the attributes evaluated. As the Appendix indicates, the critical decisions as to which attributes to include and which attribute-levels to evaluate were based on a combination of in-depth group interviews with consumers and group discussions by industry professionals. Future studies will continue to require careful attention to this phase of study design, and these group approaches continue to provide a most fruitful approach (Claxton, Ritchie, and Zaichkowsky, 1980).

The Appendix also indicates that the seven studies each evaluated the importance of from 11 to 27 attributes, and estimated from 35 to 71 attribute-level parameters. The most ambitious study, the Service Design Study done by Air Canada, divided 27 air trip attributes into 4 major groups (ground service, in-flight service, aircraft decor, and other) and asked respondents to evaluate the trade-offs associated with each group. Even with this subdivision into four groups, the number of potential trade-offs is very large. For example, each of the seven "other" attributes was specified at three levels. If respondents were asked to rank all combinations they would be faced with 3^7 or 2187 alternatives. Fortunately the use of carefully selected subsets of these alternatives makes it possible to estimate the 21 attribute-level parameters without burdening the respondent with an impossible task (Green, 1974).

The final observations to be made regarding the seven example applications are directed at the nature of attribute-level specification (Table 5 provides an example taken from the Rail Corridor Study). First, a major criterion in the selection of attribute-levels is that they encompass alternatives that are representative of marketplace possibilities. For example, the Rail Corridor Study considered travel times ranging from 1 to 9 hours, consistent with the modes and route being evaluated. Second, it can be noted that the attribute-levels can be expressed in a qualitative manner, as in the case of "quality of ride," or in a quantitative manner, as in the case of "door-to-door travel time."

In summary, the applications presented here serve to identify some of the major issues facing users of conjoint analysis. The following sections discuss these issues in greater detail and highlight the areas where user–researcher interaction is critical to the success of a conjoint analysis study.

A MANAGER'S PERSPECTIVE

For managers to be able to make effective use of conjoint analysis there must be (1) a general appreciation of the major issues involved in the implementation in this type of research study and (2) an understanding of the manager's role in this process. These two topics are discussed in the final sections of this paper. Prior to this, other reference papers on conjoint analysis are suggested.

REFERENCE DOCUMENTS

A thorough discussion of conjoint analysis was first provided by Green and Wind in their book *Multiattribute Decisions in Marketing* (1973). There also have been a number of journal articles that provide overview discussions (for example, Johnson, 1974a; Green and Wind, 1975). A more recent article (Green and Srinivasan, 1978) has discussed research concerns that have emerged since the introduction of conjoint analysis methods.

Papers specifically addressing tourism and travel have also utilized conjoint analysis. A paper in *Traffic Quarterly* (Ross, 1975) discussed these methods. A paper in *Harvard Business Review* (Green and Wind,

TABLE 5   Attribute-Level Specification Examples from Study II

ATTRIBUTE	ATTRIBUTE-LEVELS
1. On-time reliability	1. Usually arrives on time 2. Does not usually arrive on time
2. Personal comfort	1. Room to stretch out when you are sitting 2. Not much room to stretch out when you are sitting
3. Ride quality	1. Ride is smooth enough to be able to read or write 2. Not smooth enough to be able to read or write
4. Baggage arrangements	1. Baggage may be checked 2. Baggage may be stored in a special area near the entrance of the vehicle
5. Mobility during trip	1. You can leave your seat to go to another area such as a lounge 2. You cannot get up and move around during the trip
6. Door-to-door travel time	Nine attribute-levels specified as 1 hour through 9 hours inclusive
7. Mode	1. Car 2. Bus 3. Train 4. Plane

1975) indicated the use of conjoint analysis in a transatlantic air traveller study. More recently papers have been published that indicate the application of conjoint analysis in applications dealing with the performing arts (Currim, Weinberg, and Wittink, 1981) and urban transportation (Srinivasan, Flachsbart, Dajani, and Hartley, 1981).

The references indicated above were selected to provide an overview of conjoint analysis methods and applications. References in the following sections address specific aspects of conjoint analysis research.

MAJOR ISSUES IN CONJOINT ANALYSIS

The major issues involved in the application of conjoint analysis can be divided into three phases: attribute generation, data collection, and parameter estimation. These three phases are discussed next.

Attribute Generation

The identification of attributes that consumers will be asked to evaluate is part of the problem-definition process, the cornerstone of research design. What product/service attributes do consumers consider when making their purchase choices? What attributes can managers modify to achieve a more desirable product/service? These questions are clearly a central focus for many research studies.

A survey of 698 applications of conjoint analysis (Cattin and Wittink, 1981) indicated that all applications used "expert judgment" to identify relevant attributes, and that a large majority also used in-depth group interviews. It is absolutely critical that methods such as these be used to generate attributes that are relevant to consumers. Further, because of the somewhat intuitive nature of attribute generation, there is a danger that this phase of the research will be relegated to second place to more technical aspects of conjoint analysis, whereas the opposite should be the case.

Data Collection

The purpose here is not to describe the variety of data collection procedures in detail but rather to indicate the range of available alternatives. As indicated earlier, the data collection *format* may be either full profile or concept evaluation (Green, 1974). Another alternative involves pairwise comparisons of partial profiles (Johnson, 1975). A second data collection consideration is the method of *stimulus communication* with the major alternatives being to describe the stimuli in prose, to use pictures, or to show respondents actual products. In addition, Johnson (1974b) has introduced the use of interactive computer terminals.

A third consideration is the nature of *response information* to be collected. Respondents can be asked their degree of liking, preferences, and/or intentions to buy. Finally, a related consideration is *respond*

format with alternatives being paired choice, rankings, or ratings (Carmone, Green, and Jain, 1978).

Parameter Estimation

Accompanying the initial introduction of conjoint analysis procedures for data collection, computer programs were developed for data analysis. Probably the most well known, MONANOVA, was based on monatonic analysis of variance (Kruskal, 1965); another, LINMAP, was based on linear programming (Srinivasan and Schocker, 1973).

More recently, researchers have applied a variety of procedures including ordinary least squares regression (OLS), monatone regression, and logit analysis (Cattin and Wittink, 1981; Jain, Acito, Malhotra and Mahajan, 1979). A recent paper by Wittink and Cattin (1981) compared alternative estimation methods, and argued in favor of OLS on the basis of robustness and ease of interpretation.

THE MANAGER'S ROLE IN RESEARCH DESIGN

The following section raises a series of questions that should be raised by a manager when a conjoint analysis study is being designed. The reader will recognize that similar questions could be asked when evaluating a study that was already completed.

Is conjoint analysis appropriate? Whenever consumer trade-offs are a serious concern conjoint analysis presents a major research option. In parallel with conjoint analysis, respondents should be asked to provide a direct rating of the importance of each attribute. Such parallel measures will provide a useful indication of research validity. Managers would be well advised to ensure that direct measures accompany conjoint analysis methods.

What attributes should be measured? As discussed earlier, this is a critical question in the research design process. Further, it is the area where the manager rather than the researcher should provide research leadership.

Do the data collection methods seem reasonable? One aspect of this question is the extent to which the response task simulates real world decisions. In other words, the attribute-level combinations should represent alternatives that respondents will consider realistic. The second aspect of this question is the complexity of the response task. Care must be taken not to overtax respondents by asking them to evaluate an onerous set of attribute-level combinations. Careful pilot testing of the data collection methods can provide important insights in this area. A manager's major concern when evaluating data collection methods should be to ensure that consumers will consider the response task to be realistic and not tiring and/or confusing.

Will the analysis produce results that are readily

understood? This question can be divided into four subsidiary questions:

1 Does the parameter estimation procedure provide an indication of "goodness-of-fit" for the overall model? In other words, is it possible to assess how well the attribute utilities derived by the analysis capture the information contained in the respondent data? For example, in a regression analysis R^2 provides that this indication of variance is accounted for.

2 Does the analysis provide an indication of the statistical significance for each attribute utility, or only for the overall model? That is, the overall results may be highly significant when consumers consider a few of the attributes to be very important, and other attributes to be irrelevant. Again, using regression as an example, the statistics provide an indication of the significance of individual attributes.

3 Will the analysis facilitate the evaluation of differences across consumers? Although an overall indication of consumers' attribute utilities is an important starting point, it is frequently equally important to be able to identify groups of consumers with common values for purposes of market segmentation.

4 Will the analysis attempt to provide some indication of the validity of the findings? As indicated earlier, use of direct measures of attribute importance in parallel with conjoint analysis methods is one validation approach, with converging results providing confidence in the findings. Looking for similar results across split-sample analyses is another approach. A third approach that has been used with conjoint analysis is to predict market share of existing products based on the derived attribute utilities, and then to compare predicted with actual market share figures.

It is clear that a manager faced with attempting to understand relatively complex analytical techniques must draw on the expertise of their research associates. Looking for answers to the four questions outlined above should provide a useful framework for this interaction.

Since introduced in 1971 conjoint analysis has gained widespread acceptance as a method for evaluation customer trade-offs. Cattin and Wittink (1981) surveyed commercial usage in the U.S. and found 698 applications prior to 1981. As with any new technique, potential users are faced with assessing the merits of the new approach and deciding whether it is appropriate for their needs. The purpose of this paper has been to provide potential users in the field of tourism and travel with an overview of conjoint analysis, and to suggest key issues to consider when a study using these procedures seems appropriate.

APPENDIX   Applications of Conjoint Analysis

STUDY I: INTERCITY SHORT TAKEOFF AND LANDING (STOL) SERVICE
(by the Transportation Development Center)

---

1 Study objectives—to develop a model for forecasting traffic on a new STOL service and to predict the effect of changing the levels of service offered.

2 Attribute specification—in-depth group interviews with business travellers were used to identify 13 attributes of concern, each attribute specified by 2 to 4 levels.

3 Sampling—random telephone calls to quality potential users of service, followed by personal interviews.

4 Measurement approach—21 trade-off matrices supported with sketches to convey some of the attributes.

5 Attributes—(levels in brackets).

Trip time (3)	Reliability (2)
Trip cost (4)	Refreshments (4)
Reservations (3)	Baggage (3)
Other travellers (3)	Reading comfort (2)
Credit (2)	Seat width (3)
Transfers (3)	Ride comfort (3)
Departure (3)	

6 Outcome—aided in decision regarding number of aircraft needed for the introduction of new STOL service.

STUDY II: RAIL CORRIDOR STUDY
(by the Transportation Development Center)

---

1 Study objectives—to compare alternative intercity travel modes and to determine how to increase passenger rail traffic.

2 Attribute specification—in-depth group interviews used to identify 13 attributes and to specify each at 2 to 14 levels.

3 Sampling—random telephone calls to qualify corridor travellers, followed by personal interviews.

4 Measurement approach—69 paired choices specified by sets of 3 attributes (Johnson 1975).

5 Attributes—(levels in brackets).

On time reliability (2)	Food & beverage (3)
Personal comfort (2)	Travel time (9)
Ride quality (2)	Terminal convenience (3)
Baggage (2)	Reservations (3)
Mobility enroute (2)	Cost (14)
Departure times (3)	Mode (4)
Peace & quiet (2)	

6 Outcome—attribute utilities indicated that it would be extremely difficult to switch travellers from auto to rail.

STUDY III: INDEX OF AIR SERVICE QUALITY
(by the Canadian Transport Commission)

1 Study objectives—to develop a measure of quality of air service as perceived by business and pleasure travellers.

2 Attribute specification—in-depth group interviews used to identify 13 attributes and specify each at 3 to 5 levels.

3 Sampling—random selection of houses with respondents qualified for travel patterns.

4 Measurement approach—60 trade-off matrices.

5 Attributes—(levels in brackets).

Reservations (3)	Ticketing wait (3)
Flight time (3)	Reliability (3)
Airplane size (3)	Frequency (3)
Baggage service (3)	Airport access (3)
Seat width (3)	Stops (3)
Food service (3)	Fare (5)
Airport crowds (3)	

6 Outcome—provided a general description of consumer interests with respect to air travel. For example, on-time service was found to be more important than in-flight time.

STUDY IV: TRANSCONTINENTAL RAIL STUDY
(by the Canadian Transport Commission)

1 Study objectives—to study service preferences of rail travellers.

2 Attribute specification—based on expert opinion 11 attributes were identified and specified at 2 to 5 levels.

3 Sampling—on-board interviews with random sample of rail travellers.

4 Measurement approach—concept evaluation.

5 Attributes—(levels in brackets).

Sleeping accommodation (4)	Reliability (3)
Accommodation space (2)	Trip time (3)
Toilet facilities (4)	Food quality (3)
Fare supplement (5)	Meal service (3)
Departures (3)	Meal price (4)
Arrivals (3)	

6 Outcome—used to guide the modification of passenger service.

STUDY V: MARITIME RAIL SERVICE
(by the Canadian Transport Commission)

This study was very similar to Study IV.

STUDY VI: SERVICE DESIGN STUDY
(by Air Canada)

1 Study objectives—to determine the relative importance of air trip components.

2 Attribute specification—group sessions involving industry professionals identified four groups of air trip attributes: 9 ground service, 4 in-flight, 7 aircraft decor, and 7 others. The attributes were specified at 2 to 5 levels.

3 Sampling—random telephone screening from passenger list resulting in subjects qualified by route and business–pleasure. Personal interviews were conducted with qualified subjects.

4 Measurement approach—concept evaluation with pictures used to represent the various combinations of attribute levels for each of the 4 main groups of air trip attributes.

5 Attributes—(levels in brackets).

"Ground Service"	"Aircraft Decor"
Telephone answer speed (2)	Leg room (3)
Telephone voice (2)	Seat width (2)
Telephone info (2)	Overhead racks (2)
Check-in line (2)	Carry-on (2)
Check-in personnel (2)	Interior color (2)
Ground hostess (2)	Seat adjustments (2)
Personnel grooming (2)	Lavatory line-up (2)
P/A announcements (2)	
Baggage wait (2)	"Other"
	On-time (3)
"In Flight Service"	Price (3)
Attendant grooming (3)	Routing (3)
Reading material (5)	Check-in (3)
Refreshments (5)	Seating (3)
Entertainment (5)	Reservations (3)
	Scheduling (3)

6 Outcome—indicated areas of emphasis for service improvement. For example, baggage handling needed more attention than in-flight snacks and newspapers.

STUDY VII: TRANSATLANTIC AIR TRAVEL STUDY
(by I.A.T.A.)

1 Study objectives—to assess consumers' perceptions of transatlantic air fare packages for non-business travel.

2 Attribute specification—group discussions involving international representatives of I.A.T.A. identified 12 attributes and specified each at 2 to 8 levels.

3 Sampling—random telephone screening from passenger lists to qualify respondents who had travelled across the North Atlantic. Personal interviews were conducted with qualified subjects in 6 countries.

4 Measurement approach—matrix trade-offs.

5 Attributes—(levels in brackets).

Length of stay (8)	Seasons (5)
Advanced booking (6)	Stand-by (5)
In-flight service (4)	Day of week (4)
Land accommodation (5)	Group flights (5)
Flexible booking (4)	Stopovers (4)
Air fare (8)	Flight type (2)

6 Outcome—provided general guidelines for the design and promotion of new transatlantic fare packages.

REFERENCES

Carmone, Frank J., Paul E. Green, and Arun K. Jain (1978), "Robustness of Conjoint Analysis: Some Monte Carlo Results," *Journal of Marketing Research*, 15 (May), pp. 300–303.

Cattin, Philippe, and Dick R. Wittink (1981), "Commercial Use of Conjoint Analysis: A Survey," Research Paper No. 596, Graduate School of Business, Stanford University, Palo Alto, California.

Claxton, John D., J.R. Brent Ritchie, and Judy Zaichkowsky (1980), "The Nominal Group Technique: Its Potential for Consumer Research," *Journal of Consumer Research*, 7 (December), pp. 308–313.

Currim, Imran S., Charles B. Weinberg, and Dick R. Wittink (1981), "The Design of Subscription Programs for a Performing Arts Series: Issues in Applying Conjoint Analysis," *Journal of Consumer Research*, 8 (June), pp. 67–75.

Davidson, J.D. (1973), "Forecasting Traffic on STOL," *Operation Research Quarterly*, 24, pp. 561–569.

Green, Paul E. (1973), "On the Analysis of Interactions in Marketing Research Data," *Journal of Marketing Research*, 10 (November), pp. 410–419.

Green, Paul E. (1974), "On the Design of Choice Experiments Involving Multifactor Alternatives," *Journal of Consumer Research*, 1 (September), pp. 61–68.

Green, Paul E., and Vithala R. Rao (1971), "Conjoint Measurement for Quantifying Judgment Data," *Journal of Marketing Research*, 8 (August), pp. 355–363.

Green, Paul E., and V. Srinivasan (1978), "Conjoint Analysis in Consumer Research: Issues and Outlook," *Journal of Consumer Research*, 5 (September), pp. 103–123.

Green, Paul E., and Yoram Wind (1973), *Multiattribute Decisions in Marketing: A Measurement Approach*, Hinsdale, Ill: The Dryden Press.

Green, Paul E., and Yoram Wind (1975), "New Way to Measure Consumers' Judgments," *Harvard Business Review*, (July), pp. 107–117.

Hargreaves, George, John D. Claxton, and Fred H. Siller (1976), "New Product Evaluation: Electric Vehicles for Commercial Applications," *Journal of Marketing*, (January), pp. 74–77.

Jain, Arun K., Franklin Acito, Naresh K. Malhotra, and Vijay Mahajan (1979), "A Comparison of the Internal Validity of Alternative Parameter Estimation Methods in Decomposition Multiattribute Preference Models," *Journal of Marketing Research*, 16 (August), pp. 313–322.

Johnson, Richard M. (1974a), "Trade-off Analysis of Consumer Values," *Journal of Marketing Research*, 11 (May), pp. 121–127.

Johnson, Richard M. (1974b), "Measurement of Consumer Values Using Computer Interactive Techniques," in *Market Measurement and Analysis*, David B. Montgomery and Dick R. Wittink, Eds., Cambridge, Mass: Marketing Science Institute, pp. 271–177.

Johnson, Richard M. (1975), "Beyond Conjoint Measurement: A Method of Pairwise Trade-off Analysis," in *Advances in Consumer Research*, Volume 3, B.B. Anderson, Ed., Proceedings, Association of Consumer Research, pp. 353–358.

Kruskal, J.B. (1965), "Analysis of Factorial Experiments by Estimating Monotone Transformations of the Data," *Journal of the Royal Statistical Society, Series B*, 27 (No. 2), pp. 251–263.

Luce, R. Duncan, and John W. Tukey (1964), "Simultaneous Conjoint Measurement: A New Type of Fundamental Measurement," *Journal of Mathematical Psychology*, 1 (February), pp. 1–27.

Ross, Richard B. (1975), "Measuring the Influence of Soft Variables on Travel Behavior," *Traffic Quarterly*, (July), pp. 336–346.

Srinivasan, V., Peter G. Flachsbart, Jarir S. Dajani, and Rolfe G. Hartley (1981), "Forecasting the Effectiveness of Work-Trip Gasoline Policies through Conjoint Analysis," *Journal of Marketing*, 45 (Summer), pp. 157–172.

Srinivasan, V., and Alan D. Shocker (1973), "Linear Programming Techniques for Multi-dimensional Analysis of Preferences," *Psychometrica*, 38, pp. 337–369.

Strachan, Morley B. (1978), "Conjoint Measurement—Transport Model Choice," Research Paper, Center for Transportation Studies, University of British Columbia, Vancouver, British Columbia.

Wittink, Dick R., and Philippe Cattin (1981), "Alternative Estimation Methods for Conjoint Analysis: A Monte Carlo Study," *Journal of Marketing Research*, 18 (February), pp. 101–106.

PART EIGHT

SPECIAL MARKETING APPLICATIONS

This final part of the Handbook contains four chapters which describe the application of particular research approaches to increasing our understanding of four important marketing problems commonly facing managers in the travel, tourism, and hospitality industry. In Chapter 40, Thomas Davidson (Davidson-Peterson Associates) examines how managers can assess the effectiveness of advertising or other forms of persuasive communications targeted to the travel/tourism/ entertainment/hospitality marketplace. The initial part of the chapter clarifies what is meant by research designed to evaluate advertising and emphasizes that both technical and managerial dimensions are involved. The chapter goes on to review the key questions that a marketing manager must answer when attempting to assess advertising effectiveness. These questions involve ensuring that the objectives of the advertising are clear, defining when research should be conducted, ensuring that the correct factors are being studied, determining the most appropriate measurement method, and being clear on the appropriate sampling frame. The chapter concludes by reminding readers that it is critical for managers to keep clearly in mind the purpose of research related to their advertising activities.

Chapter 41 also deals with advertising research but in a very specific manner. In this chapter, Ilkka Ronkainen (Georgetown University) and Arch Woodside (Tulane University) review the use of coupon conversion research as an aid to assessing the effectiveness of this particular form of promotion. After briefly describing the use of coupons in advertising, the authors review the different research approaches that may be used to gather data for coupon studies and provide examples of the kinds of samples used, the response rates obtained, and the kind of data gathered. They subsequently provide advice concerning the appropriate types of data analysis commonly employed and the nature of the findings obtained.

Chapter 42 deals with a very fundamental research topic in the field of marketing, namely, segmentation. In this chapter, Jane Fitzgibbon (Ogilvy & Mather) examines the use of segmentation research methods as they apply to travel, tourism, and hospitality. The chapter starts off with a brief review of basic market segmentation concepts and the manner in which segmentation analysis has developed to this point in time. A particular emphasis is placed on the importance of attitudinal segmentation. In this regard, Ms. Fitzgibbon provides managers with a series of very practical guidelines for the effective use of these important segmentation criteria. It is emphasized that these guidelines have been empirically derived and represent practical lessons which the author feels are particularly relevant for individuals responsible for segmentation analysis. Readers will particularly appreciate Ms. Fitzgibbon's comments concerning the use of statistical analysis in segmentation research and her views on interpreting and using the results from segmentation analysis.

The final chapter in Part Eight and the Handbook has been prepared by Don Wynegar (United States Travel and Tourism Administration). The chapter is entitled "Estimating the Potential of International Markets." This area of research is one which has clearly grown in importance in recent years as the competition for the growing international market has risen dramatically. Mr. Wynegar, who has considerable experience in the field, provides readers with a very thorough and systematic framework for analyzing the potential and relative importance of international markets. Towards this end, the author presents a model providing the reader with a step-by-step approach to the analysis of international travel market potential. This model incorporates measures of both existing size and incremental market potential. In addition to these quantitative factors, the model includes several qualitative variables which can affect the marketability of a country in its travel markets. By incorporating a system of weighted indices into his model, the various factors are aggregated to form a Cumulative Market Evaluation Index, which provides a measurement of the relative marketing viability of each country and the basis for resource allocation. Readers responsible for undertaking the analysis of international markets will very much appreciate the rigor of the model presented by Mr. Wynegar and the level of detail he has provided.

40

Assessing the Effectiveness of Persuasive Communications in Tourism

THOMAS LEA DAVIDSON

Principal
Davidson-Peterson Associates, Inc.
New York, New York

This chapter is directed to the manager who, in the course of discharging his or her marketing responsibilities, must fund, commission, and use the results of research efforts designed to evaluate the effectiveness of advertising or other forms of persuasive communications targeted to the travel/tourism/entertainment/ hospitality marketplace. The comments are intended to help such a manager make decisions concerning advertising/communications research that will lead to more effective and cost-efficient marketing efforts. It is emphasized that the ultimate goal of evaluating advertising is to contribute to future sales and profits by increasing the effectiveness and the cost efficiency of future marketing efforts.

WHAT IS ADVERTISING EVALUATION RESEARCH?

Advertising evaluation research can be defined in two ways—technical and managerial.

- Technical: Advertising evaluation research is that body of systematic, scientific procedures employed to ISOLATE, DEFINE, MEASURE, and UNDERSTAND the relationship between advertising efforts and the influence of such advertising on the marketplace. These advertising efforts are usually specific as to copy, layout, artwork, media, timing, weight, and/or frequency.

- Managerial: Advertising evaluation research includes those procedures and techniques which may be employed to provide knowledge about the effect of advertising—which knowledge can be used by managers to make better decisions. The researcher or evaluator is attempting to replace opinion and guess with fact and thereby reduce risk.

Both definitions focus on cause-and-effect studies where advertising is the cause and some marketplace change is the effect.[1] The direct effect or influence of advertising is viewed as being a change in the mind-set of the potential buyer—that is, in attitudes, opinions, perceptions, image, desires, expectations, knowledge, awareness, or inclination to act (buy). The marketing manager anticipates that these changes in mind-set will, in turn, lead to favorable changes in buying behavior that will mean more sales of the advertiser's travel products and hence increase his profits. To influence sales, advertising must be exposed to the buyer, a message must be communicated, and a change in the buyer's thinking must occur.

Although profitable sales are the ultimate objective,

[1]For simplicity, the term "advertising" will be used herein to refer broadly to all forms of persuasive marketing efforts whereby the marketer wishes to communicate a given sales message to a specific customer audience regardless of the medium used. Such activities include point-of-purchase promotions as well as print, direct mail, broadcast, billboard, or outdoor, etc., advertising. And, the broad category of research which can be used to study any or all of these forms will be referred to as "advertising evaluation research."

advertising evaluation research has opted most of the time to study the changes in mind-set rather than actual sales performance. There are several reasons for this choice.

- Because sales are influenced by many factors besides advertising, it is frequently difficult to isolate the influence of advertising alone. There are strong influences on tourism outside the realm of advertising. Word-of-mouth discussions, currency values, the development of a destination as an "in" place, cost changes such as airline discounts, tour packages, or the infuence of "terrorism" may have more effect on tourism than advertising.

- The decision to buy a travel product is not an impulse purchase which can be triggered by a single advertisement. Rather travel buying is generally considered and planned over a period of time.

- Further, sales effect—a decision to visit a given hotel, for example—may be far removed in time and place from the advertising that influenced it and marketing needs to know effectiveness now. It can't wait for future studies.

In essence, the science of predicting human behavior—of which advertising evaluation research is a branch—is at best imprecise. The relationship between message and a change in mind-set is more direct and easier to study; and if the effect of advertising begins in the potential customer's mind then advertising evaluation research should also begin in the potential customer's mind.

One possible exception to the focus of advertising evaluation research on mind-set rather than behavior is direct response advertising such as a direct mail campaign that offers a brochure to all who mail back a coupon. The number of returned coupons can be counted directly. However, a recent study indicated the danger in assuming such a measure was a good evaluation of effectiveness. A survey of people who had returned such a coupon determined that a significant number had already decided to visit the advertiser's destination before sending back the coupon. Neither the coupon return nor their subsequent trip were a result of the advertising. These "already decideds" were requesting the coupon because they had already decided to "buy." Including them as "influenced travelers" greatly overstated the actual sales impact of this direct mail advertising effort.

The remainder of these comments will focus on research whose primary concern is studying changes in mind-set such as attitudes, opinions, perceptions, images, desires, expectations, knowledge, awareness, or inclinations to buy—changes that are influenced by advertising.

This focus should not imply that advertising evaluation research is in practice isolated from other forms of marketing research.

- Any study that provides information on what motivates travelers, who they are, and what they want or will buy will help management improve advertising effectiveness. Knowledge of the consumer will help create concepts and provide benchmarks against which future change can be assessed.

- And what we are calling advertising evaluation research can contribute to our understanding of other areas of marketing as well. Advertising evaluation research is merely a cause-and-effect-focused portion of all marketing research efforts.

In the final analysis, the effectiveness of advertising evaluation research may depend on the degree to which it is seen as part of and coordinated with the entire research program.

In essence, advertising is both very expensive and very fragile. Advertising dollars are often a major portion of the marketing budget and they should be held accountable for their performance. Advertising can be detrimental to our sales efforts if it is not believed, confuses, or conveys the wrong message. Improperly done, advertising may even sell competitive products more than the sponsor's. Managing advertising involves making many decisions and the more the manager knows, the better his decisions will be. Besides, well executed advertising evaluation research works; it helps managers spend advertising dollars more effectively. Identifying ways to make even small improvements in communications impact or preventing the repetition of mistakes can lead in the long run to substantial gains in sales and profits.

Because of the lack of precision in predicting human behavior, some marketing managers tend to question the value of doing any advertising evaluation research. It seems to me that this is somewhat like questioning the value of a flashlight because it is not a floodlight. A small bulb that at least guides one in the general direction in which one wants to go and prevents stumbling may not show all that is happening but it is better than traveling in total darkness.

WHAT ARE THE KEY QUESTIONS FOR THE MARKETING MANAGER?

In order to fulfill his responsibilities to fund, commission, and use effectively the results of advertising evaluation research, the marketing manager needs the answers to several key questions.

- For some of these questions—such as defining the advertising objectives—the burden of providing answers is the manager's. The research professional has the right to expect and the marketing manager has the obligation to provide specific advertising objectives against which the research can be planned.

- For other questions the manager's responsibility is to ask the question of a research professional and understand the answer and the implications of that answer for the study. (Thus, if someone else does not raise these questions or provide answers that are satisfactory to the manager, he should pursue them until satisfactory answers are obtained.) Only with these answers will the manager be able to judge fairly the potential gain in advertising effectiveness that will result from the spending of research dollars.

There are three ways that asking and answering these questions will contribute to the potential effectiveness of advertising evaluation research. These ways are:

- To help design the "best" study. Deciding on answers to these questions and the discussion leading to those decisions will ensure that the proposed research effort will provide the most effective, efficient, and relevant method for assessing the advertising efforts. However, it must be kept in mind that seldom is there any absolutely right or absolutely wrong answer. There is, at best, an optimum answer that combines compromise with judgement. Nevertheless, the critical issue is to be sure the answers are carefully thought out and agreed to by both research professional and marketing manager before the fieldwork begins.
- To ensure that the manager understands the research process and has confidence that he can use the results. The manager needs to be part of the evaluation process not merely the recipient of "scores" once the study is completed—"scores" which he may or may not believe. Being part of the planning process generates in the marketing manager an association with the results that will help him to be comfortable with their use.
- To determine before the research begins that all the data to be generated can, in fact, be used. The evaluation study needs to produce data that will have direct use and meaning in planning future advertising, not simply nice-to-know facts.

To reinforce these benefits and to be sure that the key questions have been satisfactorily answered, it may be useful to hold a mock presentation before the actual fieldwork begins but after the study has been designed. In this mock presentation, hypothetical results are offered and the manager is asked to discuss how he might use such data. For example, assume that a study shows that the number of people considering a cruise vacation in the next six months and who mention Cruise Line "A" unaided when asked to list all cruise lines they were considering goes from 20% to 25%. The manager might then be asked what actions he would take if that finding does indeed result. His answer and the subsequent discussion will clearly point out the value of the data, any concerns or questions the manager has, and can be a considerable aid in improving the entire study. No amount of sophisticated analysis can compensate for a study which fails to provide useful data or which contains what the manager views as critical design faults. The following pages provide detailed description of the eight key questions to include.

WHAT ARE THE OBJECTIVES OF THE ADVERTISING?

The first task in any advertising evaluation research project is to establish clearly stated, specific objectives against which the advertising's performance—or effectiveness—can be measured. These objectives are the basis for selecting the research approach, defining the sample, designing the questionnaire, and establishing the criteria for tabulation and analysis.

Advertising objectives are best set if they are based on some underlying theory or model that expresses the laws or principles by which advertising works. Several such general theories exist which, while neither the final answer nor universally accepted, do offer a beginning. Briefly, they include:

- AIDA—Attention–Interest–Desire–Action.
  This sequence purports to indicate how advertising affects consumers.
- DAGMAR (Defining Advertising Goals for Measured Advertising Results) uses the order Awareness–Comprehension–Conviction–Action.
- Some work the author has done suggests that for a tourist destination there is a consideration set through which the destination must move before a visit is planned. This sequence might be summarized: Awareness, Association, Conviction, Perceived Value, and Action.

If a theoretical construct is lacking, then objectives need to be based on a sound analysis of the marketing task being undertaken. Reference to previous research can guide the selection of changes in mind-set that should improve the predisposition to want the advertiser's travel product.

To set advertising objectives, the manager needs to understand the concept of the potential buyers' continuum from ignorance to purchase. In establishing objectives it is important to keep several guidelines in mind:

A The objective must state who is to be affected by

the advertising—essentially the target market. The definition might be those in a geographic area, those with particular past vacation habits, those of a certain age, level of affluence, or other demographic characteristics, or those who read a particular publication—or some combination of these characteristics. Essentially, the research purpose of this definition is to decide who will be interviewed when we seek to learn if the advertising has been effective. The more precise the definition of the target market, the more precise the measure of effectiveness can be.

B The objectives must state clearly and precisely what the advertising is designed to do.

The ultimate goal of the tourism marketing effort might be to increase the number of visitor days at a destination. That could mean the same number of guests who stay longer, new guests who visit for the first time, or previous guests whose frequency of visit is increased. The goal has been stated in terms of sales. It is unlikely that advertising can be measured directly in terms of sales.

Thus, the objective for the advertising—one which can be measured—must be more limited and more specific and stated in terms of the mind-set change desired. For example, the objective for a campaign might be stated as:

- To increase awareness of the destination/hotel/carrier as an option for the next decision.
- To increase the number in the target market who hold favorable attitudes toward the destination/hotel/carrier (but favorable attitudes need more precise definition).
- To broaden knowledge of the specifics of the destination/hotel/carrier and what it offers the vacationer.
- To increase the number in the target market who say they will seriously consider the destination/hotel/carrier the next time the vacation decision arises.

Consideration of the anticipated or hoped for gain can help the researcher determine the degree of precision required, the sample size, and hence cost.

C The objective must be stated in terms which allow measurement—essentially, numeric.

Without some numeric statement of objectives it is not possible to measure advertising effectiveness. Research can provide a statistically reliable measure of whether an objective has been achieved only if that objective is stated in measurable terms. For example, research cannot provide an assessment of whether a campaign has achieved its goal if that goal is stated as "get more people to think well of us." Research can provide an assessment if the objective is stated as "Increase the proportion of the target market who say they will definitely consider vacationing with us from 20% to 30%.

In sum, the objectives of the advertising must then include who is to be addressed and what is to be achieved in a way which can be measured. Once the objectives have been established, then we can proceed to develop a research program designed to measure whether these objectives have been achieved.

WHEN IN RELATION TO THE ADVERTISING WILL THE RESEARCH OCCUR?

Any given advertising can be viewed as having a life cycle lasting from the generation of the original concept to the end of the campaign. Evaluation research can occur at any time during this cycle. Research done early in the cycle will be more predictive in nature and will be designed to make the expenditure of current advertising dollars as productive as possible—that is, improve the campaign being tested. Research done toward the end of the campaign will focus more on the measurement of actual results that have occurred already in the marketplace. Here the intent should be more oriented toward making the next advertising effort more productive.

Concept Testing

Concept tests are usually small scale, qualitative studies that occur as soon as the idea of an ad or campaign has been created. The concept or concepts being studied are usually presented as a statement, possibly with rough sketches. The intent is to make some initial judgements regarding whether to proceed with development of the concept(s) and to suggest directions for improvement. Results should usually be viewed as tentative. Focused group discussions or small-sample one-on-one interviews are usually employed.

Pretesting

Pretests are more rigorous studies than concept tests and usually involve more rigorous sampling. Travelers from the target audiences are exposed to preliminary (or finished) versions of the proposed advertisements and a battery of questions is asked to measure potential response. Such research is done before the advertisements are exposed to the market using a regular media schedule.

The purpose of pretesting is to attempt to predict actual performance, identify problems, select from among alternative versions, and provide guidance for fine-tuning the advertisements themselves.

Most exposure is "artificial" in that the potential travelers are aware that they are research subjects. The extent of realism can range, however, from showing a prototype ad to employing cable television in one city as a test for the entire campaign.

Testing during the Campaign

In many respects tests conducted during the time the advertising is actually being exposed in the marketplace are merely "early" posttests. The intent of "during the campaign" studies is usually to provide an early indication of what the total impact will be. Such information can help the marketer decide whether to extend a successful campaign or to cut short one that is not working well.

These studies can also help assess wear-out—that is, after how much repetition does a given advertisement begin to lose effectiveness?

Methods and procedures are similar to those in posttesting.

Posttesting

These are studies conducted after or almost after the advertising has run its course and the scheduled media are finished. Hopefully, posttesting results will be compared with some benchmark measurements developed before the advertising began to run. The intent is to "score" the advertising by measuring how the potential travelers' mind-sets have changed.

Sampling procedures and questionnaires are designed to disguise the advertising nature of the study.

WHAT IS BEING STUDIED OR MEASURED?

The issue here is to select just which components of the advertising are being studied. Is the research to focus on some component of the advertising—headline, copy, layout, use of color, media selection, or frequency—is it to focus on a single ad in its entirety, or is the research to focus on an entire campaign? Each can be a meaningful and valid focus for a research effort. The determinant is what management needs to know to improve advertising effectiveness and what questions exist that need to be settled in planning advertising.

WHAT MEASUREMENT METHODS WILL BE EMPLOYED?

Another way to restate this question is to ask, "What (types of) questions will be asked and how will they be worded?" That is, how will the questionnaire be designed? Basically, questionnaire design is better left to the research professional and will not be discussed here in any detail. There is too much to say and there are many excellent and lengthy references that say it well.

However, several comments are in order. First, the determination of the subject matter of the questionnaire and the wording of the questions comes directly from the statement of advertising objectives. When the questionnaire is written, the relationship between it and the objectives should be clear. It may be useful to go so far as to write a rationale in which the reason for each question is shown by relating it to the objective it addresses and, conversely, for each objective the relevant questions are listed. Then we know that (the relationship is complete) all the data will be relevant and all the objectives measured.

Second, there is really no limit on the type of questionnaire nor on the type of measurement method which may be employed. Interviews can be done in person, by mail, over the telephone, or even self-administered with groups of people who congregate at one spot. Each technique has, of course, its own strengths, weaknesses, and peculiarities.

Questionnaires can be highly structured and direct or they can call for discursive answers. Frequently they rely on the subject's memory as when recall, recognition, or association questions are asked. They can use scales to measure opinions and attitudes or they can make use of projective techniques.

A typical sequence of questions might include:

1 Awareness of and preference for the travel product being advertised and key competitors would include intent to visit each if appropriate. These question are asked early in the interview so that response will not be biased by specific questions to be asked later.

2 Image of the travel product and key competitors.

3 Registration and comprehension of the message being delivered. This could include factual questions about the advertising or the travel product itself as well as measures of comprehension, believability, and clarity of message.

4 Specific buying/shopping behavior including previous travel patterns.

5 Demographic and psychographic (attitudes, intent, opinion, and lifestyle) characteristics.

6 Exposure to media. Because memory is fragile, it is not possible to develop accurate measures of previous media exposure. It is, however, possible to develop an index of impact by combining two measures: (1) a ranking of perceived exposure relative to competitive advertising possibly factored by relative dollars spent and (2) a "test" including specific questions on format and/or message content.

Finally, some techniques employ electronic or mechanical aids to assist in understanding buyer response. These aids include eye cameras (optical devices that track eye movement), a tachistoscope to control exposure time, the use of voice analysis to determine when the respondent is telling the truth, commercial lie detectors, and other devices that provide a means whereby a respondent can indicate interest or attention. The artificial nature of the test situation and an apparent lack of acceptance by many advertising executives limit the use of mechanical devices.

WHO IS BEING INCLUDED IN THE SAMPLE?

The basic issue here is to be sure of two things. First, that the sample and screening criteria reflect the target audience as specified in the objectives and, second, that the manager clearly understands who is being interviewed.

WILL THE ASSESSMENT BE MADE IN A "REAL LIFE" SITUATION OR WILL IT BE IN A LABORATORY SETTING?

A number of services are available that offer laboratory or artificial settings for conducting advertising evaluation research. They include:

- Cable television systems where ad exposure can be directed to specific households, allowing for split-run testing of two commercials simultaneously.
- Theatres where groups of people see films interspersed with commercial material.
- Minimarkets where consumers see commercials and then shop for items including those for which commercials were shown.

These laboratory settings offer more control. Real life testing occurs when the advertising is run on a limited basis such as in a single test city on one television station or in a limited number of copies of a limited edition of a magazine.

IS THE STUDY "AD HOC" OR WILL SOME EXISTING SYSTEM OR OMNIBUS TECHNIQUE BE EMPLOYED?

A number of firms offer "special" techniques for testing advertising in either television or print. The usual procedure is to expose the advertising by means of some predetermined procedure; a series of questions usually related to awareness, intention to buy, or comprehension may be asked. The result is often a "score" which can then be compared to norms for the category developed from previous comparable studies. The cost is usually less than that for "ad hoc" studies.

One problem for the tourism marketer is much the same for existing systems as for laboratory procedures.

Most of these were designed for the package goods/supermarket business and, thus, may be less effective when the advertising is for travel or tourism. Thus, the tourism marketer may be forced to employ more "ad hoc" procedures wherein the study is designed and implemented specifically for him.

ARE WE KEEPING SCORE OR DEVELOPING A GAME PLAN?

In some ways this can be one of the most critical questions. Too frequently research wastes effort documenting where a company has been in the past—documentation that often takes on the appearance of a report card or a scorecard which offers little value as a guide to how to improve. The thrust of the scorecard assessment is to tell management what they bought with their advertising dollars. Further, score-keeping research can lead to antagonism as it is used to rate the performance of the advertising agency or creative, media, or account staffs. This antagonism leads to ill will, defensive reactions, and reduced performance.

Another danger of "single-number" or score card research is that the goal becomes one of getting a better score not necessarily of creating more effective advertising. Unfortunately, a better score and more effective advertising are not necessarily synonymous.

Advertising evaluation research that will contribute to future sales should focus on developing data and analyses that help advertising/marketing decide where they should be going and how to get there. The future should be viewed as an opportunity for achievement. Game plan development based on sound diagnosis of past performance should be the hallmark of effective and contributing advertising evaluation research. Game plan research helps us learn what works and what does not work so that this knowledge can be used to make future advertising more effective. This is constructive research designed to provide creative guidance for developing advertising that is increasingly more effective.

CONCLUSION

This chapter has attempted to suggest three ideas:

- One key to the success of advertising evaluation research is the active involvement of the marketing manager in the evaluation process. The manager must provide clear, precise advertising objectives, he must understand the method being employed, and he must be prepared to use the results in planning future advertising efforts. Lacking these commitments, the ultimate value of this type of research is questionable.
- There are a great many techniques that can be

employed to assess advertising effectiveness—each with its strengths and weaknesses. A marketing manager should get competent professional research guidance to select that mix of techniques which will optimize each individual study.

- Done well, advertising evaluation research can offer continuing assistance in improving the performance of advertising. A modest increase in advertising effectiveness—generated by the intelligent use of research findings—can almost always result in sales and profits that are larger than the cost of doing the research.

BIBLIOGRAPHY

While a number of journal articles have been written on assessing advertising, almost nothing has been published on assessing tourism advertising. Probably the best general bibliography can be found in the *Handbook of Marketing Research* edited by Robert Ferber (McGraw—Hill Book Company). Certainly the Journals of *Marketing, Marketing Research*, or *Advertising* are also good sources. The only other text the author has found that stands the test of use and time is *Measuring Advertising Effectiveness* by Lucas and Britt (McGraw—Hill Book Company).

41

Advertising Conversion Studies

ILKKA A. RONKAINEN

Assistant Professor of Marketing
Georgetown University
Washington, D.C.

ARCH G. WOODSIDE

The Malcolm S. Woldenberg
Professor of Marketing
Tulane University
New Orleans, Louisiana

*C*oupon conversion studies in travel and tourism are reviewed in terms of applications and issues critical to achieving reliable results. Methodological topics include sampling, response rates, measuring expenditures, and sponsor identification. Applications beyond estimating rates of conversion of inquirers into visitors include comparisons of the relative performance of ads, advertising campaigns, and media vehicles.

With more states and specific locations awakening to tourism's potential as an economic accelerator, the advertising budgets to attract tourists have increased. During the 1982/1983 fiscal year, the average state ad budget was $937,000, with New York in the forefront with $6,800,000 earmarked for advertising production and media costs. A number of other states, such as Alaska, Florida, North Carolina, and Hawaii, are spending well in excess of $1,000,000 (U.S. Travel Data Center 1983; *Advertising Age* 1982).

These figures are not surprising when per person per visit expenditures are considered. Alaska ranks first with $1,667 per person per visit (1977 data), followed by Hawaii with $524 (1977 data) and Florida with $474 (1979 data) (Goeldner and Dicke 1981).

As both the costs and the benefits of these programs have increased, more research has been directed at the effectiveness of the advertising campaigns conducted. Most state travel offices conduct promotional campaigns which include coupons, addresses, and/or toll-free telephone numbers through which those interested can obtain brochures and travel information on the particular state's attractions and features.

The effectiveness of such campaigns is measured by using advertising conversion research. This research is conducted to answer the question of how many inquirers from travel ads convert to visitors and what their (travel) behavioral characteristics (e.g., expenditures) are. The information generated from returned questionnaires (or responses obtained by phone) permits the computation of total revenue, average revenue per inquiry (RPI), and average cost per inquiry (CPI). Since this technique was presented by Woodside and Reid (1974), a number of conversion studies have been completed. Conversion studies have been used to compare the relative performances of one ad versus another ad and one ad campaign versus another ad campaign (Woodside and Motes 1980, 1981), as well as one media vehicle versus another media vehicle (Woodside and Ronkainen 1982). Furthermore, several studies have addressed methodological issues in conversion research (Woodside 1981; Ellerbrock 1981; Ballman *et al.* 1983; Woodside and Ronkainen 1983, 1984).

The purpose of this chapter is to discuss the major issues pertaining to conversion research as well as to

481

address some of the problems inherent in the approach. Data from conversion studies are used to highlight the major points raised.

THE RESEARCH PROCESS
DATA COLLECTION MODES

Three primary modes are available: personal interviews, telephone interviews, and mail interviews. Personal interviews have not been reported as a primary mode mainly because of its cost and staff requirements. Typically, a questionnaire is mailed to (or a phone call made to) a sample of inquirers six to ten months after receiving the inquiries.

In comparing and contrasting the telephone and mail methods, the advantages of one are often the disadvantages of the other. While a general comparison (such as the one provided in Table 1) can be made, a major caveat should be emphasized. The choice of a mode is situation specific, i.e., factors such as time constraints, budget, sample size, and information requirements determine a particular mode's advantages and disadvantages in a given situation (Peterson 1982; Churchill 1983).

The per-contract cost of the mail questionnaire is generally low; e.g., Hunt and Dalton (1983) found that the cost per usable questionnaire was estimated to run approximately 40% more for the telephone method ($1.33 versus $2.05). However, if nonresponse is substantial, the cost per return can end up being high.

The introduction of computer-controlled cathode-ray terminals (CRT) has had a significant impact on the conduct of telephone interviews. In addition to assisting in sequencing of questions, results are available at a moment's notice since all replies are stored in memory. Depending on the number of follow-up mailings required, the total time needed to conduct a good mail survey can be substantial. However, as the number of required contacts increases, the attractiveness of the telephone mode decreases (with additional staff requirements and escalating costs).

Although the mail questionnaire mode allows little speed control, it represents a standardized stimulus. With telephone interviews, interviewer-induced variance can be reduced through proper selection, training, and supervision during the data collection.

The types of questions that can be asked as well as the amount and the accuracy of the information needed will influence the choice of the mode. Telephone interviews, although they usually do not allow the same quantity of data collection as mail, will enable flexibility in terms of probing respondents' comments further as well as the use of open-ended questions to a greater extent. Since respondents to a mail questionnaire are able to work at their own pace, a better thought-out response may result. The appropriateness of these responses, however, is a function of the adequacy of the questionnaire.

Mail questionnaires permit data collection from a wide geographic dispersion of individuals since the mode is relatively time and cost insensitive. With sample sizes of 5,000−10,000 (e.g., Woodside and Reid 1974; Woodside and Motes 1980), mail interviews become the only feasible mode of data collection.

TABLE 1 Comparison of Data Collection Methods[a]

	MODE	
CHARACTERISTIC	TELEPHONE	MAIL
Unit cost	Moderate	Low
Speed	Fast	Slow
Control of data collection environment	Good	None
Refusal, nonresponse problems	Moderate	Substantial
Control of data collection process	Good	Very good
Size of staff required	Moderate	Small
Quantity of data possible	Limited	Considerable
Diversity of questions possible	Limited	Moderate
Interviewer−interviewee bias	Slight	None
Flexibility in data collection	Moderate	Low
Geographical reach	Good	Very good
Perceived anonymity by subject	Moderate	High

[a]For more information consult Peterson (1982) and Churchill (1983).

SAMPLING

Since the number of inquirers is usually quite high, e.g., 73,831 inquirers from black-and-white ads placed in magazines as reported by Woodside and Ronkainen (1982), sampling is one of the major problem areas to be encountered. Random sampling in some form is the generally accepted method. Ballman *et al.* (1983) provide a thorough discussion on incorporating sampling precision to improve the quality of management decisions based on conversion studies.

RESPONSE RATE

Typically, the response rates produced from an initial mailing range from 20 to 40%. If a second mailing to nonrespondents to the first mailing is used, the response rates usually range between 30 and 50%; response rates after a third mailing have been reported at 46 to 80%. Only one study reported by Wettstein (1982) had a single mailing. The results of this study after a 40% response rate should be treated with suspicion, especially when no further sampling of nonrespondents was reported.

Ellerbrock (1981) points out that people who actually visit are more likely to respond to a survey due to the feeling that their answers are more valuable to the state than those who did not visit. It is, therefore, clear that failure to correct for nonresponse bias leads to inflated conversion estimates. Hunt and Dalton (1983) calculated that not correcting for nonresponse bias would have resulted in a 44% overstatement of conversion. Woodside and Ronkainen (1983) found that conversion rates of inquirers were substantially lower for second versus first mailing respondents, while rates were similar for third versus second mailing respondents. While demographics were found to be similar across respondent categories, travel behavior was found to differ between first, second, and third mailing respondents.

Two approaches have been proposed to correct for the nonresponse problem. Response rates between 70 and 80% should be achieved if mailings are to be used. Hunt and Dalton (1983) suggest that telephone survey methods (probably) give more accurate results than mail surveys composed of only one or two mailings. Telephone surveys are, however, subject to bias resulting from the exclusion of households without telephones. For instance, of the 498 households selected by Hunt and Dalton (1983), 100 did not list a telephone number. Furthermore, an additional 62 could not be located and another 81 had been disconnected or would not cooperate. The proportion of households with telephones increases each year, and thus the problem of bias due to the exclusion of no-telephone households should diminish in the future.

A number of studies report the use of incentives to increase response rates. These incentives have usually been posters of the region sponsoring the study or a promise to send the respondent the summary results of the study once completed.

EXPENDITURES

Respondents are typically asked how much they spent while in the location under study. Muha (1976) and Mak *et al.* (1977) have attacked conversion studies with respect to the accuracy of expenditures reported by respondents. Mak *et al.* (1977) empirically tested the relationship between data from recall surveys and diaries and found that survey respondents tend to underestimate their expenditures. Ellerbrock (1981) proposes the use of diary techniques at the minimum as a control group from which to weigh the expenditure figures reported by a large group of survey respondents. The diary technique is not recommended as the primary data collection method. Less than 20% of the persons approached agree to participate in such endeavors. Of these, less than 50% return their diaries. Also, daily and accurate entries are doubtful (Woodside 1981). The additional costs incurred by using a diary panel would not be acceptable for most state tourism offices.

Travelers do accurately respond to questions on expenditures if broad expenditure categories are used. Typically, nine to twelve categories are used (e.g., $0, $1−50, $51−100, etc.). Vehicles, media, ads, and campaigns can be evaluated and decisions made based on revenue projections using such expenditure categories.

SPONSOR IDENTITY

The identification of a state or location as the sponsor of the study should be avoided. To desensitize respondents, the questionnaire should be used to collect data on travel behavior with respect to competing travel destinations. Furthermore, the letter accompanying the questionnaire should not refer to the fact that the respondent is known to have written for travel information. Recent conversion studies have been conducted by independent research agencies identified as the sponsor of the study. However, no direct test has been reported to substantiate this proposition.

A sample questionnaire from a conversion study (Woodside 1981) is provided in Exhibit 1, which incorporates most of the recommendations made in this chapter.

DATA ANALYSIS
REVENUES

In calculating the average revenue per inquiry (RPI), the total number of parties actually visiting has to be estimated. The total number of inquiries, e.g., 4,135,

EXHIBIT 1   Vacation and Pleasure Travel in 1980

Your help is appreciated in completing this survey on vacation and pleasure travel in 1980.

1. Your city of residence: _____ State (Province): _____

2. In 1980, did you (will you) or members of your household travel for vacation or pleasure in or through Virginia, North Carolina, South Carolina, Georgia, or Florida?

    Yes ( )   No ( )   Not sure ( )

    If yes, which States did you visit or pass through in 1980, please check all that apply:

    Virginia ( )   North Carolina ( )   South Carolina ( )   Georgia ( )   · Florida ( )

3. For vacation or pleasure travel *in 1980*, did you or members of your household write for information related to travel in Virginia, North Carolina, South Carolina, Georgia, or Florida?

    Yes ( )   No ( )   Do not recall ( )

    If yes, to whom did you write? _____

    Anyone else?   Yes ( )   No ( )   If yes, who? _____

    If you did write for information on travel in the States mentioned, please check any of the following that apply:

    I did *not* receive information/material ( )
    Information received was *not* helpful ( )
    Information received was helpful ( )
    Information received was taken on trip ( )

    Additional comments: _____

    _____

4. If you did not travel in or pass through one of the following three States (Virginia, North Carolina, or South Carolina) in 1980, please skip the following questions but mail this questionnaire. Thank you.

5. For your 1980 trip in or through Virginia, North Carolina, or South Carolina, what was your major destination away from home?

    City/Location _____ State _____

6. The number of persons in your travel party for this trip:

    Adults _____   Children under 16 years of age _____

7. How many nights, if any, did you stay in each of the following States during your 1980 trips?

    Number of nights in: Virginia _____ North Carolina _____ South Carolina _____

    If you stayed overnight, what city/location did you stay at in each State?

    City/Location in: Virginia _____
                       North Carolina _____
                       South Carolina _____

    From the following list, please identify by letter the type of accommodations used, if any, in each State on your 1980 trip:

    M = Motel/Hotel   Virginia _____
    F = Friends/Relatives home
    S = State Park Campground   North Carolina _____
    C = Commercial/Private Campground
    R = Rental House/Cabin   South Carolina _____
    O = Other _____

Please continue to other side . . .

8. Which of the following best describes your activity in each of the three States in 1980? Please check *one* activity for each State:

Activity	Virginia	North Carolina	South Carolina
Did not visit or pass through this State in 1980	( )	( )	( )
Just passing through	( )	( )	( )
Visiting friends/relatives	( )	( )	( )
Beachs	( )	( )	( )
Scenery/natural attractions	( )	( )	( )
Camping	( )	( )	( )
Historical attractions	( )	( )	( )
Business meeting	( )	( )	( )
Convention/conference	( )	( )	( )
Golfing	( )	( )	( )
Fishing	( )	( )	( )
Other _____	( )	( )	( )

please name other

9. If you visited or passed through *Virginia* in 1980, please check your party's total expenditures (including lodging, food, use of car, recreation, gifts, etc.) while in *Virginia*:

$0 ( )	$101-$300 ( )	$901-$1,200 ( )
$1-$50 ( )	$301-$600 ( )	$1,201-$1,500 ( )
$51-$100 ( )	$601-$900 ( )	Over $1,500 ( )

If you visited or passed through *North Carolina* in 1980, please check your party's total expenditures (including lodging, food, use of car, recreation, gifts, etc.) while in *North Carolina*:

$0 ( )	$101-$300 ( )	$901-$1,200 ( )
$1-$50 ( )	$301-$600 ( )	$1,201-$1,500 ( )
$51-$100 ( )	$601-$900 ( )	Over $1,500 ( )

If you visited or passed through *South Carolina* in 1980, please check your party's total expenditures (including lodging, food, use of car, recreation, gifts, etc.) while in *South Carolina*:

$0 ( )	$101-$300 ( )	$901-$1,200 ( )
$1-$50 ( )	$301-$600 ( )	$1,201-$1,500 ( )
$51-$100 ( )	$601-$900 ( )	Over $1,500 ( )

If you would like a copy of the summary of the study, please provide your name, address, and complete ZIP Code below:

Name: _____

Address: _____ ZIP: _____

Thank you for your help. Please mail in the postpaid envelope.

---

is multiplied by the percentage of those respondents who visited, e.g., $0.44 \times 4.135 = 1,836$ estimated inquirers who visited as a result of the advertisement. Woodside and Reid (1974) have noted that this estimate may be inflated since the calculations are based on the assumption that the percentage of inquirers who visited is identical to that indicated by the results. This, of course, can be remedied by a high response rate.

Ellerbrock (1981) and Ballman *et al*. (1983) point out the need to use net versus gross conversion rates. They propose that a true conversion rate is one in which inquirers who decide to visit the destination before ad exposure are not included. Ballman *et al*. (1983) suggest that gross conversion rates may be overestimating conversion by 50%; in their study the gross conversion rate was 33%, while the net rate was 22%. Their results are based on answers to the following question: "Did you request information from us before or after you decided to vacation in X?" The literature received may in some cases cause the final decision, although the respondent will most likely indicate that the decision had been made before the request. Woodside (1981) calls for the use of a true experiment to meaningfully answer the question of whether or not the advertising and the literature influenced visits. Cities could be used for such research along with regional editions of magazines. For a specific magazine, some editions would include an advertisement (i.e., treatment) while some would not (i.e., control). Random samples of all subscribers in all cities could be drawn and information on their travel behavior collected. The travel behavior of the treatment versus the control groups could be compared.

The average expenditure per part, e.g., $432, is then multiplied by the estimated number of visitors (1,836) to arrive at an estimate for total revenue ($793,000). Estimated total revenue divided by the total number of inquirers results in RPI: $793,000/4,135 = $192.

The more specific the destination for which the conversion study is performed (e.g., state versus specific location), the more careful the definition of the barriers of the region to the respondents needs to be. Misunderstanding or misconception may lead to unnecessary inflation of the results.

COSTS

Average cost per inquiry (CPI) is obtained by dividing the total cost of the advertising campaign (e.g., $128,000) by the number of inquiries (4,135) for

$31.00. It is of utmost importance that *all* costs be included beyond production and insertion charges, i.e., including inquiry handling costs (e.g., postage, brochure printing, etc.). It is even appropriate to add conversion study costs to the overall costs of the campaign.

The ratio of CPI as a percentage of RPI ($31.00/$192.00 = 16%) provides a means of comparing the effectiveness of different campaigns, media vehicles, or ads. The interesting criterion for a state agency is to see if taxes as a percentage of revenue generated are greater than the cost per inquiry as a percentage of revenue per inquiry (CPI/RPI). In a recent study on South Carolina's advertising tourism campaign, CPI as a part of RPI for five advertising campaigns was less than the estimated 9.9% tax rate (Woodside and Motes 1981).

The various conversion studies are summarized in terms of critical dimensions in Table 2.

APPLICATIONS

Although conversion studies are designed primarily to estimate rates of conversions of inquirers into visitors, applications can be extended well beyond this

TABLE 2   Conversion Studies and Their Critical Dimensions

MAIL	TOTAL NO. OF INQUIRERS	SAMPLE SIZE[a]	MAILING SECOND	MAILING THIRD	RESPONSE RATE[a]	PERCENTAGE OF INQUIRERS WHO VISITED[a]	SPONSOR IDENTIFIED	INDUCEMENT[b]	DATA COLLECTION ON COMPETITIVE DEST.	STATE INVOLVEMENT
Woodside and Reid (1974)	39,502	42%	No	No	28%	53%	Yes	No	Yes	SC
Wettstein (1982)	10,000	5%	No	No	40%	50%	Yes	Yes	No	AZ
Woodside and Motes (1980)	14,075–95,664	14–16%	Yes	No	31–34%	62%	Yes	No	Yes	SC
Woodside and Motes (1981)	682–11,234	8–100%	Yes	Yes	62–65%	47–58%	Yes	Yes	Yes	SC
Woodside and Ronkainen (1982)	4,135–73,831	1–2%	Yes	Yes	74–80%	43–61%[c]	No	Yes	Yes	NC,SC VA
Hunt and Dalton (1983)	67,000	1%	Yes	No	68%	33%	Yes	No	No	UT

TELEPHONE	TOTAL NO. OF INQUIRERS	SAMPLE SIZE[a]	FOLLOW-UP CALLS	RESPONSE RATE[a]	PERCENTAGE OF INQUIRERS WHO VISITED[a]	SPONSOR IDENTIFIED	INDUCEMENT	DATA COLLECTION ON COMPETITIVE DEST.	STATE INVOLVEMENT
Ballman et al. (1983)	2,353	31%	Yes	NR[d]	22%	Yes	No	Yes	MN
Hunt and Dalton (1983)	67,000	1%	Yes	66%	23%	Yes	No	Yes	UT

[a]The range of answers is provided for studies with comparisons (e.g., of one medium against another).
[b]Inducements ranged from posters to promising respondents the results of the completed study.
[c]Percentage given is for total number of visits; the state was the major destination for 21–35% of respondents.
[d]A total of 750 completed interviews.

purpose. Woodside and Motes (1981) studied five distinct advertising strategies with different creative approaches, media schedules, and direct mail literature which were used to affect vacation behavior of five market segments. Substantial differences in estimated total revenues, costs, and net revenues produced from each market and advertising strategy were detected. The findings resulted in the advertiser's reallocation of his advertising efforts for the following year.

Woodside and Motes (1980) compared image versus direct-response advertising and found no significant profile differences between direct-response and image-ad inquirers, but data showed significant differences in cost and net revenue. The findings resulted in the reduction of the advertiser's use of image advertisements.

Woodside and Ronkainen (1982) compared the performance of black-and-white and color ads placed in newspapers versus magazines. Although substantially more national, city, and state tourism advertising expenditures are allocated to magazines, newspapers were found to outperform magazines in revenue-generating power.

SUMMARY

Conversion studies, since their introduction, have been developed with respect to controlling factors which may inflate the results. The following improvements have been made:

1 *Controlling for nonresponse bias* by ensuring response rates of 70% or better. This can be achieved by following standard methods of increasing response propensity (e.g., Heberlein and Baumgartner 1978; Kanuk and Berenson 1975), such as individualizing the letters, having a postage stamp on the envelopes, and providing incentives.

2 *Not identifying the real sponsor* (nor the reason) of the study by using an independent research agency. This avoids unnecessary sensitizing of the respondents and allows for collection of data on competing vacation destinations.

3 *Using net versus gross rates of conversion* by factoring out inquirers who had decided to visit the destination before ad exposure.

4 *Including all relevant costs*, not only inquiry-generating costs, that can be directly allocated to the project such as postage for mailing material to inquirers.

5 *Clearly defining the area(s) of vacation* especially in the case of individual locations to avoid possibility of misinterpretation and subsequent inflation of results.

6 *Striving for an accurate estimate of the expenditures* incurred by the respondents. Remedial ac-

tions include using broad expenditure categories as well as diary techniques as a complementary data collection method.

Given the approach's intuitive appeal and relative simplicity of the methodology, conversion studies enjoy increasing popularity. However, if the conversion study is not conducted properly, the results can lead to interpretive errors based on inflated results. If executed as an integral part of an advertising campaign (i.e., planning for a conversion study starts with the planning of a campaign), conversion studies can provide invaluable input in improving managerial decision making.

REFERENCES

Advertising Age (1982), "Alaska Goes after Tourists in a Big Way," (4 January), 10.

Ballman, Gary, Jim Burke, Uel Blank, and Dick Korte (1983), "'Real' Conversion Rates of Regional Advertising Programs: Working from Gross to Net Rates," *Proceedings of the XIII Annual Meeting of the TTRA*, Salt Lake City, Utah: TTRA, pp. 244–245.

Churchill, Gilbert A. (1983), *Marketing Research*, Hinsdale, Illinois: The Dryden Press.

Ellerbrock, Michael J. (1981), "Improving Coupon Conversion Studies," *Journal of Travel Research*, 19 (Spring), 37–38.

Goeldner, Charles R., and Karen P. Dicke (1981), *Travel Trends in the United States and Canada*, Boulder, Colorado: Business Research Division, University of Colorado, pp. 44–50.

Heberlein, T.A., and R.A. Baumgartner (1978), "Factors Affecting Response Rates to Mailed Questionnaires: A Quantitative Analysis of the Published Literature," *American Sociological Review*, 43 (August), 447–462.

Hunt, John D., and Michael J. Dalton (1983), "Comparing Mail and Telephone for Conducting Coupon Conversion Studies," *Journal of Travel Research*, 21 (Winter), 16–18.

Kanuk, Leslie, and Conrad Berenson (1975), "Mail Surveys and Response Rates: A Literature Review," *Journal of Marketing Research*, 12 (November), 440–453.

Mak, James, James Moncur, and David Yonamine (1977), "How or How Not to Measure Visitor Expenditures," *Journal of Travel Research*, 16 (Summer), 1–4.

Muha, S.L. (1976), "Evaluating Travel Advertising: A Survey of Existing Studies," paper presented at the Fifth Annual Educational Seminar for State Travel Officials, Lincoln, Nebraska, 4 October, 1976.

Peterson, Robert A. (1982), *Marketing Research*, Plano, Texas: Business Publications, Inc.

U.S. Travel Data Center (1983), *Survey of State Travel Offices*, Washington, D.C.: U.S. Travel Data Center.

Wettstein, Earl (1982), "Agency's Business Reply Card Survey Elicits 40% Response; Results Valuable," *Marketing News*, 15 (22 January), 20.

Woodside, Arch G. (1981), "Measuring the Conversion of Advertising Coupon Inquirers into Visitors," *Journal of Travel Research*, 19 (Spring), 38–41.

Woodside, Arch G., and David M. Reid (1974). "Tourism Profiles versus Audience Profiles: Are Upscale Magazines Really Upscale?" *Journal of Travel Research*, 12 (Spring), 17–23.

Woodside, Arch G., and William H. Motes (1980), "Image versus Direct-Response Advertising," *Journal of Advertising Research*, 20 (April/May), 31–39.

Woodside, Arch G., and William H. Motes (1981), "Sensitivities of Market Segments to Separate Advertising Strategies," *Journal of Marketing*, 45 (Winter), 63–73.

Woodside, Arch G., and Ilkka A. Ronkainen (1982), "Travel Advertising: Newspapers versus Magazines," *Journal of Advertising Research*, 22 (June/July), 39–43.

Woodside, Arch G., and Ilkka A. Ronkainen (1983), "How Serious is Non-response Bias in Advertising Conversion Research?" working paper, College of Business Administration, University of South Carolina, Columbia, South Carolina.

Woodside, Arch G., and Ilkka A. Ronkainen (1984), "Principles of Pretesting Travel Advertising," *Proceedings of the XIV Annual Meeting of the TTRA*, Salt Lake City, Utah: TTRA.

42

Market Segmentation Research in Tourism and Travel

JANE R. FITZGIBBON

Vice President
Director of Research Development
Ogilvy & Mather
New York, New York

*T*his chapter provides the travel marketing and research executive with a general overview of market segmentation. It focuses on the underlying rationales for the technique, the business utility to be derived from its thoughtful use, and the general guidelines to be employed in any successful segmentation experiment. The technical underpinnings of segmentation analysis are not covered, nor are the pros and cons of the various statistical techniques that move in and out of favor with the "experts"—this is part of the "craft" or the "how to" of segmentation and therefore beyond the purview of this chapter. The objective here is to describe the "art of segmentation" as it can be effectively used to identify key product and strategy guidelines.

It should be recognized that, while the title of this chapter makes specific reference to *travel and tourism* segmentation, the development of segmentation techniques and the application of segmentation findings have been most consistently used by consumer packaged goods companies. Accordingly, it is this experience that must be referenced in presenting the basic material, with suggested applications to the travel and tourism business contained in a separate section at the end of this chapter.

Segmentation analysis is variously seen as the complete solution to all marketing problems *or* an esoteric research exercise with little to offer in the way of practical business application or marketing utility. It is easy to understand how each of these views developed—the first, among those practitioners mesmerized by the new, the technical, and the seemingly "scientific"; the second, among those naively looking for research techniques which magically point the way to instant profits and share point increases. It goes without saying that neither view does justice to one of the most important research developments in the recent history of the field.

MARKETING VERSUS SALES AND THE ROLE OF SEGMENTATION

Prior to the 1950s, the distribution of goods and services to consumers was primarily a sales function. Selling efforts were geared to the retailer rather than to the end-user, and sales were increased by motivating the sales force. Segmentation thinking was present in that sales activity and performance was analyzed according to geographical area, type of community, large vs. small outlets, and other "territorial" considerations. For the most part, however, "moving the goods" was a question of getting them on the right shelf in the right place, and then relying on the retail merchant to complete the sales job; little attention was given to understanding the motivations of those who were eventually expected to buy the goods and take them home.

Marketing—or the discipline of applying a microscope to the end-user of a product in order to establish his or her needs and wants, and then shaping a product, and sales and advertising strategy to meet those needs—did not really emerge as an area of study until the 1950s, when *self-service* outlets (supermarkets,

489

mass merchandisers, discount stores) began to proliferate in an era of large families and sprawling suburbs. With the *personal* influence of the retail merchant "out of the picture" and the possibility of new mass markets ready to be developed and consolidated, business began to direct their thinking to the consumer—to determine:

- Which segments of the market can be expected to support a given product or service category?
- How do these segments differ in terms of their potential responsiveness to different brands? different positionings?
- How do these segments differ in their product expectations?
- What advertising and promotional strategies will be most effective in capturing new users and sustaining present users?
- What media channels should be used to maximize attention, gain awareness, reinforce interest, and stimulate purchase?
- What kinds of marketing expenditures will be necessary, and how should the dollars be allocated, in the pursuit of profitable brand franchises?

While many marketing disciplines are obviously required to complete the answers to all of these questions, the contribution of the market research industry in the fifties and sixties was to develop modes of grouping (or segmenting) the population into targets of varying susceptibility to specific product purchase.[1] Armed with detailed information as to which population groups (or segments) offered the best market opportunities, all of the key marketing functions—product development, advertising, media, sales—could launch a campaign with considerably more confidence in the final payout than was possible in the early days when the success or failure of a brand was dependent almost totally on sales force motivation techniques and gimmicks.

THE DEVELOPMENT OF SEGMENTATION ANALYSIS

The word "segmentation," as used today, almost always refers to *attitudinal* segmentation, and therefore fails to credit other forms of segmentation (demographic, behavioral) that preceded attitudinal modes and that are still being successfully used by marketers to identify and describe consumer markets. Segmentation, in its broadest sense as a method of analysis, involves disaggregation of data followed by reassembly

[1]See Daniel Yankelovich, "New Criteria for Market Segmentation," *Harvard Business Review*, March–April 1964, Volume 42, No. 2, pp. 83–90.

and synthesis. The disaggregation step can be accomplished according to any number of known (or hypothesized) independent variables.

The earliest variables used by marketers were demographic characteristics. Demographic data are easily accessible (census reports, at the very least), readily understood, and they can be universally applied (everybody has a demographic profile). For the most part, age and socioeconomic status proved to be the most useful demographic clues for marketing managers looking to develop products, packaging, advertising, and distribution strategies for specific consumer markets. While enormously valuable, demographic segmentations were simplistic by today's standards. The population was essentially viewed in terms of:

- Life cycle: youth, marrieds, elderly, and
- Household income level

with education and occupation overlaid to produce norms of "upscaleness" and "downscaleness," which were widely understood short-hand terms for specific population segments.

The next type of variable used in segmentation was behavioral. This step followed from the legitimate questions of marketing managers, who reasoned that additional insights could be contributed by the investigation of product usage habits and frequency-of-use patterns—information which, in many cases, did not "group" according to traditional demographic targets, that is, one might find that the young, upscale segment was more likely to buy or prefer your brand, but that this market was composed of the least frequent users of the product category, and further that these users were the most apt to switch brands as new options were introduced in the marketplace. From this example, it is not hard to recognize the need for a marketing approach that goes beyond a narrowly targeted appeal to upscale young consumers. In fact, the combination of demographic and behavioral modes of segmentation gave real impetus to the consideration of a *line* of products, each one designed to capture a specific and identifiable segment of the market—e.g., fickle young users, frequent older users, etc.

By the early 1960s, a growing need emerged to go even further than demographic and behavioral segmentation. Brand proliferation was such that big "blockbuster" entries were few and far between, and the pinpointing of specific targets for a multibrand strategy was often difficult on the basis of demographics and behavior alone. For example, two families of identical age, household composition, and socioeconomical status live next door to each other, each drives 15,000 miles per year under the same conditions, and yet one family chooses a small foreign model car and the other a full-sized American model. Clearly, there is, in this case, a need to probe beyond demographic and behavioral information—to understand the attitudes (the needs, the wants, the values, the desires) that consumers bring to bear in the purchase decision process.

Taking another example, and carrying it a bit further:

- We may well know that affluent, frequent travelers take a disproportionate number of international trips.
- *But*, why do some choose the Caribbean, and others choose Europe?
- *And*, knowing the "reason why," what are the opportunities for developing domestic markets that satisfy the same set of needs?
- *Or*, what are the opportunities for tapping into those same needs among less affluent travelers who, under today's lifestyle priorities, might well allocate a disproportionate amount of their discretionary dollars to travel and leisure pursuits?

All of these issues are implicit (if not explicit) in the objectives of any segmentation analysis—whether demographic, behavioral, or attitudinal modes are used. The addition of attitudinal segmentation to the mix, however, has added an enormously critical dimension to marketers' ability to pinpoint targets of opportunity. Even more importantly, attitudinal segmentation provides marketers with the rich understanding necessary to know how to talk to consumers in relevant, involving ways.

Finally, it should be noted that as the growth in marketers' hunger for more and more information on the consumer psyche (i.e., the need to consider attitudes and values, as well as demographics and behavior) was taking place, there was a concurrent development of the "hardware" necessary to handle (or correlate) the growing list of influences (i.e., variables) on decision-making and buying behavior. It is probably fair to say that the coming of the computer and appropriate programming innovations were probably no less important in reinforcing interest in attitudinal segmentation analysis than were the constant demands of the marketing people to know more about the needs of prospective customers. It is indeed technology which is, today, reviving interest in, and accessibility to, more sophisticated modes of *demographic* segmentation. As just one example, the PRIZM *geo*demographic program segments the U.S. in terms of ZIP Code neighborhood clusters, each of which can be described in terms of a matrix of over 200 socioeconomic and demographic factors (from the census), behavioral factors (travel behavior from Simmons, for example), and attitudes and values (from SRI VALS, for example). Accessed, on line, via a personal computer, consumers can be profiled in three dimensions, *and* they can be physically located on a map of the U.S.

Another key to this system is that it can be linked to any set of "outside" data with zip code information (mail response cards, travel agency locations, other syndicated data, custom studies, etc.). All of this can be done for a fraction of the cost of a customized segmentation study.

ATTITUDINAL SEGMENTATION— AN ANALYTIC TOOL, NOT THE "FINAL SOLUTION"

As with most complex statistical research techniques, attitudinal segmentation is a tool, part of the *process* of reaching conclusions or hypotheses; it is not the end product. In very basic terms, attitudinal segmentation is a form of data reduction.

- Unlike demographic and behavioral information which can be gathered via very straightforward questioning methods, people's attitudes are not "either/or," "yes/no" issues. Often, five or six questions are required simply to get a given respondent's attitudes on, for example, the issue of price/value. Multiply this by eight or ten other attitudinal issues that might be important in a specific product area (need for self-esteem, susceptibility to change, aesthetic concepts, etc.) and the sheer number of variables is overwhelming.

Accordingly, segmentation techniques (along with modern computer capabilities) permit the inclusion of vast numbers of data inputs which are then synthesized into a manageable number (usually six to eight) of describable groups (or segments).

A second basic function of segmentation is that it identifies the most "powerful" attitudinal variables (e.g., price, convenience, status, familiarity) or combinations thereof, and, further, prioritizes them in terms of the number of people who, in a given product category, share a given attitudinal framework, and who can therefore be expected to respond in a similar (or predictable) way in the marketplace.

- It is often said that attitudinal segmentation is misleading, in that it pigeonholes people into *one* segment, whereas the erraticism and unpredictability of human behavior suggests that one is *sometimes* status-oriented, *sometimes* convenience-oriented, and so forth—with respect to the same product category. This is undeniably true; however, very few research practitioners claim that the kind of precision possible in the physical sciences is yet possible in the social or human behavioral sciences. While many forward-thinking research professionals are now looking to the next step in segmentation—that of *mood* or *occasion* or differential levels of *ego-involvement*—for possible sources of new sets of product choice determinants, the kinds of attitudinal segmentation modes now being used are probably as precise in identifying overarching attitudinal mind-sets as most marketing professionals are equipped to deal with.

Along with these practical advantages of segmentation—as a tool enabling the researcher to reduce masses of data into meaningful hierarchical groups—it is somewhat gratuitous, but necessary, to state that the ultimate utility of the tool rests with the degree of creativity and analytic skill brought to bear by the analyst working with the data. The following section attempts to address some of the issues confronting the researcher in his or her consideration and conduct of a segmentation study.

TEN GUIDELINES FOR THE EFFECTIVE USE OF ATTITUDINAL SEGMENTATION ANALYSIS[2]

The following guidelines on the effective application of attitudinal segmentation analysis do not represent a definitive theory on the use of this tool. Based on the accumulation of case histories where segmentation was applied in the process of solving marketing problems, these guidelines have been *empirically* derived, and represent practical lessons learned over many years of conducting segmentation studies for leading American marketers.

GUIDELINE #1

For strategic planning purposes it is short-sighted not to consider some form of *non*demographic and *non*-behavioral segmentation.

The introduction of any new tool is often accompanied by bizarre experiments in its use. Attitudinal segmentation was no exception, having been used to derive anal/oral typologies, astrological typologies, and physiological typologies—all of which were "interesting" but few of which provided any practical utility to marketers. On balance, however, where an appropriate mode of segmentation has been formed, the benefit to the marketer has been significant.

Further, the basic theory underlying attitudinal segmentation will serve to reinforce its use even more frequently in the future, given the increasingly pluralistic directions of current consumer lifestyles and value systems.

- Prior to the 1960s, it can be said that there was basic societal consensus in this country on personal

goals (i.e., upward mobility) and the means used to reach that goal (i.e., the Puritan work ethic). So that while shrewd marketers realized the value of understanding the subtle differences in people's attitudes and value systems, it was a "given" that most people were operating under an overall umbrella of conformity, system and order, reward-based indulgences, and a plan-for-the-future orientation.

- With the inception of the New Values in the mid-1960s, dominated by the focus-on-self thrust, the United States has become a nation of individuals wherein consensus on basic life goals is not only less possible but, for most, less desirable.

- Moreover, there is no evidence of any slackening in the trends toward individualized lifestyle goals, decision-making powers, and the need for personalized options—among both young and old segments of the population.

A less conformist population, therefore, suggests that an appropriate type of attitudinal segmentation be systematically considered in the formulation of marketing programs.

GUIDELINE #2

The closer the mode of segmentation is to the product field, the greater the utility of the tool.

Given the difficulties of addressing specific marketing problems with data from segmentations that are based on *generalized* typologies (be they psychological, sociological, astrological, physical, etc.), it is widely agreed that the closer a mode of segmentation is to the attitudes, needs, and wants that are operative in a particular product category, the more useful it will be. If a marketing strategy study is being conducted by a car marketer, the segmentation has to be based on needs, wants, and problems with respect to cars. If a travel marketer is planning the research, the segmentation mode should be related to travel attitudes and motivations.

- A word about generalized typologies, because many researchers certainly use them. When used descriptively—that is, to describe what is happening in a population—generalized typologies are very useful. It is a nice tidy way of showing, for example, that there is a substantial proportion of people who are inherently aggressive; or that there is a rise in people who hold "new" social values.

But most marketers would question the use of any generalized typology for direct and specific marketing planning. Without question, an understanding of *trends* in generalized typologies offers highly valuable and increasingly essential background data for the marketer, providing a holistic view of the total envi-

[2]For this section in particular I would like to acknowledge the help and assistance of Florence Skelly, president of Yankelovich, Skelly & White, Inc, whose thoughts and words are liberally used.

ronment in which business operates—and providing a jumping-off point for target identification, benefits–needs analysis, and alternative positioning options. However, when it comes to the nuts and bolts of marketing thinking, it is almost axiomatic today that the closer the segmentation dimensions come to the product field, the more useful they are for marketing and strategic thinking.

GUIDELINE #3

Even within a product class, there is probably more than one way to segment the market, and the key to the appropriate segmentation dimension (and to whether you'll do a good job or not) is the objective of the research.

More specifically, if the objective is to look for multiple strategies, or for consumer needs-gaps to direct new product development, the segmentation analysis might be done one way. The focus here would be to identify segments within the population who do not have available to them an appropriate product. On the other hand, if the marketer is locked into a product line for one reason or another, the strategic opportunities may lie in the appropriate use of advertising. Then, a segmentation mode geared to unearthing optimum advertising strategy may turn out quite differently from a segmentation geared to strategic product planning. Similarly, if the output is a pricing strategy, the segmentation mode would, again, be quite different.

The wise marketer will not simply decide that a segmentation study would be a good idea. He/she will define the objective, and, *based on the objective*, will determine whether or not a segmentation analysis is only an analytic tool; it is not an end, it is a means.

GUIDELINE #4

It is highly desirable to exercise a considerable degree of discipline and restraint with respect to the input items in order to have a successful segmentation emerge.

At one time, there was a tendency to throw in any item that came to mind—psychological, lifestyle, product attitude, demographics. In the early 1960s some statisticians even urged that this was the best approach, since the big computers could easily sort it all out. Experience indicates that this undisciplined approach has led to confusion, and then to cynicism.

It has been learned that the better approach is to restrict the input to issues that are relevant to the objective—however great the temptation to add in other issues. Increasing numbers of practitioners of segmentation analysis confirm the fact that, based on bitter experience, they are becoming far more selective and restrained in the input for segmentation analysis.

GUIDELINE #5

The only "technical" point: experience has shown that, irrespective of the particular technique being used, if there's truth in the segments, the different segmentation techniques will produce essentially the same segments.

In other words, R&Q, CHIRP, Singleton and Johnson, etc., will produce virtually the same groupings; given the same inputs, the same insights will generally emerge. This suggests that segmentation analysis has advanced to the point where personal idiosyncracy, cost, and speed issues can govern the selection of an appropriate statistical procedure, and that the battles among statisticians may be coming to an end. As mentioned earlier, these battles are very often part of the adoption of new substantive approaches, and help call attention to the substance, even though the debate may center on techniques.

GUIDELINE #6

It is highly desirable (in fact, probably vital) to have a theory about the way a given market works—or about possible segments—*before* looking at the statistical output.

Certainly, there are practitioners who believe that taking a *tabula rasa* approach to a segmentation analysis ensures objectivity and leads to new insights. The experience of many, however, has been the reverse. The more that is known and understood about a product field—about how consumers think and act with respect to the category—the more incisive and useful will be the analyst's interpretations of the statistics.

The sources for developing an understanding of the dynamics of a given market are manifold: any and all the research that has been done, or, very appropriately, the "discovery" or qualitative step that is usually mandatory to the development of the specific product-related input for the segmentation. Also, macrosegmentation schema and systematic environmental scanning techniques are two excellent and cost-effective ways to develop a presegmentation point of view.

GUIDELINE #7

Nomenclature can be a key to the ultimate utility of segmentation analysis to marketing management.

While this principle may not be profound, it is, nevertheless, an unheralded truth. If the names assigned the segments are speakable by human beings, and if they are evocative of the character of each segment, chances are that the names—and, it follows, the *concepts*—will get the thinking of marketers.

If, on the other hand, obscure, or hyphenated, or clumsy, names are assigned to the segments (however precise they may be), the *vocabulary* hurdle seems to become a *usage* hurdle. Similarly, if, as sometimes occurs, words seem to fail, and numbers or letters are assigned to the segments, there is yet another hurdle to usage. Abstractions such as numbers or letters seem to encourage different members of the marketing team to develop their own unique ideas about the segments. This leads to misunderstandings about the inherent nature of a segment—which, of course, becomes a hurdle to usage.

It takes time and wordsmithing, but finding effective nomenclature is an important step in segmentation analysis, if ultimate utility is to be realized.

GUIDELINE #8

Presentation of the segments can also be crucial in ensuring use by marketing management.

All too often, when a segmentation analysis has been carried out by a team that is strong in statistics (but not really concerned with marketing), the very presentation of the material can mitigate against its usefulness. When the bulk of a presentation to marketing management centers on how the segmentation was done, rather than on how these new understandings of the consumer market can be used, the viability of the tool suffers, the research suffers, and the credibility of the researcher suffers.

It has to be remembered that attitudinal segments are often new concepts to marketers, and that they have to be "brought to life"—through nomenclature, presentation, example, etc. And, all-importantly, it has to be what the segments suggest in the way of practical down-to-earth marketing strategy. The goal of any research is, in the last analysis, not to make management smarter, but to help management make better decisions.

GUIDELINE #9

Linking nondemographic (optimally, product–attitude) segments to known structural data can significantly increase their utilization by marketing management.

Sometimes, attitudinal segments can be effectively described in demographic terms, i.e., one segment is younger and more upscale, another is older and blue collar, etc. When this happens, marketing *to the segments* is more feasible—since media and distribution channel data are often available only in demographic terms.

When the attitudinal segments are not linkable to demographics, it is useful to try to link them directly to market structures, e.g., types of outlets patronized, media exposure, responsiveness to promotions, etc. This type of linkage enhances the practical application of the segmentation and avoids the criticism that segmentations are interesting but not useful.

GUIDELINE #10

Good, old-fashioned demographic and/or behavioral segments are sometimes the most fruitful approaches for strategic thinking.

Most of this chapter has focused on the use and implementation of nondemographic segmentation as a marketing tool. There are, however, some markets where the most meaningful understandings of consumer needs/wants emerge from demographic or life cycle analyses. It should not be construed as a disservice to nondemographic segmentation, in the long run, to point out that cutting up a given market demographically can, in certain instances, make the most marketing sense.

Such insights will emerge from the "discovery" phase which precedes the segmentation work and can easily be checked out before a commitment to attitudinal segmentation is made.

SEGMENTATION APPLICATIONS FOR TRAVEL AND TOURISM MARKETERS

The relative slowness of many travel marketers to adopt some of the segmentation techniques long used by packaged goods marketers is not difficult to understand.

- First, up until fairly recently, the travel market was supported by two cohesive and fairly elitist groups—the business traveler and the upscale traveler—neither of which were difficult to characterize, isolate, and reach with appropriate products, services, and strategies.

- Second, given traditional sociocultural ties, combined with the unchallenged appeal of warm climate locales, the *a priori* predictability of vacation destination choices remained intact for many years.

- Third, considering the tight concentration of the business travel market—middle-aged, white collar male managers—it was not an enormous challenge to determine *his* needs, and to design appropriate products and services for *him*.

- Fourth, the widespread adherence to Puritan work ethic values tended to circumscribe most people's frequency of travel and alternatives. Travel marketers could be somewhat complacent and secure in the knowledge that their turnover share of market would remain undisturbed and unchallenged from year to year.

- And finally, the constraints of airline regulation precluded the unhampered and effective use of strategic *marketing* techniques—forcing carriers, instead, to maintain profits based on operating efficiencies and technological advances, rather than on any research-based response to consumer needs.

None of the above situations is any longer true! Marketing assumptions as to "who" is traveling "where" today, and "how" and "why," can only be educated guesses—possibly correct, depending on who is doing the guessing, but very risky inputs in deciding how to maximize one's share of a market that is estimated to represent over $100 billion in sales in the United States alone.

Briefly, to enumerate some of the recent changes in the market for travel:

- With vast numbers of the population susceptible to a psychology of entitlement and a leisure ethic, and placing new value on the pursuit of the full, rich life, *nontraditional* consumer segments are lured into the travel market. Less affluent travelers, blue collar workers, single people, and healthy and comfortably financed older people are all beginning to recognize the pleasures and rewards of taking a trip, and are adjusting their budgetary priorities in order to be able to do so. *As the population is becoming more pluralistic, so too is the market for travel and tourism.*

- Women are no longer *moving* into the workforce, *they are in it.* And, as they rise up the career ladder, they are reaching those positions where travel becomes part of their job responsibilities. For the foreseeable future, men will continue to dominate the business travel market, but the approximately two in ten business travelers who are women will have to be considered an important decision-making minority target.

- A further change in the business travel market will quite possibly come from the blue collar and open-collar segments, with conventions and travel incentives becoming as important in worker motivation rewards for these employees as for their white collar counterparts.

- As New Values lifestyles seep into the total population, the notion of travel as a once-a-year reward for 50 weeks of hard work is being superseded by the year-round inclusion of travel as part of one's total lifestyle. Travel will increasingly be seen as a "leisure hypodermic" to relieve the pressures and anxieties of modern life; it will be seen as a route to the full, rich life of experiences and adventures; and it will be required to provide constantly innovative and updated opportunities to see and do *new* things. The more frequent traveler will be a more demanding traveler, presenting the implied challenge of "Can you top this?" to airlines, hoteliers, and destinations looking to attract new markets. The predictability of market behavior will soften as the more frequent New Values traveler "uses up" the traditional destinations and looks for new places to go.

- Finally, with the solidification of airline deregulation, a leading-edge factor in the travel industry is now free to promote differential product and service benefits in strategic *marketing* efforts designed to compete for consumer preference and loyalty.

With all of these changes, the travel and tourism industry is hard-pressed to develop new markets based on outmoded assumptions about the traveling public. Updated information is needed—on demographics, on behavior, and on travel motivations.

- It should be noted here that one of the difficulties in researching people's motivations and attitudes toward travel is the fact that almost everyone likes to travel, thinks travel is a good thing, would like to travel more often, etc., etc. In other words, travel *per se* is not a highly controversial activity.

- At the same time, there are methods which can help travel marketers to sharpen their understanding of *why* different people like to travel and what underlying issues are important as consumers process "travel information" and proceed along all of the decision points that must be faced in the course of putting a trip together. Clearly, one of the most useful methods for this task is segmentation analysis.

As the travel market used to be comprised, demographic segmentation was sufficiently precise for most marketers. For others, an overlay of behavioral data (e.g., frequency of travel, preferred travel activities) strengthened and sharpened the demographic groupings. In the current climate, however, wherein travel is becoming a mass-market business, it is difficult, if not impossible, to compete on a cost-effective basis without a serious examination of exactly what different people expect from the travel experience—their attitudes, values, and priorities.

- What part does sheer hedonism or escape play in people's travel motivations?
- What do people mean when they say (as they all do) that travel is "rewarding"?
- How are notions of self-esteem and status linked to travel?
- What role does "branding" play in the travel market, e.g., Club Med, TWA Getaway, American Express?
- Is there such a thing as "brand loyalty" in travel?
- What is in travelers' minds when they talk about "good value"?
- What kinds of trade-offs, surprises, and disappointments are acceptable on a trip, and when does real disenchantment set in?

Only by asking these types of questions will the travel industry be prepared for what has been called the increasing "democratization" of the travel market. Only by researching the underlying motivations of travelers will the industry be able to sort out some of the new cross-currents in the marketplace:

- Blue collar workers who take tennis vacations.
- Single women with money to spend on activity-filled (not husband-hunting) vacations.
- Upscale travelers who foresake the luxurious comforts of a resort vacation, preferring instead to "rough it" at an "underdeveloped" destination.
- Older travelers, less interested in a simple lakeside retreat than in a "swinging trip" to a cosmopolitan city locale.

Attitudinal segmentation, applied to travel, will no doubt shatter some long-held beliefs with respect to the cohesiveness and the predictability of market targets. It will challenge the continuing viability of once-successful promotional strategies (sun, sand, and surf for the family vs. scuba, sex, and skydiving for singles); it will reinforce consideration of new communication channels (particularly direct marketing and new hi-tech media options); and it will force destinations, airlines, and hoteliers to rethink their product and service offerings in light of new markets with new priorities. The options are many—gourmet food and beautiful decor vs. fast check-in, room service, and efficient baggage handling; or the emotional, self-fulfilling appeal of a fantasy trip to the Islands vs. the rational, well-organized sightseeing trip to European cities—and the opportunities are there.

But most importantly, the consideration of segmentation as a route into the dynamics of consumer attitudes will direct the travel industry's attention to the *marketing* of travel—not the sale of travel. It will focus the industry's market development efforts on the *consumer*—not just in terms of how old or how rich he/she is, or how often he/she has travelled in the past, but in terms of his/her travel *needs and wants*. Once uncovered, these needs and wants may or may not correlate with traditional predictive norms based on demographics and behavior, but, in any case, their integration into the strategic planning process will serve to enrich the lines of effective and relevant communication between marketer and customer, and thereby promote sales. In short, attitudinal segmentation can define new targets of opportunity and/or redefine traditional targets in more meaningful terms.

Recognizing the power of the segmentation tool, the travel industry can now capitalize on the experience of packaged goods marketers; they can, at modest cost, update their consumer research methods and begin to target their marketing strategies at those segments where there is likely to be optimum congruence between consumer need and product benefit.

43

Estimating the Potential of International Markets

DON WYNEGAR

Director
Office of Research
United States Travel and
    Tourism Administration
United States Department
    of Commerce
Washington, D.C.

*T*his chapter provides a structured approach to analyzing the potential and relative importance of international travel markets. A model is developed which utilizes a weighted indexing system for evaluating the cumulative significance of pertinent variables for countries under study. The model's output provides decision-makers with an indication of the relative marketing viability of each country.

A national tourism office, other federal, state, and regional tourism agencies, and private industry concerned with promoting international travel are faced with the need for allocating often relatively minimal resources in the most cost-effective and productive manner. To accomplish an optimum distribution of marketing efforts, it is essential that an organization employ a systematic approach for objectively determining the importance and relative attractiveness of various international travel markets for the host country.

Before a government agency or, for that matter, a private business organization can accurately gauge the resource level necessary to compete effectively in a given market, some measure of the total potential of that market must be ascertained (Munsinger and Hansen 1974). Determination of this measure not only entails study of current market performance and/or historical trend analyses of travel patterns, but also evaluation of factors which provide indications of possible market demand and facility of promotional efforts. In analyzing these factors, the potential for growth, or incremental market development, can be determined.

The model outlined in this chapter provides a step-by-step approach to the analysis of international travel market potential. It incorporates measures of both existing market size and realized performance and total and incremental market potential. In addition to these quantitative factors, several qualitative variables which affect the marketability of respective country travel markets are evaluated. By incorporating a system of weighted indices, these factors are aggregated to form a Cumulative Market Evaluation Index, providing a measurement of the relative marketing viability of each country and a basis for resource allocation.

Other market potential models have been developed which address specific travel market segments, such as the Market Potential Index developed by Drs. Munsinger and Hansen of the University of Arizona for the United States Travel Service in 1971. This current model is considerably disparate, in its coverage, in the variables included in the model and in the methods of indexing utilized. An effort has been made to make this model as straightforward and easily applied as possible by research practitioners and market analysts.

In addition to providing a structural approach for

estimating the potential of international markets, a brief section is provided addressing other factors which an organization should take into consideration when studying the feasibility of establishing and funding programs/offices in foreign countries. Analysis of these "cost-of-doing-business" indicators can provide additional quantitative data for decision-makers in allocating resources in international travel markets.

As an illustration, the United States is considered as the host country in the following analysis, and the country travel markets of Canada, Mexico, Japan, the United Kingdom, West Germany, and France—the six countries in which the USTTA currently maintains offices—are included for evaluation. The model is, however, designed for possible application in other host countries and, with appropriate modifications, could be used by bodies concerned with domestic markets. Finally, as each input variable is introduced into the model, the availability and limitations of the data are also discussed.

DEFINITIONS

Two terms which are used throughout this chapter should be defined at the outset. *Potential* as employed in a marketing context refers to the sales, measured in dollars or units, that could be attained from a given market, within a certain period of time, under optimal conditions. Performance should never exceed potential, although theoretically it is possible for the two to be equal. Potential differs from a *forecast* in that the latter represents what is expected to happen, based on an analysis of demand factors coupled with the effort the organization plans to expend. Potential is not effected by company plans. Rather, it can be thought of as a quantity of which a part can be purchased through marketing efforts. In general, the greater the potential realized, the more difficult it becomes to capture the potential remaining. As a firm or agency strives to increase the share of potential it attracts, the ratio of sales to effort applied tends to decrease. For example, the first 70 percent of potential can in all probability be realized more efficiently than the next 20 percent (Munsinger and Hansen 1974, p. 6).

The term *index* as used in this text should also be clarified. For each variable or factor considered for the six countries in the illustration, an index base of 100.0 is assigned to the country displaying the most favorable rating. The remaining five countries receive index ratings which are derived by dividing each country's factor value by that of the country which has the most favorable factor value. For example, if Canada, with some 10.7 million tourists visiting the United States, ranks highest in this category, Canada would be assigned an index value of 100.0. Japan, with some 1.1 million arrivals, would achieve an index rating of 10.2

(derived by dividing the number of Japanese arrivals by the number of Canadian arrivals and multiplying the quotient by 100). An index sequence is thus determined for the six countries, which provides a direct relative ranking of each for the variable under consideration.

QUANTITATIVE FACTORS INDEX

While this model attempts to provide an objective process for determining aggregate international travel market potentials, the selection of the variables which are to be used as input factors is, at best, a subjective procedure. This chapter does not attempt to provide exhaustive "cookbook" inclusion of all pertinent variables which could possibly be used, and in that sense this particular combination should be viewed as exemplificative. Another analyst employing this method could easily substitute other variables into the model should other factors be deemed more appropriate to a particular host country.

The variable "financial capability for travel to the host country" is not included in this model, although it has been used as a measure of the overall potential of a market population for international travel in other models. This factor is excluded because use of this characteristic produces an exaggerated estimate of the true market potential. Not all persons possessing the economic capacity for international travel are inclined to venture abroad. The incidence of "nontravelers" in all socioeconomic categories is unavoidable. Further, measurements of this financial capacity cannot be arbitrarily linked to a singular, specific economic criterion, such as the proportion of a country's population classified in certain income groupings. It is reasonable to assume that, due to factors such as market contiguity and varying modes/costs of transportation used in travel to the host country, this financial capability would not necessarily be linked to the same economic criteria for each country. For example, the economic determinants affecting capacity for travel to the United States would not be the same for Canada (a contiguous, auto-oriented travel market) as it would be for West Germany (a long-haul, air-oriented travel market).

An attempt is made to include input variables which more closely reflect the actual market population which has potential for travel to the United States—by taking into account the tendency and inclination of the populations under study for international/long-haul travel. The quantitative travel potential determinants used here are grouped as follows:

A   Travel Volume Potential
  1. Competitive market potential
  2. Competitive market travel as proportion of total population travel

3. Current travel to host country
4. Potential incremental trips to host country
5. Potential for further marketing penetration

B Travel Receipts Potential
1. Current travel receipts
2. Per capita travel receipts
3. Total potential travel receipts
4. Potential incremental travel receipts.

A TRAVEL VOLUME POTENTIAL

In this section, the quantitative input variables which deal with numbers of potential travelers/trips to the host country are discussed and developed for use in the evaluative model.

1 Competitive Market Potential

Marketers concerned with promoting international tourism to a host country are most likely to concentrate their efforts on that market segment which is most inclined to travel abroad and therefore more receptive to promotional stimuli. The input variable used here as a quantitative indication of a population's marketing potential is simply the number of "competitive trips" taken by the respective populations—trips which in distance, time spent away from home, or by their international nature approximate the competitive potential market for travel to the United States.

Differing measures of "competitive trips" are used here because of inclusion of Canada and Mexico in the country inventory. Due to the proximity of these na-

tions to the United States, certain categories of domestic trips taken by their residents must be included as part of the competitive market which has real potential for travel to America. For the four overseas countries under study, only certain international trips taken by their residents are evaluated as indicators of the competitive market for travel to the United States. Table 1 provides a comparative ranking and index rating of this market potential variable for the six country travel markets.

As indicated by the various types of information used in estimating the competitive market potential and by the various sources referenced, strict comparability of the data between countries is clearly impossible. This nonconformity need not be a prohibitive drawback provided the researcher exercises care in relying only on official sources and carefully utilizes data which most closely approximate that market in which the host country must realistically compete for international travelers. In this sense, the standard of "competitive market" does provide comparability for the purposes of this analysis.

For the most reliable and up-to-date information on this market factor, the official national tourist offices of the respective countries should be referenced whenever possible. A limited amount of country departure information on a country-by-country basis is available in reports published by the World Tourism Organization (WTO) and the Organization for Economic Cooperation and Development (OECD), although these data are usually not current and are of insufficient detail for studies of this type.

TABLE 1 Variable A—Competitive Market Potential

COUNTRY	COMPETITIVE TRIPS TAKEN BY POPULATION (YEAR X) (THOUSANDS)	RANKING	INDEX RATING (I_a)
Canada	23,900[a]	1	100.0
Mexico	17,600[b]	2	73.6
Japan	4,038[c]	5	16.9
United Kingdom	7,175[d]	3	30.0
West Germany	5,100[d]	4	21.3
France	2,310[d]	6	9.7

[a]Estimated interprovincial domestic (excluding business trips) and international person-trips taken by Canadians in reference year; derived from data from the Canadian Government Office of Tourism.

[b]Estimated number of international and domestic (air) person-trips taken by Mexican residents in reference year; derived from data from the Mexican Ministry of Tourism and the Bank of Mexico.

[c]Total number of international person-trips taken by Japanese residents in reference year; Source: Japan National Tourist Office.

[d]Estimated international holiday trips (person-trips) taken by air transportation by residents in reference year; Sources: British Tourist Authority, Statistisches Bundesamt, Wiesbaden (West Germany), and Secretariat d'Etat au Tourisme (France).

2   Competitive Market Travel as Proportion of Total Population Travel

As an indication of market penetration and the incidence and preference of the population of each country for possible international tourism, travel by the competitive potential market should be compared to all travel by the residents of each nation. The resulting proportion sheds light on the general receptivity and accessibility of the target market in each country's populace. This input variable (Competitive Market Share) is derived simply by division of Variable A, competitive trips taken by population (see Table 1), by the total number of domestic and international trips taken by the residents of each country. The results of this exercise, along with comparative index ratings for this factor for the six country travel markets, are shown in Table 2.

As with the previous input data, information on total trips (domestic plus international) taken by a country's residents should be obtained either directly or indirectly from the national tourist office of that country. Domestic tourism data will likely be incomparable between countries since each national tourist office usually incorporates its own set of definitions designed to meet its individual needs in gathering and reporting statistics on intracountry travel by residents. Many countries, such as West Germany, report domestic trips as tourist arrivals at all accommodation establishments, excluding stays with friends and relatives. Other nations, such as Canada, provide domestic tourism information based on all travel exceeding a certain distance away from home (e.g., 50 miles) and/or overnight or longer. The limitations of comparisons made between such data should be taken into account in this analysis.

3   Current Travel to Host Country

Existing arrivals from a given country to the host nation are, of course, an important factor which a promotional organization should include in an evaluation of marketing potential. Current market performance in supplying international trips to the United States from each of the six countries is outlined in Table 3, as are resultant market rankings and relative index ratings.

4   Potential Incremental Trips to Host Country

This measurement refers to the arithmetic difference between the total competitive market trips taken and the number of tourist trips taken to the host country, or Variable A minus Variable C. The resulting increment reflects that market which remains to be tapped—in other words, potential incremental trips. The results of this computation for the sample countries under evaluation are illustrated in Table 4.

5   Potential for Further Market Penetration

In defining the term "potential" at the outset of this chapter, it was noted that potential should be thought of as a quantity of which a part can be attained through marketing efforts. Additionally, it was pointed out that as a firm or agency attempts to increase its share of potential, an increasing amount of marketing effort is required; in other words, the first 50 percent of potential is much easier to achieve than the next 50 percent.

Based on the theory of decreasing marginal returns, it is logical to assume that the greater the ratio of as yet unattained market potential to the total market potential, the more attractive the market would be in terms of facilitating efficient penetration through promotional efforts. In the parameters of this model, this ratio may be determined by dividing Variable D, potential incremental trips to the United States, by Variable A, total competitive trips taken by population (see Tables 1 and 4). The higher the proportion obtained, the more favorable the country market appears in terms of marketing viability. Table 5 provides the results of this exercise for the six major international travel markets to the United States.

While not included in this model, another input variable which might be considered by a host country

TABLE 2   Variable B—Competitive Market Travel as Proportion of Total Population Travel

COUNTRY	COMPETITIVE MARKET SHARE (%)	RANKING	INDEX RATING (I_b)
Canada	19.3	2	64.8
Mexico	29.8	1	100.0
Japan	2.0	6	6.7
United Kingdom	14.7	3	49.3
West Germany	11.0	4	36.9
France	4.5	5	15.1

TABLE 3 Variable C—Current Travel to Host Country

COUNTRY	TOURIST TRIPS TO THE UNITED STATES (YEAR X) (THOUSANDS)	RANKING	INDEX RATING (I_c)
Canada	10,716[a]	1	100.0
Mexico	8,770[b]	2	81.8
Japan	1,089[c]	3	10.2
United Kingdom	930[c]	4	8.7
West Germany	608[c]	5	5.7
France	303[c]	6	2.8

[a]Source is Statistics Canada; reflects the number of Canadians returning from the United States after a stay of at least one night.

[b]Estimate of Mexican travelers spending at least 24 hours in the United States. For technical reasons associated with documentation, the United States has historically counted only a portion of the Mexican tourist and excursionist trips to this country. Consequently, the true number of Mexican tourist arrivals has been understated. A USTS survey of Mexican travel to the U.S. border zone, for example, indicates that the existing data system may be excluding over six million *tourists* in U.S. tabulations of annual nonimmigrant arrivals from Mexico. This inadequacy results from a lack of data concerning the actual length of stay in the United States by total visitors. The figure for Mexican tourist trips shown here was derived for purposes of this study only and should not be confused with the arrival data generated by the existing U.S. arrival data system.

[c]U.S. Travel and Tourism Administration estimates.

TABLE 4 Variable D—Potential Incremental Trips to Host Country

COUNTRY	POTENTIAL INCREMENTAL TRIPS TO U.S. (VAR. A−VAR. C) (THOUSANDS)	RANKING	INDEX RATING (I_d)
Canada	13,184	1	100.0
Mexico	8,830	2	67.0
Japan	2,949	5	22.4
United Kingdom	6,245	3	47.4
West Germany	4,492	4	34.1
France	2,007	6	15.2

is historical growth in travel. Aggregate or average annual growth in arrivals during the past five years, for example, might be analyzed as an indicator of the trend in market demand. A country market exhibiting a pattern of strong growth in arrivals may appear more attractive as a potential market than a country displaying only marginal expansion. Conversely, marketers may prefer to stimulate latent growth in a particular marketplace which has not undergone rapid growth but, due to other influencing factors, may be ready for development.

B TRAVEL RECEIPTS POTENTIAL

The desired end results of an agency's or firm's marketing effort are, naturally, sales. The economic purpose of encouraging increased international tourism is to increase the amount of foreign exchange earnings which flow into the host country's economy as a result of spending by international visitors. The importance of these travel receipts was highlighted by a study sponsored by the U.S. Travel and Tourism Administration which indicated that in 1983, foreign tourist spending in the United States directly supported some

TABLE 5 Variable E—Potential for Further Market Penetration

COUNTRY	POTENTIAL INCREMENTAL TRIPS AS SHARE OF TOTAL MARKET POTENTIAL (VAR. D ÷ VAR. A) (%)	RANKING	INDEX RATING (I_c)
Canada	55.2	5	62.7
Mexico	50.2	6	57.0
Japan	73.0	4	82.9
United Kingdom	87.0	2	98.8
West Germany	88.1	1	100.0
France	86.9	3	98.6

313,000 U.S. jobs while generating 3.1 billion dollars in payroll (U.S. Travel and Tourism Administration and U.S. Travel Data Center 1985). In analyzing possible foreign tourism markets, it is necessary to look closely at those variables which provide indications of a market's potential economic contribution. The quantitative factors which deal with potential travel receipts from the foreign traveler are developed and discussed in this section.

1 Current Travel Receipts

The amount which travelers from individual countries currently spend in the host country should be analyzed in a straightforward comparison of total travel receipts. These data usually reflect spending while in the destination country and do not include amounts paid by foreign travelers for international transportation. A single source which provides comparable country-by-country spending estimates should be used—usually an agency in the government of the host country charged with gathering and reporting these data for purposes of balance of payments accounting. In the United States, the Bureau of Economic Analysis, U.S. Department of Commerce, carries out this function. A comparison of international travel receipts and the resultant index ratings for Canadian, Mexican, Japanese, British, German, and French visitors to the United States is illustrated in Table 6.

2 Per Capita Travel Receipts

Spending patterns of visitors from different countries vary considerably, and it is necessary to take these variances into account. For example, the average German tourist in the United States may spend three or four times as much as would the average Canadian visitor. Consequently, the marginal economic impact of the German's expenditures would be greater. It follows that the marginal return from an agency's or firm's marketing efforts would likely be greater if con-

centrated on the visitor market displaying tendencies for higher per capita spending. (This is, of course, only one consideration.)

Per capita trip spending estimates may be derived either directly from market survey results or indirectly by dividing total current foreign travel receipts (Variable F) by the current tourist trips to the host country (Variable C) for each of the country markets under consideration. Due to limitations in the U.S. systems which generate tourist arrival and spending data, both methods are used in this case study. Table 7 provides the comparative ratings for this input variable.

3 Total Potential Travel Receipts

The third quantitative variable dealing with travel receipts is the total amount of international tourism receipts a host country could possibly receive should its potential for achieving full competitive market penetration (monopoly) be realized. These total potential travel receipts are tabulated in this model by multiplying current per capita travel receipts (Variable G) by the number of competitive trips taken by the population (Variable A). The results of this exercise for the United States are outlined in Table 8.

4 Potential Incremental Travel Receipts

The arithmetic difference between total potential travel receipts (Variable H) and current travel receipts (Variable E) provides an indication of the incremental amount of potential foreign travel receipts which remains to be tapped from the competitive marketplace. This helps determine which country travel markets possess the greater potential for further economic contribution to the host country. (This input factor may also be generated by multiplying per capita travel receipts, Variable G, by potential incremental trips to the host country, Variable D.) For the six country travel markets to the United States under consideration, potential incremental travel receipts are ranked and indexed in Table 9.

TABLE 6 Variable F—Current Travel Receipts

COUNTRY	TRAVEL SPENDING IN THE U.S. (YEAR X) (MILLIONS)	RANKING	INDEX RATING (I_f)
Canada	$2,092[a]	1	100.0
Mexico	1,869[a]	2	89.3
Japan	699	3	33.4
United Kingdom	375	5	17.9
West Germany	440	4	21.0
France	180	6	8.6

Source: Bureau of Economic Analysis, U.S. Department of Commerce.
[a]Receipt data for Canada and Mexico include spending by excursionists (staying less than 24 hours).

TABLE 7 Variable G—Per Capita Travel Receipts

COUNTRY	EXPENDITURES IN THE U.S. PER TOURIST TRIP (U.S. $)	RANKING	INDEX RATING (I_g)
Canada	$155[a]	5	21.4
Mexico	101[b]	6	14.0
Japan	642[c]	2	88.7
United Kingdom	403[c]	4	55.7
West Germany	724[c]	1	100.0
France	595[c]	3	82.0

[a]Spending per Canadian person-trip (1 night or longer) to the United States in reference year; Statistics Canada.
[b]Estimated spending per Mexican person-trip to the U.S. (1 night or longer) in reference year; unofficial estimate based on USTS market survey results.
[c]Derived by dividing total travel receipts by total tourist trips to the United States (Variable F ÷ Variable C).

TABLE 8 Variable H—Total Potential Travel Receipts

COUNTRY	TOTAL POTENTIAL TRAVEL RECEIPTS (VAR. A × VAR. G)	RANKING	INDEX RATING (I_h)
Canada	$4,136[a]	1	100.0
Mexico	2,761[a]	4	66.8
Japan	2,592	5	62.7
United Kingdom	2,892	3	69.9
West Germany	3,692	2	89.3
France	1,372	6	33.2

[a]Receipt figures for Canada and Mexico have been adjusted to include expenditures by excursionists (staying less than 24 hours), since total travel spending data for these two countries reported by the Bureau of Economic Analysis, U.S. Department of Commerce, currently include these sums.

TABLE 9   Variable I—Potential Incremental Travel Receipts

COUNTRY	POTENTIAL INCREMENTAL U.S. TRAVEL RECEIPTS (VAR. H−VAR. F) (MILLIONS)	RANKING	INDEX RATING (I_i)
Canada	$2,044	3	62.9
Mexico	892	6	27.4
Japan	1,893	4	58.2
United Kingdom	2,517	2	77.4
West Germany	3,252	1	100.0
France	1,192	5	36.6

CUMULATIVE QUANTITATIVE FACTORS INDEX

Upon determination of these sets of indices for the nine quantitative input variables, the next step is development of a cumulative index for the quantitative factors. A series of weights are applied to the individual variable indices, and the resulting products are aggregated to formulate overall quantitative factors index ratings. This procedure may be notated as follows:

$$I_{qti} = w_a I_{ai} + \ldots + w_i I_{ii} \tag{1}$$

where

I_{qti} = Cumulative quantitative index rating for country i

$w_a, w_b \ldots w_i$ = Weights assigned to country i's index ratings in indices

$I_{ai}, I_{bi} \ldots I_{ii}$ = Country i's index ratings in indices $I_a, I_b, \ldots, I_i$

The determination of the individual weights (w_a, w_b, etc.) is one of the most critical steps in this system. A country travel market's final quantitative factors index rating is directly dependent on the weights assigned to the individual variable indices (I_{ai} through I_{ii}). Unfortunately, a degree of subjectivity comes into play at this stage since these weights must be derived from opinions concerning the respective importance of the nine different quantitative input variables. The most appropriate method to overcome this subjectivity, to the extent possible, is to utilize a modified Delphi technique in which a series of "expert opinions" may be obtained and averaged to achieve the distribution of index weights.

These factors' weights should be applied as proportions of one, or unity. In other words, the arithmetic sum of the weights should be 1.00. Utilizing this weighting system, the maximum cumulative index rating for a given country market would be 100.0. (This

value could only be obtained if the country market had achieved individual index ratings of 100.0 for each of the variables A through I.)

For the nine quantitative input variables, the corresponding index weights derived for this example are as follows:

w_a = 0.12 (Competitive market potential, I_a)

w_b = 0.07 (Competitive market share, I_b)

w_c = 0.13 (Current travel to the U.S., I_c)

w_d = 0.08 (Potential incremental trips to the U.S., I_d)

w_e = 0.12 (Potential for further market penetration, I_e)

w_f = 0.15 (Current travel receipts, I_f)

w_g = 0.11 (Per capita travel receipts, I_g)

w_h = 0.09 (Total potential travel receipts, I_h)

w_i = 0.13 (Potential incremental travel receipts, I_i)

1.00

For illustrative purposes, the following is the application of Equation (1) in deriving the cumulative quantitative factors index rating for the Canadian travel market to the United States:

$$
\begin{aligned}
I_{qt} &= (0.12)(100.0) + (0.07)(64.8) + (0.13)(100.0) \\
&\quad + (0.08)(100.0) + (0.12)(62.7) + (0.15)(100.0) \\
&\quad + (0.11)(21.4) + (0.09)(100.0) + (0.13)(62.9) \\
&= 12.0 + 4.5 + 13.0 + 8.0 + 7.5 + 15.0 + 2.4 \\
&\quad + 9.0 + 8.2 \\
&= 79.6
\end{aligned}
$$

Summary Table Qt provides the completed listing of cumulative quantitative factors index ratings for the six country travel markets to the United States.

TABLE Qt   Cumulative Quantitative Factors Index

COUNTRY	CUMULATIVE QUANTITATIVE FACTORS INDEX RATING (I_{qt})	RANKING
Canada	79.6	1
Mexico	63.1	2
Japan	43.5	5
United Kingdom	49.1	4
West Germany	55.8	3
France	33.8	6

QUALITATIVE/REFINING FACTORS INDEX

Quantitative factors such as outlined in the foregoing section are quite important in analyzing the potential of international tourism markets. However, they must not be considered the sole indicator of marketing viability. Other qualitative factors which directly affect demand in the marketplace must be considered in the evaluation process. In this model, these qualitative variables are applied as refining factors which, when taken together with the cumulative quantitative factors index, result in a final Market Evaluation Index.

As with quantitative input variables, the selection of the refining factors for inclusion in the study is a subjective matter. Those appearing here were chosen as important inputs for consideration of the competitive marketplace for travel to the United States and should be thought of as illustrative. Throughout this chapter, it is the *method* of analysis which should be focused on; other input variables considered more appropriate by a particular host country or analyst can be easily incorporated into the model.

The qualitative input factors used here are:

1 Cost and distance of travel to the host country—cost and distance affect/effect existing commercial transportation infrastructure, fare structures, trip itineraries, type of transportation utilized by visitors, purpose of trips, and length of stay.

2 General political/social attitude towards host country—this affects tendencies/propensities of population to consider the host country as a possible trip destination.

3 Competitive environment—the degree to which other destinations are competing for potential travelers in the marketplace affects the host country's likelihood of achieving further market penetration.

4 Market concentration—the more concentrated the potential market (i.e., in a single major urban

area), the greater the ease in reaching that market with promotional messages; marketing efforts can be more tailored and more effectively targeted and delivered.

5 Trade structure—the extent to which the market country's travel industry infrastructure (airlines, travel agencies, tour operators, etc.) is organizationally equipped to handle the type of travel which is to be promoted affects the host country's facility for success in that market.

A single refining index is developed for these five qualitative variables. A scaled grading system is first used to assign a numerical rating (from 1, representing the least favorable situation in the market for a particular variable, to 10, the most favorable rating) to an individual country for each qualitative factor. A modified Delphi procedure of averaging gradings given by a panel possessing firsthand experience in or knowledge of the individual country travel markets is suggested. For each variable under consideration, graders should attempt to assign ratings based on relativity between country markets.

For example, Canada, due to its proximity to the United States (nine of ten Canadians live within 100 miles of the U.S. border) and the high incidence of relatively low-cost auto travel to this country, would likely receive a numerical rating of 10 for the input variable of "cost and distance of travel to the host country." European countries would naturally receive lower marks for this variable. For the six subject travel markets to the United States, Table 10 provides the averaged gradings achieved for the individual qualitative refining factors.

Next, a series of weights must be applied to the five variable gradings achieved for each country, and the resulting products must be aggregated to formulate respective refining factors index ratings. In order to produce a qualitative index comparable to that achieved for the quantitative variables, with a maximum possible rating of 100.0, these weights must be five numbers which total 10.0. (If a country market should receive perfect ratings of all 10's for the five refining factors, its final index rating would be 100.0.) A modified Delphi technique may also be used to determine these weighting values.

This procedure of applying weights to the refining factor's scalar gradings and the subsequent summation of the products to formulate the qualitative/refining factors index is notated as follows:

$$I_{qli} = w_1g_{ci} + w_2g_{ai} + w_3g_{ei} + w_4g_{mi} + w_5g_{ti} \quad (2)$$

where

I_{qli} = Qualitative/Refining factor index rating for country i

TABLE 10   Qualitative Refining Factors—Grading Results

COUNTRY	COST AND DISTANCE OF TRAVEL TO THE U.S.	POLITICAL SOCIAL ATTITUDE TOWARDS U.S.	COMPETITIVE ENVIRONMENT	MARKET CONCENTRATION	TRADE STRUCTURE
Canada	10.0	9.2	6.8	7.2	5.6
Mexico	8.8	5.2	7.2	7.6	5.2
Japan	4.4	8.0	5.2	8.0	10.0
United Kingdom	5.6	8.8	4.0	7.6	8.0
West Germany	5.6	8.0	4.0	4.8	9.6
France	5.2	5.2	4.0	8.4	5.2

Note: Grading scale: 1 (most unfavorable) to 10 (most favorable).

$w_1 - w_5$ = Respective weights assigned to the five refining factors

g_{ci} = Averaged grade achieved by country i for the variable, "cost and distance of travel to host country"

g_{ai} = Averaged grade achieved by country i for the variable "general political/social attitude towards host country"

g_{ei} = Averaged grade achieved by country i for the variable, "competitive environment"

g_{mi} = Averaged grade achieved by country i for the variable "market concentration"

g_{ti} = Averaged grade achieved by country i for the variable "trade structure."

For the five qualitative/refining factors, the corresponding grading weights derived for this example are:

w_1 =   4.5 (Cost and distance of travel to the U.S.)
w_2 =   1.0 (Political/social attitude towards the U.S.)
w_3 =   2.5 (Competitive environment)
w_4 =   1.0 (Market concentration)
w_5 =   1.0 (Trade structure)
           10.0

For purposes of illustration, following is the application of Equation (2) for deriving the qualitative/refining factors index rating for the Canadian travel market:

$$I_{ql} = (4.5)(10.0) + (1.0)(9.2) + (2.5)(6.8)$$
$$+ (1.0)(7.2) + (1.0)(5.6)$$
$$= 45.0 + 9.2 + 17.0 + 7.2 + 5.6$$
$$= 84.0$$

Summary Table Q1 provides the completed refining factors index ratings for the six country travel markets to the United States under study here.

TABLE QI   Qualitative/Refining Factors Index

COUNTRY	QUALITATIVE/ REFINING FACTORS INDEX RATING (I_{ql})	RANKING
Canada	84.0	1
Mexico	76.0	2
Japan	58.8	4
United Kingdom	59.6	3
West Germany	57.6	5
France	50.5	6

CUMULATIVE MARKET EVALUATION INDEX

In order to formulate a single set of numerical country ratings, the Cumulative Quantitative Factors Index (I_{qt}) and the Qualitative/Refining Factors Index (I_{ql}) must be combined. By again applying appropriate weights to each country's I_{qt} and I_{ql} ratings and aggregating the results, a Cumulative Market Evaluation Index can be produced.

The equational notation for this combination of the two major indices is

$$I_{mei} = w_{qt}I_{qti} + w_{ql}I_{qli} \qquad (3)$$

where

I_{mei} = Cumulative Market Evaluation Index rating for country i

w_{qt} = Weight assigned to index ratings in I_{qt}

w_{ql} = Weight assigned to index ratings in I_{ql}

I_{qti} = Country i's index rating in I_{qt}

I_{qli} = Country i's index rating in I_{ql}.

For the example used in this model, the two index

weights, w_{qt} and w_{ql}, are assigned values of 0.75 and 0.25, respectively.

Using Equation (3) for the Canadian travel market, the following results are obtained:

$$\begin{aligned} I_{me} &= (0.75)(79.6) + (0.25)(84.0) \\ &= 59.7 + 21.0 \\ &= 80.7 \end{aligned}$$

Carrying out this tabulation for the six principal country travel markets to the United States results in the series of Cumulative Market Evaluation Index ratings shown in Summary Table ME.

TABLE ME   Cumulative Market Evaluation Index

COUNTRY	CUMULATIVE MARKET EVALUATION INDEX RATING (I_{me})	FINAL RANKING
Canada	80.7	1
Mexico	66.3	2
Japan	47.3	5
United Kingdom	51.7	4
West Germany	56.3	3
France	38.0	6

This final index provides a means for comparison of international tourism markets in terms of market potential and overall viability for market development. In essence, this index provides an agency or firm concerned with allocating resources in the most productive and cost-efficient manner with a decision-making tool on which to base distribution of those resources among international tourism markets.

OTHER EVALUATIVE FACTORS

The output of the foregoing model yields measurements on relative market importance and potential, providing a basic system for determination of appropriate target country markets. After these choices are made, decisions concerning promotional, budgetary, and resource requirements are necessarily affected by other external variables which are inherent in marketplace operations.

These factors, which involve "cost-of-doing-business" considerations, must be systematically included in any evaluation concerning resource allocation in international tourism markets. While this text does not attempt to develop specific quantitative data on these factors, a brief listing of the major variables to be considered is provided.

When studying the feasibility of establishing field marketing offices and/or allocating resources for marketing programs in foreign countries, an organization should quantitatively analyze the following costing variables:

1 *Cost of Advertising/Promotion*—Cost of air time and print space varies considerably from country to country.

2 *Cost of Public Relations Efforts*—Costs incurred in providing public relations materials and familiarization and product inspection tours to foreign travel writers, travel agents, and tour operators vary, due to disparate competitive environments, cost of travel, etc.

3 *Cost of Consumer Information System*—Ongoing provision of detailed travel information, either promotional or descriptive, directly to the public can vary by market, involving costs and logistical considerations for supply of informational materials, translation requirements, location and costs of facilities, etc.

4 *Cost of Trade Liaison and Support*—Market development efforts with the travel trade in the competitive marketplace involve sales calls, educational seminars, supplying promotional support materials, financial support for tour development, etc. The amount of personal and budgetary resources required to carry out comparable functions of this type varies by country market.

5 *Cost of Field Office Maintenance*—Varying expenses are incurred in renting/leasing appropriately located field office space, in maintaining employee staff support, and in meeting fixed and variable costs associated with office operations.

These variables, along with the characteristics of the marketplace and the target audience, will influence an organization's mix of marketing programs, as well as the ultimate commitment of resources to support these programs.

REFERENCES

Burkart, A.J., and S. Medlik (1974), *Tourism—Past, Present, and Future*, London: Heinemann.

Crampon, L.J., L. M. Rothfield, and Salah Wahab (1976), *Tourism Marketing*, London: Tourism International Press.

Economic Development Administration, U.S. Department of Commerce (1981), *Creating Economic Growth and Jobs through Travel and Tourism*, Washington, D.C.

Gearing, C.E., W. W. Swart, and T. Var (1976), *Planning for Tourism Development*, New York: Praeger Publishers.

Munsinger, Gary M., and Richard W. Hansen (1974), *A Market Potential Index*, Washington, D.C.: United States Travel Service, U.S. Department of Commerce.

Schmoll, G.A. (1977), *Tourism Promotion*, London: Tourism International Press.

U.S. Travel and Tourism Administration and U.S. Travel Data Center (1985), *Impact of Foreign Visitors on State Economies, 1983*, Washington, D.C.

U.S. Travel Service (1978), *Tourism USA, Volume II—Development, Assessing Your Product and the Market*, Washington, D.C.

INDEX